Radio Crime Fighters

Radio Crime Fighters

Over 300 Programs from the Golden Age

by JIM COX

McFarland & Company, Inc., Publishers
Jefferson, North Carolina, and London

All photographs provided by Photofest.

Library of Congress Cataloguing-in-Publication Data

Cox, Jim, 1939–
Radio crime fighters : over 300 programs
from the golden age / by Jim Cox.
p.   cm.
Includes bibliographical references and index.

ISBN 0-7864-1390-5 (illustrated case binding : 50# alkaline paper)

1. Detective and mystery radio programs—United States—catalogs.
I. Title.
PN1991.8.D47C69   2002   016.79144'655—dc21   2002012039

British Library cataloguing data are available

Cover photograph: Basil Rathbone as the title character in
The Adventures of Sherlock Holmes, January 1942 *(Photofest)*

Manufactured in the United States of America

*McFarland & Company, Inc., Publishers
Box 611, Jefferson, North Carolina 28640
www.mcfarlandpub.com*

For Al Hubin, Gary Mercer, Stewart Wright and Jack French—
true detectives of the modern age—
and the memories of a trio of crime fighting thespians,
personal heroes of their respective genres:
Brace Beemer, Bennett Kilpack and John Larkin

Acknowledgments

How does one convey his appreciation to individuals who may have unselfishly given away hundreds of hours of their time without any thought of personal recompense to supply and verify the massive documentation in a work like this? I shall be forever grateful to several ardent, authoritative old time radio collectors for the expertise they dispensed in an effort to substantiate the most credible permanent record of these shows anywhere. I want to thank them publicly, and extend sincere apologies to any I may inadvertently overlook.

To Al Hubin will go my undying gratitude for being a voluntary editor-in-chief. I liked Al from the moment I met him a few years ago at a Newark Friends of Old Time Radio convention. We had corresponded by email before that and I knew of his great love for crime and detective series. I was then toying with the idea of writing the book you hold in your hands. When I told him at Newark that I was going in another direction, I read the disappointment in his face. When the chance to actively pursue this topic resurfaced later, from the very start Al's unconditional aid was available. He never refused a request and patiently listened to hundreds of hours of tapes out of his vast private collection, gathering many critical details. At times he listened to me vacillate and gave me seemly advice. I gratefully salute him for the incredible commitment he made.

Gary Mercer wasn't a slacker, either. The plethora of resources in visual entertainment at his fingertips and his familiarity with so much that is film-oriented is no less than astounding. Gary supplied nearly every piece of cinematic data, and some of the television supplements, too. It's good work and I offer my sincere thanks.

Many of the little known, hard-to-find radio series are in this book as a direct result of the dogged tracking of Stewart Wright. He discovered numerous obscure shows, no small feat, and provided tidbits about many. This is a far more complete compendium as a direct result of his concerted efforts, and to him goes my unfaltering gratitude.

Another who was able to furnish considerable detail on a sizable lot of series was Jack French. Jack specializes in multiple vintage radio sectors and so was in a unique position to supply some key material, which he did generously and obligingly. I'm pleased to acknowledge it.

A host of radiophiles provided commentary or other data that substantively improved the finished product. I'm especially thankful to each of these: Jerry Austin, Kenneth Clarke, Martin Grams Jr., Larry Groebe, Michael Hayde, Michael Henry, Rand B. Lee, Allen Lingley, Patrick Lucanio, Gary McDole, Elizabeth

McLeod, Charles Niren, Arlene Osborne, Terry Salomonson, Andrew Steinberg, Tom van der Voort and Harlan Zinck.

I would be remiss if I failed to acknowledge the encouragement, inspiration and offers of assistance that were received from a number of individuals who regularly support research projects like this. Their affirmation is one of the constant reminders why this hobby is worth investing one's time in. Some probably don't realize that their influence is as powerful as it is, or that it matters, but it is and does. While that influence is certainly not limited to the following people, I'm particularly grateful to Bob Axley, Glenn Brownstein, Chris Chandler, Claire Connelly, Dennis Crow, Ted Davenport, Doug Douglass, Larry Gassman, Lou Genco, Eddie Ginsburg, Jay Hickerson, Ted Kneebone, Ken Krug, John Leasure, Tom McConnell, Ted Meland, Bob Mott, Lee Munsick, Joe Postove, Hal Sampson, Chuck Schaden, Jerry Siebel, Jim Snyder, Paul Urbahns and Robert Wheeler.

I'm also thankful for the latitude extended by my wife Sharon in appreciably assisting me so that these endeavors can come to fruition.

Preparing this volume was absolute joy. The men and women just mentioned made it so. I'm thrilled to be identified with the many who share an abiding love for old time radio.

Contents

Preface

The weed of crime bears bitter fruit ...
Crime does not pay! ...
The Shadow knows!

For a variety of reasons, the radio programmers of yesteryear clearly understood the desire for stories about evil—the evil that lurked in the hearts of men (and women and boys and girls)—and they made almost incalculable attempts to satisfy our quests for it.

Very early in their professional careers the producers, the directors and authors of radio broadcasting and those who stood behind them discerned that the public would develop an insatiable fascination with subject matter that was tinged with almost any form of wrongdoing. Audiences hungered for stories that compared right and wrong, reflected on crime and punishment, and showed the good guys upholding law and order. The outcome of that revelation was the plethora of programs destined to thrill audiences of every age for more than three decades of the twentieth century. The series emerged in many forms, most often featuring private detectives but also peopled by amateur sleuths, cops and robbers, cowboys, government spies, space travelers, and a multitude of diverse species designed primarily to amuse adults. Then there were the juvenile adventures—in the air, on land and on sea—that were selected from make-believe or authentic history, modern settings and bizarre inspirations about tomorrow. It was an abundant exposition of truth or consequences, peace and justice that American radio provided to millions of fans.

Not only were there loyal audiences for such material, those who paid the medium's bills quickly ascertained that such interest—and the high numbers of people tuning in—could provide an enormous cash cow for their varied commercial enterprises. It was an established fact, for instance, that such programming fare could be offered to the public at a mere fraction of the capital outlay required to underwrite several of radio's other entertaining formats.

In 1950 *Variety* projected that the sponsor of *The Jack Benny Program*, the American Tobacco Company at that time, was shelling out $40,000 to produce the show every week, not including the purchase of the network time to transmit it. Yet all but a handful of detective dramas were being readied for prime time broadcast for $4,000 to $7,000 per week. While admittedly these features didn't draw the crowds that *Benny* did, the fact that they delivered more listeners per sponsor dollar than the celebrated comedy and variety shows didn't escape notice. Documentation was available at that time indicating that a radio concert music series was received in 123 American homes per single sponsor dollar expended. The same dollar could corral 163 homes for a comedy-variety show, while a nondescript drama would be heard in 187 households and 215 homes would tune in a musical-variety program. An evening mystery, on the other hand, found listeners in 267 dwelling places. There could be little argument that while crime might not pay for the culprit, it usually *did* for the sponsor.

Radio Crime Fighters: Over 300 Programs from the Golden Age includes network and syndicated radio mystery and adventure series heard in the United States between 1920 and 1960 in which one or more figures regularly appeared in occupations or avocations that fought against criminal offense. Examples of such figures include private detectives, police officers, western lawmen, amateur sleuths and others with a predilection for crime prevention. Also included among the programs are juvenile serials and adventures in which a principal combated evildoers of varying types on an ongoing basis. Anthology series with a crime fighting theme are included if a recurring host narrated or presided over their dramatic tales. Single audition episodes and anthologies for which no character existed in a presiding or continuing role are generally exempted.

With these criteria in mind, I have assembled what I believe is a comprehensive guide to audio series in which crime fighting was a predominant theme. It seems inevitable, however, that a few relevant series were unintentionally overlooked. I regret any oversights. If you find errors, they are mine alone, and you may be certain that they are of the head and not the heart.

In compiling this book I had the help of several individuals with demonstrated knowledge and interest in the subject, and their expertise occasionally inspired lively debates on whether to include dramas that appeared to be borderline. *Bold Venture* is a typical example of a rejected series. Despite a media observer's contention that pirates, treasure hunters and revolutionaries could be found there, it appeared that the drama was never intended as a crime fighting show. Rather, it could more aptly be described as an adventure series. By the same token, *Fort Laramie* aired as a subdued narrative of life on the frontier. Instead of crime fighting, it focused on a cavalryman's reaction to the adversities that were part of his normal existence—boredom, cold, drowning, freezing, heat, typhoid, smallpox and other diseases. While J. B. Kendall was a gunman (in a day that required him to be), as the hero of *Frontier Gentleman* he was first and foremost a journalist covering the American West for an English newspaper. Carrying a gun was incidental in his case. While Raymond operated that squeaking door while presiding over a dramatic anthology on *Inner Sanctum Mysteries*, the episodes were just that—mysteries—and weren't presented out of an organized crime fighting perspective. Such instances may suggest why, after due consideration, some borderline series were excluded.

I wish I could say that every hole that has appeared in published accounts over the years had been plugged. Unfortunately, I cannot. Between 5 and 10 percent of the series included still lack some information. No individual may be held accountable. One simply cannot manufacture unknown details. Our research was painstaking, resolute and exhaustive. While we scrupulously examined the documented works of numerous conscientious, reliable and authoritative historiographers, tenaciously scoured the world wide web, listened to hundreds of hours of individual series recordings and requested the input of more than 1500 subscribers to a daily electronic forum devoted to vintage radio, my colleagues and I were at last unable to fill in every blank. I offer no apology, although it is a personal disappointment that we didn't solve every mystery. It seemed better to include *every* program, even with limited detail, than to ignore some for lack of complete information. I hope we have supplied future researchers with the impetus to carry on beyond present revelations.

It is probably wise to bring to the reader's attention a brief discussion of the radio networks that are designated in this text. This may eliminate some of the confusion that a neophyte in old time radio might encounter through a casual reading. From its earliest days, the National Broadcasting Company (NBC) owned two radio chains. They were easily illustrated on a United States map by red or blue lines that connected their affiliates. The dual systems thus became commonly known as the Red and Blue networks. In the early 1940s the Federal Communications Commission, with authority over all broadcasting facilities in this country, ruled—largely for competitive reasons—that the networks could not be jointly owned. The requirement forced NBC to sell one of its webs. Ultimately it kept the Red network, to be henceforth known as NBC. The Blue network was renamed the American Broadcasting Company (ABC) and was dispatched to an individual buyer. You will find references in this volume to NBC (properly understood as the Red network), NBC Blue, the Columbia Broadcasting System (CBS), the Mutual Broadcasting System (MBS), and ABC. There was also a Don Lee network, named for its owner, that largely served the Western states, one of several regional alliances. It was particularly instrumental in airing many of the programs carried by Mutual outlets elsewhere. Finally, some shows were syndicated, either live or by transcription, to independent or chain-affiliated stations in local markets.

The reader will also note under data in the listings provided on program sponsorship that many shows were "sustained." That means that they were offered as a service by their networks without the realization of any commercial remuneration in airing them. Participatory arrangements existed, too, whereby more than one underwriter paid for a show's bills in a cooperative venture.

Finally, while the material herein is intended to be informative as well as accurate, my writing style doesn't permit me to ignore all opportunities for being animated, imaginative and perhaps at times lighthearted. I do this to help the cold hard facts appeal to my readers, hoping I've not rendered a disservice in the process. If a treasure chest of data about "nameless terrors of which they [their perpetrators] dare not speak" can be a joy to read, then my efforts may have proved worthwhile.

Return with us now to those thrilling days of yesteryear!

The Series

The Abbott Mysteries

(aka *The Adventures of the Abbotts*)

On the Air: *The Abbott Mysteries*, June 10–Sept. 2, 1945, MBS, Sunday, 6 p.m.; June 9–Sept. 1, 1946, MBS, Sunday, 5:30 p.m.; June 8–Aug. 31, 1947, MBS, Sunday, 5:30 p.m.; *The Adventures of the Abbotts*, Oct. 3, 1954–June 12, 1955, NBC, Sunday, 8:30 p.m. 30 minutes.
Sponsor: Helbros Watch Co. for Helbros timepieces (MBS); Sustained (NBC).
Extant Episodes: One.

CAST & CREDITS

Directors—Roger Bower, Carlo De Angelo.
Writers—Ed Adamson, Howard Merrill.
Music—Albert Burhman, Hank Sylvern.
Announcers—Frank Gallop, Cy Harrice.
Leads—Pat Abbott, played by Charles Webster (1945, 1947), Les Tremayne (1946), Les Damon (1954–55); Jean Abbott, played by Julie Stevens (1945, 1947), Alice Reinheart (1946), Claudia Morgan (1954–55).
Support Roles—Jean Ellyn, Elspeth Eric, Ted Osborne, Luis Van Rooten, Sidney Slon, Louis Sorin.

A series of *Pat Abbott* novels by Frances Crane was the basis for this radio feature. It was a blithe tale of a young newly married couple in San Francisco who were habitually involved in various sorts of mayhem and in solving murders. Comparisons naturally abound with a couple of earlier audio triumphs, *The Adventures of the Thin Man* and *Mr. and Mrs. North*. The Abbotts, in the meantime, could only be casually balanced against those far more celebrated features.

Claudia Morgan was the heroine, Nora Charles, during the entire run of *The Adventures of the Thin Man* (1941–50). Two of *The Abbotts'* male lead actors traded the role of Nick Charles (*The Thin Man*) intermittently: Les Damon (1941–43, 1946–47) and Les Tremayne (1943–44, 1945–46, 1948–49). Tremayne and real-life wife Alice Reinheart played the leads in the summer of 1946.

ABC Mystery Time

(aka *Mystery Time*, aka *Mystery Time Classics*)

On the Air: 1957–58, ABC, Monday–Friday, 8:30 p.m. 30 minutes.
Sponsor: Multiple commercial participation.
Extant Episodes: 21.

CAST & CREDITS

Host—Don Dowd.
Support Roles—Steve Brodie, Roger De-Koven, Ivor Francis, John Gielgud, Alec Guinness, Raymond E. Johnson, Bill Johnstone, Ann Loring, Laurence Olivier, Michael Redgrave, Ralph Richardson, Orson Welles, Bill Zuckert.

This was an anthology of thriller dramatic fare offered in the waning days of radio's golden age. A different but regularly scheduled program was established for each weeknight with the same 30-minute timeslot cleared Monday through Friday. The agenda consisted of *Mike Malloy, Private Eye* (Monday) and actor Steve Brodie in the lead; *The Adventures of Sherlock*

Holmes (Tuesday) with John Gielgud in the title role; *Masters of Mystery* (Wednesday) comprised of a different story, writer and cast weekly; *Mystery Classics* (Thursday) featuring a name-dropper's holiday—narratives from the pens of gifted scribes like Guy de Maupassant, Charles Dickens, Feodor Dostoyevski, A. Conan Doyle, Alexander Pushkin, Robert Louis Stevenson and Oscar Wilde and starring such notable thespians as John Gielgud, Alec Guinness, Laurence Olivier, Michael Redgrave and Orson Welles; and finally, *Police Blotter* (Friday) with Bill Zuckert playing Sergeant Brad Peters. Tying the five-part series together in a neat little package was host Don Dowd, who narrated the show each night. In theory, perhaps it was the precursor of *The CBS Radio Mystery Theater* some two decades later—a revival of a venerated dramatic art form that appeared well after the gate to radio's final criminal's jail cell had long been slammed shut.

In the 1950s Don Dowd was one of *The Breakfast Club's* foremost announcers during that durable series' heyday, which emanated weekday mornings from Chicago over NBC Blue and (by then) ABC.

Typical titles of narratives aired during the run of *ABC Mystery Time* include: "Death Walked In," "Four Fatal Jugglers," "Four Time Loser," "The Killing in Lafayette Place," "Murder in Haste," "No One Will Ever Know," "The Overcoat," "Death Is My Caller," "Shortcut to Death," "Murder Wears a Straw Hat," "Open the Door for Murder," "Dig Your Own Grave," "I'll Dance on Your Grave," "Death Takes First Prize," "Death Rides the Storm" and "The Suicide Club."

The Adventures of Bill Lance

On the Air: April 23, 1944–Sept. 9, 1945, CBS (West Coast), Sunday, 9 p.m. PT; June 14– Aug. 9, 1947, ABC, Saturday, 9 p.m.; Sept. 15–Sept. 22, 1947, ABC, Monday, 9 p.m.; Sept. 28, 1947–Jan. 4, 1948, ABC, Sunday, 5 p.m. 30 minutes.
Sponsor: Planters Peanut Co. for Planters peanuts and other nuts (CBS); Sustained (ABC).
Extant Episodes: None known.

CAST & CREDITS

Producer—Glan Heisch (CBS), Dwight Hauser (ABC).
Director—Mel Williamson.
Writers—Martha Chapin, Sylvia Richards, Stewart Sterling, J. Donald Wilson (series creator), Maurice Zimm.
Music—Milton Charles.
Announcers—Owen James, Dick Joy.
Leads—Bill Lance, played by John McIntire (to March 1945), Pat McGeehan (March–September 1945), Gerald Mohr (1947–48); Ulysses Higgins, played by Howard McNear.
Support Roles—Frank Graham, Joseph Kearns, Cathy Lewis, Mercedes McCambridge.

Private eye Lance, working out of L. A. alongside confederate Ulysses Higgins, applied his incredibly perceptive powers to unearthing thugs of diverse orders. Introduced first to CBS West Coast audiences, the series later received wider exposure when ABC took it to national listenership.

The initial producer and author of *The Whistler*, an enormously intriguing radio tale of evildoers starting in the early 1940s, wasn't quite finished with aural crime features. J. Donald Wilson launched the fictional character Bill Lance, imbuing his new sleuth with an appetite for melody while possessing an intrepid mind. Lance's exploits took him to bizarre spots like beaches, circuses, far-flung haunts overseas and occasionally to local morgues. The vice world dubbed the protagonist "Fer-de-Lance" (a large, poisonous pit viper). He was labeled the "ace of criminologists, whose daring ... never misses."

When villains crossed his path, thoughts of escape proved utterly fruitless.

The Adventures of Charlie Chan

(aka *Charlie Chan*, aka *The Incomparable Charlie Chan*)

On the Air: *Charlie Chan*, Dec. 2, 1932–May 26, 1933, NBC Blue, Friday, 7:30 p.m.; Sept. 17, 1936–April 22, 1938, MBS, Weekdays, 5:15 p.m.; *The Adventures of Charlie Chan*, July 6–Sept. 28, 1944, NBC, Thursday, 7:30 p.m.; Oct. 5, 1944–April 5, 1945, ABC, Thursday, 7:30 p.m.; June 18–Nov. 30, 1945, ABC, Weekdays, 6:45 p.m.; Aug. 18, 1947–June 21, 1948, MBS, Monday, 8:30 p.m. 15 minutes (Sept. 17, 1936–April 22, 1938 and June 18–Nov. 30, 1945), 30 minutes (otherwise).

Sponsors: Standard Oil Co. for Esso gasoline, motor oil and other automotive products (Dec. 2, 1932–May 26, 1933); Sustained (Sept. 17, 1936–April 22, 1938); Lever Brothers Co. for Lifebuoy soap and Rinso detergent (July 6–Sept. 28, 1944); Pharmaco Inc. for Feen-A-Mint laxative chewing gum and other health care products (Aug. 18, 1947–June 21, 1948).

Extant Episodes: 42.

CAST & CREDITS

Producers—Alfred Bester, Chick Vincent.
Director—John Cole.
Writers—Alfred Bester, Judith Bublick, John Cole, Tom Curtin, James Erthein.
Music—Lew White (organ).
Sound Effects—Keene Crockett.
Announcer—Dorian St. George.
Leads—Title role played by Walter Connolly (Dec. 2, 1932–April 22, 1938), Ed Begley (July 6, 1944–Nov. 30, 1945), Santos Ortega (Aug. 18, 1947–June 21, 1948); Lee Chan, aka Number One Son, played by Rodney Jacobs and Leon Janney.

The Chinese detective supersleuth of Earl Derr Biggers' novels and of a healthy showcase of B-grade films, Chan was a master investigator working for the Honolulu Police Department. Assisted by Lee Chan, most trusted Number One Son, Chan usually traipsed over numerous corpses before fingering guilty parties. Patiently, with finesse, he considered the evidence while unraveling complex mysteries with astounding deductive powers. He also prided himself on an exhibition of impeccable manners. And a distinctive trademark he frequently demonstrated was a predilection for quoting ancient Chinese proverbs at opportune moments.

Charlie Chan was originally modeled upon a real person, Detective Chang Apana of the Honolulu Police Department. Even in the 1930s the Chan aura became the bane of civil rights activists who strongly protested alleged racial and discriminatory undertones. Had the Chan films, comic strips, comic books and broadcast series been introduced a half-century later, one could have wondered how it all might have been perceived.

In its initial radio segment, through May 26, 1933, the show aired as a portion of the *Five Star Theater*, offering a separate production every weeknight. Three Biggers novels were performed over several installments, including *The Black Camel, The Chinese Parrot* and *Behind That Curtain*.

Chan's halcyon days, according to one reviewer, were 1937 to 1940 on the silver screen—and *never* on radio: He was given "better treatment" and a "kinder reception" in movies starring Warner Oland, Sidney Toler and Roland Winters than surfaced on the air. Between 1931 and 1947 some 39 Chan full-length motion pictures were released, several of them filmed in the United Kingdom and Germany. The most recent cinematic production, *Charlie Chan and the Curse of the Dragon Queen*, appeared in 1981.

In a brief fling on the tube, 39 episodes of *The New Adventures of Charlie Chan* that were shot in Great Britain turned up in weekly 30-minute syndicated form. The series was released to U.S. TV stations in June 1957. J. Carrol Naish played Chan while James Hong was Barry Chan, a new name for Number One Son.

In 1971 another TV series was in the works. A pilot was shot featuring Ross Martin but it proved unsuccessful and was canceled. In a caricature video feature that could be pegged outrageously ludicrous, Keye Luke provided voiceovers as the master detective. William Hanna and Joseph Barbera produced *The Amazing Chan and the Chan Clan*, appearing on CBS-TV between Sept. 9, 1972, and Sept. 1, 1974. Later, in 1979, there was a TV movie offered to American viewers called *The Return of Charlie Chan*, aka *Happiness Is a Warm Clue*.

The Adventures of Christopher London

On the Air: Jan. 22–April 30, 1950, NBC, Sunday, 7 p.m.; May 8–June 5, 1950, NBC, Monday, 10:30 p.m. 30 minutes.
Sponsor: Sustained.
Extant Episodes: Three.

CAST & CREDITS

Producer/Director—William N. Robson.
Writer—Les Crutchfield.
Music—Lyn Murray.
Lead—Title role played by Glenn Ford.
Support Roles—Joan Banks, Ted de Corsia, Virginia Gregg, Alan Reed, Ben Wright, Barton Yarborough.

A globetrotting troubleshooter fulfilled the requests of his clients in far away places with strange-sounding names. His jaunts invariably led him to confront multiple forms of debauchery.

Erle Stanley Gardner, who spawned *Perry Mason*, the crusading criminal attorney in print, radio and video formats, was likewise responsible for Christopher

London. Attached to the coattails of its renowned creator, the fledgling series referred to Gardner each week as both "the world's foremost mystery writer" and "the world's most widely read mystery writer." As on other Gardner-inspired narratives, someone else actually penned the scripts.

The Adventures of Christopher Wells

On the Air: Sept. 28, 1947–Jan. 25, 1948, CBS, Sunday, 10 p.m.; Feb. 3, 1948–June 22, 1948, CBS, Tuesday, 9:30 p.m. 30 minutes.
Sponsor: DeSoto-Plymouth Division of Chrysler Corp. for DeSoto automobiles.
Extant Episodes: None known.

CAST & CREDITS

Producer/Director—Ed Byron.
Writer/Assistant Director—Robert J. Shaw.
Music—Peter Van Steeden (orchestra).
Leads—Title role played by Myron McCormick (through Jan. 25, 1948) and Les Damon (from Feb. 3, 1948); Stacy McGill, Wells' assistant, played by Charlotte Lawrence (through Jan. 25, 1948) and Vicki Vola (from Feb. 3, 1948).

A single-season caper featuring a Big Apple columnist who, despite professional duty, invariably found himself enchanted by beautiful women. A crusade against organized crime carried this bachelor to the four corners of the earth—to Tahiti one week and Timbuktu the next—where he was often mauled by the hooligans he pursued.

Newsweek published a memoir of Christopher Wells prepared by creator Ed Byron. Readers learned that the fictional newsman was born Sept. 28, 1912, which made him precisely age 35 on the day his tales debuted on the ether. With developing writing talent, Wells first sold newspapers, followed by a $16-a-week stint as a tabloid intern. He eventually earned the credentials of a bylined columnist, something akin to Dorothy Kilgallen, Ed Sullivan and others of that ilk.

Ed Byron also introduced *Mr. District Attorney* in 1939, a series commanding superior audience reception. Attempting to duplicate that success, Byron corralled several individuals who were linked with *Mr. DA* for his new entry: Robert J. Shaw wrote the scripts for both; Peter Van Steeden, who composed *Mr. DA*'s rousing theme, conducted *Wells'* music; and actress Vicki Vola, the *DA*'s secretary for its full 13-year network run, became *Wells'* assistant. Nothing saved it, however. The show went down in flames when pitted at midseason against NBC's powerhouse *Fibber McGee & Molly*, which for a decade had been firmly entrenched in the Tuesday timeslot against which *Wells* was assigned.

The Adventures of Detectives Black and Blue

(aka *Detectives Black and Blue*)

On the Air: Oct. 24, 1932–Feb. 6, 1934, Syndicated, 3 times weekly. 15 minutes.
Sponsors: Local firms in markets airing the series.
Extant Episodes: Five.

CAST & CREDITS
Uncredited.

This was an early comedy-mystery series pursuing the exploits of a couple of shipping clerks with surnames Black and Blue. While working for a Duluth market they signed up for a correspondence course in criminology. Subsequently, they opened a detective agency, setting the discipline of deductive science in reverse by at least 40 years, according to one critic. The syndicated program originated with KHJ, Los Angeles.

This was one of the first features to include music to build suspense but it added little in the way of sound effects. Most of the action was communicated via primitive dialogue. There was an overabundance of rhyming communication (e.g. "Detecatives' Black and Blue, good men tried and true") delivered in a singsong manner.

Premiums were an integral part of the production; among them, the show offered listeners badges and caps.

The Adventures of Dick Cole

(aka *Dick Cole*)

On the Air: 1942, Syndicated. 30 minutes.
Theme Song: *Farr Academy Song.*
Sponsor: *Bluebolt* magazine and *Foremost* comics.
Extant Episodes: 28.

CAST & CREDITS
Music—Lew White.
Announcer—Paul Luther.
Lead—Title role played by Leon Janney.

Out of the pages of *Bluebolt* magazine came the figure of Dick Cole, a contemporary Frank Merriwell. A cadet at Farr Military Academy, Cole and his companions Ted and Simba (who appeared to be born without surnames) competed on the football field, earned respect for dear old Farr and stalked lawbreakers as a sideline. (The institution's hackneyed fight song included the idiom "We'll always be near to Farr.") A critic assessed that Cole inevitably managed "to find excitement and help good defeat evil."

Cole offered a slight resemblance to the much more important and widely accepted *Jack Armstrong*. An obscure *Cole* in syndication could never be considered the all–American Boy, even with comic book collaboration. When *Cole* surfaced, an unassailable *Armstrong* had already ingratiated himself with a generation of juveniles. There was probably little room in the hearts of adolescents for more than one crime fighting, alma mater–singing all–American Boy from the halls of learning; that spot was already permanently occupied. *Cole* vanished quickly from the ether, never to return.

The Adventures of Dick Tracy see Dick Tracy

The Adventures of Ellery Queen

(aka *Ellery Queen*)

On the Air: June 18–Sept. 10, 1939, CBS, Sunday, 8 p.m.; Sept. 17, 1939–Feb. 18, 1940, CBS, Sunday, 10 p.m.; Feb. 25–April 21, 1940, CBS, Sunday, 10 p.m.; April 28–Sept. 22, 1940, CBS, Sunday, 7:30 p.m.; Jan. 10, 1942–Dec. 30, 1944, NBC, Saturday, 7:30 p.m. (West Coast: Thursday, 9:30 p.m. starting Jan. 8, 1942); Jan. 24, 1945–April 16, 1947, CBS, Wednesday, 7:30 p.m.; June 1–June 8, 1947 and Aug. 3–Sept. 21, 1947, NBC, Sunday, 6:30 p.m.; Nov. 27, 1947–Jan. 29, 1948, ABC, Thursday, 7:30 p.m.; Feb. 5–May 27, 1948, ABC, Thursday, 8:30 p.m. 60 minutes through Feb. 18, 1940; 30 minutes from Feb. 25, 1940.

Sponsors: Sustained (through April 21, 1940, and Nov. 27, 1947–May 27, 1948); Gulf Oil Corp. for Gulf gasoline, oil and other automotive products and services (April 28–Sept. 22, 1940, plus July–September during which previously aired shows were repeated); Bromo-Seltzer pain/discomfort reliever (Jan. 1, 1942–Dec. 30, 1944, except July–September 1943); Whitehall Pharmacal Co., a division of American Home Products Corp., for Anacin pain reliever, Kolynos toothpaste and other drug remedies and personal care items (Jan. 24, 1945–Sept. 21, 1947).

Extant Episodes: 18 plus 225 "minute mysteries."

CAST & CREDITS

Producers/Directors—Tom Victor, Dick Woollen, George Zachary.

Directors—Phil Cohen, Dwight Hauser, William P. Rousseau, Robert S. Steele.

Writers—Anthony Boucher, Frederic Dannay (née Daniel Nathan), Manfred Bennington Lee (née Emmanuel Lepofsky).

Music—Bernard Herrmann, Chet Kingsbury, Rex Koury, Lyn Murray, Charles Paul, Leith Stevens.

Announcers—Ernest Chappell, Don Hancock, Roger Krupp, Paul Masterson, Bert Parks, Ken Roberts.

Leads—Title role played by Hugh Marlowe (through Sept. 22, 1940), Carleton Young (through Aug. 14, 1943), Sidney Smith (through April 16, 1947), Lawrence Dobkin (through Jan. 11, 1948), Howard Culver (through May 27, 1948); Nikki Porter, played by Kaye Brinker, Virginia Gregg, Charlotte Keane, Helen Lewis, Marion Shockley, Barbara Terrell, Gertrude Warner.

Support Roles—Inspector Richard Queen, played by Herb Butterfield, Santos Ortega, Bill Smith; Sergeant Velie, played by Ted de Corsia, Ed Latimer, Alan Reed, Howard Smith; Medical Examiner Doc Prouty, played by Arthur Allen, Robert Strauss; also, Joan Banks, Bill Johnstone, Mandel Kramer, Charles Seel.

Queen was a professional writer of detective stories who lived in New York and whose avocation was solving criminal cases. Nikki Porter, his spirited secretary, also doubled as his love interest. Queen considered his sleuthing services as book research; thus, unlike most of his peers, the urbane sophisticate never charged for his services. He claimed that his "major purpose in life is to bring criminals to justice." He frequently sought fresh substance for his literary labors by aiding Inspector Richard Queen of the New York Police Department, his own dad, even though said progeny had no official standing with law enforcement personnel. Young Queen invariably arrived at a series of clues that led to solving cases. Shortly before the identity of an offender was revealed, the drama was interrupted to allow one or more visiting "authorities" in the studio to project the outcome. Consequently, when the final scene was then enacted, the younger Queen fingered the culprit. A critic remarked: "The real fascination of this long-lived series was in his ingenious examples of deduction." The show's opening billboard tersely proclaimed that the program was offered "in the interest of a safer America, a happier American community, a more 'united' states."

One day in 1929 while lunching together Frederic Dannay and Manfred B. Lee, cousins, hatched out the mythical figure Ellery Queen. Alongside Sherlock Holmes, Queen may have eventually become as widely recognized as any detective in literature. (Author Jim Harmon noted: "The best disguise Sherlock Holmes ever donned is Ellery Queen." A wordsmith for both series, Anthony Boucher, called him "the logical successor to Sherlock Holmes." Harmon asserted: "Queen simply is Sherlock Holmes in modern dress.") Dannay and Lee's collaboration led to a sequence of motion pictures, a series of novels more than two score in number and—as is often the case following such successes—adaptations for both radio and television.

The radio feature came about after the twin creators turned up as "plotsmiths" on an MBS quiz program called *Author, Author* (April 7, 1939–Feb. 12, 1940). Literary guests appearing there matched their story design skills with those of Ellery Queen (in actuality, facing both Dannay and Lee working in tandem). The visitors developed listener-submitted scenarios into finished plots before the pair of "plotsmiths" challenged them.

Just two months after *Author, Author* premiered director George Zachary debuted a new radio vehicle, *The Adventures of Ellery Queen*, combining the drama and quiz elements into a vastly improved format. Dannay and Lee were employed to create a new mystery narrative each week, for which they were compensated at $350 per episode. Action was terminated shy of its conclusion to permit a panel of celebrity figures (or a single personality) from venues of information and entertainment to determine a satisfactory solution, operating as "armchair detectives." Guests were paid fees ranging between $25 and $50. A documented list of more than 100 well-known names (nearly everybody who *was* anybody, in fact) appeared on the show at least once:

Jim Ameche, Peter Arno, Dorothy Arzner, Benny Baker, Lucille Ball, Red Barber, Wendy Barrie, Vicki Baum, Milton Berle, Joe Besser, Janet Blair, Mel Blanc, Ray Bolger, Shirley Booth, Margaret Bourke-Paige, Les Brown, Frank Buck, Gelett Burgess, Dale Carnegie, John Carradine, Earl Carroll, Joan Caulfield, Bennett Cerf, Ilka Chase, Agatha Christie, Jan Clayton, Marc Connelly, Ann Corio, Norman Corwin, Jack Dempsey, Howard Dietz, Paul Douglas, Alfred Drake, Ralph Edwards, Sally Eilers, George F. Eliot, Nanette Fabray, Jose Ferrer, Nina Foch, Arlene Francis, Eva Gabor, Ed (Archie) Gardner, Bernard Geis, Arthur Godfrey, Helen Hayes, Edith Head, Ben Hecht, Lillian Hellman, Harry Hershfield, (The Incomparable) Hildegarde, Celeste Holm, Edward Everett Horton, Warren Hull, Fannie Hurst, Ted Husing, George Jessel, Paul Johnson, Spike Jones, Victor Jory, Nancy Kelly, Evelyn Keyes, Dorothy Kilgallen, Princess Alexandra Kropotkin, Francis Lederer, Gypsy Rose Lee, Jerry Lester, Guy Lombardo, Vincent Lopez, Bela Lugosi, Rouben Mamoulian, Rose Marie, Eddie Mayehoff, Dorothy McGuire, Ruth McKenney, Vaughn Monroe, Henry Morgan, Willie Mosconi, Florabell Muir, Arthur Murray, Kathryn Murray, John Nanavic,

William Powell, Otto Preminger, Louise Rainer, Marjorie Rambeau, Sally Rand, Clayton Rawson, Craig Rice, Flora Robson, Lanny Ross, Jane Russell, Herb Shriner, Herman Shumlin, Lawrence E. Spivac, Bill Stern, Colonel Stoopnagle, Barry Sullivan, Ed Sullivan, Gloria Swanson, Deems Taylor, John Van Druten, Harriet Van Horne, Harry Von Zell, Fred Waring, John Wayne, Orson Welles, Richard Widmark, Cornel Wilde, Earl Wilson, Peggy Wood, Jane Wyatt.

When the panel branded only one perpetrator in the series' first four months on the air, the team was displaced and the show relied on volunteers from the studio audience. This proved even worse; not only were these nobodies invariably mistaken, the fans at home found them as dull as dishwater. Following this debacle, another panel was introduced that was comprised of mystery writers, a decision resulting in significant improvement over preceding attempts.

The Adventures of Ellery Queen was by no means the first radio feature to suspend the conclusion of a story before its final revelation. In 1929, on a local WMAQ Chicago series called *Unfinished Play*, a furniture store underwriting it offered $200 weekly to the listener who submitted the most plausible ending to the dramatic fare just presented.

In a subsequent variation on the style, during 1933-34 *The Eno Crime Club* was broadcast on both Tuesday and Wednesday nights over the NBC Blue network. On Tuesdays the hints necessary to solve the crimes were introduced; on Wednesdays, the protagonists dramatized the solutions. As the fans heard the clues one night and tested their own ideas the next along with the investigative authorities, they vicariously shared in apprehending the perpetrators of the sleaze. "In this manner," observed media analyst Fred MacDonald, "radio fostered in the impotent,

potential victims of gangsterism—the members of the radio audience—a sense of self-confidence and power in the face of crime."

For yet another variation of the same theme, see the mystery quiz *Murder Will Out*. (All separate entries.)

Before fading into obscurity for another week, the central character inevitably left his listeners with a parting shot: "This is Ellery Queen saying good night till next week and enlisting all Americans every night and every day in the fight against bad citizenship, bigotry and discrimination, the crimes which are weakening America." His message seemed quaint for a series devoted to murder and other virtually unspeakably dastardly deeds, in addition to ferreting out the responsible rapscallions. While several more years would pass before the U.S. Supreme Court handed down its sweeping anti-discriminatory decrees, this show had judged that such societal undermining was "the" offense that was weakening the nation. A direct descendant of one of the principals, Rand B. Lee, writer Manfred Lee's son and the nephew of author Frederic Dannay, may have offered the proper explanation for Ellery Queen's directive. Opined the younger Lee: "Dannay and Lee were politically liberal Jews, sensitized to the plight of minorities, owing to the prejudice they both faced as Jews living in 1920s, 1930s and 1940s America." Were the producers and writers envisioning an America of the future? While their concerns may have witnessed little impact at the moment they were expressed, the spirit of the nation would take a dramatic turn in the years that lay ahead.

Queen could become topical whenever the situation warranted. During World War II he urged listeners to go to their drug stores and buy war stamps. For two bits one stamp would provide a dozen bullets for the magazine of an American's military firearm. "The most vicious gang of international criminals in all history is loose in the world," Queen allowed. "We Americans have organized—a wrathful army of men, women and children—to track down these criminals together. You're in this army, even if you're not shouldering a gun—not everyone can. But everyone can take a shot at the Axis [powers] just the same—with no more effort than it takes to stop at your corner drug store." It sounded like a coordinated effort fostered by the U.S. government and, in this case, it probably was. Federal agencies employed many radio programs during the war years to air their messages.

On-air credit wasn't acknowledged for the actors appearing as Ellery Queen. According to a June 4, 1947, *Variety* article, their names were purposely omitted "in an effort to perpetuate the fiction that Ellery is a real character." Originators Dannay and Lee, in the meantime, considered Ellery Queen to be their mutual pen name, both there and on the earlier series *Author, Author*.

A postscript to the Dannay-Lee contribution is in order. Rand B. Lee, the son of writer Manfred Bennington Lee, said that his father and mother (actress Kaye Brinker) first met on the set of the *Ellery Queen* series on April Fool's Day in 1942. She was cast in the role of Nikki Porter, Queen's feisty secretary. The pair fell in love and were married on Independence Day that same year. "It was only after Mom was wed that she learned that the man she had married was one-half of *Ellery Queen* himself," said the younger Lee. Lee further noted: "My strong intuition is that many of the femme fatales in the *Queen* books from the early forties onward were modeled, at least in part, after my mother, Kaye Brinker."

The video chapters of *The Adventures of Ellery Queen* were scattered over more than a quarter of a century. They began with a weekly live performance on Du-

mont TV Oct. 19, 1950, continuing on Dumont until Dec. 6, 1951; the program jumped to ABC-TV Dec. 16, 1951. It lasted there to Nov. 26, 1952. A syndicated film version appeared in 1954 with Hugh Marlowe in the title role. He was the original radio actor who, of course, hadn't played the part in 14 years. In 1956 the title of the non-network series was altered to *Mystery Is My Business*. The show returned to live network television Sept. 26, 1958, under the slightly revised moniker *The Further Adventures of Ellery Queen*, shortened a month later to *Ellery Queen*. It aired on NBC-TV through Sept. 4, 1959. The show again returned to NBC-TV from Sept. 11, 1975, through Sept. 19, 1976, when it left the small screen as a regular series, presumably forever. In that final year, under the banner *Ellery Queen*, the feature was tailored to a period piece set in New York City in the late 1940s. A character playing a radio detective was permanently added to the cast; he sparred with Queen over solutions to the murders. Shortly before resolving each week's case, Queen faced the audience at home, à la George Burns' monologues on television, inquiring: "Have you figured it out? Do you know who the murderer is?" It was an obvious throwback to an earlier era. Ellery Queen was played on TV by Richard Hart (Dumont), Lee Bowman (Dumont and ABC), George Nader and Lee Philips (NBC, 1958–59) and Jim Hutton (NBC, 1975–76).

There were two made-for-TV movies—*Ellery Queen: Don't Look Behind You* (1971) and *Too Many Suspects* (1975)—in addition to more than a half-dozen theatrical films three decades earlier: *Ellery Queen, Master Detective* (1940), *Ellery Queen and the Murder Ring* (1941), *Ellery Queen and the Perfect Crime* (1941), *Ellery Queen's Penthouse Mystery* (1941), *A Close Call for Ellery Queen* (1942), *Enemy Agents Meet Ellery Queen* (1942) and *A Desperate Chance for Ellery Queen* (1942). Note that—unlike other legendary detective series that initially made a splash on the big screen with a radio series thereafter and then, perhaps, television (e.g. *Philip Marlowe, Sam Spade, The Thin Man*, et al.)—in *Queen's* case, radio *preceded* the movie magic.

In a 1981 Brownstone Books treatise, Ray Stanich and Francis Nevins chronicled Queen's aural antics. Titled *The Sound of Detection: Ellery Queen's Adventures on Radio*, the volume includes a log for the series.

Martin Grams Jr. and Francis M. Nevins Jr. co-authored *The Radio Adventures of Ellery Queen* (OTR Publishing, 2002). It includes considerable biographical information on actors and others in the cast as well as the plot developments of individual episodes, material not available elsewhere.

The Adventures of Father Brown

On the Air: June 10–July 29, 1945, MBS, Sunday, 5 p.m. 30 minutes.
Sponsor: Sustained.
Extant Episodes: Five (include four aired over the BBC).

CAST & CREDITS

Producer—Frances Shirley Oliver.
Director—William Sweets.
Music—Bill Worgen.
Announcers—Jack Irish, John Stanley.
Lead—Title role played by Karl Swenson.
Support Roles—Gretchen Davidson (Nora, the rectory housekeeper), Will Geer, Mitzi Gould, Bill Griffis (Police Detective Flambeau), Vinton Hayworth, Robert Readick, Barry Thomson, Gladys Thornton.

This was an eight-week summer replacement with an eccentric Catholic priest nabbing miscreants. The protagonist eerily, yet habitually, probed human intellect: "To understand how a criminal acts as he does," he moralized, "one must ... get inside of him, understand his every thought. When I've done this, ... reached the point of committing the crime myself, then I know who the criminal is." A felony was committed in each episode. The police or someone linked to the event enlisted the British-born Father Brown, widely recognized as an amateur sleuth with a rapaciously inquiring mind.

The drama was based on the mythical stories of G. K. Chesterton. In the epigraph Father Brown was christened "the best-loved detective of them all."

Over his career Karl Swenson was far better known for the prominent character of Lord Henry Brinhrope on radio's *Our Gal Sunday* and the namesake roles of *Lorenzo Jones* and *Mr. Chameleon* from an extensive broadcasting and theatrical repertoire. A wide-ranging capacity for deftly handling dialectal parts undoubtedly qualified him as a candidate for the role of Father Brown, a native Brit.

The Adventures of Frank Merriwell

On the Air: March 26–June 22, 1934, NBC, Monday/Wednesday/Friday, 5:30 p.m.; Oct. 5, 1946–June 4, 1949, NBC, Saturday, 10 a.m. (11 a.m. beginning in 1949). 15 minutes (1934); 30 minutes (1946–49).
Theme Song: *Boola, Boola.*
Sponsor: Dr. West's toothpaste (1934); Sustained (1946–49).
Extant Episodes: 56.

CAST & CREDITS

Directors—Harold Junkin, Ed King, Joseph Mansfield, Harold Weihe.
Writers—Gilbert and Ruth Brann, William Welch.
Music—Paul Taubman (organ).
Sound Effects—Max Russell.
Announcers—Harlow Wilcox (1934), Mel Brandt.

Lead—Title role played by Donald Briggs (1934), Lawson Zerbe (1946–49).

Support Roles—Brad Barker, Jean Gillespie (Inza Burrage), Al Hodge, Patricia Hosley (Elsie Bellwood), Lamont Johnson, Grace Keddy, Elaine Rost (Inza Burrage), Hal Studer (Bart Hodge).

Frank Merriwell, whom Jim Harmon dubbed "the original all–American boy," was a Yale athletic superstar in the latter nineteenth century. He also engaged a strong penchant for sticking his nose into dark corners as he struggled bravely on behalf of anyone endangered by evilmongers.

Some dime novels by Burt L. Standish, pseudonym of Gilbert S. Patton, formed the basis of the Merriwell character. There were nearly 800 such stories produced.

The series' latter run burst onto the ether with a colorful epigraph given over the echo of a horse-and-buggy clomping along as it rolled: "There it is, an echo of the past … an exciting past, a romantic past … the era of the horse and carriage, gaslit streets and free-for-all football games. The era of one of the most beloved heroes in American fiction, Frank Merriwell…. loved as much today as he ever was."

While not all of these episodes dealt with crime, some clearly did: "Clue of the Numbers," "The Doubtful Alibi," "The Mystery of the Iron Door," "The Mystery of the Missing Records," "The Riddle of the Wrong Answer," "Thunderstorm Mystery" and others.

Don Aston and Fred King compiled a fairly complete list of these shows.

The Adventures of Frank Race

On the Air: May 1, 1949–Feb. 19, 1950, Syndicated (East Coast); June 5, 1951–March 25, 1952, Syndicated (West Coast). 30 minutes.

Sponsor: Local advertisers in markets where it was sold.

Extant Episodes: 43 (complete run).

CAST & CREDITS

Producer/Director—Joel Murcott (for Bruce Eells Productions).
Writer—Buckley Angell.
Music—Ivan Ditmars (organ).
Announcer—Art Gilmore.
Leads—Title role played by Tom Collins (initial 22 shows), Paul Dubov; Mark Donovan, played by Tony Barrett.

Frank Race was a criminal attorney in prewar America, but from World War II's inception he became a counter espionage agent seeking to eliminate international forces of evil. With colleague Mark Donovan he infiltrated and spied on enemies of the U.S. government.

Bruce Eells Production Co. adopted a habit of introducing new shows that featured fairly prominent talents—in this case, Tom Collins, unblemished from a continuing, peerless performance in *Chandu, the Magician*—while replacing those actors shortly after the opening with lesser recognized quantities like Paul Dubov.

While there was little in *Race* to distinguish it from other dramas of its theme, the program was able to capitalize on the talents of instrumentalist Ivan Ditmars, who composed and played an artistic score for it.

Jay Hickerson prepared a log of the series.

The Adventures of Leonidas Witherall

(aka *Leonidas Witherall*)

On the Air: June 4–Oct. 1, 1944, MBS, Sunday, 9 p.m.; Oct. 8–Nov. 26, 1944, MBS, Sunday, 7 p.m.; Dec. 3, 1944–Jan. 14, 1945, MBS, Sunday, 10 p.m.; Jan. 21–May 6, 1945, MBS, Sunday, 7 p.m. 30 minutes.

Sponsor: Sustained.
Extant Episodes: Seven.

CAST & CREDITS

Producer—Roger Bower.
Music—Milton Kane.
Announcer—Carl Caruso.
Leads—Title role played by Walter Hampden; Mrs. Mollet, played by Agnes Moorehead and Ethel Remey.
Support Role—Jack MacBryde (Sergeant McCloud).

An aging New England schoolmaster—a native Brit with an uncanny resemblance to the Bard of Stratford-on-Avon, William Shakespeare himself—Leonidas Witherall was inevitably wrapped up in murder inquiries. His matronly Birch Hill housekeeper, Mrs. Mollet, was fascinated by his exploits and often was the catalyst that led him into new quests. Witherall was headmaster at the mythical Meredith School for Boys in Dalton where he also taught criminology. When he wasn't tied up with teaching and tangential investigations, he wrote a radio detective series. There were few dull moments in his life—he obviously had few of them to spare.

A mystery novel by Alice Tilden created the figure of Leonidas Witherall. An audition episode featuring Hampden and Moorehead aired over CBS on Sept. 7, 1943.

Producer Roger Bower was a versatile broadcasting insider. He had provided live commentary on the first Macy's Thanksgiving Day parade, and was well known to national radio audiences as producer-director-moderator-scorekeeper of the popular audience participation comedy game *Can You Top This?* Later he was prominently linked with *Stop Me If You've Heard This One.* Bower hosted the Paul Winchell–Jerry Mahoney variety show and directed both *The Crime Club* and *The Witch's Tale.* For nearly a quarter of a century (1928–52) he was a permanent staffer at New York City's WOR Radio. (A more extensive profile of him appears in my work *The Great Radio Audience Participation Shows,* McFarland & Company, Inc., Publishers, Jefferson, N.C.)

The Adventures of M. Hercule Poirot

(aka *Hercule Poirot,* aka *Agatha Christie's Poirot*)

On the Air: Feb. 22–Sept. 6, 1945, MBS, Thursday, 8:30 p.m.; Oct. 7–Oct. 14, 1945, MBS, Sunday, 9 p.m. 30 minutes.
Sponsor: Sustained.
Extant Episodes: Nine.

CAST & CREDITS

Director—Cecil Eastman.
Lead—Title role played by Harold Huber.

Among crime novelist Agatha Christie's many fictional conceptions, none was as enthralling and as amusing as the five-foot-four mustachioed, insufferably immodest Belgian detective M. Hercule Poirot. Transferred from London to New York for the radio series, his deductive powers intensified as he relied upon his "little grey cells." The exotic nature of things foreign provided an appropriate milieu for Poirot and he was often involved in substantive international capers.

Poirot was often depicted in films and on television while his radio run was relatively brief. His cases are still being rerun on cable television today. He was a central character in a 1994 made-for-television movie, the subject of Anne Hart's book *The Life and Times of Hercule Poirot* (Putnam, 1990) and figured in 33 novels and 55 short stories from the fertile pen of Agatha Christie.

On radio, speaking from London, Christie introduced the initial broadcast of the Poirot series via shortwave.

The Mercury Players dramatized what was reported to be the most famous of all the Poirot cases, "The Murder of Roger Ackroyd," Nov. 12, 1939, on CBS's *Campbell Playhouse.*

See separate entry, *Mystery of the Week.*

The Adventures of Michael Shayne

(aka *The New Adventures of Michael Shayne,* aka *Michael Shayne, Private Detective*)

On the Air: *Michael Shayne, Private Detective.* Oct. 16, 1944–1946, MBS-Don Lee, Monday, 8:30 p.m. PT, later Wednesday, 7 p.m. PT (West Coast); Oct. 15, 1946–Nov. 11, 1947, MBS, Tuesday, 8 p.m.; *The New Adventures of Michael Shayne.* July 15, 1948–1950, ABC or MBS, varied days, including May 5–July 25, 1949, MBS, Saturday, 5 p.m.; *The Adventures of Michael Shayne.* Oct. 14–Nov. 4, 1952, ABC, Tuesday, 8 p.m.; Nov. 6, 1952–Feb. 5, 1953, ABC, Thursday, 9:30 p.m.; Feb. 13–July 10, 1953, ABC, Friday, 8 p.m.

Sponsor: Sustained (coast-to-coast).
Extant Episodes: 30.

Cast & Credits

Producers—Bob Ney, Don W. Sharpe, Dave Taylor.
Director—Bill Russo.
Writers—Richard de Graffe, Bob Ryf.
Music—John Duffy.
Leads—Title role played by Wally Maher (through Nov. 14, 1947), Jeff Chandler (1947–50), Donald Curtis (1952), Robert Sterling and Vinton Hayworth (after Nov. 6, 1952); Phyl Knight, played by Louise Arthur, Cathy Lewis (spring 1945), Judith Parrish (1952).
Support Roles—Bob Bruce, Sharon Douglas, Jack Edwards, Joe Forte (the inspector), Hal Gerard, Virginia Gregg, Virginia Keith, Harry Lang, Charlie Lung, GeGe Pearson, Earle Ross, Anne Stone.

Getting a "handle" on this gumshoe series was one of its most persistent quirks. Several reincarnations netted a trio of monikers. The native New Orleanian and his blonde bombshell girl—and girlfriend—Friday, Phyllis (Phyl) Knight, traipsed through *Michael Shayne, Private Detective* from 1944 to 1946. In *The New Adventures of Michael Shayne* between 1948 and 1950, Knight was history. In a final reprise during 1952–53, *The Adventures of Michael Shayne* found the protagonist in New York City, once again hooked up with Knight. A common thread in all three versions was his dominant personality—brash, abrasive, skeptical, tough, relentless and generally resentful of police inspectors. For $20 a day and expenses this "reckless, red-headed Irishman" took on some pretty shady clients who frequently carried him to some terribly seedy places. Receiving a lump on the head in a dark alley was almost a given for Shayne in every episode.

The radio series had origins in literature and film. It was based on the fictional volume *Dividend on Death* by Brett Halliday (pseudonym of author Davis Dresser) and on a series of screenplays by Lloyd Nolan.

A distinguishing feature, employed by several contemporaries and perhaps most effectively by *Yours Truly, Johnny Dollar,* was Shayne's frequent asides to the radio audience. He literally narrated his own stories, filling in the action over bridge music during transitions between scenes. It provided a strong pull in drawing the listener into the story and keeping him involved. The device became widely accepted and practiced in the genre of crime drama.

The second actor to portray Shayne, Jeff Chandler, was also to win the role of the bashful biology teacher at Madison High, Philip Boynton, on the debuting *Our Miss Brooks* in 1948. His voice would be instantly recognized by most listeners to both of these shows, which ran simultaneously between 1948 and 1950.

Richard Denning, who had played Jerry North from 1952 to 1954 in television's *Mr. and Mrs. North* and in the latter days of the series' radio run, portrayed the title role of *Michael Shayne* in its video format. There the aural New Orleans-turned-New York City gumshoe waged battles on the beaches in the vicinity of Miami. Unfortunately, spectacular scenery wasn't able to sustain it and the show left the air after a single season. It was telecast on NBC between Sept. 30, 1960, and Sept. 22, 1961.

The Adventures of Mr. and Mrs. North see Mr. and Mrs. North

The Adventures of Nero Wolfe

(aka *The Amazing Nero Wolfe*, aka *The New Adventures of Nero Wolfe*)

On the Air: *The Adventures of Nero Wolfe*, April 7–June 30, 1943, ABC (New England region), Wednesday; July 5–Sept. 27, 1943, ABC, Monday, 8:30 p.m.; Jan. 21–July 14, 1944, ABC, Friday, 7 p.m.; *The Amazing Nero Wolfe*, 1946–Dec. 15, 1946, MBS-Don Lee, Sunday; *The New Adventures of Nero Wolfe*, Oct. 20, 1950–April 27, 1951, NBC, Friday, 8 p.m.; Jan. 16–April 10, 1982, CBC. 30 minutes.

Sponsor: Elgin Watch Co. for Elgin timepieces (ABC); Andrew Jergens Co. for Jergens lotions (MBS-Don Lee); DeSoto-Plymouth Division of Chrysler Corp. for Plymouth automobiles (NBC).

Extant Episodes: 45 (including 13 aired over the Canadian Broadcasting Corporation in 1982).

CAST & CREDITS

Producer/Director—Travis Wells.
Producers—Himan Brown, Edwin Fadiman.
Director—J. Donald Wilson.
Writer—Louis Vittes.
Music—Johnny Green, Lew White.
Sound Effects—Virgil Reimer.
Announcers—Jim Bannon, Carl Eastman, Don Stanley.
Leads—Title role played by J. B. Williams (New England run), Santos Ortega (1943–44), Luis Van Rooten (1944), Francis X. Bushman (1946), Sidney Greenstreet (1950–51); Archie Goodwin, played by Harry Bartell, Lawrence Dobkin, Herb Ellis, John Gibson, Lamont Johnson, Joseph Julian, Elliott Lewis, Wally Maher, Gerald Mohr.
Support Roles—Jeanne Bates, Betty Lou Gerson, William Johnstone, Peter Leeds, Grace Leonard, Howard McNear, Victor Perrin, Victor Rodman.

A prize-winning horticulturist with a proclivity for orchids, an obese epicurean with the passions of a gourmand, wallowed in eccentricities in this caper. With the aid of minion Archie Goodwin, the stay-at-home criminologist unraveled the secrets to inexplicable slayings, fingering perpetrators among an audience of suspects assembled at his fashionable New York City domicile. No detail, however seemingly insignificant it might have appeared, escaped Wolfe's notice. His analytical mind and deductive powers were second to none. (On one occasion he was branded "the smartest, and the stubbornest, the fattest and the laziest, the cleverest and the craziest, the most extravagant detective in the world" by his assistant.) Performing the legwork for hero Nero, the affable, strapping Archie was a renowned ladies' man. With an adept eye for feminine form, he could be counted on for a few amorous moments to spice up any faltering story line.

The series was based on characters inspired by Rex Stout in a series of novels dating from 1934.

An interesting ploy introduced here was in using the underling (Archie Goodwin) to narrate the action for the listeners, as opposed to having the hero do so. Wolfe then took all of the evidence Goodwin gathered and brilliantly figured everything out as the clock wound down.

Drama critic Martin Grams Jr. convincingly argued that of all the actors who played the part of Wolfe, "none so fittingly" portrayed the wily interrogator better than Sidney Greenstreet, the last to carry the role.

A one-hour video version following a premise similar to that of the radio series—simply titled *Nero Wolfe*—appeared on NBC-TV between Jan. 16 and Aug. 25, 1981. Its star was the rotund actor who played marshal Matt Dillon during the aural run of *Gunsmoke* (CBS, 1952–61), William Conrad. Conrad was engaged to perform other starring roles on the tube where obesity was hailed as a virtue, including the principal in *Cannon* in the early 1970s and *Jake and the Fatman* in the late 1980s.

The Adventures of Phil Cole see Phyl Coe Radio Mysteries

The Adventures of Philip Marlowe
(aka *The New Adventures of Philip Marlowe*)

On the Air: *The Adventures of Philip Marlowe*, June 17–Sept. 9, 1947, NBC, Tuesday, 10 p.m.; *The New Adventures of Philip Marlowe*, Sept. 26, 1948–Jan. 2, 1949, CBS, Sunday; Jan. 8, 1949–Feb. 4, 1950, CBS, Saturday, 8:30 p.m.; Feb. 7–June 6, 1950, CBS, Tuesday. 9:30 p.m.; June 14–July 26, 1950, CBS, Wednesday; July 28–Sept. 29, 1950, CBS, Friday; July 7–Sept. 15, 1951, CBS, Saturday, 8:30 p.m. 30 minutes.
Sponsors: Pepsodent toothpaste; William J.

Wrigley Co. for Wrigley's Spearmint chewing gum; Ford Motor Co. for Ford automobiles; Sustained.
Extant Episodes: 102.

CAST & CREDITS

Producer/Director—Norman Macdonnell.
Producer—Jim Fonda.
Writers—Mel Dinelli, Milton Geiger, Kathleen Hite, Gene Levitt, Robert Mitchell.
Music—Richard Aurandt, Wilbur Hatch, Lyn Murray.
Sound Effects—Clark Casey, Cliff Thorsness.
Announcers—Wendell Niles, Roy Rowan, Bob Stevenson.
Lead—Title role played by Van Heflin (1947), Gerald Mohr (1948–51).
Support Roles—Lynn Allen, Hy Averback, Parley Baer, Fay Baker, Joan Banks, Edgar Barrier, Harry Bartell, Jeanne Bates, Ed Begley, Richard Benedict, Gloria Blondell, Arthur Q. Bryan, Herb Butterfield, Lillian Buyeff, Jeff Chandler, Frances Chaney, Whitfield Connor, Hans Conried, Lois Corbett, Jeff Corey (Lieutenant Abar), Howard Culver, Olive Deering, John Dehner, Donald Diamond, Larry Dobkin (Lieutenant Matthews), Paul Dubov, Jim Eagles, Jack Edwards Jr., David Ellis, Georgia Ellis, Verna Felton, Laurette Fillbrandt, June Foray, Paul Frees, Barbara Fuller, Betty Lou Gerson, Clark Gordon, Virginia Gregg, Ken Harvey, Jerry Hausner, Wilms Herbert, Sam Hill, Bert Holland, Vivi Janiss, Byron Kane, Earl Keen, Berry Kroeger, Lou Krugman, Jack Kruschen, Mary Lansing, Charlotte Lawrence, Peter Leeds, Grace Lenard, Charles Lung, Junius Matthews, Edwin Max, Charles McGraw, Howard McNear, Eve McVey, Shep Menkin, Lee Millar (*sic*), Kay Miller, Sidney Miller, Jane Morgan, Ann Morrison, Jack Moyles, Jay Novello, Ted Osborne, Tudor Owen, Nestor Paiva, Yvonne Peattie, Vic Perrin, Peter Prouse, Don Randolph, Alan Reed, Elliott Reid, Frank Richards, Doris Singleton, Olan Soule, John Stevenson, Gil Stratton Jr., Irene Tedrow, Hugh Thomas, Cliff Thorsness, Luis Van Rooten, Sylvia Simms, Bob Sweeney, B. J. Thompson, Tom Tully, Ted Von Eltz, Stan Waxman, Jack Webb, Anne

Whitfield, June Whitley, Bud Widom, Ben Wright.

"Get this and get it straight—crime is a sucker's road and those who travel it wind up in the gutter, the prison or the grave." Actor Gerald Mohr didn't mince words at the top of the half-hour as Philip Marlowe, hard-boiled, two-fisted L. A. private eye. At his Franklin Square digs Marlowe couldn't afford liquor for his clients as the higher-priced investigators could. He made up for his lapses, perhaps, by a relentless drive to track onerous prey. And unlike some of those peers, he often reiterated that he worked in tandem with professional law enforcement.

"From the pen of Raymond Chandler, outstanding author of crime fiction, comes his most famous character in *The Adventures of Philip Marlowe*," an announcer gushed near the start of the show. Mystery novelist Chandler introduced Marlowe to readers in such stories as *The Big Sleep*, *Farewell My Lovely*, *The Lady in the Lake* and *Playback*. The character even survived a leap into cinema, turning up June 6, 1945, in a *Lux Radio Theatre* dramatization of *Murder, My Sweet* starring Dick Powell and Claire Trevor.

When Milton Geiger adapted the Marlowe character and Lyn Murray scored the music (a critic termed it "loud and stinging") for a radio series, nevertheless, Chandler—whose name, but not assistance, was inextricably linked with the show—became fairly miffed. To contemporary Erle Stanley Gardner he wrote that the initial episode was "thoroughly flat." Later, when tough-sounding Gerald Mohr replaced film actor Van Heflin in the lead, Chandler's perception slightly altered, signifying that the acting at least "packed personality."

Philip Marlowe was a "lone wolf" in his profession, as were the protagonists of *Boston Blackie*, *The Falcon*, *Michael Shayne* and, fittingly, *The Lone Wolf*. Reviewer

Fred MacDonald suggested: "Although they may have flirted or conversed with incidental characters, they wandered through civilization unable to rest because justice was incomplete. Whether they were self-righteous or casual in their approach to responsibility, ultimately they all were compelled to action. Free of restraint, save their inbred codes of justice and honor, these heroes alluringly embodied the desire of many in the audience to wander uninhibitedly."

In a brief video outing on ABC-TV from Sept. 29, 1959, through March 29, 1960, while Philip Carey played Marlowe as a loner, the character became far more gentlemanly than anybody remembered on radio. On the tube he also continued to transition freely from place to place without being encumbered by any lasting personal relationships.

Martin Grams Jr. and Jay Hickerson have both provided partial logs for this radio series.

The Adventures of Sam Spade

On the Air: July 12–Oct. 4, 1946, ABC, Friday, 8 p.m.; Sept. 29, 1946–Sept. 18, 1949, CBS, Sunday, 8 p.m.; Sept. 25, 1949–Sept. 17, 1950, NBC, Sunday, 8 p.m.; Nov. 17, 1950–April 27, 1951, NBC, Friday, 8:30 p.m. 30 minutes.

Theme Song: *Goodnight, Sweetheart* (concluding melody).

Sponsor: Wildroot Cream Oil hair preparations for men; Sustained (ABC and final NBC run).

Extant Episodes: 64.

CAST & CREDITS

Producer/Director—William Spier.

Writers—Jo Eisenger and Bob Tallman (until March 1947), Gil Doud and Tallman (through June 19, 1949), John Michael Hayes, E. Jack Neuman, Harold Swanton.

Music—Robert Armbruster, Pierre and Rene Garriguenc, Lud Gluskin, Lucien Morawek.

Sound Effects—Berne Surrey.

Announcer—Dick Joy.

Leads—Title role played by Howard Duff (through Sept. 17, 1950), Steve Dunne (subsequently); Effie Perrine, played by Lurene Tuttle.

Support Roles—Joan Banks, Bea Benaderet, William Conrad (Lieutenant Dundy, NBC), Hans Conried, Mary Jane Croft, Betty Lou Gerson, Jerry Hausner (Sid Weiss, Spade's lawyer), June Havoc, Joseph Kearns, Lois Kibbee, Cathy and Elliott Lewis, John McIntire (Lieutenant Dundy, ABC/CBS), Jeanette Nolan, Alan Reed, Elliott Reid.

Sam Spade was the epitome of a breed of case hardened, cynical radio detectives. This man for hire operated out of a drafty office in San Francisco, dictating his encounters to an effervescent, shallow-sounding, addlepated secretary, Effie Perrine. The man-hungry subordinate who could pass for radio's Corliss Archer typed his reports—Spade labeled them "capers," and always signed them with his trademark license number 137596—to file with clients, their next-of-kin or law officers. (His clients were, with some degree of consistency, bumped off during his routine investigations.) At the end of every episode Perrine matter-of-factly confirmed: "Period. End of report." A sensual dimension prevailed with a running, spicy flirting tease between Spade and Perrine.

Like some of his peers, Spade wasn't wealthy but loved his work. He maintained a wandering eye and a lingering thirst as he massaged a weakness for arch metaphors and wise-guy slang. His animated jargon was infused with labored metaphors and taut similes: "You might as well try to start a conga line in a cathedral," he once allowed; he achieved literary summits in defining a pretty girl as "118 pounds of warm smoke," a departure

from his normal references to "dames" or "blondes," "brunettes" or "redheads." Even the sponsor figured in the lighthearted humor that peppered the show, with a billboard reading: "Dashiell Hammett, America's leading detective fiction writer, and William Spier, radio's outstanding producer-director of mystery and crime drama, join their talents to make your hair stand on end with *The Adventures of Sam Spade*, presented by the makers of Wildroot Cream Oil for the hair." A modern Bay area travel writer aptly dubbed Spade "the ultimate American private eye: an unsentimental character in a cutthroat world." It would be difficult to contest.

An old gag recycled when the series was parodied on radio comedy programs went something like this: "Sam Spade—I wonder where that guy digs that stuff up!"

Novelist Dashiell Hammett himself, who was briefly employed by the San Francisco branch of the Pinkerton National Detective Agency, was the inspiration for Sam Spade. Hammett introduced the character in a series of narratives, the most famous of them *The Maltese Falcon*. ("The best detective story in the world," affirmed renowned literary and theater critic Alexander Woollcott.) That volume was turned into dual screenplays—in 1930, starring Ricardo Cortez, with Una Merkel in the role of Effie Perrine, and in 1941, featuring Humphrey Bogart as Spade and Lee Patrick as Perrine. It was the remake, and Bogart's portrayal, that inculcated *Spade* in the American entertainment psyche. It also allowed Hammett to gain widespread stature as the father of the modern American detective novel. Today summertime walking tours around San Francisco's Union Square and the Tenderloin, where Hammett sites are decorated, often attract contemporary mystery writers desiring to walk in the footsteps of greatness.

The Adventures of Sam Spade: Effie Perrine (Lurene Tuttle), perky, well-intentioned clerical help to Sam Spade (Howard Duff), took down summaries of Spade's cases and typed them up for the files. Meanwhile, the duo carried on a flirtatious rapport. Tuttle played Effie throughout the run while Duff, soon to be a Hollywood hunk, is the best recalled Spade, the San Francisco gumshoe who signed his reports with his license number, 137596.

Less than five years after the remake of *The Maltese Falcon*, *Spade* was adapted for radio. A pilot under the curious title *Sam and the Walls of Jericho* was recorded May 1, 1946. Jo Eisinger and Bob Tallman wrote the script, although they weren't publicly credited for it. While Hammett had little or nothing to do with the show's production, ABC insisted on capitalizing on his recognized acclaim by using his name up front, without acknowledging the real wordsmiths. Hammett lent his creative efforts to three successful mystery programs (*The Adventures of Sam Spade, The Adventures of the Thin Man, The Fat Man*). Not until the show shifted to CBS that fall was the work of Eisinger and

Tallman noted on the air. (At the time Eisinger assumed the pseudonym Jason James to avoid a contract dispute with Columbia Pictures.)

Meanwhile, there was another disparity in monikers yet unresolved. When producer-director William Spier cast Howard Duff—then an active Hollywood supporting player—as Spade, Duff's name developed instant recognition among radio listeners. Yet despite the show's overnight success, Duff was credited for his efforts only at the end of each show. He argued vehemently that some of the series' fame could be attributed directly to him. Spier, on the other hand, who was also producer-director of CBS's longrunning

Suspense series, scorned giving credit to actors on the air, all the while liberally marketing himself during the opening billboard of both shows (e.g. "radio's master of suspense," or some similar epithet). It took two years for Duff to hear his name at the start of the show, and the name of co-star Lurene Tuttle, at last achieving the tribute he believed he was always due. Despite the fact that casts on *The Adventures of Sam Spade* and *Suspense* were both filled with some of Hollywood's most talented radio actors, Spier refused to allow their names to be read aloud at all until very late in the run.

Duff began acting in films during this, his most important aural series. When he appeared in *Brute Force* he was billed on-screen as "radio's Sam Spade." When his career reached star status on the silver screen, he refused to jettison his weekly radio series. On journeying to New York City to film *Naked City*, he was accompanied by the entire cast of *Sam Spade*. To media historiographer Leonard Maltin, he recalled filming *Red Canyon*, a western, in that period: "I had to be taken every Saturday night over to the Twentieth Century Limited [train]. I had to stop in the middle of a one-horse place, a station out in the middle of the desert near Utah; [the train would] pick me up and take me into the city so I could work the next morning at *Sam Spade*, and then they flew me back." He waited alone in the desert, surrounded only by coyotes and jackrabbits, frequently until 4 or 5 a.m. because the train was invariably late. All of that—because he was absolutely committed to a single radio role!

When Lurene Tuttle was engaged to appear on *The Red Skelton Show* on Sunday nights—the same night *Spade* broadcast—as the Mean Widdle Kid's mom, there was a conflict in rehearsal time. She was perceived as critical to *Spade's* success, although her dialogue was normally limited to the start and close of each week's drama. Given that situation, producer-director Spier allowed her to record her repartee with Duff on Sunday afternoons during *Spade's* rehearsals so she could be available for *Skelton's* rehearsals that evening. As time went on, it appeared to some critics that Spier was beginning to thaw a little.

Tuttle, incidentally, was given high praise by Duff during a eulogy he delivered for the late actress, who died in 1986: "I think she never met a part she didn't like. She just loved to work; she loved to act. She's a woman who was born to do what she was doing, and loved every minute of it."

On Jan. 10, 1948, Hans Conried, Howard Duff, Jay Novello and Lurene Tuttle starred in "The Candy Tooth," a one-hour dramatization on *Suspense*. It was adapted from a two-part *Sam Spade* feature, "The Candy Tooth Caper," featuring Joseph Kearns, and aired Nov. 24 and Dec. 1, 1946. Both *Suspense* and *Spade*, the reader will recall, were under William Spier's direction.

The Adventures of Sam Spade was produced for about $6,000 in round figures every week. By comparison, *The Jack Benny Program* and other comedies typically ran about $40,000 weekly. Could there be any wonder why detective series proliferated during radio's golden age on the networks' schedules?

Author Fred MacDonald mused thoughtfully over *Spade* and its radio colleagues: "At the beginning of a broadcast the hero was usually found peacefully and calmly uninvolved. With the introduction of other characters, he inexorably found himself enmeshed in trouble and was physically and intellectually challenged. Accepting this new reality and eventually solving the dilemma, the detective inevitably ended his weekly adventure with a sense of self-confidence and achievement."

Spade lasted until the McCarthy hullabaloo discharged at mid century and Dashiell Hammett fell into disfavor in refusing to respond to some meddling queries of Wisconsin's junior senator. Of course, Hammett wasn't directly connected with the show; his link was solely in the use of his name, characters and concept. Nothing more. It was simply another case—and there were many—of guilt by association. Hammett's name and that of Howard Duff had both surfaced before the House Committee on Un-American Activities, which McCarthy spawned. In 1947 Duff, as Spade, had taken potshots at politicians on the trail of Communist sympathizers. While the matter lay dormant for a couple of years, in June 1950 Duff was named in the publication *Red Channels* as a sympathizer. The heat was noticeably turned up. It was more than the sponsor—and the network—could accept.

On Sept. 9 the industry tabloid *Billboard* announced that Wildroot was purging itself of *Spade* with the broadcast of Sept. 17, and that it would underwrite a new series, *Charlie Wild, Private Detective*. Meanwhile, a quarter-million written communications from the fans vigorously demurred, enough to sway NBC to renew the series minus Duff and without reference to Hammett. Two months later the show was reprised with an adolescent-sounding Steve Dunne attempting to recreate the toughness that listeners had experienced in Duff. It didn't work. Five months later the unsponsored feature was gone—a dismal ending to what, by all accounts, had been one of the best-loved shows in audio sleuthing history.

Following the show's departure, in a peculiar turn of events, Effie Perrine—the gal who faithfully aided Sam Spade as his San Francisco secretary—turned up in New York City as secretary to *Charlie Wild, Private Detective*, in the successor to the *Spade* series. And if that wasn't uncommon enough, she was included in the cast of a live *Charlie Wild* production that ran on three TV networks for an aggregate 18 months (1950–52). It may be observed that Perrine didn't achieve video notoriety working on the *Spade* show, an unequivocally more renowned series than *Wild*. Would *Spade* have continued on TV had its principals not fallen into disfavor with those that were blacklisting performers? Given the fact that many other radio sleuths *did* go to the small screen, it is fair to suppose that the answer is "yes." Howard Duff, incidentally, made a brief appearance at the opening of the *Wild* series, wishing its cast well, then was silenced from the radio microphones for the next six years.

A combination of sparkling scripts, superb direction and the exploits of the determined rough-and-tumble Spade—who took his share of lumps on the head—and the versatile thespian Duff, who breathed life into him, had carried that show. In the opinion of a coterie of critics (one called him "the most striking detective on the air"), the series was set apart from most of its contemporaries, and it became the classic detective melodrama, holding intrigued fans spellbound through its final sequence every week. Convinced of its unparalleled achievement, reviewer John Dunning averred: "This show was loved in its time and still is…. [It] had a style and class that the others all envied…. The wit and charm of the show has weathered … decades, and *The Adventures of Sam Spade* remains today the pinnacle of radio private eye broadcasts."

Jerry Haendiges prepared a log for the radio series.

The Adventures of Sherlock Holmes see Sherlock Holmes

The Adventures of Superman

On the Air: 1938–40, Syndicated, three times weekly; Feb. 12, 1940–March 9, 1942, MBS, Monday/Wednesday/Friday; Aug. 31, 1942–Jan. 1, 1943, MBS, Weekdays, 5:30 p.m.; Jan. 4, 1943–March 3, 1944, MBS, Weekdays, 5:15 p.m.; March 6–June 30, 1944, MBS, Weekdays, 5:45 p.m.; July 4–Sept. 28, 1944, MBS, Tuesday/Thursday, 5:45 p.m.; Jan. 15, 1945–June 27, 1947, MBS, Weekdays, 5:15 p.m.; Sept. 29, 1947–Jan. 28, 1949, MBS, Weekdays, 5:15 p.m.; Jan. 31–June 17, 1949, MBS, Monday/Wednesday/Friday, 5 p.m.; Nov. 5–Dec. 10, 1949, ABC, Saturday, 8:30 p.m.; Dec. 17, 1949–Feb. 4, 1950, ABC, Saturday, 8 p.m.; June 5, 1950–March 1, 1951, ABC, mixed days, 5:30 p.m. 15 minutes through Jan. 28, 1949, then 30 minutes. About half of the 30-minute episodes were originals, the other half abridged adaptations of previously aired stories.

Theme Song: *Superman March* (Sammy Timberg).

Sponsor: W. K. Kellogg Co. for Kellogg's Pep cereal (Jan. 4, 1943–Dec. 26, 1947); Sustained (otherwise).

Extant Episodes: 1250 (approximate).

CAST & CREDITS

Producers—Jessica and Robert Maxwell.

Directors—Allen Ducovny, Mitchell Grayson, Jack Johnstone, George Lowther, Jessica and Robert Maxwell.

Writers—B. P. Freeman, Mitchell Grayson, Jack Johnstone, George Lowther.

Music—John Gart.

Sound Effects—Al Binnie, Keene Crockett, John Glennon, Jack Keane.

Announcers/Narrators—Jackson Beck, Frank Knight, George Lowther, Dan McCullough.

Leads—Title role of Superman/Clark Kent played by Clayton (Bud) Collyer (through Feb. 4, 1950), Michael Fitzmaurice (June 5, 1950 to end of the run); Lois Lane, played by Joan Alexander; Jimmy Olsen, played by Mitch Evans and Jackie Kelk; Perry White, played by Julian Noa; Beanie, played by Jackson Beck; Batman, played by Matt Crowley, Stacy Harris, Richard Kolmar, Don MacLaughlin, Gary Merrill, Bret Morrison; Robin, played by Mitch Evans, Dick Grayson, Ronald Liss.

Support Roles—Mason Adams (Henry Miller, aka Atom Man), Robert Dryden, Mandel Kramer, George Petrie, Guy Sorel, Ned Wever (the Wolf).

Unable to save planet Krypton from destruction, scientist Jor-El and his wife Lara sent their small son Kal-El journeying by rocket to Earth. Krypton subsequently exploded, hurling billions of Kryptonite atoms into the ether, the only matter capable of rendering Kal-El helpless. Growing into manhood Kal-El determined "to devote his existence on Earth to helping those in need." Given enormous powers including X-ray vision and incredible strength ("Faster than a speeding bullet … more powerful than a locomotive … able to leap tall buildings at a single bound"), he applied his cosmic brawn against the forces of destruction that undermined his newly adopted world, vowing "a never-ending battle for truth, justice and the American way." In between rescues and other missions of mercy, Superman kept his identity hidden in the guise of a nerdy newspaper reporter, Clark Kent, on the *Daily Planet* in Metropolis. He was surrounded by a handful of mental lightweights who were inept at times and, more often, imperiled—including editor Perry White, reporters Lois Lane and Jimmy Olsen and office boy Beanie.

Beginning March 1, 1945, Superman was intermittently abetted in his moral indignation by a pair of well-established crusaders against underworld evildoers, Batman (also incognito; in reality, "millionaire playboy Bruce Wayne") and Batman's faithful sidekick, the "Boy Wonder," Robin. Meanwhile, for a generation, millions of school kids tuned in to Superman's adventures, first on radio, then on television, while emulating their hero and making

The Adventures of Superman: Superman, played by Clayton (Bud) Collyer, center, was incessantly flanked by "a handful of mental lightweights" more aptly associated with his alias, the nerdy newspaper reporter Clark Kent. And as it turned out, Collyer was just as comfortable announcing soap operas and emceeing game shows—two genres to which he contributed heavily—as he was portraying the Man of Steel. The actors flanking Collyer in this photograph could not be identified.

him an international marketing phenomenon. It was, indeed, a powerful farce to be reckoned with.

A youthful artist, Joe Shuster, and writer, Jerry Siegel, pooled their talents to devise the character of Superman. The Man of Steel's initial public exposure can be traced to a single story appearing in the June 1938 issue of *Action Comics*, a strip anthology fostered by fledgling DC (*Detective Comics*) Publishing Co. That single incident was to have monumental consequences on the firm and on its entire industry. Not only did the issue of *Action Comics* featuring Superman sell out at once, it was reprinted four times. Its overnight success wasn't lost on the trade, however: In a brief spell hundreds of new publishers surfaced, many intending to replicate

DC's success by introducing similar mythical figures who were capable of capturing the imagination and allegiance of young readers.

The phenomenon infused the comic book industry with enough momentum to help it thrive to the present day. While numerous other 1930s and 1940s symbols failed to survive—including radio drama, Saturday matinee movie serials, Big Little Books and pulp fiction magazine mysteries—the comic creations remain in a distribution network of limited newsstand and specialty shop displays. Jim Harmon, who devoted much of his career to a study of such media, contends: "Superman was the most influential comics character to appear in magazine format.... Without Superman, it is doubtful that the genre would still exist, except for an occasional paperback special."

Coming on the heels of its print success, the Superman radio adaptation was launched that same year (1938) in thrice weekly syndication—before there was an exclusive *Superman* comic book. At the time the savior of Metropolis was merely the lead feature in *Action Comics*.

Superman's young creators, meanwhile—like many others who inspired comic book legends, apart from syndicated newspaper producers—signed over all the rights to their most famous character for a paltry $150 plus $6 for the original drawing of their first cover. Subsequently, while the industry netted billions of dollars from the character they inspired, the pair lived in poverty for most of their lives. Artist Joe Shuster, then on welfare, experienced the added handicap of blindness. Some four decades after Superman's inception as an international entertainment icon, its originators appeared on television. Their revelations touched a sympathetic chord with the public's heart. In a magnanimous—though late—gesture, the corporation then owning the assets of the former DC Publishing Company offered to underwrite a $30,000 annual pension for each man, a sum later upgraded.

In 1941 the Man of Steel made his initial appearance on theater screens in animated short subjects produced by Dave and Max Fleisher. Clayton (Bud) Collyer, the best-remembered, most durable voice of Superman/Clark Kent, and others of the radio cast, spoke lines of the immortal hero in what was to be the first of dual caricature experiences, separated by a quarter of a century. Collyer, actress Joan Alexander (Lois Lane) and memorable narrator Jackson Beck reprised the roles that collectively provided some of their most commanding respect in radio. CBS-TV added *Superman* to its Saturday morning cartoon lineup on Sept. 10, 1966, and continued it under varied monikers—*The New Adventures of Superman, The Superman-Aquaman Hour* and *The Batman-Superman Hour*—through Sept. 5, 1970, and again from Sept. 17, 1988 to Sept. 9, 1989. In 1973 the character moved to ABC-TV on Saturday morning as part of a *Super Friends* omnibus, airing several more years there. In 1996 the WB network unveiled yet another animated *Superman* series featuring Tim Daly as the lead voice and Dana Delaney as Lois Lane. The cycle, it seems, never knows completion.

The phenomenon burst into cinema in 1948 in a serialized Columbia Pictures feature, *Superman*, its first live action attempt on the big screen. Actor Kirk Alyn, then 40 years of age, played the Man of Steel with Noel Neil as Lois Lane and Tommy Bond as Jimmy Olsen. It was the first of what would be numerous movie adventures in both serial and single feature formats.

Actor George Reeves accompanied by Phyllis Coates as Lois Lane appeared in a subsequent movie released in 1951, *Superman and the Mole Man*. It was an obvious and convincing try-out for a television series that went into production that same year with Reeves and Coates in the leads. (Coates was replaced in 1953 by Noel Neil, who had been Lois Lane in the 1948 film.) A total 104 half-hour episodes of *The Adventures of Superman* were produced for syndicated and daytime network release between July 1951 and November 1957.

The most dazzling of the Superman theatrical attempts, featuring Christopher Reeve in the title role and Margot Kidder as Lois, evolved into a string of four productions: *Superman—The Movie* (1978), *Superman II* (1980), *Superman III* (1983) and *Superman IV: The Quest for Peace* (1987). For the last of these, Reeve penned the filmography. Jim Harmon called the casting of Reeve as the Man of Steel a "masterstroke," noting that he moved from the bumbling reporter to the idolized Herculean "in a way that George Reeves had never done on television, or even Bud Collyer on radio."

There were further derivatives and marketable breaks for this superhuman hero. A Broadway play, a novel, another live television series (*Lois and Clark: The New Adventures of Superman*, which ran on ABC-TV on Sunday nights for several seasons starting in 1993), cartoons, serials, comic books and an unending barrage of merchandise bearing the man in red tights' likeness, continue to underscore his popularity in this country and around the globe. Localized versions of the character have been accepted in other cultures for more than a half-century. Nostalgia buffs satisfy their unending quests for memorabilia at an Illinois Superman museum.

The "Pep Pins" that the W. K. Kellogg Co. placed in boxes of cereal when it sponsored the radio feature in the 1940s—featuring Superman and other comic strip figures, and promoted heavily on the air—were merely the tip of the marketing iceburg that has filled "Supermerchandising" coffers with billions of dollars. Few icons, if any, have shared in as much wealth as have the owners and subsidiaries of rights to the mythical hero of Metropolis that Shuster and Siegel created in 1938.

Harmon also attested that the selection of Clayton (Bud) Collyer for the original radio role of Superman was "inspired." He cited Collyer's "impressive and unique" ability to deliver lines in a high-pitched tone as Clark Kent and to significantly alter that timbre to a commanding basal quality when the situation demanded "a job for ... Superman!" Claimed Harmon: "The difference between Kent and the Man of Steel was unmistakable, yet there was no doubt both voices came from one man. None of the many other people who have portrayed Superman in various media could duplicate this vocal duality."

Incidentally, Collyer appeared somewhat embarrassed to perform as the object of such heroic worship for a while. (He later recanted, even asking the public to send him recordings of the series.) Coming out of a decade-long career as a busy soap opera announcer and actor, plus being the sponsor's pitchman on *Truth or Consequences*, he downplayed his involvement with *Superman*. The Mutual network, meanwhile, was happy to oblige for it didn't want the true identity of its legendary idol released. Not until a hungry reporter from *Time* magazine revealed the discovery by publishing an interview with Collyer in 1946 did the public discover the real truth—that the Man of Steel absolutely had feet of clay.

Collyer continued with his soap opera successes before transitioning to game shows as a host, first on radio, then television. His most notable triumphs included *Beat the Clock, Break the Bank, Feather Your Nest, To Tell the Truth* and *Winner Take All*. Having headed the New York chapter of the American Federation of Radio Artists previously, he was elected to a two-year stint as AFRA's national president in 1948. He also worked tirelessly to flush out those in the industry who were acknowledged or alleged Communist and/or nazi sympathizers during the McCarthy un-American activities frenzy in the early 1950s. It was something, perhaps, the fans of Superman—had they been older—might have anticipated.

In full costume, Collyer made some personal appearances as Superman. But when a child sneaked up on him and swung a baseball bat at his head to determine just how "super" he really was, Collyer added a football helmet to his regalia for successive outings among the public.

The aural *Superman* series maintained one of the most distinctive openings in radio:

> ANNOUNCER: Kellogg's Pep, the super delicious cereal, presents *The*

Adventures of Superman.... Faster than a speeding bullet!...

SFX: *A gunshot bullet richochets*

ANNOUNCER: More powerful than a locomotive!...

SFX: *A speeding train*

ANNOUNCER: Able to leap tall buildings in a single bound!...

SFX: *A mighty gust of wind*

ANNOUNCER: Look! Up in the sky!...

MALE VOICE: It's a bird!...

FEMALE VOICE: It's a plane!...

MALE VOICE: (*loudly*) It's Superman!

Hardly a child who lived through that era and who is an adult today could not continue to recite that program opening readily. It was that impressive and memorable.

In those days the various networks issued inviolable edicts to those using their airwaves. Some pertained to children's features such as *Superman*: "Cowardice, malice, deceit, selfishness, and disrespect for the law must be avoided ... the hero and heroine must be portrayed as intelligent and morally courageous.... Cruelty, greed, and selfishness must not be presented as worthy motivations ... conceit, smugness or unwarranted sense of superiority over others less fortunate may not be presented as laudable...."

By enlisting its fans in a moral decency campaign against racial and religious bigotry during the postwar years—the first juvenile fare to cultivate such heavy themes—*Superman* earned a reputation as an "explicitly progressive" children's series.

Earlier, when Mutual canceled the then-sustaining show on March 9, 1942, failing to realize the magnitude of what it had developed, an outpouring of thousands of fan letters returned the series to the air within a few months. A short time later Kellogg's bought the show as one of its principal advertising conduits.

While Superman's continuing nemesis in the celluloid productions featuring Christopher Reeve was mad scientist Lex Luthor, in radio his earliest major combatant was a figure known merely as the Wolf. In later years his most consistent opponent was contemporary journalist Henry Miller, aka Atom Man, in a classic duel of wits between good and evil.

The writers discovered soon enough that Superman lacked true friendship—preferably someone he could consider an equal, a colleague. The introduction of Bob Kane's Batman and Robin (who also appeared in DC Publishing's comics) in early 1945 filled that bill. In Batman the Man of Steel confided his true identity without fear of revelation. He even allowed the black-caped mortal to stand in for him when he couldn't be Superman and a situation demanded it. Batman and Robin also provided a ready "antidote" for the deadly radioactive Kryptonite, which contemptuous evilmongers employed to halt Superman in his tracks.

Regarding radio's not-so-apparent romantic tryst between Superman and Lois Lane (unlike developments in much later theatrical and television productions), author Gerald Nachman's judgment was delivered tongue in cheek: "An unwritten radio rule was that superheroes were ... asexual beings ... that lingering, halfhearted relationship between wet noodle Clark Kent and Lois Lane, radio's most ruthless tease, seemed not just sexless but pointless. It never occurred to kids (boys, anyway) that there was anything romantic in the air.... It was also hard to figure how Lois could hunger for Superman but refuse to give Clark Kent the time of day when it was obvious that they were the same guy, except that Clark wore glasses. Superman was oblivious to Lois Lane, of course, because it was a firm given that radio superheroes never messed with women."

A final assessment, from Jim Harmon, puts this superior being—and others of his ilk—in perspective: "Those who were the correct age at the time loved both the … show and the comics, but from the distance of adulthood, one must objectively say that the stories, both broadcast and printed, were often silly and trivial. According to them, Superman's greatest problems came from being a celebrity in demand. He was famous for being famous."

Fred Shay prepared a partial log of the radio series.

The Adventures of the Abbotts
see *The Abbott Mysteries*

The Adventures of the Falcon
(aka *The Falcon*)

On the Air: April 10–Aug. 28, 1943, NBC Blue, Saturday, 7 p.m.; Sept. 1–Dec. 29, 1943, NBC Blue, Wednesday, 7:05 p.m.; July 3, 1945–Sept. 23, 1947, MBS, Tuesday, 8:30 p.m.; Jan. 5–Dec. 27, 1948, MBS, Monday, 8 p.m.; Jan. 2, 1949–Jan. 1, 1950, MBS, Sunday, 7 p.m.; Jan. 7–March 25, 1950, MBS, Saturday, 7 p.m.; April 2–April 30, 1950, MBS, Sunday, 7 p.m.; May 7–June 18, 1950, NBC, Sunday, 7 p.m.; June 21–Aug. 30, 1950, NBC, Wednesday, 8:30 p.m.; Sept 3, 1950–May 27, 1951, NBC, Sunday, 4 p.m.; June 6–Aug. 29, 1951, NBC, Wednesday, 8:30 p.m.; Oct. 21, 1951–June 8, 1952, NBC, Sunday, 4 p.m.; June 19–Aug. 28, 1952, MBS, Thursday, 8 p.m.; Sept. 7–Sept. 14, 1952, NBC, Sunday, 4 p.m.; Jan. 5, 1953–Sept. 27, 1954, MBS, Monday, 8 p.m.; Nov. 1–Nov. 29, 1954, MBS, Monday, 8 p.m. 30-minute segments except for 25 minutes from Sept. 1–Dec. 29, 1943.

Sponsors: Sustained (April 10–Dec. 29, 1943, Jan. 5–Jan. 1, 1950, April 2–June 18, 1950, Oct. 21, 1951–Sept. 14, 1952); Gem blades and razors (July 3, 1945–Sept. 23, 1947); Anahist antihistamine spray and similar health care goods (Jan. 7–March 25, 1950); Kraft Foods Co. for Kraft cheese, mayonnaise and other edible products (June 21, 1950–Aug. 29, 1951); Participating concerns including General Mills Inc. for its food wares, plus several other firms (Jan. 5, 1953–Nov. 29, 1954).

Extant Episodes: 87.

Cast & Credits

Producer—Bernard L. Schubert Jr.
Directors—Stuart Buchanan, Carlo De Angelo, Richard Lewis.
Writers—Jay Bennett, Bernard Dougall, Stanley Niss, Palmer Thompson, Eugene Wang.
Music—Emerson Buckley, Bob Hamilton (organ), Harry Sosnik.
Sound Effects—Adrian Penner.
Announcers—Jack Costello, Russ Dunbar, Ed Herlihy.
Lead—Title role of Mike Waring/the Falcon played by Berry Kroeger (April 10–Dec. 29, 1943), James Meighan (July 3, 1945–Sept. 23, 1947), Les Tremayne (Jan. 5, 1948–Aug. 29, 1951), Les Damon and George Petrie (Oct. 21, 1951–Nov. 29, 1954).
Support Roles—Joan Alexander (Nancy, Michael's girlfriend), Joan Banks, Robert Dryden, Elspeth Eric, Ethel Everett (Renee), John Gibson, Mandel Kramer (Sergeant Johnny Gleason), Ken Lynch (Sergeant Corbett), Everett Sloane.

"Ready with a hand for oppressed men and an eye for repressed women." Big Apple freelance private investigator Michael Waring—like so many of his contemporaries—had origins in pulp fiction. Michael Arlen created the character in *Gay Falcon*, a tale RKO quickly turned into a series of motion pictures. Waring—for reasons best known to himself, and certainly for reasons more dramatic than practical was identified by both kind and evil creatures as the Falcon. Mere mention of that term put the fear of God into many a hooligan's heart, setting the scoundrel to trembling.

Waring had a taste for details, helping him detect what might have gotten by the typical sleuth. He could also be acerbic in both demeanor and dialogue. He

The Adventures of the Falcon: A critic's hint that aural private eyes often sustained an aversion for their law enforcement counterparts may have applied in the case of Mike Waring, aka the Falcon, and Sergeant Corbett. Their rivalry could have stemmed from both men seeking solutions to the same crime. Actors Ken Lynch (Corbett), at left, and Les Damon (the Falcon) appeared to personify those assumptions.

found most professional law enforcement to be a little slow on the uptake and ill-equipped much of the time, and he seldom minded saying so. As he pursued his quarry—like several of his audio peers—he was sometimes in the company of an attractive dish, most often a charming secretary-girlfriend, Nancy (whose last name was usually disregarded). Late in the run the Falcon worked for Army Intelligence, ferreting out espionage agents, saboteurs and other foreign subversives. The unusual thing, which may have crossed the thoughtful listeners' minds on occasion, was that this detective dragonfly—who had acquired a special title and a matching aura to accompany it—possessed no

cape or mask, maintained no rapid transportation and had nothing with which he could cloud men's minds and become invisible. Somehow, if you thought about it for a while, even in that age of innocence it all seemed a little hokey.

The series was highly successful in generating sponsor identification. While Gem blades was associated with the drama only a couple of its almost dozen years on the air, the firm's snappy commercial jingle lingers today with listeners who heard it in that era. Speaking against the ticking and tolling of a loud clock, an announcer ominously whispered between strikes, followed by a mighty chorus touting the sponsor's product in triplicate: *Avoid ... five ...*

o'clock ... shadow! [Speech Choir]: *Use Gem blades! Use Gem blades! Use gem blades!*

Citing Mike Waring's ongoing wise-cracking quarrel with both a lieutenant and a sergeant on the police force, radio historiographer Fred MacDonald opined: "Many private detectives [on the air] and amateur sleuths exhibited a distaste for police officers. This caustic relationship ranged from sarcasm to open contempt. Such tension usually emanated from the rivalry of the two investigatory units seeking a solution to the same crime."

In cinematic productions the Falcon was known by identities other than Michael Waring. Initially he was Gay Stanhope Falcon in Michael Arlen's short story and on the screen. When Gay died at the hand of assassins (because the actor playing him wanted out), the mission, mantle and nomenclature fell upon a surviving sibling, Tom Lawrence, who carried on adroitly in Gay's stead. A dozen Falcon motion pictures were released in the five years between 1941 and 1946: *A Date with the Falcon* (1941); *The Falcon's Brother* and *The Falcon Takes Over* (both 1942); *The Falcon and the Coeds*, *The Falcon in Danger* and *The Falcon Strikes Back* (all 1943); *The Falcon in Hollywood*, *The Falcon in Mexico* and *The Falcon Out West* (1944); *The Falcon in San Francisco* (1945); and *The Falcon's Adventure* and *The Falcon's Alibi* (1946). Another trio of theatrical releases was produced after that era: *Falcon Claw* (1981), *The Falcon and the Snowman* (1984) and *Falcon Down* (2000).

In a 1955 syndicated TV series, *The Adventures of the Falcon*, Charles McGraw starred as Mike Waring.

The Adventures of the Thin Man

(aka *The New Adventures of the Thin Man*, aka *The Thin Man*)

On the Air: July 2, 1941–Dec. 23, 1942, NBC, Wednesday, 8 p.m.; Jan. 8–Sept. 24, 1943, CBS, Friday, 8:30 p.m.; Oct. 3, 1943–June 11, 1944, CBS, Sunday, 10:30 p.m.; June 23–Sept. 8, 1944, NBC, Friday, 8:30 p.m.; Sept. 15, 1944–Sept. 7, 1945, CBS, Friday, 8:30 p.m.; Sept. 16, 1945–June 9, 1946, CBS, Sunday, 7 p.m.; Aug. 9, 1946–May 30, 1947, CBS, Friday, 8:30 p.m.; Aug. 1–Dec. 26, 1947, CBS, Friday, 8:30 p.m.; *The New Adventures of the Thin Man*, June 22–July 20, 1948, NBC, Tuesday, 9 p.m.; July 21–Sept. 22, 1948, NBC, Wednesday, 10:30 p.m.; Oct. 28, 1948–Jan. 20, 1949, MBS, Thursday, 10 p.m.; June 23–Sept. 1, 1950, ABC, Friday, 9 p.m. 30 minutes.

Sponsors: Woodbury soap (through Dec. 23, 1942); General Foods Inc. for Post cereals and Sanka coffee (Jan. 8, 1943–Dec. 26, 1947); Pabst Brewing Co. for Pabst Blue Ribbon beer (June 22–Sept. 22, 1948); Sustained (MBS); H. J. Heinz Co. for Heinz ketchup and many other food products (June 23–Sept. 1, 1950).

Extant Episodes: Five.

CAST & CREDITS

Producer/Director—Himan Brown.
Writers—Denis Green, Ruth Hawkins, Milton Lewis, Robert Newman, Louis Vittes, Eugene Wang.
Music—Fred Fradkin.
Sound Effects—Hal Reid.
Announcers—Ed Herlihy, Ted Pearson, Ron Rawson, Tom Shirley, Jimmy Wallington, Joe Weeks, Dwight Weist.
Leads—Nick Charles, played by Les Damon (through Sept. 24, 1943, and again May 5, 1946–Dec. 26, 1947), Les Tremayne (Oct. 3, 1943–Feb. 1944, Feb. 2, 1945–April 28, 1946, June 22, 1948–Jan. 20, 1949), David Gothard (Feb. 1944–Jan. 26, 1945), Joseph Curtin (June 23–Sept. 1, 1950); Nora Charles, played by Claudia Morgan.
Support Role—Parker Fennelly (Crabtree County Sheriff Ebenezer Williams).

This lighthearted romp in time turned up on all four major networks. It centered on novelist Dashiell Hammett's character Nick

Charles, ex-private detective-turned-mystery editor for a publishing house in the Big Apple, and his wife, Nora. Nora was an attractive but trouble-prone dame with a creepy flair for incessantly stumbling into felonies. (Was their uncanny resemblance to *Mr. and Mrs. North*, then paralleling the Charleses on the air, sheer coincidence?) Believing that her feminine intuition was more perceptive than Nick's professional experience as a private eye, Nora often leaped into danger head first, involving Nick who invariably came to her rescue and solved the dilemmas.

To assist the pair of urbane sophisticates in their deductive endeavors, Nick periodically cavorted with offbeat figures like Big-Ears Benny, Charlie the Creep and Dippy Danny, the Pickpocket. And while the series was titled *The Thin Man*, that didn't apply to Nick but to another character who was murdered in an earlier theatrical film. The moniker stuck, however, becoming a hook for Nick and Nora's escapades. They were accompanied in many episodes by their little dog Asta, a wire-haired terrier on which they doted. The Charleses were introduced to audiences each week as "the happiest married couple in radio." Their shenanigans were never taken solemnly by fans; instead of a mystery, their adventures could have almost qualified as comedy surrounded by occasional dark edging.

Dashiell Hammett's novel *The Thin Man* coincidentally appeared in the year (1934) a motion picture starring William Powell and Myrna Loy bearing the same appellation was released. (Subsequently, there were five more theatrical productions based on these characters: *After the Thin Man* [1936], *Return of the Thin Man* [1939], *Shadow of the Thin Man* [1941], *The Thin Man Goes Home* [1945] and *Song of the Thin Man* [1947].)

Powell and Loy went before the *Lux Radio Theatre* microphones on June 8, 1936. There they reprised their roles from the original film in a performance featuring supporting actors Theda Bara, Barbara Luddy, Wally Maher, Bret Morrison and W. S. Van Dyke.

Hammett wasn't a copious scribe, yet his few short stories and still fewer novels were bound into hard cover volumes. Some of his more obscure radio scripts were models of a style that typified the American language, comparing favorably with the writings of Ernest Hemingway. A few of Hammett's works appeared elsewhere. A *Thin Man* script, for one, turned up in a 1942 issue of *Click*, a photo magazine similar to its better-known contemporaries *Life* and *Look*.

Metro-Goldwyn-Mayer initially purchased all of the rights to *The Thin Man* from Dashiell Hammett except the radio rights, bungling the job by apparently never considering that possibility as a valid one. It was an obvious gaffe. When producer-director Himan Brown was seeking an aural vehicle for the makers of Woodbury soap, he stumbled upon this happy discovery and the rest became history. He paid Hammett $750 per week for broadcast privileges, a hefty sum by early 1940s standards.

Radio historiographer John Dunning dubbed Nick and Nora Charles the "sexiest" married couple in radio. With Powell and Loy firmly entrenched in his brain, producer-director Himan Brown cast Les Damon and Claudia Morgan as leads for the radio adaptation. The pair emulated the celluloid stars so well that some fans were convinced it *was* Powell and Loy, not Damon and Morgan, delivering those lines across the airwaves. The brilliantly deductive Nick acquired a charming, peculiarly "sexually suggestive purr" (Dunning's words). Nora, on the other hand, "cooed invitingly," mouthing long, drawn-out caresses while mercilessly jesting with "Nickeee-darling" over his selection of bizarre sleepwear. "When she preened, he purred," Dunning noted. Despite that, *Life* observed that Nora could readily "step across pools of blood with all the calm delicacy of a lady-in-waiting." She was thus capable of keeping her mind preoccupied with more than simple lust of the flesh! (A *Radio Life* critic, to the contrary, was incensed by the squeaky-clean romantic interludes between Nora and Nick, even offering profound gratitude that their series aired during the pre-TV days: "No censor on earth would allow scenes enacted that would tie in with the noises that come out of our radio on *Thin Man* night," scolded the reviewer.)

When Parker Fennelly was added to the cast well after the feature was firmly established, he contributed enormously to the show's jocular façade. Portraying a New England pessimist whose annotations were fortified with dry wit and humor, he appeared to listeners as virtually the same Titus Moody so familiar to many, a popular resident of Allen's Alley on *The Fred Allen Show*.

The principals in *The Thin Man* were all deeply mired in radio soap opera, maintaining multiple daytime jobs while the nighttime series aired on various networks. Les Damon kept running roles on *Portia Faces Life*, *The Right to Happiness*, *This Is Nora Drake* and *Young Doctor Malone*. When Damon was called away to the service during World War II, he was replaced as Nick Charles by actor Les Tremayne. Tremayne's career credits in the serials included service on *Ma Perkins*, *One Man's Family*, *The Romance of Helen Trent*, *The Second Mrs. Burton* and *Wendy Warren and the News*. His replacement, David Gothard, was not only Helen's longtime swain, Gil Whitney, on *The Romance of Helen Trent*, but also won parts on *Big Sister*, *Hilltop House*, *The Light of the World* and *The Right to Happiness*. Finally, the last actor to play Nick Charles was Joseph Curtin, who por-

trayed the male half of *Mr. and Mrs. North* and turned up in *Backstage Wife*, *David Harum*, *Hilltop House* and *Our Gal Sunday*.

On the distaff side, Nora Charles's alter ego, Claudia Morgan, was—for the entire 21-year run of *The Right to Happiness*—the lead, Carolyn Allen Walker Kramer Nelson MacDonald, the most married heroine in radio! She also appeared regularly in *David Harum*. Morgan, incidentally, took the part of Nora Charles so seriously that she was fired from a show business job because of it. When her radio role delayed the start of the stage play *Ten Little Indians* every Friday night, she lost her portrayal in the theatrical production to honor her broadcast contract.

Seven years after the radio series faded, *The Thin Man* was telecast as a Friday night half-hour over NBC-TV from Sept. 20, 1957, through June 26, 1959. Peter Lawford and Phyllis Kirk played the principals. The network reran these episodes in the daytime between September 1959 and February 1960.

Jay Hickerson prepared what he termed a "sketchy log" of the radio series.

The Adventures of Wild Bill Hickok see Wild Bill Hickok

The Affairs of Ann Scotland

On the Air: Oct. 30, 1946–Oct. 22, 1947, ABC, Wednesday, 9 p.m. Continued beyond the network run on an NBC western regional hookup. 30 minutes.

Sponsor: Richard Hudnut Co. for Richard Hudnut women's hair care products.

Extant Episodes: None known.

Cast & Credits

Director—Helen Mack.
Writer—Barbara Owens.

Music—Del Castillo (organist).
Announcer—Ken Niles.
Lead—Title role played by Arlene Francis.
Support Roles—Howard Duff, David Ellis, Cathy Lewis, Howard McNeer.

An affable lady detective, considered a "satin-tongued cutie," combined her merry manner and feminine allure to catch crooks in frothy chases.

Arlene Francis' career spanned several decades and included everything from soap operas (she and future real-life husband Martin Gabel were on *Big Sister* together in the 1930s and 1940s) to CBS-TV's long-running *What's My Line?* on which she appeared weekly and where Gabel showed up sporadically as a panelist. She was a hostess on radio's *Blind Date, Fun For All, It Happens Every Day, Monitor, What's My Name?* and many other features, and did a variety of daytime TV duties, most prominently as *Home* show hostess on NBC-TV (1954–57) and in the subsequent *Arlene Francis Show* (1957–58) on the same chain. A charming sophisticate, Ms. Francis was expecting when her radio detective series was on the ether: "I could have been called Scotland Yard because that's how wide I was," she jubilantly recalled. In an autobiography, tongue in cheek, she characterized Ann Scotland as "a sort of private eyelash." Ms. Francis died in 2001.

The Affairs of Peter Salem

On the Air: May 7–June 4, 1949, MBS, Saturday, 2:30 p.m.; June 13, 1949–April 17, 1950, MBS, Monday, 8:30 p.m.; April 23, 1950–March 25, 1951, MBS, Sunday, 7 p.m.; April 15–June 17, 1951, MBS, Sunday, 8:30 p.m.; Jan. 6–Oct. 5, 1952, MBS, Sunday, 7 p.m.; Dec. 28, 1952–Jan. 18, 1953, MBS, Sunday, 7 p.m.; Jan. 24–April 18, 1953, MBS, Saturday, 1 p.m. 30 minutes.
Sponsor: Sustained.
Extant Episodes: None known.

CAST & CREDITS
Producer—Himan Brown.
Director—Mende Brown.
Writer—Louis Vittes.
Sound Effects—Adrian Penner.
Lead—Title role played by Santos Ortega.
Support Roles—Jean Ellyn, Jack Grimes (Marty, Salem's minion), Ann Shepherd, Everett Sloane, Luis Van Rooten.

Using mental gymnastics to outwit the big boys from the big city, a cool, calculating, debonair gumshoe from the hinterlands took a passive, non-violent course in catching urbane varmints.

In 1943 Santos Ortega originated the namesake role in *The Adventures of Nero Wolfe*, a portly crime solver and accomplished orchid cultivator who seldom left his own digs. Later, *Inner Sanctum Mysteries* director Himan Brown introduced Ortega as Peter Salem, in direct contrast to the eccentric hero he had earlier portrayed. Luis Van Rooten, who became prominent in the *Salem* cast, succeeded Ortega as Wolfe in 1944.

One of the major problems with *Salem*, which contributed to a diminishing audience, was the unreliability of its scheduling. It was, like so many other shows of its era, caught in a time warp. Instead of allowing it to build fans after a 94-week run between 1949 and 1951 (which was interrupted at midpoint by a day and time change), the drama left the air for a few weeks. It returned for 10 weeks at a new time, was again canceled for several months, then aired for several more months at a new hour. It was off the air for a few weeks and resumed to finish the run with 17 more weeks, four on one day plus 13 on a different day at a different hour. There was little continuity—the fans simply couldn't find their program easily and many may have decided to skip it after a while, thinking it was no longer worth the effort.

Neglect was one of the contributing factors in *Salem's* demise. It could have been one of the strongest and most durable detective dramas in the final decade of radio's golden age. Such unsponsored series tended to plug holes in network schedules when advertisers pulled out to shift their money elsewhere. The fact that this dramatic fare was still aired at all is a credit to the broadcasting chains, which could have easily dumped them long before they eventually vanished.

Agatha Christie's Poirot see *The Adventures of M. Hercule Poirot*

The Air Adventures of Jimmie Allen

(aka *Jimmie Allen*)

On the Air: Three shows weekly, 1933–34 and 1935–36, and repeated for many years by syndicated transcription; summers of 1942 and 1943, transcriptions re-released; 1946 and for several years thereafter, a new cast performed re-creations of minimally altered scripts. 15 minutes.

Sponsor: Skelly Oil Co. for Skelly oil, gasoline and other vehicle products and services, and aired on local stations throughout Skelly's marketing territory, principally the Midwest and Southwest regions—and also syndicated to additional markets beyond that area by World Broadcasting Co.

Extant Episodes: 135 (approximately).

CAST & CREDITS

Producer—Russell C. Comer.

Writers—Robert M. Burtt, Wilfred (Bill) G. Moore.

Announcer—Ed Prentiss.

Leads—Title role played by John Frank (1933–36), Jack Schlicter (1946–47); Speed Robertson, played by Shelby Storck and Robert Fiske.

Support Roles—Al Christi, Twila Comer, Art Ellison.

More than just a juvenile adventure that simply stirred the imaginations of youngsters (especially boys) about flying, this Cleveland-originated series (later from Chicago) delved into danger and occasional criminal activity. At 16, Allen was a messenger for the Kansas City Air Terminal during aviation's earliest years and—in his series' formative stages—a novice pilot for National Airways. Along with his instructor and idol, ace pilot Speed Robertson, the pair tackled dangerous global aerial missions.

When Jimmie received his "wings," he flew daredevil expeditions on a plane christened the Blue Bird Special. Jimmie and pal Speed solved crimes of varied descriptions, including at least one murder. Their enemies went under the tags of Black Pete and Digger Dawson. Jimmie and Speed faced a sky full of airmail robbers, kidnappers, spies, saboteurs, bandits, swindlers, espionage agents and a few mad scientists. For diversionary relief, Flash Lewis, an anecdote-laden plane mechanic, could distract them, and so could Jimmie's lithe, raven-haired love interest, Barbara Croft. It was presumably the stuff that rudimentary imaginations were made of in the 1930s.

Burtt and Moore, who penned this fictional series, made a mint by perfecting aviation tales. While *The Air Adventures of Jimmie Allen* was never as popular as some other aerial adventures (e.g. *Captain Midnight, Hop Harrigan, Sky King* and possibly *Tailspin Tommy*), *Allen* was the first of the form. Burtt and Moore eventually honed their talents to bring all but the last of those subsequent heavenward heroes to radio's youngest ears.

More than three million adolescents joined a Jimmie Allen Flying Club created to foster fan interaction and loyalty. Copious premiums were offered at the addresses of local Skelly service stations: comic books and other printed adventures, maps, a pilot's creed, photos, identification bracelets, flight wing pins, membership emblems, "personal" greetings by mail from Jimmie Allen himself, picture puzzles, secret service whistles and an Allen album. A club newsletter was mailed to 600,000 youngsters weekly. Tens of thousands of fans, parents, siblings, grandparents, friends and neighbors attended Jimmie Allen air races in major markets in which the show aired. Flying lessons, model planes and other promotions were byproducts at those events.

The show debuted over just three stations on Feb. 23, 1933: KLZ, Denver; KDAF, Kansas City; and KVOO, Tulsa. The project quickly drew another seven stations with more added sporadically.

A real 16-year-old lad, Murray McLean, was engaged to make personal appearances as Jimmie. By 1936 the character was so popular that Paramount made a Jimmie Allen film, *Sky Parade*, directed by Otho Lovering, in which the *real* Jimmie Allen starred.

There was also a Big Little Book about Jimmie Allen co-authored by Burtt and Moore.

A reviewer may have hit the nail on the head when he assessed: "The heyday of Jimmie Allen was 1933 to 1936, when boys from coast to coast had great dreams of piloting one of those double-winged beauties themselves someday."

Alias Jimmy Valentine

On the Air: Jan. 18–April 12, 1938, NBC Blue, Tuesday, 9:30 p.m.; June 6, 1938–Feb. 27, 1939, NBC Blue, Monday, 7 p.m. 30 minutes.
Theme Song: *If I Should Lose You.*
Sponsors: Larus & Brothers Co. for Edgeworth pipe tobacco (through April 1938); Sterling Drugs Inc. for Dr. Lyons tooth powder and a myriad of other health and beauty aids (from June 1938).
Extant Episodes: None known.

CAST & CREDITS

Producers—Anne Hummert, Frank Hummert.
Writer—Doris Halman.
Announcer—Dick Joy.
Lead—Title role of Lee Randall ("Alias Jimmy Valentine") played by Bert Lytell, James Meighan.

An ex-con and reformed safecracker applied his talents and enormous underworld contacts to abet the forces of law and order. In serialized format he became a bank clerk, creating a stir by falling for the banker's daughter, already the object of another clerk's intentions. That peer decided to wreak havoc on Valentine, prompting the never-to-be-resolved query: "Can a protagonist go straight and overcome his impasse?" It was true formulaic Hummert.

Short story writer O. Henry introduced this mythical hero in *The Retrieved Reformation.* The tale was adapted for a stage play by Paul Armstrong in 1909 under the same handle as the later radio series.

James Meighan, the second actor to play Valentine, became one of radio's (and the Hummerts') most prolific thespians. Over a long career he played the leading man or a support player in numerous daytime dramas, and is perhaps best recalled as Larry Noble in *Backstage Wife* and Kerry Donovan in *Just Plain Bill.* Other series in which he had recurring parts: *Against the Storm, By Kathleen Norris, City Desk, Death Valley Days, Dot and Will, The Adventures of The Falcon, Flash Gordon, I Love Linda Dale, Lone Journey, Lora Lawton, Marie the Little French Princess, Mohawk Treasure Check, Orphans of Divorce, The Romance of Helen Trent, Second Husband, Special Agent.*

The Amazing Adventures of Flash Gordon see Flash Gordon

The Amazing Interplanetary Adventures of Flash Gordon
see Flash Gordon

The Amazing Mr. Malone
(aka *Murder and Mr. Malone*, aka *John J. Malone for the Defense*, aka *Attorney John J. Malone*)

On the Air: *Murder and Mr. Malone.* Jan. 11, 1947–April 17, 1948, ABC, Saturday, 9:30 p.m.; *The Amazing Mr. Malone.* April 24–May 29, 1948, ABC, Saturday, 9:30 p.m.; June 5–Dec. 4, 1948, ABC, Saturday, 8:30 p.m.; Dec. 11, 1948–March 26, 1949, ABC, Saturday, 9:30 p.m.; Sept. 21–Nov. 2, 1949, ABC, Wednesday, 8 p.m.; Nov. 6, 1949– Sept. 24, 1950, ABC, Sunday, 7:30 p.m.; May 25–July 13, 1951, ABC, Friday, 9 p.m. 30 minutes.
Sponsor: Guild Wines (Jan. 11, 1947–March 26, 1949); Sustained (Sept. 21, 1949–July 13, 1951).
Extant Episodes: 11.

CAST & CREDITS
Producer—Bernard L. Schubert.
Directors—Bill Rousseau, Richard Lewis (starting May 15, 1951).
Writers—Craig Rice (pen name of Georgiana Ann Randolph), Eugene Wang.
Music—Dick Aurant, John Duffy, Rex Koury.
Sound Effects—Jack Robinson.
Announcers—Dresser Dahlstead, Arthur Gary, Art Gilmore, Dick Tufeld.
Lead—Title role played by Frank Lovejoy, Gene Raymond (starting Sept. 21, 1949), George Petrie (starting May 25, 1951).
Support Roles—Tom Collins, William Conrad, Betty Lou Gerson, Frank Graham, Larry Haines (Lieutenant Brooks), Peter Leeds, Frances Robinson (Malone's secretary).

A Chicago criminal attorney, John J. Malone, was the central figure, purportedly "fiction's most famous criminal lawyer"—

a claim *Perry Mason* and several more counselors could easily challenge. Potential culprits in an as-yet-uncommitted felony were named at the launch of the weekly episodes. When the crime became fact, a suspect was arrested and John J. Malone, "the best mouthpiece in Chicago," defended the individual. Turning detective, Malone questioned all of the aforementioned suspects, snaring the perpetrator in the final moments.

Based on a character created by novelist Craig Rice, the program initially appeared as *Murder and Mr. Malone*, changing to the better-recalled title in 1948. Before it was finished the moniker shifted to *John J. Malone for the Defense*, then to *Attorney John J. Malone* and—near the end of the run—reverted to *Murder and Mr. Malone*, creating a true identity crisis.

Speaking of Frank Lovejoy, the Hollywood star who was first to play Malone, one reviewer wrote: "Lovejoy played the kind of part he did best—that of a cynical, somewhat humorless man with a keen analytical mind sharpened by years of courtroom fencing."

From Sept. 24, 1951, through March 10, 1952, Lee Tracy starred as the famous Chicago barrister in a live half-hour video performance of *The Amazing Mr. Malone*. It alternated weeks on ABC-TV with *Mr. District Attorney*.

The Amazing Mr. Smith

On the Air: April 7–June 30, 1941, MBS, Monday, 8 p.m. 30 minutes.
Sponsor: American Can Co.
Extant Episodes: One.

CAST & CREDITS
Director—George McGarrett.
Writers—Martin Gosch, Howard Harris.
Music—Harry Salter.
Announcer—Harry Von Zell.

Leads—Title role of Gregory Smith played by Keenan Wynn; Herbie, Smith's butler, chauffeur and valet, played by Charlie Cantor.

Support Roles—John Brown, Cliff Carpenter, Santos Ortega, Elizabeth Reller.

A former G. I., independently wealthy, having the wherewithal to go anywhere and do anything, evolved into an amateur sleuth in this droll comedy-mystery. Gregory Smith became "a carefree young man who runs into trouble galore and becomes an involuntary detective," according to the program's epigraph.

Of nearly a dozen published sources that reliably offer data on obscure, short-run series such as *The Amazing Mr. Smith*, one—and only one—purports that the feature was reprised during the 1946–47 radio season on CBS. It supposedly included Alan Johnston in the title role with Ed Brophy as Herbie. Ken Niles announced, Lud Gluskin conducted the orchestra and former writers Martin Gosch and Howard Harris produced. When about 1500 subscribers to an old time radio website were asked to confirm or deny if there was a "second season" for the program, none could respond affirmatively. Rather than perpetuate a potential myth, we must state that no authentic proof of a reported CBS run has surfaced to date.

The Amazing Nero Wolfe see *The Adventures of Nero Wolfe*

The American Adventures of Bulldog Drummond see *Bulldog Drummond*

American Agent
(aka *Bob Barclay, American Agent*)

On the Air: Dec. 6, 1950–Sept. 26, 1951, ABC, Wednesday, 8 p.m. 30 minutes.
Sponsor: Mars Candy Co. for Milky Way, Mars, Snickers, Forever Yours and other confectionery treats.
Extant Episodes: 58 (complete run), plus all rehearsals and two audition tapes.

CAST & CREDITS
Producer—George W. Trendle.
Announcer—Jay Michael.
Lead—Bob Barclay, played by Jack McCarthy.
Support Roles—WXYZ, Detroit, extensive drama company members.

A brief, little-recalled tale of a double agent who attempted to filter out anti-government subversives under the guise of being a legitimate foreign correspondent for the mythical *Amalgamated News*. This soldier of fortune, Bob Barclay, took his share of lumps, albeit more of the stressful kind rather than physical abuse.

Newsmen everywhere, it seemed, took potshots at this well-intentioned series, hurling brickbats at both the network and the sponsor. No respectable newsman, they claimed, would ever stoop to becoming an undercover double agent. The situation intensified for an American journalist, William Oatis, who was imprisoned at the time in Czechoslovakia on an espionage charge. The show was viewed as hurting his case. Probably in no small measure due to these sustained, vitriolic outbursts—despite decent ratings—the network allowed the drama to slip away quietly after only a few months.

This series was considered one of the lesser lights attributed to producer George W. Trendle. Trendle had a hand in the creation and production of *The Lone Ranger*, *The Green Hornet* and *Sergeant Preston and the Challenge of the Yukon*, among several better known productions.

Ann of the Airlanes

On the Air: Mid 1930s, Syndicated, Week-days. 15 minutes.
Sponsor: The series was sold in local markets.
Extant Episodes: 65 (complete run—13 weeks).

CAST & CREDITS

Producer—Comer Productions.
No credits given for individual cast performers.

Ann was the heroine of a transcribed day-time juvenile adventure show. She enlisted in an airline stewardess-training program. Upon completion, her professional duties led her to cross paths with multiple facets of political intrigue as she encountered subversive agents and diamond smugglers. The series was one of the earliest adolescent broadcast features with a heroine instead of a hero as its protagonist.

Ann Scotland see The Affairs of Ann Scotland

Are These Our Children?

On the Air: Sept. 29, 1946–Dec. 28, 1947, ABC, Sunday, 4 p.m.; Jan. 8–22, 1948, ABC, Thursday, 10 p.m.
Sponsor: Sustained.
Extant Episodes: Five.

CAST & CREDITS

Director/Writer—Gilbert Thomas.
Music—Phil Bovero.
Announcer—John Galbraith.
Support Roles—Herbert Ellis, Helen Kleeb, Norma Jean Rose.

An obscure dramatic series that covered issues of juvenile delinquency—and how to cope with them. Its narratives were accompanied by live exchanges on given themes including divorce, the mother complex, parental neglect and racial prejudice.

Juvenile delinquency court case files supplied the foundation for the scenarios and discussions. While names were altered, the incidents "occurred today and yesterday and the day before to people who didn't ask 'Are these our children?'" Humanity, taken together, it was surmised, was often due whatever culpability was assessed.

Created by Gilbert Thomas, the radio series was based on a 1931 RKO theatrical production under the same banner. In that Wesley Ruggles-directed film with screenplay by Howard Estabrook and minus prominent stars, a good kid with a clean record committed a robbery, killed a man and wound up on death row. Authorities sought to understand why he had chosen such a disappointing route, irrefutably a prelude to the later radio series.

Armstrong of the SBI

On the Air: Sept. 5, 1950–June 28, 1951, ABC, Tuesday/Thursday, 7:30 p.m. 30 minutes.
Sponsor: General Mills Inc. for Wheaties "breakfast of champions" cereal.
Extant Episodes: One.

CAST & CREDITS

Producer/Director—James Jewell.
Writers—Thomas Elvidge, Paul Fairman, Alan Fishburn, Donald Gallagher, James Jewell (chief writer and story editor), Jack Lawrence, Kermit Slobb.
Announcers—Ken Nordine, Ed Prentiss.
Leads—Title role played by Charles Flynn; Vic Hardy (director of the SBI and a reformed criminal), played by Ken Griffin, Carlton KaDell; Billy Fairfield, played by Dick York; Betty Fairfield, played by Patricia Dunlap.

Hudson High alumnus Jack Armstrong abruptly grew up in 1950 and departed his traditional pre-supper hour juvenile adventure timeslot as he approached two decades on the air. In a bold stroke of folly he landed in an after-supper fantasy thriller after undergoing an overnight metamorphosis. By then the chief investigator for the Scientific Bureau of Investigation (a federal organization that all but echoed the FBI), he was thrust into twice weekly sagas of suspenseful counterintelligence. There, according to one critic, he brought "the gigantic forces of government down not only on gangsters and killers, but on people guilty of such nefarious crimes as game poaching on federal land and falsifying weather reports!" It was to be a dismal end to a promising adolescent who had earlier held legions of youngsters in the palm of his hand, youngsters who must have surely inquired of parents and guardians: "Why can't we have [the old] Jack back?"

The significantly more prominent *Jack Armstrong, the All-American Boy* adventure show (one observer dubbed the title character "radio's champion teenage globetrotter"), of which this was a derivative, aired between July 31, 1933, and June 1, 1950. It was a late afternoon juvenile serial broadcast over CBS, MBS, NBC Blue and ABC. Its longtime sponsor was General Mills, closely identified with Wheaties cereal. (See separate entry below, *Jack Armstrong, the All-American Boy.*)

Author Jim Harmon, noting the differences between *Jack Armstrong, the All-American Boy* and *Armstrong of the SBI*, drew this comparison from his own adolescent age: "The illusion of reality was gone forever. It was disillusioning to find that the stories about people like Jack Armstrong were just *stories* and could be hacked and crammed into thirty minutes, instead of having to be *lived* day by day.... I listened to the complete half-hour stories of Jack Armstrong more faithfully than I had the serial.... Now I knew Jack

wasn't real, and he was no longer a threat to me with his smug superiority. I was more comfortable with the phony half-hour Jack Armstrong than I had been with his 'real' fifteen-minutes-a-day self."

On the final episode of *Armstrong of the SBI* titled "The Deadliest of the Species," Jack warred against a feminine drug pusher. When her male companion failed to surrender to him, the model, fair-haired, morally straight arrow Jack Armstrong drew his gun and plugged the felon. There was no mention following the incident that that was the finale of an 18-year run featuring Jack on the air—merely a statement that a new show (short-lived circus detective *Mr. Mercury*) would occupy the time period the following week. It was, regrettably, the way radio kissed off a lot of its former instruments of grandeur.

Fred King wrote a book and prepared a log on this series.

Attorney at Law
(aka *Terry Regan, Attorney at Law*)

On the Air: Jan. 3–May 27, 1938, NBC Blue, Weekdays, 10:30 a.m.; May 30–June 29, 1938, NBC Blue, Weekdays, 3 p.m.; July 5–Aug. 30, 1938, NBC, Tuesday, 9:30 p.m. 15 minutes (Jan. 3–June 29, 1938), 30 minutes (thereafter).

Sponsor: S. C. Johnson and Sons Co. for Johnson's wax and an extensive line of household, business and automotive cleaning products.

Extant Episodes: Two.

CAST & CREDITS

Producer—Cecil Underwood.
Writer—Milton Geiger.
Music—Billy Mills (orchestra).
Announcers—Fort Pearson (through June 29, 1938), Harlow Wilcox (July 5–Aug. 30, 1938).
Leads—Title role played by Jim Ameche (through June 29, 1938), Henry Hunter,

pseudonym for actor Arthur Jacobson (July 5–Aug. 30, 1938); Sally Dunlap (Regan's secretary), played by Fran Carlon (through June 29, 1938), Betty Winkler (July 5–Aug. 30, 1938).

Support Roles—Lucy Gilman (Regan's sister), Grace Lockwood (Regan's mother), June Meredith (Dorothy Wallace Webb), Fred Sullivan (Regan's father).

In 1938 a youthful, single, suave criminal lawyer, Terry Regan, became the precursor of a line of audio courtroom counselors. In atypical but formulaic soap opera tradition he interrupted the homemakers' day with mystery, mayhem and murder on behalf of S. C. Johnson and Sons. When the firm's ballyhooed *Fibber McGee & Molly* departed its venerated evening timeslot for a two-month hiatus that summer, Johnson plugged the half-hour with *Regan*, its new matinee defender. Expanding his daily 15 minutes of fame to a weekly half-hour, the move boosted *Regan's* audience significantly. Meanwhile, his resolve for truth and righteousness remained steadfast, as it had before he switched from daylight to dark. Thirty minutes allowed him to tidy up each case in a single episode. But when *McGee & Molly* returned refreshed from their vacation, unfortunately, *Regan* had nowhere to go. Johnson was overjoyed with the McGees and Terry Regan had bowed out as a ladies man weeks earlier. In less than nine months since his radio debut, the crusading counselor was washed up. The legacy he instituted, however, was to impressively outshine his brief sojourn by many years.

Drama mama Irna Phillips, one of the most powerful forces to be reckoned with in soap opera, with tremendous creative ability, recognized the possibilities of populating the genre with professionals (physicians, ministers, nurses, lawyers and similar occupations) quite early. In *Attorney at Law* she honed her technique, refining it for several more series to follow.

Regan was the first of a quartet of daytime dramas to introduce the courtroom as their centerpiece. Others: *Her Honor, Nancy James* (Oct. 3, 1938–July 28, 1939), *Portia Faces Life* (Oct. 7, 1940–June 29, 1951), *Perry Mason* (Oct. 18, 1943–Dec. 30, 1955). Of the foursome, none was nearly as influential or as well remembered as *Mason*, "defender of human rights … champion of all those who seek justice." The crusading crime counselor—who later became television's best-recalled criminal attorney—took matinee murder to new extremes: on radio, he offered some of the most suspenseful tales ever to cross the ether, in sunlight or in moonlight.

Attorney for the Defense

(aka *Jonathan Brixton's Murder Cases*)

On the Air: June 9–July 28, 1946, MBS, Sunday, 5 p.m. 30 minutes.
Sponsor: Sustained.
Extant Episodes: Two.

Cast & Credits

Producer—Herbert Rice.
Director—Ernest Ricca.
Writer—Milton Kramer.
Lead—Roger Allen (initially, then Jonathan Brixton), played by Michael Raffetto and Al Hodge.
Support Player—Barton Yarborough.

In an all-too-brief eight-week summer stint, this barrister-laden crime drama focused on heroic young lawyers: initially there was Roger Allen, but he was soon succeeded by Jonathan Brixton. Based in San Francisco, they attempted to identify guilty parties in the slayings for which their clients were charged. Weekly they confronted an uncompromising, politically assertive district attorney who seldom allowed the defense team any breathing room.

Alumni of *One Man's Family* and *I Love a Mystery* blended their talents once again during the early episodes of this series. Michael Raffetto and Barton Yarborough were both permanent fixtures in several well-received Carlton E. Morse drama creations.

Attorney John J. Malone see The Amazing Mr. Malone

The Avenger

On the Air: Oct. 25, 1945–April 18, 1946, Syndicated. 30 minutes. (Earlier this series appeared weekly on New York City's WHN, between July 18, 1941 and Nov. 3, 1942.)
Sponsor: Local advertisers in each market.
Extant Episodes: 26 (complete run).

CAST & CREDITS
Producer—Charles Michelson.
Writers—Gil and Ruth Braun, Walter B. Gibson.
Music—Doc Whipple.
Announcer—George Ansbro.
Leads—Jim Brandon, played by James Monks and Dick Janaver; Fern Collier, played by Helen Adamson.

Could more than one radio figure "know what evil lurks in the hearts of men"? In this copycat version of the infinitely more memorable disappearing act integrated into *The Shadow*, elements of that superior wizard's powers allowed biochemist Jim Brandon to conquer vice without revealing himself, too. A drop-dead gorgeous subordinate, Fern Collier, who alone knew his true identity, accompanied Brandon on missions against those evil denizens.

Through "numerous scientific experiments," the mythical Jim Brandon developed a couple of supernatural innovations that assisted him in his battle against corruption—a secret diffusion capsule that shrouded him "in a black light of invisibility," and a telepathic indicator, permitting him to interpret the "thought flashes" of other people. While the show was purely a charade, fans that couldn't get enough of *The Shadow* every week could pick up a second dose of its antics here.

The astonishing similarities with *The Shadow*, a forerunner, contemporary and successor crime series (1930–54), are readily explained by the connection of Walter B. Gibson to each. He created and inspired both dramas. Both were an outgrowth of fictional tales originally appearing in magazines issued by Street and Smith, a widely respected publisher of pulp fiction periodicals.

The radio series is not to be confused with a spy drama, *The Avengers*, that appeared on ABC-TV between 1966 and 1969 starring Patrick Macnee. Despite the similarity in titles, their premises were altogether disparate.

B-Bar-B Ranch see Bobby Benson and the B-Bar-B Riders

B-Bar-B Songs see Bobby Benson and the B-Bar-B Riders

Bandwagon Mysteries
(aka *Rogue's Gallery*)

On the Air: *Bandwagon Mysteries.* June 24–Sept. 16, 1945, NBC, Sunday, 7:30 p.m.; *Rogue's Gallery*, Sept. 27, 1945–June 20, 1946, MBS, Thursday, 8:30 p.m.; *Bandwagon Mysteries.* June 23–Sept. 22, 1946, NBC, Sunday, 7:30 p.m.; June 8–Sept. 28, 1947, NBC, 7:30 p.m.; *Rogue's Gallery.* Nov. 29, 1950–Nov. 21, 1951, ABC, Wednesday, 9 p.m. 30 minutes.

Sponsor: F. W. Fitch Co. for Fitch shampoo and other hair care properties (summer series and 1945–46); Sustained (ABC).
Extant Episodes: 22 (*Rogue's Gallery*).

CAST & CREDITS

Producer—Charles Vanda.
Directors—Clark Andrews, Dee Engelbach, Jack Lyman.
Writer—Ray Buffum.
Music—Milton Kay (organ), Leith Stevens (orchestra).
Announcers—Carl Caruso, Jim Doyle.
Leads—Richard Rogue played by Dick Powell (1945–46), Barry Sullivan (1947), Chester Morris and Paul Stewart (1950–51); Eugor (Rogue's alter ego), played by Peter Leeds.
Support Roles—Tony Barrett, Gloria Blondell, Staats Cotsworth (District Attorney), Robert Dryden, Bill Lipton, Lou Merrill, Gerald Mohr, Bryna Raeburn, Lurene Tuttle, Ted von Eltz, Lawson Zerbe.

Wisecracking private detective Richard Rogue was the drama's central figure. Rogue stalked luscious dames, spied on unfaithful spouses, solved slayings and sheltered eyewitnesses, commonly displaying a tough façade. In one episode, he alleged: "I collect murders." When he was knocked out (and that was frequently), his awareness ascended to "cloud eight." There he interacted with a tittering alter ego, Eugor (or *Rogue* in reverse), "a nasty little spook." The duo cogitated over the hero's current plight. Regaining awareness, Rogue shook off his stupor, well aware of the pathway he must follow. If such trivia seemed ludicrous, it was, but it allowed the detective's subconscious to consider important elements he might have disregarded. He lacked a mortal trusted confidant, and so the series' sideline eccentricity offered an engaging twist.

In deference to its sponsor, which underwrote *The Fitch Bandwagon* (1938–48)—initially a showcase for the nation's big bands—*Bandwagon Mysteries* was launched as a warm weather filler for the venerable series. Although the dramatization pursued similar notions on shifting to other networks in cold weather extensions, its title was altered to *Rogue's Gallery* there.

Dick Powell, who before that was singularly acclaimed as a vocalist, exploited this dramatic outing as a step to a serious acting career. From 1949 to 1953 Powell was to become even more firmly entrenched in that arena as the star of radio's *Richard Diamond, Private Detective*.

Jay Hickerson produced a log for the *Rogue's Gallery* series.

Barry Craig, Confidential Investigator

(aka *Barry Crane, Confidential Investigator* [initial title])

On the Air: Oct. 3, 1951–April 2, 1952, NBC, Wednesday, 10 p.m.; March 18–Sept. 9, 1952, NBC, Tuesday, 8:30 p.m.; Sept. 24–Oct. 15, 1952, NBC, Wednesday; Oct. 19, 1952–Sept. 6, 1953, NBC, Sunday, 10:30 p.m.; Sept. 15, 1953–Sept. 7, 1954, NBC, Tuesday, 8:30 p.m.; Oct. 3–Dec. 26, 1954, NBC, Sunday, 8:30 p.m.; Jan. 5–April 27, 1955, NBC, Wednesday, 8:30 p.m.; May 5–June 30, 1955, NBC, Thursday, 9 p.m. 30 minutes.
Sponsor: Sustained except for three brief associations with commercial enterprises—Lewis-Howe (March 18–June 10, 1952), Knomark (March 15–May 17, 1953), Coleman Co. (Sept. 15–Oct. 13, 1953).
Extant Episodes: 59.

CAST & CREDITS

Producer—Van Woodward.
Directors—Himan Brown, Jaime Del Valle, Arthur Jacobson, Ed King, Andrew C. Love.
Writers—George Lefferts, John Roeburt, Louis Vittes.
Leads—Title role played by William Gargan; Lieutenant Travis Rogers, played by Ralph Bell.
Support Roles—Parley Baer, Ralph Bell, Elspeth Eric, Parker Fennelly, Betty Lou

Gerson, John Gibson, Mitzi Gould, Virginia Gregg, Vivi Janiss, Joseph Kearns, Jan Miner, Arnold Moss, Jack Moyles, Santos Ortega, Barney Phillips, Byrna Raeburn, Lurene Tuttle.

This New Yorker, one of many introduced on the air as "America's number one detective" or similar sobriquets, pledged to keep his clients' business securely classified, hence the title of his series. Working alone (but narrating his own adventures) out of his Madison Avenue digs, Craig primarily made money assisting individuals who—for one reason or other—couldn't involve professional law enforcement in their dilemmas. Complained a media critic, his cases "seldom rose above B-grade detective fare."

William Gargan, who for a couple of years carried the title role of predecessor sleuth *Martin Kane, Private Detective*, had a weird experience in his personal life. He was employed previously by a legitimate detective agency. While there, he poked fun at the bungling that he perceived was performed by the radio detectives.

Barry Crane, Confidential Investigator see Barry Craig, Confidential Investigator

Behind Prison Bars see Twenty Thousand Years in Sing Sing

The Big Guy

On the Air: May 7–Nov. 5, 1950, NBC, Sunday, 5 p.m.
Sponsor: Sustained.
Extant Episodes: Three.

CAST & CREDITS
Director—Thomas Mattigan.
Writer—Peter Barry.
Music—Jack Ward, George Wright.
Announcers—Fred Collins, Peter Roberts.
Leads—Joshua Sharp, played by John Henry Calvin; Debbie Sharp, played by Denise Alexander and Joan Lazer; Joshua Sharp Jr., played by David Alexander.
Support Roles—Anita Anton, Joseph Bell, Burford Hampden, Peggy Laughton, Sandy Strauss (Risky Skinner), Lyle Sudrow, Linda Watkins, Bill Zuckert.

Working on a cash-only basis, PI Joshua Sharp, a widower, minded his "nearest and dearest"—his children—while satisfying his clients. (To the kids, he was "the friendly magician ... the fabulous hero ... the giant among giants ... the big guy.") Unlike some in his business, he leaned on deductive reasoning instead of taking a violent stance in crimesolving. This straight arrow prided himself on the integrity he brought to the job, too: "There are some things that even the biggest of big guys can't do," he averred, when urged to run afoul of the law.

John Henry Calvin, the actor portraying the hero in the drama, faded from radio about as quietly as he arrived. The obscure thespian's name is unrecorded by all of the major audio historiographers that traditionally document the comings and goings of program leads. Calvin apparently drifted into radio for this feature and departed, and is believed to have never played on any network series again.

The Big Story

On the Air: April 2, 1947–July 2, 1952, NBC, Wednesday, 10 p.m. (until 1951, when it shifted to 9:30 p.m.); Aug. 27, 1952–June 17, 1953, NBC, Wednesday, 9:30 p.m.; Sept. 23, 1953–June 2, 1954, NBC, Wednesday, 9:30 p.m.; Sept. 8, 1954–March 23, 1955, NBC, Wednesday, 9:30 p.m. 30 minutes.

Theme Song: *Prowess in Battle* from *Ein Heldenleben* (Richard Strauss).

Sponsors: Brown & Williamson Tobacco Co. for Pall Mall cigarettes (through June 2, 1954); American Tobacco Co. for Lucky Strike cigarettes (Sept. 8, 1954–March 16, 1955).

Extant Episodes: 34.

CAST & CREDITS

Producer—Bernard J. Prockter.
Directors—Harry Ingram, Thomas F. Vietor, Jr.
Writers—Max Erlich, Gail Ingram, Arnold Perl.
Music—Vladimir Selinsky.
Sound Effects—Al Scott.
Announcers—Ernest Chappell, Cy Harrice.
Narrator/Lead—Robert Sloane as himself.
Support Roles—Robert Dryden, Alice Frost, Betty Garde, Bernard Grant, Craig McDonnell, William J. Smith, Bill Quinn.

This was an anthology that was absorbed in violent crime cases from the past exposed by honest-to-goodness journalists. While murder was at the core of many of the dramatizations, an NBC puff piece rallied behind each featured newsman, proclaiming him to be "a reporter who has solved a crime, exposed a corrupt political administration, smashed a racket, or performed some other notable public service." To avoid accusations of pretrial publicity, vintage cases alone were brought to life on the sound stage. And only the reporter and his newspaper were unmistakably identified; names of the other figures on the program were carefully disguised. At the conclusion of the weekly episodes the sponsor presented a $500 check to the newsman whose story had been aired. Along the way the series wallowed in realism to a fault, a trait particularly in short supply on most other theatrical broadcasts.

In its first year on the air *The Big Story* leaped into a challenging race for dominance in listenership standings with Bing Crosby's *Philco Radio Time*, then aired over ABC on the same day at the same hour (Wednesday, 10 o'clock). When Crosby switched to CBS two years later—having been burned by the NBC drama during several strategic ratings periods—he opted for a 9:30 slot, out of harm's way, giving him the ability to croon without the danger of being topped by an unfamiliar newspaperman again.

When producer Bernard J. Prockter envisioned a show based on the exploits of actual journalists, he concluded that their big stories would almost indubitably be limited to murder mysteries, political corruption cases, et cetera. In addition to developing an appealing vehicle for introducing the weekly narratives, Prockter liked the idea of extolling correspondents who had been ignored by Pulitzer prize panels. Old newspaper files and referrals provided grist for the episodes.

Narrator Bill Sloane took his role to the tube on Sept. 16, 1949, when NBC-TV began running a Friday night televersion lauding courageous journalists. The show lasted longer than Sloane did; the network run ended June 28, 1957, but Sloane departed in 1954. Norman Rose replaced him and was followed by Ben Grauer a year later. In a one-year syndicated edition in 1957–58, Burgess Meredith hosted the series' finale.

Big Town

On the Air: Oct. 19, 1937–July 12, 1938, CBS, Tuesday, 8 p.m.; Sept. 20, 1938–July 18, 1939, CBS, Tuesday, 8 p.m.; Sept. 19, 1939–June 11, 1940, CBS, Tuesday, 8 p.m.; Oct. 9, 1940–July 2, 1941, CBS, Wednesday, 8 p.m.; Oct. 8, 1941–Jan. 14, 1942, CBS, Wednesday, 8 p.m.; Jan. 22–July 2, 1942, CBS, Thursday, 9:30 p.m.; Oct. 5, 1943–June 22, 1948, CBS, Tuesday, 8 p.m.; Sept. 14, 1948–Dec. 25, 1951, NBC, Tuesday, 10 p.m.; Dec. 12,

1951–June 25, 1952, CBS, Wednesday, 8 p.m. 30 minutes.

Theme Song: *Tell the Story.*

Sponsors: Lever Brothers Co. for Rinso detergent (Oct. 19, 1937–July 2, 1942); Sterling Drugs Inc. for Ironized Yeast supplement, Bayer aspirin pain reliever and other health care products (Oct. 5, 1943–June 22, 1948); Lever Brothers Co. for Lifebuoy soap (Sept. 14, 1948–June 25, 1952).

Extant Episodes: 45.

CAST & CREDITS

Producers—Clark Andrews, Phil Cohen.

Producer/Director/Writer—Jerry McGill.

Directors—Joseph Bell, William N. Robson, Richard Uhl, Crane Wilbur.

Music—John Gart (organ), Leith Stevens.

Sound Effects—Ray Erlenborn, John Powers.

Announcers—Carlton KaDell, Ken Niles, Dwight Weist.

Leads—Steve Wilson, played by Edward G. Robinson (1937–42), Edward Pawley (after 1942), Walter Greaza (final few months of the run); Lorelei Kilbourne, played by Claire Trevor, Ona Munson (c1940), Fran Carlon (after 1942).

Support Roles—Bill Adams, Mason Adams, Casey Allen, Helen Brown, Ted de Corsia, Robert Dryden, Howard Duff, Gale Gordon (District Attorney Miller), Larry Haines, Jerry Hausner, Tommy Hughes, Cy Kendall, Ross Martin, Donald MacDonald, Ed McDonald (Reporter Tommy Hughes), Lou Merrill, Michael O'Day, George Petrie, Thelma Ritter, Jack Smart, Dwight Weist, Bobby Winkler, Paula Winslowe, Lawson Zerbe.

One reviewer acclaimed it "the most famous series of reporter dramas." Steve Wilson, managing editor of *The Illustrated Press* in Big Town, U.S.A., was its central character. Proving "the pen is mightier than the sword," Wilson relentlessly and fearlessly applied the power of the press while crusading against the denizens of the underworld. Embroiled in Wilson's daring was society editor Lorelei Kilbourne, a pawn in the hands of dubious creatures. The tales were purportedly derived from real newspaper accounts, contributing a note of authenticity and relevance to radio drama. Adding to their believability, the program intermittently explored such themes as racial and religious intolerance.

At its inception the series attracted a compelling staff of cinematic celebrities, quickly landing it among radio's top 10 shows. It would have been a tremendous boost for any drama to add Edward G. Robinson *or* Claire Trevor to the cast; to corral *both*, with the enormous prestige of their names and talent, gave the program incredible status.

Trevor (Lorelei Kilbourne) and producer Clark Andrews, who worked simultaneously on the show, experienced a real-life romance that culminated in marriage.

For many years the monthly newsletter of the Old Time Radio Club based in western New York state has appeared under the banner *The Illustrated Press.* The organization is one of a liberal number of similar groups fostering memories of vintage radio while circulating and preserving its historical data. Address (at the time this manuscript was prepared): Old Time Radio Club, 56 Christen Court, Lancaster, NY 14086.

While faintly censuring *Big Town* as "mundane" in a 1992 book, 25 years earlier—in a 1967 volume—author Jim Harmon esteemed the drama in near-reverential tones: "The *Illustrated Press* was a rugged training ground for aspiring newspapermen. I wouldn't be surprised if Brit Reid [*The Green Hornet*] and even Clark Kent [*Superman*] may have taken their early training there, dodging bullets, catching crooks, and writing a feature story on the back of a matchbook while hanging on to the rear bumper of a black sedan. Surely, if any newspaperman wanted to learn how to be a superman, he could do far worse than follow the example of Editor Steve Wilson."

The show originated from Hollywood from 1937 to 1942 before it was transferred to New York. Dramatic productions were usually staged without onlookers. However, Edward G. Robinson insisted that *Big Town* must be performed in front of a live studio audience. While it aired from Hollywood, the show's venue was the Wilshire Ebell Theatre, allowing for a large crowd of spectators. In this regard the drama's performances were similar to those of the eminently admired *Lux Radio Theatre*.

Actor Jerry Hausner provided some discerning insights when questioned by Leonard Maltin about his days on *Big Town*: "We would rehearse from 9:00 in the morning until ... 5:00 in the afternoon,... and while we were rehearsing, Edward G. Robinson had a card table with a typewriter on it. The author of that week's script had to sit there all day long, every day, and rewrite as we went along. He'd read a line and Eddie'd say, 'I don't like that one, cut that out, change this, change that.'... We had to sit there while this was being done. They rewrote and rewrote all week long, and if you were cut out, they waved you good-bye and you didn't get any money at all.... If your part stayed in and it was a minor supporting role, you wound up with $15, $20 for the week, $35 if you had a good part."

Big Town landed on the small screen in half-hour segments premiering over CBS-TV on Oct. 5, 1950. Repeating episodes ran concurrently from February to July 1953 on Dumont Television under the moniker *City Assignment*. Departing CBS in Sept. 16, 1954, the show relocated the next month, Oct. 11, at NBC-TV, appearing there through Oct. 2, 1956. In April 1952 it transferred from New York to Hollywood (reversing its radio pilgrimage), and became a filmed rather than a live production. From 1950 to 1954 actor Patrick McVey playing Steve Wilson was reduced to a mere reporter at *The Illustrated Press*. On video society columnist Lorelei Kilbourne was obviously sweet on Wilson. That part rotated among a cadre of actresses—Mary K. Wells, Julie Stevens, Jane Nigh, Beverly Tyler and Trudy Wroe. When the show moved to NBC, Mark Stevens became its producer and director and was cast as Wilson; his role was upgraded to its radio status (imagine!), managing editor. By 1955 Lorelei Kilbourne was gone, replaced by reporter Diane Walker, who was also romantically involved with Wilson. The show was widely syndicated then and later under multiple names—*Byline Steve Wilson*, *Headline* and *Heart of the City*.

After decades in which the series sponsor's product was not available in this country, an English company is now distributing the original red Lifebuoy soap with its characteristic "pure, clean, healthy aroma" (as depicted by product literature). It may be found on the Internet at www.lifebuoy.co.uk.

Billy Swift, Boy Detective

On the Air: 1938–39, Syndicated regionally in Arizona, California and adjacent Southwest territory, Saturday.
Sponsor: Sunkist Growers for Sunkist fruits and juices.
Extant Episodes: Two.

CAST & CREDITS
Announcers—Ken Carpenter, Bill Goodwin. Other cast members uncredited.

In a sense this was a series within a series. Syndicated by World Broadcasting System, *Sunkist Time* was distributed during the late 1930s as a weekday wake-up morning program. It featured recorded music and chatter. On Saturday mornings the emphasis shifted to the juvenile set, the same sponsor then offering the adventures of *Billy Swift, Boy Detective* to the same regional outlets. Swift fought crime with underpinnings of moral and ethical bromides. In a marketing ploy, he urged his young radio fans to join his Sunkist Secret Service club.

The Bishop and the Gargoyle

On the Air: Sept. 30–Dec. 2, 1936, NBC Blue, Wednesday, 9:30 p.m.; Jan. 11–Feb. 22, 1937, NBC Blue, Monday, 9 p.m.; July 7–Aug. 25, 1940, NBC, Sunday, 8 p.m.; Sept. 6–Oct. 4, 1940, NBC Blue, Friday, 8 p.m.; Oct. 8–Dec. 31, 1940, NBC Blue, Tuesday, 9:30 p.m.; Jan. 18, 1941–Jan. 3, 1942, NBC Blue, Saturday, 8:30 p.m. 30 minutes.
Sponsor: Standard Brands Inc. for Chase and Sanborn coffee and other victuals (July 7–Aug. 25, 1940); Sustained (otherwise).
Extant Episodes: None known.

CAST & CREDITS

Director—Joseph Bell.
Writer—Frank Wilson.
Leads—The bishop, played by Richard Gordon; the gargoyle, played by Milton Herman, Ken Lynch.

With a dilettante's interest in crime, a retiring bishop accepted a post on the parole board at Sing Sing prison in Ossining, New York. In the course of his duties he met a prisoner known only as the gargoyle. The bishop had occasion to befriend the convict and the two found they shared common ideals for the future. With the gargoyle's release imminent, the duo paired up to track criminals and bring them to justice. On occasion, when physical force was necessary to coerce an unwilling subject, the bishop deferred to the gargoyle, who supplied the necessary brawn.

In an early attempt to televise drama, NBC-TV experimented by presenting a single episode of this program to the na-

tion's handful of video set owners on Nov. 29, 1941. That chapter's title was "The Item of the Scarlet Ace."

The Black Hood

On the Air: July 5, 1943–Jan. 14, 1944, MBS, Weekdays, 5:15 p.m. 15 minutes.
Sponsor: Sustained.
Extant Episodes: One.

CAST & CREDITS

Leads—Kip Burland, played by Scott Douglas; Barbara Sutton, played by Marjorie Cramer.

The feature opened with an authoritative voice admonishing: "Criminals beware! The Black Hood is everywhere!" The hooded hero—actually rookie cop Kip Burland incognito—bellowed: "I, the Black Hood, do solemnly swear ... that neither threats ... nor bribes ... nor bullets ... nor death itself ... shall keep me from fulfilling my vow: to erase crime ... from the face of the earth!" While acquiring his powers from the hood he wore, Burland conjured up images of Lamont Cranston (*The Shadow*) clouding men's minds and Clark Kent (*Superman*) exchanging his business suit for a cape, and a long list of draped aural do-gooders (*Mr. Chameleon, The Green Hornet*, et al) whose costume changes allowed them to cleverly outwit the rapscallions they pursued. Several of these wizards took a companion—most often, a woman—into their confidence, revealing themselves and divulging the details of their supernatural abilities. Burland/Hood was no exception: he chose newswoman Barbara Sutton as his confidante; like the others, she assisted him in waging war on anyone with diabolical intents.

The Black Hood grew out of a popular comic strip, although its audio dimensions made it—according to one critic—"about the corniest [program] of old-time radio ... hokey-plus." Aimed at strictly juvenile fans, it joined a wave of "secret identity" shows launched on radio during the war years.

The Black Museum

On the Air: Jan. 1–June 24, 1952, MBS, Tuesday, 8 p.m.; Sept. 30–Oct. 21, 1952, Tuesday, 8 p.m.; Oct. 29, 1952, MBS, Wednesday, 8 p.m.; Nov. 11–Dec. 30, 1952, MBS, Tuesday, 8 p.m. 30 minutes.
Sponsor: F. Savor Co. (Sept. 30–Dec. 23, 1952); Sustained (otherwise).
Extant Episodes: 52.

CAST & CREDITS

Producer—Harry Alan Towers.
Host/Narrator—Orson Welles.

Narrator Orson Welles sifted through the Black Museum, Scotland Yard's "repository of death," picking up ordinary-looking artifacts that had figured in major crime investigations. As he held a length of twine, a hammer, a straight-edged razor or a silk scarf, he relayed the gory details behind them in this "gallery of death," while launching into another thriller narrative.

The British Broadcasting Corporation originated the series in London in 1951. Transcriptions were later aired over Mutual for an American audience.

Astute vintage radio buffs will handily recall that Orson Welles probably presided over the best remembered and most-talked-about radio broadcast of all time: "The War of the Worlds," a presentation on the *Mercury Theater* on Oct. 30, 1938. Mass hysteria set in across the nation as a consequence; millions panicked, believing the reports in the show to authentic, and that the eastern U.S. seaboard was being invaded by unfriendly aliens from Mars.

The Black Museum pursued a similar concept to NBC's *Whitehall 1212*, the two programs airing concurrently for most of their runs. (See separate entry below, *Whitehall 1212*.)

Blackstone, the Magic Detective
(aka *Blackstone, the Magician*)

On the Air: Oct. 3, 1948–April 3, 1949, MBS, Sunday, 2:45 p.m. 15 minutes.
Sponsor: Sustained.
Extant Episodes: 55.

CAST & CREDITS
Director—Carlo De Angelo.
Writers—Joan Webb, Nancy Webb.
Music—Bill Meeder (organ).
Announcer—Alan Kent.
Leads—Title role of Harry Blackstone played by Ed Jerome; John, played by Ted Osborne; Rhonda, played by Fran Carlon.

Former stage magician Harry Blackstone applied his talents to helping those in trouble. He performed magical tricks for his young friends John and Rhonda each week after overwhelming them with a baffling mystery case that soon drew to a magical conclusion. Narratives were retold in flashback sequences with the children given a chance to figure out the ending before "the world's greatest living magician" revealed it.

Ed Jerome, the master magician of this show, was lucky enough to land numerous recurring parts elsewhere in radio. His credits include *Aunt Jenny's Real Life Stories, By Kathleen Norris, The Cavalcade of America, Carol Kennedy's Romance, The Chase, Dimension X, The Man I Married, The March of Time, Mystery in the Air, Rich Man's Darling, The Theatre Guild on the Air, Trouble House, When a Girl Marries, A Woman of America* and *The Wonder Show*.

Blair of the Mounties

On the Air: c1935, Syndicated. 15 minutes.
Sponsor: Underwritten by entities in markets
 where it aired.
Extant Episodes: 28 (first 28 episodes).

CAST & CREDITS
Producer—Audisk Corp.
Director—G. Donald Grey.
Writer—Colonel Rhys Davies.
Leads—Title role played by Colonel Rhys
 Davies; Constable Marshall, played by Jack
 Abbott.

This tale of 39 episodes produced by Audisk Corp. was distributed by Conquest Alliance Co. of New York City to broadcast outlets in the U. S., Canada and Australia. It recalled the crime fighting adventures of a member of the famous Royal Canadian Mounted Police. The series was quite possibly inspired and influenced by an earlier one, *With Canada's Mounted Police.* (See separate entry below, *With Canada's Mounted Police.*)

Jack French, who did some serious exploratory research into radio series about the Royal Canadian Mounted Police, assessed: "Blair is not restricted to Canada, as other Mounties would be; in a few episodes we find him solving cases in Great Britain. Overall, the whole series is amateurishly written while the actor playing Blair comes across a trifle stuffy. Sound effects are minimal and Blair spends a lot of time in his office telling [Constable] Marshall what has already transpired."

The Blue Beetle

On the Air: May 15–Sept. 13, 1940, Syndicated, Wednesday and Friday. 30 minutes through June 21, afterwards 15 minutes.
Sponsor: Commercial ventures in markets where the show aired.
Extant Episodes: 36 (complete run).

CAST & CREDITS
Lead—Dan Garrett, played by Frank Lovejoy
 (through June 7).

An early comic book superhero's adventures formed the basis for this juvenile crime drama. Rookie cop Dan Garrett was near death after being gunned down when a mystical wizard known as Dr. Franz appeared. Franz provided the fallen patrolman with a secret liquid formula (2X) that could be ingested and which would magically impart superhuman powers. In so doing it transformed its user into the Blue Beetle, complete with blue chain armor regalia. Furthermore, Franz—the only individual to know Garrett's true identity—bestowed invisibility fluid on him, plus a poison detector ring and Franz's formula X4 to be applied in melting locks. Garrett waged ongoing war against gangsters in York City and left a recognizable calling card behind—some blue beetles. No silver bullets for him. One simply *had* to be a juvenile to comprehend and appreciate such drivel.

Typical episode titles were "Sabotage and Liquidation," "Murder for Profit," "The Frame Up," "Asylum of Dr. Drear" and "Jewel Mystery of Channel Island." After Frank Lovejoy departed, the series left its run of single episode stories behind, presenting only two-part tales. Part one was introduced on Wednesday with part two concluding that tale on Friday of the same week. The ploy may have increased listenership.

Chuck Juzek prepared a log of this series.

Bob Barclay, American Agent
see *American Agent*

Bobby Benson and Sunny Jim
see *Bobby Benson and the B-Bar-B Riders*

Bobby Benson and the B-Bar-B Riders

(aka *Bobby Benson's Adventures*, aka *Bobby Benson's H-Bar-O Rangers*, aka *B-Bar-B Ranch*, aka *B-Bar-B Songs*, aka *Songs of the B-Bar-B*, aka *Bobby Benson and Sunny Jim*)

On the Air: (Note: Due to conflicting data provided by usually dependable sources, it is impractical to confirm some of the days and times this series aired with authenticity. Over Mutual it routinely shifted between late afternoon time slots on weekdays, at times airing two, three or five episodes per week for only a few weeks. Recurrently the program moved in and out of multiple Sunday afternoon time slots, turning up briefly on other days for occasional runs.) *Bobby Benson's Adventures*, aka *Bobby Benson's H-Bar-O Rangers*. Nov. 14, 1932–March 24, 1933, CBS, Monday/Wednesday/Friday, 5 p.m.; Oct. 2, 1933–Dec. 11, 1936, CBS, Weekdays, 6:15 p.m.; *Bobby Benson and the B-Bar-B Riders*, et al. June 21–Sept. 15, 1949, MBS, Tuesday/Thursday, 5 p.m.; Sept. 19, 1949–Jan. 27, 1950, MBS, Monday/Wednesday/Friday, 5 p.m.; Feb. 6–Dec. 18, 1950, MBS, Monday, 8 p.m.; March 25–May 13, 1950, MBS, Saturday, 3 p.m.; April 2, 1950–Jan. 28, 1951, MBS, Sunday, 3 p.m.; Jan. 2–June 7, 1951, MBS, Tuesday/Thursday, hour unsubstantiated; May 19–July 21, 1951, MBS, Saturday, 5 p.m.; July 8, 1951–March 9, 1952, MBS, Sunday, 4 p.m.; Dec. 30, 1951–June 29, 1952, MBS, Sunday, hour unsubstantiated; June 9–Sept. 12, 1952, MBS, Weekdays, 5:30 p.m.; Nov. 17, 1952–June 4, 1954, MBS, Monday/Wednesday/Friday, hour unsubstantiated; June 14, 1954–June 17, 1955, MBS, Monday/Wednesday/Friday alternating with Tuesday/Thursday, 5:30 p.m. CBS, 15 minutes; MBS, mostly 30 but some 25-minute episodes from June 9, 1952.

Sponsor: Heckers H-O Oats cereal (Nov. 14, 1932–Dec. 11, 1936); Sustained (June 21, 1949–Jan. 28, 1951, May 19, 1951–March 9, 1952, June 9–Sept. 12, 1952, June 14, 1954–June 17, 1955); Kraft Foods Co. (Jan. 2–June 7, 1951, Nov. 17, 1952–June 4, 1954); Adams Chewing Gum Co. for Chiclets and Dentyne brands (Dec. 30, 1951–June 29, 1952).

Extant Episodes: 20, plus five of *Songs of the B-Bar-B*.

CAST & CREDITS

Creator/Producer—Herbert C. Rice.
Director—Bob Novak.
Writers—John Battle, David Dixon, Peter Dixon, James McMenemy (*Songs of the B-Bar-B*), Jim Sheehan.
Music—Ernestine Holmes (organ), Milton Kay (orchestra).
Sound Effects—Barney Beck, Frank Milano, Al Schaffer.
Announcers—"Two Gun" Andre Baruch, Carl Caruso, Bob Emerick, Art Millet, "Dangerous" Dan Seymour, "Cactus" Carl Warren.
Leads—Title role played by Richard Wanamaker (1932–March 1933), Billy Halop (October 1933–36), Ivan Cury (1949–50), Clyde Campbell (pseudonym for Clive Rice, April 1951–55); Tex Mason (aka Buck Mason), played by Herbert C. Rice (1932–36), Charles Irving (1949–51), Bob Haig (1952–55), and sporadically by Al Hodge, Neil O'Malley and Tex Ritter.
Support Roles—Jim Boles (multiple character roles), Florence Halop (Polly Armstead), Don Knotts (Windy Wales), Craig McDonnell (Harka, an Indian ranch hand, and Irish), Larraine Pankow (Aunt Lilly), Herbert C. Rice (unnamed Chinese cook), Tex Ritter (Diogenes Dodwaddle), Eddie Wragge (Black Bart).

When his parents died, 12-year-old Bobby Benson inherited their ranch in the Big Bend country of south Texas. A plethora of name-changing series ensued, capturing the imagination of little tykes and older adolescents as Bobby and his ranch hands stumbled upon exploits well beyond an ordinary youngster's reach. Most of Benson's escapades involved the pursuit and capture of contingents of bandits and desperadoes of diverse sorts. Rustlers, smugglers, bank and stagecoach robbers dotted the scripts like cactus spread across the Western plains. Straddling his faithful mount, Amigo, the youngster appeared fearless as he tracked down those who practiced evil. To relieve the suspense, music and humor were routinely introduced into the story lines. Bobby and the ranch hands sang campfire tunes while handyman Windy Wales, an incurable liar, shared "wild tales" that invariably eased the stress with laughter.

On more serious assignments— which in the early days took the youthful landowner far from home, including at least once to China—Benson was accompanied by ranch foreman Ted Mason (who was originally called "Buck"). Having an adult squire the preteen on his perilous missions was a pattern adopted by multiple radio juvenile crime fighters. (The model may have reached its pinnacle in *Jack Armstrong, the All-American Boy*, who was flanked by a couple of peers and their Uncle Jim from 1933 on. Jim was superseded in 1946 by an even better prepared investigator, Vic Hardy, who definitely expanded the role of mentor.) Mothers in those days surely felt more comfortable with globetrotting youngsters venturing on treacherous missions when they were in the care of an adult male than they might have been with kids traveling to such faraway destinations alone!

During its reincarnation (1949–55), the program offered one of the most stirring and memorable billboards of audio juvenile fiction, bursting onto the airwaves with an announcer shouting above a stampede of galloping stallions: "Here they come! They're riding fast and they're riding hard. It's time for excitement and adventure in the modern West with *Bobby Benson and the B-Bar-B Riders*. And out in front, astride his golden palomino Amigo, it's the cowboy kid himself, Bobby Benson." After which the tenderfoot hero roared: "BEEEEE-BAR-BEEEEE!"

During the series' latter years it simultaneously offered a five-minute musicale featuring cowboy and western ballads sung around a campfire setting. This interlude usually followed *Sky King*'s 25-minute aerial exploits.

This show capitalized on the radio premium-baiting frenzy that swept the nation during the epoch of the Great Depression. While discretionary funds were often nonexistent in the homes of many fans, enterprising Benson marketing pros offered options for those without cash. Typically, during its first four years on the air, the series' listeners could swap a boxtop from H-O Oats cereal accompanied by a nickel for a ranger's badge or bandanna, or receive the same commodity for two boxtops. A rodeo rope with printed instructions on how to spin it or a ranger's holster, gun or cartridge belt could be ordered for a boxtop and 15 cents or for five boxtops. Other early premiums and their values: ranger's chaps, one boxtop and $1.45 or 25 boxtops; ranger's hat, one boxtop and 85 cents or 20 boxtops; ranger's spurs, one boxtop and 35 cents or 10 boxtops; ranger's cuffs, one boxtop and 30 cents or eight boxtops. It was a prime method of tying young listeners to their heroes and their series while selling more of the sponsor's product, a practice followed by virtually every juvenile mystery adventure on the air. The same theory was widely practiced by many of the soap operas, as housewives were proffered trinkets—autographed pictures of a program's heroine, a simple piece of jewelry, flower seed packets, recipes, etc.—in exchange for boxtops or labels from the sponsor's product, often accompanied by a dime or a quarter.

An assessment by *Variety*, sometimes considered the show business bible, stipulated that the latter *Benson* series—between 1949 and 1955—was seldom as "entertaining" as its original form, aired between 1932 and 1936.

Radio historiographer Fred Mac-Donald noted the incongruity of placing a child in an adult's world as the lead in an aural mystery-adventure. "His [Benson's] colleagues called him 'son' and 'kid,' and he was sheltered from the occasional brutalities of mature life," MacDonald declared. One day, for instance, as Benson neared the site of a gruesome homicide, the adults surrounding the lad protected him from witnessing the blood-stained scene. There was always something "unbelievable" about a preteen owning a ranch and solving crimes, MacDonald insisted. Despite that, youngsters took charge in several adolescent-centered shows other than this.

In late 1932 and early 1933, when George W. Trendle (who was destined to bring *The Lone Ranger* to the airwaves) was seeking a new dramatic vehicle to entice more listeners to the station he owned, Detroit's WXYZ, he lamented that there was no prominent western on the air. Curiously, he disregarded *Bobby Benson and His H-Bar-O Rangers*, gaining widespread popularity at that very moment.

Bobby Benson's Adventures see *Bobby Benson and the B-Bar-B Riders*

Bobby Benson's H-Bar-O Rangers see *Bobby Benson and the B-Bar-B Riders*

The Border Patrol

On the Air: Feb. 6, 1941–unknown date, MBS, Thursday, 8:15 p.m. 15 minutes.
Sponsor: Sustained.
Extant Episodes: Six.

CAST & CREDITS
Uncredited.

This was an adventure series of G-Men guarding the borders of our nation. Calling themselves "Uncle Sam's sentinels," they patrolled 12,000 miles of U.S. boundaries by land and sea from Canada to Mexico and the Gulf of Mexico and from the Atlantic to the Pacific. The officers dealt with immigration matters, drug smuggling and similar concerns.

The series was based on actual exploits of the immigration-border patrol. Names of characters other than border patrolmen were fictitious.

Boston Blackie

On the Air: June 23–Sept. 15, 1944, NBC, Friday, 10 p.m.; April 11–June 6, 1945, MBS, Wednesday, 10 p.m.; June 11–Sept. 3, 1945, MBS, Monday, 8:30 p.m.; Sept. 13–Sept. 20, 1945, MBS, Thursday, 8:30 p.m.; Oct. 4, 1945–Jan. 3, 1946, ABC, Thursday, 7:30 p.m.; Jan. 8, 1946–April 29, 1947, ABC, Tuesday, 7:30 p.m.; May 7, 1947–Oct. 25, 1950, MBS, Wednesday, 8:30 p.m.; Sept. 11, 1949–Sept. 3, 1950, CBS, Sunday, 7:30 p.m. 30 minutes.
Sponsors: Lever Brothers Co. for Rinso detergent and Lifebuoy soap (June 23–Sept. 15, 1944); Lucerna milk (Sept. 11, 1949–Sept. 3, 1950); Sustained and/or participating enterprises, including Champagne Velvet beer and R & H beer (during other segments).
Extant Episodes: 200 plus.

CAST & CREDITS
Producer—Jeanne K. Harrison.
Writers—Kenneth Lyons, Ralph Rosenberg.
Music—Charles Cornell and Hank Sylvern (organists).
Sound Effects—Walt Gustafson.
Announcers—Larry Elliott, Ken Roberts, Harlow Wilcox.
Leads—Title role played by Chester Morris (NBC), Richard Kollmar (beginning April 11, 1945); Mary Wesley, played by Jan Miner, Lesley Woods (NBC); Inspector Faraday, played by Richard Lane (NBC),

Frank Orth, Maurice Tarplin; Shorty, played by Tony Barrett.

When he decided to play it straight, former master thief Boston Blackie—who claimed "I can open any vault in the world with these fingers"—applied his wizardry to capturing criminals. Each week he was introduced to listeners as an "enemy to those who make him an enemy ... friend to those who have no friends." Assisting a dim bulb Inspector Faraday of the New York Police Department's homicide squad, Blackie was tagged with a couple of cohorts to help him pass the time and embroiled them in his cavorting escapades against Big Apple gangsters: Shorty (identified only by that handle), an ex-con, small in stature yet reliable in Blackie's hour of need; and a love interest as exhibited in most similar fare—in Blackie's case, nurse Mary Wesley filled that function. Alas, despite the fact that Blackie appeared to dote on getting the last laugh on the cops, he was so intimate with public law enforcement that in one show he even assisted them in raising funds for disadvantaged kids. Perhaps it was a witness to his Robin Hood nature. One critic's assessment of the show—"high in corn content, but hardly one of radio's schedule stoppers"—spoke volumes.

Based on the fictional detective created by Jack Boyle, Boston Blackie initially appeared in the early 1900s in the pages of *Cosmopolitan* and *Redbook* magazines. One account suggests that the figure could have been fashioned from Blackie Daw, a chic con man in George Randolph Chester's "Get-Rich-Quick Wallingford" narratives that surfaced after 1907. Boyle's Blackie was a common thief with expertise in knocking over banks. While he was both astute and scholarly, he ultimately could not outsmart the police. As a result, he spent a lot of time in prison as Mary Wesley tolerantly dawdled. Following an especially harsh confinement, Blackie opted to go straight and shifted his modus operandi from *committing* to *solving* crimes.

Two silent films brought *Blackie* to theater-goers in the World War I and pre-Depression era: *Boston Blackie's Little Pal* (1918) and *The Return of Boston Blackie* (1923). In the former, Bert Lytell played Blackie in a screenplay written by Jack Boyle, the originator. William Russell was the hero in the 1923 motion picture penned by Paul Schofield. But it was in the 1940s that the character achieved near-universal status via a series of 11 B-grade silver screen features starring Chester Morris in the title role. (Morris was to introduce Blackie to radio audiences in 1944, the reader will recall.) The Morris releases included *Meet Boston Blackie* and *Confessions of Boston Blackie* (1941), *Alias Boston Blackie* and *Boston Blackie Goes Hollywood* (1942), *After Midnight with Boston Blackie* (1943), *Boston Blackie Booked on Suspicion* and *Boston Blackie's Rendezvous* (1945), *Boston Blackie and the Law* and *A Close Call for Boston Blackie* (1946), *Trapped by Boston Blackie* (1948) and *Boston Blackie's Chinese Venture* (1949).

Following its original NBC 1944 run as a summer replacement for vacationing *Amos 'n' Andy*, the radio drama went into transcribed syndication. Circulated by the production house of Frederic W. Ziv, it was broadcast by other networks. Eventually the series aired over all four national chains, three of them via transcription.

Fifty-eight syndicated episodes of *Boston Blackie* were produced for television between 1951 and 1953. They starred Kent Taylor as Blackie, Lois Collier as Mary Wesley and Frank Orth (from the radio cast), who re-created the role of Inspector Faraday. That time around the setting was Los Angeles, not New York. Produced by Ziv TV, the show was directed in succession by Eddie Davis, Sobey Martin and George M. Cahan.

Jay Hickerson has prepared a log of all shows currently in circulation.

Box 13

On the Air: March 15, 1948–March 7, 1949, MBS West Coast Network, Monday; Aug. 22, 1948–Aug. 14, 1949, MBS, Sunday. 30 minutes.
Sponsor: No information.
Extant Episodes: 52 (complete run).

CAST & CREDITS

Producer—Richard Sanville.
Director—Vern Carstenson.
Writers—Russell Hughes, Alan Ladd.
Music—Rudy Schrager.
Announcer—Vern Carstenson.
Leads—Dan Holiday, played by Alan Ladd; Suzy, played by Sylvia Picker.
Support Roles—John Beal, Betty Lou Gerson, Marsha Hunt, Frank Lovejoy, Alan Reed, Luis Van Rooten, Lurene Tuttle.

Newspaper reporter-turned-fiction writer Dan Holiday placed an ad in the *Star-Times* stating: "Adventure wanted. Will go anywhere, do anything. Box 13." To pay the rent, he capitalized on those responses by latching onto hot topics that could be introduced into his fictionalized tales. Those replies came from psychotics, blackmailers, cultists—"screwballs of all kinds," as one wag put it—who took him down roads he had never been, where he bumped into danger and battled vice in diverse forms as he railed against the odds. Suzy—without a surname—an addle-brained secretary (who was "just a little too well-baked and the show's weakest link," according to a reviewer), fetched and checked his mail from Box 13, cultivating the most stimulating replies to that intriguing classified. Despite the comment about Suzy, the critic allowed that the series presented "a fine piece of radio for the listener."

Alan Ladd, a popular Hollywood screen legend who often appeared in westerns, and a business associate formed an audio syndication outfit, Mayfair Productions. The pair had operated a string of Mayfair restaurants earlier. Ladd simply wasn't enamored with television and decided to cast his broadcasting lot in radio, transcribing and distributing his own shows.

An interesting sidenote: In 1935, Russell Hughes hired Ladd as a $19-a-week actor for station KFWB, where Ladd steadily performed. The same Hughes would eventually pen the bulk of scripts for *Box 13*.

Broadway Cop

On the Air: Oct. 11, 1954–Oct. 10, 1955, MBS, Monday, 8:30 p.m.; Oct. 18, 1955–Jan. 3, 1956, MBS, Tuesday, 8:30 p.m. 30 minutes.
Sponsor: No information.
Extant Episodes: None known.

CAST & CREDITS

No information.

No tapes or added printed data surrounding this series have been recovered. A request to hundreds of readers of a popular web site, regretfully, resulted in obtaining no further detail.

Broadway Is My Beat

On the Air: Feb. 27–June 12, 1949, CBS, Sunday, 5:30 p.m.; July 7–Aug. 25, 1949, CBS, Thursday, 8 p.m.; Nov. 5, 1949–Jan. 21, 1950, CBS, Saturday, 9:30 p.m.; Jan. 31, 1950, CBS, Tuesday; Feb. 3–June 23, 1950, CBS, Friday, 9:30 p.m.; July 3–Aug. 21, 1950, CBS, Monday, 8:30 p.m.; Oct. 13–Dec. 8, 1950, CBS, Friday, 9:30 p.m.; April 7–June 30, 1951, CBS, Saturday, 9:30 p.m.; July 8–Aug. 26, 1951, CBS, Sunday, 9 p.m.; Sept.

15, 1951–May 24, 1952, CBS, Saturday, 9:30 p.m.; June 2–July 21, 1952, CBS, Monday, 9:30 p.m.; Aug. 2–Sept. 27, 1952, CBS, Saturday, 9:30 p.m.; Oct. 4, 1952–Oct. 3, 1953, CBS, Saturday, 7 p.m.; Oct. 7–Nov. 4, 1953, CBS, Wednesday, 9:30 p.m.; Nov. 13–Nov. 27, 1953, CBS, Friday; July 11–Aug. 1, 1954, CBS, Sunday, 6:30 p.m. 30 minutes.

Theme Song: *I'll Take Manhattan.*

Sponsors: Sustained, yet occasionally various commercial enterprises underwrote portions, including Lever Brothers Co. for Lux soap, and William J. Wrigley Co. for its lines of chewing gum.

Extant Episodes: 100 (approximately).

CAST & CREDITS

Producer—Lester Gottlieb (New York).
Director—John Dietz (New York).
Producer/Director—Elliott Lewis (Hollywood).
Writers—Morton Fine, David Friedkin.
Music—Robert Stringer (New York), Alexander Courage, Wilbur Hatch (Hollywood).
Sound Effects—Ralph Cummings, David Light, Ross Murray.
Announcer—Bill Anders.
Leads—Danny Clover, played by Anthony Ross (Feb. 27, 1949–June 23, 1950), Larry Thor (July 3, 1950–Aug. 1, 1954); Gino Tartaglia, played by Charles Calvert; Mugowen, played by Jack Kruschen.
Support Roles—Hy Averback, Tony Barrett, Edgar Barrier, Harry Bartell, Bill Bouchey, Herb Butterfield, Mary Jane Croft, Lawrence Dobkin, Sam Edwards, Herb Ellis, Eddie Fields, Betty Lou Gerson, Sammie Hill, Lamont Johnson, Byron Kane, Charlotte Lawrence, Sheldon Leonard, Truda Marson, Junius Matthews, Eva McVeagh, GeGe Pearson, Barney Phillips, Mary Shipp, Irene Tedrow, Herb Vigran, Martha Wentworth, Anne Whitfield, Paula Winslowe, Ben Wright.

"From Times Square to Columbus Circle ... the gaudiest ... the most violent ... the lonesomest mile in the world" summarily expressed plainclothes detective Danny Clover's beat for the New York Police Department. Assisting Clover in criminal detection while he encountered the difficulties of living in a large city were Gino Tartaglia, an at times comical officer, along with Sergeant Mugowen, the city coroner.

In the 1950s radio producers brought to the air police dramas that could be called anything but alluring. Although informative, they witnessed a forbidding side of law enforcement in the harsh realities of an urban backdrop. *Broadway Is My Beat, Dragnet* and *Twenty-First Precinct* fell into this category. "Listeners could not help reacting to the fearful picture that these detectives presented," noted a radio historian. "In their purview, the greatest cities of the country ... were criminal cesspools with only a cadre of depressed public and private investigators defending them from anarchy."

Fred MacDonald added: "If murder continued to be the criminal's favorite act, it was now accomplished with noisy pistol shots interrupted by morbid groans and punctuated by the explicit thud of bodies collapsing to the floor." He observed that nontraditional crimes were also investigated. *Broadway Is My Beat* occasionally introduced topics like juvenile delinquency and anti-Semitism in some of its narratives, subjects that hadn't been profoundly heard earlier.

MacDonald believed the "most colorful" writers of such neo-realistic police dramas were Morton Fine and David Friedkin, authors of *Broadway Is My Beat* (and earlier, *Bold Venture*). He cited their superior literary style as "a striking example of a writing flare which was generally absent from radio."

Producer/director Elliott Lewis was one of a handful of multitalented individuals in the radio business. At one and the same time he produced and directed *three* shows airing *in succession* on Sunday evenings over CBS: *Broadway Is My Beat, On Stage* and *Crime Classics.* Furthermore, he and then-wife Cathy Lewis co-starred in the middle series while he intermittently wrote openings and scripts for this trio as the occasion demanded. To anyone else it might have been maddening; to Lewis, reflecting on it three decades later, it was simply "marvelous."

Broadway Is My Beat shifted into and out of as many as 16 different days and time periods across a five-year broadcast run. Its shortest appearance in a given time-slot was a single episode (Jan. 31, 1950). Some other segments ran but a few weeks longer. The longest continuing extension lasted for 53 episodes, from Oct. 4, 1952, through Oct. 3, 1953.

The program originated from New York through May 29, 1949, and from Hollywood starting July 7, 1949.

Jay Hickerson compiled a log of this show.

Buck Rogers in the Twenty-Fifth Century

On the Air: Nov. 7, 1932–June 16, 1933, CBS, Weeknights, 7:15 p.m.; Oct. 2, 1933–June 28, 1934, CBS, Monday–Thursday, 6 p.m.; Sept. 3, 1934–Dec. 26, 1935, CBS, Monday–Thursday, 6 p.m.; Dec. 30, 1935–May 22, 1936, CBS, Monday/Wednesday/Friday, 6 p.m.; April 5–July 31, 1939, MBS, Monday/Wednesday/Friday; May 18–July 27, 1940, MBS, Saturday, 12 noon; Sept. 30, 1946–March 28, 1947, MBS, Weekdays, 4:45 p.m. All 15 minutes, except 30 minutes (May 18–July 27, 1940).
Theme Song: *Les Préludes* (Franz Liszt).
Sponsors: W. K. Kellogg Co. for its cereal brands (Nov. 7, 1932–June 16, 1933); Cocomalt beverages (Oct. 2, 1933–June 28, 1934, and Sept. 3, 1934–Dec. 26, 1935); Cream of Wheat cereal (Dec. 30, 1935–May 22, 1936); Popsicle, Fudgesicle and Cremesicle frozen confection treats (April 5–July 31, 1939); Sustained (May 18–July 27, 1940); General Foods Corp. for Post cereals and a diversified line of foodstuffs (Sept. 30, 1946–March 28, 1947).
Extant Episodes: 23.

CAST & CREDITS

Producer/Director/Writer/Announcer— Jack Johnstone. **Writers—**Dick Calkins, Joe A. Cross, Tom Dougall, Albert G. Miller.
Sound Effects—Ora D. Nichols.
Announcers—Paul Douglas, Jack Johnstone, Fred Uttal, Kenny Williams.
Leads—Title role played by Matt Crowley (Nov. 7, 1932–Dec. 26, 1935), Carl Frank, John Larkin (Sept. 30, 1946–March 28, 1947); Wilma Deering, played by Adele Ronson (from the start), Virginia Vass (Sept. 30, 1946–March 28, 1947).
Support Roles—Curtis Arnall, Matt Crowley, Carl Frank, Alice Frost, Joe Granby (Black Barney, a likable but dimwitted Martian), Walter Greaza, Henry Gurvey, Ronald Liss, Junius Matthews, Elaine Melchior (Ardala Valmar, archvillainess), John Monks, Dan Ocko (villain Killer Kane), Frank Readick, Jack Roseleigh (Black Barney), Bill Shelley (Killer Kane), Everett Sloane, Edgar Stehli (Dr. Huer, scientific inventor and Rogers' confidant), Paul Stewart, Walter Tetley, Fred Uttal, Walter Vaughn, Arthur Vinton, Vicki Vola, Dwight Weist, Eustace Wyatt.

This was a futuristic juvenile adventure yarn with demonstrated leanings toward crime and injustice. The youthful Rogers, a fighter pilot in World War I, was trapped in suspended animation, waking up 500 years later. Journeying on spaceship missions with him was constant companion Wilma Deering, a lieutenant in the Space Corps. The incredibly amazing scientist and inventor Dr. Huer, literally the "brain" behind the organization, was forever dreaming up worthy creations, yet he had a hard time holding onto them. Frequently his ingenious designs fell into enemy territory—most often, into the hands of the notorious Killer Kane and his accomplice, Ardala Valmar, a gruesome twosome who

Buck Rogers in the Twenty-Fifth Century: Matt Crowley in full costume regalia might be all dressed up with nowhere to go, his character of Buck Rogers having been newly released from suspended animation—"just an ordinary human being who keeps his wits about him." The tenderfaced Crowley, who originated the role, played a juvenile hero living 500 years after his birth, outwitting celestial troublemakers fighting desperately to control the universe.

schemed to disrupt the interplanetary status quo. Kane, in particular, was viewed as a madman, intent on controlling the universe. With time on his hands (no pun intended), Rogers was summoned to outwit him and keep tabs on his next moves. Rogers was—as the announcer reminded his little friends every day—"just an ordinary human being who keeps his wits about him." In a world of advanced skill and knowledge, keeping one's wits could make a big difference for mere mortals suddenly arriving from the twentieth century.

Buck Rogers originated in a 1929 newspaper comic strip that syndicator John D. Dille thought up, Dick Calkins sketched and Phil Nowlan wrote. The early story there paralleled the one told later on radio. In 1919 in Pittsburgh young Rogers, an Air Corps vet, was surveying the lower levels of an abandoned mine. When the timber supports crumbled and the roof fell in, he was overcome by gaseous fumes that quickly enveloped the chamber where he was, rendering him unconscious. He was held in a suspended state for five centuries. Awakening in the year 2430 when the earth shifted and fresh air entered the mine, Rogers found that society as he knew it was gone. The capital was now Niagara and he soon qualified as a member of the Space General's staff to fight evil of multiple kinds. The show made use of many forms of fantasy marvels to assist him.

One critic noted "the propriety of Buck's long space flights with Wilma Deering was debated by parents, who were also fretting over what Tarzan and Jane were doing alone in the jungle together." (Innocently, before a flight, Buck would inquire of his copilot: "Wilma, does all your equipment check out?" Apparently nobody thought of double entendres then.) While their journeys had come across as antiseptic in the comics, adding the dimension of live voices made a difference. Marooned once on an Arctic ice cap, the duo was far from cold. Observing the heavens at night, the voices drifted lower and lower, more cozy sounding than before. Irate moms fired off communiqués disapproving of such intimacy. Yet it all appeared destined for pure bliss as the series' finale approached, the pair of star-crossed lovers heading for Niagara—a honeymooners' paradise in the world Rogers recalled. Legitimacy would win the final battle.

The series capitalized on the premium hysteria among boys and girls of listening age. For a boxtop from the sponsor's product and "one thin dime" it offered the fans rings, badges, games, cutout adventure books, paper guns and helmets, planetary maps and sketches of the principal characters among a wide array of trinkets. Fans could become "Solar Scouts" by merely responding to the premium offers.

Versatile professional Jack Johnstone would, a few years later, apply his penmanship to another supernatural intergalactic series, *The Adventures of Superman*. Did Johnstone's talents, like his heroes, simply know no bounds?

Leonard Maltin recalled how Johnstone got into the business, worth noting in connection with this show. Like many others, Johnstone became a director by chance: "He was working at an advertising agency earning $32 a week, when one of his colleagues was assigned to write … *Buck Rogers*. After a while, his friend asked if Jack would like to take a crack at it, and he did; before long he was sharing scriptwriting chores on a regular basis. Then one morning the show's director, Carlo De Angelo, called to say he couldn't make it in time for rehearsal and asked if Jack would run through the show with the actors. He did, and before long, De Angelo recommended that he be promoted to the director's post full-time. 'Later,' Johnstone recalled, 'when Kellogg's canceled the series, a friend of mine was a salesman for CBS and I told him that I could write and direct—the whole schmear—if he could sell it. And he did. A few weeks later I started doing the whole job on it, and my take-home pay was not $32 a week but $300 a week.'" Beyond that, when Johnstone supplied for an announcer who failed to arrive on one occasion, he was recommended to take on *that* job permanently as well!

Years later a network professional sound effects specialist, Robert L. Mott, remembered how difficult it was to produce the imaginative noises that complemented science fiction series like *Buck Rogers in the Twenty-Fifth Century*: "The problems confronting the sound-effects artists on those shows were enormous. It was their responsibility to come up with all the futuristic sounds that were only in the imagination of the writers and directors. The scripts were overflowing with such sounds as rocket belts, ray guns, rocket ships, sparkle static, dream water, repellent guns, reducer rays, and various and sundry zips and zaps to ward off Killer Kane or dispose of all those hideous outer-space monsters." Mott recollected that the show's opening and closing theme was a combined drum roll on the sound-effects thunder drum and the announcer's voice echoing: "Buck Rogerrrrrs ... in the twenty-fifth century!" To accomplish the desired effect the announcer said the line into a microphone placed near the strings of a grand piano. This made the strings vibrate in a way that gave the voice precisely the eerie, futuristic tone the show needed. Mott added: "It is interesting to note that more than 50 years later, this piano effect is still being used in Hollywood for such films as *Raiders of the Lost Ark*."

Jack Johnstone reminisced about the sounds for Rogers' rocket ship: "CBS New York had an excellent air conditioning system.... There were huge grates, perhaps four by four, for exhaust and intake; the sound effects man took a spare script and plastered pages over the whole thing, which stuck because of the draw of the air, except for a small spot in the middle of it, out of which he placed a microphone. The air conditioning system provided the sound for the rocket. Where we had Killer Kane flying a different ship..., the engineer sent it through a filter, to give a little different sound."

Screen actor Buster Crabbe parlayed the role of Buck Rogers into a Saturday-matinee idol. He also doubled in the namesake part in *Flash Gordon* serials, boosting his image among the adolescents who in the 1930s were caught up in all things interplanetary.

Bulldog Drummond

(aka *The American Adventures of Bulldog Drummond*)

On the Air: April 13–June 22, 1941, MBS, Sunday, 6:30 p.m.; Sept. 28, 1941–March 22, 1942, MBS, Sunday, 6:30 p.m.; May 25, 1942–April 19, 1943, MBS, Monday, 8:30 p.m.; Sept. 26, 1943–April 23, 1944, MBS, Sunday, 3:30 p.m.; April 30–Aug. 27, 1944, MBS, Sunday, 5:30 p.m.; Sept. 4, 1944–Sept. 17, 1945, MBS, Monday, 7:30 p.m.; Sept. 24, 1945–Oct. 14, 1946, MBS, Monday, 8 p.m.; Dec. 6, 1946–Sept. 19, 1947, MBS, Friday, 9:30 p.m.; Dec. 31, 1947–Jan. 12, 1949, MBS, Wednesday, 10 p.m.; Oct. 14–Dec. 23, 1953, MBS, Wednesday, 9:30 p.m.; Jan. 3–March 28, 1954, MBS, Sunday, 6 p.m. 30 minutes.

Sponsors: Howard clothes (April 13, 1941–March 22, 1942); Tums antacid tablets (Sept. 24, 1945–Oct. 14, 1946); American Transit (Feb. 28–July 11, 1947); Chrysler Corp. for Dodge automobiles and trucks (Feb. 7–March 14, 1954); Sustained (other time periods).

Extant Episodes: 23.

CAST & CREDITS

Producer/Director—Himan Brown.
Writers—Edward J. Adamson, Jay Bennett, Leonard Leslie, Allan E. Sloane.
Music—Lew White (organ).
Sound Effects—Walt Gustafson, Adrian Penner, Walt Shaver.
Announcers—Ted Brown, Henry Morgan, Dan Seymour.
Leads—Title character played by George Coulouris (April 13, 1941–March 22, 1942), Santos Ortega (May 25, 1942–March 8, 1943), Ned Wever (March 15, 1943–Jan. 12, 1949), Sir Cedric Hardwicke (Oct. 14, 1953–March 28, 1954); Denny, his assistant, played by Rod Hendrickson, Everett Sloane, Luis Van Rooten.

Support Roles—Ray Collins, Ted de Corsia (District Attorney), Mercedes McCambridge, Agnes Moorehead, Paul Stewart.

With an echo of footsteps and a foghorn drifting out of the radio speaker, a couple of shots fired and a trio of sharp blasts from a cop's whistle, an announcer brought this whodunit to the air with a memorable billboard: "Out of the fog ... out of the night ... and into his American adventures ... comes ... *Bulldog Drummond!*" Captain Hugh Drummond was a charming British police inspector who practiced his occupation in *this* nation. His relentless pursuit of felons allowed the handle of "Bulldog" to be hung on him. One critic evaluated the series as "a B-grade detective on the screen and on the air," claiming it was "remembered for years by people who thought it better than it was." Aided by his valet/assistant Denny (characters seemed more imposing with single-word names!), he fought counterfeiters, racketeers, thieves of all sorts and just plain killers. It was a jolly good time, and most of the series' fans wouldn't have recognized a B-grade composition anyway.

The character Bulldog Drummond originated in books by H. C. McNeile.

A total of 19 Drummond motion pictures, from the silent movie era through the middle of the twentieth century, were released. Most were by Paramount. The first and last of these productions, in 1923 and 1952, were simply titled *Bulldog Drummond* (there was one more by that precise name, in 1929). A dozen films were issued in the 1930s but only three in the 1920s and two in the 1940s and 1950s each—the latter two decades being when the radio show aired.

The show's distinctive opening turned up nearly three decades after it was introduced on radio in a parody ("out of the fog, into the smog") by the Firesign Theatre comedy troupe. Their detective adventure was released on a 1969 long-playing album titled *How Can You Be in Two Places at Once When You're Not Anywhere at All?*

Bunco Squad

On the Air: 1950, CBS.
Sponsor: Sustained.
Extant Episodes: Two.

CAST & CREDITS
No credits given on available recordings.

Each week Captain Trumble, an authority on bunco schemes, not only narrated the dramatizations but also advised his listeners about methods of avoiding being taken by the scams of bunco artists (e.g. swindlers, con men). A bunco artist "can make a sucker out of you!" warned an announcer. "Be on guard! For the protection of you, the American public, CBS presents these authentic cases drawn from the police records of the nation," continued the billboard.

Existing recordings are of a rare program rehearsal and an audition tape. To date no solid confirmation has emerged proving that these efforts resulted in an ongoing series, although that is categorically possible.

Calamity Jane

On the Air: March 31–April 14, 1946, CBS, Sunday, 8 p.m. 30 minutes.
Sponsor: Tums antacid distress reliever.
Extant Episodes: None known.

CAST & CREDITS
Announcer—Ken Niles.
Leads—Title role played by Agnes Moorehead; her grandfather, the publisher, played by Dan Wolfe.
Support Roles—Bill Johnstone, Cathy Lewis.

Lasting just three broadcasts and featuring one of radio's megastars, this crime drama focused on a cunning newspaper reporter who often fumbled the ball while trying to expose local con artists and other lawbreakers. The series was played semi-humorously.

Agnes Moorehead was one of radio's most respected thespians. Her impeccable performance in novelist Lucille Fletcher's "Sorry, Wrong Number" was aired on *Suspense* a total of eight times by popular request across that prominent thriller's durable run.

Call the Police

On the Air: June 3–Sept. 23, 1947, NBC, Tuesday, 9 p.m.; June 1, 1948, NBC, Tuesday, 9 p.m.; June 8–Sept. 28, 1948, NBC, Tuesday, 9:30 p.m.; June 5–Sept. 25, 1949, CBS, Sunday, 7:30 p.m. 30 minutes.
Sponsor: Lever Brothers Co. for Rinso detergent and Lifebuoy soap (June 3, 1947–June 1, 1948, June 5–Sept. 25, 1949); S. C. Johnson and Sons Co. for Johnson's wax and other home, business and automotive cleaning agents (June 8–Sept. 28, 1948).
Extant Episodes: Six.

Cast & Credits

Producer/Director—John Cole.
Writer—Peter Barry.
Music—Ben Ludlow.
Announcers—Jay Sims (1947), Hugh James (1948, 1949).
Leads—Bill Grant, played by Joseph Julian (1947), George Petrie (1948, 1949); Libby Tyler, played by Joan Tompkins (1947) and Amzie Strickland (1948, 1949); Sergeant Maggio, played by Robert Dryden.
Support Roles—Ed Jerome, Mandel Kramer, George Matthews, Bill Smith, Alice Reinheart.

Bill Grant was the son of a police sergeant who was killed while on duty. The younger Grant, fresh out of the FBI academy, returned home from the Marines in World War II to discover that con artists had overrun his town of Ashland. He decided to clean up the city, accepting the reigns of responsibility from a maturing police captain. To help him in his ongoing battle with gangsters, Grant turned to criminal psychologist Libby Tyler. He also had a rather clumsy subordinate in Sergeant Maggio. The drama's billboard set the tone for serious subject matter: "Between you and the evil outside the law stands the policemen of your community. He gives up his safety so you may be safe and sometimes he gives up his life to protect yours." There were tough-sounding reincarnations of ghastly offenses, and law enforcement's uphill struggles to solve those crimes.

When Lever Brothers sponsored the series, at the end of each episode an "Award of Valor" was presented to a real police officer that had demonstrated courage in the line of duty. With it went a $100 check to the individual and a plaque to his law enforcement unit.

Calling All Cars

On the Air: Nov. 29, 1933–Sept. 8, 1939, CBS Pacific network stations, Wednesday, 9 p.m. PT. 30 minutes. (The show was also sent by transcription to Southwestern markets served by the sponsor but beyond the reach of the Western CBS circuit. There it was aired at different times and on different days apart from the regional network broadcasts.)
Sponsor: Rio Grande Oil Co. for its oil, gasoline and other vehicle products and services.
Extant Episodes: 299 (of 302 total episodes).

Cast & Credits

Producer/Writer—William N. Robson.
Director—Robert Hixson.
Sound Effects—Clark Casey, Ray Erlenborn.
Narrator/Host—Charles Frederick Lindsley (a college speech professor), Chief James E. Davis, L.A.P.D.

Support Roles—Elvia Allman, Jackson Beck, Charles Bickford, Robert Dryden, John Gibson, Richard LeGrand, Lindsay MacHarrie, Henry Niles, Hanley Stafford, Martha Wentworth, William Zuckert. (Cast members were uncredited on the air, however.)

One of radio's initial police dramas, this one was rooted in true police case histories. Aside from the series' host, Sergeant Jesse Rosenquist of the Los Angeles Police Department was cited as the only ongoing character and he did not appear in every episode.

This was an unsophisticated prototype of a breed of audio dramatic fare that achieved its summit with *Dragnet* more than 15 years later. The style allowed listeners to overhear the unmitigated and thankless task of tracing thieves and murderers. The punishment for these crimes was often revealed in a summary at the end of an episode.

A monthly periodical, *Calling All Cars News*, available gratis from the sponsor's service stations, paralleled the radio series. It frequently included stories that were about to be aired, augmenting fans' appetites in dual media.

An in-depth article in the Nov. 1, 1934, issue of *Broadcasting* magazine by producer William N. Robson depicted the program's history until that time.

Writing for an OTR electronic mail forum, radio historiographer Elizabeth McLeod cited *Calling All Cars* as "an excellent example of what a well-produced dramatic show was like in the mid thirties." She continued: "Early radio drama tends to get a bad rap from people who've only heard the really cheap syndicated serials of the 1930s, but given a decent budget and a good production team, I think thirties drama stands up quite favorably."

Jerry Haendiges provided a log for this series.

Calling All Detectives

On the Air: April 7–Aug. 25, 1945, MBS, Saturday, 9:30 p.m. 30 minutes. From 1947 to 1950 the series was reduced to 15-minute syndicated shows in which Paul Barnes played all parts in a brief mystery melodrama. Following that—appearing then as private detective Jerry Browning—he randomly telephoned numbers asking fans some pertinent questions related to the action just broadcast.

Sponsor: Sealy Bedding Co. (MBS); Commercial ventures in markets where the show was syndicated.

Extant Episodes: 200 plus two audition tapes.

CAST & CREDITS

Music—Dick Platt (organ).
Announcer—George Bower.
Leads—Robin, played by Vincent Pelletier; Detective Browning, played by Paul Barnes.
Support Roles—Owen Jordan, Frank Lovejoy.

This game show began with a whodunit narrative. Crime guide Robin (no surname) offered clues from which listeners were to cull the perpetrator. At its apex the program was interrupted. Five minutes of air time was handed to local stations for their announcers to telephone fans—chosen by postal card drawings—within the calling territory. When the show resumed, correct guessers received war bonds, with the bonds' values determined by local stations.

The formula of interrupting a live network show to return a portion for local feedback or participation did not originate here. By 1945 quite a few programs had adopted some variation of the style.

Martin Grams Jr. prepared a log of this series.

Canada's Mounted on the Air see *With Canada's Mounted Police*

Candy Matson

(aka *Candy Matson, YUkon 2-8209*)

On the Air: June 29, 1949–May 20, 1951, NBC
West Coast stations. Various days and times.
30 minutes.
Theme Song: *Candy.*
Sponsor: No information.
Extant Episodes: 15.

CAST & CREDITS

Producer/Director/Writer—Monte Masters.
Music—Eloise Rowan (organ).
Sound Effects—Jay Rendon.
Announcers—Bud Heidi, Dudley Manlove.
Leads—Title role played by Natalie Masters;
Ray Mallard, played by Henry Lemp; Rembrandt Watson, played by Jack Thomas.
Support Role—Montgomery the Mole
(Candy's informant), played by Jerry Walter.

A critic observed that Candy Matson was
the most successful feminine detective
radio produced. Operating out of her San
Francisco penthouse apartment on Telegraph Hill, Matson—whose telephone
number was YUkon 28209, an important
piece of business in every episode—was a
dazzling doll. Her looks didn't get in the
way of her duties, however: She handled
guns with expertise and recalcitrant antagonists with dispatch. Matson possessed
"an intriguing, brassy voice that conveyed
good humor and a hard edge," one critic
observed. A somewhat soft Rembrandt
Watson, whom she nicknamed "Ducky,"
assisted with her cases. Lacking in some
departments, he offered more smiles than
strength. Matson's love interest, who addressed her merely as "Cupcake," was a
police lieutenant—Ray Mallard—whose
base of operations was the Hall of Justice.
In the final episode he was promoted to
police captain, then proposed to Candy,
informing her—and her audience—that
she had solved her last case.

Natalie Masters, who carried the
starring role, was married to Monte Mas-

ters, the producer/director/writer. As a
consequence, the pair tightly controlled
the entire series. It was broadcast from San
Francisco's KNBC.

Candy Matson, YUkon 2-8209 see Candy Matson

Captain Midnight

On the Air: Autumn 1938–spring 1939 (specific dates unsubstantiated) as a syndicated
series dispersed largely to local Midwest stations covering territory in which then-sponsoring Skelly Oil Co. maintained operations,
Weekdays, various time slots; Oct. 16, 1939–
March 29, 1940, WGN, Chicago, and transcribed for markets chiefly in the Midwest
and Southwest where Skelly Oil Co. operated service outlets, Weekdays, various time
slots; Sept. 30, 1940–July 3, 1942, MBS,
Weekdays, 5:45 p.m.; Sept. 28, 1942–June
25, 1943, NBC Blue, Weekdays, 5:45 p.m.;
Sept. 27, 1943–June 23, 1944, NBC Blue,
Weekdays, 5:45 p.m.; Sept. 25, 1944–June
22, 1945, NBC Blue, Weekdays, 5:45 p.m.;
Sept. 24, 1945–June 20, 1947, MBS, Weekdays, 5:30 p.m.; Sept. 29, 1947–June 17, 1949,
MBS, Weekdays, 5:30 p.m.; Sept. 20–Dec.
15, 1949, MBS, Tuesday/Thursday, 5:30 p.m.
15 minutes, except 30 minutes (Sept. 20–
Dec. 15, 1949).
Theme Song: *Flying Dutchman Overture* from
The Flying Dutchman (Richard Wagner).
Sponsors: Skelly Oil Co. for its gasoline, oil
and other vehicle products and services
(Oct. 16, 1939–March 29, 1940); Wander
Co. for its Ovaltine brand breakfast drink
(Sept. 30, 1940–Dec. 15, 1949).
Extant Episodes: 127.

CAST & CREDITS

Producers/Directors—Alan Wallace, Russell
Young, Kirby Hawkes.
Writers—Robert M. Burtt, Wilfred (Bill) G.
Moore.
Sound Effects—Harry Bubeck, Michael
Eisenmenger, Robert J. Graham.

Announcers—Pierre Andre, Don Gordon, Tom Moore.

Lead—Title role played by Ed Prentiss (1938–39, 1940–49, Bill Bouchey (1939–40), Paul Barnes (1949).

Support Roles—Bill Rose, Jack Bivens, Johnny Coons (Chuck Ramsey), Angeline Orr, Marilou Neumayer (Joyce Ryan), Hugh Studebaker, Art Hern, Sherman Marks (Ichabod Mudd), Boris Aplon (Ivan Shark), Rene Rodier, Sharon Grainger (Fury Shark), Maurice Copeland (Dr. Glazer), Earl George (Gardo), Marvin Miller (Rogart and Captain Einman, a Nazi), Olan Soule (SS-11).

For years bizarre yarns of sightings of "a shadowy plane and a mysterious pilot who—whenever trouble started in any part of the world—was certain to come diving furiously from the night sky" were repeated. A secret government agency combating evil around the globe was commanded by Captain Jim (Red) Albright, dubbed Captain Midnight, for his World War I aerial activities. Into Midnight's hands the nation entrusted a large share of its peacekeeping concerns on the very precipice of World War II. One reviewer acknowledged that the figure was conceived as "a man of mystery, whose job in the war was so important that not even his superiors knew his identity."

To assist in his monumental endeavors, the masquerading captain picked a trio of indefatigable young accomplices— Chuck Ramsey and Joyce Ryan (in pre-network days, named Patsy Donovan) and master mechanic Ichabod (Ikky) Mudd. Joyce could barely express a thought without uttering the one-word phrase "Gee-men-eee!" Ikky's pet idiom was "Loopin' loops!" Together the quartet collided in serialized narratives with the world's foremost criminal mind, sinister Eurasian spy Ivan Shark, and his lovely but lethal daughter, an aptly named Fury. The pair were flanked by a wide assortment of lesser menaces, all with the ambition of ruling the world.

During World War II the good guys unremittingly pursued the Axis powers' saboteurs and espionage agents wherever they were found in an all-out attempt to rid the world of threats to universal tranquility. The tale promised young listeners "a story of real adventure in the air and on the ground." Yet its billboard urged adults to also consider linking up: "*Captain Midnight* is written for red-blooded young Americans, both boys and girls; yes, for mother and dad, too; for everyone who's young in spirit." That harmonized with promotional messages that cited sponsoring Ovaltine as "a favorite with millions of Americans, young and old."

Radio Life recorded the auspicious origins of *Captain Midnight*, retelling U.S. airman Robert M. Burtt's exploits during World War I. Serving with the Lafayette Escadrille, Burtt once met eight enemy aircraft during combat over European skies. Unable to withstand those odds, Burtt's plane was shot down. Yet the pilot brought it to a safe belly-flop landing between opposing ground troops. With tommy guns spraying shells far and wide, Burtt managed to slither into American-held trenches. There, he would later note, "*Captain Midnight* was born." The ex-airman collaborated with Wilfred G. (Bill) Moore to put the image onto paper and bring it to the air. (The pair became renowned for their contributions to radio aerial drama. They were responsible for creating and penning *The Air Adventures of Jimmie Allen*, contributed to the scripts of *Hop Harrigan* and, later, developed the even more popular *Sky King*.)

Actor Ed Prentiss announced *The Air Adventures of Jimmie Allen* during its transcribed aural run between 1933 and 1937, also on behalf of the Skelly Oil Co. When auditions were held in 1938 in Chicago for the leading role of a new aviation adventure developed by the creative spirits who had inspired *Jimmie Allen*, virtually every nearby "leading male" thespian turned up. Upon Prentiss' selection, it was as if Jimmie Allen had matured to become Captain Midnight. Prentiss was featured during the fall, winter and spring of 1938–39.

Hearing that new auditions were scheduled for the show in the fall of 1939, Prentiss mistakenly believed he needn't reapply—the part *belonged* to him. As a result an aspiring Bill Bouchey was awarded the namesake role from that tryout. Despite that, Prentiss remained determined: When Bouchey left the syndicated series after that season to pursue Hollywood film acting, Prentiss made certain he was present at the *next* audition. He won the coveted role a second time, assuming it for the final transcription season, 1939–40, and becoming the first actor to play the part when the series was beamed to a national audience the following year. He claimed the role, in fact, through June 17, 1949. The quarter-hour daily episodes gave way that fall to half-hour narratives aired twice weekly and presenting Paul Barnes in the featured role. But in just three months the series left radio forever.

A curious oddity occurred in this juvenile crime fighting series, applicable to several of its peers. Why was it necessary for Captain Midnight to take summers off? Did he need to regroup and rest from his labors and tension of the other months? Were there perhaps fewer villains to subdue in the summertime? Maybe *they* needed a rest from their relentless efforts to conquer the world and decided to take time off to regroup between June and September every year. In only three of the 11 radio seasons that *Captain Midnight* aired did the program continue without interruption. Surely the kid fans must have wondered why their hero predictably went away for a few weeks annually, only to return as if months of time hadn't intervened.

It was an incongruity for a child's perceptive mind to ponder.

Members of the Secret Squadron were assigned a membership number to accompany the initials "SS" (Captain Midnight was SS-1; Chuck, SS-2; Joyce, SS-3; Ikky, SS-4, for instance). It presented a novel opportunity for Ovaltine to entice young fans to become faithful listeners as well as loyal to the sponsor's product by applying for club membership with a dime and a seal from inside an Ovaltine lid. Each applicant was given a personal number and sent a membership card and Secret Squadron decoder. The decoders were good for a year, then replaced by an "updated" model that required yet another dime and seal. Some of these were reportedly clumsy affairs that didn't work very well but others were well worth their price and the wait for them. (See *The Great Radio Heroes* by Jim Harmon for a fuller description. Harmon was among thousands of juveniles who regularly ordered those premiums. For a listing of scores of premiums offered by the show, consult his volume *Radio Mystery and Adventure and Its Appearances in Film, Television and Other Media*.)

Stuntman/writer/B-western cowboy actor Dave O'Brien was selected to play the role of Captain Midnight in 1942 when Columbia Pictures brought the aerial hero to the silver screen via the matinee serial. Featured alongside him were Guy Wilkerson as Ichabod Mudd, Sam Edwards as Chuck Ramsey, Dorothy Short as Joyce Edwards (a name and background change from the radio series) and James Craven as Ivan Shark. They kept juvenile theater-goers spellbound through 15 chapters, at the conclusion of which Ivan (the Terrible) was trounced for good by accidentally electrocuting himself.

Two years earlier, in 1940, Captain Midnight turned up in *The Funnies*, a Dell comic book that included many mythical stalwarts adapted from juvenile radio heroes. Within a year the stunning aerialist was the subject of a daily newspaper comic strip. Some of those strips later appeared in Whitman's Big Little Books novels. By 1942, obviously at peak frenzy surrounding the character, Fawcett acquired some of the pulp fiction publishing rights and premiered an exclusive *Captain Midnight* comic book. All of the extensions had the effect of perpetuating the familiar series that thrilled adolescent fans on radio.

Captain Midnight's Adventure Theatre, consisting of edited chapters of Republic movie serials, introduced the character to TV audiences in 1951. A young, handsome, nameless actor played the title role, yet he was seen sparingly. He introduced the filmed features and delivered plugs for Ovaltine along with a barrage of premium offers. Following a brief run, the series departed, never to return.

The Wander Company, makers of Ovaltine, wasn't ready to banish Captain Midnight to never-never land just yet. It was convinced that video was ripe for continuing the airman's exploits and reaching potential new consumers for its product. A half-hour black-and-white series simply titled *Captain Midnight* debuted over CBS-TV on Sept. 4, 1954. It ran continuously in various midday Saturday time slots through May 12, 1956. Richard Webb starred as Captain Midnight, with Sid Melton as Ikky Mudd and Olan Soule as Aristotle Jones (aka Tut), an eccentric lab scientist of the Secret Squadron. Soule had played a recurring role in the radio series and was the only known holdover. Ovaltine, meanwhile, never ceased to pitch a long cycle of premiums to its newly acquired fans on the tube, as it had done earlier on radio.

In the 1970s and again in the 1980s Richard Webb made several futile attempts to revive the televised series. He reappeared in some Ovaltine commercials that aired in 1988 featuring the image of Captain Midnight.

Simultaneously in the 1950s, the Screen Gems production company offered a syndicated version of the same televised property under a different moniker—*Jet Jackson, Flying Commando*. It was small-screened in about 130 markets that didn't receive the network feed. The change in names resulted because Wander Company owned exclusive rights to the *Midnight* appellation.

Captain Starr of Space see Starr of Space

Carolyn Day, Detective

On the Air: Syndicated.
Sponsor: Local advertisers in markets where the series aired.
Extant Episodes: 10 (including six five-minute features).

CAST & CREDITS

Leads—Title role played by Mary McConnell; Larry Bixby, played by Howard McNear.

Gangsters were a common foe in Carolyn Day's crime fighting exploits. She turned out to be a victim about as often as she did a crimestopper, frequently finding herself on the wrong end of a gun as she tracked down ruthless mobsters who displayed little compunction over their shooting sprees. Despite the title, Day was an avocational sleuth; yet her father, Randolph Day, was a trained professional detective. Police lieutenant Larry Bixby of the homicide squad usually assisted Ms. Day on her killer-trailing escapades.

The Casebook of Gregory Hood

On the Air: June 3, 1946–May 26, 1947, MBS, Monday, 8:30 p.m.; March 2–June 22, 1948,

MBS, Tuesday, 9:30 p.m.; June 28, 1948–Jan. 31, 1949, MBS, Monday, 8:30 p.m.; June 1–Oct. 11, 1949, MBS, Tuesday, 8 p.m.; Oct. 15–Oct. 29, 1949, MBS, Saturday, 8:30 p.m.; Nov. 13–Dec. 25, 1949, MBS, Sunday, 5 p.m.; Jan. 25–May 3, 1950, ABC, Wednesday, 8:30 p.m.; May 9–Sept. 3, 1950, ABC, Tuesday, 8 p.m.; Oct. 3–Oct. 10, 1951, ABC, Wednesday, 8:30 p.m. 30 minutes.

Sponsors: Petri wine (most of the run); Sustained (Jan. 25–May 3, 1950); American Chicle Co. for Adams Dentyne and Chiclets chewing gums (Oct. 3–10, 1951).

Extant Episodes: 18.

CAST & CREDITS

Producer—Frank Cooper.
Directors—Martin Andrews, Lee Bolen, Ray Buffum, Frank Cooper, Ned Tollinger.
Writers—Anthony Boucher, Ray Buffum, Dennis Green.
Music—Dean Fossler.
Sound Effects—Art Sorrance.
Announcer—Harry Bartell.
Leads—Title role played by Jackson Beck, Martin Gabel, Gale Gordon, Elliott Lewis, Paul McGrath, George Petrie; Sandor (Sandy) Taylor, played by Carl Harper, Bill Johnstone, Howard McNear; Harry, played by Harry Bartlett.
Support Roles—Art Carney, Kathleen Cordell, John McGovern.

In a lavish flat fronting San Francisco's Golden Gate Bridge, Gregory Hood resided—a debonair gentleman, amateur composer and celebrated lady-killer. Hood operated an import concern in which he transacted exchanges in curios and artifacts. The very nature of the business saw him frequently crisscrossing the globe in search of rare commodities. Some objects had distinguishing features or trivia from their past that could be tied to a contemporary mystery. Each week Hood wove a narrative around an object, recalling it to his friend Harry. The caper brought up incidents surrounding the item that occupied both Hood and his assistant, Sandor (Sandy) Taylor.

The method of retelling the preceding action employed by *Hood* was one of several adopted for the airwaves. For 18 years *Mr. Keen, Tracer of Lost Persons*—ardent fans of that venerable series will remember—took from his files and brought to *his* radio audiences "one of his most widely celebrated missing persons' cases." Creative people in the industry sought untapped techniques on main themes to apply to their dramas, hopefully infusing them with a distinctive edge.

A genuine San Francisco importer, Richard Gump, was the archetype for Gregory Hood. The writers approached him when they were confused over importing ambiguity.

The Cases of Mr. Ace

On the Air: 1945, ABC, Monday. 30 minutes. Specific dates and time unidentified.
Sponsor: No information.
Extant Episodes: Three.

CAST & CREDITS

Producer/Director—Jason James.
Music—Del Castillo.
Announcer—Carlton KaDell.
Lead—Title role played by George Raft.
Support Roles—Lorraine Beaumont, Leo Cleary, Mary Jane Croft, Stanley Farrar, Frances Huffman, Joseph Kearns, Cathy Lewis, Charlie Lung, Jeanette Nolan, Barney Phillips, Elliott Reed, Theodore von Eltz, Peggy Webber.

The homicide investigations of PI Edward Ace formed the nucleus of this little crime drama. Ace maintained an office on Manhattan's Sixth Avenue. His gruff exterior was two-fisted and tough as nails; he was the archetype of a substantial segment of his profession.

Casey, Crime Photographer

(aka *Flashgun Casey*, aka *Casey, Press Photographer*, aka *Crime Photographer*)

On the Air: *Flashgun Casey*. July 7–Aug. 4, 1943, CBS, Wednesday, 11:30 p.m.; Aug. 12–Oct. 21, 1943, CBS, Thursday, 11:30 p.m.; Oct. 30, 1943–July 8, 1944, CBS, Saturday, 11:30 p.m. (with name change to *Casey, Press Photographer* effective April 8, 1944); July 15–Sept. 9, 1944, CBS, Saturday, 5 p.m.; Sept. 12, 1944–June 26, 1945, CBS, Tuesday, 11:30 p.m.; *Crime Photographer*. July 11–Sept. 5, 1945, CBS, Wednesday, 9 p.m.; Sept. 12–Sept. 26, 1945, CBS, Wednesday, 10:30 p.m.; Oct. 20–Dec. 1, 1945, CBS, Saturday, 1:30 p.m.; Dec. 3, 1945–March 4, 1946, CBS, Monday, 10:30 p.m.; March 12–May 28, 1946, CBS, Tuesday, 10 p.m.; June 3–July 22, 1946, CBS, Monday, 8:30 p.m.; Aug. 8, 1946–Nov. 16, 1950, CBS, Thursday, 9:30 p.m. (with name change to *Casey, Crime Photographer* effective March 20, 1947); *Crime Photographer*. Jan. 13–Sept. 29, 1954, CBS, Wednesday, 9 p.m.; Oct. 8, 1954–April 22, 1955, CBS, Friday, 8 p.m. 30 minutes.

Sponsors: American Hocking Glass Corp. for Anchor Hocking glassware (Aug. 8, 1946–March 25, 1948); Toni Division of the Gillette Co. for Toni home permanents, shampoos and other hair care commodities (April 1, 1948–July 28, 1949); Philip Morris Co. for Philip Morris cigarettes (Aug. 4, 1949–Oct. 19, 1950); Sustained (all other time periods).

Extant Episodes: 72.

CAST & CREDITS

Producers—R. L. Landy, A. Renier.
Directors—John Dietz, Albert Ward.
Writers—Alonzo Dean Cole, Gail Ingram, Harry Ingram, Milton J. Kramer.
Music—Archie Bleyer (orchestra), Lew White (organ).
Sound Effects—Jerry McCarthy, James Rogan, Art Strand.
Announcers—Bill Cullen, Bob Hite, Tony Marvin, Ken Roberts.
Leads—Title role played by Matt Crowley, Jim Backus (first few months), Staats Cotsworth (late 1943–April 22, 1955); Annie Williams, played by Jone Allison, Alice Reinheart, Lesley Woods, Betty Furness, Jan Miner.
Support Roles—Jackson Beck, Bernard Lenrow (police Captain Bill Logan), John Gibson (Ethelbert), Herman Chittison, Juan Hernandez and Teddy Wilson (pianist); also, Bill Adams, Ed Begley, Ralph Bell, Peter Capell, Art Carney, Ted de Corsia, Roger De Koven, Joe Di Santis, Robert Dryden, Hope Emerson, John Griggs, Jack Hartley, Raymond Edward Johnson, Joseph Julian, Mandel Kramer, James Kreiger, Abby Lewis, Arnold Moss, Santos Ortega, Bryna Raeburn, Karl Swenson, Miriam Wolfe.

Jack Casey, a photojournalist for the fictitious *Morning Express*, hung around the Blue Note Café with Annie Williams, fellow reporter and romantic distraction, in between assignments. "When not solving murders," noted a radio reviewer, "he was mostly concerned with negotiating small loans to tide him over to payday and trying to keep his stomach calm with soothing liquids." The locale's ambiance was enhanced by Casey's exchanges with bartender-pal Ethelbert (no last name) and the Blue Note piano, with proportions exceeding those of a simple backdrop.

Casey and Williams were actively involved in the newspaper stories that they covered, which were predominantly homicides. The hero could turn into an amateur detective by merely studying a photo he had shot at a crime scene. Predictably he derived clues that the police missed and, thus, caught killers who might have escaped. Casey and Williams often crossed with local law enforcement officials—in particular, police captain Bill Logan. The program was a kind of laid-back mystery drama without the startling revelations and intense action inherent in many other series. The soothing melody from tickling those ivories contributed immeasurably to its rest-easy approach.

Casey, the character, was originated in the novels of George Harmon Coxe. When Alonzo Dean Cole adapted the figure for radio, he (Cole) had already been distinguished by his literary contributions to *The Witch's Tale* during the crystal-set age of the 1930s. His *Casey* scripts, claimed a reviewer, "contained wit and naturalism missing from many radio thrillers."

Over its long run *Casey, Crime Photographer* aired in 14 time periods, several of them in post-bedtime hours for much of the nation's East Coast, on six broadcast days and with four title changes reflecting as many different names. Yet when CBS left *Casey* in one timeslot on the same day of the week for more than four years (1946–50), the drama drew a loyal following and maintained sponsorship for all but the final month of that period. Those claims couldn't be substantiated throughout the series' usual onerous and haphazard scheduling. Little wonder, then, that advertisers and audiences stayed away—many of them probably couldn't find the feature on the dial or weren't sure it was the same series, due to those frequent moniker switches.

One trivia expert recalled that a character named Walter, whose voice was never heard on the air, was employed in the Blue Note Café kitchen. Although he had no lines to speak, Walter was often summoned for more olives by bartender Ethelbert. Walter's "appearances" were a cost-cutting method, extending the bistro facade, adding to the authenticity of the setting by developing (non) action that the listener only perceived.

Professional sound effects technician Robert L. Mott recalls in one of his books how footsteps gave radio drama movement and perspective, especially if a scene had little dialogue. On such occasions it was critical for every step to be heard distinctly for that helped an audience envision precisely what was transpiring at the moment. Once during a live broadcast of *Casey, Crime Photographer*, Mott recounted, "An actor carelessly stepped out his cigarette near the sound-effects area. Later, during a scene requiring a long pattern of footsteps, the sound man accidentally stepped on the cigarette butt, causing it to stick and silence the effectiveness of one of his heels…. As Casey hurried down the long hallway…, audiences at home wondered how he could move so rapidly on just one leg." Mott concluded: "Obviously, the effects of cigarette smoking to the health and sanity of sound men were known many years before it was announced by the surgeon general's office."

CBS-TV brought a new series, *Crime Photographer*, to the small screen on April 19, 1951, based on the exploits of crusading newspaperman Jack Casey. Richard Carlyle originated the role on the tube but departed from the live production within two months. Darren McGavin replaced him, playing his first starring role on TV. McGavin persisted until the series left the air on June 5, 1952. John Gibson, radio's Ethelbert, carried his part to TV but within two months he was also gone, replaced by Cliff Hall. Jan Miner, one of the radio actresses playing Annie Williams, reprised her role during the full video run. The popular piano of radio's Blue Note Café was taken up by Tony Mottola on the video version.

Jay Hickerson has developed a log of all the radio performances of this series.

Casey, Press Photographer
see Casey, Crime Photographer

The Challenge of the Yukon
(aka *Sergeant Preston of the Yukon*)

On the Air: *The Challenge of the Yukon*—Between Feb. 3, 1938, and May 28, 1947, the series aired over Detroit's WXYZ on various weekdays. (Note: Where time cannot be verified it has been omitted.) June 12–July 3, 1947, ABC, Thursday; July 12–Sept. 6, 1947, ABC, Saturday; Sept. 11–Oct. 23, 1947, ABC, Thursday; Nov. 1, 1947–July 24, 1948, ABC, Saturday, 7:30 p.m.; July 28–Sept. 1, 1948, ABC, Wednesday; Sept. 6, 1948–June 10, 1949, ABC, Monday/Wednesday/Friday, 5 p.m.; June 15–Sept. 7, 1949, ABC, Wednesday; Sept. 12–Dec. 30, 1949, ABC, Monday/Wednesday/Friday, 5 p.m.; Jan. 2–Dec. 15, 1950, MBS, Monday/Wednesday/Friday, 5 p.m.; Jan. 1–Jan. 8, 1951, MBS, Monday, 5:30 p.m.; Jan. 20, 1951, MBS, Saturday, 5:30 p.m.; Jan. 27–July 8, 1951, MBS, Saturday and Sunday, 5:30 p.m.; July 10, 1951–Jan. 3, 1952, MBS, Sunday/Tuesday/Thursday, 5 p.m.; *Sergeant Preston of the Yukon* (effective Nov. 13, 1951)—Jan. 8–June 26, 1952, MBS, Tuesday/Thursday, 5 p.m.; June 29–Sept. 7, 1952, MBS, Sunday; Sept. 16, 1952–May 14, 1953, MBS, Tuesday/Thursday, 5 p.m.; May 19–June 9, 1953, MBS, Tuesday; Sept. 15, 1953–June 10, 1954, MBS, Tuesday/Thursday, 5 p.m.; Sept. 14, 1954–June 9, 1955, Tuesday/Thursday, 5 p.m. 15 minutes (Feb. 3, 1938–May 28, 1947), 30 minutes (June 12, 1947–June 10, 1954), 25 minutes (Sept. 14, 1954–June 9, 1955).

Theme Song: *Donna Diana Overture* (Von Reznicek) (Note: This melody was part of the background and bridge music heard between the scenes of *The Lone Ranger*.)

Sponsor: Sustained (Feb. 3, 1938–May 28, 1947); The Quaker Oats Co. for Quaker Puffed Rice and Quaker Puffed Wheat cereals (June 12, 1947–June 9, 1955).

Extant Episodes: 250 plus.

CAST & CREDITS

Creator—Thomas Dougall.

Producer—George W. Trendle.

Directors—Al Hodge, Charles D. Livingston, Fred Flowerday.

Writers—Dan Beattie, Tom Dougall, Bob Green, Felix Holt, Betty Joyce, Jim Lawrence, Steve McCarthy, Mildred Merrill, Fran Striker.

Sound Effects—Dewey Cole (who could bark, whine and growl appropriately on cue),

Jimmy Fletcher, Fred Flowerday, Fred Fry, Bill Hengsterbeck, Ken Robertson.

Announcers—Fred Foy, Bob Hite, Jay Michael.

Lead—Title role played by Brace Beemer (1941, 1953–54), Jay Michael (1941–46), Paul Sutton (1947–53).

Support Roles—Lee Allman, Harry Goldstein, Paul Hughes, Rollon Parker, Frank Russell, Bill Saunders, John Todd (Inspector Conrad), Ernie Winstanley.

A series readily identified by dual monikers, this drama focused on the efforts of Sergeant William Preston of the Royal Northwest Mounted Police and his wonder dog, Yukon King. Preston exhibited fine form in his smart red uniform, broad-brimmed hat and pencil-thin mustache. While in the warmer months he mounted his stallion, Blackie (later called Rex), it was inevitably King, an Alaskan husky, who saved the day, ferrying his master by dog sled to most of the far reaches of the frozen North. King was permitted to run "free lead" with the team, dashing in and out of the line, nipping at the other dogs to keep them pulling ahead. Man and canine employed every ingenious tracking device offered to follow the trails—often cold, both figuratively and literally—to capture miscreants who opted to carry out sinister plots in howling winds and deepest snows.

Sometimes the sergeant and his companion were merely called upon to tote serum to victims of epidemic outbreaks, or rescue gold-seekers from bandits and blizzards, or capture fur pelts and the thieves who pilfered them. Whatever their mission, the pair was prepared to meet the odds, King justifiably receiving most of the credit for their successes: "Well, King, thanks to you, this case is closed," a grateful sergeant routinely acknowledged, with great solemnity at the conclusion of their dramatic rescues.

Launched by George W. Trendle, the series emanated from Detroit's WXYZ where a trio of famous dramatic heroes broadcast their pursuit-and-capture escapades. Besides Sergeant Preston there was *The Green Hornet* and—still more famous and undoubtedly more durable than all other juvenile radio features—*The Lone Ranger*. One analyst characterized the Trendle dramas as having "the common trademarks of simple, vigorous adventure plotting, a staunchly bigger-than-life male hero, and lively music cribbed from the classics." Casts on one routinely turned up on the others. Author Gerald Nachman, referring to the Northwest Mountie as a "Canadian cowboy," concisely assessed his heritage this way: "Sergeant Preston, with his trusty husky, was really the Lone Ranger on ice."

The name change from *The Challenge of the Yukon* to *Sergeant Preston of the Yukon* occurred after 946 performances; there were 1,260 dramatizations altogether during the dual-moniker run.

The best recalled premium offered by this program was a deed to a square inch of Yukon land, at $25 in 1955. For a complete listing of the numerous premiums the show provided, the reader is directed to Jim Harmon's book *Radio Mystery and Adventure and Its Appearances in Film, Television and Other Media*.

In a clever reversal of roles, Inspector Conrad, Preston's superior officer, stationed at Dawson City, was played by actor John Todd, who appeared simultaneously in the prominent part of the Lone Ranger's "faithful Indian companion" Tonto. During a portion of *Yukon*'s run, actor Brace Beemer—best remembered as the Lone Ranger—played Sergeant Preston. Is this a fair example of true poetic justice?

Every Thursday night at 7:30 p.m. ET between Sept. 29, 1955, and Sept. 25, 1958, CBS-TV screened *Sergeant Preston of the Yukon* for its video audiences. Played by actor Richard Simmons, the Mountie was accompanied by his horse Rex and the wonder dog, King. Of the series, one reviewer averred: "Preston seemed to spend most of his time by himself, trudging through the snow to apprehend fugitives." Shot in black-and-white, the 78-episode series was largely filmed at Ashcroft, Colorado, by the Wrather Corp. When the network run ended another 26 episodes were filmed in color and syndicated to local TV markets. NBC-TV replayed some of the previously aired episodes on Saturday afternoons during the 1963–64 television season.

Terry Salomonson prepared a log of the radio series.

Chandu the Magician

On the Air: Oct. 10, 1932–1936, Don Lee Network, MBS and independents—originating from KHJ, Los Angeles, over 77 stations initially and from Chicago in 1935–36, Weekdays, various time periods; June 28, 1948–Jan. 28, 1949, MBS, Weekdays, time unsubstantiated; Feb. 3–April 28, 1949, MBS, Thursday, time unsubstantiated; Oct. 15, 1949–June 10, 1950, ABC, Saturday, 7:30 p.m.; June 14–Sept. 6, 1950, ABC, Wednesday, 9:30 p.m. 15 minutes (Oct. 8, 1932–Jan. 28, 1949), 30 minutes (Feb. 3, 1949–June 6, 1950).

Sponsors: White King Granulated soap (West) and Beech Nut chewing gum (East) (1932–36); White King Granulated soap (1948–49); Sustained (1949–50).

Extant Episodes: 148.

CAST & CREDITS

Creators—Harry A. Earnshaw, Raymond R. Morgan.
Producer/Director—Cyril Armbrister.
Director—Blair Walliser.
Writers—Sam Dann, Vera Oldham.
Music—Felix Mills, Raymond Paige, Korla Pandit (pseudonym for Juan Rolando).
Sound Effects—Keene Crockett.
Announcer—Howard Culver.
Lead—Frank Chandler, played by Jason

Robards Sr., Gayne Whitman (1932–35), Howard Hoffman (1935–36), Tom Collins (1948–50).

Support Roles—Dorothy Regent (Chandler's sibling), played by Margaret MacDonald (1932–35), Cornelia Osgood (1935–36), Irene Tedrow (1948–50); Bob Regent (his nephew), played by Bob Bixby (1932–35), Olan Soule (1935–36), Lee Miller (1948–50); Betty Regent (his niece), played by Betty Webb (1932–35), Audrey McGrath (1935–36), Joy Terry (1948–50); also Roger deKoven, Carl Emory, Peter Griffith, Leon Janney, Lou Krugman (the storyteller), Ian Martin, Tudor Owen (Ahmad), Bryna Raeburn, Susan Thorne, Luis Van Rooten (Roxor), Veola Vonn (Princess Nadji, Chandler's love interest), Gertrude Warner, Ben Wright.

Endowed with supernatural powers, San Francisco covert agent Frank Chandler, armed with little more than a crystal ball, subdued global forces of evil. In the Far East he had mastered the mysterious secrets of a Hindu yogi. Dubbed "Chandu," he roamed the world in search of despots dedicated to enslaving the universe if left to their own devices. Invariably, nearly every juvenile thriller's hero had a single recurring nemesis; in Chandler's case it was the villainous Egyptian Roxor, whose devious mind frequently matched wits with the American mystic who was enhanced with abstruse capabilities. Like contemporary shows, this one offered a primarily youthful audience premiums galore, a great percentage of them, not surprisingly, consisting of magic tricks.

Writer Vera Oldham became so indispensable to the series that on one occasion the production agency compensated her with a trip to the Orient and a new automobile. Until she applied to write the new radio dramatization, her true gifts had largely gone unnoticed while she idled in a clerical position. So respected was Oldham's talent that—when the series left the air—she received calls to pen scripts for the *Maxwell House Show Boat, Those Websters* and other features.

Charlie Chan see *The Adventures of Charlie Chan*

Charlie Wild, Private Detective

On the Air: Sept. 24–Nov. 5, 1950, NBC, Sunday, 6:30 p.m.; Nov. 12–Dec. 17, 1950, NBC, 5:30 p.m.; Jan. 7–July 1, 1951, CBS, Sunday, 6 p.m. 30 minutes.
Sponsor: Wildroot cream oil hair tonic and similar hair preparations for men (NBC); Sustained (CBS).
Extant Episodes: None known.

CAST & CREDITS

Producers—Edwin Marshall, Lawrence White.
Directors—Carlo De Angelo, Stanley Niss.
Writer—Peter Barry.
Music—C. Sherrill.
Announcer—William Rogers.
Leads—Title role played by George Petrie (Sept. 24–Dec. 17, 1950), Kevin O'Morrison (Jan. 7–March 18, 1951), John McQuade (March 25–July 1, 1951); McCoy, played by Peter Hobbs. (The actress's name who played Effie Perrine remains an unsolved mystery to radio historians.)

The central figure here was a Big Apple PI whom *Billboard* dubbed a "hard-guy hero" spouting lots of "tough talk and vivid similes." While branded for his original sponsor (Wildroot), Wild apparently lived up to his name—another reviewer pointed out that he was good for at least a "knockdown drag-out brawl every week." The show inherited *Sam Spade's* timeslot and some of his audience; it was a weird turn of events when Effie Perrine—Spade's loyal but addlepated San Francisco secretary—turned up in New York to win a similar spot with Charlie Wild. (Perrine even landed on a subsequent televised series of the *Wild* show, a pinnacle Spade never trespassed! Talk about walking on the wild side!) Meanwhile, McCoy (only known name) assisted the driven detective in his sleuthing exploits.

Wildroot introduced this show as a replacement for *Sam Spade* when that series got into trouble. *Spade* lasted until the Eugene McCarthy melee discharged at mid century, and novelist Dashiell Hammett fell into disfavor for refusing to respond to some queries of Wisconsin's junior senator. Hammett wasn't directly connected with the radio program; his link was solely in the use of his appellation, characters and concept. Yet Hammett's name and that of Howard Duff, who was playing Spade, had both surfaced before the House Committee on Un-American Activities, which McCarthy's followers ran. In 1947 Duff, as Spade, took potshots at politicians on the trail of Communist sympathizers. While the matter lay dormant for a couple of years, in June 1950 Duff's moniker appeared in the publication *Red Channels* making him out to be a sympathizer. The heat was appreciably turned up. It was more than the sponsor—and the network—could handle.

On Sept. 9 *Billboard* announced that Wildroot was purging itself of *Spade* with the broadcast of Sept. 17, and that it would underwrite a new series, *Charlie Wild, Private Detective*. Duff appeared as Spade one last time at the inception of the new series with felicitations for his aural successor. According to John Scheinfeld, who chronicled the *Spade* show, Duff's voice wasn't heard on the air again for six years. A quarter of a million written communications from fans, meanwhile, vigorously protested the demise, enough to sway NBC to renew the *Spade* series sans Duff and lacking any reference to Hammett. Two months later the show was reprised with an adolescent-sounding Steve Dunne attempting to recreate the toughness that listeners experienced in Duff. It didn't work. Within five months the unsponsored feature was gone—a dismal ending to what, by all accounts, had been one of the most-loved shows in audio gumshoe history.

Peter Hobbs, who played Charlie Wild's assistant, McCoy, became the first actor to star as protagonist Peter Ames on a new CBS-TV soap opera, *The Secret Storm*, which debuted Feb. 1, 1954. He appeared in that part until 1960.

The live TV series alluded to—*Charlie Wild, Private Detective*—premiered Dec. 22, 1950, on CBS-TV, having just left NBC Radio five days earlier. It was telecast there into the following June. Returning to the air in September 1951 it resurfaced on ABC-TV, remaining until it switched to Dumont Television in March 1952. The drama left the air forever on June 19, 1952. Kevin O'Morrison and John McQuade, who were also giving live performances on radio during the months the show was on CBS-TV, filled the title role. McQuade assumed the part in May 1951 and carried it to the end of the run. Cloris Leachman played Effie Perrine on TV.

Jay Hickerson produced a log of the *Wild* radio show.

Chick Carter, Boy Detective

On the Air: July 5, 1943–July 6, 1945, MBS, Weekdays, floating time periods between 5 and 6 p.m. 15 minutes.
Sponsors: No information.
Extant Episodes: Two.

CAST & CREDITS
Director—Fritz Blocki.
Writers—Fritz Blocki, Walter Gibson, Ed Gruskin, Nancy Webb.
Announcer—Ken Powell.
Leads—Title role played by Bill Lipton, Leon Janney (as of July 3, 1944); Sue, played by

sisters Jean McCoy, Joanne McCoy; Tex, played by Gilbert Mack.

Support Roles—Bill Griffis (Rufus Lash), Stefan Schnabel (the Rattler).

More than a mere adventure series, this crime drama for adolescents grew from the eminently more popular *Nick Carter, Master Detective*, which preceded it to the air by only three months. Chick was the adopted son of Nick, an infamous detective of pulp fiction and the ether that picked up his father's sleuthing habits. There were, in fact, occasional tries at joining the two shows' story lines. Chick's nemesis, an imperious villain and crime lord known only as The Rattler, appeared with some regularity. And like the more mature investigators, Chick Carter had a pretty female accomplice, Sue (no last name), to fill in the gaps when dialogue was required. Tex (another one-name-only figure), their friend, shared the duo's adventures. The show arrived each day to a distinctive billboard. Over the clicking of telegraph keys, an announcer would beckon: *Mutual to Y… O… U… Sending … Are you ready?* An unidentified voice would respond: *Y… O… U to Mutual … Go ahead.* The kiddies could immediately tell that this was their kind of gumshoe.

Nick Carter, Master Detective, from which this show emanated, developed considerably greater appeal among its mature radio audiences. It lasted a dozen years as opposed to *Chick's* mere two seasons with the juvenile set.

Jay Hickerson prepared a partial log of the *Chick Carter* series.

Chip Davis, Commando

(aka *Commando*)

On the Air: *Commando*—July 18–Sept. 26, 1942, CBS, Saturday, 8:30 p.m.; Oct. 4, 1942–July 18, 1943, CBS, Sunday, 7 p.m.

(title change to *Chip Davis, Commando*, March 28, 1943); July 24–Oct. 9, 1943, CBS, Saturday, 5:30 p.m. 30 minutes.

Sponsor: Sustained.

Extant Episodes: Two.

CAST & CREDITS

Producer—Robert Louis Shallot.

Director—John Dietz.

Music—Charles Paul (organ).

Lead—Title role played by Clayton (Bud) Collyer, Carleton Young.

Chip Davis was a courageous American identified with the London-based Commandos, "Britain's famous fighting unit." Those troops were reportedly made up of highly skilled, comprehensively-prepared Allied forces during World War II. Their sole purpose was to overcome the Nazis through a determined, coordinated combat effort.

The Cisco Kid

On the Air: Oct. 2, 1942–April 23, 1943, MBS, Friday, 8:30 p.m.; May 4–July 6, 1943, MBS, Tuesday, 8 p.m.; Oct. 8–Dec. 17, 1943, MBS, Friday, 8:30 p.m.; Jan. 22–Oct. 7, 1944, MBS, Saturday, 8:30 p.m.; Nov. 1, 1944–Feb. 14, 1945, MBS, Wednesday, 9:30 p.m.; 1947–56, Syndicated, multiple days, aired in local markets in various time slots. 30 minutes.

Sponsors: Sustained (network run); local underwriters (in syndication).

Extant Episodes: 313 (minimum).

CAST & CREDITS

Producer—J. C. Lewis.

Directors—Jeanne K. Harrison, Fred Levings, Jock MacGregor.

Writers—Bill Gordon, Larry Hays, Kenny Lyons, Ralph Rosenberg, John Sinn.

Sound Effects—Jack Dick, Dick James, Ray Kemper, James Murphy, Ross Murray.

Announcers—Marvin Miller, Michael Rye (pseudonym for Rye Billsbury).

Leads—Title role played by Jackson Beck (1942–45) and Jack Mather (1947–56); Pan Pancho played by Louis Sorin (1942–45), Harry Lang and Mel Blanc (1947–56).

Support Roles—Jean Ellyn, Marvin Miller, Bryna Raeburn, Mark Smith, Vicki Vola.

Slackly centered in O. Henry's classic romantic character Robin Hood, Cisco was a Latin adaptation of the tenderhearted guy who stole from the haves to share with the have-nots. In this version he encountered banditos galore and an assortment of other rampaging, mean-spirited hombres. They had to be suppressed in order for the Hispanic avenger to rectify wrongs, pillage the plunderers and restore the underdogs to their rightful spots. By his side was a stereotypical gringo, a laughing, paunchy cohort named Pan Pancho (Cisco called him "Chico") who apparently came along for the ride and not much else. While a master of the bullwhip, Pancho offered little more than conversation—usually humorous—to the adventurous Cisco. A perceptive wit typified the sidekick: "Pancho was a Mexican buffoon whose strong dialect and penchant for malaprops seemed more appropriate to vaudeville than evening radio." Although Cisco could rebuke his friend for sheer idiocy, no one else was ever so permitted to malign the cohort.

Almost invariably, near the end of every episode—before the pair rode off into the sunset and to their next adventure—Cisco, fancying himself a ladies' man, kissed that episode's leading feminine figure goodbye. The Latin lover would consider it unthinkable not to take advantage of such a moment! And while Cisco might be considered to be a philanderer by the parents of small fry listeners, radio standards hampered his going further. When a senorita swooned to his adoring affections ("Oh-h-h-h, Ceesco!") it was—as author Gerald Nachman matter-of-factly pointed out—"the closest thing to an orgasm on radio." Cisco's relationships with his opposite gender were always punctuated by insincerity. Thus the Casanova of the old West turned out to be an OK kind of guy, to the adults as well as the youngsters, who cared very little for a lot of mush in their juvenile narrative plots.

Although Cisco was eventually able to shake off a badman image he had been saddled with when the series premiered, a favorite plot device regularly found the sheriff and his posse mistakenly suspecting Chico and Pancho of the misdeeds of hooligans on the trail. But *Radio Life* explained in a 1947 article: "The two perpetuate the hoax so the real cowboy-crooks will let down their guard." Astride their trusty mounts, Diablo and Loco, "the Cisco Kid and Pancho were modeled after common stereotypes of the Latin American as a rascalish lover and a lazy clown," a wag noted. "It was as if the Frito Bandito had joined up with Sancho Panza," allowed another. Despite such put-downs, a third assessment correctly assessed: "The ready, fun-loving camaraderie between Cisco and Pancho was what made the series work."

The origins of the Cisco Kid figure may be found in O. Henry's short story *The Caballero's Way*. He debuted there as a disheveled bandito who victimized the rich to help the poor. Cisco next turned up in early silent films, then in numerous sound features starting in 1929 with *In Old Arizona*. For his portrayal of the part there Warner Baxter received one of the very first Academy Awards to be delivered. There were dozens of subsequent films, with Cesar Romero, Gilbert Roland and Duncan Renaldo starring in the role.

Membership in The Cisco Kid Rancher Club was but one of a myriad of trinkets held out to adolescent listeners of the radio series. Such novelties as masks, puzzles and secret compartment rings were offered as enticements for young fans to maintain close ties to both the radio series and its local sponsors.

When Jackson Beck signed for the aural lead in *The Cisco Kid* in 1942 at $50 weekly, he exclaimed: "I thought I was in fat city. My God, fifty bucks for a half-hour; you came in and did two, three hours of rehearsal and you got fifty bucks. Wow, that was a lot." America had not totally recovered from the Great Depression by then and was in the throes of a second global conflagration within a couple of decades, commanding not only the nation's attention but diverting much of its economic resources. Fifty dollars easily would have exceeded the top pay in most professions for a few hours of work.

Duncan Renaldo and Leo Carillo starred as Cisco and Pancho, respectively, when the radio series inspired a syndicated video version produced by Ziv TV. Critics Tim Brooks and Earle Marsh claimed the tube's feature was "the first big syndicated film hit," observing that it was "in fact one of the first popular filmed programs on TV." Most shows then were telecast live. Launched in 1950, some 156 half-hour episodes were released by 1956. Because the series was shot in color (though most stations in the 1950s screened it in black-and-white), it was repeated over local television outlets for more than two decades.

From 1950 to 1968 a *Cisco Kid* comic strip appeared in daily newspapers.

On Feb. 6, 1994, both lead characters turned up in a made-for-television movie shown on the TNT cable network. In that version, Jimmy Smits played Cisco and Cheech Marin was Pancho.

Terry Salomonson prepared a partial log of the radio series.

City Desk

On the Air: Jan. 2–June 26, 1941, CBS, Thursday, 8:30 p.m.; July 5–Sept. 27, 1941, CBS, Saturday, 8:30 p.m. 30 minutes.
Sponsor: Colgate-Palmolive-Peet Inc. for Palmolive soap and Colgate brushless shave cream.
Extant Episodes: None known.

CAST & CREDITS

Directors—Himan Brown, Kenneth W. MacGregor.
Writers—Frank Dahm, Frank Gould, Stuart Hawkins.
Music—Charles Paul (organ).
Leads—Jack Winters, played by Donald Briggs, James Meighan, Chester Stratton; Linda Webster, played by Gertrude Warner.
Support Roles—Geoffrey Bryant (editor Dan Tobin), George Coulouris, Jimmy McCallion (Caruso), Ethel Owen (Mrs. Cameron), Karl Swenson.

A couple of crack newspaper reporters, Jack Winters and Linda Webster, trailed murderers and gangsters in a metropolitan area riddled by crime. The twosome maintained a sterling reputation for solving the mayhem that inevitably bewildered local law enforcement authorities.

Listeners must have wondered how journalism school grads invariably gained an edge when performing the jobs of alumni of the police academies as such themes were quite prevalent in radio. It was the same premise adapted by several other aural fictional newspaper series (e.g. *The Big Story, Big Town, Casey Crime Photographer, Front Page Farrell,* et al ad infinitum) and done better—based on the tenures on the air alone—elsewhere.

Cloak and Dagger

On the Air: May 7–Aug. 27, 1950, NBC, Sunday, 4 p.m.; Sept. 1–Oct. 6, 1950, NBC, Friday, 8 p.m.; Oct. 15–22, 1950, NBC, Sunday, 4 p.m. 30 minutes.
Sponsor: Sustained.
Extant Episodes: 22 (complete run).

CAST & CREDITS

Producers—Louis G. Cowan, Alfred Hollander.
Director—Sherman Marks.
Writers—Jack Gordon, Winifred Wolfe.
Music—John Gart.
Announcers—Karl Weber, Robert Warren.
Host—Corey Ford.
Support Roles—Inge Adams, Jone Allison, Michael Artist, Boris Aplon, Martin Balsam, Luise Barclay, Brad Barker, Jackson Beck, Ralph Bell, Lili Darvas, Eric Dressler, Janice Gilbert, Larry Haines, Eileen Heckart, Irene Hubbard, Leon Janney, Jerry Jarrett, Raymond Edward Johnson, Joseph Julian, Berry Kroeger, Ross Martin, Mel Ferrer, Jan Miner, Virginia Payne, Bill Quinn, Bryna Raeburn, Guy Repp, Grant Richards, Arnold Robertson, Francis Robinson, Stefan Schnabel, Everett Sloane, Guy Sorel, Lou Sorin, Lotte Stavisky, Maurice Tarplin, Les Tremayne, Karl Weber, Chuck Webster, Bill Zuckert.

This anthology of surveillance tales from behind enemy lines was adapted from a book titled *Cloak and Dagger*. Its co-author Corey Ford hosted the radio feature, focusing on the operation of the U.S. Office of Strategic Services (OSS)—forerunner of the CIA—during World War II. Ford, himself, was an ex–OSS officer. "Are you willing to undertake a dangerous mission for the United States knowing in advance you may never return alive?" he inquired at the inception of every broadcast. It was a question put to those volunteering for OSS duty on behalf of their nation.

The show billed the OSS as our "top secret intelligence agency" during wartime. "It was this country's first all-out effort in black warfare—dropping undercover operatives behind enemy lines, organizing local partisans to blow bridges and dynamite tunnels, outwitting the best spy systems of Europe and Asia," Ford explained to listeners. Continuing lengthy epigraphical remarks, he added: "The success of the OSS is known but the story be-hind that success—the story of the everyday, average Americans of every race, creed and color who risked their lives knowing all too well that if they were caught they would face torture and probably death—is what Alistair McBain [his co-author] and I have tried to tell in *Cloak and Dagger*. We feel it is a story in which every American can take deep pride."

A critic called this drama "a gripping show with every story an unpredictable departure from formula." Unfortunately, he advised that the program was lost in a seasonal schedule when it was placed in the midst of "several other shows of far inferior quality."

Jerry Haendiges prepared a log of this series.

Cohen, the Detective

On the Air: Aug. 17–Sept. 21, 1943, NBC Blue, Wednesday. Sept. 27–Oct. 18, 1943, NBC Blue, Tuesday. Air times and length unsubstantiated.
Sponsor: No information.
Extant Episodes: None known.

CAST & CREDITS
No information.

This was a fleeting, lighthearted mystery combining comedy with criminal sleuthing.

Commando see *Chip Davis, Commando*

Confession

On the Air: July 5–Sept. 13, 1953, NBC, Sunday, 9:30 p.m. 30 minutes.
Sponsor: Sustained.
Extant Episodes: Eight.

CAST & CREDITS

Producer—Warren Lewis.
Producer/Director—Homer Canfield.
Music—J. Frederick Albech.
Announcer—John Wald.
Special Guest—Richard McGee.
Lead—Correctional Officer Richard A. McKee, played by Paul Frees.
Support Roles—Parley Baer, Herb Butterfield, Don Diamond, Sam Edwards, Virginia Christine, Virginia Gregg, Stacey Harris, Jonathan Hole, Peter Leeds, Joyce McCluskey, Marvin Miller, Jack Moyles, Barney Phillips.

Richard A. McGee, the director of the California State Department of Corrections, was impersonated weekly as he participated in a dramatic anthology drawn from the archives of several state correctional institutions. At the series' inception, the voice of an alleged criminal read these lines: "I make this confession of my own free will because it is true. There wasn't any force or violence used upon my person to induce me to make these statements. Without promise of immunity or gratuity, I confess." An announcer inquired: "You understand, of course, your statements will be made public to the radio program *Confession*?" "I do," was invariably the reply. The announcer responded: "You are listening to *Confession*. This confession is a matter of documented record. You will hear the story of this crime experience told in the person's own words. This is *Confession*."

The names, of course, were altered to protect the subjects' legal rights. All the while it sounded very much like the program it was filling in for then on summer hiatus, *Dragnet*. The listeners were once again treated to some authentic adventures in crime and punishment. The big difference in the dual dramas was that, whereas *Dragnet* began with a felony, *Confession* examined the experience after a perpetrator

had been apprehended. The work of law officers was revealed through the words of the confessor who recounted his tale, often with an air of indisposed acceptance to his plight. Dramatic action frequently took over from his monologue, highlighting some of the detail for the listener. The *real* Richard McGee turned up midway through the broadcast to make a pitch that—beyond any doubt—became the series' overriding theme: "Crime does not pay." No unexpected surprises there.

Confidentially Yours

On the Air: July 7–Oct. 27, 1950, NBC, Friday, 9:30 p.m. 30 minutes.
Sponsor: Sustained.
Extant Episodes: None known.

CAST & CREDITS

Writer—David Harmon.
Music—Jack Miller (orchestra).
Announcer—Bob Warren.
Host/Narrator—Jack Lait.
Support Roles—Peter Capell, Ethel Everett, Joe Julian.

Jack Lait, variously assigned by radio historians as both a reporter and editor (actually, he may have been both) of the now extinct *New York Daily Mirror*, offered a dramatic anthology. Professional journalists working for the paper pursued a wide variety of crime cases that were recounted to the listening audience in narrative form. Those wordsmiths had a responsibility to ferret out criminal activity as they conducted their investigations into serious matters, sometimes exposing corruption and other lapses in the course of duty. As a result, the scribes could be considered partially instrumental in determining that justice was ultimately meted out where it was due.

The Count of Monte Cristo

On the Air: 1944–45, Don Lee Network (West Coast stations), Tuesday; Dec. 19, 1946–June 26, 1947, MBS, Thursday, 8:30 p.m.; Summers, 1947 and 1948, MBS, Sunday; June 12–Sept. 18, 1949, MBS, Sunday, 9 p.m.; Oct. 18, 1949–Jan. 1, 1952 (intermittently, not continuously), MBS, Tuesday, 8 p.m.
Theme Song: *The Sylvia Ballet* (Delibes).
Sponsor: Sustained.
Extant Episodes: 24, plus 12 of a series bearing the same name with similar theme broadcast over the BBC Jan. 3–March 21, 1938.

CAST & CREDITS

Director—Thomas Freebairn-Smith (1944–45), Jaime del Valle (1946–52).
Writer—Anthony Ellis.
Announcers—Rod O'Connor (1944–45), Charles Arlington, Dick Wynn.
Music—Dean Fossler (orchestra).
Sound Effects—Ray Kemper.
Leads—Edmond Dantes, played by Carleton Young; René Michon, played by Ferdinand Munier (1944–45), Parley Baer (1946–52); Marie Duchene, played by Anne Stone (1944–45).
Support Roles—William Conrad, John Dehner, Virginia Gregg, Joseph Kearns, Barbara Lee, Paul Marion, Howard McNear, Jay Novello, Jack Petruzzi, Vic Rodman.

Edmond Dantes has been described as "one of literature's great crusaders for justice." The adventurous French patriot, born in the fertile mind of novelist Alexandre Dumas, was imprisoned for life in the 1830s at Chateau d'If on a false charge of treason. A cellmate informed him of a buried treasure on the island of Monte Cristo. A determined, enterprising Dantes subsequently dug his way out of confinement, fled to Monte Cristo, located the treasure and established himself as an inscrutable, blustering, very powerful count.

In so doing he dedicated his life to meting out justice to the victims of injustice, and fighting evildoers wherever they might be found. He battled corruption across his native land, making intense applications of his fortune, his sword and his resolve. Dantes was assisted in all of his escapades by a faithful minion, René Michon, who held the aristocrat in highest esteem, and by the lovely Marie Duchene, who was both a devoted confidante and an ardent co-conspirator.

The famous swashbuckling figure was the subject of a quartet of theatrical motion picture productions. Three of those preceded the character's 1944 transition from pulp fiction to the airwaves. Details of a fourth, scheduled for release in 2002, were not available when this manuscript was completed for publication.

The first movie, in 1912, simply titled *Monte Cristo*, starred Eugenie Besserer, Hobart Bosworth, Herbert Rawlinson and Tom Santschi. It was written and directed by Colin Campbell.

In *The Count of Monte Cristo*, released the following year, Joseph A. Golden and Edwin S. Porter directed and the writing credits were assigned only to the original author, Alexandre Dumas. James O'Neill played Edmond Dantes and Eugenie Besserer and Hobart Bosworth returned in supporting roles.

The last of the black-and-white films surfacing in the twentieth century was a 1934 remake of *The Count of Monte Cristo*. Directed by Rowland V. Lee with screenplay by Philip Dunne, the movie starred Robert Donat as Edmond Dantes. A long list of poorly recalled actors accompanied him.

In a 1955 half-hour series syndicated for TV titled *The Count of Monte Cristo*, George Dolenz portrayed Edmond Dantes and Faith Domergue appeared as Princess Anne. Hal Roach Jr. was executive producer.

Counterspy

(aka *David Harding, Counterspy*)

On the Air: May 18–July 27, 1942, ABC, Monday, 10 p.m.; Aug. 31, 1942–Jan. 8, 1945, ABC, Monday, 9 p.m.; Jan. 17–June 20, 1945, ABC, Wednesday, 8:30 p.m.; June 27–Dec. 19, 1945, ABC, Wednesday, 10 p.m.; Feb. 3, 1946–Dec. 5, 1948, ABC, Sunday, 5:30 p.m.; Jan. 11–Oct. 20, 1949, ABC, Tuesday–Thursday, 7:30 p.m.; Dec. 1–Dec. 29, 1949, ABC, Thursday; Jan. 3–Aug. 31, 1950, ABC, Tuesday–Thursday, 7:30 p.m.; Oct. 13–Oct. 27, 1950, NBC, Friday; Nov. 3, 1950, NBC, Friday, 9:30 p.m.; Nov. 12, 1950–Jan. 21, 1951, NBC, Sunday, 5 p.m.; Feb. 1, 1951–Sept. 25, 1952, NBC, Thursday, 9:30 p.m.; Oct. 5, 1952–June 28, 1953, NBC, Sunday, 5:30 p.m.; July 2–Sept. 24, 1953, NBC, Thursday, 9 p.m.; Oct. 5–Dec. 28, 1953, MBS, Monday, 8:30 p.m.; Jan. 3–March 14, 1954, MBS, Sunday, 4 p.m.; April 2, 1954–Nov. 29, 1957, MBS, Friday, 8 p.m. 30 minutes.

Sponsors: Mail Pouch pipe tobacco (Sept. 28, 1942–June 20, 1945); Pharmacraft (June 27–Dec. 19, 1945); Schutter Candy Co. (Feb. 3, 1946–Dec. 5, 1948); Pepsi Cola Co. for Pepsi Cola soft drink (Jan. 11–Oct. 20, 1949, and Jan. 3–Aug. 31, 1950); Anahist decongestant nasal spray (Dec. 1–Dec. 29, 1949); Gulf Oil Corp. for Gulf gasoline, oil and other automotive products and services (Feb. 1, 1951–Sept 24, 1953); Multiple commercial ventures (Jan. 2, 1954–Nov. 29, 1957); Sustained (all other times).

Extant Episodes: 69.

CAST & CREDITS

Producer—Phillips H. Lord.
Directors—Leonard Bass, Marx B. Loeb, Victor Seydel, Robert Steen, Bill Sweets.
Writers—Edward J. Adamson, Arva Everitt, Morton Friedman, Milton J. Kramer, Phillips H. Lord, Peggy Lou Mayer, John Mole, Stanley Niss, John Roeburt, Emile C. Tepperman, Palmer Thompson, Jacqueline W. Palmer, Jacqueline W. Trey.
Sound Effects—Joe Cabbibo, Walt Gustafson, Harry Nelson.
Announcers—Roger Krupp, Lionel Rico, Bob Shepherd, Ed White.
Leads—David Harding, played by House Jameson (first episode only), Don MacLaughlin; Peters, played by Mandel Kramer.
Support Roles—Larry Haines, Bryna Raeburn, Lawson Zerbe.

David Harding was a detective as American as apple pie and baseball. A critic viewed him and his tribe of national protectors as "by-the-book, humorless, heavy-footed, hard-nosed, unromantic federal agents." Their unambiguous mission was to combat threats to the nation's security. Harding, their leader, was abetted by special agent Peters (who apparently had no first name). The series began during the war years by spotlighting the German Gestapo, the Italian Zobra and the Japanese Black Dragon. In the postwar epoch it turned to the cold war, Communist antagonists and others who sought to undermine the welfare of the United States.

In a sense these were international detectives and—while their tales were highly fictionalized—the efforts of behind-the-scenes officials who persevered in the nation's behalf were brought to the public forefront. Over the clicking of the Morse code, each episode traveled across the ether, introduced by this inimitable opening—Announcer: *Washington ... calling counterspy*. David (after a pause, in calm, firm, reassuring tones): *Harding ... counterspy ... calling Washington*. (Some in the industry conceded that the radio actor long associated with Harding, Don MacLaughlin, possessed "the 'most American' voice on the air.")

Although no federal agency existed under the moniker "United States Counterspies," many listeners were convinced that the narratives presented by *Counterspy* were authorized cases. Audiences believed that the tales that were aired on another Phillips H. Lord creation, *Gangbusters*,

Counterspy: "Humorless and Heavy-Footed" is how one critic assessed the counterintelligence officials under the made-up moniker Counterspies. Their objective was to ferret out subterfuge involving U.S. enemy agents. Principals in the cast included (l–r) Mandel Kramer as special agent Peters; Don MacLaughlin, the "most American" voice on the air, chief agent David Harding; and series director Marx B. Loeb.

were also literal. (In addition Lord was responsible for bringing to the air *G-Men, Mr. District Attorney, Policewoman* and *Treasury Agent.*) As *Gangbusters* was a substitute term for *G-Men* during peacetime pursuits, so *Counterspies* was a euphemism for the FBI performing counterintelligence during World War II. G-Men were actually represented on the CBS series *The FBI in Peace and War*. This show was disdained by agency director J. Edgar Hoover and was never an official program of the FBI. The feds received their come-uppance at last by introducing their own publicly endorsed feature, *This Is Your FBI.* Yet the latter program never achieved the prestige, popularity or respect that the trio of "unofficial" dramas that had pre-ceded it enjoyed with the fans.

Crime and Peter Chambers

On the Air: April 6–Sept. 7, 1954, NBC, Tues-day, 9:30 p.m. 30 minutes.
Sponsor: Sustained.
Extant Episodes: 21.

CAST & CREDITS

Producer/Writer—Henry Kane.
Director—Fred Weihe.
Announcer—Fred Collins.
Leads—Title role played by Dane Clark; Lieu-tenant Louis Parker, played by Bill Zuckert.
Support Roles—Fran Carlon, Roger De-Koven, William Griffis, Leon Janney, Bryna Raeburn, Elaine Rost, Everett Sloane, Edgar Stehli, Evelyn Varden, Patricia Wheel, Les-ley Woods, Lawson Zerbe.

New York-based PI Chambers, whose fee was $500 per day—unlike many of his counterparts—always cooperated with local law enforcement authorities. He even considered police Lieutenant Louis (Louie) Parker his best friend. Chambers and Parker sometimes labored in concert while solving a crime, although infrequently they worked autonomously on a single case. Among Chambers' peculiarities, and there were a few, was that he professed to be—not a private eye or a confidential investi-gator—a "private Richard" (his term). No matter how innocently an exchange with one of his clients might begin, somebody's murder was the inevitable outcome.

The character of Peter Chambers first appeared in novels penned by Henry Kane, who later produced the radio show.

Radio historiographer John Dunning minced few words in a clipped assessment of this series: "*Peter Chambers* was an undistinguished half-hour, filled with glib dialogue that played into Dane Clark's image as a screen tough guy."

Crime Cases of Warden Lawes see *Twenty Thousand Years in Sing Sing*

Crime Classics

On the Air: June 15–Sept. 7, 1953, CBS, Mon-day, 8 p.m.; Sept. 30, 1953–June 30, 1954, CBS, Wednesday, 9:30 p.m. 30 minutes.
Sponsor: Sustained.
Extant Episodes: 49.

CAST & CREDITS

Producer/Director—Elliott Lewis.
Director—Ken McManus.
Writers—Morton Fine, David Friedkin.
Music—Bernard Herrmann.
Announcers—Bob Lemond, Roy Rowan, Larry Thor.
Host—Thomas Hyland, played by Lou Mer-rill.
Support Roles—Hy Averback, Parley Baer, Tony Barrett, Edgar Barrier, Harry Bartell, Jeanne Bates, Dick Beals, Julie Bennett, Bill Bissell, Herb Butterfield, Lillian Buyeff, Charles Calvert, Bob Cole, Whitfield Con-nor, William Conrad, Hans Conried, Mary Jane Croft, Charles Davis, Dix Davis, Jerry Deamond, Ted de Corsia, John Dehner, Larry Dobkin, Alistair Duncan, Jimmy Ea-gles, Jack Edwards, Sam Edwards, Georgia Ellis, Tony Ellis, Norman Field, Paul Frees, Betty Lou Gerson, Roy Glenn, Joe Granby, Virginia Gregg, Betty Harford, Alec Har-ford, Jerry Hausner, Sam Hill, Gladys Hol-land, Jean Howell, Lamont Johnson, Bill Johnstone, Miliza Kahlke, Byron Kane, Joseph Kearns, Terry Kilburn, Lou Krug-man, Jack Kruschen, Charlotte Lawrence,

Raymond Lawrence, Alma Lawton, Donald Lawton, Truda Marsden, Kurt Martell, Junius Matthews, Howard McNear, Eve McVey, Shepard Menken, Lee Miller, Marvin Miller, Gary Montgomery, Ellen Morgan, Jeanette Nolan, Jay Novello, Tudor Owen, Richard Peel, Vic Perrin, Barney Phillips, Clayton Post, Steve Roberts, Benny Rubin, Sarah Selby, Fred Shields, Russell Simpson, Eric Snowden, Irene Tedrow, Walter Tetley, Dee J. Thompson, Larry Thor, Norma Varden, Florence Walcott, Jane Webb, Martha Wentworth, Paula Winslowe, Jean Wood, Ben Wright, Dave Young.

While admittedly an anthology originally subbing in the summertime absence of *Suspense*, *Crime Classics* preserved a recurring character in Thomas Hyland. Hyland, who narrated tales into the depths of human depravity, was presented as a "connoisseur of crime, student of violence and teller of murders." In other words, he kept his mind in the gutter. The narratives were purportedly authentic, adapted "from the records and newspapers of every land — from every time." Some slayings were well renowned, the assassination of Abraham Lincoln and the infamous exploits of ax murderer Lizzie Borden among them; most were centered on pre-twentieth century occurrences, leaving modern killings (and their anticipation and results) to *Suspense* and peer anthologies.

Mike Ogden prepared a log for this series.

Crime Club see
Eno Crime Club

Crime Doctor

(aka *Max Marcin's Crime Doctor*)

On the Air: Aug. 4, 1940–Oct. 19, 1947, CBS, Sunday, 8:30 p.m. 30 minutes.

Sponsor: Philip Morris Tobacco Co. for Philip Morris cigarettes.
Extant Episodes: Three.

CAST & CREDITS

Producer/Writer — Max Marcin.
Directors — Jack Johnstone, Paul Monroe.
Music — Ray Bloch (orchestra).
Sound Effects — Al Binnie, Jimmy Dwan, Al Hogan, Jerry McCarty, Charles Range.
Announcers — Charles O'Connor, Ken Roberts.
Lead — Dr. Benjamin Ordway, played by Ray Collins, House Jameson, Hugh Marlowe, John McIntire, Everett Sloane.
Support Roles — Edith Arnold, Elspeth Eric, Walter Greaza (Inspector Ross), Jeanette Nolan, Edgar Stehli (District Attorney Miller), Walter Vaughn (Harold Sayers), Vicki Vola.

The protagonist was a reformed criminal, not initially by choice but by circumstance. Sustaining a jolt to the head, psychiatrist Benjamin Ordway fell victim to what would have been, if it had occurred in radio soap opera, that genre's most likely oldest and widely practiced malady — amnesia. Subsequently he attended medical school and specialized in criminal psychology.

At some point, while aggressively fighting corruption, he learned that he, too, had been a crime lord in his "other life." Ordway vowed to continue on the straight and narrow path he had so recently adopted, claiming his experiences with the underworld, joined with his newly acquired knowledge in medicine, greatly aided in subduing evil. His proficiency proved useful to police Inspector Ross and District Attorney Miller in solving offenses that initially appeared to be totally impenetrable. Earlier in the run Ordway was a member of the parole board, hearing the pleas of cons requesting release. A related case was the source of each episode.

Jeanette Nolan, portraying several support roles while John McIntire was in the lead, was in actuality Mrs. John McIntire.

Listeners were apprised of a killer's identity from the start; what they didn't know was how he would give himself away. Before that disclosure, a message informed the audience: "Ladies and gentlemen, in exactly 57 seconds Dr. Ordway will be back to tell you the piece of evidence overlooked by the suspect." With bated breath the fans awaited his startling revelation.

Warner Baxter played Dr. Ordway in a 1943 film simply titled *Crime Doctor*. It was the first of 10 based on the radio character. Subsequent releases: *Crime Doctor's Strangest Case* (1943), *Shadows in the Night* (1944), *Crime Doctor's Courage* and *Crime Doctor's Warning* (both 1945), *Just Before Dawn* and *Crime Doctor's Manhunt* (1946), *The Millerson Case* and *Crime Doctor's Gamble* (1947), *Crime Doctor's Diary* (1949).

Crime Does Not Pay

On the Air: Jan. 7–Dec. 22, 1952, MBS, Monday, 8:30 p.m. 30 minutes.
Sponsor: Various commercial enterprises in local markets where the series aired.
Extant Episodes: 64 (includes earlier WMGM series).

CAST & CREDITS

Director—Marx B. Loeb.
Writer—Ira Marion.
Music—John Gart.
Lead—An anthology series featuring a different "star" in each episode. Some of these were Diana Barrymore, Anne Baxter, Ed Begley, Donald Buka, Ronald Colman, Parker Fennelly, Betty Furness, Martin Gabel, Joan Lorring, Bela Lugosi, Myron McCormick, Ralph Meeker, Cameron Mitchell, Jean Muir, George Reeves, Everett Sloane.

Plots were similar to those heard on the more widely embraced *Gangbusters*. They ran the gamut from murder to thefts to espionage to racketeering, portraying the detective force in unwavering pursuit. The route leading down the path of destruction in a juvenile offender's life was frequently examined. These narratives promoted the theme "crime does not pay" and the lead actors often returned to the microphone at the end of the episodes to offer personal appeals to younger listeners.

The radio show evolved out of a series of two-reel short-subject films released by movie producer Metro-Goldwyn-Mayer between 1935 and 1947 titled *Crime Does Not Pay*. One theatrical analyst termed them the "most successful" dramatic dual-reel films produced during the sound era.

This was a transcribed aural series that aired twice before its network debut on New York City's WMGM, a station owned by Metro-Goldwyn-Mayer. It initially ran from Oct. 10, 1949 to April 11, 1951, and was repeated there from April 18 to Oct. 10, 1951. While 78 episodes were originally recorded, not all of them were rerun for the second and third broadcasts. The third airing appeared as the network run.

Jay Hickerson prepared a log of this radio series.

Crime Fighters

On the Air: Nov. 7–Nov. 28, 1949, MBS, Monday, 9:30 p.m.; April 24, 1950–Sept. 22, 1952, MBS, various days and times; Jan. 7–Sept. 30, 1953, MBS, Wednesday, 8:30 p.m.; Feb. 4, 1954–Aug. 2, 1956, MBS, Thursday, 8:30 p.m. 30 minutes.
Sponsor: No information.
Extant Episodes: Nine.

CAST & CREDITS

Producer/Director—Wynn Wright.
Writer—Paul Milton.
Music—Nelson Ray (organ).

Sound Effects—Joe Keating.
Announcer—Durward Kirby.
Support Roles—Raymond Edward Johnson, Abby Lewis, Ian Martin, Allan Stevenson.

These cops were introduced as "master manhunters to match master criminals ... shrewd experts in a thousand rackets ... or simple men who study human nature ... the city dicks who work in teams ... county sheriffs covering lonely regions ... federal men with a nation to police ... or scientists whose weapon is the laboratory." Was any segment of law enforcement overlooked? Not so intentionally. One well-respected critic labeled it "rather a hokey Mutual series," however.

The Crime Files of Flamond

On the Air: Initially emanating from Chicago's WGN, a transcribed syndicated version of the show existed from 1946 to 1948 preceding the network run. Jan. 7–April 1, 1953, MBS, Wednesday, 8 p.m.; May 20–July 1, 1953, MBS, Wednesday, 8 p.m.; April 4–Oct. 3, 1956, MBS, Wednesday, 8:30 p.m.; Oct. 10, 1956–Feb. 27, 1957, MBS, Wednesday, 8 p.m. 30 minutes.
Sponsors: Local sponsorship in markets where broadcast (1946–48); General Mills Inc. for an extensive food products line (Jan. 7–April 1, 1953); Lever Brothers Co. for an extensive line of personal care and home cleaning products (May 20–June 3, 1953); Multiple participation (June 10–July 1, 1953); Sustained (April 4, 1956–Feb. 27, 1957).
Extant Episodes: Nine.

CAST & CREDITS

Producer—W. B. Lewis.
Director—Myron Golden.
Writer—George Anderson.
Announcer—Bob Cunningham.
Leads—Myron (Mike) Wallace in the title role (in the transcribed syndicated run, 1946–48), Everett Clark (network run, 1953–57); Sandra Lake, played by Patricia Dunlap (1946–

48), Muriel Bremner (1953–57). (The latter actress' name is sometimes spelled Bremmer.)
Support Roles—Maurice Copeland, Harry Elders, Ben Younger.

A potentially overzealous author dubbed this single-named sleuth "the most unusual detective in criminal history." To distinguish him, he was granted some uncommon characteristics. Flamond was equipped by training as both a psychologist and a character analyst. His cases were presented as "card files." He was assisted—as were so many of his contemporaries—by a secretary (Sandra Lake) with an avid interest in unlawful behavior, and he approached crimesolving by learning *why* a felony was executed. Flamond probed "beyond laughter and tears, jealousy and greed" in attempting to discover the real reasons. (Unlike some of his peers, however, his liaison with his secretary was kept strictly platonic—he even summoned her with "Miss Lake.")

The audience could summarily dismiss the "basic clue," while obvious, appearing in every one of the dramatizations. Yet for those listeners with keen insights, there were chances to work alongside Flamond in cracking a case. Many did so often before the answer was publicly revealed. Flamond at last interpreted the basic clue, giving the culprit away as he drew each case to conclusion.

Myron (Mike) Wallace's was the same voice that delivered the Peter Pan commercials for radio's *Sky King* in the late 1940s. He extended a seemingly never-ending broadcast career over a multiplicity of decades as a popular interviewer on CBS-TV's *60 Minutes*. As 2002 arrived he was showing no signs of abandoning that capacity. (See separate entry, *Crime on the Waterfront*.)

A Crime Letter from Dan Dodge

On the Air: Oct. 31, 1952–Feb. 27, 1953, ABC, Friday, 8 p.m. 30 minutes.
Sponsor: Toni Division of the Gillette Corp. for Toni home permanents and other women's hair care preparations.
Extant Episodes: None known.

CAST & CREDITS

Directors—Charles Irving, Donald Painter.
Writer—Harold Swanton.
Leads—Title role played by Myron McCormick; secretary played by Shirley Eggleston.

PI Dan Dodge dictated a detailed letter to his secretary in the reminiscent vein of mythical detective Sam Spade. Through his communications he shared accounts of his cases in step-by-step revelations of the investigations. To accomplish this, flashback sequences of the action were employed.

Surprisingly, generally authoritative radio historiographers that normally substantiate information on dramatic series have been unable to record a name for Dan Dodge's secretary. As no tapes of the series are known to exist, her name can't be identified at present.

Crime on the Waterfront

On the Air: Feb. 24–March 1, 1949, NBC, Thursday and Tuesday. 30 minutes. (These were audition performances that weren't continued as a permanent series.)
Sponsor: Sustained.
Extant Episodes: Two.

CAST & CREDITS

Announcer—George Stone.
Leads—Lou Kagel, played by Myron (Mike) Wallace; Muriel Bremner, played by June Sherman. (The actress's name is sometimes spelled Bremmer.)

This charming ladies man, a New York City police lieutenant, was assigned the harbor as his regular beat. Most often his cases naturally pertained to events occurring on and around ships. Assisting in his quests was his newspaper reporter/girlfriend, June Sherman. There was lots of inconsequential talk about fog and liners and piers and tugs and whistles amid his attempts to rid the shoreline of its criminal elements.

The two actors in the leads in this series also appeared in *The Crime Files of Flamond* (see that entry), although in different periods.

Crime Photographer see Casey, Crime Photographer

Criminal Case Histories with Warden E. Lawes see Twenty Thousand Years in Sing Sing

The Curley Bradley Show see Tom Mix

D-24

On the Air: Aug. 2, 1954–Jan. 10, 1955, MBS, Monday, 9:30 p.m. 30 minutes.
Sponsor: Sustained.
Extant Episodes: None known.

CAST & CREDITS

No information.

These narratives were based upon authentic Australian police files.

Dan Dunn, Secret Operative 48

On the Air: Syndication. 15 minutes.
Sponsor: Local advertisers in markets where the series was aired.
Extant Episodes: Four.

CAST & CREDITS

Writer—Maurice Zimm.
Lead—Title role played by Lou Marcelle.
Support Roles—Hans Conried, Myron Gary, Lucille Meredith, Gerald Mohr, David Sterling.

A prominent media critic labeled this juvenile adventure-detective series a "cheap imitation" of the more prestigious and much better established *Dick Tracy.* In copycat fashion Dan Dunn and his portly and humorous sidekick, Irwin Higgs, left the funny papers (where the principal figure was launched Oct. 16, 1933, by cartoonist Norman Marsh) to fight the enemies of righteousness on all fronts.

Dunn was a detective hero in the U.S. Secret Service. He owned a pet "wolf dog," appropriately a German shepherd known as Wolf, who could be counted upon to attack a hood when ordered. Dunn also befriended and adopted an orphan named Babs. She and Wolf were pals, which was somewhat reminiscent of *Little Orphan Annie* of both radio and comic strip fame. One reviewer mused that "*Dan Dunn* provided a wilder and stranger story mix than *Dick Tracy* much of the time." The show featured master villains like a Fu Manchu double, Wu Fang, and a death-ray wielder named Eviloff, who lived on an island of mystery and piloted a dirigible, of all things.

This syndicated feature has been variously assigned by three different radio historiographers to 1937, 1944 and 1948. Nothing currently on record signifies which of these dates is accurate, or if more than one is correct.

When the series was about to be launched, syndicators ordered 13 scripts for it. A stable of authors submitted material that was rejected, however, and just four days before the debut, producers found themselves without a script. At that moment an impoverished Ruth Henning arrived at the studio to audition as an actress. Overhearing their dilemma, she volunteered that she and her husband, Paul, were scriptwriters and could meet their deadline demands. Years later she recalled that they were promised $15 per episode. While the Hennings met their part of the bargain, the producers paid only about half of *their* commitment. It was enough, however, to get the pair home to Kansas City for Christmas and they decided to overlook the rest. Paul Henning went on to become associated with some very large broadcast enterprises, eventually writing for Rudy Vallee, Burns and Allen and other major names, and producing TV series like *The Beverly Hillbillies.*

The *Dan Dunn* comic strip lost favor after 1940, primarily when its subscribing newspapers indicated a willingness to pay higher fees for the more popular competitive strip, *Dick Tracy.* (Publishers' Syndicate had offered *Dunn* as an inexpensive alternative to *Tracy.*) When creator Norman Marsh enlisted in the Marines in 1942 the strip passed into the hands of cartoonist Paul Pinson and subsequently to Alfred Andriola. Continuing its downhill spiral, the illustration disappeared altogether in 1943.

Marsh, meanwhile, returned from the war to create a direct imitation of *Dan Dunn* for King Features in 1946 that he labeled *Hunter Keene.* After a year of producing it, he developed another short-lived strip titled *Danny Hale.* The *Dunn* strip, incidentally, had been the basis for a dime novel pulp titled *Dan Dunn* that ran for two issues in autumn 1936. A cartoon critic opined: "*Dan Dunn* deserves at least partial reprinting as an often amusing record of the taste in strips during its time."

Danger, Dr. Danfield

On the Air: Aug. 18, 1946–Feb. 9, 1947, ABC, Sunday, 3 p.m.; Feb. 16–April 13, 1947, ABC, Sunday, 2 p.m.; 1947–51, Syndicated, Thursday, then Wednesday timeslots. 30 minutes.
Sponsor: Knox Co. for a line of "scientifically compounded" pharmaceutical products.
Extant Episodes: 26.

Cast & Credits
Producer—Wally Ramsey.
Writer—Ralph Wilkinson.
Lead—Title role played by Michael (Steve) Dunne; Rusty Fairfax, played by JoAnne Johnson.

Dr. Daniel Danfield was a criminal psychologist who launched into each episode by dictating the results of one of his cases to Rusty Fairfax, his secretary. (Does that sound familiar?) Using flashbacks, his tales were recounted in dramatic sequences. (That sounds familiar, too.) When a crime didn't fit a meticulous blueprint, law enforcement would request Danfield's services. He often met with the criminals, analyzing them from a vantage point outside their prison cells and sometimes on their own terrain. In the meantime Rusty Fairfax appeared more concerned about Danfield's safety than did the good doctor himself. She had an innate ability to complicate matters, contributing heightened anxiety for him. In the opening billboard Danfield claimed that the human mind was "like a cave," filled with "dark passages and mysterious recesses." Yet he assured the fans he had explored "those unknown retreats and know their secrets." An erudite reviewer panned the drama "as one of the worst detective shows ever to curse the ABC airwaves."

One critic tabbed the character Rusty Fairfax as "pert and sassy" and suggested that she "usually had too much to say and said it badly." This analyst, in another bit of prose, declared: "What made Rusty especially obnoxious was her penchant for telling everybody off and sticking her foot squarely into her mouth. Danfield couldn't have cared less. Rusty was allegedly beautiful."

Danger with Granger

On the Air: July 23, 1956–Feb. 25, 1957, MBS, Monday, 8:30 p.m. 30 minutes.
Sponsor: Sustained.
Extant Episodes: 24.

Cast & Credits
On-air identifications and credits weren't given.

PI Steve Granger unavoidably spent much of his time looking over his shoulder for the baddies he had previously placed behind bars. Most of them had vowed that they would collect for it big time. Thus, while pursuing new cases, the hero was somewhat distracted while he defied such personal peril. He was also known to strike a woman when a situation warranted, something nearly all of his peers refused to do. Could there be any wonder why this guy attracted so many foes?

Dangerous Assignment

On the Air: July 9–Aug. 20, 1949, NBC, Saturday, 9:30 p.m.; Feb. 6–April 24, 1950, NBC, Monday, 10:30 p.m.; May 3–June 7, 1950, NBC, Wednesday, 8 p.m.; July 19–Sept. 27, 1950, NBC, Wednesday, 8 p.m.; Nov. 18, 1950–May 5, 1951, NBC, Saturday, 8 p.m.; May 11–18, 1951, NBC, Friday, 9 p.m.; June 26–Sept. 18, 1951, NBC, Tuesday, 8:30 p.m.; Oct. 13–Dec. 22, 1951, NBC,

Saturday, 10 p.m.; Dec. 31, 1951–Jan. 28, 1952, NBC, Monday, 10:30 p.m.; Feb. 4, 1952–Feb. 23, 1953, NBC, Monday, 10:35 p.m.; Feb. 25–July 8, 1953, CBS, Wednesday, 10:35 p.m.; 1953–54, Syndicated. 30 minutes, except 25 minutes (Feb. 2, 1952–Feb. 23, 1953), and 15 minutes (Feb. 25–July 8, 1953).

Sponsors: Sustained, with two exceptions—Ford Motor Co. for its automobiles and trucks (c1949–50) and General Mills Inc. for a wide line of foodstuffs (May 3–Sept. 27, 1950).

Extant Episodes: 106.

CAST & CREDITS

Producer—Don Sharpe.
Director—Bill Karn.
Writer—Bob Ryf.
Music—Steve Ashley (orchestra).
Announcer—John Storm.
Leads—Steve Mitchell, played by Brian Donlevy (1949–53), Lloyd Burrell (1953–54); Commissioner, played by Herb Butterfield; Secretary to the Commissioner, played by Helen Choate, Betty Moran.
Support Roles—Paul Frees, Betty Lou Gerson, Dan O'Herlihy, GeGe Pearson, Ken Peters.

International troubleshooter Steve Mitchell investigated criminal activity in glamorous locales: "Baghdad! Martinique! Singapore! And all the places of the world where danger and intrigue walk hand in hand," an announcer barked (in syndication) at the drama's inception. "There you will find Steve Mitchell on another *Dangerous Assignment*." In the epigraph, Mitchell exclaimed: "Yeah, danger is my assignment—I get sent to a lot of places I can't even pronounce. They all spell the same thing, though—trouble." Narrating his tales in the first person present tense, the private eye constantly watched his back: Those culprits he had earlier nailed, it seemed, frequently threatened to do him bodily harm. Working without the protection or intervention of the U.S. gov-

ernment, at least in theory, Mitchell was engaged to perform independently in sustaining the interests of the nation. Each week an unnamed commissioner of an unidentified federal agency dispatched the soldier of fortune on missions to prevent or put out fires in foreign fields. Most of the plots were similar, sadly, leading the audience to figure an outcome before a narrative reached its peak. Noting that, a radio critic tagged it "just another spy show," hinting that the drama proffered little to distinguish it or permit it to become compelling; therefore, it remained lackluster to the ears of some potentially faithful hearers.

With Harold Knox producing, radio lead Brian Donlevy starred in a 39-week syndicated TV series that was released in early 1952 under the banner *Dangerous Assignment*. In 30-minute episodes Donlevy played Steve Mitchell, then an undercover U.S. government agent instead of a private detective as he was then still on radio. He continued to dabble in foreign intrigue on missions abroad, on radio and TV. "The scenery was nice, but only a backdrop for violence," read one assessment.

Dangerous Paradise

On the Air: Oct. 25, 1933–Sept. 14, 1934, NBC Blue, Wednesday/Friday, 8:30 p.m.; Sept. 17, 1934–Dec. 13, 1935, NBC Blue, Monday/Wednesday/Friday, 7:45 p.m. 15 minutes.
Sponsor: Woodbury soap.
Extant Episodes: None known.

CAST & CREDITS

Leads—Dan Gentry, played by George (Nick) Dawson; Gale Brewster, played by Elsie Hitz.

When this series premiered, it was clearly one thing; but in a few months, it was totally something else altogether. At its debut Dan Gentry and Gale Brewster were a couple of castaways on a deserted island (hence, the series title). But by 1934 the pair had shifted locales to the Canadian northwest where Gentry signed up for duty as a member of the elite Royal Canadian Mounted Police. (Until 1920 that body was known as the Royal Northwest Mounted Police; from 1873–1904 it had been called the Northwest Mounted Police.) Gentry fought crime in the bleakest of conditions, similar to a number of mythical contemporaries on more than a dozen Mountie series broadcast over U.S. and CBC radio networks—a distant cry from the deserted island they originally occupied.

At the drama's inception, Brewster was an American newspaperwoman who had been sent on assignment to The Philippines. When she rented an aircraft to fly to another island, the plane developed engine trouble and ditched into the Pacific, fatally wounding the pilot. At that juncture Gentry arrived in his dinghy and ferried Brewster to an island that only he and three other men occupied. Love blossomed for Gentry and Brewster. (One wag insisted that they may have been "radio's first romantic adventure duo.") The show was soon receiving a thousand letters a week from fans, a large percentage of those addressed to Elsie Hitz, claimed by radio columnists to possess "the most beautiful speaking voice on the air." When all of the mileage had been milked out of the deserted island theme, the lovebirds escaped to Canada to begin a new life together.

Before and after this feature aired, Dawson and Hitz appeared as the leads in a quarter-hour serialized drama, *The Magic Voice*. It was carried over CBS on Tuesday and Saturday evenings at 8:15 p.m. between Nov. 15, 1932, and June 27, 1933. The show became a true soap opera when Chipso flakes underwrote it and transferred it to 4:45 p.m. five weekday af-

ternoons on NBC Blue from March 30 to Aug. 28, 1936. The pair wasn't done with soap opera yet, however. Their next collaboration placed them in the leads of the serialized *Follow the Moon* between Jan. 4 to July 2, 1937, at 4:30 p.m. over NBC, and from Oct. 4, 1937 to April 1, 1938, at 5 p.m. over CBS.

Dantro the Planet Man

On the Air: 1952–53, Syndicated by Palladium Radio Productions Inc., New York (78 episodes). 15 minutes.
Sponsor: Advertising time sold in local markets.
Extant Episodes: 78.

CAST & CREDITS
No identifications known.

The billboard of this transcribed science fiction adventure summarized the premise thus: "This is the fascinating story of Dantro the Planet Man, troubleshooter for the League of Planets organization, the law enforcement body for peace and justice in the celestial world, whose headquarters and center of operations are situated in the capital of all the planets—Planeteria Rex. From Mercury to Pluto, wherever danger threatens the universe, you will find Dantro the Planet Man fighting for fair play." Intrepid young cadets Billy and Jane (no last names, please) accompanied Dantro on his peacekeeping journeys into celestial orbits, a characteristic of comic book-type kiddie science fiction series. One wag called it "A Captain Video swipe translated to radio."

Chapter titles, which may or may not be authentic, according to more than one collector that provided them, serve as a fairly strong indicator of program content, nonetheless. They include "Let's Orbit the Moon," "Marston of Mars Planning Attack on Earth," "Hoping for a Miracle to

Stop Marston," "Billy and Jane in Space on a Scout Ship" and "Captured on Venus by the Dusters." A media critic, meanwhile, acquiesced: "The program was not one of the strongest adventure series on the air." It disappeared after a moderately brief run.

David Harding, Counterspy
see *Counterspy*

David Harum

On the Air: Jan. 27–March 27, 1936, NBC Blue, Weekdays, 10:45 a.m.; March 30, 1936–Sept. 27, 1940, NBC, Weekdays, 11 a.m.; Sept. 30, 1940–Jan. 10, 1947, NBC, Weekdays, 11:45 a.m.; Jan. 13, 1947–June 25, 1948, CBS, Weekdays, 10:45 a.m.; June 28, 1948–Jan. 6, 1950, CBS, Weekdays, 3 p.m.; Jan. 9, 1950–Jan. 5, 1951, NBC, Weekdays, 11:45 a.m. Also: 1937–38, MBS, Weekdays, 3:45 p.m.; Feb. 2, 1942–May 14, 1943, CBS, Weekdays, 3 p.m. 15 minutes.

Theme Song: *Sunbonnet Sue* (initially hummed by Stanley Davis to his own guitar accompaniment, later played on the studio organ).

Sponsor: B. T. Babbitt Inc. for Bab-O cleanser, Best soap and Lycons home soap-making recipes and farm products.

Extant Episodes: 15.

CAST & CREDITS

Producers — Anne Hummert, Frank Hummert.

Directors — Martha Atwell, Himan Brown, John Buckwalter, Arthur Hanna, Ed King, Lester Vail.

Writers — Peggy Blake, John DeWitt, Noel B. Gerson, Charles J. Gussman, Johanna Johnston, Mary W. Reeves.

Music — Stanley Davis.

Sound Effects — Jack Anderson, Bill Brown.

Announcer — Ford Bond.

Lead — Title character played by Craig McDonnell, Cameron Prud'homme (1944–47, 1950–51), Wilmer Walter.

Support Roles — Charme Allen and Eve Condon ("Aunt Polly" Benson), Bennett Kilpack (James Benson), Peggy Allenby, Joan Tompkins, Gertrude Warner (Susan Price Wells); Donald Briggs, Philip Reed, Ken Williams (Brian Wells), plus Ray Bramley (Silas Finke), Joseph Curtin (John Lennox), Marjorie Davies (Clarissa Oakley), Ethel Everett (Elsie Anderson), Roy Fant (Deacon Perkins), Paul Ford (Mark Carter), Florence Lake (Tess Terwilliger), Arthur Maitland (Zeke Sweeney), Junius Matthews (Grandpa Eph), Richard McKay (Henry Longacre), Claudia Morgan (Clarissa Oakley), Billy Redfield (Willy), William Shelley (Lish Harem), Paul Stewart (Charlie).

While clearly a soap opera, this washboard weeper packed a powerful punch by promoting an unmistakable dark edge. Beyond the melodrama was "the kindly little country philosopher who makes life worth living by helping those who need help and by outwitting those who are too clever and scheming in helping themselves"—with strong emphasis on the latter group. David Harum was truly a private eye in banker's clothing, banking being the profession that paid his salary. Portraying the friend of all decent citizens of his little New England hamlet of Homeville, the confirmed bachelor set out to right the wrongs that were perpetrated against his invariably vulnerable townsfolk. In so doing he routinely encountered mighty rapscallions performing their dastardly deeds: He searched for kidnapped damsels in distress with some regularity while nailing crooks of many persuasions and exposing diabolical schemes that law enforcement authorities somehow overlooked.

The common sense he employed— along with the perceptive abilities he acquired which everybody else in Homeville obviously missed—turned the banker-hero into a trusted friend of the righteous and a despised nemesis of the evildoers.

Never bewildered by those who used debauchery to achieve fortune, he vigilantly pursued piety, becoming the epitome of rectitude within the heart and soul of small-town America. A minor habitat never produced a more sagacious, tenacious crimefighter than the dedicated servant David Harum.

In the mid 1930s advertising executive Duane Jones, operating on behalf of B. T. Babbitt, bought the rights to a bestselling novel released in 1898 on which a 1934 motion picture had been based starring America's legendary super entertainer Will Rogers. The novel, *David Harum*, and the movie featured a homespun New England banker who offered practical advice while providing vigilant surveillance over his clients' finances.

Jones enlisted the aid of Frank and Anne Hummert, two of his most trusted former business associates (at Blackett-Sample-Hummert advertising agency), to adapt the tale to a serialized radio play. When the drama debuted in 1935 on New York City's powerful WOR, it acquired an immediate following. Encouraged, Jones decided there was potential for a much larger market beyond the confines of New York. He took the series to network radio and Babbitt underwrote it for the next 15 years, the full length of the run.

No other serial integrated the mailhook into its story line more frequently or more effectively than *David Harum*. Its messages were often straightforward appeals to listeners to respond in order to receive a premium offer. *Harum* was one of three dramas underwritten by B. T. Babbitt. The others were *Lora Lawton* (1943–50) and the short-lived *Nona from Nowhere* (which succeeded *Lawton*, 1950–51). All vigorously exploited the premium but *Harum* was the champion at consistently and unabashedly combining it with the story line to help marketing efforts. For 10 cents and a label from the sponsor's prod-

uct, listeners might receive a packet of flower seeds "just like those planted by David Harum in his very own garden." The response to that bait brought about some unanticipated pandemonium: The show's fans mailed in over 275,000 labels, each accompanied by a dime.

Deadline Mystery

On the Air: April 20–Aug. 31, 1947, ABC, Sunday, 2 p.m. 30 minutes.
Sponsor: Knox Co. for Cystex Nerve tonic and Mendaco Asthma medication.
Extant Episodes: Four.

CAST & CREDITS

Creator—Frank Neville.
Director—Dave Titus.
Writers—Fred Howard, Wallace K. Norman.
Music—Len Salvo (orchestra).
Announcer—Frank Hemingway.
Lead—Lucky Larson, played by Steve Dunne.
Support Roles—Neil Browers, Sam Edwards, John Frank, Virginia Gregg, Fred Howard, Byron Kane, Jack Kruschen, Herbert Rawlinson, Hugh Studebaker, June Whitley.

Investigative newspaper reporter Lucky Larson often found himself running into rackets, scandals, frame-ups, murders, kidnappings and a myriad of odd, unexplained circumstances that bore a distinctly smelly taint. Larson's nose for news coupled with a resolute determination led him to turn the spotlight on the less-than-honorable intentions of a variety of rogues.

Dear Margie, It's Murder

On the Air: Jan. 11–Oct. 4, 1953, MBS, Sunday, 4:30 p.m. 25 minutes.
Sponsor: Sustained.
Extant Episodes: None known.

CAST & CREDITS

Producer/Director—Cyril Armbruster.

Leads—The student, played by Mason Adams; the inspector, played by Ian Martin.

This was the tale of an American vet studying in England under the G. I. Bill who found time to assist a Scotland Yard inspector in crimesolving. The show's title was derived from letters he sent home to his girlfriend, Margie, in which he recalled for her his sleuthing experiences.

Death Valley Sheriff see The Sheriff

Defense Attorney

(aka *The Defense Rests*)

On the Air: Aug. 31–Sept. 28, 1951, ABC, Friday, 8 p.m.; Oct. 11–Dec. 20, 1951, ABC, Thursday, 8 p.m.; Dec. 27, 1951–Oct. 30, 1952, ABC, Thursday, 8:30 p.m.; Nov. 18–Dec. 30, 1952, ABC, Tuesday, 8 p.m. 30 minutes.

Sponsors: Clorets chlorophyll breath mints and gum (Aug. 31, 1951–Dec. 30, 1952); General Mills Inc. for Kix cereal (Feb. 21–June 26, 1952); Goodyear Tire and Rubber Co. for Goodyear tires and other automotive products and services (April 24–May 15, 1952).

CAST & CREDITS

Producer—Warren Lewis.
Director—Dwight Hauser.
Writers—Cameron Blake, Bill Johnston, Joel Murcott.
Music—Rex Koury.
Leads—Martha (Marty) Ellis Bryan, played by Mercedes McCambridge; Judson (Jud) Barnes, played by Howard Culver.
Support Roles—Tony Barrett, Harry Bartell, Paul Fries, Bill Johnston, Irene Tedrow, Kay Wiley.

While San Francisco lawyer Martha (Marty) Ellis Bryan insisted that conducting an investigation was "out of my line," she invariably found herself doing substantial detective work while attempting to defend her clients in criminal cases. On those occasions she usually worked alongside her love interest, Judson (Jud) Barnes, a newspaper reporter for *The Dispatch*. Bryan was recognized as a woman of impeccable integrity and assured listeners: "I submit the facts, fully aware of my responsibility to my client and to you as defense attorney."

Even a gifted and highly respected actress like Mercedes McCambridge could be patronizing. At the close of her weekly drama, she announced: "This is Mercedes McCambridge reminding you to stay tuned to your ABC station for that entertaining program, *The Original Amateur Hour*, emceed by that great showman and grand person, Ted Mack." Such munificent descriptions suggested that even the best thespians could be buttonholed for a price!

The Defense Rests see Defense Attorney

Detective Drama

On the Air: April 13–Sept. 28, 1955, MBS, Wednesday, 8 p.m. 15 minutes.
Sponsor: No information.
Extant Episodes: None known.

CAST & CREDITS
No information.

Regrettably, no responses arrived when additional information on this program was solicited at a prominent web site routinely perused by hundreds of radiophiles.

Detective Stories

On the Air: 1937–38, NBC Blue, Sunday, 8 p.m.

Sponsor: No information.
Extant Episodes: None known.

CAST & CREDITS

No information.

Detectives Black and Blue see *The Adventures of Detectives Black and Blue*

Detectives Dalt and Zumba

On the Air: 1938.
Sponsor: No information.
Extant Episodes: Two.

CAST & CREDITS

No information.

No new data resulted when hundreds of readers of a web site devoted to old time radio were asked to post details they might have pertaining to this series.

Dick Tracy

(aka *The Adventures of Dick Tracy*)

On the Air: The full network run was preceded by a brief 1934 try-out on NBC stations in New England. Feb. 4–July 11, 1935, CBS, Monday–Thursday, 5:45 p.m.; Sept. 30, 1935–1937, MBS, Weekdays, 5 p.m.; Jan. 3–June 3, 1938, NBC, Weekdays, 5 p.m.; Sept. 26, 1938–April 28, 1939, NBC, Weekdays, 5 p.m.; April 29–May 27, 1939, NBC, Saturday, 7 p.m.; June 3–July 29, 1939, NBC, Saturday, 8 p.m.; Aug. 7–Aug. 28, 1939, NBC, Monday, 8 p.m.; Sept. 9–Sept. 30, 1939, NBC, Saturday, 7 p.m.; March 15–June 4, 1943, ABC, Monday/Wednesday/Friday, 5:15 p.m.; Sept. 13–Oct. 1, 1943, ABC, Monday/Wednesday/Friday, 5:15 p.m.; Oct. 4, 1943–Oct. 25, 1946, ABC, Weekdays, 5:15 p.m.; Sept. 15, 1945–June 1,

1946, ABC, Saturday, 7:30 p.m.; Oct. 28, 1946–Nov. 14, 1947, ABC, Weekdays, 4:45 p.m.; Nov. 17, 1947–July 16, 1948, ABC, Weekdays, 5 p.m. 15 minutes (Feb. 4, 1935–April 28, 1939, March 15, 1943–Oct. 25, 1946, Oct. 28, 1946–July 16, 1948); 30 minutes (all other time periods).
Theme Song: *Toot-Toot Tootsie* (an unlikely number, unless one recalls it occurred in the era that Tootsie Rolls candy sponsored the show).
Sponsors: Sterling Products (Feb. 4–July 11, 1935); Sustained (Sept. 30, 1935–1937, Oct. 28, 1946–July 16, 1948); the Quaker Oats Co. for Quaker Puffed Wheat and Quaker Puffed Rice cereals (Jan. 3, 1938–Sept. 30, 1939); Sweets Co. for Tootsie Roll confectionery treats (March 15, 1943–Oct. 25, 1946).
Extant Episodes: 58.

CAST & CREDITS

Producer/Directors—Mitchell Grayson, Charles Powers, Frank Shinn, Bob White.
Writers—Maurice Brachhausen, Everett S. Crosby, George Lowther, Sidney Slon, John Wray.
Music—Ray Carter.
Sound Effects—Maurice Brachhausen, Keene Crockett, Al Finelli, Bill McClintock, Walt McDonough.
Announcers—Don Gardiner, George Gunn, Ed Herlihy, Dan Seymour.
Lead—Title character played by Bob Burlen (1934 in New England), Matt Crowley, Barry Thomson, Ned Wever (1940–45).
Support Roles—Andy Donnelly and Jackie Kelk (Junior Tracy), Walter Kinsella (Pat Patton), Howard Smith (Police Chief Brandon), Helen Lewis (Tess Trueheart), Beatrice Pons (Tania); plus Curtis Arnall, Ralph Bell, John Griggs, Mandel Kramer, John Larkin, Gil Mack, Mercedes McCambridge, Craig McDonnell, James Van Dyk, Lawson Zerbe.

Richard (Dick) Tracy was a master police detective in an unspecified, metropolitan crime-ridden area. He was fair and honest and never aimed his weapon with the intent to kill. Married to Tess Trueheart, he was the father of Dick Tracy Jr., commonly referred to as "Junior Tracy." Tracy's assistant was Patrick (Pat) Patton. The juvenile mystery-adventure's closing epigraph was highly graphic: "Any tough detective lives the life of danger. He must be on the alert at all times because tough characters know that the best way of keeping out of his clutches is to get him first. Well, Tracy fans, I guess you know that goes double for Dick Tracy because he's so very tough. That's one of the reasons you can be sure that the adventures of Dick Tracy will keep you on the edge of your seats."

This juvenile adventure was based on the comic strip created by Chester Gould that first hit the newspapers in 1931. Its action moved swiftly and included a gritty realism that lifted it above most of its peer comics of that day. As a result it quickly became one of the most prominent cartoon strips of pulp fiction.

A little known fact: Himan Brown, whose name isn't usually linked with *Dick Tracy*—according to Leonard Maltin—negotiated for the radio rights to the hugely popular comic strip and put the show on the air—while he was still in college! A *true* entrepreneur!

Dick Tracy was one of a handful of hero-studded serials for adolescents aired during World War II on which the fans were encouraged to help in subduing America's enemies. A child's cooperation was solicited in several ways—planting victory gardens, writing to servicemen each month, purchasing war bonds and collecting commodities such as newspapers, rubber, tin, used fats and scrap metal. In a 1943 five-point pledge to fight waste, *Dick Tracy* listeners agreed to conserve water, gas and electricity; fuel oil and coal; their own clothing; their Mom's furniture; and their playthings. Obedience didn't bring the only reward; informing the network of one's pledge guaranteed a child

that his name would be placed on a victory honor roll to be sent to Allied military headquarters in North Africa and, as the announcer confidently assured hearers, there to be read by General Dwight D. Eisenhower, commander-in-chief, himself.

There was a Dick Tracy Club offering many premiums. A top article, reportedly requiring more than 50 cereal box tops, was an inspector general badge.

Republic Pictures put Dick Tracy in a quartet of movie serials that turned out to be the most popular chapterplays ever made about a fictional detective. The first, titled *Dick Tracy*, was released in 1937 and was comprised of 15 episodes. Surprisingly it was produced for under $200,000, a paltry sum in theatrical productions by then. For this on-screen series Tracy was no longer a city policeman but a Federal Bureau of Investigation agent. With both the comic strip and the radio adaptation already well established, the serial gained instant favor with the Saturday matinee crowd. Rounding out the quartet of continuing cinematic narratives were *Dick Tracy Returns* (1938), *Dick Tracy's G-Men* (1939) and *Dick Tracy vs. Crime Inc.* (1941). An actor whose physical features closely resembled those of the angular character in the pulp fiction sketches, Ralph Byrd, was selected to play Tracy in the four serials.

RKO acquired the screen rights to Charles Gould's character next and released a full-length feature film in 1945 titled *Dick Tracy, Detective.* Morgan Conway was featured as the popular police officer, though he never acquired the acclaim that his predecessor earned. RKO produced several sequels: *Dick Tracy vs. Cueball* (1946), *Dick Tracy's Dilemma* and *Dick Tracy Meets Gruesome* (both 1947). Ralph Byrd, who was featured in the earlier movie serials, starred as Tracy in the latter two films.

Byrd was to have one more shot at the part that had typecast him in his professional career, on television. He played the master detective in 26 installments on ABC-TV between Sept. 13, 1950, and Feb. 13, 1951, in what one media reviewer termed a "very violent" production. Byrd's untimely death from a heart attack in 1952 at age 43 canceled the plans to revive the show in syndication.

The character returned in dual TV cartoon series in 1961 and 1971 (the latter as part of *The Archie Show*).

In a 1990 Disney feature film that opened to rave reviews, Warren Beatty starred as Tracy and Madonna was included in the supporting cast. In the wake of the Beatty picture, two Tracy documentaries were released: *Dick Tracy— America's #1 Crimestopper* and *Dick Tracy— Saga of a Crime Fighter*.

"Dick Tracy may never again return to the screen," wrote Jim Harmon in 1992. "Yet his history in the movies is rich enough to keep his memory alive in the minds of movie buffs as it lives in the minds of Dick Tracy fans of the comics and of golden age radio."

Doc Savage

(aka *Doc Savage, Man of Bronze*)

On the Air: Feb. 10–Aug. 4, 1934, Don Lee Network, Saturday, 9 p.m.; Oct. 6, 1934–March 30, 1935, Syndicated. 15 minutes.
Sponsor: Knox Co. for Cystex Nerve tonic and Mendaco Asthma medication.
Extant Episodes: None known.

Cast & Credits

Creator/Writer—Lester Dent.
Performers' names were not announced on the air during the initial dual runs.

A media critic described Doc Savage as a "preserver of law and order." Typical

chapter titles included "The Sniper in the Sky," "The White Haired Devil," "Death Had Blue Hands" and "The Too-Talkative Parrot." The radio series was an adaptation that extended from *Doc Savage Magazine*, premiering in 1933. The shows that aired starting in October 1934 were repeats of the 26 original performances.

A half-hour revival of the original series, retitled *Doc Savage, Man of Bronze*, was broadcast over New York City's WMCA between Jan. 6 and June 30, 1943, on Wednesdays at 5 p.m. Three additional repeats were aired on Thursdays, June 17 to July 1, 1943. Edward Gruskin penned the scripts that featured Bernard Lenrow and Earl George. Charles Michaelson produced and Garrett E. Hallihan directed the drama.

Long after radio's golden age ended, *Doc Savage* was reprised yet again via a couple of serialized attempts ("The Thousand Headed Man" and "Fear Cay"). It was carried over National Public Radio Mondays between Sept. 30 and Dec. 23, 1985.

Martin Grams Jr. prepared a log for the series.

Doc Savage, Man of Bronze
see Doc Savage

Dr. Sixgun

On the Air: Sept. 2–Oct. 21, 1954, NBC, Thursday, 8:30 p.m.; Oct. 24, 1954–April 17, 1955, NBC, Sunday, 8 p.m.; April 21–Aug. 11, 1955, NBC, Thursday, 8:30 p.m.; Aug. 18–Oct. 13, 1955, NBC, Thursday, 8 p.m. 30 minutes.
Sponsor: Sustained.
Extant Episodes: 16.

Cast & Credits

Directors—Harry Frazee, Fred Weihe.
Writers—Ernest Kinoy, George Lefferts.

Announcer—Fred Collins.
Leads—Title role of Dr. Ray Matson played by Karl Weber; Pablo, played by William Griffis.

While Dr. Ray Matson was a practicing physician at Frenchman's Fork, his exploits with a sixgun and a desire to right the wrongs of bushwhackers, self-appointed vigilantes and white supremacists might have momentarily called his dedication to patching up wounds into question. Even though he claimed to put "healing before killing," Matson was pretty good with the snub-nose derringer he carried beside a medical bag stuffed with bandages, a stethoscope and pills. The physician was sometimes accompanied on the trail by a wandering peddler, his faithful compatriot Pablo. The sidekick also verbalized their encounters in suspense and danger with radio listeners through flashback narratives. One of Pablo's eccentricities was his ownership of a pet raven that talked.

Citing the protagonist as a "legendary figure," a tell-all epigraph introduced Matson to audiences as "the gun-toting frontier doctor who roamed the length and breadth of the old Indian territory—friend and physician to white man and Indian alike—the symbol of justice and mercy in the lawless West of the 1870s." The feature was considered a *mature* western due to its subject matter and audience appeal, part of a wave of adult cowboy thrillers introduced to aural fans in the early 1950s. The most famous of these, of course, was *Gunsmoke*.

Dr. Standish, Medical Examiner

On the Air: July 1–Aug. 19, 1948, CBS, Thursday, 8 p.m. 30 minutes.
Sponsor: Sustained.
Extant Episodes: None known.

CAST & CREDITS
Announcer—Lee Vines.
Leads—Title character played by Gary Merrill; his assistant, played by Audrey Christie; the homicide inspector, played by Eric Dressler.

This series was undoubtedly broached in recognition of a commonly disregarded service profession. Here local law enforcement officials routinely requested the assistance of Dr. Peter Standish, a public officer responsible for conducting autopsies. Standish applied his training and experience to probe for clues from the corpses of crime victims, thereby helping the police to fathom arcane murders that had absolutely stumped them. A couple of other figures with running roles in the series included Standish's feminine assistant and a homicide inspector, whose appellations have not been preserved.

Dr. Tim, Detective

On the Air: 1948. 15 minutes. The series aired 13 episodes.
Sponsor: No information.
Extant Episodes: Seven.

CAST & CREDITS
No information given on extant recordings.

This detective series combined the medical profession with investigative discoveries and was directed toward adolescents. Dr. Tim was a bachelor physician who lived by himself in a rooming house and therein maintained a crime laboratory. Like so many other series targeted to this age group, Dr. Tim featured a couple of juvenile protégés, Jill and Sandy. His investigations of criminal offenses, which often had educational aspects, were shared with those precocious youngsters and sometimes involved them. On one episode, when Dr. Tim provided an emergency blood transfusion to a man that had been shot, he related several facts about human blood to the children. Another time, when a character developed tuberculosis, he led a frank discussion in small fry terms on the disease's characteristics and treatment.

Meanwhile, Dr. Tim drew on his knowledge to identify culprits in such crimes as arson, bodily harm and theft while discovering the source of such rare illnesses as Rocky Mountain spotted fever. Disease prevention, food poisoning acquired by eating contaminated food and alleged sabotage of the physician's X-ray equipment were subjects pursued in some of the episodes. Chapter titles were intriguing: "The Mystery of the Man from Trouble Creek," "The Mystery of the Guest in Number Two," "The Mystery of the Dog That Did and Didn't" and "The Mystery of the Man from Hiroshima," et al.

Don Winslow of the Navy

On the Air: Oct. 18, 1937–June 17, 1938, NBC Blue, Weekdays, 5:15 p.m.; May 2–Aug. 12, 1938, NBC, Weekdays, 7 p.m.; Aug. 15, 1938–March 24, 1939, NBC Blue, Weekdays, 7 p.m.; March 27–May 26, 1939, NBC Blue, Weekdays, 5:30 p.m.; Oct. 5, 1942–Jan. 1, 1943, NBC Blue, Weekdays, 6:15 p.m. 15 minutes.
Sponsors: Sustained (Oct. 19, 1937–June 17, 1938); W. K. Kellogg Co. for its cereal brands (May 2, 1938–March 24, 1939); Bristol-Myers Inc. for Ipana toothpaste (March 27–May 26, 1939); General Foods Inc. for Post brand cereals (Oct. 5, 1942–Jan. 1, 1943).
Extant Episodes: Two.

CAST & CREDITS

Director—Ray Kremer.
Writers—Albert Aley, Al Barker.
Leads—Title role of Commander Don Winslow played by Bob Guilbert (1937–39),

Raymond Edward Johnson (1942–43); Lieutenant Red Pennington, played by Edward Davison (1937–39), John Gibson (1942–43).
Support Roles—Ruth Barth, Betty Lou Gerson, Betty Ito, Lenore Kingston.

This was a juvenile adventure series derived from Frank Martinek's comic strip of the same name. Supported by his trusty colleague, Lieutenant Red Pennington, U.S. Naval Intelligence commander Don Winslow conducted a never-ending war through many of the chapters with a diabolical crime czar identified simply as the Scorpion. He also fought other subversive types whose scheming could lead to control of the universe.

A "Squadron of Peace" club was one of the premiums hawked to its adolescent fans by the show. Joining up entitled a member to receive a printed membership card, manual and Don Winslow Creed.

Douglas of the World

On the Air: 1950s. No additional information.
Sponsor: Sustained.
Extant Episodes: Three.

CAST & CREDITS

Producer/Directors—Steven R. Callahan, Robert M. Young. **Writer**—John Blayhos, William Sundberg.
Music—Earl Lawrence, Mishel Perrier.
Announcer—Bill Woodson.
Lead—Title role of Bradford Douglas played by Jack Moyles.

Bradford (Brad) Douglas was a foreign correspondent for the mythical *New York World* newspaper. Coincidentally, he also had a hard time resisting beautiful women. Wherever he went they appeared to fall at his feet from the sky. By the very nature of his investigative assignments he was thrust into international political intrigue on a steady basis. Small matters like preventing suicides and kidnappings engaged him in the course of his daily routine.

Some tasks, however, required even more: At times, in far-flung locales, he'd encounter such activities as espionage, stealing atomic secrets and fending off villains who'd like nothing better than to screw the universe. Douglas had to halt them in their tracks, single-handedly or with assistance from local authorities by putting the spotlight of the *World* on their diabolical intents. It was dirty stuff but the denizens of the globe could undoubtedly rest easier knowing Douglas was on the job, taking it all seriously—at least, when not distracted by a lecherous female. That predicament, it seemed, simply went naturally with the turf.

Dragnet

On the Air: June 3–June 24, 1949, NBC, Friday, 10 p.m.; July 7–Sept. 1, 1949, NBC, Thursday; Sept. 3–Oct. 1, 1949, NBC, Saturday; Oct. 6, 1949–Sept. 11, 1952, NBC, Thursday, 10:30 p.m. (moved to 9 p.m. in 1950); Sept. 14, 1952–June 28, 1953, NBC, Sunday, 9:30 p.m.; Sept. 1, 1953–Sept. 20, 1955, NBC, Tuesday, 9 p.m.; (repeats) Sept. 27, 1955–June 26, 1956, NBC, Tuesday, 8:30 p.m.; (repeats) Sept. 18, 1956–Feb. 26, 1957, Tuesday, 8:30 p.m. 30 minutes.

Theme Song: *Dragnet March*, originally known as *Danger Ahead* (Walter Schumann).

Sponsors: Sustained (June 3–Oct. 1, 1949); Liggett & Myers Tobacco Co. for Fatima cigarettes (Oct. 6, 1949–Sept. 11, 1952); Liggett & Myers Tobacco Co. for Chesterfield cigarettes (Sept. 14, 1952–Sept. 20, 1955); Multiple participation (Sept. 27, 1955–Feb. 26, 1957).

Extant Episodes: 288.

CAST & CREDITS

Directors—Bill Rousseau, Jack Webb.
Writers—Ben Alexander, Richard L. Breen, Frank Burt, James E. Moser, Jack Robinson, Jack Webb.
Music—Walter Schumann (orchestra).
Sound Effects—Wayne Kenworthy, Jack Robinson, Bud Tollefson.
Announcers—George Finneman, Hal Gibney.
Leads—Joe Friday, played by Jack Webb; Friday's partners: Sergeant Ben Romero, played by Barton Yarborough (1949–51); Sergeant Ed Jacobs, played by Barney Phillips (1951–52); Officer Bill Lockwood, played by Martin Milner (1952); Officer Frank Smith, played by Harry Bartell, Vic Perrin, Herb Ellis (all 1952), Ben Alexander (1952–57).
Support Roles—Tol Avery (Chief of Detectives Thaddeus Brown), Raymond Burr and Charles McGraw (Chief of Detectives Ed Backstrand), Herb Butterfield (crime lab lieutenant Lee Jones), Olan Soule (Lieutenant Ray Pinker), Peggy Webber (Ma Friday); plus Parley Baer, Richard Boone, Lillian Buyeff, Virginia Christine, Whit Connor, Sam Edwards, Georgia Ellis, Virginia Gregg, Stacy Harris, Bill Johnstone, Helen Kleeb, Jack Kruschen, John McIntire, Tyler McVey, Marvin Miller, Harry Morgan, Jeanette Nolan, Kenneth Patterson, Ken Peters, Sarah Selby.

Sergeant Joe Friday of the Los Angeles Police Department robotically displayed a cool, calculated temperament. His drama projected a fraudulent society defended by committed but dispirited cops and limited by the vastness of imperfection. Set in a semi-documentary style, it stressed precise references to numbered regulations in the police code. With frequent intrusions of extraneous material, the narrative seemed quite real. Its chief interrogator, Friday, became something of a believable hero to fans. He was ultimately as much a part of the police force as any real-life officer, a quality missing in most earlier crime presentations. Assisting him was a series of partners. Paired together, they made formidable inroads into quelling the violence and mayhem surging in metropolitan Los Angeles.

The program's billboard was explicit: "The story you are about to hear is true; the names have been changed to protect the innocent: *Dragnet*, the documented drama of an actual crime. For the next 30 minutes, in cooperation with the Los Angeles Police Department, we will travel step by step on the side of the law through an actual case transcribed from official police files. From beginning to end, from crime to punishment, *Dragnet* is the story of your police force in action." Technical assistance, a concluding statement noted, was provided by the office of Chief of Police W. H. Parker of the Los Angeles Police Department.

While earlier radio detectives failed to demonstrate integrity and respect in their quest to right civil wrongs, the sleuths of the neo-realistic era (including those of *Dragnet* and several series that followed it) flaunted a kind of halting crudeness themselves. Persistently drawn into conflict, they functioned in a vacuum within the lapses created by social failure and criminal behavior. In doing so they clearly performed their tasks in a mechanical, often repetitious fashion.

Nontraditional themes were inserted into the story lines of these dramas. Abandoned kids, children running from home, child molestation, drug addiction and female juveniles posing for pornography turned up as subjects of *Dragnet* episodes. Attacks on police officers, contract murders, muggings, anti-Semitism, juvenile delinquency, strangling the elderly and political retribution were all a part of this new wave of dramatizations. None of these topics would have been covered in depth on most crime series before this time. *Dragnet* unquestionably became radio's

most influential police drama in the 1950s and was later to be hailed by a couple of distinguished TV reviewers in 1988 as "the most successful police series in the history of television."

Jack Webb starred in a *Dragnet* theatrical film in 1954. He carried the radio show to NBC television on Dec. 16, 1951, where it became even more popular, continuing through Sept. 6, 1959. It made a comeback on that network from Jan. 12, 1967, through Sept. 10, 1970. A syndicated, but totally undistinguished re-creation, *The New Dragnet*, appeared in the 1990-91 TV season starring Jeff Osterhage as Sergeant Vic Daniels. By then the bloom was off the rose; Jack Webb had died on Dec. 23, 1982. His persona simply couldn't be duplicated.

Randy Eidemiller, Chris Lembesis and Terry Salomonson compiled a log for the radio series.

Dyke Easter, Detective

On the Air: Audition tape aired March 19, 1949, NBC, Saturday. 30 minutes.
Sponsor: Sustained.
Extant Episodes: One (audition tape).

CAST & CREDITS
Producer/Director—Alan M. Fishburn.
Lead—Title role played by Albert Hecht.

This hard-boiled, tough-minded gumshoe appeared to dislike what he did for a living and spent about as much time depreciating himself as he did actively pursuing miscreants. It was obvious that Easter despised his very existence and perhaps this was a partial explanation as to why no continuing series followed.

Opposite: In *Dragnet*, "the story of your police force in action," crime investigation got down where people lived, without any glamour as witnessed on some other cops-and-robbers series. This was nitty gritty, "just the facts." A couple of officers at its forefront included series star Jack Webb, left, as Sergeant Joe Friday, and an early partner, Sergeant Ben Romero, played by Barton Yarborough.

Radio historiographer Fred Mac-Donald was blunt in his assessment of Dyke Easter and his peer band of neo-realistic investigators: "Like all such sleuths, Easter lived with a pain he was unable to share. This type of hero had no such companion as a girl friend or a flirtatious secretary—love in the world of these detectives was contemptuous, since revealing an openness to human warmth was only a sign of exploitable vulnerability. Should such a character make an attempt at developing a relationship with a woman, he was doomed to failure; and a collapsed love affair meant only more self-castigation."

Ellery Queen see *The Adventures of Ellery Queen*

Eno Crime Clues see *Eno Crime Club*

Eno Crime Club

(aka *Eno Crime Clues*, aka *Crime Club*)

On the Air: *Eno Crime Club*. Feb. 9–July 4, 1931, CBS, Monday–Saturday, 6:45 p.m.; July 6–Sept. 30, 1931, CBS, Monday and Wednesday; Oct. 7–Dec. 30, 1931, CBS, Wednesday; Jan. 5–Oct. 26, 1932, CBS, Tuesday and Wednesday, 9:30 p.m.; Nov. 9–Dec. 21, 1932, CBS, Wednesday; *Eno Crime Clues*. Jan. 3, 1933–July 24, 1934, NBC Blue, Tuesday and Wednesday, 8 p.m.; Sept. 4, 1934–June 30, 1936, NBC Blue, Tuesday, 8 p.m.; *Crime Club*. Dec. 2–Dec. 30, 1946, MBS, Monday, 8 p.m.; Jan. 2–Oct. 23, 1947, MBS, Thursday, 10 p.m. 15 minutes (Feb. 9–July 4, 1931); 30 minutes (other time periods).
Sponsor: Eno effervescent antacid salts (1931–36); Sustained (1946–47).
Extant Episodes: 10.

CAST & CREDITS

Directors—Carlo De Angelo, Jay Hanna.
Writers—Albert G. Miller, Stewart Sterling.
Leads—Spencer Dean, played by Clyde North, Edward Reese; Danny Cassidy, played by Walter Glass, Jack MacBryde; Jane Elliott, played by Helen Choate; Barry Thompson, the "librarian" in a revised version.
Support Roles—Georgia Backus, Arline Blackburn, Linda Carlon-Reid, Ray Collins, Brian Donlevy, Helene Dumas, Gloria Holden, Elaine Melchior, Adele Ronson, Ralph Sumpter, Ruth Yorke.

One of radio's earliest mystery anthologies changed formats and names several times, beginning as a six-a-week thriller, then progressing to a weekly half-hour to a twice-a-week half-hour that required two episodes to resolve a tale. Spencer Dean, identified as "The Manhunter," was the ongoing detective who solved heinous crimes in "another Manhunter mystery." Listeners were encouraged to "match wits with the Manhunter" and to join the club he founded devoted to sorting out corruption that the law couldn't unravel. Danny Cassidy was Dean's partner; Jane Elliott was Dean's love interest. In one format change, the Crime Club "librarian" recounted the story of a mystery adventure involving detectives in pursuit.

Radio historiographer Fred Mac-Donald claimed *The Eno Crime Club* was "eminently popular" with radio audiences, noting that—by early 1932—the program was heard in more American homes than such broadcasting giants as bandleader Paul Whiteman or newsmen Walter Winchell and Lowell Thomas. Conversely, MacDonald observed: "Although *The Eno Crime Club* and *The Adventures of Sherlock Holmes* were among the top-rated shows in 1931, most dramatic series made little lasting impact on listeners and soon faded in popularity. Many reasons could be suggested for such a development: the paucity of good writers, the still-maturing art of sound effects, the preference of Americans for drama in motion pictures rather than radio. But the most pressing reason was the lack of big-name talent. Movie personalities avoided radio…. As a new form of programming, broadcast drama had little experienced talent upon which to draw."

Some of these stories were adapted from novels published under the Doubleday Crime Club imprint.

The Falcon see The Adventures of the Falcon

The Fat Man

On the Air: Jan. 21, 1946–Jan. 6, 1947, ABC, Monday, 8:30 p.m.; Jan. 10, 1947–Aug. 4, 1950, ABC, Friday, 8 p.m.; Oct. 6–Dec. 29, 1950, ABC, Friday, 8 p.m.; Jan. 10–Sept. 26, 1951, ABC, Wednesday, 8:30 p.m. 30 minutes.
Theme Song: *Fat Man Polka* (Bernard Green, pseudonym for Bernard Greenwald).
Sponsors: Sustained (Jan. 21, 1946–Feb. 7, 1947); the Norwich Pharmacal Co. for Pepto-Bismol stomach distress remedy and Unguentine skin ointment (Feb. 14, 1947–Aug. 4, 1950); R. J. Reynolds Tobacco Co. for Camel cigarettes (Oct. 6–Dec. 29, 1950); American Chicle Co. for Adams Dentyne and Chiclets chewing gum brands (Jan. 10–Sept. 26, 1951).
Extant Episodes: 10 (U.S.), 36 (Australian).

CAST & CREDITS

Producer—Ed Rosenberg.
Directors—Clark Andrews, Charles Powers, Robert Sloane.
Writers—Richard Ellington, Dashiell Hammett (creator), Lawrence Klee, Daniel Shuffman, Robert Sloane, Harold Swanton.

Music—Bernard Green (orchestra), Joseph Stopak, Mark Winston.
Sound Effects—Ed Blainey.
Announcers—Charles Irving, Gene Kirby, Don Lowe.
Leads—Brad Runyon, played by J. Scott Smart; Lila North (his secretary), played by Mary Patton; Cathy Evans (his love interest), played by Amzie Strickland; police Sergeant O'Hara, played by Ed Begley.
Support Roles—Inga Adams, Rolly Bester, Jim Boles, Sarah Burton, Robert Dryden, Alice Frost, Betty Garde, Nell Harrison, Jimmy McCallion, Dan Ocko, Margot Stevenson, Paul Stewart, Vicki Vola, Linda Watkins.

A New York bachelor who tipped the scales at 237 pounds, portly PI Brad Runyon was dubbed "a cross between Sam Spade and Nick Charles"—a sleuthing trio created by novelist Dashiell Hammett. Each episode began with a distinctive opening as a penny was dropped into a pharmacy scale, followed by a declaration of the hero's weight. Such a memorable billboard conjured up images of a jolly fellow whose girth alone could make him an ample threat to the rogues he pursued and brought to justice. The jocular nature often associated with heavy individuals could be overlooked, however; Runyon was tough as nails and sometimes dispensed little frivolity along the way.

John Dunning recalled that producer Ed Rosenberg believed a realistic narrative could be derived from Dashiell Hammett's figure Gutman in *The Maltese Falcon*. Chapter 11 of that classic was designated *The Fat Man*. "Gutman's resemblance to the character who emerged on the air began and ended with the title," noted Dunning. "Gutman was sinister and brooding; radio's *Fat Man* was a charmer, a witty ladykiller." Dunning also cited Brad Runyon as "the one gumshoe of the air who couldn't be copied," based on his hard-boiled methods of dealing with criminals. In practical application, that assessment might be given of multiple aural detectives.

The Fat Man: A charmer, a witty ladykiller—that was radio's Fat Man, Brad Runyon, who was also characterized as "as tough as nails." Don't be fooled by his true 270-pound frame—he could sit down on his prey and hold them for the cops if he had to! Playing a scene with J. Scott Smart (center), the enduring actor who surely took plenty of kidding about his portly role, are thespians Jim Boles and Inga Adams.

Interestingly J. Scott Smart, who often appeared in bow tie and suspenders while portraying the 237-pound fat man, weighed 270 pounds at that time. Both Smart and Runyon shared a size 58 belt. The thespian was just 57 when he died. Smart was multi-talented, combining gifts in art, music and dance with his onstage and radio acting persona. He appeared frequently on a variety of comedy shows (including *Fred Allen, Jack Benny, Blondie, Bob Hope* and more) and turned up in serious parts on *The March of Time* and *Theatre Guild*. Residing in a simple fisherman's hut on the coast of Maine, he commuted weekly to New York for radio performances and otherwise painted picturesque seascapes at his Maine retreat. He starred in *The Fat Man* in a 1951 theatrical release, a film that introduced Rock Hudson

to cinematic audiences while adding Julie London and Emmett Kelly in supporting roles. Yet Smart "was better behind the microphone than in front of the camera," a media critic pronounced.

While contributing little to the radio series, Dashiell Hammett's name was employed in the epigraphs each week until 1950 when his perceived sympathies with subversive national security elements negated his broadcasting utility. For a more comprehensive background of that development, you can read the details under *The Adventures of Sam Spade*.

Comparing *The Fat Man* to another Hammett alter-ego investigator, *The Thin Man*, author Jim Harmon avowed that the latter was "a better show" and the former was "a poor imitation." Publishing his appraisal in 1967, Harmon suggested: "After Hammett's first few scripts 'setting' the series, the program sank into pedestrian mediocrity and only the great booming voice and sly intonations of the man we knew as the Fat Man still bring the series to mind after nearly a score of years."

There was also an Australian version of *The Fat Man* complete with an altogether different cast.

Charles Laughlin wrote a biography about J. Scott Smart, published by Three Faces East Press.

Father Brown see The Adventures of Father Brown

Federal Agent

On the Air: 1947, Syndicated. 15 minutes.
Sponsor: Music filled time for local commercial inserts.
Extant Episodes: Four.

CAST & CREDITS

No information.

The Federal Agent showed up wherever there was trouble on the international scene and his support was needed. In one episode he assisted the Royal Canadian Mounted Police when a trainload of expensive furs was dynamited. In another he helped the French Sûreté locate a valuable work of art pilfered from the Louvre. In England he aided Scotland Yard in bringing an end to the careers of an infamous gunman and his moll.

The FBI in Peace and War

On the Air: Nov. 25, 1944–June 30, 1945, CBS, Saturday, 8:30 p.m.; Aug. 23, 1945–June 27, 1946, CBS, Thursday, 8:30 p.m.; Aug. 29, 1946–June 26, 1947, CBS, Thursday, 8:30 p.m.; Aug. 22, 1947–June 24, 1948, CBS, Thursday, 8 p.m.; Aug. 26, 1948–June 30, 1949, CBS, Thursday, 8 p.m.; Sept. 1, 1949–June 29, 1950, CBS, Thursday, 8 p.m.; Aug. 31, 1950–June 5, 1952, CBS, Thursday, 8 p.m.; June 12–Sept. 25, 1952, CBS, Thursday, 8:30 p.m.; Oct. 1, 1952–Sept. 28, 1955, CBS, Wednesday, 8 p.m.; Oct. 5, 1955–July 4, 1956, CBS, Wednesday, 8:30 p.m.; July 8, 1956–Sept. 20, 1957, CBS, Sunday, 6:05 p.m.; Oct. 6, 1957–Sept. 28, 1958, CBS, Sunday, 5:30 p.m. Most shows 30 minutes; 25 minutes late in the run.
Theme Song: March from *Love for Three Oranges* (Sergei Prokofiev).
Sponsors: Procter & Gamble Co. for Lava soap (Nov. 25, 1944–Dec. 28, 1950); Multiple participation for Wildroot Cream Oil and Brylcreme hair groom preparations, Lucky Strike cigarettes, Nescafé instant coffee, Wrigley's chewing gum, Wheaties cereal, CBS Radio, and others, and Sustained (Jan. 4, 1951–Sept. 28, 1958).
Extant Episodes: 40.

CAST & CREDITS

Producer/Directors—Max Marcin (1940s), Betty Mandeville (c. 1949 and beyond).
Writers—Ed Adamson, Fred Collins, Jacques Finke, Louis Pelletier.
Music—Vladimir Selinsky.
Sound Effects—Ed Blainey, Al Hogan, Byron Wingett.
Announcers—Andre Baruch, Hugh Holder, Dick Noel, Len Sterling, Warren Sweeney.
Leads—Adam Sheppard, played by Martin Blaine; FBI field agent supervisor Andrews, played by Donald Briggs.
Support Roles—Edith Arnold, Charita Bauer, Jackson Beck, Ralph Bell, Joe DeSantis, Robert Dryden, Elspeth Eric, Walter Greaza, Larry Haines, Pat Hosley, Harold Huber, John M. James, Paul McGrath, George Petrie, Frank Readick, Rosemary Rice, Grant Richards, Bob Sloane, William J. Smith, Luis Van Rooten.

These narratives, where rackets and swindles proliferated, were based upon Frederick L. Collins' copyrighted book *The FBI*

The FBI in Peace and War: Field service agent supervisor Andrews and top field agent Sheppard share a scene while on the trail of elusive crooks. Donald Briggs (left) played Andrews and Martin Blaine was featured as the authoritative voice in charge of the tracking. Their series was made forever memorable to its fans by its theme song and ringing commercials touting "L-A-V-A, L-A-V-A."

in Peace and War, as audiences were reminded in every episode. While the show in theory depicted actual cases pursued by the federal agency, those who listened closely near the end each week may have been disappointed to learn that "any similarity to persons living or dead is purely coincidental." (That embedded tagline was adopted by numerous crime shows.) Perhaps sadly the fans may have also discovered that their series wasn't "an official program of the FBI." The tales were heavily dramatized to present action out of each criminal's experience. Field Agent Adam Sheppard and a team of disciplined cohorts followed clues the culprits left behind that led them to identify and ultimately capture their prey. Even the long sentences meted out to the guilty, announced at the close of each drama, tended to make the "reenactments" appear as both highly appealing and authentic to the millions who tuned in regularly. Sheppard and his counterparts were described as "by-the-book, humorless, heavy-footed, hardnosed, unromantic federal agents" by one critic. Notwithstanding, the drama's realism made it a fan favorite for 14 years, approaching the very end of the radio's golden age.

The show developed one of the most distinctive and memorable theme songs on the air: a dramatic rendition of the march from Prokofiev's *Love for Three Oranges*. The long-running sponsor's name was announced while a baritone voice pronounced a drum-pounding "L-A-V-A, L-A-V-A" from an echo chamber. The familiar music, in step with those four letters, immediately followed. The advertising phrase was recited by millions of Americans who added it to their everyday vernacular. Could a sponsor have asked for anything more?

Shortly before signing off each week, the announcer declared: "The broadcast does not imply endorsement, authorization or approval of the Federal Bureau of Investigation." Actually, FBI director J. Edgar Hoover reportedly never was enamored by this series, even though it raised his agents to lofty plateaus. Hoover later endorsed an "official broadcast of the Federal Bureau of Investigation," *This Is Your FBI*, that debuted in 1945 and ran for eight seasons over ABC. (See separate entry.) That one probably never gained the audience and popularity of the "unautho-rized" program, however. Prokofiev's charm was tough to beat.

For a while Betty Mandeville was the only feminine producer-director of a nighttime crime series in network radio. Her broadcasting credits include similar duties on the game show *Take It or Leave It*.

Flash Gordon

(aka *The Amazing Adventures of Flash Gordon*, aka *The Amazing Interplanetary Adventures of Flash Gordon*)

On the Air: *The Amazing Adventures of Flash Gordon*. April 27–Oct. 26, 1935, MBS, Saturday; Oct. 28, 1935–Feb. 6, 1936, MBS, Monday through Thursday, 5:30 p.m.; *The Amazing Interplanetary Adventures of Flash Gordon*, 1939, Syndicated, weekly chapters aired in a myriad of time slots. 15 minutes.
Theme Song: *The Storm*. The same selection was also continued on the successor series, *Jungle Jim*. It came from a 1927 RCA Black Seal recording by maestro Rosario Bourdon and the Victor Symphony.
Sponsors: Hearst Newspaper Corp. for its *Comic Weekly* supplement and Groves Laboratories Inc. for Groves Emulsified nose drops (network run); Local sponsors in markets carrying the syndicated show.
Extant Episodes: 30.

CAST & CREDITS

Producer—Himan Brown.
Lead—Title role played by Gale Gordon, James Meighan.
Support Roles—Dr. Zarkoff, played by Owen Jordan (1935–36), Maurice Franklin (1939); Dale Arden, played by Irene Watson (1935–36), Franc Hale (1939); Bruno Wick (Ming); Alan Reed (Teddy Bergman); Charlie Cantor, Ray Collins, Everett Sloane.

In the original radio adaptation, emperor Flash Gordon went the distance for his people in their ocean floor kingdom of Atlantis. He fought legions of sinister figures that attempted to control his people.

Crusading alongside him were Dr. Zarkoff, a prominent and gifted scientist, and Flash's beautiful and resourceful love interest, Dale Arden. Their cause came to a rather ignoble ending after a few months on the air when Gordon and company managed to crash into a remote forest. Rendered helpless, they were heroically rescued by Jungle Jim, a character that the sponsoring Hearst newspaper syndicate had preordained as Gordon's aural successor.

When the series was reincarnated in syndication three years later, Gordon and his tribe left their underwater confines to dispel evil forces of the universe, just like many of their peers were doing. Out in planetary space they encountered Ming the Merciless, chief of the warring planet Mongo. Ming became a recurring nemesis in ongoing confrontations with the Atlantis trio.

Flash Gordon was conceived in the mind of Alex Raymond, an illustrator who created a weekly tabloid comic strip in advance of the radio series. The widely popular feature appeared for several years in the Hearst Sunday newspaper section *Comic Weekly* and was later regularly mentioned on the radio broadcasts in a developing trend toward multimedia plugs. The artist, Raymond, was also illustrator for the Hearst comic strip *Jungle Jim*, successor to *Flash Gordon* on network radio.

Gordon himself had a bigger career on screen via a Saturday matinee serial starring Larry (Buster) Crabbe. He also appeared in the title role in the weekly film installments of *Buck Rogers in the Twenty-Fifth Century*.

Flashgun Casey see Casey, Crime Photographer

Flying Patrol

On the Air: Sept. 29, 1941–Aug. 28, 1942, NBC Blue, Weekdays, 5:30 p.m. 15 minutes.
Sponsor: Sustained.
Extant Episodes: One.

CAST & CREDITS

Leads—Skip Donovan, played by Hugh Rowlands; Pat Moran, played by Sharon Grainger.
Support Roles—Kay Campbell, Mary Frances Desmond, Sidney Ellstrom, Willard Farnum, Bob Guilbert, Pat Murphy, Norma Jean Ross, Cliff Soubier.

This juvenile thriller narrative exploited the adventures of the U.S. Coast Guard Air Corps fliers. On peacekeeping missions, Pat Moran, the girlfriend of unit commander Skip Donovan, frequently accompanied him in his battles with smugglers and other enemy agents hoping to infiltrate our country along its coastlines.

Forbidden Cargo

On the Air: 1950s, Syndicated. 30 minutes.
Sponsor: Local underwriters in markets where the show was sold.
Extant Episodes: 33.

CAST & CREDITS

On-air credits were omitted from several episodes that we heard in preparing this entry. Accents were distinctly British, however.

These narratives involved unscrupulous elements surreptitiously importing and exporting various commodities, and invariably running afoul of the existing customs laws. Perpetrators were tracked, identified and captured by law enforcement authorities whose job was to stop illegal smuggling. The show's billboard read: "By ship, by plane, by road ... goods are smuggled dangerously out of one country into another—goods which are *Forbidden Cargo!*" Surprisingly, few sound effects were included, suggesting the feature was perhaps a low-budget affair.

Jerry Haendiges prepared a partial log of this series.

Foreign Assignment

On the Air: July 24, 1943–Jan. 8, 1944, MBS, Saturday, 8:30 p.m. 30 minutes.
Sponsor: Sustained.
Extant Episodes: One.

CAST & CREDITS

Director—Chick Vincent.
Writer—Frank H. Phares.
Music—Henry Sylvern (orchestra).
Announcer—Joe Julian.
Leads—Brian Barry, played by Jay Jostyn; Carol Manning, played by Vicki Vola.
Support Roles—Guy Repp, Bartlett Robinson, Maurice Wells.

A foreign correspondent for the mythical *American Press*, Brian Barry, battled the Gestapo in occupied France. An attractive feminine assistant, Carol Manning, accompanied him on his crusades to counter Nazi espionage.

At the same time they were performing here, Jay Jostyn and Vicki Vola were appearing over NBC's far more durable *Mr. District Attorney*. Jostyn was featured in the title role while Vola played his secretary, Edith Miller. (See separate entry.)

The Front Page

On the Air: May 6–Sept. 16, 1948, ABC, Thursday, 8 p.m. 30 minutes.
Sponsor: Sustained.
Extant Episodes: None known.

CAST & CREDITS

Director—Bill Rousseau.
Writers—Morton Fine, David Friedkin.
Leads—Hildebrand (Hildy) Johnson, played by Dick Powell; Walter Burns, played by William Conrad.

In 1931 Ben Hecht and Charles MacArthur saw their play *The Front Page* make its stage debut. Set in 1920s Chicago, the lighthearted drama centered on star reporter Hildebrand (Hildy) Johnson, rescued from the brink of retirement and marriage by a quick-talking editor who required his services in covering "one last case," the politically charged execution of a cop-killing radical. The "killer" turned out to be a blameless fall guy. The editor was more interested in getting the story than in saving the guy's neck, however.

Following stage and theatrical productions of *The Front Page* that played to widely approving audiences, in 1948 the comedic crime drama was limply adapted for a summer stint on radio. The result was biting reviews, primarily due to its major departures from the original premise. On the air, at times it dissolved into a love-hate relationship between reporter Hildy Johnson and his managing editor, Walter Burns. A highly competitive Burns barked orders and found some of Johnson's actions difficult to accept. While exposing corruption and catching culprits was their mission in the process of putting out a paper, the pair were never as grimfaced about it as were their journalistic peers over at *Big Town*, *The Big Story* and *Front Page Farrell*. In many regards, Johnson and Burns offered a humorous tack on what would usually be considered some pretty serious stuff.

A critic offered a synopsis of the 1931 black-and-white Lewis Milestone-directed movie production. Adapted by Bartlett Cormack, it starred Adolphe Menjou as Walter Burns and Pat O'Brien as Hildy Johnson: "This story portrays the alluring, wise-cracking, mob mentality of the modern press corps. The excitement is so addicting that Hildy has a hard time leaving it even for a great woman, who is everything he wants. The anarchist is a political pawn, and the corruption of big-city politics is apparent."

In a technicolor movie remake in 1974, directed by Billy Wilder with screenplay by I. A. L. Diamond, Jack Lemmon was featured as Johnson and Walter Matthau as Burns. In supporting roles were Susan Sarandon and Martin Gabel.

The Front Page went to CBS-TV on Sept. 29, 1949, occupying the Thursday-at-eight half-hour slot that it had held a year earlier on radio. The televersion ran through Jan. 26, 1950, with John Daly as Burns and Mark Roberts as Johnson. Three weeks after the program's demise Daly launched a new "career" as moderator of the CBS-TV panel show *What's My Line?* He'd be doing that live nearly every Sunday night for the next 17.5 years! He also was ABC-TV's first major evening news anchor. Daly was selected for his role in *The Front Page* from his experience as an authentic newsjournalist, the producers thinking that would add a ring of authenticity to the dramatic series.

A couple of newspaper crime stories with similar monikers subsequently appeared on television. There was a syndicated feature, *Front Page Detective*, starring Edmund Lowe as newsman David Chase, with Paula Drew as his girlfriend, making it onto the Dumont Television network's schedule between 1951 and 1953. In 1993–94 five young reporters (Andria Hall, Tony Harris, Vicki Liviakis, Josh Mankiewicz, Ron Reagan) appeared in a Fox TV investigative drama simply titled *Front Page*.

Front Page Farrell

On the Air: June 23, 1941–March 13, 1942, MBS, Weekdays, 1:30 p.m.; Sept. 14, 1942–

June 29, 1951, NBC, Weekdays, 5:45 p.m.; July 2, 1951–March 26, 1954, NBC, Weekdays, 5:15 p.m. 15 minutes.

Theme Song: *You and I Know.*

Sponsor: American Home Products Corp. which rotated its commercials among a long line of personal-care and household commodities including Kolynos toothpaste and tooth powder dentifrice, Anacin pain reliever, Kriptin antihistamine, Bi-So-Dol analgesic, Freezone corn remover, Heet liniment, Dristan and Primatene cold remedies, Preparation H hemorrhoidal medication, Neet hair remover, Infrarub balm, Sleep-Eze calmative, Black Flag and Fly-Ded insect repellents, Aerowax and Olde English floor cleaners, Wizard room deodorizer, Sani-Flush toilet cleanser, Easy-Off oven cleaner, etc. (June 23, 1941–March 26, 1954).

Extant Episodes: 13.

Cast & Credits

Producers—Anne Hummert, Frank Hummert.

Directors—John Buckwalter, Arthur Hanna, Frank Hummert, Richard Leonard, Ed Slattery, Bill Sweets, Blair Walliser.

Writers—Alvin Boretz, Harold Gast, Box Saxon, Robert J. Shaw.

Music—Ann Leax, Rosa Rio (organ).

Sound Effects—Ross Martindale, Manny Segal.

Announcers—Bill Bond, Larry Elliott, Ed Fleming, Don Hancock.

Leads—David Farrell, played by Richard Widmark, Carleton Young and Staats Cotsworth; Sally Farrell, played by Virginia Dwyer and Florence Williams.

Support Roles—Peter Capell, Frank Chase (George Walker, managing editor of *The New York Daily Eagle*), Robert Donley (police lieutenant Carpenter), Katherine Emmet, Elspeth Eric, Betty Garde (reporter Kay Barnett), Ethel Intropide, Sylvia Leigh, Athena Lorde, James Monks, William Shelley, Eleanor Sherman, Vivian Smolen, George Sturgeon, James Van Dyk, Evelyn Varden (Sally's mother, Mrs. Howard), Sammy Warner (George Sturgeon, newspaper copy boy).

Centering on a newspaper reporter and his wife, David and Sally Farrell, *Front Page Farrell* was launched as a daytime melodrama, heavy on domestic crises and thin on journalistic exposés—precisely what anyone would expect from the Hummert (Frank and Anne) production factory. Somewhere in the late 1940s, however, the serial took a bolder stance toward thugs in the Big Apple. David's efforts intensified, his persistence in uncovering the truth turning relentless as he sought to unveil legions of evildoers and place them behind bars. Perhaps in an effort to combat audience slippage to television, this "get-tough" policy became even more pronounced as time went on, moving almost exclusively from matters of the heart to hysteria and homicide. By the 1950s new five-part episodes were launched every Monday. David was on a tear to solve mysteries, expose corruption and deal with crooks of every persuasion. By Friday evening he and Sally had helped remove that week's culprit from the city's streets, giving him another page-one byline. Infrequent listeners who missed an episode now and then found it simpler to keep up with the story line when the serial offered a new case every week. Because *Farrell* aired well within the hearing range of millions of men, it enjoyed the added benefit of being followed by male commuters, too.

In 1941 this became the first live serial on the Mutual Broadcasting System to air from New York City. It was also one of the first pieces of business that the renowned Blackett-Sample-Hummert advertising agency gave to Mutual.

Possibly at the forefront of a wave of newfound carnage that surfaced on daytime radio in the late 1940s stood *Front Page Farrell*, a drama that could shed its staid domesticity rather easily to concentrate on fighting crime. For three or four years after reinventing itself, the series resulted in a hard-hitting investigative style.

Though the change didn't ultimately save the show, it probably staved off its demise, squeezing out a few extra years of fast-paced action and dialogue. The drama focused on such weekly case titles as "The Man Who Knew All the Angles," "The Case of the Mysterious Killer," "High Explosives" and "Fatal Smile."

The most memorable David Farrell, actor Staats Cotsworth, who played the part longer than contemporaries, provided—apparently unintentionally—some fascinating insights into the compensation of radio actors in a 1948 magazine interview. The prospect certainly existed for some rather lucrative incomes in the business; most outsiders had no idea just how rewarding those were, however, until the slick newsjournal hit the stands. Over a few drinks on the terrace of his penthouse apartment, Cotsworth loosened up to a *Newsweek* reporter's inquiry. Just how had an actor who began his career in the repertory theater of Eva Le Gallienne, and who had also played on Broadway with such luminaries as Judith Anderson, Maurice Evans and Flora Robson, turned to *Casey, Crime Photographer* and *The Second Mrs. Burton* for a livelihood? When the full-page text of his answer appeared under the banner "Cotsworth in the Chips," radio actors everywhere cringed. The deep, dark secret surrounding their rather generous occupational recompense, a matter they had closely guarded across the years, came to light. As a consequence, a few who weren't intimidated by all the publicity decided to meet the press too, sharing similar accounts of large salaries.

The periodical estimated Cotsworth's weekly wages at $1,000, an immense sum in 1948 when incomes from all trades and professions were considered. He flatly acknowledged that he received $250 weekly for the half-hour *Casey* series. In addition, he portrayed the title role in *Front Page Farrell* every day and was the male lead in the daily *Lone Journey.* An average of three times weekly his recurring role was written into the story line of *The Second Mrs. Burton.* Beyond that, he appeared each week, without billing, on one or more other nighttime shows. With union scale then at $18.15 plus $7.26 for each hour of rehearsal per fifteen-minute show, anyone could easily calculate his approximate income. So why did he act on soap operas? "Giving up a daytime show is like turning in your insurance policy," Cotsworth freely admitted. Although he hadn't intended to release a financial statement to the press, his comments offered fresh insights into a gray area that the public could only speculate about until then. After all, those penthouses, servants and Cadillacs were coming from somewhere!

Frontier Town

On the Air: 1952–53, Syndicated. 30 minutes.
Sponsor: Sold to various sponsors in local markets.
Extant Episodes: 47 (complete run).

CAST & CREDITS

Producer—Bruce Ellis.
Music—Ivan Ditmars (orchestra).
Announcer—Bill Forman.
Leads—Chad Remington, played by Jeff Chandler (23 episodes), Reed Hadley (24 episodes); Cherokee O'Bannon, played by Wayne Crosby.

Chad Remington was a nineteenth century attorney living in imaginary Dos Rias, situated on the Western border of American civilization. With his hard-drinking Irish companion, who could at times be quite humorous—Cherokee O'Bannon—Remington and his series challenged the fine line between adventure and mystery. Sometimes he was a mere force demonstrating courage, and moral and ethical integrity within his community; otherwise, he might be risking his life to overtake desperadoes who were attempting to enrich themselves at the expense of law-abiding citizens. At all times "he combined physical strength and legal expertise and thereby presented a formidable opponent to antagonists," noted an analyst. Individual chapter titles testified to his crimefighting connection: "Six Gun Justice," "The Return of the Badmen," "The Valley of Lawless Men," "The Guns of Wrath," "Land Grab," "The Jailbird Rangers," "Valley of the Varmints," "The Six Gun Lawyer," "Canyon of Wanted Men" and "The Badlands."

Calling *Frontier Town* "the first adult western," J. Fred MacDonald claimed the series never achieved the distribution and popularity it deserved by being a syndicated program. "The themes, dialogue, and characterizations of *Frontier Town* clearly separated it from adolescent westerns," he averred. None of the heroes in juvenile westerns, for instance, ever warned a bad guy, as Chad Remington did in one installment: "If you try to pick up that gun, I'm promising you this much: I'll jump you and bang your head until it goes clean through that floor!" The age of real violence in the aural western was surely in the incubation period.

An insightful MacDonald claimed: "It was an irony that radio did not develop the genre [of the mature western] until creative broadcasting was in ebb. Several reasons help account for this condition. Among them were the reluctance of sponsors to underwrite a western for primarily adult audiences, network economics which mitigated [*sic*] against sustaining series, the lack of creativity among script writers who chose to remain with proven formats rather than experiment, and the general inertia in radio programming which over the decades created patterns of imitation and variation rather than produce the widest possible range of shows for listeners' tastes."

Jay Hickerson prepared a log of this show.

Fu Manchu see *The Shadow of Fu Manchu*

G-Men see *Gangbusters*

Gangbusters
(aka *G-Men*)

On the Air: *G-Men.* July 20–Oct. 19, 1935, NBC Blue, Saturday, 9 p.m.; *Gangbusters.* Jan. 15, 1936–June 15, 1938, CBS, Wednesday, 10 p.m.; Aug. 17, 1938–June 28, 1939, CBS, Wednesday, 8 p.m.; Oct. 21, 1939–June 15, 1940, CBS, Saturday, 8 p.m.; Oct. 11, 1940–April 4, 1941, NBC Blue, Friday, 9 p.m.; Oct. 10, 1941–April 3, 1942, NBC Blue, Friday, 9 p.m.; May 1–Sept. 11, 1942, NBC Blue, Friday, 9 p.m.; Sept. 18, 1942–July 9, 1943, ABC, Friday, 8 p.m.; July 16, 1943–April 6, 1945, ABC, Friday, 9 p.m.; Sept. 15, 1945–Feb. 28, 1948, ABC, Saturday, 9 p.m.; March 13–Dec. 25, 1948, ABC, Saturday, 9 p.m.; Jan. 8, 1949–June 12, 1954, CBS, Saturday, 9 p.m.; July 5, 1954–June 27, 1955, CBS, Monday, 9:30 p.m.; Oct. 5, 1955–Nov. 27, 1957, MBS, Wednesday, 8 p.m. 30 minutes.

Sponsors: General Motors Corp. for its Chevrolet Division (July 20–Oct. 19, 1935); Colgate-Palmolive-Peet Inc. for Palmolive brushless shaving cream, soap and additional personal care products (Jan. 15, 1936–June 28, 1939); *Cue* magazine (Oct. 21, 1939–June 15, 1940); Sloan's liniment (Oct. 11, 1940–April 3, 1942, Sept. 18, 1942–April 6, 1945); Sustained (May 1–Sept. 11, 1942, June 15–Sept. 7, 1946, Aug. 16–Sept. 6, 1947); Waterman Pen Co. for Waterman writing instruments, ink and related supplies (Sept. 15, 1945–June 8, 1946, Sept. 14, 1946–Aug. 9, 1947, Sept. 13, 1947–Feb. 28, 1948); Procter & Gamble Co. for Tide detergent (March 13–Dec. 25, 1948); General Foods Corp. for Grape Nuts flakes, plus partially Sustained, particularly in summers (Jan. 8, 1949–June 12, 1954); William J. Wrigley Co. for its chewing gum brands, and Sustained (July 5, 1954–June 27, 1955); Multiple participants (Oct. 5, 1955–Nov. 27, 1957).
Extant Episodes: 66.

CAST & CREDITS
Producer/Director—Phillips H. Lord.
Directors—Leonard Bass, Ted Corday, Harry Frazee, Jay Hanna, Paul Munroe, Bill Sweets, George Zachary.
Writers—Richard Dana, Brice Disque, Phillips H. Lord, John Mole, Stanley Niss.
Sound Effects—Ed Blainey, Harry Bubeck, James Flynn, Ray Kremer, Jerry McCarty, Robert L. Mott, Harry Nelson, Bob Prescott, James Rogan, Orval White, Byron Wingett.
Announcers—Frank Gallop, Don Gardiner, Roger Forster, Art Hannes, H. Gilbert Martin, Charles Stark.
Narrators—Dean Carlton, John C. Hilley, Phillips H. Lord, H. Norman Schwarzkopf, Lewis J. Valentine.
Support Roles—Mason Adams, Joan Banks, Ralph Bell, Art Carney, Roger DeKoven, Joe DeSantis, Robert Dryden, Helene Dumas, Elspeth Eric, Louise Fitch, Anne-Marie Gayer, Gale Gordon, Robert Haag, Larry Haines, Leon Janney, Raymond Edward Johnson, Adelaide Klein, Mandel Kramer, Barbara Lee, Bill Lipton, Athena Lorde, Frank Lovejoy, Ken Lynch, Don MacLaughlin, James McCallion, Mercedes McCambridge, Santos Ortega, Ethel Owen, George Petrie, Bryna Raeburn, Alice Reinheart, Grant Richards, Elaine Rost, Bill Smith, Julie Stevens, George Tiplady, Linda Watkins, Richard Widmark, Lawson Zerbe, Bill Zuckert.

Giving rise to the popular expression "coming on like gangbusters" (e.g. anything with a robust start), this was indisputably the most piercing half-hour in radio. It arrived to whistle blasts, shuffling feet, gunshots, broken windows, burglar alarms and police sirens—and all of that *before* the sound effects were added to the weekly narratives! It was a no-holds-barred law enforcement drama billing itself as "the only national program that brings you authentic police cases."

Each week creator Phillips H. Lord interviewed an actor pretending to be an actual lawman (introduced "by proxy"). It was that officer's story that was presented to the fans via flashback sequences that week. Cases were initially drawn from FBI files. In addition to the more obscure criminals, the tales of such well-known individuals as John Dillinger, Arthur Flegenheimer aka Dutch Schultz, Charles A. (Pretty Boy) Floyd, George (Machine Gun) Kelly, George (Baby Face) Nelson, Bonnie (Parker) and Clyde (Barrow) were offered.

At the conclusion of each drama—following the apprehension of those notorious thugs—the program offered bulletin-style advisories about miscreants then at large. Complete descriptions including scars, moles, tattoos, hair, eye and skin color were dispatched along with instructions on how to report sightings or their whereabouts. ("Not me!" exclaimed author Jim Harmon as he listened to those clues in his youth. "If I saw that man, I was going to run like hell!") Broadcasting every week, decades before the inception of TV's popular *America's Most Wanted* series, *Gangbusters* was instrumental in locating literally hundreds of hooligans while facilitating their arrests. A 1990s TV series, *Unsolved Mysteries*, effectively incorporated the same idea into its dramatic plots.

Radio historiographer John Dunning labeled *Gangbusters* the "best-remembered of all police shows," an argument that *Dragnet* fans would likely challenge.

The son of Colonel H. Norman Schwarzkopf gained international acclaim in 1991 while directing American combat forces during the Persian Gulf War. The elder Schwarzkopf was a celebrated figure in his own right, having played a major role earlier in the infamous Lindbergh kidnapping case while directing the New Jersey State Police.

Actress Elspeth Eric was deemed so credible as a *Gangbusters* gun moll—a role in which she was frequently cast—that at least two fan clubs were organized by inmates of maximum-security penitentiaries in tribute to her talents. Bryna Raeburn and Alice Reinheart regularly appeared in similar parts.

Federal Bureau of Investigation director J. Edgar Hoover reportedly was unhappy with producer-director Phillips H. Lord's insistence upon frequent gunplay rather than stable investigative activity while bringing criminals to justice. Hoover abruptly terminated the agency's ties to Lord's production following a 1935 introductory series, *G-Men*. No matter. Lord distributed city police badges to the officers in his narratives instead of FBI credentials at that juncture, carrying on unfazed under a new moniker of *Gangbusters*. Residing at ease along the Maine coast, Lord was sent a transcription disk of *Gangbusters'* rehearsals a few days before the weekly shows aired. It allowed him to appraise and officially validate each program prior to its broadcast, a practice he insisted upon.

Gangbusters ostensibly engaged the largest contingent of sound effects technicians, equipment and turntables in all of radio. For additional reading, Robert L. Mott offers some absorbing anecdotes about working on this series as a sound technician in his book *Radio Sound Effects*.

When Bill Sweets directed *Gangbusters* he not only drew from a cadre of seasoned New York actors but insisted on hiring those who were also adept at playing poker. The card game filled the long void the cast experienced in the two-and-a-half-hour gap between the dual live performances for the Eastern and Pacific time zones.

When tapes of *Gangbusters* were syndicated to air on local stations during a 1970s nostalgia craze that swept the nation, the drama didn't fare well at all. Surprisingly, some of the most vocal objectors argued that the program elevated law enforcement officials to a higher status than complaining listeners could abide.

A video version of *Gangbusters* surfaced on NBC-TV from March 20 to Dec. 25, 1952, alternating weeks with Jack Webb's *Dragnet* performances. Phillips H. Lord introduced the episodes of *Gangbusters* and at their conclusion a picture of an at-large criminal was flashed on the screen. A verbal description of the individual was given, similar to clues provided on the radio program. The TV drama achieved an average 42 rating among the four national chains and reached eighth place among all series then on the air. Tube chroniclers Tim Brooks and Earle Marsh pointed out that *Gangbusters* was "probably the highest-rated program ever to be canceled in the history of television." As much as viewers liked the show, they were even more infatuated by *Dragnet*, it turned out. When Jack Webb was able to offer the network a new film every week, *Gangbusters* suddenly disappeared.

The Gargoyle see The Bishop and the Gargoyle

The Gene Autry Show see Gene Autry's Melody Ranch

Gene Autry's Melody Ranch

(aka *The Gene Autry Show*, aka *Melody Ranch*)

On the Air: Jan. 7, 1940–Aug. 1, 1943, CBS, Sunday, 6:30 p.m.; Sept. 23, 1945–June 9, 1948, CBS, Sunday, 5:30 p.m.; June 16, 1946–Dec. 19, 1948, CBS, Sunday, 7 p.m.; Dec. 25, 1948–June 24, 1950, CBS, Saturday, 8 p.m.; July 29, 1950–June 30, 1951, CBS, Saturday, 8 p.m.; Aug. 4, 1951–July 25, 1953, CBS, Saturday, 8 p.m.; Aug. 2, 1953–May 13, 1956, CBS, Sunday, 6 p.m. (later 6:05 p.m.). Mostly 30-minute formats but some 45-, 25- and 15-minute segments.

Theme Song: *Back in the Saddle Again* (Gene Autry, Ray Whitley).

Sponsor: William J. Wrigley Co. for Doublemint chewing gum (all shows).

Extant Episodes: 117 (approximately).

CAST & CREDITS

Producer/Director—Bill Burch.

Writers—George Anderson, Irwin Ashkenazy, Carroll Carroll, Doris Gilbert, Ed James.

Music—Johnny Bond, the Cass County Boys (trio), Carl Cotner (instrumentalist/band), Mary Ford, the Gene Autry Blue Jeans, the King Sisters (quartet), Frankie Marvin (instrumentalist), the Melody Ranch Six, The Pinafores, Alvino Rey, Paul Sills (band), Jimmy Wakely.

Sound Effects—Gus Bayz, Ray Erlenborn, David Light, Jerry McCarty, Gene Twombly.

Announcers—Lou Crosby, Tom Hanlon, Charles Lyon, Wendell Niles.

Host/Star—Gene Autry (appearing as himself).

Support Roles—Sara Berner, Jim Boles, Pat Buttram, Scotty Harrel, Wally Maher, Frank Mahoney, Nancy Mason, Tyler McVey.

This was a variety show majoring in Western ballads and light banter featuring Republic Pictures B-movie cowboy legend Gene Autry. The weekly series included a 12- to 15-minute dramatic sketch in which "America's favorite cowboy," as Autry billed himself, brought another coyote of the human kind—a cattle rustler, bank robber, horse thief or murderer—to justice. From around a purported campfire setting at Autry's ranch in the San Fernando Mountains of southern California, flashback sequences helped the star tell his

Gene Autry's Melody Ranch: **Flanked by instrumental and singing group the Cass County Boys, "America's favorite cowboy" Gene Autry sang and interacted with the ranch hands around a campfire at his southern California spread. As a part of each week's half-hour show he narrated a tale in which he was instrumental in restoring peace within the community and in bringing the lawless to justice.**

tales of pursuit and capture. Each improvisation recalled an adventure on the untamed prairie where Autry, ever the hero, used his fists instead of his guns to settle a score.

Aimed at juveniles as much as adults, these adventurous snippets unmistakably witnessed the good guys triumphing over evildoers. Themes illustrating that crime not only doesn't pay but that transgressions lead to one's undoing were espoused. Autry's "Cowboy Code," which he frequently called upon to promote his moral precepts, began: "A cowboy never betrays a trust; a cowboy is kind to small children, animals and old folks; a cowboy is clean about his person, and in thought, word and deed; a cowboy is a patriot...." While all of this sounds mild-mannered, when

the situation required it, Autry could be just as fearless and rough-and-tumble on radio as he appeared for years at the Saturday matinees.

Announcer Charlie Lyons opened the show weekly by introducing "the boss man himself ... America's favorite cowboy ... Gene Autry," who received a raucous accolade from the audience and ranch hands before bursting into a ballad.

Autry joined the Army Air Corps in 1942, taking his show off the air to serve. He was administered an oath while on the air in July 1943. Two years later when his tenure was completed, he returned to the same network for the same sponsor, which indicated a favorable appraisal of his earlier performances.

On CBS Television between July 23, 1950, and Aug. 7, 1956, *The Gene Autry Show* offered 104 half-hour episodes in which the singing cowboy tamed the West by catching outlaws while in the company of radio sidekick Pat Buttram. The series was so successful that it fostered a couple of spinoffs: *Annie Oakley*, video's initial Western heroine (syndicated, 1952–56), and *The Adventures of Champion*, featuring Autry's horse (CBS-TV, Sept. 30, 1955–Feb. 3, 1956).

Gentleman Adventurer see Special Agent

The Great Merlini

On the Air: 1950, NBC. 30 minutes.
Sponsor: No information.
Extant Episodes: None known.

CAST & CREDITS

Leads—Title role played by Chester Morris; Julie Boyd, played by Barbara Cook; police Inspector Gavigan, played by Robert Noe.

A master illusionist and escape artist, the Great Merlini pursued an avocation of battling criminals and exposing fake mystics. These narratives depicted his assists of law enforcement officers in solving arcane felonies. Julie Boyd was usually beside him offering right-handed assistance.

The Green Hornet

On the Air: (Jan. 31–Feb. 14, 1936, WXYZ, Detroit, Friday; Feb. 18, 1936–April 7, 1938, WXYZ, Detroit, Tuesday/Thursday); April 12, 1938–Nov. 9, 1939, MBS, Tuesday/Thursday, 8 p.m.; Nov. 16, 1939–Jan. 20, 1940, NBC Blue, Thursday/Saturday, 8 p.m.; Jan. 24–25, 1940, NBC Blue, Wednesday/Thursday; Jan. 29–Aug. 28, 1940, NBC Blue, Monday/Wednesday, 8 p.m.; Sept. 2–Oct. 23, 1940, MBS, Monday/Wednesday, 8 p.m.; Sept. 20–Sept. 27, 1940, NBC Blue, Friday; Oct. 3–Oct. 10, 1940, NBC Blue, Thursday; Dec. 28, 1940–Dec. 13, 1941, MBS, Saturday, 8 p.m.; Jan. 3–July 11, 1942, NBC Blue, Saturday, 8 p.m.; July 18–Nov. 28, 1942, NBC Blue, Saturday, 8:30 p.m.; Dec. 6, 1942–April 18, 1943, ABC, Sunday, 4:30 p.m.; April 20–Aug. 24, 1943, ABC, Tuesday, 7 p.m.; Sept. 2, 1943–March 16, 1944, ABC, Thursday, 8:30 p.m.; March 21, 1944–Jan. 23, 1945, ABC, Tuesday, 7:30 p.m.; Feb. 1–Dec. 20, 1945, ABC, Thursday, 7:30 p.m.; Dec. 25, 1945–Feb. 12, 1946, ABC, Tuesday, 7:30 p.m.; Feb. 16–Oct. 19, 1946, ABC, Saturday, 7:30 p.m.; Oct. 27, 1946–March 2, 1947, ABC, Sunday, 4:30 p.m.; March 11–Dec. 30, 1947, ABC, Tuesday; Jan. 6–Aug. 24, 1948, ABC, Tuesday, 7:30 p.m.; Sept. 14, 1948–June 9, 1949, ABC, Tuesday/Thursday, 5 p.m.; June 13–Sept. 12, 1949, ABC, Monday; Sept. 20, 1949–June 6, 1950, ABC, Tuesday, 5:30 p.m.; June 16–Sept. 8, 1950, ABC, Friday, 5:30 p.m.; Sept. 10–Dec. 5, 1952, ABC, Wednesday/Friday, 5 p.m. 30 minutes.
Theme Song: *Flight of the Bumblebee* (Nicolai Rimsky-Korsakov).
Sponsors: On WXYZ it was underwritten by Detroit Creamery and United Shirt shops. On the networks it was Sustained, except for General Mills Inc. for its various cereal brands (Jan. 6–Aug. 24, 1948) and Orange Crush soda (Sept. 10–Dec. 5, 1952).
Extant Episodes: 500 plus.

CAST & CREDITS

Producer—George W. Trendle.
Directors—James Jewell, Charles Livingstone.
Writers—Dan Beatie, Leo Boulette, Tom Dougall, James Jewell, Jim Lawrence, Steve McCarthy, Lee Randon, Fran Striker.
Sound Effects—Tony Caminito, Dewey Cole, Jimmy Fletcher, Fred Flowerday, Fred Fry, Bill Hengsterbeck, Ken Robertson.
Announcers—Fielden Farrington, Fred Foy, Bob Hite, Hal Neal, Mike Wallace, Charles Woods.

Leads—Title role played by Al Hodge (1936–43), A. Donovan Faust (1943), Robert Hall (1943–46), Jack McCarthy (1946–52); Kato, played by Raymond Hayashi (renamed Raymond Toyo by director James Jewell), Rollon Parker and Michael Tolan.

Support Roles—Lee Allman (Lenore "Casey" Case, Reid's secretary and low-key romantic interest), Patricia Dunlap (photographer Clicker Binney), Harry Goldstein, Paul Hughes, Jim Irwin, Gil Shea (an ex-cop, originally a bodyguard, Michael Axford, hired by Dan Reid to oversee his son's pursuits; Axford later assumed the role of a dense police reporter), Lois Kibbee, Jack Petruzzi (ace reporter Ed Lowry), Rollon Parker (a newsboy), Bill Saunders, John Todd (Dan Reid), Ernest Winstanley.

This was one of a trio of exceptional adventure series created under the watchful eye of producer George W. Trendle and writer Fran Striker that produced *The Lone Ranger* and *The Challenge of the Yukon*. On turning the *Daily Sentinel* into one of the nation's premier newspapers, publisher-editor Dan Reid, nephew of the Lone Ranger (alias John Reid), transferred the administrative reins to his son Britt. A bachelor playboy, the younger Reid exuded many of the sterling qualities that marked his family members as fierce advocates for justice. Carrying on tradition, to augment the practice Britt Reid—like his great uncle before him—wore a mask, separating his identity from the forces of evil that he pursued. And like the Lone Ranger, he revealed himself to a single companion: Kato, in his case, an oriental valet and the driver of his powerful automobile that he named the Black Beauty. (At some point, however, he would confirm to his father and his secretary who he really was, which they had long ago deduced.)

Reid was known to the underworld simply as the Green Hornet, considered the deadliest of all insects when aroused. He hunted "the biggest of all game, pub-

lic enemies that even the G-Men cannot reach." (Federal Bureau of Investigation director J. Edgar Hoover, who had a habit of injecting his personal stance into radio crime series, was chagrined by the latter phrase. In 1939 it was thus altered to accommodate his views: "…public enemies who try to destroy our America!") Using a gas gun that left victims unconscious preceding the culprits' capture by paid law enforcement, the Green Hornet and Kato inevitably vanished before officers could arrive asking questions about the Hornet's identity or thinking he was a criminal, too.

One critic called them a pair of "avenging angels" whose ends justified their means: Sometimes they intruded on police investigations in progress and aggravated professional lawmen by frequently circumventing protocol and even legal procedure in their determined battle to put away crooks. Their quarry included racketeers, saboteurs, murderers, burglars, thieves and con artists of every persuasion, sometimes none too bright. The concluding billboard noted "the events depicted in the drama are fictitious" and "any similarity to persons living or dead is purely coincidental." The show obviously demonstrated an essential staying power over a very long run.

A strong argument, debated by some sources, advanced the notion that—after Pearl Harbor Day, Dec. 7, 1941—Kato's nationality instantly shifted from Japanese to Filipino. If that could be substantiated, it appeared to have occurred to avoid raising doubts about the loyalty and intent of the Green Hornet's sidekick.

Over its long run the program occupied no less than 25 different network time periods. This could account for the fact that an aggregate of less than a year's episodes was subscribed by commercial firms. Some potential sponsors might have viewed the many transfers in time slots as awkward, being convinced fans would have difficulty in locating their show long term, and thus shy away. At best so many schedule changes were daunting to anyone trying to faithfully track a broadcast series.

The Green Hornet's Secret Seal Ring, one of many premiums the show offered, reportedly has become extremely valuable to modern trivia collectors.

A number of thespians in the series were also cast in important roles on George W. Trendle's other programs, among them John Todd, the Lone Ranger's "faithful Indian companion" Tonto and the inspector in *The Challenge of the Yukon*, and character actors Paul Hughes, Rollon Parker and Jack Petruzzi, who turned up in multiple series. All the network broadcasts of these programs originated at Detroit's WXYZ.

Radio historiographer John Dunning submitted that WXYZ was no ordinary radio station, noting *The Lone Ranger* singularly placed that local outlet on the nation's broadcasting map. "A remarkable aggregation of creative talent worked there," observed Dunning—a contingent of acting, writing, musical and sound artists capable of generating fare "worthy of any network." Sound specialist Robert L. Mott recalled that WXYZ assigned five sound effects artists to *every one* of its shows. This practice would have been a rare occurrence for a network, let alone for a single station. It attests the extent that WXYZ was willing to go to achieve superior quality for its productions.

Al Hodge, then playing the Hornet on radio, spoke that heroic figure's lines in the 1939 Universal serial *The Green Hornet* on the silver screen. While Fran Striker was an advisor to that production, four other writers penned its scripts. Perhaps more than any similar venture, that one closely resembled the radio show on which it was based. Gordon Jones appeared as Britt Reid while various stuntmen under mask and hat disguise drew the more dangerous assignments required of the Hornet. Charlie Chan's Number One Son, Keye Luke, was Kato and actress Anne Nagel appeared in the part of Miss Case.

In a subsequent serial release in 1944, *The Green Hornet Strikes Again*, future *Strike It Rich!* radio-TV master of ceremonies Warren Hull portrayed the Hornet, with support actors from the initial serial reprising their roles. This time out Universal repeated much of the stock footage from the earlier series, regretfully, which a critic noted was still fresh in moviegoers' minds.

On ABC-TV *The Green Hornet* ran for a single season, Sept. 9, 1966, through July 14, 1967. That cast included Van Williams as Britt Reid/The Green Hornet, Bruce Lee as Kato, Wende Wagner as Lenore Case, Walter Brooke as District Attorney Frank Scanlon and Lloyd Gough as Mike Axford, the newspaper's police reporter. Richard Bluel produced. "The Flight of the Bumblebee," previously thought to be a violin classic, was curiously played as the show's theme by trumpeter Al Hirt.

Jay Hickerson and Terry Salomonson collaborated in producing a log for the radio series.

The Green Lama

On the Air: June 5–July 3, 1949, CBS, Sunday, 5:30 p.m.; July 9–Aug. 20, 1949, CBS, Saturday, 7 p.m. 30 minutes.
Sponsor: Sustained.
Extant Episodes: Three.

CAST & CREDITS

Producer/Director—James Burton, Norman Macdonnell.
Writers—Richard Foster, William Froug.
Music—Richard Aurandt.
Announcer—Larry Thor.

Leads—Title role played by Paul Frees; Tulku, played by Ben Wright.

Support Roles—Harry Bartell, Gloria Blondell, Lillian Buyeff, William Conrad, Larry Dobkin, Paul Dubov, Georgia Ellis, Laurette Fillbrandt, Jack Kruschen, Nestor Paiva, Herb Vigran.

Spending a decade in a Tibetan monastery, prosperous young Jethro Dumont of New York City subsequently traversed the globe accompanied by a native minion, Tulku, applying newly acquired supernatural powers to fight evil wherever he encountered it. Having been exalted with honorary status as a Tibetan Lamaist monk, Dumont christened himself the Green Lama—the hue representing justice in Tibet. Dumont was known to radio listeners for his relentless efforts to conduct a "single-handed fight against injustice and crime."

The show was based on pulp magazine articles written by Richard Foster. The hero also appeared in a comic strip.

A log for this series was prepared by Jay Hickerson.

Gunsmoke

On the Air: April 26, 1952–Dec. 26, 1953, CBS, Saturday, 9:30 p.m.; Jan. 2–July 3, 1954, CBS, Saturday, 8 p.m.; July 5–Sept. 27, 1954, CBS, Monday; Oct. 2, 1954–Oct. 8, 1955, CBS, Saturday, 12:30 p.m.; Oct. 9, 1955–June 18, 1961, CBS, Sunday, 6:30 p.m. (6:35 p.m. as of 1960). 30- and 25-minute versions.

Theme Song: *The Old Trail* (Rex Koury).

Sponsors: Sustained (April 26, 1952–Sept. 26, 1953; Jan. 2–July 3, 1954); General Foods Inc. for Post Toasties cereal (Oct. 3–Dec. 26, 1953); Liggett & Myers Tobacco Co. for Chesterfield and L&M cigarettes (July 5, 1954–April 7, 1957); Sustained and multiple participation (April 14, 1957–June 18, 1961).

Extant Episodes: 476 (of 480 broadcasts), plus three audition tapes.

CAST & CREDITS

Producer/Director/Co-creator—Norman Macdonnell.

Writers—Marian Clark, Les Crutchfield, John Dunkel, Antony Ellis, Kathleen Hite, John Meston (head writer and co-creator), Herb Purdum.

Music—Del Castillo, Rex Koury.

Sound Effects—Tom Hanley, Bill James, Ray Kemper, David Light.

Announcers—George Fenneman, Roy Rowan, George Walsh.

Leads—Marshal Matt Dillon, played by William Conrad; townsman Chester Proudfoot, played by Parley Baer; Charles (Doc) Adams, played by Howard McNear; Kitty Russell, played by Georgia Ellis.

Support Roles—Lynn Allen, Irene Andres, Michael Ann Barrett, Edgar Barrier, Harry Bartell, Charles Bastin, Jeanne Bates, Dick Beals, Butch Bernard, Eleanor Berry, Ted Bliss, Lillian Buyeff, Frank Cady, Virginia Christine, Hans Conried, Tommy Cook, Joe Cranston, Richard Crenna, Howard Culver, Richard Deacon, John Dehner, Don Diamond, Larry Dobkin, Frances Drew, Paul Dubov, Joe DuVal, Robert Easton, Jack Edwards, Sam Edwards, Barbara Eiler, Herb Ellis, Louise Fitch, Joe Forte, Paul Frees, Frank Gerstle, Clark Gordon, Tim Graham, Virginia Gregg, Bob Griffin, James Griffith, Tom Hanley, Louis Jean Heydt, Sammie Hill, Jonathan Hole, Tom Holland, William Idelson, Vivi Janiss, Jill Jarmyn, Byron Kane, Joseph Kearns, Jess Kirkpatrick, Helen Kleeb, Lou Krugman, Jack Kruschen, Bill Lally, Mary Lansing, Charlotte Lawrence, Peter Leeds, Ken Lynch, Fred MacKaye, Kathy Marlowe, Junius Matthews, Joyce McCluskey, Pat McGeehan, Johnny McGovern, John McIntire, Eve McVey, Lee Millar [*sic*], Ralph Moody, Ann Morrison, Jack Moyles, Jeanette Nolan, Jim Nusser, James Ogg, William Oiler, Nestor Paiva, Edward Penney, Vic Perrin, Barney Phillips, Clayton Post, Peggy Rea, Bartlett Robinson, Paul Savage, John Stephenson, Gil Stratton Jr., Bob Sweeney, Eleanore Tanin, Irene Tedrow, Tom Tully, Herb Vigran, Patricia Walter, Stan Waxman, Anne Whitfield,

Elaine Williams, Paula Winslowe, Ben Wright, Will Wright.

Set in Dodge City, Kansas, in the 1870s, which was proclaimed "a suburb of hell," *Gunsmoke* was the epic drama of marshal Matt Dillon—"the first man they look for and the last they want to meet"—who had come to Dodge to repress that outpost on the prairie. Interacting with the marshal was a strong cast of recurring support players including the whiny but faithful townsman Chester Proudfoot, the crusty country physician Doc Adams and the saloon gal Kitty Russell, who eventually evolved into Dillon's subdued love interest. Dillon exuded integrity while he was equipped with an inordinate amount of courage and strength, often in the face of great odds, as he combated the outlaws of the old West. Standing six-foot-seven, he was an imposing figure with an indomitable will. The narratives delved into human experience on the frontier, often incorporating a test of an individual's character.

The opening billboard established that out West "there is just one way to handle the killers and the spoilers and that is with the U.S. marshal and the smell of *Gunsmoke* ... the transcribed story of the violence that moved West with young America and the story of a man who moved with it." One radio reviewer certified it as "among the best shows of any kind and any time."

There can be little doubt that the true radio adult western was inaugurated with *Gunsmoke*, the grandfather of a breed. With the exception of *Have Gun, Will Travel*, no new western besides *Gunsmoke* lasted for more than a season. The fact that it appeared at a time when Americans were, by and large, turning off their radios and turning on their TVs, categorically blunted its potential. Yet *Gunsmoke* became so popular with radio lovers that

CBS carried it for several months beyond the outer limits of the traditionally accepted end of radio's golden age (November 1960). When the series was discontinued with the 480th broadcast, it had already completed the sixth of a 20-season run on CBS-TV, during which it became one of the most respected dramatic series ever televised. *Gunsmoke* on radio defined the adult western genre and set a lofty standard for all other entries that followed. Cited by one critic as the style's "highest achievement," it was identified by another as "a classy western, with more mature plots, writing, and characterization than almost anything on radio."

When talk of a TV series began, the radio cast was auditioned but bypassed in favor of James Arness (Matt), Dennis Weaver (Chester), Milburn Stone (Doc) and Amanda Blake (Kitty). John Meston was engaged to carry on the tradition he had begun in scripting the radio epic.

Weaver eventually claimed he despised the role he played as Chester. Parley Baer, who performed it for nine years on radio, seemed satisfied. The idea was later advanced that the part that became the apex of Baer's professional life had—to his TV successor (Weaver)—become "a limiting, confining trap, like the picture tube itself."

Bill Conrad, on the other hand, took his loss of the leading role to Arness quite personally, refusing interviews for a while. While he would later be given the chance to direct some of the *Gunsmoke* episodes on the tube, for a spell he slipped into obscurity. Eventually he reappeared in TV guest slots while acquiring several voiceover roles in a medium that had little use for a middle-aged, pudgy, balding, mustachioed actor. Some starring roles for him were finally discovered on the tube anyway: He is recalled as the portly detective *Cannon* on CBS-TV from 1971 to 1976 and as a tough district attorney in

Jake and the Fatman on the same network in the late 1980s. Cannon died in North Hollywood, Calif., on Feb. 11, 1994, at the age of 73.

On CBS Television, between Sept. 10, 1955, and Sept. 1, 1975, *Gunsmoke* became not only that medium's longest running western but also video's most durable primetime series with continuing characters. Two made-for-TV movies appeared late in the following decade: *Gunsmoke— Return to Dodge* (Sept. 26, 1987) and *Gunsmoke—The Last Apache* (March 18, 1990). Several more such films appeared in the early 1990s, all starring James Arness in his heroic role: *Gunsmoke—To the Last Man* (1992), *Gunsmoke—The Long Ride* (1993) and *Gunsmoke—One Man's Justice* (1994).

Jay Hickerson produced a radio log of the series. A log is also included in the volume by SuzAnne and Gabor Barabas titled *Gunsmoke: A Complete History and Analysis of the Legendary Broadcast Series with a Comprehensive Episode-by-Episode Guide to Both the Radio and Television Programs* (McFarland, 1990).

Hannibal Cobb

On the Air: Jan. 9, 1950–May 11, 1951, ABC, Weekdays, 3:30 p.m. 15 minutes.
Sponsor: Sustained.
Extant Episodes: Two.

CAST & CREDITS

Producer/Directors—Martin Andrews, William D. Hamilton, Roy LaPlante, Charles Powers.
Writers—Bernard Dougall, Louis Heyward, Ira Marion, Lillian Schoen.
Music—Rosa Rio (organ).
Announcer—Les Griffith.
Lead—Title role played by Santos Ortega.
Support Roles—Wendy Drew, Ethel Everett, Barry Kroeger, Amy Sedell, Jimmy Van Dyke.

Reported from the client's perspective, these were tales of a private eye who took an intense personal interest in those for whom he worked. Cobb's adventures were highlighted in "the photocrime pages of *Look* magazine."

Something unique going on here was that this PI operated wholly in the sunshine, at a time when much of the listening audience was tuning in to soap opera melodrama elsewhere.

Hashknife Hartley

On the Air: July 2, 1950–Dec. 30, 1951, MBS, Sunday, 3:30 p.m. (2:30 p.m. later in the run). 30 minutes.
Sponsor: Sustained.
Extant Episodes: Two.

CAST & CREDITS

Producer/Director—Tom Hargis.
Writer—Fred Luke.
Music—Harry Zimmerman (orchestra).
Announcer—Don McCall.
Host/Narrator—Wilbur C. Tuttle.
Leads—Title role played by Frank Martin; Sleepy Stevens, played by Barton Yarborough.

In a rather easygoing adventure, gypsy cowboy Hashknife Hartley and his partner, Sleepy Stevens, spelled victory in the troubles they encountered on the Western plains. One could tell by their names, of course, that they weren't immediately recognized as the type of two-fisted, guntotin' heroes of similar tales on the frontier. Despite that, and their rather laid-back manners, the billboard identified the twosome as "rough and tumble cowboys," and they got the job done in restoring law and order to the old West. In one episode they were called upon to quell a range war and to locate stolen cattle; in another, they set out to discover the secret identity of a pinto bandit. Novelist W. C. Tuttle, who created the characters, offered a verbal prologue and epilogue to their weekly exploits on the trail.

Have Gun, Will Travel

On the Air: Nov. 23, 1958–Nov. 27, 1960, CBS, Sunday, 6:05 p.m. 25 minutes.
Sponsors: Multiple participation, including American Telephone and Telegraph Co., R. J. Reynolds Tobacco Co. for Camel and Winston cigarettes, CBS Radio, Columbia phonographs, Dristan nasal allergy medication, Ex-Lax medication, F. W. Fitch Shampoo Co. for Fitch shampoo and other hair care preparations, Frito snack foods, Guardian Maintenance, W. K. Kellogg Co. for Kellogg's cereals, *Look* magazine, Pepsi-Cola Co. for Pepsi-Cola soda pop, Super Sixty hearing glasses, Sylvania flash bulbs, Yardley perfume.
Extant Episodes: 106 shows (complete run).

CAST & CREDITS

Producers/Directors—Norman Macdonnell, Frank Paris.
Writers—Albert Aley, Marian Clark, Les Crutchfield, John Dawson, Ann Doud, Herb Meadow, Frank Michael, William N. Robson, Gene Roddenberry, Sam Rolfe.
Sound Effects—Tom Hanley, Ray Kemper.
Announcer—Hugh Douglas.
Lead—Paladin, played by John Dehner.
Support Roles—William Alice, Lynn Allen, Russell Arms, Edgar Barrier, Harry Bartell, Jeanne Bates, Dick Beals, Eleanor Berry, Lillian Buyeff, Frank Cady, Virginia Christine, Perry Cook, Joseph Cranston, Richard Crenna, Howard Culver, Joel Davis, Donald Diamond, Larry Dobkin, Paul Dubov, Jack Edwards, Sam Edwards, Barbara Eiler, Waldo Emerson, Patty Gallagher, Frank Gerstle, Clark Gordon, Tim Graham, Virginia Gregg (Missy Wong), Betty Harper, Blanche Hawkins, Bill Idelson, Frank Katy, Joseph Kearns, Jess Kirkpatrick, Helen Kleeb, Lou Krugman, Jean Landsworth, Forrest Lewis, Charles Lung, Ken Lynch, Eve McVey, Marvin Miller, Shirley Mitchell, Ralph Moody, Ann Morrison, Jack Moyles, Norma Jean Nilsson, Jeanette Nolan, James Nusser, Richard Perkins, Vic Perrin, Barney Phillips, Clayton Post, William Redfield, Tracy Roberts, Robert Robertson, Bartlett Robinson, Olan Soule, Walter Stocker, Eleanor Tanin, Herb Vigran, Peggy Webber, James Westerfield, Anne Whitfield, Roy Woods, Ben Wright (Heyboy).

Have Gun, Will Travel was, in one reviewer's perception, the "chief prototype of a rash of dapper heroes invented by TV [where it initially appeared] to populate the Old West." Who knows what effect it ultimately might have had on radio had it not surfaced in the medium's fading days? Ironically, it ran there only two years and two days before the end of radio's golden age.

Created by Herb Meadow and Sam Rolfe, Paladin—its central figure—wasn't an illiterate run-of-the-mill gunslinger. Instead he was a man of culture, college-educated, preferring the finer things of life. Following a stint in the Civil War he moved to San Francisco, became a high-priced gun for hire and was able and willing to journey wherever his services were required. Operating out of the Hotel Carlton in 1875, he performed the perilous tasks that others would not or could not handle. While he did them for high personal recompense, it didn't diminish his intentions as a man of lofty principles and integrity. When the occasion warranted that he act as a crime fighter, Paladin invariably responded magnificently. He often found himself in the company of an oriental bellhop at his headquarters hotel that he referred to as "Heyboy." "Heyboy" had a girlfriend named Missy Wong.

Have Gun, Will Travel arrived on radio by a most improbable method. When this adult western premiered on CBS Radio it had been appearing in video form for a little more than a year. The tube's half-hour rendering of *Have Gun, Will*

Travel starred Richard Boone and debuted on CBS-TV Sept. 14, 1957. There it continued as a Saturday night staple (and as a lead-in to CBS-TV's *Gunsmoke*) for six seasons, through Sept. 21, 1963. *Travel* became one of only a handful of televised series, and arguably the most successful, that made the jump to radio. It was a route diametrically opposed to that adopted by most series in which switches between the mediums transpired.

Jay Hickerson prepared a log for the radio series.

Hawk Durango see Hawk Larabee

Hawk Larabee

(aka *Hawk Durango*)

On the Air: *Hawk Durango.* July 12–Aug. 16, 1946, CBS, Friday, 10:30 p.m.; *Hawk Larabee.* Oct. 3–Dec. 12, 1946, CBS, Thursday, 5:30 p.m.; May 31–June 7, 1947, CBS, Saturday, 7 p.m.; June 20–Aug. 1, 1947, CBS, Friday, 8 p.m.; Aug. 9, 1947–Feb. 7, 1948, CBS, Saturday, 7 p.m. 30 minutes.
Sponsor: Sustained.
Extant Episodes: Eight.

CAST & CREDITS

Producer/Director—William N. Robson.
Assistant Director—Richard Sanville.
Writers—Gomer Cool, E. Jack Neuman, Arthur E. Orlock, Dean Owen, Kenneth Perkins.
Music—Wilbur Hatch.
Announcer—James Matthews.
Leads—Title role played by Elliott Lewis (as Hawk Durango), Barton Yarborough (as Hawk Larabee); Brazos John, played by Barton Yarborough; Somber Jones, played by Barney Phillips.
Supporting Roles—William Conrad, Charlie Lung.

The Hawk's whistle accompanied by hoofbeats and an announcer's shrill "The hawk is on the wing!" marked the inception of this aural narrative. Its original concept featured Hawk Durango as a frontier barkeep with a partner named Brazos John but the show's format was overhauled after a six-week summer stint. In its reincarnation it focused on the exploits of Black Mesa Ranch owner Hawk Larabee of Sundown Wells, who had a wisecracking sidekick, Somber Jones. Hawk told the tales himself. An epigraph offered "stories of the men and women, famous and infamous, who loved and hated, lived and died in the colorful drama of the American West."

Hawk (by either surname) nourished a penchant for getting into mischief, even to the point of being almost lynched by the local citizenry for crimes he didn't commit. Inevitably it became his duty to prove his innocence on those occasions by locating the real culprits and pinning the misdeeds on them inconclusively. At least once Durango/Larabee had to thwart the scheming of a railroad company that was using underhanded tactics to complete a length of track before a competitor did. Another time his investigating ferreted out the killer of a local merchant. While by trade Durango/Larabee may have been a tavern owner or a cattle rancher, in practice he was largely an old West sleuth, although frequently finding himself running just ahead of a noose. Curiously, he was never able to acquire the undying confidence of many of the townspeople—certainly not the respect that those in Grover, Arizona, afforded fellow cattle rancher *Sky King*, nor those in many other radio westerns gave to their local law-abiding heroes.

This was one of the first programs to employ vocal bridges between scenes. To the tune of "The Old Chisholm Trail," lyrics often hinted at future plot twists. Two different ensembles performed—the Texas Rangers initially, comprised of Bob

Crawford, Tookie Cronenbold, Rod May and Fran Mahoney, and then Andy Parker's Plainsmen.

Hearthstone of the Death Squad

On the Air: Aug. 30, 1951–Jan. 10, 1952, CBS, Thursday, 9 p.m.; Jan. 13–Feb. 10, 1952, CBS, Sunday, 5:30 and 9:30 p.m.; Feb. 17–Feb. 24, 1952, CBS, Sunday, 4:30 p.m.; March 2–June 1, 1952, CBS, Sunday, 8 p.m.; June 3–Sept. 17, 1952, CBS, Tuesday and Wednesday, 8 p.m. 30 minutes.
Sponsor: No information.
Extant Episodes: Three.

CAST & CREDITS

Producers—Anne Hummert, Frank Hummert.
Director—Henry Howard.
Writer—Frank Hummert.
Announcer—Harry Cramer.
Leads—Title role played by Alfred Shirley; Sam Cook, played by James Meighan.

A spinoff of a better-recalled series, *The Molle Mystery Theater*, aka *Mystery Theater*, this drama focused on consummate Scotland Yard detective Inspector Hearthstone. The wily Hearthstone was revered as the "implacable manhunter" of the homicide (Death Squad) division of London's Metropolitan Police Department. Frequently he resorted to a ruse to trounce the killers he sought, and was capably supported in his intellectual and corporeal pursuits by Detective Sam Cook.

This series was introduced as a portion of the earlier *Mystery Theater*.

Jay Hickerson prepared what he termed a "sketchy log" of the *Hearthstone* series.

Helen Holden, Government Girl

On the Air: March 3–June 27, 1941, MBS, Monday–Saturday, 1:30 p.m.; June 30, 1941–

March 20, 1942, MBS, Monday–Saturday, 1:15 p.m. 15 minutes.
Sponsor: No information.
Extant Episodes: None known.

CAST & CREDITS

Announcer—Frank Blair.
Leads—Title role played by Nancy Ordway; Mary Holden, played by Nell Fleming; David, played by Robert Pollard.

Upon the rise of the Second World War, a young, single G-woman faced tough challenges in Washington, D.C. in one of the first daytime radio serials dealing with war themes. (Outside *Helen Holden, Government Girl* and the far more successful *Against the Storm*, matinee dramas were reluctant to broach war themes for a while following U.S. entry into the global conflagration.) Holden was sworn to protect the homeland against enemy infiltration and aggression, and faithfully carried out her tasks. Her boyfriend, David, and an aunt, print newsjournalist Mary Holden, were on hand to add a domestic touch to the melodrama.

Helen Holden appeared along with a minor wave of single-minded young debutantes that Mutual introduced to its daytime listeners during that epoch. Others: *Edith Adams' Future* and *I'll Find My Way*. None was successful. "The never-married heroine was simply a poor risk as a daytime-serial protagonist," noted Raymond William Stedman, whose published observations on drama-by-installment are a classic.

Helen's specific assignments as a global crime fighter are unknown. Even a modern collector of data on feminine vintage radio detectives, Jack French, himself a retired professional G-man, admitted defeat and was unable to provide more facts about this heroine's experience. While French found a theme about a G-girl "fascinating" and alliteration in the program's title "delightful," he couldn't add to the sketchy data supplied by audio historians. Such lapses exist when historiographers are unable to acquire or substantiate records, and particularly when no known tapes of a drama exist to enhance contemporary appreciation for a series that may have aired decades earlier.

Hercule Poirot see The Adventures of M. Hercule Poirot

Here Comes McBride

On the Air: Spring, 1949, NBC. 30 minutes.
Sponsor: Sustained.
Extant Episodes: One.

CAST & CREDITS

Producer/Director—Warren Lewis.
Music—Hank Sylvern (organ).
Announcer—Art Ballinger.
Lead—Title role of Rex McBride played by Frank Lovejoy.

Novelist Cleave F. Adams unveiled *Rex McBride* to pulp fiction readers before introducing the character to radio listeners. McBride was an L.A. private insurance investigator (though in no way a threat to the popularity of contemporary *Johnny Dollar*, then airing over CBS). McBride obviously attended the school of hard knocks for he encountered a fair number of the physical kind. Somehow law enforcement officials were often persuaded that he was a culprit in the matters he probed; adding insult to injury, women didn't seem to find his manner irresistible, either. For both reasons McBride approached his assignments with enough baggage to wear out a normal sleuth. Despite the producers' casting of a major Hollywood thespian as the lead, *McBride* still died a quick death. Perhaps two private insurance investigators proved to be one too many.

Highway Patrol

On the Air: April 5–July 2, 1943, MBS, Weekdays. 15 minutes.
Sponsor: No information.
Extant Episodes: None known.

CAST & CREDITS

Director—Allen Ducovny.
Leads—Steve Taylor, played by Michael Fitzmaurice; Mike Gallager, played by John McGovern.

Troopers Steve Taylor and Mike Gallager risked their lives to keep the highways of an unidentified state safe in this dramatic series.

A syndicated video version of *Highway Patrol* was released by Ziv TV between 1955 and 1959. It starred Broderick Crawford as Captain Dan Matthews with narration by Art Gilmore. While only 156 episodes were produced, the show was so popular that for years it was run and rerun on local stations.

An earlier version of the radio series, in the 1930s, which also appeared under the appellation *Highway Patrol*, starred Jack Kirkwood. Four tapes of that show survive.

Hollywood Mystery Time

On the Air: July 20–Sept. 7, 1944, CBS, Thursday; Sept. 15–Oct. 13, 1944, CBS, Friday; Oct. 15, 1944–Dec. 16, 1945, ABC, Sunday, 9:15 p.m. 30 minutes.
Sponsor: Sustained (CBS); Woodbury soap (ABC).
Extant Episodes: Two.

CAST & CREDITS

Music—Ernest Gill.
Announcer—Jim Doyle.

Leads—Jim Laughton, played by Carleton Young, Dennis O'Keefe (as of mid 1945); Gloria Dean, played by Gloria Blondell, Constance Moore (as of mid 1945).

The sideline pursuit of Hollywood independent mystery movie producer Jim Laughton was sleuthing as a private detective. His secretary, Gloria Dean, facilitated his efforts. When the series premiered, its dual original stars—Carleton Young and Gloria Blondell—were featured as leads in an anthology of dramatic presentations. The concept was altered in a mid-series metamorphosis to reflect a detective format. A critic labeled the program "a poor man's *Mr. and Mrs. North.*"

Honor the Law

On the Air: 1938, Syndicated. 15 minutes.
Sponsors: Sold in local markets where it aired.
Extant Episodes: 39.

CAST & CREDITS

Producer—Conquest Alliance Co., New York City.
Director—Ralph Scott.
Writers—Eugene Alford, Virginia Barber.
Acting Company—Joseph J. Franz, Barbara Luddy, Frank Nelson, Paul Norby, Ralph Scott, Frederick Shields.

With each of its 39 installments complete unto itself, *Honor the Law* focused upon the exploits of two police pals who were partners on the force—a senior officer, Kemp, and a junior officer, Benton. Benton possessed serious ambitions for promotion in rank. A nervy newspaperman, Larry Stevens, who was perpetually seeking a news scoop, monitored their radio calls as well as their adventures. He was also a foil for the cops' humor. Wit and wisecracks were regularly inserted to relieve the tensions of the moment. Meanwhile, Julia Allen, described by a producer-generated

puff piece as a "beauteous theatre cashier," was the object of affection of both Benton and Stevens, offering an intriguing dimension.

A police radio dispatcher identified merely as Wallace—and branded in the marketing promo as a criminal's "deadliest enemy," which seems altogether unlikely—sent the radio patrol team into action "to make all citizens *honor the law.*" The melodrama was so convoluted that, in typical quarter-hour stints, there wasn't a whole lot of time to commit a crime, gather the evidence, track a criminal and bring him to justice.

Hop Harrigan

On the Air: Aug. 31, 1942–Sept. 29, 1944, NBC Blue, Weekdays, 5:15 p.m., later 5 p.m.; Oct. 2, 1944–June 29, 1945, ABC, Weekdays, 4:45 p.m.; Oct. 1, 1945–Aug. 2, 1946, ABC, Weekdays, 4:45 p.m.; Oct. 1, 1946–Jan. 31, 1947, MBS, Weekdays, 5 p.m.; Feb. 3–May 2, 1947, MBS, Monday–Wednesday–Friday, 5 p.m.; May 6–June 19, 1947, MBS, Tuesday–Thursday, 5 p.m.; June 23–Sept. 26, 1947, MBS, Weekdays, 5:30 p.m.; Sept. 29, 1947–Feb. 6, 1948, MBS, Weekdays, 5 p.m. 15 minutes.
Sponsors: Sustained (Aug. 31, 1942–Sept. 29, 1944; Oct. 1, 1946–Jan. 31, 1947); General Foods Inc. for Grape Nuts Flakes cereal (Oct. 2, 1944–Aug. 2, 1946); Taylor-Reed for Cocoa-Malt chocolate drink mix (Feb. 3–June 19, 1947); Lever Brothers Co. (June 23, 1947–Feb. 6, 1948).
Extant Episodes: 177 plus 16 Australian shows.

CAST & CREDITS

Directors—Jay Clark, Allen Ducovny, Jessica Maxwell.
Writers—Albert Aley, Bob Burtt, Wilfred Moore.
Sound Effects—Ed Blainey.
Announcer—Glenn Riggs.
Leads—Title role played by Albert Aley,

Chester Stratton; Tank Tinker, played by Jackson Beck, Ken Lynch; Gail Nolan, played by Mitzi Gould.

Daring juvenile air ace Hop Harrigan of DC comic book fame fought a never-ending warfare with the enemies of freedom and upheld the values many U.S. citizens cherished. Assisting the 18-year-old flying warrior were Tank Tinker, his buddy, copilot and mechanic (whom one critic viewed as "a bit slow in the brainpower department, but a good guy to have along in a fight"), and Hop's girlfriend, Gail Nolan. The Second World War was raging as the serial debuted, offering perfect background scenarios for Hop and Tank's aerial escapades. The bombing missions they performed and dogfights they encountered with America's adversaries—often behind enemy lines—turned their runs into perilous adventures. As they risked their lives to sustain peace, the youthful pair was sometimes captured, subjected to concentration camps and then beat the odds through rescue and escape measures. Their detecting and crime fighting enthralled the adolescents for whom it was intended, creating a loyal following that clung to every new action-packed crisis. When the hostilities ceased, the themes of sabotage and espionage endured as America—and Hop Harrigan—encountered the nation's subsequent Cold War.

Writers Bob Burtt and Wilfred Moore also penned *Captain Midnight*, a rival late-afternoon juvenile serial. There was, as one might anticipate, a recognizable resemblance between Harrigan and his pals and the Secret Squadron crew on Midnight's show.

Dual Hop Harrigan organizations existed that young fans were invited to join. They naturally perpetuated the kid camaraderie while advancing a growing association with the show. One group was known as the All American Flying Club

while the other was called the American Observation Corps.

Throughout the war years announcer Glenn Riggs reminded the homefront audience to aid the nation's preparedness by taking waste fats, paper, tin and rubber to salvage depots. There were ongoing announcements that the Red Cross needed blood and almost daily reminders that "America needs fliers." During the show's years without paid sponsorship, such public service announcements dovetailed with similar patriotic themes espoused by many other radio features of that epoch.

Jerry Haendiges prepared a partial log of this series.

Hopalong Cassidy

On the Air: Jan. 1–Sept. 24, 1950, MBS, Sunday, 4 p.m.; Sept. 30, 1950–June 30, 1951, CBS, Saturday, 8:30 p.m.; Sept. 22, 1951–March 15, 1952, CBS, Saturday, 8:30 p.m.; April 26–Dec. 27, 1952 (repeated episodes), CBS, Saturday, 9:30 p.m. (Mountain States regional network). 30 minutes.

Sponsors: General Foods Corp. for Post cereals brands (Jan. 1, 1950–March 15, 1952); Cella Vineyards (April 26–Dec. 27, 1952).

Extant Episodes: 104 (complete run through March 15, 1952).

Cast & Credits

Producers—Shirley White, Walter White Jr.
Director—Ted Bliss.
Writers—Buckley Angel, John Barkley, Dean Owen, Robert T. Smith, Harold Swanton, Howard Swart, Wayne Yarnell.
Music—Albert Glasser.
Sound Effects—David Light.
Leads—Title role played by William Boyd; Jack (California) Carlson, played by Andy Clyde, Joe Duval.

B-western 1930s movie star William Boyd—once again as Hopalong Cassidy—owned the Bar-20 Ranch near the mythical hamlet of Blackton Bend. His zealous preoccupation with law and order, righteousness and integrity led him to be more widely accepted as a hero-detective instead of a cattle rancher. Astride his powerful mount, Topper, Hoppy was aided and abetted in his laudable deeds by a clumsy sidekick, Jack (California) Carlson. Carlson's presence added comic relief and not a whole lot else. Hoppy challenged cattle rustlers, bank and stagecoach robbers, cold-blooded killers, swindlers of every description and other greedy scoundrels on the Western frontier.

Hopalong Cassidy—long a genuine celebrity in American amusement before the middle of the twentieth century—was introduced as "the same Hoppy you cheer in motion pictures ... a name to be feared, respected and admired." His belly laugh was as distinguishing on radio as the all-black outfit he wore on-screen. His show's billboard claimed he was "the most amazing man ever to ride the prairies of the early West," an assertion that would likely have caused hair to bristle on the heads of Gene Autry, Lone Ranger, Roy Rogers and Wild Bill Hickok fans and those of similar plains hero legends.

The character Hopalong Cassidy was the inspiration of western novelist and short story author Clarence E. Mulford. In Mulford's pulp fiction the protagonist was presented as a "belching, snorting, drinking, chewing relic of the Old West." One reviewer saw him as a "profane, unwashed, gimpy-legged cowpoke." Harry Sherman displaced that when he brought Hoppy to the silver screen, then hired veteran silent movie talent Bill Boyd to play him and turned the character into a heroic sensation. One of the byproducts was a comic strip based on the national prodigy.

At one point the Hoppy phenomenon became so pervasive that *Time* magazine observed that a rush for shirts and slacks similar to those the infamous fictional cowboy wore resulted in a national shortage of black dye. At the peak of the mania, product endorsements by Bill Boyd thrust him into multimillionaire status, earning royalties from comic books, lunch pails, candy bars, clothing, bicycles, roller skates, furniture and a whole lot more. There were, in fact, more than 2,000 Cassidy commodities merchandised.

Between 1935 and 1948 Boyd made 66 movie features with either Andy Clyde or Gabby Hayes as his sidekick. Sensing that TV was just around the corner, the entrepreneur began acquiring rights to those films, editing them into 30- and 60-minute segments. When television emerged, he gained enormous profits as a prime source for action reels, helping to supply video's voracious appetite. His show appeared on NBC-TV from June 24, 1949 (predating the radio series by six months) through Dec. 23, 1951. He filmed 52 additional episodes that were then syndicated across the land, playing on local TV stations between 1952 and 1954. Edgar Buchanan appeared with him in the latter series as sidekick Red Connors.

The TV features were rerun many times throughout the 1950s but faded in the 1960s as more sophisticated westerns took to the small screens. Yet in June 1966 *Variety* noted that a station in Fresno, Calif., KJEO-TV, had rerun the *Cassidy* series continuously since June 8, 1953. When Bill Boyd died in South Laguna Beach, Calif., on Sept. 12, 1972, at age 74, so did most TV exposure of a feature that media observer Wesley Hyatt claimed was once "the top filmed show on television." Old Hoppy movies, however, shown in matinee theaters in the 1930s, 1940s and 1950s, are still randomly screened as features on contemporary cable networks such as AMC.

The "success story of 1950," the radio series was a "commercial juggernaut that defied all reason to become the radio and

TV triumph of its day," John Dunning believed. Hoppy's first appearance on the aural medium occurred on CBS's *Forecast* on Aug. 11, 1941, an audition in which the network advanced potential radio series, urging listeners to respond. It was an initial attempt to transfer the nation's fascination with the hero horseman of the screen to the airwaves. On that occasion *Hopalong Cassidy* featured Lou Merrill and Gerald Mohr but no Bill Boyd. While the venture proved unsuccessful, by Jan. 1, 1948, Commodore Productions and Artists Inc. was transcribing radio dramas with Boyd in the lead, ultimately producing 144 episodes. Two years to the day passed before the series premiered to a national audience over Mutual through 517 local outlets.

Bernard Drew prepared a log of the radio show.

Hot Copy

On the Air: Oct. 4, 1941–June 27, 1942, NBC, Saturday, 10:30 p.m.; July 27–Aug. 10, 1942, NBC, Monday, 11:30 p.m.; Aug. 29–Sept. 26, 1942, NBC, Saturday, 9:30 p.m.; July 18, 1943–June 18, 1944, NBC Blue, Sunday, 3:30 p.m.; June 25–Nov. 19, 1944, NBC Blue, Sunday, 5:30 p.m. 30 minutes.
Sponsor: Sustained (NBC); O'Cedar floor and furniture polish (NBC Blue).
Extant Episodes: None known.

CAST & CREDITS

Director—Albert Crews.
Writer—Nelson Bond.
Music—Roy Shield (orchestra).
Leads—Anne Rogers, played by Betty Lou Gerson, Eloise Kummer, Fern Parsons; Sergeant Flannigan, played by Hugh Rowlands.

Syndicated newspaper columnist-reporter Anne Rogers dabbled in murder investigations as a kind of avocational diversion while plying her salaried craft as a journalist. To the humiliation of a bewildered Sergeant Flannigan, she often not only fingered the killers but also patiently interpreted the clues that should have been obvious to the rather obtuse professional lawman.

The protagonist was originally named Patricia Murphy, also a newspaper columnist.

Howie Wing

On the Air: Oct. 3, 1938–June 30, 1939, CBS, Weekdays, 6:15 p.m. 15 minutes.
Sponsor: W. K. Kellogg Co. for various cereal brands (Oct. 3, 1938–June 30, 1939).
Extant Episodes: None known.

CAST & CREDITS

Writer—Bill Moore.
Sound Effects—Al Binnie.
Leads—Title role played by William Janney; Captain Harvey, played by Neil O'Malley.
Support Roles—Richard Bishop (the Chief), Raymond Bramley (Burton York), John Griggs (Zero Smith), Mary Parker (Donna Cavendish), Robert Strauss (Typhoon Tootel).

"An aviator and do-gooder who usually encountered crime and brutality," Howie Wing—at 21—was considered a "junior pilot." (Ironically, one of his contemporaries, Hop Harrigan, was dubbed "America's ace of the airways" at 18. It may be all in one's perspective.) Wing, whose name seemed more than appropriate for his profession, was shepherded in his quests as a Cadet Aviation Corps member by Captain Harvey, mythical ace pilot of World War I. While managing a South American airline, Harvey was Wing's instructor, mentor and friend. Others in the cast included Howie's girlfriend, Donna Cavendish; his mechanic, Typhoon Tootel; an obstinate pilot named Zero Smith; and the fiendish Burton York, whose cover as an insurance agent was a hoax to hide his true intent as a saboteur. Howie and Harvey were constantly in conflict with their challenging nemesis.

The show was loosely based on the real-life experiences of writer Bill Moore who had been a World War I pilot.

A large number of premiums were offered during the series' brief run.

While *Howie Wing* was a forerunner of *Hop Harrigan* and in some important ways quite similar, *Wing* was unable to sustain the audience and gain the durability over the years that its successor did. Airing before the start of the Second World War, *Wing* didn't have the in-built fixation with fighting enemies in the air that *Harrigan*—debuting three years later, merely a few months after the U.S. joined the fray—was capable of attracting.

I Deal in Crime

(aka *Ross Dolan, Detective*)

On the Air: *I Deal in Crime.* Jan. 21–Oct. 14, 1946, ABC, Monday, 9 p.m.; Oct. 19, 1946–May 24, 1947, ABC, Saturday, 8:30 p.m.; May 31–Oct. 18, 1947, ABC, Saturday, 8 p.m.; *Ross Dolan, Detective.* Oct. 25, 1947–Sept. 4, 1948, MBS, Saturday, 8 p.m. 30 minutes.
Sponsor: Sustained (Jan. 21–Oct. 14, 1946, Oct. 25, 1947–Sept. 4, 1948); Hastings (Oct. 19, 1946–Oct. 18, 1947).
Extant Episodes: Four.

CAST & CREDITS

Director—Leonard Reeg.
Writer—Ted Hediger.
Music—Skitch Henderson (orchestra).
Announcer—Dresser Dahlstead.
Lead—Ross Dolan, played by William Gargan.
Support Roles—Hans Conried, Ted de Corsia, Betty Lou Gerson, Mitzi Gould, Joseph Kearns, Lurene Tuttle.

Ex-seaman Ross Dolan experienced a decade as a Los Angeles private eye before serving a brief hitch in "Uncle Sugar's Navy." Suddenly cut from nautical duty, he returned to the profession he had practiced earlier. Selling his services for $25 a day plus expenses, the hard-boiled investigator operated out of room 404 in the Melrose Building. Dolan solicited clients via ads in *The Chronicle* and often found those clients inexorably linked to murder. Furthermore, he sustained a proclivity demonstrated in almost every episode for running afoul of professional lawmen. It wasn't an altogether unbelievable circumstance for there were many examples of that among those who selected his chosen occupation.

I Love a Mystery

(aka *I Loved an Adventure*)

On the Air: Jan. 16–Sept. 29, 1939, NBC West Coast network, Weekdays, 3:15 p.m. PT; Oct. 2, 1939–March 29, 1940, NBC, Weekdays, 7:15 p.m.; April 4–June 27, 1940, NBC, Thursday, 8:30 p.m.; Sept. 30, 1940–June 30, 1941, NBC Blue, Monday, 8 p.m.; Oct. 6, 1941–June 29, 1942, NBC Blue, Monday, 8 p.m.; March 22, 1943–Dec. 29, 1944, CBS, Weekdays, 7 p.m.; Oct. 3, 1949–Dec. 26, 1952, MBS, Weekdays, 7:45 p.m. (moved to 10:15 p.m. in 1950). Weekday series, 15 minutes; weekly episodes, 30 minutes.
Theme Song: *Valse Triste* (Sibelius).
Sponsors: Sustained (Jan. 16–Sept. 29, 1939; April 4–June 27, 1940; Oct. 3, 1949–Dec. 26, 1952); Standard Brands Inc. for Fleischmann's yeast and Chase and Sanborn coffee (Oct. 2, 1939–March 29, 1940; Sept. 30, 1940–June 29, 1942); Procter & Gamble Co. for Ivory soap and Oxydol detergent (March 22, 1943–Dec. 29, 1944).
Extant Episodes: 35 plus (some only in segments).

CAST & CREDITS

Producer/Director—Carlton E. Morse.

Assistant Producer—Buddy Twiss.

Director—Mel Bailey.

Writers—Carlton E. Morse, Michael Raffetto, Barton Yarborough.

Music—Paul Carson, Rex Corey (organists).

Sound Effects—Ralph Amati, Barney Beck, George Cooney, Al Span.

Announcers—Jim Bannon, Dresser Dahlstead, Frank McCarthy.

Leads—Doc Long, played by Jim Boles, Barton Yarborough; Jack Packard, played by Robert Dryden, John McIntire, Jay Novello, Michael Raffetto, Russell Thorson; Reggie Yorke, played by Tom Collins, Walter Paterson, Tony Randall; Jeri Booker, played by Gloria Blondell.

Support Roles—Ben Alexander, Cliff Arquette, Tommy Cook, Don Douglas, Jack Edwards, Sarah Fussel, John Gibson, Page Gillman, Richard LeGrand, Cathy Lewis, Elliott Lewis, Forrest Lewis, Althena Lorde, Mercedes McCambridge, Wally Maher, Lal Chand Mehra, Jeanette Nolan, Edgar Norton, Luis Van Rooten, Naomi Stevens, Les Tremayne, Kathleen Wilson, Barbara Jean Wong.

This drama was centered around triple figures who formed the A-1 Detective Agency in Hollywood and whose exploits led the fans on merry chases that were characterized by heavy doses of thrills, often taking them to exotic locales. (One sage felt they had more depth than most hard-boiled private eyes, calling them "soft-boiled lugs.") Doc Long invariably favored the distaff side, never encountered a skirt he didn't chase, yet was mesmerized by unsolved homicides. Jack Packard, their acknowledged leader, was the consummate strategist-detective—a mental heavyweight with extraordinary deductive powers. Englishman Reggie York, on the other hand, contributed the brawn often required by the intrepid trio.

Theirs could not be classified as tales geared solely to the juvenile set for their murders and other grisly charades kept mature audiences entranced. After all, commercials for Fleischmann's yeast, Chase and Sanborn coffee, Ivory soap and Oxydol detergent could hardly be pitched to an audience comprised solely of youngsters. The series proved to be popular nighttime fare separated from the purely adolescent adventures of late afternoon by more than just a meal. "No job too tough, no mystery too baffling" was the watchword of these dedicated zealots who combed the world to banish evil and put away guilty parties for the betterment of mankind.

Critics have been extremely kind to this series for its timeless, universal appeal. Jim Harmon dubbed it "the greatest radio program of all time" and John Dunning certified it as "the most-sought of all radio shows." Harmon compared it favorably to both Conan Doyle's *Sherlock Holmes* and Robert Louis Stevenson's *Treasure Island*, labeling it "a true classic, a work of art." Gerald Nachman suggested that the series "neatly interwove two related radio genres, the private eye and the suspense program, into a seamless original that became the most respected show of its type."

When actor Walter Paterson took his own life in 1942, the figure of Reggie Yorke vanished from the story line. The A-1 Detective Agency's charming and shapely secretary, Jeri Booker, succeeded him. From that point the show was introduced as "The adventures of Jack, Doc and Jeri." It abruptly left the air in 1944 as Doc and Jack shut down the agency, allegedly to enter the service of Uncle Sam. The original threesome (Doc, Jack, Reggie) resurfaced in their established haunts under a new banner—*I Love Adventure*—in 1948. (See separate entry.) They were again reunited when *I Love a Mystery* made a comeback from 1949 to 1952. Those shows on the Mutual Broadcasting System utilized scripts that had been previously aired from Hollywood but were performed by an East Coast troupe then.

The cast may have sounded familiar to radio audiences for, indeed, several of its members carried leading roles in Carlton E. Morse's most memorable, legendary, award-winning epic, *One Man's Family*. The latter appeared first on radio (for 27 years) and briefly on television; most episodes aired live weekly or on weekdays. Among the actors in dual dramas: Michael Raffetto (eldest Barbour son, Paul), Russell Thorson (successor as Paul when Raffetto assumed heavy responsibilities in the show's writing and directing), Barton Yarborough (one of the Barbour twins, Clifford), Page Gilman (youngest son, Jack), Walter Paterson (twin Claudia's second husband), Tom Collins (following Paterson as Claudia's second husband), Jay Novello (Judge Hunter), director Buddy Twiss, organist Paul Carson and a large contingent of support players who shifted back and forth between Morse's various audio creations.

Morse himself once explained that—between *I Love a Mystery* and *One Man's Family*—he was churning out 15 pages of script every day, seven days a week, while single-handedly directing and producing both shows. He also cast each role, and furthermore supervised the music and sound effects on both shows. This left him with no time for anything else, he admitted. "The minute I started to write I was lost to the world for two-and-a-half hours," Morse reminisced. He further confessed, "I get more pleasure than anybody else I know, doing what I'm doing."

For many years he refused to add a co-writer—never finding anyone capable of penning the shows the way he heard them in his head. Early in his radio career the master author, clucking like a mother hen over each page of every script, would have found any assistance an abomination. He later admitted that even he frequently had no idea where the drama's circuitous plots, which normally ran through a three-

or four-week thread, were headed. Announcer Dresser Dahlstead attested to Morse's sense of propriety: "We rehearsed very religiously…. We did it right … with Carlton in the booth there wasn't anything else you could do. You *had* to be right." (Other Morse broadcast creations: *His Honor the Barber, Adventures by Morse, Family Skeleton* and *The Woman in My House*.)

Columbia Pictures released a trilogy of *I Love a Mystery* films in 1945. Jim Bannon, who had delivered the Oxydol commercials for Procter & Gamble during the radio dramas, replaced Michael Raffetto as Jack Packard; Raffetto was reportedly deemed too diminutive. While Barton Yarborough played Doc Long in the screenplay, the part was significantly diminished and he was given fourth billing. Both radio actors took it personally and departed the cast of the broadcast series for about a year. The series of films included *I Love a Mystery, The Unknown* and *The Devil's Mask*. None of the movies was a box office smash.

No matter how unlikely the circumstances in which the three principals found themselves, the cast always accepted things as absolutely plausible. Yet a comic-book style movie offered by Universal Studios to TV audiences in the 1970s based on the exploits of the *I Love a Mystery* characters dissolved into the less than believable: David Hartman was cast as Doc, Hegan Beggs played Reggie and Les Crane appeared as Jack. "Crane was awful," noted media critic Harmon, "but … Laurence Olivier could not have saved the script." The TV film could be appreciated only "on the level of a *Mad* magazine parody," wrote Harmon, "not a reasonable adaptation of the real thing."

In the 1980s, three decades after the series' appeal to radio fans, Carlton E. Morse allowed syndicated cartoonist Don Sherwood to draw a comic strip based on the faintly remembered radio drama. Results were mixed: Limited numbers of American newspapers agreed to run it although it appeared for a time in some European periodicals.

Late in life Carlton E. Morse began authoring novels which he self-published, his first two being *Killer at the Wheel* and *A Lavish of Sin*, both of them well received by his adoring fans. Encouraged, he turned out what he intended to be the first in a series of *I Love a Mystery* fictional tales titled *Stuff the Lady's Hatbox*. Unfortunately, he died at 91 on May 24, 1993, before completing any more.

For anecdotes, cast photos and expanded verbiage behind the scenes, the reader is referred to the chapter on "I Love a Mystery" in Jim Harmon's authoritative volume *Radio Mystery and Adventure and Its Appearances in Film, Television and Other Media* (McFarland, 1992).

Jay Hickerson created a log of the radio series.

I Love Adventure

On the Air: April 25–July 18, 1948, ABC, Sunday, 7 p.m. 30 minutes.
Theme Song: *Valse Triste* (Sibelius), the same as that used on *I Love a Mystery*.
Sponsor: Sustained.
Extant Episodes: 13 (complete run).

CAST & CREDITS

Producer/Director/Writer—Carlton E. Morse.
Writer—John Paul Schofield.
Music—Rex Koury (organ).
Announcer—Dresser Dahlstead.
Leads—Jack Packard, played by Michael Raffetto; Doc Long, played by Barton Yarborough; Reggie Yorke, played by Tom Collins.
Support Roles—Jeanne Bates (secretary Mary Kay Jones), Henry Blair, Lillian Buyeff, Dix Davis, Betty Lou Gerson, Everett Glass, Lou Krugman, Harry Lang, Alma Lawton, Earl Lee, Janet Logan, John McIntire, Lal Chand Mehra, Donald Morrison, Jeanette Nolan, Frank Richards, Rolfe Sedan, Russell Thorson, Luis Van Rooten, Peggy Webber, Barbara Jean Wong.

This fleeting feature was a conduit that linked West and East Coast renderings of *I Love a Mystery*. Yet, according to reviewer John Dunning, it was minus both the "dramatic tension" and "cohesion" of either one. At best it was an uneven version of the more infamous and superior predecessor/successor drama. Jack, Doc and Reggie were reunited by teams—initially Jack with Reggie, then Jack with Doc (and without illumination on Reggie's abrupt departure). While their illustrious author had them pursuing crime thriller sagas overseas, "Carlton E. Morse couldn't decide from week to week what to do with the show," allowed Dunning. The protagonists joined a London-based alliance that was committed to combating worldwide adversaries of global harmony. Meanwhile, the principals faded in and out; the detective agency didn't resume until the midpoint of the run; and the show dissolved into "a jerky mishmash."

Author Jim Harmon offered some perceptive asides regarding this brief series: "[Carlton E.] Morse thought the late Mr. [Tom] Collins did a bad job of playing Reggie." While Harmon described Collins' portrayal as both "youthful" and "carefree," he assessed it as that of a "competent professional." Harmon suggested that the shift in participating lead figures halfway through the run was due to both a diminished audience and a lack of interest in tales penned during the global conflagration dealing with wartime intelligence. He believed that listeners didn't want to be reminded of the hostilities.

Harmon also observed a major shift in the predilections of Jack and Reggie. Having been virtually blind to the feminine form in the prior series—unlike their colleague, Doc—Jack and Reggie's testosterone kicked into high gear and all three subjects displayed lecherous tendencies in spare moments. Had times changed that quickly since the servicemen had begun returning home?

Jay Hickerson prepared a log.

I Loved an Adventure see *I Love Adventure*

I Was a Communist for the FBI

On the Air: 1952–54. Originally aired by transcription over WIP, Philadelphia, Penn., Sunday at 6 p.m. 78 episodes distributed to more than 600 markets by broadcast syndicator Frederic W. Ziv Co. 30 minutes.
Sponsor: Kingston Cake Co. (WIP, Philadelphia) and sold to local underwriters in each market where the series aired.
Extant Episodes: 78 (complete run).

CAST & CREDITS
Director—Henry Hayward.
Lead—Matt Cvetic, played by Dana Andrews.

With U.S. anti–Red panic amounting to a national state of frenzy at the middle of the twentieth century, a syndicated show like this one was readily purchased by more local stations than the number that would have carried it as a network series. Double agent Matt Cvetic infiltrated the U.S. Communist Party on behalf of the Federal Bureau of Investigation to gain information that would ultimately protect freedom-loving citizens from the party's avowed intent to subjugate the globe.

Unable to divulge his personal role to family or friends, Cvetic found himself frequently ostracized. While attending cell meetings and carrying out his party-issued mandates, he could never be certain whose

suspicion he might provoke or who was already spying on him. It was a highly hazardous mission as he gathered incriminating evidence and exposed insider secrets that could have thwarted our system of government. The severity of the cold, calculating, deadly serious opportunists who were determined to bring the country to its knees was implied in the tone of Cvetic's opening lines: "You can read it in the official report, the whole story of my life as a Communist for the FBI. I was in the party. I saw it work. For nine years I recorded the Communist conspiracy against the United States from within." There was no margin for error. It was a frenetic existence and the risk of tipping his hand kept listeners on edge as they, too, feared for his life.

Real-life double agent Matt Cvetic revealed his true identity following his service to the FBI by authoring a book along with magazine articles detailing some of his close encounters. Subsequently, a 1951 movie titled *I Was a Communist for the FBI* surfaced. Directed by Gordon Douglas with screenplay by Crane Wilbur, the production starred Frank Lovejoy as Matt Cvetic. Also appearing in the cast were Dorothy Hart, Philip Carey, James Millican, Richard Webb and Konstantin Shayne.

Frederic W. Ziv, a big name among early television syndicators, distributed the radio features *Boston Blackie, Bright Star* and *Freedom, U.S.A.* in addition to this series.

A similar tale formed the basis of a popular syndicated TV show distributed by Ziv, *I Led Three Lives*. A total of 117 half-hour episodes were filmed for release between 1953 and 1956 and were repeated on local stations for many years. The tube version starred Richard Carlson as the indefatigable Herbert A. Philbrick, who had infiltrated U.S. Communist Party ranks for nine years as a spy. A Boston advertising executive, Philbrick met many of the same frightening exploits that were simultaneously experienced by his radio contemporary Matt Cvetic. Upon completing his assignment, Philbrick also reported his undercover mission by way of a book. Ziv officials, meanwhile, confided: "Our chief purpose is to find good story properties, turn them into good films, and sell them." Their concern was first and foremost their own bottom line instead of rendering some meaningful public service.

In the Name of the Law

On the Air: May 31–Aug. 16, 1936, Syndicated.
Sponsor: Sold to advertisers in each local market where it was aired.
Extant Episodes: 12 (complete run).

CAST & CREDITS
Performers uncredited on taped episodes.

The show's opening billboard lauded it as "thrilling stories" in an "exciting series taken from actual police file cases." A narrator introduced the dramatizations that were drawn from local law enforcement agencies across the United States and Canada. Most titles of the individual episodes were unusual and included among their number "I Dreamed Mother was Poisoned," "Narcotics in the Trunk," "I Bumped Off Hubby" and "He Did It. Or Did He?"

The Incomparable Charlie Chan see The Adventures of Charlie Chan

Indictment

On the Air: Jan. 29, 1956–Jan. 4, 1959, CBS, Sunday, 5:05 p.m. 25 minutes.

Sponsor: Sustained and participating enterprises.
Extant Episodes: Seven.

CAST & CREDITS
Producer—Nathan Kroll.
Directors—Ira Ashley, Paul Roberts.
Writers—Robert Corcoran, Allan Sloane.
Leads—Edward McCormick, played by Nat Polen; Tom Russo, played by Jack Arthur.

Actual murder probes previously conducted by former New York City assistant district attorney Eleazar Lipsky offered the backdrop of this pragmatic narrative. For the listening audience, fictional investigators Edward McCormick, as assistant D. A., and police Detective Tom Russo pursued the true cases that Lipsky had earlier investigated over his professional career. McCormick and Russo plodded through an enormous amount of tedium required to bring an arraignment against an accused individual. As the billboard stated: "It is the assistant district attorney who directs criminal investigations, assembles facts and witnesses and brings the case to a just indictment." Procedures detailing the intricacies of the courts and the law—not that familiar to most radio fans, and certainly not before the medium reached its twilight years—were the basis of an intriguing feature.

After a three-year run, this series departed the airwaves on the same weekend that CBS deleted four of radio's most durable soap operas. *Backstage Wife, Our Gal Sunday, Road of Life* and *This Is Nora Drake*—collectively airing weekdays for more than three-quarters of a century—bowed out on Friday, Jan. 2, 1959. In retrospect it was an omen of things to come: Less than 23 months later CBS conducted another housecleaning over a single weekend (Nov. 25–27, 1960), that time disposing of virtually all of radio's remaining dramatic and scripted dialogue features. They included *The Couple Next Door, The*

Right to Happiness, Whispering Streets, Ma Perkins, Young Doctor Malone, The Second Mrs. Burton, The Amos 'n' Andy Music Hall and *Have Gun, Will Travel.* Of the chain's popular, longstanding dramatic fare, only three series remained—*Gunsmoke, Suspense* and *Yours Truly, Johnny Dollar.* That November weekend became the widely accepted conclusion of radio's golden age.

Inspector Mark Sabre see Mystery Theater

Inspector Thorne

On the Air: July 20–Aug. 31, 1951, NBC, Friday, 9 p.m.; Sept. 6–Sept. 27, 1951, NBC, Thursday, 9 p.m. 30 minutes.
Sponsor: Sustained.
Extant Episodes: 11 (complete run).

CAST & CREDITS

Producers—Anne Hummert, Frank Hummert.
Director—Kenneth MacGregor.
Writer—Eugene Edward Francis.
Lead—Title role played by Karl Weber (first 10 programs), Staats Cotsworth (final one); Sergeant Muggin, played by Dan Ocko.

There were only 11 episodes in the full run of this British-produced feature, and the titles of all 11 were something or other murder case (e.g. "The Golden Girl Murder Case," "The Two Fiancées Murder Case"), which divulged a great deal about the severity of the investigations. Police Inspector Thorne of the Homicide Bureau of New Scotland Yard applied extraordinary deductive skills to capturing the prey that committed such heinous crimes. The opening billboard cited the revered professional's conquests via a circuitous route, claiming that his accomplishments "rank with many of the most celebrated ones in the annals of crime fiction" while noting that he was "an investigator smart enough to claim he is dumb and modest enough to believe it." Sergeant Muggin helped Thorne in his conquests in fingering cold-blooded killers.

Luther Sies reported that in the premier episode as the victim was murdered, he fell to the floor, screaming at his assailant: "You killed me!" That superfluous line was typical of all Hummert-produced melodrama, in their vast daytime and primetime series, and was often a laughingstock among critics. Upon solving the same case, the renowned Inspector Thorne summarized it with this less-than-sensational statement: "Murder is murder and the price is execution." Sies observed: "With dialogue of this nature, the cast had a serious obstacle to overcome." This appears to be an understatement, and the problem may have substantially contributed to the brevity of the program's life.

A log was prepared by Jay Hickerson.

Inspector White of Scotland Yard

On the Air: 1936–37, MBS, 5:30 p.m., Tuesday/Thursday. 15 minutes.
Sponsor: Sustained.
Extant Episodes: None known.

CAST & CREDITS

No information.

This was another of a seemingly endless procession of police detectives conducting their investigations out of London's widely renowned Scotland Yard. This drama, however, was offered by installment and was pointed directly at an audience comprised principally of small fries. Thus, it was aired in the accepted pre-dinner juvenile adventure hour.

It's a Crime, Mr. Collins

On the Air: Aug. 9, 1956–Feb. 28, 1957, MBS, Thursday, 8:30 p.m.
Sponsor: Sustained.
Extant Episodes: 24.

CAST & CREDITS

Leads—Title role played by Mandel Kramer; Gail Collins, played by namesake Gail Collins; Uncle Jack, played by Richard Denning.

San Francisco private eye Greg Collins vigorously sought to prove the innocence of his clients, who were often accused of murder. Gail Collins, the gumshoe's gorgeous spouse—with green-eyed predilections emerging as curvaceous damsels in distress frequently petitioned her husband—shared his investigative exploits with her Uncle Jack, and thereby, with the listeners at home.

The bulk of Collins' cases were assigned titles bearing colors, e.g. "The Blue Steel Fountain Pen," "The Brown Alligator Briefcase," "The Chrome Yellow Death," "The Clue of the Ivory Thread," "The White Black Boat," "The Fabulous Redhead," "The Pink Lady," "The Red Hot Mama," "White Plumes, Red Blood."

It's Murder

On the Air: June 8–July 6, 1944, NBC Blue, Thursday, 11:15 p.m. 15 minutes.
Sponsor: National Safety Council.
Extant Episodes: One.

CAST & CREDITS

Leads—Rex A. Starr, played by Edgar Stehli.
Support Roles—Joan Alexander, Parker Fennelly.

A novice connoisseur of criminal activity, Rex A. Starr, probed into homicides.

Jack Armstrong, the All-American Boy

On the Air: July 31, 1933–Nov. 3, 1934, CBS, Monday–Saturday, 5:30 p.m.; Nov. 5, 1934–April 24, 1936, CBS, Monday–Friday, 5:30 p.m.; Aug. 31, 1936–April 23, 1937, NBC, Monday–Friday, 5:30 p.m.; Sept. 27, 1937–April 22, 1938, NBC, Monday–Friday, 5:30 p.m.; Sept. 26, 1938–April 28, 1939, NBC, Monday–Friday, 5:30 p.m.; Sept. 25, 1939–May 30, 1941, NBC, Monday–Friday, 5:30 p.m.; June 2–Sept. 26, 1941, NBC, Monday–Friday, 5:45 p.m.; Sept. 29, 1941–July 3, 1942, MBS, Monday–Friday, 5:30 p.m.; Aug. 31, 1942–May 28, 1943, NBC Blue, Monday–Friday, 5:30 p.m.; May 31, 1943–May 31, 1946, NBC Blue/ABC, Monday/Wednesday/Friday, 5:30 p.m.; Sept. 2, 1946–Aug. 29, 1947, ABC, Monday/Wednesday/Friday, 5:30 p.m.; Sept. 1, 1947–June 17, 1948, ABC, Monday/Wednesday/Friday and Tuesday/Thursday alternate weeks, 5:30 p.m.; Sept. 6, 1948–May 5, 1949, ABC, Monday/Wednesday/Friday and Tuesday/Thursday alternate weeks, 5:30 p.m.; Sept. 5, 1949–June 1, 1950, ABC, Monday/Wednesday/Friday and Tuesday/Thursday alternate weeks, 5:30 p.m. 15 minutes. (Continued on ABC in 30-minute evening episodes twice weekly Sept. 5, 1950–June 28, 1951, under the title *Armstrong of the SBI*. See separate entry.)
Theme Song: *Wave the Flag for Hudson High*, same tune as the gridiron fight melody of Chicago University, *Wave the Flag for Old Chicago*.
Sponsor: General Mills Inc. for Wheaties cereal (entire run).
Extant Episodes: 139.

CAST & CREDITS

Producers—James Jewell, David Owen.
Directors—James Jewell, Ted MacMurray, Ed Morse, Pat Murphy, David Owen.
Writers—Irving Crump, Robert Hardy Andrews, James Jewell, Lee Knopf, Talbot Mundy, Colonel Paschal Strong.
Vocalists—The Norsemen (Ted Kline, Ed Lindstrom, James Peterson, Al Revere, Kenneth Schon).

Sound Effects—Harry Bubeck, Robert J. Graham, Ed Joyce, Curt Mitchel.

Announcers—Truman Bradley, Paul Douglas, Norman Kraft, Jack Lester, Franklyn Mac-Cormack, Bob McKee, David Owen, Ed Prentiss, Tom Shirley.

Leads—Title role played by Jim Ameche (1933–38), St. John Terrell (1938), Stanley (Stacy) Harris (1938), Frank Behrens (1939), Charles Flynn (1939–43, 1944–50), Michael Rye (Billsbury) (1943); Billy Fairfield, played by John Gannon (1933–43, c1945–46), Roland Butterfield (c1943–45), Milton Guion, Murray McLean, Dick York; Betty Fairfield, played by Shaindel Kalish (1933), Sarajane Wells (1933–41), Loretta Poynton (1941–43), Naomi May (c1943–46), Patricia Dunlap (c1946–50); Uncle Jim Fairfield, played by Jim Goss; Vic Hardy, played by Ken Griffin.

Support Roles—Don Ameche, Frank Dane and Jack Doty (Captain Hughes), Robert Barron (Blackbeard Flint), Frank Behrens (Babu and Michael), Herb Butterfield (master spy Weissoul and villain Lorenzo), Ken Christy (Sullivan Lodge and Talia-San), Ed Davidson, Olan Soule, Les Tremayne and Arthur Van Slyke (Hudson High Coach Hardy), Naomi May and Sarajane Wells (Gwendolyn Devol), Art McConnell (Pete), Michael Romano (Lal Singh), Dick York (Dickie); also William Green, Butler Manville, Marvin Miller, William Rath.

While prominently dubbed a preadolescent adventure series that aired in the traditional late afternoon children's hour, *Jack Armstrong, the All-American Boy* unmistakably delved into villainy and criminal deceit. Eventually that expanded into tracking down Communists and fascists and more espionage agents in addition to mere gangsters, thieves, counterfeiters and other ill sorts who were clearly out-of-step with the law.

The serial focused on the global exploits of youthful Jack Armstrong, star athlete, honor student and all-around big man on campus at Hudson High School in the mythical city of the same name. (He was certified by one wag as "the *perfect* American boy," although no criteria were given.) Accompanying Jack on his thrilling escapades were young Billy and Betty Fairfield and their piloting uncle Jim, until Jim was replaced in 1946 with criminal investigator Vic Hardy. For years Hardy had been a nemesis to Armstrong and company, precisely the opposite of what he turned out to be upon regaining his memory following a decade-long bout with amnesia. Completely forgiven for his past indiscretions, Hardy's transformation was explained to the satisfaction of young listeners by noting that he "has dedicated the remainder of his life to the readjustment of criminals and the prevention and correction of crime…. In this way, he intends to repay society for those ten years in which he lived outside the law." ("Ah ha!" other jailbirds must have been thinking: "I'll just do that!")

Late in the 1930s Jack Armstrong's training rules were routinely advocated by the show. Fans were urged to get plenty of sleep, fresh air and exercise, to apply plenty of soap and water and to eat healthy foods like Wheaties (the sponsor's product).

There were some marks to distinguish this series from *The Adventures of Frank Merriwell* (1934, 1946–49) that are worthy of comparison. (See separate entry.)

The creative genius behind Jack Armstrong—Charles Robert Douglas Hardy Andrews (*one person!*)—was already established as a radio writer when assigned the task of devising "a soap opera for kids." Born at Effingham, Kansas on Oct. 19, 1903, Andrews produced a 100,000-word serialized story for a newspaper competition by the time he was 16. Within four years he was the city editor of *The Minneapolis Journal*. He penned features-by-installment for *The Chicago Daily News* before an appointment to the Blackett-Sample-Hummert advertising agency staff to create radio serials.

Andrews' first drama, *The Stolen Husband*, was about (a) a handsome young businessman, (b) a voluptuous secretary who was eager to advance her boss's career and (c) a dim but attractive spouse who would learn much too late that a man spending nights at the office with a dazzling, wily assistant could be occupied beyond his occupation. While *The Stolen Husband* wasn't an overnight success, it gave agency principals Frank Hummert, his assistant Anne S. Ashenhurst (the future Mrs. Hummert) and Andrews invaluable insights. In rapid-fire order it led Andrews to contribute to three extremely appealing serials against which almost all others would be measured over succeeding decades: *Just Plain Bill* (1932–55), *The Romance of Helen Trent* and *Ma Perkins* (a duo airing 1933–60).

Andrews, in fact, became the most fluent author of soap opera before or since—labeled by one scribe as a writing "syndicate." He single-handedly churned out five quarter-hour scripts weekly for as many as seven different serials running concurrently. For a decade, working in a penthouse apartment on New York's Central Park West, he consumed 40 cups of coffee and chain-smoked 100 cigarettes between the hours of noon and midnight seven days a week while typing scripts. His weekly production rate habitually surpassed 100,000 words. As a diversion, he wrote numerous novels and dozens of movies, alone or with other writers. The Hummerts never replaced him and when Andrews died on Nov. 11, 1976, it was the passing of an era among serial-writing wordsmiths.

In October 1934 an independent chain of local stations began airing prerecorded transcription discs of the *Armstrong* show. Of course this significantly boosted the number of outlets broadcasting the series. The drama's underwriter, General Mills, insisted that the episodes on discs be aired on the same day as the live performances. In that way the characters' various exploits were carried simultaneously across the country. Scripts had to be prepared several weeks in advance to make that happen; and transcriptions were recorded at least three weeks before air dates to allow time for them to arrive at the stations broadcasting by disc.

When the *Armstrong* show formed the Write-a-Fighter Corps during World War II, more than a million fans joined up, promising to become pen pals to overseas service personnel by sending a minimum of a letter per month. The club also advocated sales of war bonds, planting victory gardens and collecting tin, paper and rubber scraps as a contribution from the homefront to the war effort.

The program capitalized on the premium concept, too. For a few cents and a Wheaties boxtop, cereal manufacturer General Mills offered rings, medallions, bombsights, pedometers, stamps, planes, photos and a vast array of other memorabilia carefully crafted to tie in with the dramatic plotlines. Sales of Wheaties soared. The initial premium, a shooting plane, pulled in a reported 424,441 requests in the show's first year, while for months depleting the supply of Wheaties on grocers' shelves. The cereal maker was ready the next time a premium offer was proffered, however—carloads of the food product were methodically stashed in warehouses scattered about the country before anything was publicly announced.

The show enjoyed one of the greatest sponsor identifications in juvenile adventure history. The whole wheat cereal Wheaties, "breakfast of champions," bought the quarter-hour and a spinoff series for 18 years. Commercials and musical jingles reinforced the notion that Wheaties was *all* that growing youngsters like Jack Armstrong ever needed to start their day, as in this ditty's message: "Try Wheaties, they're whole wheat with all of the bran ... Jack has them, never tires of them and neither will you ... Just buy Wheaties, the best breakfast food in the land." The opening billboard created enthusiasm by underscoring that theme, promising "Wheaties brings you a story of champions in action." Could kids who were routinely urged to remind their mothers to buy Wheaties expect anything less? Endorsements by prominent sports figures were routinely introduced into sales pitches, celebs like Bob Feller and Joe DiMaggio, who sometimes read their copy in appalling fashion. (At age 80 actor Charles Flynn, who played the title role for most of the run, told author Gerald Nachman that he still consumed Wheaties: "It put my kids through school," said he. "By golly, I owe 'em something.")

Fifteen chapters of a 1947 theatrical serial titled *Jack Armstrong, the All-American Boy* played on Saturday matinee bills across the country. Produced by Sam Katzman and directed by Spencer Bennet, the sequences featured John Hart as the youthful hero adventurer. Joe Brown appeared as Billy, Rosemary La Planche as Betty, Pierre Watkin as Uncle Jim and Hugh Prosser in a diminished role as Vic Hardy.

While there was discussion in the 1980s of transporting *Jack Armstrong* into a Saturday morning TV cartoon series, it never happened. An Armstrong adapted to a contemporary setting—with possibly a bent toward modern rock—simply appeared implausible to the prospective producers.

A *Jack Armstrong* comic book hit the newsstands in November 1947 but within two years, after 13 issues, it vanished. The hero of Hudson High was also briefly featured in his own syndicated comic strip.

Jack Armstrong and the Ivory Treasure, released in print in 1937 by Whitman Publishing Co., was an original tale in Whitman's Big Little Books series. Written by Leslie N. Daniels Jr., the story was based on radio scripts by Talbot Mundy and illustrated by Henry E. Vallely. A second Whitman volume, *Jack Armstrong and the Mystery of the Iron Key,* included in Whitman's subsequent Better Little Books series, appeared in 1939. While no author was credited, Mundy's scripts were the basis for the plots with illustrations by Vallely.

Fred King prepared both a log and added detail on the radio show.

Jeff Regan, Investigator
(aka *The Lion's Eye*)

On the Air: July 10–Dec. 18, 1948, CBS West Coast region, Saturday, 9:30 PT; Oct. 5, 1949–Aug. 27, 1950, CBS West Coast region, starting Wednesday but later shifted to Sunday. 30 minutes.
Sponsor: Sustained.
Extant Episodes: 34.

CAST & CREDITS

Producers—Sterling Tracy, Gordon D. Hughes.
Writers—Jackson Gillis, E. Jack Neuman, Larry Roman (1948), William Fifield, William Froug (1949–50).
Music—Richard Aurandt, Del Castillo, Milton Charles (organists).
Announcers—Marvin Miller, Bob Stephenson.
Leads—Title role played by Jack Webb (July 10–Dec. 18, 1948), Frank Graham and Paul Dubov (Oct. 5, 1949–Aug. 27, 1950); Anthony J. Lyon, played by Herb Butterfield (1948), Wilms Herbert (1948), Frank Nelson (1949–50); Melody, Lyon's receptionist, played by Laurette Fillbrandt.
Support Roles—Ken Christy, Paul Dubov, Paul Frees, Betty Lou Gerson, Lon Krugman, Harry Lang, Mary Lansing, Eve McVeagh, Marvin Miller, Sidney Miller, Jack Petruzzi, Charles Seel, Theodore von Eltz.

After five months in dress rehearsal, actor Jack Webb relinquished the lead role as an undercover detective who traveled the world to focus on being a big city cop in an infinitely more promising *Dragnet*. But before that he reprised yet another detective role he had earlier brought to radio, *Pat Novak for Hire*. The more noteworthy *Dragnet* debuted June 3, 1949, over NBC and as history assertively records, the actor made a wise choice in leaving his other series behind.

In this particular farce Webb, as Jeff Regan, took orders from a miserly little despot who ran the mythical International Detective Bureau in Los Angeles—Anthony J. Lyon. The latter's money-grubbing disposition led friend and foe to dub his lair "the Lyon's Den." Clients, meanwhile, often labeled the hard-nosed Regan, who earned a paltry $10 per day plus expenses for his services, "the Lyon's Eye." It was true that when boss Lyon had an especially tricky assignment, he'd call Regan. Regan appeared up for any challenge, however, and obviously knew how to keep his mouth shut. The opening and closing billboards tagged him "radio's most exciting private detective," a judgment possibly better deferred to the mystery fans tuned in at home. While Jack Webb acted in the part and E. Jack Neuman penned it, the Regan figure characteristically carried a chip on his shoulder. On their departure, however, the lead personality was softened and turned into an empathetic figure that fought assiduously for the little guy's interests.

One reviewer noted that Jack Webb developed an "almost cult following" for his portrayal of the "hilarious hard boiled" detective *Pat Novak for Hire*. That drama, the first of a quartet in which the actor was to portray a detective, appeared from 1946 to 1947 over ABC's West Coast stations and during the winter and spring of 1949 over the full ABC network. *Novak* coast-to-coast followed Webb's brief tenure as *Johnny Madero, Pier 23* and as *Jeff Regan,*

Investigator, all of them leading to the debut of *Dragnet*.

Original *Regan* author E. Jack Neuman, who worked with Webb in that series for the first time, recalled some advice that the noted actor gave the scriptwriter: "You've got to climb the mountain and plant a flag in every scene. Every scene can be like the ending of an act." In an interview with Leonard Maltin, Neuman remembered: "He [Webb] tried to hit a home run every time he came to bat, and he did it almost every time. And he was a very hard taskmaster. But he created the idea of dramatizing reality, and the film and television industry owes him a lot."

Jay Hickerson prepared a radio log.

Jimmie Allen see *The Air Adventures of Jimmie Allen*

Jimmy Valentine see *Alias Jimmy Valentine*

John J. Malone for the Defense see *The Amazing Mr. Malone*

Johnny Dollar see *Yours Truly, Johnny Dollar*

A Johnny Fletcher Mystery see *Johnny Fletcher*

Johnny Fletcher
(aka *A Johnny Fletcher Mystery*)

On the Air: May 30–Sept. 5, 1948, ABC, Sunday, 7:30; Sept. 11–Nov. 27, 1948, ABC, Saturday, 8 p.m. 30 minutes.

Sponsor: Sustained.
Extant Episodes: Two.

CAST & CREDITS

Writer—Frank Gruber.
Music—Buzz Adlam.
Announcers—Owen James, John Storm.
Leads—Title role played by Albert Dekker, Bill Goodwin; Sam Kragg, played by Mike Mazurki, Sheldon Leonard.

An inept amateur detective, Johnny Fletcher was frequently drunk. He and his brawny partner, Sam Kragg—both unemployed and residents of the Eagle Hotel—thought up unusual ruses for obtaining income. Their clients often took them into murder and other mayhem of many sorts. A damsel in distress was absolutely certain to pique their curiosities.

A couple of normally authoritative sources list the series as airing over NBC during the 1945–46 radio season. The preponderance of reliable researchers in this field make no mention of an earlier run, however, giving way to the prospect that one chronicler may have inadvertently provided unsubstantiated information, then copied it in a more recent publication. Regretfully, we are left with nothing to corroborate the fact that the program may have aired prior to 1948.

Johnny Madero, Pier 23

On the Air: April 24–Sept. 4, 1947, MBS, Thursday, 8 p.m. 30 minutes.
Theme Song: *I Cover the Waterfront*.
Sponsor: Sustained.
Extant Episodes: Two.

CAST & CREDITS

Creator/Producer—Richard Breen.
Director—Nat Wolff.
Writers—Herb Margolis, Louis Markheim.
Music—Harry Zimmerman.
Announcer—Tony LaFrano.

Leads—Title role played by Jack Webb; Gale Gordon as Father Leahy.
Support Roles—Francis X. Bushman, William Conrad (Officer Warchek).

This private dick, a refugee from the street wars, covered the Embarcadero waterfront of San Francisco (as did several of his contemporaries). He was depicted as "a carbon copy of *Pat Novak*" (*for Hire*), another tough detective on the air during his era and also played by actor Jack Webb. Madero's adventures often began in the boat shop that he operated at Pier 23. Working largely by himself, not infrequently did he compare notes with a bayfront priest, Father Leahy, not your typical man of the cloth. Leahy networked with underworld contacts and maintained a watchful eye on the throbbing heartbeat of Frisco's teeming coastline. This twosome was forever hassled by police officer Warchek, who invariably smelled something fishy when the pair plotted together. Madero's language was clipped, his demeanor rough and his exterior façade appeared evenly matched for the environment he had staked out.

Media critic Leonard Maltin referred to the Jack Webb features *Johnny Madero, Pier 13* and *Jeff Regan, Investigator* as "soundalike shows" following *Pat Novak for Hire*. None of this triumvirate, however, held a candle to the eminently better produced, better written *Dragnet*, which was to follow, turning Webb as Sergeant Joe Friday into an American entertainment icon. Gerald Nachman compared Madero and Friday: "Johnny, who prowled the San Francisco waterfront, was far more of the wise guy than Joe, though clearly his ancestor—a transitional figure between the hard-bitten Sam Spade school of private eyes and the even harder-bitten Joe Friday police academy."

Within a week of the series' premiere *Variety* informed readers that *Madero* was "a hard-hitting, fast-moving item that carries a good deal of punch in its dialog." Those exchanges soon led to the show's collapse, however. With little warning the Mutual Broadcasting System withdrew the series because the chain's CEO wasn't happy when the writers refused to restrain the characterizations. "The most striking feature of the series—beyond the incessantly rude banter the hero carried on with everyone he encountered—was the hatred for society which he betrayed in all his undertakings," one media historiographer observed.

Jonathan Brixton's Murder Cases see *Attorney for the Defense*

The Judge

On the Air: June 5–June 26, 1952, CBS, Thursday, 9:30 p.m. 30 minutes.
Sponsor: Sustained.
Extant Episodes: One (audition show, Feb. 13, 1952).

CAST & CREDITS

Producer/Director—Norman Macdonnell.
Writers—Henry Lee, Richard Pedicini.
Music—Leith Stevens.
Announcer—Dan Cubberly.
Leads—Title role played by John Dehner; police lieutenant played by Lawrence Dobkin. (Actual names of both have not survived.)
Support Roles—Georgia Ellis, Vivi Janis, Byron Kane, Sarah Selby, June Whittley.

A judge with years of experience on the bench came out of retirement to assist a police lieutenant in his pursuit of criminals. The concept failed to impress enough listeners and the series was discontinued the same month it premiered.

Jungle Jim

On the Air: Nov. 2, 1935–Aug. 1, 1954. Transcribed and syndicated weekly to local markets and offered on varying days often at erratic times there. 15 minutes.
Theme Song: *The Storm*, from *The William Tell Overture* (Gioacchino Rossini). Featured on the predecessor series, *Flash Gordon*, it was continued on the successor program. It came from a 1927 RCA Black Seal recording by maestro Rosario Bourdon and the Victor Symphony Orchestra.
Sponsor: Hearst Syndicate *Comic Weekly* newspaper supplement.
Extant Episodes: 525.

CAST & CREDITS

Producer—Jay Clark.
Directors—Stuart Buchanan, Irene Fenton.
Writers—Jay Clark, Gene Stafford.
Announcers—Roger Krupp, Glenn Riggs.
Leads—Title role of Jungle Jim Bradley played by Matt Crowley, Gerald Mohr (briefly in 1938); Kolu, played by Juano Hernandez.
Support Roles—Kenny Delmar, Franc (pronounced *France*) Hale (Shanghai Lil), Arthur Hughes (Singh-Lee), Owen Jordan (Tom Sun), Jack Lloyd (Van), Vicki Vola, Irene Winston (Tiger Lil).

Simultaneously airing the same narratives that were appearing in newspaper comic sections, the radio serial also urged fans to follow the print illustrations as the dual mediums interacted. Jungle guide Jim Bradley, accompanied by his native companion, Kolu, of Africa's darkest interiors, sought to abolish evil in every form, including some sinister forces that would reduce the globe to a mere acquisition, controlled by insidious lunatics. Shanghai Lil became their most persistent foe as the pair sought to adopt resourceful modes of overcoming her diabolical scheming.

The series began when Jim rescued an existing radio crime fighter—*Flash Gordon*—then in ratings trouble, as the sponsoring Hearst Corp. shifted its allegiance from one juvenile adventurer to another. Both appeared in Hearst comics created by Alex Raymond, but only one would continue for a sustained period on the air.

One of the few non-comedic Negro actors performing regularly in radio during the *Jungle Jim* epoch was the versatile Juano Hernandez. He played disparate parts on several adolescent series. In *Jungle Jim* he appeared as the faithful African sidekick Kolu. He was the black subordinate, Lothar, in *Mandrake the Magician* and portrayed a myriad of Indian figures in *Tennessee Jed*.

A quartet of black-and-white movie projects based on the comic strip and radio sequel hit the big screen a few months after the character's aural debut. In 1936 the first, named simply *Jungle Jim*, was a 12-chapter serial. Starring Grant Withers in the title role, it was directed by Ford Beebe and Clifford Smith. Wyndham Gittens and Norman S. Hall co-authored it. A plethora of unknowns teamed up in the supporting roles.

The remaining trio of silver screen features were full-length movies, all featuring a stereotyped jungle actor and former Olympian, Johnny Weissmuller, as the namesake hero.

In 1948 a second theatrical production was also released under the simple banner of *Jungle Jim*. Directed by William A. Berke, it was unique because Alex Raymond, the protagonist's creator and comic strip illustrator, penned the screenplay. Again a string of unknowns appeared in the lesser roles.

Jungle Jim and the Captive Girl, in 1950, allowed Berke to again direct Weissmuller. Carroll Young wrote the script. A couple of emerging Hollywood actors, Larry (Buster) Crabbe and John Dehner, were included in the cast. Crabbe appeared as an evil treasure hunter while Dehner was a witch doctor.

The final big screen offering, in 1952—*Jungle Jim in the Forbidden Land*—was directed by Lew Landers with script by Samuel Newman. Lesser quantities filled the screen once more in utility roles.

A 1955 syndicated television rendering of *Jungle Jim*, not to be confused with the 1952–53 non-network series of similar qualities, *Ramar of the Jungle*, also starred Johnny Weissmuller as the infamous African guide. By his side for 26 episodes were Martin Huston as his son, Skipper; Norman Fredrick as his aide, Kassim; and a chimpanzee, Tamba. It was an unmistakably Africanized tale.

A manufacturing firm acquired the rights to play upon the name of the familiar hero figure from comics, radio, movies and TV. It created a line of Jungle Gym exercise equipment for children.

A *Jungle Jim* radio log was prepared by Jay Hickerson.

Junior G-Men
(aka *True Adventures of Junior G-Men*)

On the Air: March 1, 1936–March 18, 1938, MBS, Monday–Friday, 6:30 p.m. (moved to 5:45 p.m. in 1937). Also syndicated by Donald Peterson Radio Programs. 15 minutes.
Sponsor: Fischer Baking Co.; General Foods Corp. for Post Toasties cereal; Local advertisers (in syndication).
Extant Episodes: 65 (13 weeks in syndication).

CAST & CREDITS
Announcer/Host—Melvin Purvis.
Other identifications not announced on the air.

A small boy and his pals united their efforts to fight crime in this adventure series strictly for adolescents. Stories were normally serialized over two or three chapters with intriguing titles designed to capture the imaginations of younger hearers like: "The Secret of the Locked Room," "The Footprints That Solved a Crime," "The League of One-Legged Men," "The Clue in the Mirror," "The Secret That Had to Be Kept" and "Mystery of Cemetery Hill." Murders, burglaries, smuggling, bribery, narcotics, kidnapping, escaped cons, jewel heists, blackmailers and hijackings figured into the plots. Wherever crime was rampant, it seemed that a junior G-man inevitably appeared to crack down on the offender.

Newspaperman Harold Schindler, writing in *The Salt Lake Tribune*, quoted radio premium-historian Jim Harmon in regard to the program's appealing patriotic trinkets: "Junior G-Man members were issued a Manual of Instructions to All Operatives (obtained with Post Toasties box tops) right from the Chief Special Agent-in-Charge, Melvin Purvis. Purvis described secret codes and signals, passwords, whistles and 'danger' code signs. He detailed instructions for solving crimes and apprehending criminals, how to 'shadow' a suspect and how to judge and compare fingerprints."

Suggesting the typical effusive tone of such marketing ploys aimed at tender ears, Harmon continued: "Yes sir, with Melvin Purvis heading up the corps, how could a red-blooded American youngster go wrong? After being cautioned never to reveal the secrets of the Junior G-Man Corps, Purvis went on to explain how he made it a rule to eat Post Toasties for breakfast every morning, why he thought all Junior G-Men ought to follow his example: Because it was good for you (and what better way to collect box tops for other Junior G-Man equipment?)."

The newspaper article noted that Purvis had been the FBI agent in charge of the bureau's Chicago office in the early 1930s, confronting gangsters Baby Face Nelson and John Dillinger. He reportedly killed Dillinger in an ambush, pushing FBI Director J. Edgar Hoover off the front page of the nation's newspapers, a big no-no for which he was reprimanded and, in 1935, ultimately asked to resign from the force.

Purvis, who took his own life in 1960,

also played a significant role in another short-lived radio series, *Top Secrets of the FBI*. While professing to be based directly on FBI files, that drama had no direct linkage to the national police-keeping organization. (See separate entry.)

Just Plain Bill

On the Air: Sept. 19, 1932–June 16, 1933, CBS, 6:45 p.m.; June 19, 1933–1935, CBS, 7:15 p.m. (Nighttime performances discontinued in 1935 with a daytime version added in 1933.) Oct. 16, 1933, CBS; 1935–June 12, 1936, CBS, 11:45 a.m.; Sept. 14, 1936–March 15, 1940, NBC, 10:30 a.m.; March 25, 1940–July 31, 1942, NBC Blue, 3:45 p.m.; Sept. 14, 1942–June 29, 1951, NBC, 5:30 p.m.; July 2, 1951–March 25, 1954, NBC, 5 p.m.; Sept. 26, 1954–July 1, 1955, NBC, 5 p.m.; July 4–Sept. 30, 1955, NBC, 3:45 p.m. 15 minutes.

Theme Songs: *Darling Nellie Gray* (early opening and bridges); *Polly Wolly Doodle* (closing, also later opening).

Sponsors: Sustained (Sept. 19, 1932–Jan. 13, 1933; July 4–Sept. 30, 1955); American Home Products Corp. (AHP) for its packaged drug division, Whitehall Pharmacal Co., including Kolynos toothpaste and tooth powder dentifrice, Anacin pain reliever, Kriptin antihistamine, Bi-So-Dol analgesic, Freezone corn remover, Heet liniment, Dristan and Primatene cold remedies, Preparation H hemorrhoidal medication, Neet hair remover, Infrarub muscle relaxing balm, Sleep-Eze calmative, interspersed with AHP's Boyle-Midway household products division, including Black Flag and Fly-Ded insect repellents, Aerowax and Olde English floor cleaners and furniture polishes, Wizard room deodorizer, Sani-Flush toilet cleanser, Easy-Off oven cleaner and more (Jan. 16, 1933–March 25, 1954, except for brief interruptions); Miles Laboratories Inc. for its pharmaceutical line including Alka-Seltzer acid-indigestion reliever and other brand name drugs like Tabcin, One-A-Day, Bactine and Miles Nervine (Sept. 26, 1954–July 1, 1955).

Extant Episodes: 19.

CAST & CREDITS

Producers—Anne Hummert, Frank Hummert.
Directors—Martha Atwell, Gene Eubank, Arthur Hanna, Ed King, Norman Sweetser, Blair Walliser.
Writers—Robert Hardy Andrews, Barbara Bates, Peggy Blake, Evelyn Hart, Jack Kelsey.
Music—Hal Brown (harmonica and banjo).
Sound Effects—Max Miller.
Announcers—Andre Baruch, John Cornell, Fielden Farrington, Ed Herlihy, Roger Krupp.
Leads—Title role of Bill Davidson played by Arthur Hughes; Nancy Davidson Donovan, played by Ruth Russell (1932–51), Toni Darnay (1951–55); Kerry Donovan, played by James Meighan; Sarah Fussell, Madeleine Pierce (Wiki Donovan).
Support Roles—Curtis Arnall, Macdonald Carey (Jonathan Hillery), Cliff Carpenter, Ray Collins, Clayton (Bud) Collyer, Elizabeth Day (Margaret Burns), Audrey Egan (Shirley King), Charles Egleston (Humphrey Fuller), Anne Elstner, Ara Gerald (Kathleen Chatton), Teri Keane, Elaine Kent, Joe Latham (Elmer Eeps), Charlotte Lawrence (Reba Britton), Bill Lytell, Bill Quinn, Ann Shepherd (pseudonym for Scheindel Kalish, as Pearl Sutton), Guy Sorel, George Tiplady, Helen Walpole, William Woodson (John Britton).

Ostensibly one of radio's most durable soap operas, this daytime classic's story line appeared to dwell more in darker undertones than lighter ones. While melodrama and humor were included, the plot lines—unlike most contemporary dishpan dramas—were at their best when Bill Davidson, "the barber of Hartville," tracked down some conniving rapscallion whose shady deeds ranged from petty larceny to murder. Davidson, a widower, often unraveled devious schemes that would otherwise have resulted in questionable ends for hapless victims. Arson, poisonings, stabbings, shootings, robberies, burglaries and the like were typical fare for a small town barber to pursue while being the unchallenged social conscience of his community. Assisting Davidson—and often the intended targets of those dastardly deeds—were his daughter and son-in-law, Nancy and Kerry Donovan, and his grandson, Wiki.

Davidson was properly branded as "a good-natured, soft-spoken, homespun country philosopher, sensitive to the needs of friends and relatives, [who] offered level-headed advice to help them straighten out their tangled lives.... He gave reassurance that even when the clouds are darkest, there is a silver lining if one searches diligently for it." Sometimes he faced far more dangerous situations than the domestic crises on which most washboard weepers thrived. In one sequence he discovered that an operator of rest homes for the aged was finishing off clients for their insurance. His own life was threatened. In the mid 1940s he became the target of vicious Judith Seymour and Leslie Groves, her son-in-law. At one point he was knocked unconscious and nearly killed. Evelyn Groves, Seymour's daughter and Leslie Groves' wife, had drowned under questionable circumstances. Offered a basket of fruit, Davidson accepted it, never realizing it was poisonous. When he shared some with Wiki, his grandson, a near-fatal tragedy resulted.

These were the catastrophes on which *Just Plain Bill* revolved. Yet the central figure's personal philosophy saw him through, even in his most trying situations. "You have to stand up to evil and fight it. You have to be ready for it when it strikes, and never give in to it. If you do them things, ... you can never be whipped by evil men," he allowed. Against this superior daytime series many of its followers came to be measured, with some lacking the quality that made it an enormous favorite with America's housewives.

Considered by his colleagues to be

"an actor's actor," Arthur Hughes, who starred in the role of Bill Davidson for nearly 6,000 performances, used to take a radio script, mark his lines in red pencil, and go off to a corner by himself to memorize those lines before broadcasts. Unlike most other soap opera thespians, he was much like the character he portrayed in *Just Plain Bill*: serious, thoughtful, depicting an "old school." As he aged in real life he became even more like Davidson, observers suggested. He was 39 when he assumed the role and carried it all the way to the end of the run 23 years later. When he died in New York City on Dec. 28, 1982, a half-century had elapsed since he inaugurated the part for which he would forever be remembered.

Just Plain Bill was a forerunner of radio drama by installment. For all intents and purposes it was the first serial with staying power, a permanent model for all other soap opera. It commanded a loyal following and endured into the mid 1950s, long beyond the time most serials arriving after its 1932 debut had faded.

King of the Royal Mounted

On the Air: 1943. 15 minutes.
Sponsor: Sustained.
Extant Episodes: Two.

CAST & CREDITS

No identifications (but a West Coast origination).

In stark contrast to another show with a related title (see *King of the Royal Mounties*), this one could be clearly identified as a juvenile adventure series. The extant recordings are audition tapes, therefore do not conclusively indicate that the drama developed into a series. A media critic who heard them suggested that it was "a shame" if the show never made it to the air. Terming the effort "excellent," the reviewer cited crisp writing, fast-moving plots and "great characterizations from a fine group of actors."

In an old time radio club's newsletter published in the mid 1990s, researcher Jack French revealed some enlightening discoveries about the origins of the central figure (Sergeant David King) in the twin radio series. Stephen Slesinger, a U.S. promoter of newspaper comic strips (instrumental in introducing *Red Ryder* in an illustrated form), noted that *The Toronto Telegram* was dropping its "Men of the Mounted" cartoon. That strip had appeared in Canadian newspapers from Feb. 13, 1933, to Feb. 16, 1935, and featured several red-coated heroes, one of them a Corporal King. "Slesinger obtained the rights to it, promoted King to sergeant, hired Allen Dean to draw the strip and paid Zane Grey for the rights to put his name on the top of the title (e.g. *Zane Grey's King of the Royal Mounted*)," French observed. "To encourage Grey to do this, Slesinger hired Grey's son, Romer, to script the story."

The strip was published in U.S. newspapers for the next 20 years, to 1955, daily and/or Sundays. In the process it spawned a Dell comic book series, a hard cover novel from Whitman Publishing, some Big Little Books and the pair of similarly named radio features. (A modern reviewer, Al Hubin, discerned that the radio series repeatedly pushed Zane Grey's stories down the throats of listeners. Pronouncements admonished them to buy his work in book, film and comic strip forms.)

The series at last made it to the small and large screens.

Between 1955 and 1958 there was a syndicated TV feature. That followed two theatrical productions. *King of the Royal Mounted* was first, released in 1936. Directed by Howard Bretherton, the writing credits were garnered by Zane Grey and Earle Snell. Sergeant King was played by

Robert Kent with a long line of forgotten names alongside him. In 1940 a 12-chapter serialized *King of the Royal Mounted* was released to cinemas. Directed by John English and William Witney with screenplay by Franklin Adreon, the production starred Allan Lane as Sergeant Dave King. The remainder of the cast was also less than memorable.

King of the Royal Mounties

On the Air: c1942–45. 30 minutes.
Sponsor: No information.
Extant Episodes: Four.

CAST & CREDITS

Music—Al Sack (orchestra and male chorus).
Lead—Title role of Sergeant David King played by Richard Dix.

This was one of two radio series with similar monikers and native to the same era and heritage. (For a fuller description of how the dual series were conceived, see the detail under the previous entry, *King of the Royal Mounted.*) The *Mounties* series opened with a male chorus giving a robust rendition of *Stouthearted Men* from Sigmund Romberg's *New Moon*. It was followed by the dramatic action in which the Mountie, Sergeant David King, pursued his prey.

Hollywood actor Richard Dix (1894–1949) was born Ernest Carlton Brimmer in Minnesota. He played King as a smiling, robust redcoat, said one theorist who observed that King was fond of emoting such glib lines as: "Just a few winks and I'll be back in the pink!"

Kitty Keene see Kitty Keene, Incorporated

Kitty Keene, Incorporated

(aka *Kitty Keene*)

On the Air: Sept. 13–Dec. 31, 1937, CBS, Weekdays, time unsubstantiated; May 30, 1938–May 31, 1940, MBS, Weekdays, 8:30 a.m.; Oct. 28, 1940–April 25, 1941, MBS, 8:45 a.m. 15 minutes.
Theme Song: *None but the Lonely Heart* (Tchaikovsky).
Sponsor: Procter & Gamble Co. for Dreft dishwashing detergent.
Extant Episodes: Four.

CAST & CREDITS

Creator—Wally Norman.
Producers—George Fogle, Anne Hummert, Frank Hummert, Alan Wallace.
Directors—Win Orr, Roy Winsor.
Writers—Lester Huntley, Day Keene, Wally Norman.
Announcers—Jack Brinkley, Dan Donaldson.
Lead—Title role played by Fran Carlon, Gail Henshaw, Beverly Younger.
Support Roles—Bob Bailey, Dick Wells (Bob Jones); Dorothy Gregory, Janet Logan (Jill Jones); Bill Bouchey, Ken Griffin, Carlton KaDell (Charles Williams); plus Cheer Brentson (Leddy Fowley), Herb Butterfield (Preacher Jim), Patricia Dunlap, Louise Fitch (Anna Hajek), Josephine Gilbert (Miss Branch), Chuck Grant (Buzzer Williams), Chuck Harris, Stanley Harris (Neil Perry), Peggy Hillias (Clara Lund), Ginger Jones (Dimples), Ian Keith (Humphrey Manners), Janet Logan, Phil Lord (Jefferson Fowley), Angeline Orr (Norma Vernack), Mary Patton, Loretta Poynton (Pearl Davis).

Kitty Keene was an ambiguous female. Having been in the chorus line of the Ziegfeld Follies, precious little else is known about her background. She was the wife of Bob Jones and they had a daughter, Jill. Professionally, Keene operated a detective agency to which she lent her maiden name. A critic labeled her "an honest-to-bubbles female detective." But regretfully, her fight for happiness was limited almost to the crises she encountered every day involving her husband and daughter; seldom did they involve her clients. The job and its accouterments, then, were hardly more than a ruse. With the moguls of melodrama—Frank and Anne Hummert—calling most of the off-microphone shots, could anyone have expected more?

In 1971 Raymond William Stedman wrote: "After the appearance of [The Romance of] Helen Trent, no serial motif was more in evidence than that featuring a woman alone against the world, be she married, single, divorced, or widowed." Into this category he put several of the daytime radio heroines who were introduced in the late 1930s, including Kitty Keene. He also noted that most of them were single and that housewives weren't interested in keeping company with "the never-married heroine ... [she was] simply a poor risk as a daytime-serial protagonist." Several of the dramas Stedman cited left the air after only brief on-air stints.

Lady in Blue

On the Air: May 5–Dec. 8, 1951, NBC, Saturday, 8:30 a.m. 15 minutes.
Sponsor: No information.
Extant Episodes: Two.

CAST & CREDITS
No information.

Pitched to adolescents, this series' central figure was a striking, well-to-do woman who sallied from her penthouse apartment to reduce crime. Inevitably she was garbed in an azure mask and dress and heavily laden with sapphires. "The plotting was childish," wrote a critic. Her identity was intended to be kept top secret, but the po-

lice, crime victims and cab drivers—in fact, *everybody*—knew where she lived. In her own beleaguered way Harriet Higgins, her maid, attempted to assist the Lady in Blue in her escapades.

One radiophile, who downloaded the available episodes from the Internet, said he "listened to about the first five minutes of one episode, which struck me as so very very bad (and I'm not talking about the sound quality) that I couldn't bring myself to listen to the rest."

Meanwhile, a specialist in juvenile radio series, Jack French, suggested that *Lady in Blue* was probably adapted from a character named Lady Luck in a comic strip. She was an attractive socialite who fought criminals while attired in a green veil and green dress. The emerald-clad heroine attracted enough attention in Sunday supplements to warrant her own comic book (in December 1949), but that was suspended after only five issues. "While it can't be proven that she was the inspiration for *Lady in Blue*," noted French, "the resemblance is undeniable."

Lady of the Press, Sandra Martin see *The Story of Sandra Martin*

Latitude Zero

On the Air: Feb. 11–May 27, 1941, NBC West Coast Network, Tuesday; June 7–Aug. 30, 1941, NBC, Saturday, 8 p.m.; Sept. 6–Sept. 27, 1941, NBC, Saturday, 10:30 p.m. 30 minutes.
Sponsor: Sustained.
Extant Episodes: Two.

CAST & CREDITS
Writers—Ann Sherdeman, Ted Sherdeman.
Lead—Lou Merrill as Captain Craig McKenzie.

Support Roles—Charlie Lung (Simba), Ed Max (Bert Collins), Bruce Payne (Captain Brock Spencer), Anne Stone (Lucretia), Jack Zoller (Tibbs Canard).

Presented as "a story of five men against the world—heroic men with ideals and courage and strength to fight for them in Latitude Zero," these science-fiction tales focused on the awful human creatures inhabiting the treacherous zones beneath the surface of the sea. An amazingly indefatigable Captain Craig McKenzie, an alien—commander of a submarine (the *Omega*) from Latitude Zero—was their fearless leader. He fashioned the sub in the unknown port in 1805, some 136 years earlier, fueling speculation that by then he might be 200 years old. A six-foot, five-inch black bodyguard, Simba, who possessed enormous strength and was capable of taking on multiple vengeful thugs at once, shadowed McKenzie's every move. Assisting with McKenzie's missions for peace and freedom were the skipper of the Hope, a small fishing vessel in the Bering Sea, Captain Brock Spencer. A two-man crew of Tibbs Canard and Bert Collins accompanied him. Together they made a formidable quintet in their serialized battles against the wicked Lucretia and Moloch, a couple of dastardly evildoers with whom they fought relentlessly in the subterranean sea. The opening billboard assured listeners that they had tuned in to "the most exciting and fabulous adventure story you've ever heard." Its images were unparalleled for an exciting narrative on the air in that period, and established an atypical realism for its day.

Latitude Zero was "the first serious attempt to break the science fiction story out of the category of juvenile entertainment," according to one radio critic. Regretfully, the network gave the series short shrift, leading the reviewer to add: "It was remarkable in many ways, deserving of a better run than its one partial season."

Law West of the Pecos

On the Air: 1944. (No additional information substantiated.)
Sponsor: No information.
Extant Episodes: One.

CAST & CREDITS

Music—Wilbur Hatch (orchestra).
Announcer—Fort Pearson.
Leads—Judge Roy Bean, played by Walter Brennan; Buck, played by Andy Devine; Jim Grant (the Pecos Kid), played by Lou Crosby.

Judge Roy Bean of Vinegar Roan held high court in his own saloon for "killin', thievin' and other such fracas" for—as he assured listeners in the opening billboard—"I'm the law out west of the Pecos" (referring to the Pecos River in southwest Texas). An announcer added that the series was "a thrilling new radio program recalling the rough and tumble life of the old West as it was really lived." The story was presented in a weekly installment format, setting Jim Grant, aka the Pecos Kid, against Judge Roy Bean. Bean went after the Kid who "dared to defy his strange brand of justice."

As only the audition tape is known to exist, it's possible this show never made it past its initial broadcast on Feb. 3, 1944, although that hasn't been verified in any conclusive way.

Leonidas Witherall see The Adventures of Leonidas Witherall

Let George Do It

On the Air: Oct. 18, 1946–1954, MBS West Coast-Don Lee Network, Friday, then Monday (c1948), 8 p.m.; transcribed repeats Jan.

20, 1954–Jan. 12, 1955, in New York City only, Wednesday, 9:30 p.m. 30 minutes.

Sponsor: Standard Oil Co. of California for Chevron and Standard service stations throughout the West during the original years on MBS West Coast-Don Lee Network; otherwise unknown.

Extant Episodes: 199.

CAST & CREDITS

Producers—Owen Vinson, Pauline Vinson.
Director—Don Clark.
Writers—Jackson Gillis, Polly Hopkins, David Victor.
Music—Charles "Bud" Dant, Eddie Dunstedter (organ).
Announcers—John Easton, John Hiestand.
Leads—Title role of George Valentine played by Bob Bailey, Olan Soule (c1954); Brooksie, played by Lillian Buyeff, Virginia Gregg, Shirley Mitchell, Frances Robinson; Sonny, played by Eddie Firestone Jr.; Caleb, played by Joseph Kearns; Lieutenant Riley, played by Wally Maher.
Support Roles—Ed Begley, Howard McNear, Horace Murphy, Frances Robinson.

Ex-cop turned private eye George Valentine maintained a fifth floor office on Manhattan Island. In his early years on the air he soft-pedaled muscle, instead placing his optimism and confidence in his mental dexterity. Eventually he evolved into a tough, gutsy investigator with a nose for trouble and a reputation that coincided. Valentine didn't work alone—the animated, audacious P. I. surrounded himself with a trio of figures that allowed him to dialog about his current cases: his secretary, Clair Brooks, ("Brooksie," he called her); office boy Sonny Brooks, Brooksie's younger sibling; and an elevator operator with a single name, Caleb.

Brooksie's ambiguous relationship with Valentine was never clearly defined—she was something more than a "girl Friday," which permitted her to accompany him on business and pleasure trips while gathering critical data to help him solve cases. While Valentine had no partner or associate as did some of his peers, Brooksie aptly filled the bill. The question of any romantic entanglement was chiefly left to the fans' imaginations, although Brooksie acquired something of a distinct "man-chasing" aura in the latter chapters.

Normally Valentine enlisted his clients by way of inquiries that they made into a classified ad he had submitted to the local tabloid, adapted as the opening lines of the weekly series: "Personal notice. Danger is my stock in trade. If the job's too tough for you to handle, you've got a job for me. George Valentine." The promo provided enough murders and misdemeanors to intrigue listeners and turn them into avid fans for several years, even though his escapades never made it to the ears of a national audience.

Surveying a list of feminine confederates and confidantes attached to radio's private eyes, including Brooksie, author Gerald Nachman offered this assessment of the group: "None of these sidekicks did a whole lot of typing, but they could plug a gangster at a hundred feet, were always available for hair-raising assignments, had witty rejoinders, and sounded incredibly stylish. It was easy to be seduced by these older Real Women, whose knowing repartee dripped with what even a twelve-year-old boy recognized as innuendo. (Aural sex, you could call it.)"

A Life in Your Hands

On the Air: June 7–Sept. 13, 1949, NBC, Tuesday, 10:30 p.m.; June 27–Sept. 12, 1950, NBC, Tuesday, 10:30 p.m.; June 29–Sept. 21, 1951, ABC, Friday, 9 p.m.; July 10–Aug. 21, 1952, NBC, Thursday, 8 p.m. 30 minutes.

Sponsors: Brown & Williamson Tobacco Co. for Raleigh cigarettes (June 7, 1949–Sept. 12, 1950); H. J. Heinz Co. for a wide line of foodstuffs (June 29–Sept. 21, 1951); Sustained (July 10–Aug. 21, 1952).

Extant Episodes: 14.

CAST & CREDITS

Producer/Directors—John Cowan, Homer Heck, Patrick Murphy, Jack Simpson.
Writers—Doug Johnson, Billie McKee, Bob McKee.
Music—Bernard (Whitey) Berquist, Adele Scott.
Announcer—Ken Nordine.
Narrators—Carlton KaDell, Myron (Mike) Wallace.
Lead—Jonathan Kegg, played by Lee Bowman (1951), Carlton KaDell (1950, 1952), Ned LeFevre (1949).
Support Roles—Boris Aplon, Marianne Berthrand, Maurice Copeland, Everett Clark, Harry Eders, Carl Grayson, Art Hern, Geraldine Kaye, Ed Prentiss, Beverly Younger.

This was an unusual series created by Erle Stanley Gardner who then washed his hands of it. When fairness was in jeopardy during criminal proceedings at the hall of justice, Jonathan Kegg was called in. Kegg's role was as an *amicus curiae*—friend of the court—not a party to the litigation in progress, yet possessing expertise that was useful in helping the legal minds, acting as a disinterested third party on matters related to a given case. The affluent Kegg had been a seasoned attorney prior to his retirement from the profession. Without bias, he would register his opinions, often interrogating those who had testified during a trial, in an effort to determine the truth and render an appropriate verdict. In his own way, then, Kegg fought crime in a unique manner that most citizens would have seldom contemplated.

This series was limited exclusively to a summer replacement and never given the opportunity to become a season-long drama. It supplanted *People Are Funny* in its first two years, and was followed in order by *The Adventures of Ozzie and Harriet* and *Father Knows Best*.

Lightning Jim

On the Air: 1940s, West Coast only; 1950s, Syndicated.
Sponsor: Commercials added in local markets.
Extant Episodes: 42.

CAST & CREDITS

Leads—Title role of Jim Whipple played by Francis X. Bushman; Whitey Larson, played by Henry Hoople.

This yarn related tales of the adventures of U.S. marshal Lightning Jim Whipple and his deputy, Whitey Larson, in a never-ending chase to remove bad guys from the dusty trails of the old West. Cattle rustlers, murderers, arsonists, renegade Indians, kidnappers, stagecoach thieves, vigilante committees, smugglers, jailbreakers, horse thieves, train robbers, claim jumpers, Pony Express crooks, army deserters, bank bandits, a feminine gang leader and more were among the desperadoes Whipple and Larson faced on the American frontier as part of an ongoing quest to rid the territory of undesirables. The pair even came into contact with the legendary Wild Bill Hickok at least once, and on another occasion the notorious bank-robbing James brothers.

Whitman Publishing Co. of Racine, Wis.', produced at least a single volume, *Lightning Jim: U. S. Marshal Brings Law to the West*, "Based on the Famous Radio Program," c1940s–1950s. The release was included among Whitman's vast repertoire of illustrated pulp fiction tales known as Better Little Books, successor to the firm's Big Little Books series that was launched in 1932 with a highly successful *The Adventures of Dick Tracy, Detective*.

The Line Up

On the Air: July 6–Aug. 24, 1950, CBS, Thursday, 8 p.m.; Sept. 9–Sept. 23, 1950, CBS, Saturday, 8:30 p.m.; Sept. 28,

1950–March 1, 1951, CBS, Thursday, 10 p.m.; March 6–July 3, 1951, CBS, Tuesday, 10 p.m.; July 12–Aug. 23, 1951, CBS, Thursday, 9 p.m.; Sept. 5–Sept. 26, 1951, CBS, Wednesday, 9 p.m.; Oct. 4–Nov. 29, 1951, CBS, Thursday, 10 p.m.; Jan. 8–May 27, 1952, CBS, Tuesday, 10 p.m.; June 3–Aug. 5, 1952, CBS, Tuesday, 9 p.m.; Sept. 10–Dec. 24, 1952, CBS, Wednesday, 10 p.m.; Dec. 26, 1952–Feb. 20, 1953, CBS, Friday, 9:30 p.m. 30 minutes.

Sponsor: Sustained (most episodes, except) William J. Wrigley Co. for its chewing gum brands (some winter, spring, summer 1952 episodes), and the Chrysler Corp. for Plymouth automobiles (some autumn 1952 shows).

Extant Episodes: 61.

CAST & CREDITS

Producers/Directors—Elliott Lewis, Jaime del Valle (c1951).

Writers—Blake Edwards, Morton Fine, David Friedkin, David Light, Sidney Marshall, Jack Newman.

Music—Eddie Dunstedter (organ).

Sound Effects—David Light.

Announcer—Dan Cubberly.

Leads—Lieutenant Ben Guthrie, played by Bill Johnstone; Sergeant Matt Grebb, played by Joseph Kearns, Wally Maher (c1951); Sergeant Peter Carter, played by John McIntire, Jack Moyles.

Support Roles—Hy Averback, Ed Begley, Raymond Burr, Walter Catlett, Sam Edwards, Sheldon Leonard, Howard McNear, Jeanette Nolan, David Young.

The police headquarters of "a great American city" (never identified, though traced by some exponents to San Francisco, site of a subsequent televersion) was at the apex of this gritty crime narrative. Lieutenant Ben Guthrie, assisted by plainclothes detective sergeants Matt Grebb and Peter Carter, were on the cutting edge of ushering in a new breed of realism in audio police drama. For the first time radio listeners were presented with brutal dimensions of criminal activity like strangling an elderly spinster, muggings, contract murders, attacks on police officers and bombings at the homes of people in the public eye. In *The Line Up*, "Under the cold, glaring lights pass the innocent, the vagrant, the thief, the murderer," fans were alerted at the start of each episode. Speaking in measured tones, officer Grebb gave the following calculated discourse:

> May I have your attention, please? You people on the other side of the wire out there in the audience room, may I have your attention, please? Thank you. My name is Grebb. Sergeant Matt Grebb. I'll explain the line up to you. Each of the suspects you will see will be numbered. I'll call off the number, their name and charge. If you have any questions or identifications, please remember the number assigned to the prisoner as I call his name. At the end of each line when I ask for questions or identifications, call out the number. If you're sure or not too sure of the suspect, have him held…. The questions I ask these suspects are merely to get a natural tone of voice, so do not pay too much attention to their answers, as they often lie. All right, bring on the line.

The same speech was recited a second time on each show during the close, fading under the theme. It was Guthrie's assignment to investigate and solve the cases in which perpetrators appeared in a line up to be recognized by victims and witnesses of their alleged criminal activities. Following cross-examination, the program pursued the step-by-step procedures one might anticipate to advance the case to a just end. The radio adaptations were purportedly purely fictional.

The inauguration of several sophisticated detective series in the late 1940s and early 1950s introduced a programming trend that was unfamiliar to radio listeners. Police dramas like *Broadway Is My*

Beat with Anthony Ross as Detective Danny Clover (1949–54); *Dragnet* starring Jack Webb as detective Sergeant Joe Friday (1949–57); *The Line Up* featuring Bill Johnstone as police lieutenant Ben Guthrie (1950–53); and *Twenty-First Precinct*—including Everett Sloane, James Gregory and Les Damon at varying times as Captain Frank Kennelly (1953–56)—were instructive, albeit foreboding productions giving their listeners straightforward, though dismal, examinations of law enforcement in metropolitan settings. While earlier audio detectives appeared to demonstrate integrity and respect in their quest to right civil wrongs, the sleuths of the neo-realistic era flaunted a kind of halting crudeness themselves. Persistently drawn into conflict, they functioned in a vacuum created by social failure and criminal behavior. In doing so they clearly performed their tasks in mechanical, often repetitious fashion.

Nontraditional themes were inserted into the story lines of these dramas. On *Broadway Is My Beat*, anti-Semitism and juvenile delinquency were addressed. Abandoned kids, children running from home, drug addiction and female juveniles posing for pornography turned up in *Dragnet* tales. Attacks on police officers, contract murders, muggings, strangling the elderly and political retribution were typical fare on *Twenty-First Precinct* and *The Line Up*. None of these topics would have been covered in depth on most crime series before this time.

The Line Up, a Desilu production, arrived on CBS-TV on Oct. 1, 1954, and continued there through Jan. 20, 1960. For five years it was a half-hour Friday night staple at 10 o'clock. In its final season it became a Wednesday night hour-long entry at 7:30. Repeats were then circulated to local stations under the banner *San Francisco Beat*. Warner Anderson appeared as Lieutenant Ben Guthrie and Tom Tully as Inspector Matt Grebb. They were soon joined by Marshall Reed as Inspector Fred Asher. In a final few months on the tube Tully and Reed departed and four new police officers were added—Rachel Ames as policewoman Sandy McAllister, Tod Burton as Inspector Charlie Summers, William Leslie as Inspector Dan Delaney and Skip Ward as Officer Pete Larkins. Unlike its radio counterpart, where the stories were mythical creations, the televised version presented actual cases from the files of the San Francisco Police Department.

The Lion's Eye see *Jeff Regan, Investigator*

The Lone Ranger

On the Air: Jan. 31, 1933, originating with Detroit's WXYZ and beamed to seven more outlets of a newly formed Michigan Radio Network, Tuesday/Thursday/Saturday, 9 p.m.; in January 1934 three more powerful outlets signed up (Chicago's WGN, New York's WOR, Cincinnati's WLW), forming the nucleus of the Mutual Broadcasting System, which adopted *The Lone Ranger* as its flagship series from 1934, and shifting the series to Monday/Wednesday/Friday evenings, feeding it to the West Coast via the Don Lee Network in 1937 and to the Northeast that same year via Colonial and Yankee networks; Feb. 13, 1939–May 1, 1942, MBS, Monday/Wednesday/Friday, 7:30 p.m.; May 4–Oct. 30, 1942, NBC Blue, Monday/Wednesday/Friday, 6 p.m.; Nov. 2, 1942–Sept. 3, 1954, NBC Blue with name change to ABC in mid 1940s, Monday/Wednesday/Friday, 7:30 p.m.; Sept. 6, 1954–May 27, 1955, ABC, Monday/Wednesday/Friday, 7:30 p.m.; May 30, 1955–May 25, 1956, NBC, Weekdays, 5:30 p.m. New episodes ended Sept. 3, 1954, with transcribed repeats aired through May 25, 1956. 30 minutes through Nov. 28, 1952; 25-minute episodes aired Dec. 1, 1952–May 25, 1956.

Theme Song: *The William Tell Overture* (Gioacchino Rossini).

Sponsors: Sustained (Jan. 31–Nov. 27, 1933); Silvercup bread (Nov. 29, 1933–Feb. 10, 1939); Bond bread (Feb. 13, 1939–Aug. 9, 1940); General Mills Inc. for Cheerios cereal (c May 1941–May 25, 1956). Not all areas broadcast the commercials for these concerns—regional bakeries were often underwriters, including Merita bread in the South, Gingham bread in the West and Silvercup bread elsewhere through Feb. 10, 1939. During the General Mills years Merita continued to sponsor the program in markets in the South.

Extant Episodes: In excess of 1,050 originals plus 410 repeat shows (1954–56).

Cast & Credits

Executive Producer—George W. Trendle.
Producer—James Jewell.
Directors—Al Hodge, James Jewell, Charles D. Livingstone, Ted Robertson.
Writers—Dan Beattie, Leo Boulette, Tom Dougall, Gibson Scott Fox, Ralph Goll, Bob Green, Felix Holt, James Jewell, Betty Joyce, Steve McCarthy, Bob Shaw, Shelly Stark, Fran Striker (head writer/story editor).
Sound Effects—Tony Caminito, Dewey Cole, Bert Djerkiss, Jimmy Fletcher, Fred Flowerday, Fred Fry, Bill Hengsterbeck, Ken Robertson, Ernie Winstanley.
Announcers—Brace Beemer, Fred Foy, Harry Golder, Bob Hite, Harold True, Charles Wood.
Leads—Title role played by George Stenius, pseudonym for George Seaton (Jan. 31–May 9, 1933), Jack Deeds (May 11, 1933), James Jewell (May 13, 1933), Earl Graser (May 16, 1933–April 7, 1941), Brace Beemer (April 18, 1941–May 25, 1956); Tonto, played by John Todd (full run).
Support Roles—Lee Allman, Elaine Alpert (Clarabell Hornblow, a citizen the Lone Ranger often relied upon); Dick Beals, James Lipton and Ernie Winstanley (Dan Reid, nephew of The Lone Ranger); Paul Hughes (Thunder Martin, friend of The Lone Ranger, and in scores of parts as haughty Army colonels and lawbreakers);

Jay Michael (Butch Cavendish, nemesis to the Lone Ranger); plus Bertha Forman, John Hodiak, Amos Jacobs (pseudonym for Danny Thomas), Ted Johnstone, Beatrice Leiblee, Bob Maxwell, Herschel Mayall, Jack McCarthy, Malcolm McCoy, Mel Palmer, Rollon Parker, Jack Petruzzi, Ruth Dean Rickaby, Fred Rito, Frank Russell, Bill Saunders, Ernie Stanley.

Without any embellishment, this giant of the airwaves was destined to become a drama of epic proportions. *The Lone Ranger* was the bedrock upon which a radio production empire sprang. Conceived in the mind of George W. Trendle, the mythical knight on a shining white steed replaced criminal activity with justice as the Lone Ranger and a faithful Indian companion, Tonto, spread peace to the settlers of the old West. Theirs was the genesis play of a line of so-called adolescent tales that included *The Green Hornet* (1938–52) and *The Challenge of the Yukon* (1947–55). (This trio of adventures was beamed across North America from the tower of Detroit's WXYZ, a CBS station originating as WGHP where Trendle became managing partner in 1930. By 1934 the operation was instrumental in forming the Mutual Broadcasting System.)

Sensing enormous promise, and having in place a radio repertory company and a large musical library, Trendle led his station to pursue the route of independency in 1932, generating its own programming. Fran Striker, a writer then living in Buffalo, New York, came to Trendle's attention at about that time. Trendle shared with Striker an inspiration he had envisioned previously: to develop a fictional narrative of the Western plains that would center on a do-good figure that would be admired by people far and wide.

It was the start of a personal relationship that was to continue for decades, resulting in the character that would represent the antithesis of greed and hate as

The Lone Ranger: A Boy Scout pins on one of the numerous awards actor Brace Beemer received for his sterling portrayal of the Lone Ranger. Truly, nowhere in the pages of history could one find a greater champion of justice. For generations this unblemished, heroic character was an idol to legions of American youngsters who profited from his examples of unshakable integrity in many diverse situations.

early Americans advanced westward. Their hero became, in millions of homes across the land, a symbol of righteousness representing moral and ethical decency toward which every individual—young and old—might aspire. While some would randomly label the series as juvenile-oriented, a proportional sector of its audience would always be adults—people of all ages, really—who were transfixed as easily as preteens by the magnitude of its unblemished heroic character.

The Lone Ranger burst onto the air to the theme of Rossini's *William Tell Overture*, a composition that the narrative soon came to immortalize. To this day anyone who followed the program on the air (on radio or television), on hearing that music, cannot help but recall the masked man—who traveled incognito to facilitate his honorable pursuits, riding the white stallion Silver as the music resounded—or the stirring words of its narrator: "Nowhere in the pages of history can one find a greater champion of justice. Return with us now to those thrilling days of yesteryear. From out of the paths come the thundering hoofbeats of the great horse Silver! The Lone Ranger rides again!" That epigraph was followed by the ranger's shout: "Let's go big fella! Hi-Yo, Silver! Hiiiiii!" And sidekick Tonto then commanded his own mount: "Getumup, Scout!" (Tonto addressed the Lone Ranger as "Kemosabay," believed to signify "Trusted Friend.") The formidable pair rode against lawlessness thrice weekly, playing to 12 million listeners every week.

Reportedly working 14 hours daily for six days a week, author Striker not only turned out 156 scripts annually but also 365 daily comic strips as well as a dozen juvenile novels while reigning over 30 episodes of a couple of *Lone Ranger* movie serials. "Trendle and Striker deserve some kind of posthumous literary recognition for their inspired creation," one sage protested.

At last the durable tale vanished from the air as suddenly as it had appeared. In its wake it left a generation of adventurers imbued with noble ideals that profoundly contributed to the moral fiber of a nation. At the same time, they were left wondering what had become of the masked man to whom they had sworn their absolute allegiance.

The voice of Brace Beemer, formerly an announcer for this series, who stepped in to fill the void when Earl Graser died in a traffic accident in 1941, is readily recalled by millions of fans as *the* Lone Ranger. (Beemer was also cast in the role of Sergeant Preston in *The Challenge of the Yukon* during that series' final season on the air, ending June 9, 1955. It extended his opportunity to use those widely recognized, authoritative intonations in an adventure tale.) The WXYZ repertory company, with a contingent of well-trained radio actors, routinely appeared in the plots of all three of that station's major celebrated dramas. Home audiences instantly identified many of their vocal inflections.

The first Lone Ranger theatrical serial was made by Republic in 1938 under the co-direction of William Witney and John English. Billy Bletcher portrayed the ranger and an actor named Chief Thundercloud appeared as Tonto. A second serial, *The Lone Ranger Rides Again*, was issued by Republic in 1939. Robert Livingstone and Chief Thundercloud portrayed the masked man and his Indian companion, respectively. Republic released an edited full-length feature version of the initial serial that same year under the banner *Hi-Yo Silver*. There were to be no more Lone Ranger films for a full decade, until a TV series premiered in late 1949.

The Lone Ranger debuted on ABC-TV on Sept. 15, 1949, in Thursday night episodes that extended through Sept. 12, 1957. When the A. C. Nielsen Co., a national ratings service, began compiling its nationwide viewer statistics in 1950, *The Lone Ranger* was the only ABC-TV entry to find its way into the top 15 programs. Clayton Moore starred in 221 half-hours with John Hart featured as the hero in 26 episodes between 1951 and 1953. Jay Silverheels, a poker-faced, mixed-blood Mohawk Native American, appeared as Tonto throughout the TV run. The radio series' announcer, Fred Foy, narrated the televersion. After it left the tube, Moore made personal appearances as the Lone Ranger. In 1970 a subsidiary of the Wrather Corp., Lone Ranger Television, Inc., obtained a court injunction forbidding Moore from wearing his mask in public. Wrather had produced a feature film in which another actor appeared in the lead. By 1985, however, Moore won a legal challenge and was once again granted the privilege of freely wearing the mask.

Reruns of the original series aired over CBS-TV during the daytime on Saturdays from June 1953 to September 1960. From 1960–61 repeats were carried by NBC-TV in Saturday daytime. Reruns were screened on ABC-TV Sunday afternoons from 1957 to 1960 and on that network Wednesday afternoons from 1960–61.

An animated rendering titled *The Lone Ranger* appeared on CBS-TV between Sept. 10, 1966, and Sept. 6, 1969. Michael Rye read the hero's part while Shep Menken spoke Tonto's lines. Even dignified actress Agnes Moorehead turned up to read the role of the Black Widow, one of the characters the ranger encountered in that illustrated adaptation.

CBS-TV aired a couple of subsequent cartoon series in which the masked man (voiced by William Conrad) was combined with other popular comic characters: *The Tarzan/Lone Ranger Adventure Hour*, Sept. 13, 1980, through Sept. 5, 1981, and *The Tarzan/Lone Ranger/Zorro Adventure Hour*, Sept. 12, 1981, through Sept. 11, 1982.

Additional theatrical productions featuring the masked man and his faithful companion appeared in 1952 (*The Legend of the Lone Ranger*), 1956 (*The Lone Ranger*), 1958 (*The Lone Ranger and the Lost City of Gold*), 1961 (*Return of the Lone Ranger*) and 1981 (*The Legend of the Lone Ranger*). One reviewer, praising the competence of Michael Horse as Tonto in the 1981 feature-length film, was unforgiving in panning youthful actor Klinton Spilsbury's rendering of the superhero, branding him "unaccepable." Said the critic: "His ineffectual voice was dubbed by Jim Keach.... when he [Spilsbury] put on the tight-fitting shirt of the Lone Ranger ... he looked too limp and wasp-waisted to get the job done.... At one *Legend* showing, when at the end of the movie President Grant (Jason Robards) wonders 'Who was that masked man?' a theater patron yelled out, 'Well, it sure as hell wasn't the Lone Ranger!'" It was to be Spilsbury's first and last acting job on the big screen— and he never performed on the small one.

That portrayal was a far cry from TV's Clayton Moore, and still further from Brace Beemer, who was firmly entrenched in the American psyche four decades earlier as *the* ranger. Legions of die-hard fans still insist that no man before or after Beemer ever superseded his commanding portrayal. The famous actor died at Lake Orion, Michigan, on Feb. 28, 1965. He was about 62.

Warner Brothers, which owns its own cable TV network, announced in late 2001 that it would produce a new two-hour pilot film featuring The Lone Ranger for screening in 2002. Early speculation indicated that—if the project met with widespread public acceptance—it could possibly result in a new continuing video series or additional sporadic attempts on small screens that recalled the famous masked rider of the plains.

For an insightful appraisal, leading to a deeper appreciation and understanding of this series' impact, the reader is directed to John Dunning's *On the Air: The Encyclopedia of Old-Time Radio*. An extensive treatise on *The Lone Ranger* awaits the reflective researcher. Dunning places in perspective the magnitude of this drama on American thought and life in the epoch in which it appeared. He is also sensitive to the ample broadcasting achievements of the individuals who contributed to the landmark series.

Not to be missed for absorbing detail on the early beginnings of the narrative is *The Lone Ranger* chapter in Jim Harmon's discerning volume *Radio Mystery and Adventure and Its Appearances in Film, Television and Other Media*. The author gives attention to a wide range of associated premiums (badges, bandanas, belts, billfolds, masks, guns, rings, et cetera ad infinitum) proffered over the air, as well as newspaper comic strips and novels based on the famous masked champion of justice in the early American West.

The Lone Wolf

On the Air: June 29–Aug. 24, 1948, MBS, Tuesday, 9:30 p.m.; Dec. 4, 1948–Jan. 1, 1949, MBS, Saturday, 2 p.m. 30 minutes.
Sponsor: Sustained.
Extant Episodes: One.

CAST & CREDITS

Producer—Frank Danzig.
Director—Larry Hays.
Writer—Louis Vittes.
Music—Rex Koury (organ).
Announcers—Bob Anderson, Dick Winn.
Leads—Michael Lanyard, played by Gerald Mohr, Walter Coy; Jameson (Lanyard's butler), played by Jay Novello.
Support Role—Dick Aurandt.

Michael Lanyard, tall, single, dashingly debonair, was a reformed jewel thief-turned-private eye whose good looks lured

him into frequent cavorting with young women. An eye-catching female facing difficulties was a perpetual turn-on for Lanyard, even while admitting that such a creature usually spelled trouble for him. Renowned for solitary sleuthing, he was branded as a "lone wolf." When he wasn't up to his neck in corpses, Lanyard frequently imbibed highballs at a favorite watering hole, the Silver Seashell Bar and Grill. "It was more than a little reminiscent of another detective series, *The Falcon*," a radio historian noted. (Or possibly *Casey, Crime Photographer*? Casey wiled away untold hours gulping liquid refreshment at the Blue Note Café.) And although Lanyard abhorred brutality, he resorted to it when it became apparent that he had exhausted every other alternative. Unfortunately, he didn't have long to ply his craft as an audio gumshoe: He was inserted into the schedule as a summer replacement and given only a month's winter reprieve (14 performances total) before banishment from the airwaves—and all those beauties—forever.

This classic figure evolved from the published fiction of novelist Louis Joseph Vance.

A chain of mostly B movies was released over a 58-year time frame: *The Last of the Lone Wolf* (1930), *The Lone Wolf in Paris* (1938), *The Lone Wolf Meets a Lady* (1940), *The Lone Wolf Keeps a Date* (1941), *The Lone Wolf in London* (1947), *The Lone Wolf in Mexico* (1947), *The Lone Wolf and His Lady* (1949), *Lone Wolf McQuade* (1983) and *Lone Wolf* (1988).

A contingent of radio detectives operated as independent lone wolves, author Fred MacDonald confirmed. In addition to Lanyard, he included protagonists on *The Adventures of Philip Marlowe, Boston Blackie, The Falcon* and *The New Adventures of Michael Shayne*. "Although they may have flirted or conversed with incidental characters," wrote MacDonald, "they wandered through civilization unable to rest because justice was incomplete.... Ultimately they were all compelled to action. Free of restraint, save their inbred codes of justice and honor, these heroes alluringly embodied the desire of many in the audience to wander uninhibitedly." MacDonald continued: "Sex was another adventure vicariously experienced by listeners.... This was especially the case when virile and unattached young heroes of [such] programs ... were relating their stories." It was one of the behaviors Michael Lanyard demonstrated in nearly every chapter.

The Loser

On the Air: May 5–Aug. 4, 1955, NBC, Thursday, 9:30 p.m. 30 minutes.
Sponsor: Sustained.
Extant Episodes: 12.

CAST & CREDITS

Lead—Richard McGee.
No further identifications made public.

In this documentary on penal institutions and their residents, the overriding objective was to demonstrate to the public that crime doesn't pay. It began with this billboard over appropriate background din: "You are listening to *The Loser* and the sound of prisoners being locked up for the night. On this program you will hear the actual voice of the prisoner as he tells his crime story." The names were changed, of course, to protect the crooks; but these authentic narratives told in the first person would have made any God-fearing, law-abiding citizen do everything he or she could to stay out of the slammer.

Lucky Smith

On the Air: April 29–July 22, 1935, NBC, Monday, 10:30 p.m. 30 minutes.

Sponsor: The Gillette Co. for Gillette Blue Blades for men's razors.
Extant Episodes: None known.

CAST & CREDITS

Lead—Title role played by Max Baer.
Support Role—Peg La Centra.

The star of this brief detective series, Max Baer, was heavyweight boxing champion of the world at the time it debuted. To the show he lent not only the mystique surrounding him but the aura of his profession in a day in which prize-fighting was considered among the nation's chief forms of sports entertainment. Regrettably, little has been preserved about the 13-week private eye show in which he was featured.

In 1934 Baer starred in an NBC Blue series titled *Max Baer*. There he played a taxi driver hoping to become a boxer. At the close of each episode he appeared as himself, relaying his personal preparation for an upcoming bout with the current heavyweight champion, Primo Carnera. Baer took the title from Carnera; then he went on to become the lead in *Lucky Smith*. His new show created a contest in which winners received free transportation to New York City and tickets to a Baer-Braddock match. When Baer lost both the fight and the heavyweight title to underdog James J. Braddock, *Lucky Smith* was immediately dropped.

Luke Slaughter of Tombstone

On the Air: Feb. 23–June 15, 1958, CBS, Sunday, 2:05 p.m. 25 minutes.
Sponsor: Sustained.
Extant Episodes: 16.

CAST & CREDITS

Producer—Lucian Davis.
Director—William N. Robson.
Writers—Robert Stanley, Fran Van Hartesveldt.
Music—Wilbur Hatch (orchestra).

Leads—Title role played by Sam Buffington; Wichita Bagby, played by Junius Matthews; Clint Wallace, played by Charles Seel.
Support Role—Vic Perrin.

In the fading days of radio's golden age, this series appeared briefly—just 16 weeks—joining a line-up of adult westerns that the major networks introduced to their listeners in the 1950s. (For a while it shared the same hour with one of its contemporaries, *Frontier Gentleman*.) The protagonist in *Luke Slaughter* was a Civil War calvaryman who returned to Arizona in the postwar years to settle near the town of Tombstone. There he purchased a cattle ranching spread.

Slaughter was more than a mere cattleman, however. By the time his story unfolded in the 1880s, 15 or 20 years *after* the Civil War, he was firmly entrenched in the public's mind as a compelling political influence across the Grand Canyon State. He not only operated a prosperous commercial enterprise; friends and neighbors turned to him for answers in their times of crisis. As an amateur historian, Slaughter collected wanted posters and maintained a keen awareness of outlaws still running free. A man of honor, decency and moral justice, he probably spent more time tracking down lawbreakers than he did pursuing his core business.

Wichita Bagby, a ranch hand, was a sidekick to Slaughter. Together they worked as a team with the local sheriff, Clint Wallace, to clean up their portion of the West in order to make it a decent place for newcomers to settle.

The program's opening billboard postulated: "Slaughter's my name, Luke Slaughter. Cattle's my business. It's a tough business … it's a big business. I've got a big stake in it. There's no man west of the Rio Grande big enough to take it from me." And an announcer clarified: "His name was respected or feared—depending which side of the law you were on."

Jay Hickerson prepared a log for this series.

Major North, Army Intelligence see *The Man from G-2*

A Man Named Jordan see *Rocky Jordan*

Man Against Crime

On the Air: Oct. 7, 1949–Aug. 3, 1951, CBS, Friday, 8:30 p.m. 30 minutes.
Sponsor: No information.
Extant Episodes: None known.

CAST & CREDITS
Producer—Edward J. Montagne.
Director—Paul Nickell.
Writer—Lawrence Klee.
Lead—Mike Barnett, played by Ralph Bellamy; Pat Barnett (Mike's brother), played by Robert Preston (during Bellamy's absence in the summer of 1951).

Mike Barnett was a hardy private eye who operated out of the Big Apple. Unlike some peers who toted guns and possibly other weapons, he was unarmed as he valiantly pursued gangsters and other lawbreakers whom he encountered while aiding and abetting his clients. Working alone, Barnett applied brains and brawn where bullets might have been an answer for some contemporary gumshoes. Relying heavily upon his fists, Barnett nonetheless managed to pull off a frequently violent show. Yet his failure to carry firearms, in his opinion, worked for him at least as often as it might have worked against him.

The series had the distinction of premiering on both CBS Radio and CBS Television on the same night, and was simulcast live for 22 months. By comparison, few other dramas were broadcast live in dual mediums. Ralph Bellamy, who also played the video lead, took a summer vacation after June 22, 1951, a few weeks before the audio-only version was withdrawn. Robert Preston temporarily replaced Bellamy in the role. After the program faded from radio, Bellamy returned and continued with his TV part for two additional years. The show went to film in the autumn of 1952.

Following a four-year run on CBS-TV ending Oct. 2, 1953, the program shifted to not one but *two* networks: for six months, between Oct. 11, 1953, and April 4, 1954, it appeared at 10:30 p.m. Sundays on Dumont Television while from Oct. 18, 1953, through July 4, 1954, it was screened at the same hour on the same day on NBC-TV. After a two-year sabbatical, the feature returned to NBC-TV Sundays at 10 p.m. starting July 1, 1956, with Frank Lovejoy playing Mike Barnett. That summer replacement series lasted through Aug. 26, 1956. Under the banner *Follow That Man*, the show was circulated in syndication several more years.

For years *Man Against Crime* author Lawrence Klee had penned one of the great aural sleuths for the Frank and Anne Hummert factory of radio dramas, *Mr. Keen, Tracer of Lost Persons*. That series was on the air almost continuously between 1937 and 1955, although Klee did not become its chief dialoguer until the drama reached its zenith in the 1940s and early 1950s. Undoubtedly his experiences there prepared him to be a leading contender for the task of writing a new private eye narrative (*Man Against Crime*) to be aired in two media simultaneously. While still a young man, Klee died at the age of 42 on Jan. 1, 1957, only four months after the televersion ended.

The Man Called X

On the Air: July 10–Aug. 28, 1944, CBS, Monday, 9:30 p.m.; Sept. 9–Dec. 30, 1945, NBC Blue/ABC, Saturday, 10:30 p.m.; Jan. 6–March 3, 1945, ABC, Saturday, 10 p.m.; June 12–Sept. 4, 1945, NBC, Tuesday, 10 p.m.; June 18–Sept. 17, 1946, NBC, Tuesday, 10 p.m.; April 3–Oct. 16, 1947, CBS, Thursday, 10:30 p.m.; Nov. 2, 1947–Sept. 26, 1948, CBS, Sunday, 8:30 p.m.; Oct. 13–Nov. 3, 1950, NBC, Friday, 8:30 p.m.; Nov. 11, 1950, NBC, Saturday, 8 p.m.; Nov. 18, 1950–April 28, 1951, NBC, Saturday, 8:30 p.m.; May 4–July 13, 1951, NBC, Friday, 9:30 p.m.; July 20–Aug. 31, 1951, NBC, Friday, 8 p.m.; Sept. 7–Sept. 28, 1951, NBC, Friday, 9:30 p.m.; Oct. 1–Dec. 24, 1951, NBC, Monday, 10:30 p.m.; Jan. 1–May 20, 1952, NBC, Tuesday, 10:30 p.m. 30 minutes, except 25 minutes Nov. 2, 1947–June 13, 1948.

Sponsors: Lockheed Aircraft Corp. (July 10, 1944–March 3, 1945); Pepsodent toothpaste (June 12, 1945–Sept. 17, 1946); General Motors Corp. for Frigidaire appliances (April 3, 1947–Sept. 26, 1948); Multiple sponsorship, including Ford Motor Co. for its automobiles, Radio Corp. of America for its entertainment devices, American Home Products Corp. for its Whitehall Pharmacal Co.—makers of Anacin pain reliever and other drug products, Liggett & Myers Tobacco Co. for Chesterfield cigarettes (Oct. 13, 1950–July 13, 1951); Sustained (July 20, 1951–May 20, 1952).

Extant Episodes: 103.

Cast & Credits

Producer—Jack Richard Kennedy.
Directors—William N. Robson (1944), Jack Johnstone, Dee Engelbach (late run).
Writers—Sidney Marshall, Milton Merlin.
Music—Milton Charles, Johnny Green, Gordon Jenkins, Felix Mills, Claude Sweeten (orchestras).
Sound Effects—David Light, Wayne Kenworthy, Bud Tollefson.
Announcers—Jack Latham, John McIntire, Wendell Niles.
Leads—Ken Thurston, played by Herbert

Marshall; Pagan Zeldschmidt, played by Leon Belasco.

Support Roles—Joan Banks, William Conrad, Barbara Fuller, Harry Lang, Peter Leeds, Lou Merrill, George Niese, GeGe Pearson, B. J. Thompson, Stanley Waxman, Will Wright, Carleton Young.

"Wherever there is mystery, intrigue, romance in all the strange, dangerous places of the world, there you will find *The Man Called X*," an announcer recounted in introducing this intelligence agent series. Troubleshooter Ken Thurston was the agent, operating for America under the code name "X," and being sent to exotic spots on dangerous quests around the world. Listeners were informed that Thurston "crosses the ocean as readily as you and I cross town. He is the man who fights today's war in his unique fashion so that tomorrow's peace will make the world a safe neighborhood for all of us." His favorite retreat, in his own words, was the Café Tambourine in Cairo, Egypt.

Originally the program was to be an FBI adventure series but that all shifted when Thurston became a globetrotter. In his missions he frequently encountered a beautiful female with a mysterious, sometimes dubious, history. Accompanying Thurston was a somewhat ambiguous ally, a man tagged with an unusual moniker—Pagan Zeldschmidt—and that alone could speak volumes about him. Frequently tempted in the face of opportunity, at the last moment Zeldschmidt inevitably reined in a powerful weakness for thievery that sometimes reared its ugly head.

Each week the narrator signed off with a disclaimer that was popularly employed by many contemporary dramas: "All characters and incidents in this program are fictitious and any resemblance of incidents is purely coincidental." Somehow the statement had a strange ring to it, after admiring fans had been informed that these were exploits of a man who

fought diligently "so that tomorrow's peace will make the world a safe neighborhood for all of us." The perceptive listener, while entertained by it, may have realized the whole thing was a great farce perpetrated on the American public—and that they were no safer than they would have been if the series had never existed. It was offered, pure and simple, as amusement and nothing more.

In a 1956 syndicated half-hour television version that was also titled *The Man Called X*, the escapades continued where the radio drama had left off. Barry Sullivan portrayed Ken Thurston in a 39-week series produced and directed by Leon Benson and William Castle. Ladislas Farago, a former agent of the U.S. Office of Naval Intelligence, rendered technical assistance. Lee Berg provided the screenplay. Actual government files were reportedly the basis of the TV cases. No matter, Thurston was free to roam the world as he sought to save damsels in distress while rescuing gifted scientists who had been captured by enemy agents.

The Man from G-2

(aka *Major North, Army Intelligence*)

On the Air: April 12–May 24, 1945, ABC, Thursday, 7:30 p.m.; June 29–Aug. 24, 1945, ABC, Friday, 10 p.m.; Sept. 1, 1945–Feb. 2, 1946, ABC, Saturday, 8:30 p.m. 30 minutes.
Sponsor: Sustained.
Extant Episodes: None known.

CAST & CREDITS

Music—Bernard Green.
Leads—Major Hugh North, played by Staats Cotsworth; "the girl," played by Joan Alexander.

Major Hugh North, a U.S. intelligence agent, was the protagonist in an espionage thriller combating Nazi-Fascist plotting.

Radio historians identified North's feminine assistant by simply referring to her as "the girl," an unusual reference for a key figure. Paradoxically, by the time the series debuted, the Second World War—on which it was based—was rapidly winding down. When the Axis powers surrendered to the Allies months before the program left the air, the radio drama was left with little mission to be achieved, based on its original thesis.

This series was adapted from mysteries created by Van Wyck Mason.

Two of radio's busiest thespians, both with readily identifiable voices, appeared in the leads of the drama. In 1946 Staats Cotsworth was tagged as "radio's busiest actor." In addition to weekly nighttime performances in the namesake roles of *Casey, Crime Photographer*, *The Man from G-2*, *Mark Trail*, *Rogue's Gallery* and as the police lieutenant on *Mr. and Mrs. North*, he was prominent among repertory casts of *The Cavalcade of America* and *The March of Time Quiz*. Furthermore, Cotsworth played the title role in the weekday afternoon soap opera *Front Page Farrell* and maintained more running parts in several additional daytime serials: *Amanda of Honeymoon Hill*, *Big Sister*, *Lone Journey*, *Lorenzo Jones*, *Marriage for Two*, *Stella Dallas* and *When a Girl Marries*. He was all over the dial, of course, but no more so than Joan Alexander.

She appeared in daytime radio as Lois Lane in *Superman*, as Della Street in *Perry Mason* and also garnered running roles in several other washboard weepers: *Against the Storm*, *Bright Horizon*, *David Harum*, *The Light of the World*, *Lone Journey*, *Rosemary*, *This Is Nora Drake*, *Woman of Courage* and *Young Doctor Malone*. At night she turned up on a recurring basis in *Columbia Presents Corwin*, *Dimension X*, *Leave It to Mike*, *The Man from G-2*, *The Open Door*, *Philo Vance* and *Quick as a Flash*. Busy, busy actors, these two.

The Man from Homicide

On the Air: June 25–Oct. 1, 1951, ABC, Monday, 8:30 p.m. 30 minutes.
Sponsor: No information.
Extant Episodes: Three.

CAST & CREDITS

Producer—Helen Mack.
Director—Dwight Hauser.
Writers—Louis Bitties, Dick Powell.
Music—Basil Adlam (orchestra).
Announcer—Orville Anderson.
Leads—Lew Dana, played by Dan Duryea; Inspector Sherman, played by Bill Bouchey; Sergeant Dave, played by Larry Dobkin.
Support Roles—Jim Backus, Joan Banks, Tony Barrett, Arthur Q. Bryan, Herb Butterfield, Jo Gilbert, Lamont Johnson, Maggie Morley, Barney Phillips, Tom Tully.

Plainclothes police Lieutenant Lew Dana, working the homicide beat, possessed a well-earned reputation as a hard-boiled cop. "If I'm tough," he advised a thug while beating him mercilessly to extract the critical data he had requested, "it's because guys like you have made me tough." (Obviously, this transpired long before it was fashionable to appear in courtrooms alleging police brutality.) One culprit labeled him "the bitter Lieutenant Dana," confirming the detective's proud boast at the start of every episode: "I don't like killers." Inspector Sherman was Dana's intrepid sidekick.

On an audition show transcribed in 1950 and directed by Helen Mack, Charles McGraw appeared as Dana. Supporting actors included Jim Backus, Joan Banks, Lawrence Dobkin, Arthur Q. Bryan and Tom Tully.

Mandrake, the Magician

On the Air: Nov. 11, 1940–1941, MBS, Monday/Wednesday/Friday, 5:30 p.m.; 1941–Feb.

6, 1942, MBS, Weekdays, 5:15 p.m. 15 minutes.
Theme Song: *The Sorcerer's Apprentice* (*L'Apprenti Sorcier*) (Paul Dukas).
Sponsor: Sustained.
Extant Episodes: 28.

CAST & CREDITS

Producer—Henry Souvaine.
Director—Carlo De Angelo.
Leads—Title role played by Raymond Edward Johnson; Lothar (Mandrake's servant), played by Juano Hernandez; Princess Narda, played by Francesca Lenni.
Support Role—Laddie Seaman.

Mandrake was a mystic educated in a remote Tibetan valley by a foremost master of wizardry, Theron. Theron was steeped in the magic of China and the ancient secrets of Egypt that Tibetans had been preserving for centuries. As his tutor, he passed his knowledge to Mandrake. By chanting *invoco legem magicarum* ("I invoke the law of magic"), Mandrake was able to summon paranormal hypotheses that gave him supernatural powers, allowing him to accomplish great feats. Mandrake's minion, Lothar, a black man of gigantic proportions and incredible strength, regularly accompanied him on his journeys. Admirers claimed that Lothar could "rip a crocodile's jaws apart or break the back of an anthropoid ape." Assisting both of them was the glamorous Princess Narda from an unidentified geographic territory, whose mere presence invited respect as she exuded allure and grace.

The radio sequel was adapted from the King Features comic strip by Phil Davis and Lee Falk.

Juano Hernandez was one of few non-comedic Negro thespians consistently acting in radio drama throughout the 1940s. Not only did he appear as Lothar, he turned up as the African Kolu on *Jungle Jim* and with a myriad of Indian dialects on *Tennessee Jed*. On *Casey, Crime*

Photographer he was Ernie, a non-stereotyped black photojournalist.

Manhunt

On the Air: 1945–46, syndicated, 39 15-minute episodes produced.
Sponsor: Local advertisers in markets where the series aired.
Extant Episodes: 18.

CAST & CREDITS

Producer—Frederic Ziv.
Leads—Bill Morton, played by Maurice Tarplin; Drew Stevens, played by Larry Haines; Pat (only identification), played by Vicki Vola.

This syndicated, transcribed Ziv series—with each drama complete in a single episode—featured a couple of high profile police detectives. Each man represented a specific area of expertise; together they offered a formidable duo capable of tracking down alleged perpetrators of heinous crimes. Detective Bill Morton, of the homicide squad, could be classified as an overachiever: always tense, he pushed hard to solve crimes as rapidly as possible. Partner Drew Stevens was more subdued. While lacking no zeal for solving crimes, as a police lab technician, he painstakingly applied scientific methods of examining all facets of evidence in a case. Adding a unique twist to the pair's effort was Pat, Stevens' assistant and romantic interest, who regularly accompanied Morton on his investigative pursuits. Fearing for the girl's personal safety, Stevens discouraged her, taking a dim view of her overly enthusiastic support.

Screen Gems released 78 episodes of a similar syndicated police drama titled *Manhunt* to television stations between 1959 and 1961. Victor Jory portrayed a detective lieutenant with the San Diego

Police Department and Patrick McVey was a police reporter for a mythical local newspaper, similar to an earlier role he played in *Big Town*. The series is not to be confused with the detective drama *The Manhunter* that ran on CBS-TV from Sept. 11, 1974, through April 9, 1975, starring Ken Howard as an Idaho-based private investigator.

Mark Sabre see *Mystery Theater*

Mark Trail

On the Air: Jan. 30–June 30, 1950, MBS, Monday/Wednesday/Friday, 5 p.m.; Sept. 18, 1950–June 8, 1951, MBS, Monday/Wednesday/Friday, 5 p.m.; Sept. 10, 1951–Jan. 4, 1952, ABC, Monday/Wednesday/Friday, 5:15 p.m.; Jan. 7–June 27, 1952, ABC, Weekdays, 5:15 p.m. 30 minutes (MBS); 15 minutes (ABC).

Sponsor: W. K. Kellogg Co. for Kellogg's Corn Flakes and Pep cereal brands (MBS); Sustained (ABC).

Extant Episodes: 42.

CAST & CREDITS

Director—Drex Hines, Frank Maxwell.
Writers—Albert Aley, Gilbert Braun, Max Ehrlich, Elwood Hoffman, Donald Hughes, Palmer Thompson.
Music—John Gart.
Sound Effects—Bill Hoffman, Jack Keane.
Announcers—Jackson Beck, Glenn Riggs.
Leads—Title role played by Matt Crowley, John Larkin, Staats Cotsworth; Scotty, played by Ben Cooper, Ronald Liss; Cherry, played by Joyce Gordon, Amy Sidell.

Forest ranger Mark Trail was an outdoorsman at heart and a conservationist by choice. Decades before that concept caught the attention of mainstream Americans, Trail ranked protecting the environment a foremost activity for all U.S. citizens. To that end he gave himself unselfishly in a relentless pursuit to detain nature spoilers and lawbreakers who invaded the wilderness. His exploits in the wilds often involved malcontents, bullies and criminals of every persuasion, and Trail had the tenacity to cut them down to size. The show's memorable opening encompassed volumes: "Battling the ranging elements ... fighting the savage wilderness ... striking at the enemies of man and nature ... one man's name resounds from the snow-capped mountains down across the sun-baked plains ... [*from echo chamber*]: Mar-r-r-rk Trail-l-l-l!" He was properly tabbed a guardian of the forests, protector of wildlife and champion of man and nature.

The task of caring for the whole environment was entirely too much for one man working alone, of course. Like many of his late afternoon counterparts, while bringing the show down to its average listener's age level, Mark Trail was aided by a couple of young eager beavers, Scotty and Cherry (without last names). They, too, constantly risked their lives to battle the evils that lurked in the wilderness, at last bringing to justice many foes of the natural habitat.

The radio adaptation was an outgrowth of a comic strip by Ed Dodd that accentuated the value of protecting forests and wildlife.

Concerning Scotty and Cherry, Trail's companions, inquiring minds might have pondered: Where are the little darlings' mothers, that they could allow them to traipse around the wilderness with this woodsman every day rather than doing their homework and chores? And how did *they* feel about their offspring risking life and limb to rescue a giant oak tree from the clutches of an anxious developer's saber-toothed saw? Inquiring minds were few in radio days, certainly not enough to change a premise that was the basis of a well-received adolescent series.

Martin Kane, Private Detective see Martin Kane, Private Eye

Martin Kane, Private Eye

(aka *Martin Kane, Private Detective*)

On the Air: Aug. 7, 1949–June 24, 1951, MBS, Sunday, 4:30 p.m.; July 1, 1951–Dec. 21, 1952, NBC, Sunday, 4:30 p.m. 30 minutes.
Sponsor: U.S. Tobacco Co. for Old Briar pipe tobacco and Encore and Sano cigarettes.
Extant Episodes: 29.

CAST & CREDITS

Producer—Edward L. Kahan.
Director/Writer—Ted Hediger.
Music—Charles Paul (organ).
Sound Effects—Jim Goode, Jack Keane.
Announcer—Fred Uttal.
Leads—Title role played by William Gargan, Lloyd Nolan, Lee Tracy; Tucker (Hap) McMann, played by Walter Kinsella; Sergeant Ross, played by Nicholas Saunders; Captain Burke, played by Frank M. Thomas.

This tough-sounding New York gumshoe, possessed of cunning mind and an affinity for danger, was incessantly caught up in quick-tempered exploitation. Operating out of a small office in Manhattan, Kane met every dilemma head on. A popular entertainment magazine of his day observed that he had been "drugged, beaten, locked in a chamber with poison gas seeping in, thrown in the river, stabbed, shot, tied up in a burning building and locked unarmed in a room with a homicidal maniac bearing a meat cleaver." And that was merely in his first year on the air! His was unquestionably an action-packed half-hour. Kane commanded a top fee of $500

plus expenses for his most problematical cases, not a bad haul for a PI at mid twentieth century.

In his spare moments he relaxed at Happy McMann's Tobacco Shop, exchanging pleasantries with proprietor Tucker (Hap) McMann. Sponsoring U.S. Tobacco had to love that for it provided a ubiquitous platform for assimilating some of the program's commercials into the plot lines, especially with Kane being a pipe smoker. Sergeant Ross and Captain Burke, both representatives of the New York City Police Department, with whom Kane frequently exchanged inside information about various cases, aided him in his unofficial quests.

The series became one of the first radio detective programs conceived as a TV series that appeared in dual media. It premiered on NBC-TV Sept. 1, 1949, just 25 days after its radio launch, and was seen live on Thursdays at 10 p.m. for four years. In the fall of 1953 the same chain screened *The New Adventures of Martin Kane*, a filmed version shot in Europe, with Mark Stevens in the lead. It continued through June 17, 1954.

William Gargan, the actor who originated the part of Martin Kane on radio and television in 1949, turned up in the same role in a syndicated comeback in 1958. Titled *The Return of Martin Kane*, the United Artists series was also filmed in Europe.

Prior to a career in show business Gargan had been a real private investigator. He later disclosed in an autobiography (*Why Me?*) that the early TV shows were little more than "a vehicle for the flesh parade." Starlets were "pretty and empty-headed," he noted, and were cast for "cleavage" rather than talent. When Gargan urged the producers to "get decent scripts or get another boy," Lloyd Nolan replaced him on both radio and television in August 1951. That didn't end his broadcast career, of course—he debuted in the name-sake role of radio's *Barry Craig, Confidential Investigator* on Oct. 3, 1951. *Craig*, lasting nearly four years on radio, offered another brash New York gumshoe working independently. The similarities between that series and *Martin Kane, Private Eye* were strikingly uncanny. But in *Craig's* audio-only medium, the cleavage dynamic was never a problem.

Actually there *was* a real-life Martin Kane, who was an official with the J. Walter Thompson advertising agency, the series' producer. While working there Kane lent his moniker to the new drama's hero. Before his career ended, however, the authentic Kane became a senior editor at *Sports Illustrated* magazine.

Matthew Slade, Private Investigator

On the Air: Early 1950s. Syndicated by Briad Productions in conjunction with Pacifica Players.
Sponsor: Sold in local markets to a myriad of underwriters.
Extant Episodes: 13.

CAST & CREDITS

Producer—Brian Adams.
Directors—Michael Dayton, Ruth Hershman.
Writer—Robert Frederick.
Announcer—David Osman.
Leads—Title role played by William Wintersole; "Jonesy," played by Sylvia Watson; Sergeant Dinelli, played by Norman Belkin.
Support Roles—John Anniston, Mary Kate Denny, Barton Heyman, Maureen McElroy, Bill O'Connell, Joyce Reed.

At $200 per day plus expenses, San Francisco PI Matthew Slade got involved in performing the dirty work of his clients. As he related it in the show's billboard: "In my job the hours are hard. So are the circumstances and the people I meet. You could even call some of them dangerous." While he usually didn't physically beat up anybody, it was still a violent show for he was often attacked and frequently left for dead. His secretary, Rowena Jones (frequently tabbed as "Jonesy"), and police Sergeant Sid Dinelli completed the ongoing cast. To make matters still more interesting, Dinelli's supervisor didn't attempt to hide the fact that he didn't like Slade even a little bit.

Maverick Jim

On the Air: 1934, MBS, Monday. 30 minutes.
Sponsor: No information.
Extant Episodes: None known.

CAST & CREDITS

Lead—Title role played by Artells Dickson. No further credits established.

This was a half-hour juvenile western drama starring the same actor (Artells Dickson) who had been simultaneously playing Tom Mix on NBC since that crime fighter's debut on Sept. 25, 1933. Regrettably, most details about this series haven't been preserved.

Max Marcin's Crime Doctor see *Crime Doctor*

The McCoy

On the Air: 1950–51, NBC. 30 minutes.
Sponsor: Sustained.

CAST & CREDITS

Producers—Milton Fine, David Friedkin.
Music—Walter Schumann (orchestra).
Leads—Title role of Mike McCoy played by Howard Duff; Judy, played by Joan Banks; Sergeant Koska, played by Sheldon Leonard.

Theme Song: *I'll Be Seeing You.*
Extant Episodes: One.

L. A. private detective Mike McCoy's digs consisted of a fleabag hotel room in Las Palmas and a Hollywood office formerly rented to a Persian rug hawker. McCoy earned his living because "people sneak up alleys, people hate, people rob, people strangle." Unpretentiously he concluded, "I got a crummy license and I'm in a crummy business." At least once in most episodes the unhappy solider of fortune could be found passing the time at a key address, the Sunset Strip's Chez Maison. Two other figures routinely appeared: Judy, his contact with Preston Call Service, a firm he employed to take his telephone messages when he was away; and Los Angeles Police Department Sergeant Koska. The drama relied on a unique routine for relating McCoy's cases: Having no secretary, he typed them himself for his personal files, sharing them through verbal recollections and flashback sequences.

McGarry and His Mouse

On the Air: June 26–Sept. 25, 1946, NBC, Wednesday, 9 p.m.; Jan. 6–March 31, 1947, MBS, Monday, 8 p.m. 30 minutes.
Sponsors: Sustained (NBC); General Foods Inc. for a wide line of foodstuffs (MBS).
Extant Episodes: Three.

CAST & CREDITS
Writer—Milton J. Kramer.
Music—Peter Van Steeden (orchestra).
Announcer—Bert Parks.
Leads—Title role of Dan McGarry played by Roger Pryor, Wendell Corey, Ted de Corsia; Kitty Archer (the mouse), played by Shirley Mitchell, Peggy Conklin, Patsy Campbell.
Support Roles—Carl Eastman (Joe), Betty Garde (Margaret "Mom" Archer), Jerry Hartley and Jerry Macy (Inspector Matthew "Matt" McGarry, Dan's uncle and police

headquarters supervisor), Thelma Ritter (Bernice, Kitty's best friend).

A funny cop? Dan McGarry was a bumbling rookie detective with the New York City Police Department who was shadowed by a romantic companion, Kitty Archer, whom he dubbed "the Mouse." Actually, a string of regular characters turned up in this little farce, literally qualifying it as melodrama as much as it was crime drama. Kitty worked for an airline but wherever McGarry went she tagged along, in essence "to watch out for him," since his usual inclination involved the pair in danger. The steady listener soon learned that if there was any brains behind this organization, Kitty owned them—McGarry was normally dependent upon her to devise a plan for their escape out of tight situations. Like some of their contemporaries, they had a favorite dive for hanging out, too: Charlie's Tavern qualified for lounging in the off hours. McGarry was introduced to audiences weekly as "handsome as ever, brave as ever, and confused as ever." He simply wasn't your typical police detective; one could make no mistake about that.

The radio sequel was inspired by a fictional article series appearing in *This Week* magazine penned by Matt Taylor.

Radio detective series that incorporated substantial quantities of comedy into their mix were seldom given extensive chances to derive large followings on the air. There were some notable exceptions, in which eager listeners enjoyed combining sizable doses of mirth with murder. *Mr. and Mrs. North* was among the few doing it effectively. That series blended a strong dose of reality and commonplace into the day-to-day experiences of its two amateur sleuths.

McLean of the Mounties see McLean of the Northwest Mounted

McLean of the Northwest Mounted

(aka *McLean of the Mounties*)

On the Air: Mid 1930s. 15 minutes.
Sponsor: No information, but if syndicated, probably sold to advertisers in local markets.
Extant Episodes: Two.

CAST & CREDITS

Lead—Title role of Corporal Mclean played by Francis X. Bushman.
Support Role—Monte Blue.

Introducing this show, an announcer saluted the "Royal Canadian Northwest Mounted Police." While the Force had several titles, according to researcher Jack French, that wasn't one of them. Although each episode lasted only a quarter of an hour, French insisted: "It seems much longer because of the snail-paced plot and stilted acting." He noted that the story line in the initial episode precisely paralleled the plot of the musical *Rose Marie*. Thus the radio narrative could be interpreted as rudimentary at best, unrefined when compared to Mountie dramas that followed.

Bushman and Blue were both silver screen actors, leading to the belief that this series was produced on the U.S. West Coast.

Meet Miss Sherlock

On the Air: July 3–Sept. 26, 1946, CBS West Coast Network, Wednesday/Thursday; Sept. 28, 1946–Oct. 25, 1947, CBS West Coast Network, Saturday. 30 minutes.
Theme Song: *A Little Bit Independent.*
Sponsor: Sustained.
Extant Episodes: Two.

CAST & CREDITS

Producer—Dave Vale.
Writers—E. Jack Neuman, Don Thompson.

Music—Milton Charles.
Announcer—Murray Wagner.
Leads—Title role played by Sondra Gair (July 3–Sept. 26, 1946), Betty Moran (Sept. 28, 1946), Monty Margetts (Oct. 5, 1946–Oct. 26, 1947); Captain Dingle, played by Bill Conrad.

Jane Sherlock wasn't a private investigator but she did possess sleuthing tendencies. Her actual job was as a buyer for the exclusive Blossom Department Store. Her fiancée, lawyer Peter Blossom, was the son of the emporium's feminine proprietor. Sherlock's exuberance for prying into other folks' concerns might have indicated that she was *My Friend Irma* "undercover." Almost invariably her mischievous snooping thrust her into certain dilemmas at best and occasionally even into certain danger. An announcer positioned Sherlock as "a smart little gal who has stumbled across a real live clue." Captain Dingle, a member of the local police force, frequently appeared to help her in these amateurish detective escapades.

Noting an absence of very many feminine detectives on radio, astute author Fred MacDonald claimed: "While women were featured in the [crime drama] broadcasts as stenographers and sex objects, in only a few instances were they the principal characters. In these rare cases, however, the programs were either so cliché-ridden or denigrating that they were short-lived and insignificant." He pointed out that—because Sherlock's livelihood was derived from an occupation other than sleuthing—she couldn't be considered a serious detective in a traditional sense.

Melody Ranch see Gene Autry's Melody Ranch

Michael and Kitty

(aka *Michael Piper, Private Detective*)

On the Air: Oct. 10, 1941–Feb. 6, 1942, NBC Blue, Friday, 9:30 p.m. 30 minutes.
Sponsor: Canada Dry Bottling Co. for Canada Dry Ginger Ale soft drink beverage.
Extant Episodes: One.

CAST & CREDITS

Music—Lyn Murray.
Leads—Michael Piper, played by John Gibson; Kitty Piper, played by Elizabeth Reller.

What was it about combining comedy and mystery in the 1940s and naming the feminine love interest Kitty? (See earlier entry on *McGarry and His Mouse*.) In this show, which aired fewer months than that one and fits a dubious pattern, a private detective and his wife were at the apex of trouble. Yet they, too, experienced it in humorous ways.

The reader is especially directed to the final paragraph included under *McGarry and His Mouse*.

Michael Piper, Private Detective see Michael and Kitty

Michael Shayne, Private Detective see The Adventures of Michael Shayne

Mike Malloy, Private Eye

On the Air: July 16–Sept. 24, 1953, ABC, Thursday, 9 p.m.; Oct. 12, 1953–April 23, 1954, ABC, Weekdays, 8:45 p.m.; April 30, 1956–March 18, 1957, CBS, Monday, 7:30 p.m. 30 minutes, except 15 minutes (Oct. 12, 1953–April 23, 1954).
Sponsor: Sustained.
Extant Episodes: None known.

CAST & CREDITS

Lead—Title role played by Steve Brodie.

Mike Malloy gained a reputation as a tough-minded, hard-hitting PI. During most of the run, except when it was aired weekdays, the stories were presented in completed accounts. These narratives were serialized when they were offered in quarter-hour weeknight episodes. Surprisingly, radio historians preserved little about this late and fairly durable detective drama surfacing in the final decade of the medium's golden age.

Steve Brodie, who was featured in the lead role in all three segments of this show, isn't believed to have acted in any other radio series. An established performer in Hollywood movies as early as 1944, Brodie was usually cast in film roles as a rugged outdoors type of figure. He played in *Only the Valiant, This Man's Navy* and *Winchester 73*, among several cinematic triumphs.

Miss Pinkerton, Incorporated

On the Air: 1941, NBC. 30 minutes.
Sponsor: No information.
Extant Episodes: One.

CAST & CREDITS

Producer—J. Donald Wilson.
Music—Lenny Conn.
Announcer—Art Gilmore.
Lead—Mary Vance, played by Joan Blondell.
Support Roles—Gale Gordon, Ed Max (Bingo Doherty), Dick Powell (Dennis Murray), Hanley Stafford (Mr. Parker).

Mary Vance, a graduate scholar at Cornell University in Ithaca, New York, interrupted her law studies when informed she had inherited her late uncle's Manhattan detective agency. Her first thought was to sell it, but to prove a woman's capacity for professional achievement she decided to operate the business herself. Mr. Parker, who had managed the firm for Vance's late uncle, continued to advise. She also had an assistant, Bingo Doherty.

Vance's day-to-day pursuits led her into frequent entanglements with a charming and unattached New York police detective, Dennis Murray. Yet she soon developed a love-hate relationship with him. Much of the tension between the duo resulted from her stirring the pot too often in matters pertaining to criminal cases involving police surveillance.

While the program was introduced as a "comedy detective drama," it was also presented as "situations of adventure, thrills and romance," giving fairly wide latitude for it to experiment in a multiplicity of directions. Despite that ability, it aired only briefly.

The infamous Pinkerton Detective Agency, widely recognized as a standard in its industry, lent its moniker to the title of the radio series, emphasizing the fact that few women played radio detectives.

See the comments under the entry on *McGarry and His Mouse* for a discussion of the success of shows that attempted to combine comedy and detectives.

Joan Blondell and Dick Powell, who carried out that love-hate relationship in this series, were at that time married to one another in real life. Powell would soon also play the leading roles in radio crime dramas *Rogue's Gallery* and *Richard Diamond* while Blondell—a wisecracking, tough-minded, sexy broad on the silver screen, according to radio critic Jack French—played Mary Vance in the same manner.

Mr. Aladdin

On the Air: July 7–Sept. 8, 1951, CBS, Saturday, 9:30 p.m. 30 minutes.

Theme Song: *Bewitched, Bothered and Bewildered.*
Sponsor: No information.
Extant Episodes: One.

CAST & CREDITS
Producer/Director—Elliott Lewis.
Writer—Dick Powell.
Music—Marlin Skiles (orchestra).
Announcer—Bill Anders.
Leads—Title role of Robert Aladdin played by Paul Frees; Jeannie Mobley, played by Sylvia Sims; Sam, played by Sidney Miller.

Robert Aladdin was a marvel-making Manhattan Island criminologist. A private detective by trade, he promoted himself as "the man who can do anything," offering some pretty astonishing cases and clients to back up his assertion. Aladdin, whose very name conjured up images of baffling phenomena, literally performed miracles while solving crimes, a feat most of his peers dared not attempt. It was never quite clear to listeners how he acquired such powers, either. (*Variety* was highly critical of the series for providing "too many utterly fantastic elements.") Every good gumshoe needs somebody with whom he can dialogue—Aladdin had two individuals with whom he readily conversed—a secretary, Jeannie Mobley, and Sam the bartender at the Taj Mahal, where Aladdin overindulged during his free time.

Mr. and Mrs. North
(aka *The Adventures of Mr. and Mrs. North*)

On the Air: 1941, CBS, single audition transcription, specific time and date unsubstantiated; Dec. 30, 1942–Dec. 18, 1946, NBC, Wednesday, 8 p.m.; July 1, 1947–May 30, 1950, CBS, Tuesday, 8:30 p.m.; Sept. 5, 1950–June 22, 1954, CBS, Tuesday, 8:30 p.m.; Sept. 5–Sept. 26, 1954, CBS, Sunday; Oct. 4–Nov. 19, 1954, CBS, Weekdays; Nov.

29, 1954–April 18, 1955, CBS, Monday, 8 p.m. 30 minutes, except 15 minutes (Oct. 4–Nov. 19, 1954).

Theme Song: *The Way You Look Tonight.*

Sponsors: Andrew Jergens Co. for Jergens lotion and Woodbury cold cream (1942–47); Colgate-Palmolive-Peet Inc. for Colgate toothpaste and tooth powder, Halo and Lustre Crème shampoos, Cashmere Bouquet and Palmolive soap, Palmolive shave cream (1947–54); Sustained (1954–55).

Extant Episodes: 32.

CAST & CREDITS

Producers/Directors—S. James Andrews, Martin Gosch (1941), Howard Harris (1941), John W. Loveton.

Writers—Hector Chevigny, Jerome Epstein, Martin Gosch (1941), Howard Harris (1941), Frances and Richard Lockridge, Michael Morris, Robert Sloane, Louis Vittes.

Music—Donald Voorhees (orchestra, 1941), Charles Paul (orchestra).

Sound Effects—Al Binnie, Al Hogan, Jerry McCarthy, Sam Monroe.

Announcers—Art Ballinger, Ben Grauer, Joseph King, Charles Stark.

Leads—Jerry North, played by Carl Eastman (1941), Joseph Curtin (1942–54), Richard Denning (1954–55); Pam North, played by Peggy Conklin (1941), Alice Frost (1942–54), Barbara Britton (1954–55).

Support Roles—Homicide lieutenant Bill Weigand, played by Frank Lovejoy, Staats Cotsworth, Francis DeSales; also, Walter Kinsella (a harried, inept Sergeant Aloysius Mullins), Mandel Kramer (Brooklyn taxi driver Mahatma McGloin), Betty Jane Tyler (Susan, the Norths' 14-year-old niece).

Although this amateur sleuthing series premiered as a comedy show—a fact that most of its subsequent fans have probably never realized—to become successful, its bent for domesticity and romantic adventures was shelved and its focus made deadly serious. Even at that, the New York yuppies who passed themselves off as a publisher and his homemaker-spouse continued to make lighthearted wisecracks as they stepped over bodies in dark alleys and were rendered unconscious by unknown assailants dispensing blows to the head almost every week. In *Mr. and Mrs. North* (as in *The Thin Man*) the feminine half of the twosome was at least equal to the husband in solving cases that often baffled law enforcement officers with years of training and practice—except in reading clues. No explanation was given, of course, as to why a couple of misfits could be so successful in their preoccupation while the professionals thrashed about ineffectually.

One reviewer noted: "Pam was ... [a] 'normal' housewife who loved cats, talked in riddles and usually managed through clever detection and women's intuition to figure out the killer's identity just ahead of the men." Jerry North, himself, once acknowledged to his rattle-brained spouse: "Since I married you, disrupted plans in life are the one thing I can count on." By accidentally bumping into a minimum of one murder per week and slayings in duplicate or triplicate on occasion, the Greenwich duo's stock prospered among fans. Their droll approach to what would have been gory business for some invariably made them aficionados to the common man and woman tuning in, permitting the pair to challenge radio's foremost established mystery series for first place in audience appeal.

When the radio feature was launched with a fervent comedic motif, its inspiration was rooted in a series of fictional tales having appeared in 1930s issues of *The New Yorker* magazine. Based on "a lighthearted, comfy couple" set in "amusing domestic adventures," those narratives were originally penned by Richard Lockridge. Joined by his own spouse, Frances, in 1940, together they turned the focus of the mythical young affluent couple into "the most successful amateur husband-wife crime fighting team of the time," as one critic said. Their book, *The Norths Meet Murder*, was published and the popularity of the

Mr. and Mrs. North: (l–r) unidentified thespian, Alice Frost, Joseph Curtin. Frost and Curtin turned *Mr. and Mrs. North* into "the most successful amateur husband-wife crime fighting team of the time." Throughout their lengthy run the gruesome twosome challenged radio's foremost established mystery series for first place in audience appeal. Stepping over bodies and getting knocked in the head were all in a day's work for the sleuthing pair.

proletarian sleuths increased when they were introduced to wider audiences by way of stage and celluloid venues. All of this happened before the Norths hit the airwaves, initially and ironically reverting to situation comedy there without traipsing over bodies and the whodunit elements. Carl Eastman and Peggy Conklin played Jerry and Pam as humorous figures in that ill-fated distraction. It was only when the Norths turned their attention to murder and mayhem that 20 million listeners became habitually addicted to the sheer escapism they provided each week.

Robert B. Sinclair directed a black-and-white feature-length movie release in 1941 titled *Mr. and Mrs. North*. Based on the stage production by Owen Davis, S. K.

Lauren penned the screenplay and the film starred William Post Jr. and Gracie Allen in namesake parts. Paul Kelly appeared as Detective Lieutenant Luke Weigand with Millard Mitchell as Detective Mullins.

NBC-TV brought a test film featuring *Mr. and Mrs. North* to the small screen on Monday, July 4, 1949, with Joseph Allen Jr. and Mary Lou Taylor in the title roles. That effort failed to spawn a series. But in a subsequent try, CBS was successful in creating filmed episodes starring Richard Denning and Barbara Hale as the amateur crime-solvers. *Mr. and Mrs. North* ran on Fridays at 10 p.m. on CBS-TV from Oct. 3, 1952, to Sept. 25, 1953. It shifted in 1954 to Tuesdays at 10:30 p.m. over NBC-TV between Jan. 26 and July 20. Francis

DeSales reprised his aural role as Lieutenant Bill Weigand, radio's John W. Loveton produced the video version and Ralph Murphy directed. In the final season of the audio-only drama, which was still airing after the tube version departed, TV stars Richard Denning and Barbara Britton were brought in to complete the radio run.

CBS dispensed with a pair of its listeners' longtime sleuthing favorites during a single week in the spring of 1955. After killing off *Mr. and Mrs. North* on Monday night, April 18, the chain proceeded to drop the long-term *Casey, Crime Photographer* on Friday, April 22. Within five days perhaps the abandonment of two of the most imposing detective series in the history of radio occurred, signaling CBS's strong intention to place its future primary preferences elsewhere—possibly in other genres, and still more pointedly in television. The pair of crime dramas departing that week had each aired for more than a dozen years. After that debacle, the next week CBS cut *Mr. Keen, Tracer of Lost Persons*, banishing it to a 25-minute time zone in a final gasp before its quick exit after 18 years. If radio's fate hadn't been sealed before, the handwriting for its prospects was clearly visible to most observers in 1955.

Jay Hickerson prepared what he called a "sketchy" log of this series.

Mr. Chameleon

On the Air: July 21, 1948–June 20, 1951, CBS, Wednesday, 8 p.m.; Aug. 29–Dec. 5, 1951, CBS, Wednesday, 8 p.m.; Dec. 9, 1951–Jan. 6, 1952, CBS, Sunday, 5:30 p.m.; Jan. 17–Aug. 28, 1952, CBS, Thursday, 9 p.m.; Oct. 7–28, 1952, CBS, Tuesday, 10:05 p.m.; Nov. 7, 1952–Jan. 9, 1953, CBS, Friday, 9 p.m.; March 13–Aug. 7, 1953, CBS, Friday, 8:30 p.m. 30 minutes, except 25 minutes (Oct. 7–28, 1952).

Theme Song: *Masquerade* (John Jacob Loeb, Paul Francis Webster).

Sponsors: Sterling Drugs Inc. for Bayer aspirin pain reliever, Dr. Lyon's tooth powder and a multitude of other health care commodities (July 21, 1948–June 20, 1951); Sustained (Aug. 29, 1951–Jan. 6, 1952, Oct. 7, 1952–Aug. 7, 1953); General Foods Inc. for a wide line of foodstuffs (Jan. 17–June 26, 1952); William J. Wrigley Co. for its various chewing gum lines (July 3–Aug. 28, 1952).

Extant Episodes: Three.

CAST & CREDITS

Producers—Anne Hummert, Frank Hummert.

Director—Richard Leonard.

Writer—Mary Baumer.

Music—Victor Arden (orchestra).

Sound Effects—Jack Amrhein, Robert L. Mott, Byron Wingett.

Announcers—George Bryan, Howard Claney, Roger Krupp.

Leads—Title role played by Karl Swenson; Dave Arnold, played by Frank Butler.

Support Role—Richard Keith (police commissioner).

Operating out of "Central Police Headquarters" in New York City, the "dreaded detective" Mr. Chameleon was billboarded as "the man of many faces." At all times, as the narrator informed the fans, the listener would be able to immediately distinguish when Chameleon slipped incognito into one of his myriad alternative speech dialects. But the poor devil he hoped to trick usually didn't recognize him, tripping himself up and giving himself away for his foul deeds. A bumbling accomplice traveled with Chameleon: Detective Dave Arnold was reminiscent of Mike Clancy, accessory to *Mr. Keen, Tracer of Lost Persons*, whose primary function seemed little more than to dialogue with the "boss" and thus be certain ongoing developments were revealed to the audience at home. "It was a trick dating back to Sherlock Holmes and Watson, perhaps beyond—that of giving the brilliant hero a none-too-bright sidekick to ask the dumb questions and make sure the Great One had plugged all the holes," a critic observed.

Having gathered the goods on an alleged killer, with masterful artistry Chameleon would confront his suspects in disguise to confirm his suspicions, allowing the culprit to nail himself while he thought Chameleon was elsewhere. It was a predictable whodunit, yet the concept of deceiving the murderer was an intriguing device that kept the faithful mesmerized for a fairly durable run.

Clarity was a hallmark of the Frank and Anne Hummert production factory and the dialog exchanges between Detective Arnold and Inspector Chameleon were frequently inserted to satisfy this insatiable Hummert imperative. ("The show had a Hummert sound," noted a reviewer, "from the music to the sponsor." The tune that introduced it could have been as relevant in soap opera. And Sterling Drugs, manufacturer of Bayer aspirin, underwrote four of the Hummerts' most popular serials that appeared back-to-back in a single hour on weekday afternoons over NBC—*Backstage Wife, Stella Dallas, Lorenzo Jones* and *Young Widder Brown*.) One writer classified the nighttime series as "painfully contrived," based on the producers' well-understood repetitive patterns. Especially was this true when it came to a Hummert requirement for the listener to be absolutely certain who was speaking and about whom he or she was speaking. Characters' names were repeated dozens of times to avoid any misunderstanding; the dialogue, meanwhile, often appeared mired within plots that sometimes seemed to be going nowhere.

Master radio soundman Bob Mott allowed, in an anecdote in his insightful little volume *Radio Sound Effects*: "When I worked on *Mr. Chameleon*, I asked the star, Karl Swenson, why he did just about every show [on radio] that required a Scandinavian accent. He told me it wasn't

because he was that extraordinarily good (he lied; he was), it was because of his reputation: Directors were notoriously insecure about taking a chance with someone new. Besides, Swenson added, North Country voices were probably the trickiest to do. And if the directors put an ad in *Daily Variety* asking for auditions, there would be 10,000 actors knocking down the door, while probably only 50 would be acceptable. Here he paused and smiled, 'What director has the time or inclination to find that fifty out of ten thousand?'"

In 1935 Karl Swenson, then only 27, debuted on radio's *The March of Time*. The full range of his versatile talents flourished in an aural medium, making him indispensable on many shows. In addition to *Lorenzo Jones* where he played the hero, he was a *veddy veddy* British Lord Henry Brinthrope, male lead in *Our Gal Sunday*. Those two daily soap operas kept Swenson employed for many years. It has been speculated that the producing Hummerts also created the role of *Mr. Chameleon* especially for Swenson because he made assuming the dialect called for by his weekly disguise—Irish, Norwegian, German, Mexican, Yankee, Southerner, and so on—sound so easy. Other series on which Swenson regularly appeared included *Aunt Jenny's Real Life Stories, The Cavalcade of America, The Court of Missing Heirs, Father Brown, The Ford Theater, Grand Central Station, Inner Sanctum Mysteries, Joe Palooka, Lawyer Q, Linda's First Love, Little House on the Prairie* (TV), *The Mighty Show, Mrs. Miniver, Portia Faces Life* (radio and TV), *Rich Man's Darling, Spy Secrets, There Was a Woman, This Is Your FBI, The Whisper Men* and *World's Great Novels*. Married to soap heroine Joan Tompkins (who played title roles in both *Lora Lawton* and *This Is Nora Drake*), Swenson died at Torrington, Conn., on Oct. 8, 1978.

A log for this series was prepared by Jay Hickerson.

Mr. District Attorney

On the Air: April 3–June 16, 1939, NBC, Weekdays, 7 p.m.; June 27–Sept. 19, 1939, NBC, Tuesday, 10 p.m.; Oct. 1, 1939–April 7, 1940, NBC Blue, Sunday, 7:30 p.m.; April 11–June 27, 1940, NBC, Thursday, 8 p.m.; July 3, 1940–Sept. 19, 1951, NBC, Wednesday, 9:30 p.m.; Sept. 28, 1951–June 13, 1952, ABC, Friday, 9:30 p.m. 1954 in syndication. 15 minutes (April 3–June 16, 1939), 30 minutes otherwise.

Theme Song: Original music by composer/conductor Peter Van Steeden, followed later by *Ein Helden Lieben* (Richard Strauss).

Sponsors: Sustained (April 3–June 16, 1939); Pepsodent toothpaste (June 27, 1939–April 7, 1940); Bristol-Myers Inc. for Vitalis men's hair preparation, Bufferin pain reliever, Ipana toothpaste, Sal Hepatica stomach distress antidote, Mum deodorant and a wide assortment of added personal and health care goods (April 11, 1940–June 13, 1952).

Extant Episodes: 81.

CAST & CREDITS

Producers—Edward C. Byron, Phillips H. Lord.

Director—Edward C. Byron, Jerry Devine.

Writers—Edward C. Byron, Jerry Devine, Finis Farr, Harry Herman, Phillips H. Lord, Robert J. Shaw (chief).

Music—Gil Markel, Harry Salter, Peter Van Steeden (orchestras).

Sound Effects—John Powers.

Announcers—Ben Grauer, Mark Hawley, Ed Herlihy, Bob Shepherd, Fred Uttal.

Leads—Title role played by Dwight Weist (1939 weeknight serial), Raymond Edward Johnson, Jay Jostyn (starting October 1940), David Brian (syndication); Len Harrington, played by Len Doyle; Miss Edith Miller, played by Vicki Vola; Miss Rand, played by Arlene Francis, Eleanor Silver.

Support Roles—Joan Banks, Geoffrey Bryant, Maurice Franklin, Jay Jostyn, Walter Kinsella, Frank Lovejoy, Craig McDonnell, Thelma Ritter, Amy Seidell, Paul Stewart.

District Attorney Paul Garrett (whose name was never documented until he reached syndication, 13 years after his debut on radio) was portrayed as "champion of the people, defender of our fundamental rights to life, liberty, and the pursuit of happiness." The credo of *Mr. District Attorney* was offered at the start of every program through ringing stentorian tones emanating from what sounded like an enormous marbled cave: "And it shall be my duty, not only to prosecute to the limit of the law all those charged with crimes perpetrated within this county, but to defend with equal vigor the rights and privileges of all its citizens." Favorably compared to another popular radio hero, a critic viewed the D. A. as "a staunch authority figure cut from the frills of Lone Ranger cloth."

The D. A. was augmented in his efforts by a not-so-Irish-sounding ex-cop, Len Harrington, who received most of the muscle-required assignments as the D. A.'s special investigator; a faithful secretary, known only to network audiences as Miss Miller (but Edith Miller in syndication); and a receptionist, Miss Rand. (Wrote one reviewer: "The depth of the relationship between the D. A. and Miss Miller seemed deeper than most between employer and employee. After office hours, perhaps there was a time when they did use their first names.")

Because the producer and writer spent a lot of time reading about con artists, evil masterminds and average killers in the real world, and rubbed elbows with some of them on a frequent basis in the New York ghettos, the end result was a "startling realism" acquired by their show during that epoch. At times they even successfully anticipated actions that developed into headlines in real life. As a result, the series soon found itself among radio's top 10 features, a spot it occupied consistently for several years.

In chatting with creator Edward C. Byron, successful radio producer Phillips H. Lord (of *Gangbusters* and similar series fame) toyed with a concept for a weekday serial focused on a district attorney. No specific name was readily assigned to the lead figure. As some early scripts were plotted, the hero was neutrally referenced as "Mr. District Attorney." That designation clicked and was permanently adopted before the show reached the airwaves.

The original inspiration was a figure drawn from real life, the late 1930s racketbusting Gotham D. A., Thomas E. Dewey. His headline-grabbing battle with racketeers and corruption of many sorts propelled him into the Empire State governorship and a couple of tries for the presidency (1944, 1948). During the Republican National Convention in 1940 a solid corps of delegates held out for Dewey over eventual convention pick Wendell Willkie, reportedly "on the strength of the radio show alone." Wrote one reviewer: "Almost singlehandedly Dewey had changed the image of the district attorney from the incompetent inquisitor portrayed by Hollywood to the white-collar sleuth of news flashes and banner headlines."

In 1949 *Mr. District Attorney* became the first and—according to an authority— *only* radio mystery series to move to live television with its original cast intact: Jostyn, Doyle and Vola. Directed by Edward C. Byron who brought it to radio, the drama was telecast live, alternating Mondays with *The Amazing Mr. Malone*, over ABC-TV from Oct. 1, 1951, to June 23, 1952. Frederic W. Ziv Productions revived it in 1954 for a brief filmed syndicated television stint, that time minus its established leads: David Brian appeared as the redoubtable D. A. alongside Jackie Loughery as Miss Miller. Said Val Adams, in a *New York Times* review: "David Brian is a big, broad-shouldered fellow who looks powerful enough to rip a whole gang of criminals apart singlehanded. Mr. Brian's D. A. is a man fervently devoted to serv-ing the public interest and rarely does he have time to smile."

Ziv further syndicated a new 52-week radio series of *Mr. District Attorney* after the network show ended in the early 1950s. David Brian also played the lead there. In its Sept. 18, 1954, issue *Billboard* reported that the radio version had become Ziv's most successful venture in that medium, by then heard in 201 markets. Ziv had entered into an agreement with Phillips H. Lord on Sept. 24, 1953, to secure the radio and TV rights to *Mr. District Attorney*. Ziv agreed to pay Lord $20,000 per year for three years for the radio rights and $30,000 for a one-year option for TV. If the program sold, Ziv would pay Lord an added $170,000 over five years for exclusive TV rights, according to film scholar Patrick Lucanio, who has devoted a substantial portion of his professional life to researching the Ziv organization.

Mr. I. A. Moto see Mr. Moto

Mr. Keen, Tracer of Lost Persons

On the Air: Oct. 12, 1937–Oct. 22, 1942, NBC Blue, Tuesday/Wednesday/Thursday, 7:15 p.m.; Oct. 28, 1942–Nov. 5, 1943, CBS, Monday/Wednesday/Friday, 7:45 p.m.; Nov. 11, 1943–June 26, 1947, CBS, Thursday, 7:30 p.m.; Sept. 11, 1947–July 12, 1951, CBS, Thursday, 8:30 p.m.; July 20–Aug. 31, 1951, CBS, Friday, 9:30 p.m.; Sept. 13, 1951–May 1, 1952, NBC, Thursday, 8:30 p.m.; May 8–29, 1952, NBC, Thursday, 9:30 p.m.; June 5–Sept. 25, 1952, NBC, Thursday, 8 p.m.; Oct. 3, 1952–Oct. 1, 1954, CBS, Friday, 8 p.m.; also May 24, 1954–Jan. 14, 1955, CBS, Weekdays, 10 p.m.; Feb. 22–April 19, 1955, CBS, Tuesday, 8:30 p.m.; April 25-Sept. 26,

1955, CBS, Monday, 8 p.m. 15 minutes (Oct. 12, 1937–Nov. 5, 1943; May 24, 1954–Jan. 14, 1955); 25 minutes (Sept. 11, 1947–July 12, 1951; April 25–Sept. 26, 1955); 30 minutes (most other segments).

Theme Song: *Someday I'll Find You.*

Sponsors: American Home Products Corp. for its Whitehall Pharmacal Co. packaged drug division, including Anacin pain reliever, Kolynos toothpaste and tooth powder, Bi-So-Dol stomach analgesic "and many other fine, dependable pharmaceutical products" (Oct. 12, 1937–July 12, 1951); Radio Corp. of America for RCA phonographs, radios and records (July 20–Aug. 31, 1951); Liggett & Myers Tobacco Co. for Chesterfield and L & M cigarette brands (Sept. 13, 1951–Sept. 25, 1952); Procter & Gamble Co. for a wide line of personal care and cleaning aids (May 1, 1952–Oct. 1, 1954); Multiple sponsors, e.g. American Chicle Co. for Dentyne chewing gum, and Sustained (May 24, 1954–Jan. 14, 1955, Feb. 22–Sept. 26, 1955).

Extant Episodes: 59.

CAST & CREDITS

Producers—Anne Hummert, Frank Hummert.
Director—Richard Leonard.
Writers—Barbara Bates, Stedman Coles, David Davidson, Charles J. Gussman, Lawrence Klee (chief), Robert J. Shaw.
Music—Al Rickey (orchestra), John Winters (organ).
Sound Effects—Jack Amrhein.
Announcers—George Ansbro, Larry Elliott, James Fleming.
Leads—Title role played by Bennett Kilpack, Philip Clarke; Mike Clancy, played by Jimmy Kelly.
Support Roles—Arline Blackburn, Anne Elstner, Mary Jane Higby, Adelaide Klein, Joseph (Joe) Latham, Florence Malone (Miss Maisie Ellis, Keen's secretary, early in the run), William J. Smith, Vivian Smolen, Ned Wever.

Mr. Keen, Tracer of Lost Persons was one of the most durable gumshoes in broadcast history, airing for 18 years, part of that time in isolated weekly and weeknight features. Practically speaking, there were *two* separate and distinct *Mr. Keen* series. In the first, premiering as a thrice-weekly quarter-hour serial between 1937–43, the "kindly old investigator" literally traced the unexplained disappearances of individuals who had suddenly dropped out of sight from their homes, families, jobs and established routines. Working alongside an inept—at times, incompetent—partner, Mike Clancy, Keen tracked "one of his most widely celebrated missing persons cases" through several installments until he was able to unravel the baffling mystery. Sometimes a subject appeared to have vanished into thin air to fulfill unknown purposes. Other times, seditious plotting by an extra party resulted in someone's hasty departure. Whatever the origins of the case, Keen persevered until the secrets came out. (The show's fan mail in those days often requested Keen's personal assistance in helping to locate missing beaus, kids, spouses and other relatives who seemingly evaporated, too, much like the mythical subjects had done in the radio play.)

In late 1943 the program implemented some radical changes as it transitioned from a quarter-hour serial to a half-hour format. Each narrative was brought to conclusion in a single episode beginning then. While the billboard concerning the missing citizens and celebrated cases remained a portion of the spiel proclaimed by the narrator at the inception of each performance—with Keen even then prominently cited as the "tracer of lost persons"—the investigator began to look exclusively into murders.

Each tale opened with a brief vignette in which a slaying was committed and a victim frequently declaring something like: "Why, it's you!" And then, momentarily, after a shot had rung out: "Why, you— you've killed me!" followed by a thud as a body hit the floor. The scriptwriter was

Mr. Keen, Tracer of Lost Persons: Saints preserve us! When "the kindly old investigator" takes from his files and presents one of his most widely celebrated missing persons' cases, *Mr. Keen, Tracer of Lost Persons* and his partner, Mike Clancy, share some fascinating (and at times, unintentionally humorous) dialogue. Bennett Kilpack (facing camera) originated the part of the respected sleuth while Irishman Jim Kelly played Clancy.

cautious enough to avoid having the target release the name of the killer before he died, however, or else there would have been little for Keen to do. Someone close to the victim would subsequently visit Keen's office to plead for his assistance in solving the homicide. That friend or relative's effusive gratitude to Keen for taking on the case had a hollow ring to it—after all, that was the job he was engaged by clients to do, and since he was readily able to drop everything and visit the crime scene at once, it habitually appeared that he was awaiting a new case to provide his bread and butter.

It consistently seemed a bit awkward, in addition, that the victim's caring acquaintance never waited for the police to solve the crime, hiring Keen at an undisclosed sum (money was *never* mentioned) within a few hours of the body being warm. Were law enforcement officials with their years of professional training and experience simply inept? Such questions probably wandered through the minds of many fans now and then.

Searching for those who had polished off a relative, former lover, business associate or other contact, especially anyone who could make trouble for the perpetrator, Keen interrogated three or four high profile suspects who were close to the victim. Applying minimal logic—often only mere coincidence, slips of the tongue and twists of fate would prove key—Keen then unraveled the clues, fingered the assassin and brought him to face a waiting justice "in the electric chair." While the narrative ran for more than 11 years in that pursuit, the haunting refrain of the series' original theme, *Someday I'll Find You*, persisted as the crime drama wafted on and off the airwaves. In those days, of course, there was no searching for missing persons; the only thing missing was whodunit.

Keen possessed extraordinary deductive powers (apparently more than the local New York police). He could be charming and persuasive but his voice modified into a harsh tenor as he confronted cold-blooded killers. Mike Clancy, in the meantime, was a nimble-headed buffoon whose Irish brogue immediately distinguished him from all other members of the cast. While providing brawn as needed, his presence tended to defuse tense situations on a steady basis but offered little more.

An observer noted that such radio crime drama sidekicks offered "a warm and comical personality to counteract the business-like efficiency toward which the series' heroes tended." Clancy frequently made startling revelations that astonished only him, seldom the audience. In his most telling line, delivered almost weekly, he'd allow: "Saints preserve us, Mr. Keen! He's got a gun!" Carrying out the directives of the producing Hummert serial factory, every piece of dialogue was required to unmistakably identify speakers and subjects, which often dissolved the most banal scripts into simple charades.

One wag suggested that *Mr. Keen* might qualify as the grandfather of *Mr. Chameleon*, another Hummert radio detective. Keen had been airing for 11 years when Chameleon arrived; the progenitor was estimated to be about age 60 at that time (1948): "Keen and Chameleon were almost exactly alike, both drawn from the joint well of Frank and Anne Hummert, both working on the same kinds of murder cases, both using simple methods of catching killers and both using dumber-than-thou assistants," claimed the astute reviewer.

Mr. Keen—who was apparently born without a first name—could break all the rules that everyone else was subject to in a murder investigation:

(1) He visited crime scenes that should have been cordoned off from all but the police, while examining objects with disregard for possible fingerprints. He even removed articles at will from the scenes.

(2) He didn't have to report conversations with suspects and any knowledge he'd gained to investigative authorities.

(3) He bypassed search warrants, forcing illegal entry into victims' or suspects' homes or businesses while in search of clues that the police might have overlooked.

(4) In the end, he arrested those he fingered as killers, notwithstanding the fact that he had no power to do so.

"We usually work along with the police" was the prime justification given to anyone inquiring of Keen and Clancy's involvement in a murder case.

Typical titles of some of Mr. Keen's most widely celebrated missing persons cases during the catch-a-killer epoch (1943–55): "The Rented Cottage Murder Case," "Murder at a Mile a Minute," "The Poison Sandwich Murder Case," "The Silver Candlestick Murder Case," "Murder with a Thousand Witnesses," "The Quicksand Murder Case," "The Broken Window Murder Case," "The Case of the Two-Faced Murderer," "The Case of Murder and the Revengeful Ghost," "The Case of Murder and the Star of Death," "The Case of Murder and the Bloodstained Necklace," "The Country Club Murder Case," "The Forgotten Cave Murder Case" and "The Case of Murder and the Lady in Blue."

Radio comedians Bob (Elliott) and Ray (Goulding) capitalized on the melodramatic moments in the Keen scripts. Their parodies, under the wistful title of *Mr. Trace, Keener Than Most Persons*, amplified the unintentional clowning of Mike Clancy and kept listeners in stitches throughout the 1950s.

Mr. Mercury

On the Air: July 10–Dec. 25, 1951, ABC, Tuesday, 7:30 p.m. 30 minutes.
Sponsor: General Mills Inc. for its cereal brands and cooking aids.
Extant Episodes: None known.

CAST & CREDITS

Writers—Ken Pettus, Lou Scofield.
Music—John Gart.
Lead—Title role played by John Larkin.
Support Roles—Raymond Edward Johnson, Teri Keane, Gil Mack.

Amateur sleuths, it appeared, did a little of everything in their professional careers.

Mr. Mercury, christened a "secret investigator," pursued a livelihood as a circus acrobat. Yet the versatile physical specimen doubled as a private eye, applying his unique talents in crimesolving capers. The lore of the circus interwoven into the plots appealed especially to the younger listener, who found that battling evil under the big top was a happy circumstance that most other detectives simply ignored.

While short-lived, this series filled half of the timeslot previously occupied by *Armstrong of the SBI* (1950–51), the successor to the legendary juvenile adventure feature *Jack Armstrong, the All-American Boy* (1933–50).

Mr. Moto

(aka *Mr. I. A. Moto*)

On the Air: May 20–Sept. 23, 1951, NBC, Sunday, 9:30 p.m.; Sept. 30–Oct. 7, 1951, NBC, Sunday, 10 p.m.; Oct. 13–Oct. 20, 1951, NBC, Saturday, 10:30 p.m. 30 minutes.
Sponsor: Sustained.
Extant Episodes: 15.

CAST & CREDITS

Producer—Harry W. Junkin.
Leads—Title role played by Peter Lorre, James Monks; Major Grant, played by John Larkin.
Support Roles—Gavin Gordon, Scott Tennison.

Japanese-born detective I. A. Moto, who had become a U.S. citizen, battled international espionage agents who were dedicated to bringing down the government of his adopted homeland. Despite maintaining an eye for the fairer gender, he proved his ability as a crime fighter while pursuing global assignments under the direction of Major Grant. When outwitted, in typical Japanese style, he acknowledged, "I must not lose face." Thereupon he rekindled his efforts to capture the evildoers.

The show's original billboard introduced him as "the world's greatest international detective-philosopher ... a man of mystery, of culture and sensitivity, a man who, while hating violence, fights communism ruthlessly both at home and abroad with his courage, his brains and his fabulous knowledge of international persons, places and things." That epigraph was later toned down to qualify him merely as "the inscrutable, crafty and courageous little oriental whose exploits have endeared him to millions of Americans." He could still be, as modestly as his author could state it, all things to all people.

The series was based on a fictional character created by Pulitzer Prize-winning author J. P. Marquand.

Consider the fact that less than a half-dozen years before this program premiered on the airwaves, Japanese-Americans were considered unfriendly to the U.S. (many were detained in federal prisons). Dropping the A-bomb on Hiroshima and Nagasaki lay just ahead. The attitudes of the American people and acceptance of those of many ethnic persuasions were significantly altered in a brief postwar period, as the possibility of airing a program like this attests.

Murder and Mr. Malone see The Amazing Mr. Malone

Murder by Experts

On the Air: June 11–July 30, 1949, MBS, Saturday, 2:30 p.m.; July 31–Sept. 18, 1949, MBS, Sunday, 10 p.m.; Sept. 26, 1949–Dec. 17, 1951, MBS, Monday, 9 p.m. 30 minutes.
Sponsor: Sustained.
Extant Episodes: 13.

CAST & CREDITS

Producer/Directors—Robert A. Arthur, David Kogan.
Music—Emerson Buckley.

Sound Effects—Mario Siletti.
Announcer—Phil Tonkin.
Hosts—John Dickson Carr (1949), Brett Halliday, Alfred Hitchcock (1951).
Support Roles—Cameron Andrews, Frank Behrens, Ralph Camargo, Ian Martin, Byrna Raeburn, Ann Shepherd (pseudonym for Scheindel Kalish), Lawson Zerbe, Bill Zuckert.

In a sense this series was a play within a play. Each week it dramatized the works of a different mystery writer, possibly unknown or of some repute, whose work was introduced by a widely celebrated "master of mystery," the program's recurring host. These narratives were often spine-tingling cops-and-killers tales of murder most foul and usually with highly charged plots of crime and passion. Notable mystery authors—the "experts" in the series title—were said to have personally selected the dramas that were aired. Those scribes were depicted as "masters of the art of murder" who could "hold tensity at its highest." For a given week's show the host announced that a renowned author (e.g. Hugh Pentecost) "has selected a story by a young newcomer you'll do well to watch" (e.g. Andrew Evans). The action and dialogue ensued, based on a thriller penned by that week's featured mystery novelist.

Robert A. Arthur and David Kogan also wrote, produced and directed *The Mysterious Traveler* (1943–52) over MBS.

Jay Hickerson prepared a log for this series.

Murder Is My Hobby

On the Air: Oct. 14, 1945–July 14, 1946, MBS, Sunday, 4 p.m. 30 minutes.
Sponsor: Knox gelatin dessert mixes.
Extant Episodes: None known.

CAST & CREDITS

Writer—Richard Wilkinson.
Sound Effects—Dorothy Langley.

Announcer—Rod O'Connor.
Lead—Barton Drake, played by Glenn Langan.

Barton Drake, a mystery writer who earned the core of his income as a police detective investigator, pursued the perpetrators of many diverse atrocities. He also successfully turned his professional exploits into a series of published volumes under the banner *Mystery Is My Hobby*. A certain contingent of broadcast gumshoes, it seemed, couldn't get along without generating a sideline income.

An outgrowth of this series was a slightly augmented crime drama titled *Mystery Is My Hobby*. It was the same appellation as the books in which mythical criminologist Barton Drake was the protagonist. This follow-up show subsequently appeared in syndication between 1949 and 1951. (See separate entry.)

Murder Will Out

On the Air: Jan. 30, 1945–June 25, 1946, ABC West Coast Network, Tuesday. 30 minutes.
Sponsor: Ranier Brewing Co. for Ranier ale and beer.
Extant Episodes: One.

CAST & CREDITS

Producer/Director/Writer—Lew Lansworth.
Host/Announcer—Larry Keating.
Leads—Inspector Burke, played by Edmund MacDonald (early 1945), William Gargan (1945–46); Detective Nolan, played by Eddie Marr.

In these authentic crime narratives, Inspector Burke and Detective Nolan faced schemers who cheated copyrighted music owners, a plethora of bribers, killers and those behind other none-too-nice vices. Before the solutions were revealed, two men and two women were plucked from a live studio audience and asked to identify the perpetrators. Correct answers to the

clues put to these amateur sleuths earned them five bucks in war stamps. If anyone picked the right clue *and* named the slayer, he earned a fifty-dollar war bond for himself, plus a framed gold detective diploma.

The Adventures of Ellery Queen (see separate entry) adopted the mystery quiz formula, and several other unique variations are clustered at that site.

The Mysteries in Paris

On the Air: Jan. 4, 1932–April 10, 1933, CBS, Monday, 9:30 p.m. 30 minutes.
Sponsor: Bourjois Perfume Co. for Evening in Paris fragrances.
Extant Episodes: None known.

CAST & CREDITS

Music—Billy Artzt (orchestra).
Support Company—Elsie Hitz, John McGovern, Agnes Moorehead.

The object of an ongoing, persistent and tenacious chase in this early crime drama was a creepy, forceful leader of the Paris underworld known only by the trade name of "The Octopus." Tracking his movements were a resolute American heiress and a titled Englishman (but not Lord Henry Brinthrope, the spouse of *Our Gal Sunday*), a member of the British Secret Service.

Mystery in the Air

On the Air: July 5–Sept. 27, 1945, NBC, Thursday, 10 p.m. 30 minutes.
Sponsor: R. J. Reynolds Tobacco Co. for Camel cigarettes.
Extant Episodes: None known (although eight of the anthology series described below survive).

CAST & CREDITS

Director—Kenneth MacGregor.
Writer—Robert Newman.

Leads—Stonewall Scott, played by Stephen Courtleigh; Dr. Alison, played by Joan Vitez.
Support Roles—Geoffrey Bryant (Tex), Ed Jerome (Dr. Dietrich).

Private detective Stonewall Scott combined strong logic powers with the precise systematic approaches practiced by attractive pathologist Dr. Alison (who possessed a dynamite figure and personality) in Scott's ongoing quest to capture bad guys and gals. Like many others in radio fiction, Dr. Alison was apparently born without a first name, giving rise to some terribly formal dialogue exchanges. Nor was there any hint that hanky-panky was taking place between the two principals; perhaps this was due to the language chasm.

A far cry from this little saga, a series also aired under the same moniker on NBC Thursday nights in the summer of 1947 (July 3–Sept. 25) that starred Peter Lorre. He presided over a terror-packed anthology of nineteenth century horror tales. Both features under this title were summer replacements for the vacationing *Abbott and Costello Show* but professed little similarities. While the Lorre expedition was given major attention by radio historiographers, regretfully most of them ignored the earlier detective series.

Mystery Is My Hobby

On the Air: 1949–51, Syndicated. 30 minutes.
Sponsor: Sold to local underwriters in markets where it was aired.
Extant Episodes: 64.

CAST & CREDITS

Producer—Dave Titus.
Announcer—Bruce Buell.
Music—Len Salvo.
Sound Effects—Bill Hoffman, Adrian Penner.
Leads—Barton Drake, played by Glenn Langan (who had also portrayed that role in an

earlier series, *Murder Is My Hobby)*; Inspector Danton, played by Ken Christy, Norman Field; Mike (Barton's houseboy), played by Charles Lung.

Wealthy fictional novelist Barton Drake probed the shady sides of the Big Apple on a regular basis to acquire fodder for his mystery volumes. Working alongside police Inspector Danton, he had little trouble turning up illicit and illegal activities of multiple persuasions. He often found himself the crimesolver, the police inspector making excuses for his own personal deficiencies. The drama was an extension of an earlier series (on MBS, 1945–46) featuring Drake, titled *Murder Is My Hobby*. (See separate entry.)

The Mystery Man

On the Air: March 24, 1941–March 13, 1942, NBC, Weekdays, 2:15 p.m. 15 minutes.
Theme Song: *Swan Lake* (excerpts).
Sponsor: General Mills Inc. for Wheaties cereal and Gold Medal flour.
Extant Episodes: None known.

CAST & CREDITS

Lead—Jay Jostyn as host/narrator for the anthology dramas.
Support Roles—Vera Allen, Brad Barker, Charita Bauer, George Baxter, Ray Bramley, Joseph Branby, Sarah Burton, Delma Byron, MacDonald Carey, Teresa Dale, Doris Dalton, H. Davis, Margaret Douglas, Malcolm Dunn, Morgan Farley, Neil Fitzgerald, Templeton Fox, Mercedes Gilbert, Claire Granville, Stanley Harrison, Joe Helgeson, Winfield Hooey, Eunice Howard, Mona Hungerford, Dick Janaver, Edward Jepson, Alexander Kirkland, Bernard Lenrow, Basil Longhrane, Donald MacDonald, Jerry Macy, Adrienne Marden, Don McLaughlin, Beatrice Miller, Marilyn Miller, Frances Oliver, Florence Pendleton, Bartlett Robinson, Sid Smith, Hester Sondergaard, Chester Stratton, Kay Strozzi, Elizabeth Sutherland,

Gladys Thornton, Vicki Vola, Gertrude Warner, Ethel Wilson, Margaret Wycherly, Lawson Zerbe.

Complete tales in multiple episodes, these detective narratives were drawn from popular suspense novels of the era. They included, in order: *The Window at the White Cat*, by Mary Roberts Rinehart; *The Bannister Case*, by Jonathan Stagg; *The Circular Staircase*, by Mary Roberts Rinehart; *The Mystery of the Priceless Ambergris*, by Phoebe Atwood Taylor; *The Black Curtain*, by Cornell Woolrich; *The Glass Slipper*, by Mignon Eberhart; *Red Roses and White Roses*, by Q. Patrick; *A Woman Named Smith*, by Marie Conway Demler; and *The Dark Garden*, by Mignon Eberhart.

Raymond William Stedman, author of *The Serials: Suspense and Drama by Installment*, commented: "*The Mystery Man* was a good escapist series, inserted in a favorable position within The Gold Medal Hour [2–3 p.m. weekdays on NBC]. It failed, nevertheless. Respectable but not spectacular ratings were not enough for a prime broadcasting spot when Irna Phillips stood ready with a new, and open-end, drama needing a home."

A log for this series was prepared by David Easter.

Mystery of the Week

On the Air: April 1, 1946–Nov. 21, 1947, CBS, Weekdays, 7 p.m. 15 minutes.
Sponsor: Procter & Gamble Co. for Ivory soap and Dreft dishwashing detergent.
Extant Episodes: None known.

CAST & CREDITS

Writers—Alfred Bester, Louis Vittes.
Announcers—Nelson Case, Ron Rawson, Richard Stark.
Lead—M. Hercule Poirot, played by Harold Huber.

Among crime novelist Agatha Christie's many fictional conceptions, none was more enthralling nor amusing than the five-foot-four mustachioed, insufferably immodest Belgian detective M. Hercule Poirot. Transferred from London to New York for the radio series, his deductive powers intensified as he relied upon his "little grey cells." The exotic nature of things foreign provided an appropriate milieu for Poirot who was often involved in substantive international capers.

The Adventures of M. Hercule Poirot appears as a separate entry.

Mystery Theater

(aka *Inspector Mark Sabre*, aka *Mark Sabre*)

On the Air: Oct. 3, 1951–June 11, 1952, ABC, Wednesday, 8 p.m.; Oct. 8, 1952–July 1, 1953, ABC, Wednesday, 8 p.m.; Oct. 7, 1953–June 30, 1954, ABC, Wednesday, 9:30 p.m. 30 minutes.
Sponsor: Sterling Drugs Inc. for Phillips Milk of Magnesia laxative, Bayer Aspirin pain reliever, Ironized Yeast energy supplement, Dr. Lyon's tooth powder, Double Danderene hair preparation and a long line of other personal and health care goods.
Extant Episodes: 49 *Mystery Theater* plus four *Mark Sabre*.

CAST & CREDITS

Producers—Anne Hummert, Frank Hummert, Gene Patterson.
Director—Frank Papp.
Writers—Jay Bennett, Ken Field, Edward Francis, Peter Lyon, Lawrence Menkin, Joseph Russell, Charles Tazewell, Bill Wyman.
Music—Clark Whipple.
Sound Effects—Charles Grenier.
Announcer—Roger Forster.
Leads—Title role played by Robert Carroll, Les Damon, Bill Johnstone; Tim Maloney, played by Walter Burke, James Westerfield.

Support Roles—Joan Alexander, Walter Burke, Bob Hague, Santos Ortega, Luis Van Rooten.

A little history is in order for *Mark Sabre* evolved from earlier inspirations that simply kept reproducing themselves into offshoots. At its inception on Sept. 7, 1943, over NBC, the progenitor series was sponsored by Molle shaving cream and was thereby popularly known as the *Molle Mystery Theater*. It consisted of mystery and detective fiction selected and introduced by Geoffrey Barnes, a pseudonym of actor Bernard Lenrow. Its content included adaptations by popular fiction authors Raymond Chandler, Dashiell Hammett, Edgar Allen Poe, et al. until the program eventually began airing original works of contemporary authors. When Molle no longer underwrote the anthology, the Molle name was discarded effective Oct. 5, 1945, and the feature continued simply as *Mystery Theater* with Sterling Drugs Inc. paying its bills. Throughout this period the narrator changed several times.

Eight years into the run a couple of spin-off series developed. The first of those, *Hearthstone of the Death Squad*, aired over CBS between Aug. 30, 1951, and Sept. 17, 1952, and featured Alfred Shirley as a consummate Scotland Yard homicide detective. (See separate entry.)

A month after that launch the series took another twist when Inspector Mark Sabre was installed as a member of the homicide bureau of the Los Angeles Police Department. At that juncture, the mystery anthology ceased to focus dually upon the exploits of these brilliant achievers. Instead of beating answers out of informants and potential suspects, Mark Sabre much preferred quieter methods of obtaining data. He could, however—when an occasion called for it—strike a mean wallop with his left fist. (Obviously, no one was aware of police brutality in those days, and lawsuits for aggravated assaults were decades into the future.)

While tracking the down and dirty, mean and ugly of L.A., Sabre was shadowed by Sergeant Tim Maloney, his cohort. A critic pointed to Maloney's "likable awkwardness which meshed harmoniously with the intelligent and coy qualities of Inspector Mark Sabre."

Mystery Time see ABC Mystery Time

Mystery Time Classics see ABC Mystery Time

Mystery Without Murder

On the Air: July 5–Aug. 23, 1947, NBC, Saturday, 10 p.m. 30 minutes
Sponsor: Sustained.
Extant Episodes: None known.

CAST & CREDITS

Producer—Joseph F. Mansfield.
Writer—Alfred Bester.
Lead—Peter Gentle, played by Luther Adler.
Support Role—Gentle's secretary, played by Teri Keane.

No homicides here. Peter Gentle, admittedly a strange moniker for a private detective, actually lived out the quality suggested by his surname. This unusual series was absolutely devoid of slayings; it was, in fact, a respite for those listeners who wanted their mysteries without the blood and gore found elsewhere. Gentle was nonviolent to the core; when tense moments erupted, he usually went to his office to contemplate all the risks and consequences that lay before him.

While the program was a summertime replacement for the *Judy Canova Show*, it never returned to the air after its eight-week stint, possibly suggesting that most fans weren't that enthralled by its nonviolent thesis.

Ned Jordan, Secret Agent

On the Air: The series began on an undisclosed 1938 date over WXYZ, Detroit. Nov. 30–Dec. 28, 1939, MBS, Thursday, 10 p.m.; Jan. 4–May 2, 1940, MBS, Thursday, 9:30 p.m.; May 9–June 6, 1940, MBS, Thursday, 8:30 p.m.; Dec. 28, 1941–March 15, 1942, MBS, Sunday, 10:30 a.m.; April 5–May 10, 1942, MBS, Sunday, 2 p.m. 30 minutes.
Sponsor: Sustained.
Extant Episodes: Two plus four audition tapes.

CAST & CREDITS

Producer—George W. Trendle.
Director—Al Hodge.
Writer—Fran Striker (chief).
Announcers—Bob Hite, Rollon Parker, Jack Petruzzi.
Leads—Title role played by Jack McCarthy; Judy Medwick, played by Lee Allman, Shirley Squires; Agent Proctor, played by Dick Osgood.
Support Roles—A large company of WXYZ drama stock players.

Ned Jordan operated incognito. People thought he labored for the fictitious Consolidated American Railroad as an insurance investigator. That's just what he wanted them to think; undercover, he was gathering data on espionage agents working against the U.S. government. The "Federal Express," a long distance train plying a route between the Atlantic and Pacific seaboards—and a hotbed for adversaries of our nation—provided cover for Jordan as he probed into treasonable offenses. Agent Proctor, Jordan's link to the "Federal Department" (aka FBI), in-

cessantly bellowed at the conclusion of every pursuit: "This is an arrest! Uncle Sam wants *you!*" In addition to Proctor, only one other individual, J. B. Medwick, railroad president, knew Jordan's real identity and mission. Even Medwick's stunning daughter, Judy—Jordan's love interest *and* his personal assistant—at times seemed unaware of the contrived skullduggery.

In two-and-a-half years there were just 46 performances of this series in five time slots, or a median of nine shows per period. This radically reduced the odds of creating fan loyalty—the show was difficult to locate and some of those scheduled spots were infinitely less than desirable. One wonders: Could the network have been trying to kill it for reasons known only to itself?

The New Adventures of Michael Shayne see The Adventures of Michael Shayne

The New Adventures of Nero Wolfe see The Adventures of Nero Wolfe

The New Adventures of Philip Marlowe see The Adventures of Philip Marlowe

The New Adventures of the Thin Man see The Adventures of the Thin Man

Nick Carter, Master Detective

(aka *The Return of Nick Carter*)

On the Air: April 11–18, 1943, MBS, Sunday, 5:30 p.m.; April 27–July 6, 1943, MBS, Tuesday, 9:30 p.m.; July 12–Oct. 25, 1943, MBS, Monday, 9:30 p.m.; Nov. 3–24, 1943, MBS, Wednesday, 8:30 p.m.; Dec. 4, 1943–April 15, 1944, MBS, Saturday, 7 p.m.; April 17–21, 1944, MBS, four undisclosed weekdays; April 24–June 9, 1944, MBS, Weekdays, 9:15 p.m.; June 12–Sept. 1, 1944, MBS, Weekdays; Oct. 1, 1944–April 15, 1945, MBS, Sunday, 3:30 p.m.; April 22, 1945–Feb. 24, 1946, MBS, Sunday, 6 p.m.; March 5–Aug. 13, 1946, MBS, Tuesday, 8 p.m.; Aug. 18, 1946–Sept. 21, 1952, MBS, Sunday, 6:30 p.m.; Sept. 28, 1952–July 12, 1953, MBS, Sunday, 6 p.m.; July 19, 1953–Sept. 25, 1955, MBS, Sunday, 4:30 p.m. 30 minutes, except 15 minutes (April 17–Sept. 1, 1944).

Sponsors: Sustained (April 11, 1943–Sept. 1, 1944, April 22, 1945–Sept. 8, 1946, June 12, 1949–Sept. 21, 1952, July 19, 1953–June 5, 1955); Acme Paints and Lin-X Home Brighteners (Oct. 1, 1944–April 15, 1944); Old Dutch cleanser (Sept. 15, 1946–June 5, 1949); Libby, McNeill and Libby Packing Co. for Libby canned fruits and vegetables (Sept. 28, 1952–July 12, 1953); Harrison Products (June 12–Aug. 14, 1955).

Extant Episodes: 106.

CAST & CREDITS

Producer/Director—Jock MacGregor.
Writers—Alfred Bester, Norman Daniels, Ferrin N. Fraser, David Kogan, Milton J. Kramer, John McGreevey.
Music—Hank Sylvern, Lew White, George Wright (organists).
Sound Effects—Adrian Penner, Mario Siletti.
Announcers—Michael Fitzmaurice, Ken Powell.
Leads—Title role played by Lon Clark; Patsy Bowen, played by Helen Choate, Charlotte Manson (from mid 1946); Scrubby Wilson, played by John Kane; Sergeant Mathison, played by Ed Latimer.

Support Roles—Mary Jane Higby, Raymond Edward Johnson, Bill Johnstone, James Kreiger, Joseph Latham, Bill Lipton (Chick Carter), John Raby, Bryna Raeburn.

Urbane, sophisticated private investigator Nick Carter was commonly abetted by a trio of supporters who helped him flush out clues in his criminal cases. As the skilled investigator rummaged through the evidence they amassed, he'd painstakingly expound on each item during an epilogue, revealing how it figured in pointing a finger at a given suspect. At the end the culprit often made a dash to get away, shouting something like, "You'll never take me alive, Carter," then succumbing in some ghastly demise. One reviewer could have been on target when chiding that the dialogue "contained much of the Keen-Chameleon triteness," a punishing remnant from a couple of Frank and Anne Hummert-inspired gumshoe features.

Within Carter's inner circle were charming-yet-adroit protégée Patsy Bowen, his efficient secretary-assistant who often suffered emotional and physical distress at the hands of her mentor; "demon" news-journalist Scrubby Wilson, who really wasn't a demon after all; and local police Sergeant "Matty" Mathison. Bowen and Wilson found bliss in making life hell for Mathison as they sought opportunities to undercut his aid by spotlighting the dazzling triumphs of Nick Carter.

The drama proffered a distinctive opening, making excellent use of its sound effects technicians. Following five tumultuous raps in rapid succession on Carter's Brownstone office door, there was a slight pause followed by a subsequent number of wallops. After another brief pause, five more whacks ensued, this time louder and with some acceleration. At that juncture—as if she had been asleep inside—Carter's right hand, Patsy Bowen, yanked open the door with a surprised: "What's the matter—

what is it?" To which an unidentified male voice would excitedly, in rapid-fire exclamation, respond: "Another case for *Nick Carter, Master Detective!*" Then a slightly jovial interlocutor would inject: "Yes, it's another case for that most famous of all man-hunters—the detective whose ability at solving crime is unequaled in detective fiction." (One simply had to overlook the writers' tendency to embellish with editorial license.) And then ominously, the topic of "today's case" would be announced.

The show was another radio play in which the audience was reminded: "This program is fictional and any resemblance to actual persons, living or dead, or to actual names or places, is purely coincidental." So much for Carter's "unequaled" ability in crimesolving.

The mythical character of Nick Carter created by John Russell Coryell initially appeared in 1886 in pulp fiction detective stories. Street and Smith published these dime novel Victorian classics collectively known as *New York Weekly*. In March 1940 Carter turned up again in the first issue of Street and Smith's *Shadow Comics*, a compendium of most of that firm's prominent mythical heroes of the past. So successful was the concept that Carter regularly emerged in subsequent issues of this same illustrated periodical.

This radio series had the misfortune of being handed one of the most convoluted schedules in broadcast drama. After its initial couple of appearances, it was shifted in its third week to a new day and time and surprisingly retitled *The Return of Nick Carter*. The new moniker stuck until Dec. 8, 1946, when it reverted to the original *Nick Carter, Master Detective*. In the meantime, the drama was playing short runs all over Mutual's schedule. In its first year it was heard in five different time slots on as many separate days.

When it went to serialization in 1944, it aired four days and then five days while shifting in and out of timeslots. Until the program hit an extended streak in 1946, more than three years beyond its premiere, it bumbled around at 11 different schedule stops. That had to be distracting to the fans and make it difficult for the show to secure loyal audiences. Yet in its final nine years on the air the show found staying power, moving only twice, boosting the profile of its namesake figure into a significant audio gumshoe.

A spinoff series for adolescents, *Chick Carter, Boy Detective*, emerged only three months after *Nick Carter, Master Detective*, arrived on the ether. Chick was Nick's adopted son and, as such, acquired considerable interest in becoming an investigator himself. That series lasted just two years, however, also on Mutual. (See separate entry.)

Never say die. In 1972 the *Adventures of Nick Carter* surfaced as a single TV Movie of the Week in technicolor. Directed by Paul Krasny with screenplay by Ken Pettus, the film starred Robert Conrad as the legendary sleuth. Hollywood luminaries with contributing roles included Shelley Winters, Broderick Crawford, Neville Brand, Pernell Roberts, Pat O'Brien, Dean Stockwell and Jaye P. Morgan.

Night Watch

On the Air: April 5, 1954–May 24, 1954, CBS, Monday, 10:05 p.m.; May 28–July 9, 1954, CBS, Friday, 9:30 p.m.; July 17–Sept. 18, 1954, CBS, Saturday, 8:30 p.m.; Sept. 30, 1954–April 21, 1955, CBS, Thursday, 8:30 p.m. 30 minutes, except 25 minutes (May 3–24, 1954).
Sponsor: Sustained.
Extant Episodes: 46 plus two audition tapes.

CAST & CREDITS
Producer—Sterling Tracy.
Announcer—Dan Cubberly.
Host—Don Reed, portraying himself.

Support Roles—Voices of law officers, perpetrators, victims, witnesses and others were those of real subjects. William Froug was CBS supervisor; Vernon McKenney, engineer; Ray Gerhardt, editor.

In this reality-based series police reporter Don Reed traveled the environs of Culver City, Calif., between 6 p.m. and 2 a.m. alongside a couple of detectives. With the aid of a portable recorder, Reed taped on-the-scene reports from crime venues as the detectives responded to radio calls and conducted their investigations. Reed then introduced what he recorded to radio audiences through ad-lib narration: "You will actually ride with this detective unit and follow the activities of the police officers in this car," he informed listeners in an opening billboard. "You'll watch and listen to me as the cases unfold." Professional actors, scripts, music and sound effects were conspicuously absent, adding significantly to the believability and authenticity, which of course was just what it demonstrated. In some ways this effort was a precursor to the contemporary *Cops* series filmed for modern TV.

The program was presented with the cooperation of the Culver City police department. Chief W. N. Hildebrand was given on-air credit in every installment.

The Notorious Tarique

On the Air: Aug. 16, 1947, ABC, Saturday. Time and cancellation unsubstantiated although the run was brief. 30 minutes.
Sponsor: Sustained.
Extant Episodes: One.

CAST & CREDITS

Producer—Milton Merlin.
Director—Dwight Hauser.
Writer—Milton Merlin.
Music—Basil Adlam (orchestra).
Lead—Title role played by Turhan Bey.

François Tarique, a Frenchman, while a debonair continental sophisticate, was considered by adversaries to be "one of the most dangerous men in the world." His ongoing search for valuables and one-of-a-kind objects of all types—in particular, jewels and rare, priceless artifacts—had him combing the globe, exposing him to intrigue and mystery, romance, corruption, thievery and criminal activity of many sorts in far-flung, exotic locales. Working with local law enforcement, Tarique frequently assisted in recovering stolen art, antiquities and other loot and saw that their pilferers were put away. He also discovered that it was difficult for him to resist the charms of a fetching damsel, even when she might be on the questionable side of the law.

Official Detective

On the Air: Jan. 19–March 30, 1947, MBS, Sunday, 2:15 p.m.; June 24–Sept. 23, 1947, MBS, Tuesday, 8:15 p.m.; Sept. 30, 1947–July 13, 1948, MBS, Tuesday, 8:30 p.m.; July 20–Nov. 2, 1948, MBS, Tuesday, 8:30 p.m.; Nov. 20, 1948–April 2, 1949, MBS, Saturday, 1:30 p.m.; April 9–June 4, 1949, MBS, Saturday, 2 p.m.; June 7, 1949–Jan. 15, 1952, MBS, Tuesday, 8:30 p.m.; Jan. 20–June 29, 1952, MBS, Sunday, 8 p.m.; Sept. 28, 1952–Jan. 4, 1953, MBS, Sunday, 6:30 p.m.; Jan. 8, 1953–March 7, 1957, MBS, Thursday, 8 p.m. 15 minutes (Jan. 19–Sept. 23, 1947), 25 minutes (Sept. 30, 1947–July 13, 1948; Jan. 20–June 29, 1952), 30 minutes (all others).
Sponsors: Sustained (Jan. 19–Sept. 23, 1947, July 20, 1948–Jan. 4, 1953); Pharmaco Inc. for Feen-a-Mint chewing gum laxative and other pharmaceutical products (Sept. 30, 1947–July 13, 1948); Participating sponsorship (Jan. 8, 1953–March 7, 1957).
Extant Episodes: 19.

CAST & CREDITS

Director—Wynn Wright.
Writers—Jack Bentkover, William Wells.

Music—Chet Kingsbury (organist), Sylvan Levin (orchestra).
Sound Effects—Al April, Ron Harper.
Announcers—Jack O'Riley, Dwight Weist.
Leads—Dan Britt, played by Joe McCormack, Ed Begley, Craig McDonnell; Al Bowen, played by Tom Evans, Louis Nye.
Support Roles—Frank Barton, Charlotte Dembo, Joe DeSantis, Dana Hardwicke, Eileen Palmer, Alan Stevenson, Luis Van Rooten, Chuck Webster, Bill Zuckert.

Harvested from the pages of *Official Detective* magazine, this drama offered behind-the-scenes examinations of a metropolitan police department—"the men who guard your safety and protect your home." Hard-boiled Detective Lieutenant Dan Britt, assisted by Sergeant Al Bowen, offered adaptations of real cases as their own, going after killers, arsonists and gangsters of many stripes.

Assessing the series, one reviewer claimed: "The same thing was done better on *The Lineup* and much better on *Dragnet.*"

In a brief TV release of this anthology series in 1957 via syndication under the radio series title, Everett Sloane hosted. Stories were still derived from the magazine of the same name.

The Orange Lantern

On the Air: Oct. 2, 1932–July 2, 1933, NBC Blue, Sunday, 10:30 p.m. 30 minutes.
Theme Song: Original melody (Sven von Hallberg).
Sponsor: Sustained.
Extant Episodes: None known.

CAST & CREDITS

Director—Joseph Bell.
Writer—Innes Osborn.
Music—Sven von Hallberg.
Leads—Richard Norris, played by William Shelley; Olga Nesheim, played by Georgia Backus; Botak, played by Arthur Hughes.

Support Roles—Peggy Allenby, Johnny McGovern, Agnes Moorehead, Bill Shelley, Bruno Wick.

For District Attorney Richard Norris, bringing criminals to justice was all in a day's work. Together with his love interest, Olga Nesheim, Norris crusaded against some of the most ferocious bad guys of the air. The most formidable and persistent of their lot was Botak, an amusing but clever Javanese jewel thief who plainly had more diabolical schemes up his sleeve than mere heists. Indeed, the contemptible Botak's plotting has been compared to that of crafty conniver Fu Manchu, who was simultaneously appearing over on rival network CBS. Both were oriental madmen who conspired to snuff out the freedoms of individuals everywhere, and perhaps threaten the very existence of life itself. At all costs, then, Botak's intents must fail; it was ultimately up to Norris to see that he was unsuccessful.

For an interesting contrast, read the entry under *The Shadow of Fu Manchu*, the much more widely appreciated evil character.

Our Secret Weapon

On the Air: Aug. 9–Oct. 18, 1942. CBS, Sunday, 7 p.m.; Oct. 16, 1942–Oct. 8, 1943, CBS, Friday, 7:15 p.m. 15 minutes.
Sponsor: Sustained (Aug. 9–Oct. 18, 1942); Philco Corp. for Philco household appliances (Oct. 16, 1942–Oct. 8, 1943).
Extant Episodes: None known.

CAST & CREDITS

Writer—Paul Luther, Rex Stout.
Researcher—Sue Taylor White.
Host—Rex Stout.
Support Roles—Paul Luther (Adolph Hitler); Ted Osborne (Hirohito); Guy Repp (Mussolini).

In this bizarre feature, Rex Stout, the author of the Nero Wolfe detective novels, refuted current German-Italian-Japanese propaganda broadcasts. To assist him in his crime fighting, CBS staffers collected actual material aired each week. An announcer read some of the Axis powers' claims on this show, only to be interrupted by Stout, who offered a response from the Allied powers' point of view. Occasionally major addresses given in other languages were included in brief narratives, in order to make emphatic points.

Pat Novak for Hire

On the Air: Launched as a regional series over KGO, San Francisco, in 1946 and expanded to the ABC West Coast network shortly thereafter (1946–47). Feb. 13–March 27, 1949, ABC, Sunday, 7 p.m.; April 2–May 7, 1949, ABC, Saturday, 9:30 p.m.; May 14–June 18, 1949, ABC, Saturday, 8 p.m. 30 minutes.
Sponsor: Gallan Kamps shoe stores (1946–47); Sustained (1949).
Extant Episodes: 24.

CAST & CREDITS
Producer/Director—William P. Rousseau.
Writers—Richard Breen, Gil Doud.
Music—Basil Adlam.
Announcers—Franklyn Evans, George Fenneman.
Leads—Title role played by Jack Webb, Ben Morris; Jocko Madigan, played by Jack Lewis, Tudor Owen; Inspector Hellman, played by John Galbraith, Raymond Burr.

Despite its annoying proclivity for overindulging in similes ad nauseam—(e.g. "The guy had a face like three pounds of warm putty," "Everything was in place like a mixmaster in a bride's kitchen," "I had about as much chance as a bottle of scotch at a cocktail party," "He was creeping up the stairs like a stallion with a broken leg")—*Pat Novak for Hire* was the series that literally thrust actor Jack Webb into national prominence as radio's inveterate rowdy. As first cousin to *Johnny Madero* (of San Francisco's *Pier 23*), Novak also covered the Embarcadero waterfront. A moody, acid-tongued rebel, he had a nasty disposition and—like his soul mate just a couple of piers away—rented fishing vessels to earn an income. The dual figures were mirror images—hard-boiled, tough-minded, with Webb's voice to match.

The same offbeat, atypical hulking man of the cloth, Father Leahy, prominent in *Madero's* scripts, turned up on occasion in *Novak's* narratives. Leahy networked with underworld contacts while keeping a watchful eye on the throbbing heartbeat of Frisco's teeming coastline. But without exception it was Jocko Madigan, Novak's hard-drinking waterfront pal, who gathered data for him when he was sober: "Risking my life is one of the bravest things you do," Madigan reminded Novak. Police Inspector Hellman, on the other hand, was Novak's nemesis, despising him for unenumerated trespasses. Incessantly, the plots always led to a knockout blonde, brunette or redhead and thereafter to Novak's acquiring a rap on the head, then waking up to explain his presence alongside a dead body to a curious bunch of cops.

It was campy and predictable; fans may have tuned in for the merciless metaphors and their sure-fire delivery. "I'll dirty you up like a locker-room towel," Novak advised an attractive femme fatale, spiraling from ambivalent flirtation into reckless warning. The truth was, you never knew what would spew out of his mouth—and maybe that was what made it the fleeting success that it was.

One reviewer noted that Jack Webb developed an "almost cult following" for his portrayal of the "hilarious hard boiled" detective *Pat Novak for Hire*. It was the first of a quartet of dramas in which the actor was to portray a detective. *Novak* coast-to-coast followed Webb's brief tenure as *Johnny Madero, Pier 23* and as *Jeff Regan, Investigator*, all of them leading to the debut of the eminently more popular *Dragnet*.

When Jack Webb departed from San Francisco for Los Angeles in 1947, ABC recast the *Novak* lead to continue airing the series. Ben Morris, who followed Webb, "played it straight and died trying," noted a critic. *Radio Life* published many letters inquiring of the whereabouts of Webb. Webb and writer Richard Breen then collaborated on Mutual's *Johnny Madero, Pier 23*. By early 1943 the pier pair was back at the familiar stand on *Novak*, then going out to a national ABC audience, which opened the door to *Dragnet* only a few months beyond.

One reviewer claimed the *Novak* series offered little but a showcase for Webb's quips: "He was the ultimate radio hardboiler." So unique was he that he was satirized by yet another detective series. *Richard Diamond* acquired a "funny-rude rival" in 1949 when a figure named "Pat Cosak" (note the similarity in names) appeared in a single episode. Cosak's behavior bore a striking resemblance to a heap of gestures displayed by Webb/Novak.

Perry Mason

On the Air: Oct. 18, 1943–March 31, 1944, CBS, Weekdays, 2:45 p.m.; April 3, 1944–March 13, 1945, CBS, Weekdays, 2:30 p.m.; March 26, 1945–Dec. 30, 1955, CBS, Weekdays, 2:15 p.m. 15 minutes.
Sponsor: Procter & Gamble Co. for Camay soap and Tide detergent.
Extant Episodes: 324 (280 without commercials).

CAST & CREDITS

Producers—Leslie Harris, Tom McDermott.
Directors—Hoyt Allen, Ralph Butler, Carlo De Angelo, Carl Eastman, Arthur Hanna.

Writers—Ruth Borden, Erle Stanley Gardner, Dan Shuffman, Irving Vendig (head), Eugene Wang.
Music—William Meeder (organist and pianist), Paul Taubman.
Sound Effects—Jimmy Lynch.
Announcers—Bob Dixon, Alan Kent, Richard Stark.
Leads—Title role played by Donald Briggs, Santos Ortega, Bartlett Robinson, John Larkin (1947–55); Della Street, played by Joan Alexander, Jan Miner, Gertrude Warner.
Support Roles—Paul Drake, played by Matt Crowley, Charles Webster; Lieutenant Tragg, played by Frank Dane, Mandel Kramer; also Maurice Franklin, Betty Garde, Mary Jane Higby, Arthur Vinton (Sergeant Dorsett).

While *Perry Mason* on radio could ostensibly be classified as a soap opera, arriving as it did each weekday afternoon in the midst of matinee melodrama, in its heyday it was as good as any nighttime thriller and superior to many. While its criminal activity was meted out on the installment plan, in reality it was the tale of a brilliant young attorney whose practice was a potboiler of intriguing capers that often required months to resolve, one case at a time. Reaching far beyond simple domestic homicides, Mason's convoluted plots inevitably led him to cases delving into organized crime. The average citizen sometimes found it tough to remain honest, and even alive at the hands of legions of underworld figures. Mason would be called upon to defend his clients outside the courtroom—perhaps protect them from sinister forces determined to eradicate them—as frequently as he was to defend them in the hall of justice.

It was a chilling quarter-hour with one episode leading directly into another. For die-hard fans, missing a daily dose was at times unimaginable. Della Street was Mason's right hand, secretary and confidante. He employed the services of private

Perry Mason: Theirs was an intense quarter-hour of murder and mayhem as dapper young attorney Perry Mason (John Larkin) and secretary-confidante Della Street (Joan Alexander) fought evil in the streets of "the city." As "defender of human rights ... champion of all those who seek justice," Mason introduced thrills and chills to matinee melodrama. Larkin and Alexander were longrunning principals in the cast.

investigator Paul Drake as needed. There was also police lieutenant Tragg, at times Mason's adversary, at other times his colleague. But the central figure was always the captivating, debonair, masculine pro-

fessional admired by women of all ages whose exploits for righteousness while defending the innocent carried those housewives far from the mundane of their normally simple existences. Even though it was pure fantasy, big doses of the formula became addictive to a fault.

By the time *Perry Mason* reached radio in 1943 the character had already become familiar to millions of mystery-novel fans. In the late 1920s Erle Stanley Gardner, a southern California lawyer, tried writing as a diversion. Creating an imaginary alter ego whom he called Perry Mason, Gardner was successful in turning his sideline craft into something more lucrative than a mere pastime. By the early 1930s he had earned widespread public acclaim for a series of *Mason* mystery novels that attracted large reading audiences. An unanswered question remained: Could a collection of avid crime readers and simple housewives be persuaded to transfer their loyalties from pulp fiction to a daytime drama exploiting the escapades of the lawyer-turned-supersleuth? An advertising agency (Pedlar and Ryan) and network programmers were optimistic, believing a little daytime mayhem would offer milady an attractive alternative to the steady domestic misery she experienced from other washboard weepers. For a dozen years the serial became one of CBS's best-received daytime dramas.

In a trilogy of formats (pulp fiction, radio, television) portraying the best-recalled fictional lawyer of all time, the populace seems to least remember the radio drama. Perhaps because *Perry Mason* was generally heard by a few million homemakers, there is a tendency to ignore the fact that he was ever on radio. Yet for a dozen years he carried on the tradition of the earlier print hero on radio, becoming a forerunner of the "defender of human rights" admired on TV by people of both genders and still seen internationally in cablevision reruns.

Under head writer Irving Vendig, *Perry Mason* flourished on the ether, reaching its stride by the late 1940s. Vendig developed the central character into one whose prolonged, yet absorbing action-packed exigencies caught the fancy of millions. As America's housewives attended to their ironing boards, dishpans and diapers, murder and mayhem in the afternoon may have been welcome relief. Vendig also heavily influenced a couple of TV's earliest soap operas, both with darker sides than the typical melodrama. He initially infused huge doses of mystery and intrigue accompanied by frequent organ stings into *Search for Tomorrow*, applying characteristic trademarks of the *Mason* radio series. And when Erle Stanley Gardner was reluctant to allow CBS to transform *Mason* into a TV soap opera, Vendig created *The Edge of Night*. For that latter enterprise John Larkin, radio's best identified *Mason*, was cast as the protagonist-star, initially as a detective, eventually as an attorney, in a thinly veiled copy of *Mason*.

When at last Gardner gave his blessing to a primetime TV *Mason* series, Raymond Burr was cast in the role—and played him magnificently from Sept. 21, 1957, through Sept. 4, 1966. Barbara Hale appeared as Della Street, with William Hopper as Paul Drake, William Talman as prosecutor Hamilton Berger and Raymond Collins as Lieutenant Arthur Tragg. The televersion differed radically from the radio play by presenting courtroom confessions—usually from the witness stand—at the close of each episode. In the radio drama the real culprit was usually known by the listener months before a trial, frequently even before Mason knew the guilty party's true identity.

Reruns of the TV series were widely syndicated after 1966. By 1973 CBS revived the show under the moniker *The New Perry Mason*, lasting just 14 weeks, Sept. 16, 1973, through Jan. 27, 1974. Monte Markham played Mason with Sharon Acker as Della and Albert Stratton as Paul.

However, there were several successful TV movies starring Burr as Mason, beginning with *Perry Mason Returns* on NBC-TV Dec. 1, 1985. Even after Burr died in 1993 more films with some of the living *Mason* characters were screened (e.g. *A Perry Mason Mystery: The Case of the Grimacing Governor*, over NBC-TV Nov. 9, 1994). It was a testimony to the power of the great character Erle Stanley Gardner had created nearly seven decades earlier.

A chapter on the radio series appears in the book *Perry Mason: The Authorship and Reproduction of a Popular Hero* by J. Dennis Bounds (Greenwood Press, 1996).

Pete Kelly's Blues

On the Air: July 4–Sept. 19, 1951, NBC, Wednesday, 8 p.m. 30 minutes.
Sponsor: Sustained.
Extant Episodes: Eight.

CAST & CREDITS

Creator—Richard Breen.
Writers—Jo Eisinger, James Moser.
Music—Meredith Howard (as Maggie Jackson, vocalist), "Pete Kelly's Big Seven" combo: Marty Carb (bass), Dick Cathcart (cornet), Nick Fatool (drums), Matty Matlock (clarinet), Bill Newman (guitar), Elmer Schneider (trombone), Ray Schneider (piano).
Announcer—George Fenneman.
Leads—Title role played by Jack Webb; George Lupo, played by Jack Kruschen.
Support Roles—Herb Butterfield, Whitfield Connor, William Conrad, Stacy Harris, Vic Perrin, Peggy Webber.

At first glance this series came across as more Dixieland music mixed with adventure and infinitely less crime drama than most of the shows in the pages of this volume. But jazz musician Pete Kelly frequently found himself facing personal danger as he attempted to thwart the plans of potential murderers, kidnappers, swindlers and other ill-willed denizens of 1920s Kansas City.

Kelly blew a cornet in a jazz ensemble that he put together. Their principal venue was George Lupo's smoke-filled lounge, a bar that served illegal drinks, defying the law during the Roaring Twenties era. The band offered a couple of sizzling numbers on every show.

Despite Kelly's own at-times debatable ethical virtues, he could be depended upon to help a friend in need, especially when criminal activity of a more serious nature was involved. For various reasons he was also regularly in conflict with gangsters, doing well to come out alive. In a colorful first-person epigraph at the start of each program, he stated: "My name's Pete Kelly ... I play cornet. You'll find us at 417 Cherry Street, Kansas City, on the Missouri side, just wide enough to frame a suspicious eye and the bottom of shot glasses aren't quite thick enough to reach the top. It's a well-run, orderly club, the kind of place the local prohibition agents can bring their wives to. The lease is owned by George Lupo ... he's a fat, friendly little guy who always has his hand in his pocket. We start grinding every night about ten and we play until Lupo runs out of inventory, but that's all right with us—he lets us play the kind of music we like."

A critic who viewed this drama as a return to actor Jack Webb's earlier *Pat Novak for Hire* series nevertheless cited *Kelly* as "one of Webb's best shows." Although it aired only one summer, it became a pet project for Webb, affording him the chance to integrate his love of jazz into his acting career. He had already become a mega media star, having launched *Dragnet* on radio in 1949, with several lesser series preceding it.

One authority recognized some alternative artists in the musical ensemble on this show: Jud DeMotto (bass), Ray Sherman (piano), George Van Eps (guitar).

Luther F. Sies observed: "Only a program such as the *Chamber Music Society of Lower Basin Street* consistently offered jazz as good as that broadcast weekly on *Pete Kelly's Blues.*"

In 1955 Jack Webb directed and starred in a color theatrical motion picture that was derived from the radio series, also titled *Pete Kelly's Blues.* Written by Richard L. Breen, the character's creator, the movie included a plethora of Hollywood celebrities including Andy Devine, Ella Fitzgerald, Peggy Lee, Janet Leigh, Jayne Mansfield, Lee Marvin, Martin Milner and Edmond O'Brien. Dick Cathcart, the cornet player from the radio days, dubbed in Kelly's solos off-screen while also conducting the band.

When the concept was carried to television, William Reynolds was cast in the lead with Jack Webb producing. The show debuted on NBC-TV Sundays at 8:30 p.m. on April 5, 1959, shifting to Fridays at 7:30 p.m. in July and departing forever on Sept. 4 of that year. A popular radio singer of that epoch, Connee Boswell, appeared as vocalist Savannah Brown. Others in the recurring cast included Phil Gordon as George Lupo and actor Fred (Anthony) Eisley as a cop, Johnny Cassiano. Dick Cathcart again reprised his off-camera work at the cornet and was also musical director.

Peter Quill

On the Air: April 14, 1940–March 30, 1941, MBS, Sunday, 4 p.m. 30 minutes.
Sponsor: Beich Candy Co. for various Brach brand confection treats.
Extant Episodes: None known.

CAST & CREDITS
Director/Writer—Blair Walliser.
Music—Ray Herbeck (orchestra).
Leads—Title Role played by Marvin Miller;

Gail Carson, played by Alice Hill; Roger Dorn, played by Ken Griffin.

Saboteurs, traitors, spies and espionage agents were all among Peter Quill's targets. Specializing in scientific technology, the detective used his multiple skills as weapons against those who would bring our nation to its knees. A novel diversion resulted with the romantic entanglement of Gail Carson, his assistant, and police captain Roger Dorn.

Philco Mysteries of the Air see *Phyl Coe Radio Mysteries*

Philo Vance

On the Air: July 5–Sept. 27, 1945, NBC, Thursday, 7:30 p.m.; beginning July 23, 1946, the series with an unidentified cast aired for a while over the ABC West Coast Network; 1948–50, Syndicated by Frederic W. Ziv Co. 30 minutes.
Sponsors: Lever Brothers Co. for Lifebuoy soap (1945); sold to local sponsors in various markets later.
Extant Episodes: 84 plus.

CAST & CREDITS
Producer—Frederic W. Ziv.
Director—Jeanne K. Harrison.
Writers—Kenny Lyons, Robert J. Shaw.
Music—Henry Sylvern (organist).
Sound Effects—Walt Gustafson.
Leads—Title role played by Jose Ferrer (1945), Jackson Beck (1948–50); Ellen Deering, played by Frances Robinson (1945), Joan Alexander (1948–50); Ernest Heath, played by Humphrey Davis; District Attorney Frank Markham, played by George Petrie.

Based on the detective character originated in mystery novels by S. S. Van Dine, Philo Vance pursued Van Dine's formula of scrupulous clue-gathering and last-minute disclosure. He had a secretary-love interest, Ellen Deering (one wag christened theirs a "flirtatious relationship"). Whatever it was, she insisted that—during work hours—he address her as "Miss Deering" and she refer to him as "Mr. Vance." Because, as a rule, Vance figured out the clues quicker than police sergeant Ernest Heath, Heath wasn't very friendly toward the perceptive private detective, leaving Vance with some disdain for the sergeant. In a syndicated version there was also a district attorney, Frank Markham, whom Vance highly respected. Vance approached his cases with an overriding dogma: "Somewhere along the line a murderer makes a mistake—it's my job to find that mistake." Many of the homicides he solved occurred at such fashionable venues as backstage at an opera house and at high-society events.

A quartet of Philo Vance B-movies made it to the big screen, one surfacing before the radio show was created and the others after its public exposure on the air. In none of the four, however, were there actors who have been revered by most theater-goers over the years and whose names have been memorable across the decades. The 1940 movie *Calling Philo Vance* starred James Stephenson as the master gumshoe and was directed by William Clemens with screenplay by Tom Reed. In the first of a trio of 1947 feature-length productions, *Philo Vance Returns*, William Wright portrayed Vance, William Beaudine directed and Robert E. Kent authored. Basil Wrangell directed and Eugene Conrad and Arthur St. Claire co-wrote the subsequent *Philo Vance's Gamble* starring Alan Curtis. In the final film, *Philo Vance's Secret Mission*, Curtis was again cast in the lead. The production was directed by Reginald Le Borg and penned by Lawrence Taylor.

Phyl Coe Radio Mysteries

(aka *The Adventures of Phil Cole*, aka *Philco Mysteries of the Air*)

On the Air: Feb. 29–May 16, 1936, Syndicated. 15 minutes.
Sponsor: Philco Corp. for Philco radios, tubes and other home appliances and parts.
Extant Episodes: 12.

Cast & Credits

Producer—Geare-Marston Inc. (syndication house).
Leads—Some celebrated radio personalities rotated their participation, including Clayton (Bud) Collyer, House Jameson, Jay Jostyn.

According to reviewer Jack French, Phyl Coe, a pun pointing to sponsor Philco Radio Corp., was the ether's initial feminine crimestopper. In those quarter-hour transcribed installments "the beautiful girl detective" appeared in a narrative that stopped short of revealing a crime's solution. Listeners, instead, were asked to submit their outcomes on official entry forms offered by local Philco dealers, with cash prizes awarded to lucky winners. Actual revelations were given on subsequent broadcasts.

The detective's gender, name and program title were subsequently altered in midstream, shifting during the program's second year on the air to Phil Cole.

Policewoman

On the Air: May 6–June 17, 1946, ABC, Monday, 10:45 p.m.; July 7, 1946–June 29, 1947, ABC, Sunday, 9:45 p.m. 15 minutes.
Sponsor: Carter Co. for Carter's Little Liver pills.
Extant Episodes: Three.

Cast & Credits

Producer/Director—Phillips H. Lord.
Music—Jesse Crawford (organist).

Announcers—Dick Dunham, Walter Herlihy.
Host/Narrator—Betty Garde in the role of Mary Sullivan.
Support Roles—Frances Chaney, Grace Keddy, Mandel Kramer.

True occurrences from the life of Sergeant Mary Sullivan, an ex-New York City cop, formed the basis for these narratives. Sullivan, former director of the Police Woman's Bureau, was a 35-year veteran of the NYC force's homicide squad. At the end of each weekly episode the broadcast gained a greater stamp of authenticity when the real Sergeant Sullivan added her personal reflections.

Policewoman is believed to be the first feminine crime fighter on radio who was sheer sleuth, devoid of humor, fancy or soap opera derivation.

Private Eye

On the Air: No information.
Sponsor: Sustained.
Extant Episodes: One.

CAST & CREDITS
Producer—Richard Aurandt.
Writer—Doug Hayes.
Music—Richard Aurandt.
Leads—Steve Mallory, played by Doug Hayes.
Support Roles—Paul Frees, Buddy Gray, Tom Holland, Rosemary Kelly, Monty Margetts, Stanley Waxman.

Steve Mallory jumped into an automobile, barking: "Follow that man!" as the series launched its merry chase. An announcer exclaimed: "Yes, follow that man! Follow him into danger, into romance and high adventure! Follow his trail wherever it leads—through a maze of thrills and spine-tingling intrigue! Yes, follow that man, because it's Steve Mallory, the *Private Eye!*" L. A.-based Mallory possessed a bent for saving damsels in distress while hunting for the hoodlums who put them in compromising spots. The story line could be violent at times but Mallory was infinitely up to the task.

It's feasible, although unsubstantiated, that only an audition tape for this series was produced. Almost all radio historians have ignored the feature, giving rise to the possibility that it never aired as a continuing series.

The Private Files of Matthew Bell

On the Air: March 16–June 8, 1952, MBS, Sunday, 4:30 p.m.; Sept. 7–Dec. 21, 1952, MBS, Sunday, 4:30 p.m. 30 minutes.
Sponsor: Seabrook Farms for a wide assortment of frozen foods.
Extant Episodes: None known.

CAST & CREDITS
Producer/Director—Himan Brown.
Writer—John Roeburt.
Announcer—Phil Tonken.
Lead—Title role played by Joseph Cotten.
Support Role—Fran Carlon.

In addition to his principal job as a police surgeon, Matthew Bell found ways of drawing upon his medical skills to pursue crimesolving. In the course of it he tended to engage the best and worst of humanity; they included innocent crime victims and violent offenders as well as celebrities and wealthy individuals. Bell drew upon the perception and empathy a physician needs to perform his work in assisting him in bringing criminals to justice.

The Private Files of Rex Saunders

On the Air: May 2–Aug. 8, 1951, NBC, Wednesday, 8:30 p.m. 30 minutes.

Sponsor: Radio Corp. of America for RCA Victor televisions, radios, phonographs and recordings.

Extant Episodes: 16.

CAST & CREDITS

Director—Himan Brown.

Writer—Ed Adamson.

Announcer—Kenneth Banghart.

Leads—Title role played by Rex Harrison; Alec, played by Leon Janney.

Support Roles—Alice Frost, Anne Seymour, Everett Sloane.

One couldn't help but think of *Bulldog Drummond* (1941–54), a better-known British detective, in following this series. The two dramas adopted identical music and both were launched with similar foghorns and footsteps. The British-born detective Rex Saunders had left his homeland, however, and was living at 643 West 69th Street in New York City. His single-named assistant, Alec, accompanied him on his righteous quests.

This fleeting summer replacement quite obviously attempted to capitalize on the success of the better-known *Bulldog Drummond*. That drama had left the air in early 1949 but was recalled by millions of fans. It was later revived on radio, in late 1953.

Pursuit

On the Air: Oct. 28, 1949–Jan. 13, 1950, CBS, Friday, 10 p.m.; Jan. 31–May 9, 1950, CBS, Tuesday, 10:30 p.m.; July 1–22, 1950, CBS, Saturday, 8 p.m.; July 10–Aug. 21, 1951, CBS, Tuesday, 9 p.m.; Sept. 18, 1951–March 25, 1952, CBS, Tuesday, 9:30 p.m. 30 minutes.

Sponsor: Sustained and Ford Motor Co. for its automotive products (Oct. 27, 1949–May 9, 1950); William J. Wrigley Co. for its chewing gum brands (July 1, 1950–Aug. 21, 1951); Molle shaving cream and Sterling Drugs Inc. for a line of personal and health care products like Dr. Lyon's tooth powder, Energine cleaning fluid, Double Danderine shampoo, Bayer aspirin, Phillip's Milk of Magnesia and Haley's M-O stomach analgesics (Sept. 18, 1951–March 25, 1952).

Extant Episodes: 11.

CAST & CREDITS

Producer/Directors—Elliott Lewis, William N. Robson.

Writers—Antony Ellis, E. Jack Neuman.

Music—Leith Stevens (orchestra, 1949–50), Marlin Skiles (orchestra, 1950–51), Eddie Dunstedter (organ, 1951–52).

Sound Effects—Clark Casey, Ross Murray, Berne Surrey.

Announcers—Don Baker, Bob Stevenson.

Lead—Peter Black, played by Ted de Corsia (1949–50), John Dehner (1950–51), Ben Wright (1951–52).

Support Roles—Herb Butterfield, Jack Edwards, Eileen Erskine, Harold Hughes, Bill Johnstone, Byron Kane, Joseph Kearns, Raymond Lawrence, Jeanette Nolan, Tudor Owen.

Chief inspector Peter Black of London's Scotland Yard went after the bad guys with a vengeance. The epigraph of the show spelled out both his mission and his tactics in no uncertain terms: "A criminal strikes and fades quickly back into the shadows of his own dark world. And then the man from Scotland Yard, the relentless, dangerous *pursuit* ... when man hunts man!"

Raffles

On the Air: 1942–43, CBS West Coast Network, Weekdays; Summer, 1945, Syndicated.

Sponsor: Sold to underwriters in local markets.

Extant Episodes: Five.

CAST & CREDITS

Producer—Jock MacGregor.

Lead—Title role of A. J. Raffles played by Horace Braham.

A. J. Raffles was a gentleman detective. An ex-burglar and safecracker, the rehabilitated rapscallion decided to toe the line, to live for justice. He also sought to bring others who had deviated from the straight and narrow to his new point of view. A native Englishman living in America, on the side Raffles gained a reputation as something of a gourmet chef, maintaining an office at Felipo's Restaurant. The show's opening and closing billboards invited listeners to tune in to where "there's danger, there's mystery, there's action on the way."

Raffles was the creation of E. W. Hornung, who saw his figure come to life in a series of mystery novels published around the turn of the twentieth century.

Red Ryder

On the Air: Feb. 3, 1942–1951, originally NBC Blue West Coast but later on the Mutual-Don Lee Network over much of the same region, Tuesday/Thursday/Saturday, 7:30 p.m.; May 20–Sept. 9, 1942, MBS, Wednesday, 8:30 p.m.; 1948–49, MBS, Tuesday/Thursday, 7:30 p.m. 30 minutes.
Theme Song: *The Dying Cowboy* ("Oh bury me not on the lone prairie"...).
Sponsor: Langendorf bread (Mutual-Don Lee Network); others unsubstantiated.
Extant Episodes: 56.

Cast & Credits

Producer—Brad Brown.
Producer/Director/Writer—Paul Franklin.
Writer—Albert Van Antwerp.
Music—Robert Armbruster (orchestra).
Sound Effects—Jack Dick, Monty Fraser, Tom Hanley, Ray Kemper, Norm Smith, Bob Turnbull.
Announcers—Ben Alexander, Art Gilmore.
Leads—Title role played by Reed Hadley (1942–44), Carlton KaDell (c1945), Brooke Temple (1946–51); Buckskin Blodgett, played by Horace Murphy; Little Beaver, played by Tommy Cook (1942–44), Franklin

Bresee (an alternate, 1942–46), Henry Blair (1944–47), Johnny McGovern (1947–50), Sammy Ogg (1950–51).
Support Roles—Arthur Q. Bryan (Roland "Rawhide" Rolinson), Charles Lung, Jim Mather (Indian dialects), Lurene Tuttle, Fred Shields.

"America's famous fighting cowboy" was a double-fisted, red-haired cyclone living in the Colorado Rockies' Painted Valley. A cattle rancher by trade, Ryder became an unofficial lawman by choice. He tracked down outlaws and troublemakers of every type, among them cattle rustlers, bank robbers, claim-jumpers, arsonists and many more in a series that promised "stories of the West that'll live forever."

The protagonist, always wearing a red shirt, shared the Red Ryder Ranch with three companions: his Aunt Duchess, a hard-working woman "who keeps thinkin' she's an iron man"; a faithful sidekick, Buckskin Blodgett; and a young Navajo ward, Little Beaver (who was fond of offering the expression "you betchum, Red Ryder" repetitiously). The existence of Little Beaver as Ryder's adopted son provided one of radio's first racially mixed families. Speaking pidgin English and frequently tabbed as "Injun" and "redskin," Little Beaver was an affectionate figure, accepted by both children and adults in Anglo-American culture.

"The writers ... used the relationship between Ryder and Little Beaver as an analogy for all father-son relationships," a critic observed. "If Red remonstrated or punished the child, it was for transgressing standards that were familiar to youthful listeners." A rifle shot and a ricochet that sounded at the show's opening became so identified with that series that the directors of other shows refused to allow their soundmen to duplicate it.

Red Ryder initially appeared in a series of short stories penned by Fred Harman, followed in 1938 by a comic strip in

The Los Angeles Times. National syndication ensued a short time later with 13 million readers receiving the strip in 600 newspapers nationwide. After that came illustrated periodicals. When the character later moved to the airwaves, one wag assessed it and several companion features as "comic books for the ear."

A 12-part B-movie serial, *The Adventures of Red Ryder*, was released to theaters in 1940. Directed by John English and William Witney with screenplay by Franklin Adreon and Ronald Davidson, the narrative starred Don (Red) Barry as Red Ryder. Tommy Cook (of radio fame) played Little Beaver, Maude Pierce Allen was Duchess and several less-than-familiar names filled in the remainder of the cast.

Obviously writing with tongue in cheek, Gerald Nachman recounted: "*Red Ryder* was a sort of seedy *Lone Ranger* clone: Red wore red shirts and had an Indian as a faithful companion, a mini-Tonto named Little Beaver.... Red's horse was called Thunder, as opposed to the Lone Ranger's 'great white horse with the speed of light,' and his cornball cry was, 'Roll-1-1-1 on-n-n-n, Thunder!' Nice try, Red."

Tommy Cook, the original actor playing Little Beaver, was a busy man. He simultaneously portrayed the children's voices of Alexander on *Blondie* and Junior on *The Life of Riley* while turning up regularly in the casts of *I Love a Mystery* and *The Mercury Theatre on the Air*. In an interview in the late 1990s, Cook—then in his mid sixties—recalled: "I was a totally natural actor. I would just become that kid, whoever it was, and the words just flowed."

Red Trails

On the Air: Feb. 7–April, 1935, NBC Blue, Thursday, 8:30 p.m.; April–July 16, 1935, NBC Blue, Tuesday, 9 p.m. 30 minutes.

Theme Songs: *Drum Roll, Bugle Call, Pomp and Circumstance March No. 1* (latter by E. Elgar).

Sponsor: American Tobacco Co. for Lucky Strike cigarettes.

Extant Episodes: None known.

CAST & CREDITS

Director—Willis Cooper.

Writer—Stewart Sterling.

Music—Graham Harris conducting a military band.

Leads—Tim Clone, played by Warren Colston; Eric Lewis, played by Victor McLaglen; Genevieve Clone, played by Arline Blackburn; Louis Riel, played by Alfred Corn.

This early feature highlighting the Royal Canadian Mounted Police was based on fact. It related incidents stemming from a real uprising in 1895 to form an independent Republic of the Northwest. Louis Riel, a powerful and persuasive leader, pushed local renegades of mixed ancestry, called the Metis, in an attempt to overthrow the crown in Canada's Northwest Territories. A heroic Sergeant Tim Clone and Constable Eric Lewis were among the RCMP officers sent to quell the disturbance. Their resolve and daring were clearly established in listeners' minds. Clone's daughter, Genevieve, also appeared in the narratives with some regularity.

An unsponsored program bearing the same title with dramatizations based on the northwest Canadian territorial rebellion of 1895 aired over NBC Radio in 1929, Tuesdays at 9 p.m.

In radio's golden age Canada and, indeed, the Royal Canadian Mounted Police itself, became a familiar theme of the aural westerns. This development was encouraged when several 1920s pulp magazines (e.g. *Adventure, All-Story, Argosy*) popularized the country and the federal law enforcement agency that facilitated the settling of a vast Canadian wilderness. Such attempts there easily paralleled what transpired across the Western plains and ridges of our own nation, undoubtedly adding to a public fascination and, perhaps, even an obsession. *Red Trails* was one of the earliest radio features based on the area but certainly not the last—there were about a dozen in all. In future years fans would thrill to added RCMP adventures like *Renfrew of the Mounted, Silver Eagle* and undoubtedly the best remembered of the species, the classic *Challenge of the Yukon,* aka *Sergeant Preston of the Yukon.* (See separate entries.)

Actor Victor McLaglen was a native of England, born in 1886. Before moving to Hollywood, where he appeared in films, he actually lived in Canada for several years.

Renfrew of the Mounted

On the Air: March 3–28, 1936, CBS, Tuesday/Friday/Saturday, 6:45 p.m.; March 30–April 11, 1936, CBS, Monday/Tuesday/Friday/Saturday, 6:45 p.m.; April 13, 1936–March 5, 1937, CBS, Weekdays, 6:45 p.m.; 1937–38, NBC Blue, Weekdays, 6:45 p.m.; Dec. 24, 1938–Oct. 19, 1940, NBC Blue, Saturday, 6:30 p.m. 15 minutes, except 30 minutes (Dec. 24, 1938–Oct. 19, 1940).
Sponsor: Wonder bread (March 3, 1936–1938); Sustained (Dec. 24, 1938–Oct. 19, 1940).
Extant Episodes: Seven.

Cast & Credits

Director/Writer—Laurie York Erskine.
Writer—George Ludlum.
Sound Effects—Brad Barker (expert animal sound imitator, e.g. Renfrew's dog and the opening/closing mournful wolf call).
Announcer—Bert Parks.
Leads—Title role played by House Jameson; Carol Girard, played by Joan Baker.
Support Roles—Joseph Curtin, Robert Dryden, Carl Eastman.

This tale followed the exploits of law-enforcement officer Douglas Renfrew, an inspector with the Royal Canadian Mounted Police. Initially serialized—later in complete half-hour episodes—the sober, committed sergeant tracked terrorizing criminals and located youngsters lost in the wilderness of Canada's vast north. Sometimes the scarlet-clad Renfrew was aided by his love interest, Carol Girard, on his taxing missions of mercy and justice.

Books and short stories by Laurie York Erskine (1894–1976) introduced this character to fiction readers long before he reached their ears. A native Brit, Erskine spent nearly all of his adult life in the United States. Although some readers could be turned off by his effeminate-sounding name, Erskine was a true warrior in real life, fighting in the U.S. armed services in dual world wars. Ultimately he penned several hundred magazine articles and no less than 20 books. In 1925 he and three outdoorsmen buddies founded Solebuy School for boys in New Hope, Pennsylvania, still in operation. Erskine provided most of the institution's start-up funding, including $25,000 he earned from the sale of movie rights to a magazine serial.

A couple of black-and-white feature-length B-films were released during the *Renfrew* radio epoch, each starring James Newill as Sergeant Renfrew. Both were directed by Albert Herman and co-written by Laurie York Erskine and Charles Logue. *Renfrew of the Royal Mounted* (1937) was followed by *Renfrew on the Great White Trail* (1938). Each featured a list of poorly recalled supporting actors.

Renfrew of the Mounted was the first audio series to exploit the tales of the Royal Canadian Mounted Police with any demonstrated staying power. Several of the show's predecessors—notably *With Canada's Mounted, Blair of the Mounties* and *McLean of the Northwest Mounted*—

reached quick conclusions. *Renfrew*, on the other hand, couldn't have been a copy of the better-recognized *Challenge of the Yukon* for *Challenge* arrived on the air two years after *Renfrew's* inception. *Renfrew* never kept pace with that immortal drama, even though both followed the daring acts of a Mountie. Sergeant Preston, of *Challenge*, was a popular and enduring hero to adolescent fans for 17 years.

So what made the difference? There could have been several traits that compared unfavorably. A reviewer, listening to a *Renfrew* episode, hinted at one possibility: "The background contained sparse, bleak sound effects and no music." Fade-outs provided for elapsed time bridges. And Renfrew had a girlfriend, a distraction the all-business Preston would have been loath to pursue, a possible turnoff to a juvenile audience. The self-effacing Preston invariably credited the wonder dog King for most of that pair's good deeds. And if nothing else, *Challenge* had the superior fortune of drawing upon the pool of talented artists at Detroit's WXYZ, who provided the familiar voices and sounds on *The Lone Ranger, The Green Hornet* and several other audio dramatizations.

Results, Incorporated

On the Air: Oct. 7–Dec. 30, 1944, MBS, Saturday, 9 p.m. 30 minutes.
Sponsor: Sustained.
Extant Episodes: Two.

CAST & CREDITS

Creator—Lawrence E. Taylor.
Producer/Writer—Don Sharpe.
Music—Russ Trump.
Announcer—Bob O'Connor.
Leads—Johnny Strange, played by Lloyd Nolan; Terry Travers, played by Claire Trevor.

In this "lively, fun series" (a critic's opinion), Johnny Strange and his secretary,

"irrepressible" Theresa (Terry) Travers, pooled their talents to open a detective agency. It was a lighthearted romp that appeared to be more about funny business than the more serious stuff. While the pair joked that they would accept any case for cash, when CEO Strange was ambivalent about one, vice-president Travers usually felt no compunction about taking on all comers: She was obviously in it for the money. The duo attempted to deliver precisely what their firm's name implied: results. In getting there, however, they were open to more mirthful techniques than those normally applied by most of their ilk.

Few detective pairs succeeded on the air with lighthearted banter as a major ingredient. Among the handful who did were *Mr. and Mrs. North, The Adventures of the Thin Man* and *Two on a Clue.*

The Return of Nick Carter see Nick Carter, Master Detective

Richard Diamond, Private Detective

On the Air: April 24–June 26, 1949, NBC, Sunday, 7 p.m.; July 2–Dec. 31, 1949, NBC, Saturday; Jan. 8–March 26, 1950, NBC, Sunday, 5 p.m.; April 5–Aug. 30, 1950, NBC, Wednesday, 10 p.m.; Sept. 6–Dec. 6, 1950, NBC, Saturday, 8:30 p.m.; Jan. 5–June 29, 1951, ABC, Friday, 8 p.m.; Oct. 5, 1951–June 27, 1952, ABC, Friday, 8 p.m.; May 31–Sept. 20, 1953, ABC, Sunday, 7:30 p.m. (last timeslot included repeats of 1950 series). 30 minutes.
Theme Song: *Leave It to Love* (Henry Russell).
Sponsors: Sustained (April 24, 1949–March 26, 1950); Rexall Drug Co. for Rexall drug stores (April 5–Dec. 6, 1950, Oct. 5, 1951–June 27, 1952, May 31–Sept. 20, 1953); R. J.

Reynolds Tobacco Co. for Camel cigarettes and Prince Albert pipe tobacco (Jan. 5–June 29, 1951).

Extant Episodes: 119.

CAST & CREDITS

Producer—Don Sharpe.

Producer/Director—Jaime del Valle.

Directors—Blake Edwards, Jack Johnstone, Helen Mack, William P. Rousseau, Richard Sanville.

Writers—Harvey Easton, Blake Edwards.

Music—David Baskerville, Frank Worth (orchestras).

Sound Effects—Virgil Reimer.

Announcer—Bill Forman.

Leads—Title role played by Dick Powell; Walt Levinson, played by Ed Begley, Arthur Q. Bryan; Helen Asher, played by Virginia Gregg, Frances Robinson; Otis Ludlum and Francis, both played by Wilms Herbert.

Support Roles—Hy Averback, Jeanne Bates, Gloria Blondell, Herb Butterfield, Ted de Corsia, Steve Dunne, David Ellis, Betty Lou Gerson, Jack Kruschen, Betty Moran, Jane Morgan, Jay Novello.

Richard Diamond, an alumnus of the New York Police Department's fifth precinct, decided to take his training, experience and contacts into business for himself. As a wisecracking PI he was labeled "a charming mix of slick sophistication and two-fisted action." Diamond rented an office at the intersection of Broadway and Fifty-First Street and espoused the philosophy: "If trouble is around, yours truly will most likely get a chunk of it." In practice, muggings, knifings, bombings, shootings and threats of many types were the staples he regularly stumbled upon.

To facilitate matters, a quartet of added figures supported him, including an often agitated homicide lieutenant, Walt Levinson; an incredibly dim-witted desk sergeant, Otis Ludlum; Diamond's personal love interest, well-heeled and red-headed Helen Asher; and Asher's butler, the single-named Francis, who had a propensity to

surface just as Diamond was pitching woo. While the gumshoe's attitude about the police force could be typified as sarcastic—one wag termed it "mocking disdain"—he usually cooperated with Lieutenant Levinson, perhaps even admired him discreetly under a brash facade.

Richard Diamond was radio's "first singing detective," Gerald Nachman deduced. Dick Powell, who played Diamond, was transformed from a dewy-eyed, pomaded Warner Brothers tenor into a lighthearted but tough-talking PI who never took himself seriously. On the way to radio Powell played Philip Marlowe in the movie *Murder, My Sweet*. In *Diamond* Powell not only whistled the theme but occasionally crooned to his girlfriend, establishing credence for Nachman's pronouncement. In *On the Air*, John Dunning provided a more complete walk down memory lane for Powell's career, transitioning from Warner Brothers to Paramount to RKO, then leaping into radio with *Rogue's Gallery* (1945–46) and *The Front Page* (1948) before sealing his success in the medium as Richard Diamond.

A totally different effect resulted as David Janssen was cast in the starring role of *Richard Diamond, Private Detective* on television. There was, in fact, little parallel between the audio and video series. Dick Powell's own Four Star Productions brought the crime drama to the tube. When the show premiered on CBS-TV July 1, 1957, Diamond played the traditional New York ex-cop who became a PI. His familiarity with the force and his friends on it allowed him to access assistance and data that most private detectives would never receive. Lieutenant Levinson had been traded for Lieutenant McGough (played by Regis Toomey). The show aired in the summer of 1957 and returned in January 1958, continuing to September.

But when it resurfaced in February 1959, everything had changed. New York was out and with it Lieutenant McGough; Diamond then lived in Hollywood, had picked up a new semiregular girlfriend (Karen Wells, played by Barbara Bain in her first TV role), and used an answering service to retrieve messages, his contact being a sultry-voiced female whom he tagged "Sam." The audience saw Sam's legs and heard her speak but never saw her face. Mary Tyler Moore and then Roxanne Brooks were the leggy, unbilled actresses portraying her. Sam was important to the plots for she often reached the gumshoe in his telephone-equipped automobile (imagine *that* in 1959!), where she warned him of lurking dangers. Russ Conway rounded out a cast of regulars as Lieutenant Kile. The program continued on CBS-TV through September 1959, then began a disjointed run on NBC-TV, from October 1959 to January 1960 and again from June 1960 through Sept. 6, 1960, then departing network broadcasting forever. It was repeated in syndication under the title *Call Mr. D.*

Jay Hickerson prepared a log of the radio series.

Rocky Fortune

On the Air: Oct. 6, 1953–March 30, 1954, NBC, Tuesday, 9:30 p.m. 30 minutes.
Theme Song: *Puffing Willy.*
Sponsor: Sustained.
Extant Episodes: 26 (complete run).

CAST & CREDITS

Directors—Andrew C. Love, Fred Weihe.
Writers—Ernest Kinoy, George Lefferts.
Announcer—Eddie King.
Leads—Title role played by Frank Sinatra; Hamilton J. Finger, played by Barney Phillips.
Support Roles—Jeanne Bates, Carl Betz, Betty Garde, Hollis Irving, Leon Janney, Jack Mather, Charlotte Munson.

Rocky Fortune, aka Rocco Fortunato, was a street-tough private detective in the Big

Apple who solved crimes for a hodge-podge of colorful clients. This soldier of fortune (no pun intended) was frequently between jobs; when the Gridley Employment Agency didn't find some assignments for him, he fell back on unemployment insurance for sustenance. A "footloose and fancy free young gentleman"—according to the show's billboard—he was the adventurous type. When he *was* working, the challenges he faced often led him into deep trouble. Adding to his miseries was Sergeant Hamilton J. Finger of the NYPD, a permanent thorn in his side. Finger was repeatedly convinced that Fortune was guilty of some misdemeanor, if not worse, which simply hadn't yet been exposed. He dedicated himself to working tirelessly to reveal it and to nail Fortune for it.

The reviews of this series—and particularly its star, Frank Sinatra—by radio historiographers weren't very flattering. One noted that the show arrived during a low ebb for the popular singer-actor, between bobby-soxer and box-office boom eras. Of the drama itself: "It was an undistinguished, low-budget affair. Even Sinatra sounded bored with it." *Variety* compared Sinatra to "a skinny Sam Spade." Another appraisal may have expressed it for many: "It was sustained, so everybody came out losers except the sponsor who didn't take it."

Rocky Jordan

(aka *A Man Named Jordan*)

On the Air: Oct. 31, 1948–Sept. 10, 1950, CBS West Coast Network, Sunday. 30 minutes.
Sponsor: Del Monte Foods for a wide line of fresh canned and packaged frozen vegetables and fruits.
Extant Episodes: 95.

CAST & CREDITS

Producer/Director—Cliff Howell.
Writers—Gomer Cool, Larry Roman.

Music—Richard Aurandt.
Announcer—Larry Thor.
Leads—Title role played by Jack Moyles; Sam Sabaaya, played by Jay Novello.

A most inimitable detective program, this one capitalized on its colorful locale, providing a mood, sound and authenticity like none other in radio. Rocky Jordan ran the Café Tambourine in beautiful downtown Cairo, Egypt, "gateway to the ancient East where modern life unfolds against the backdrop of antiquity," so the listeners were reminded each week. In a typical episode, Jordan encountered a crime, a mystery, a stunning female or any combination of that trio. It probably wasn't his intention to become a sleuth in the first place. Yet his response to "dames in trouble to lost souls seeking help" was invariably: "I gotta help. I like it here in Cairo." What the two had in common wasn't explained. But it was enough to propel him into another escapade in which the amateur detective eventually found himself contacting the Cairo police. Captain Sam Sabaaya of that force would be called upon to help out, finally handcuffing a miscreant at the conclusion of Jordan's latest caper.

This series appeared in the middle of a trilogy of Jordan adventures.

The first, *A Man Named Jordan*, aired over the CBS West Coast network between Jan. 8, 1945, and April 20, 1947, and also starred Jack Moyles as Rocky Jordan. In this weeknight serialized tale Jordan owned the Café Tambourine, the same as later, but it was situated in beautiful downtown Istanbul instead of Cairo. His drive to increase profit potential often led him into terrifying adventures, with diminished emphasis on sleuthing.

When the *Jordan* series ended in 1950, a third branch of the same tree took to the air on June 27, 1951, as George Raft portrayed Jordan over the full CBS network. In the summer series, ending Aug. 22, 1951, Jordan was merely an average citizen trying to run a business—initially, the Grand Bazaar Café in Istanbul, reverting shortly thereafter to the Café Tambourine in Cairo. There much of his time was spent trying to talk his way—or a friend's way—out of murder allegations.

Meanwhile, in such a mishmash of convoluted concepts about the only thing the ambitious restaurateur didn't try was to establish offshoots of his dining emporiums in the cities in which he lived. He might have become a true entrepreneur then with little time for murder and mayhem on the sidelines.

Roger Kilgore, Public Defender

On the Air: April 27–Oct. 12, 1948, MBS, Tuesday, 7 p.m. 30 minutes.
Sponsor: Sustained.
Extant Episodes: Four.

CAST & CREDITS

Director—Jock MacGregor.
Writer—Stedman Coles.
Music—Sylvan Levin (orchestra).
Leads—Title role played by Raymond Edward Johnson, Santos Ortega; Miss Carpenter, played by Bryna Raeburn; Sam Howe, played by Staats Cotsworth.
Support Roles—Charita Bauer, Donald Buka, Humphrey Davis, Andy Donnelly, Robert Dryden, Earl George, Bernard Grant, Bill Griffis, Bill Lipton, Bill Smith, Lawson Zerbe.

District Attorney Sam Howe was the nemesis to Roger Kilgore, public defender, called by one critic a "stubborn rival." Kilgore's secretary was Miss Carpenter (no first name). With scripts drawn from actual cases, he represented indigent clients in and out of court, working hand in hand with the D. A. and police. He attempted to resolve cases before they went to trial. Employing flashback dramatizations, Kilgore recounted how he had arrived at his findings in each client's situation.

At first listeners may have thought they had tuned into the wrong program. An unidentified voice opened the show reciting part of the Declaration of Independence in a style reminiscent of the traditional oath read by *Mr. District Attorney* at the start of *his* show: "We hold these truths to be self-evident that all men are created equal ... that they are endowed by their creator with certain inalienable rights ... that among these are life, liberty and the pursuit of happiness." (*Variety* even suggested that Raymond Edward Johnson, while portraying the role of Kilgore, "acted like *Mr. District Attorney* in reverse.") This series sought to recognize an often overlooked public service position, that of the public defender, as much as series like *Special Investigator* and *Dr. Standish, Medical Examiner* tended to add visibility to some other arcane professions. Despite that, a radio historian lamented: "*Kilgore* was an obscure 1948 Tuesday-night flash in the pan ... never really had the appeal of the crime-busting *Mr. D. A.*, and was soon forgotten."

Rogue's Gallery see Bandwagon Mysteries

Ross Dolan, Detective see I Deal in Crime

The Roy Rogers Radio Show see The Roy Rogers Show

The Roy Rogers Show
(aka *The Roy Rogers Radio Show*)

On the Air: Nov. 21, 1944–May 15, 1945, MBS, Tuesday, 8:30 p.m.; Oct. 5, 1946–March 29, 1947, NBC, Saturday, 9 p.m.; Aug. 29, 1948–June 25, 1950, MBS, Sunday, 6 p.m.; Aug. 6, 1950–May 13, 1951, MBS, Sunday, 6 p.m.; Oct. 5, 1951–June 27, 1952, NBC, Friday, 8 p.m.; Aug. 28, 1952–Aug. 20, 1953, NBC, Thursday, 8 p.m.; Aug. 25–Sept. 29, 1953, NBC, Tuesday, 6 p.m.; Oct. 1–Dec. 24, 1953, NBC, Thursday, 8 p.m.; Jan. 28, 1954–July 21, 1955, NBC, Thursday, 8 p.m. 30 minutes, except 25 minutes (Aug. 28, 1952–Aug. 20, 1953, and Oct. 1–Dec. 24, 1953).

Theme Songs: *Smiles Are Made Out of Sunshine; It's Roundup Time on the Double R Bar; Happy Trails to You* (Dale Evans).

Sponsors: Goodyear Tire and Rubber Co. for Goodyear tires and other automotive products (Nov. 21, 1944–May 15, 1945); Miles Laboratories Inc. for Alka-Seltzer stomach distress reliever and an assortment of other health care products (Oct. 5, 1946–March 29, 1947); Quaker Oats Co. for various breakfast cereals (Aug. 29, 1948–May 13, 1951); General Foods Inc. for various Post brand breakfast cereals (Oct. 5, 1951–Aug. 20, 1953, Oct. 1–Dec. 24, 1953); Sustained (Aug. 25–Sept. 29, 1953); Chrysler Corp. for Dodge automobiles and trucks (Jan. 28, 1954–July 21, 1955).

Extant Episodes: 89.

CAST & CREDITS

Producer/Director—Tom Hargis.
Producer—Art Rush.
Directors—Fran Van Hartesfeldt, Ralph Rose.
Writer—Ralph Rose, Ray Wilson.
Music—Perry Botkin (orchestra), Milton Charles (orchestra), Pat Friday (vocalist), the Mello Men (vocal ensemble), Riders of the Purple Sage (vocal ensemble), Frank Smith (orchestra), Sons of the Pioneers (vocal ensemble), the Whipporwills (vocal ensemble), Foy Willing (vocalist), Frank Worth (orchestra).
Sound Effects—Bob Conlan.

Announcers—Lou Crosby, Verne Smith.

Leads—Roy Rogers, Dale Evans, Gabby Hayes, Pat Brady (the latter succeeding Hayes as comedian Oct. 5, 1951), each playing himself/herself.

Support Roles—Herb Butterfield, Pat Buttram, Leo Curley, Frank Hemingway, Forrest Lewis, Pat McGeehan, Marvin Miller, Ralph Moody, Ken Peters, Stan Waxman.

The self-styled "King of the Cowboys," Roy Rogers, and his future bride, Dale Evans (the "Queen of the West")—whom he married Dec. 31, 1947—earned an approving reputation in Republic Pictures' Saturday matinees long before the duo brought their brand of western shoot-em-up tales and variety to radio. Rogers was one of only a handful of juvenile adventure stars who were actual living persons, not actors playing mythical character roles. Accompanied by the Sons of the Pioneers and, in 1948, the Riders of the Purple Sage, he and Evans burst into a ballad (e.g. *Cool Water, Don't Fence Me In* or *Tumbling Tumbleweeds*) when tensions mounted on the plains.

He was a throwback to another successful media contemporary, Gene Autry, who billed himself "America's favorite cowboy." Autry, too, starred in multiple B-movies and arrived on radio nearly five years prior to Rogers. Both of their shows were knee-deep in variety acts, majoring in music and comedy, with dramatic sketches tossed in. The narratives were almost always based on the good guys vs. bad guys motif, the former finally subduing the latter. *Radio Life*, in 1948, called it "typical western drammer," suggesting that Rogers and sidekick Gabby Hayes almost always would "meet villainous adversity, save Miss Evans' ranch-home, or her father, or her younger brother, and ride off in a swirl of dust."

In the final 18 months the program aired it was retitled *The Roy Rogers Radio Show*. New sponsor Dodge shifted the emphasis from variety in brief sketches to what it viewed as a more attractive theme for adult listeners—whom it was seeking to charm—that of mystery thriller plots with minimal singing on the side. Hence, Rogers went after the bad guys with a vengeance, concentrating two-thirds or more of the half-hour on a myriad of malcontents. Weekly he signed off with a tagline "to all of you from all of us" that became familiar to millions of fans: "Goodby, good luck and may the good Lord take a likin' to ya."

Roy Rogers appeared in approximately 120 motion pictures and made numerous TV guest appearances late in his career. His image turned up in comic books as well as on hundreds of premiums and other merchandise items for sale.

At least one notable audio historiographer believed the *Rogers* show extended the margins of the traditional radio western to its limits in its final epoch on the air. Fred MacDonald observed that the plots in those days (1954–55) focused upon "the adversities encountered by Roy and Dale Evans when they visited Washington, D.C.; prospecting for uranium with Geiger counters; investigating a stolen stamp collection; resolving the tensions that arose at a roadside diner during a tornado; and breaking a smuggling ring which used railroad refrigerator cars to transport diamonds from Mexico." MacDonald intimated that the program possibly moved from a traditional western format to a detective series in its quest for more mature listeners.

The Roy Rogers Show, including Rogers, Evans, Pat Brady and the Sons of the Pioneers, premiered on NBC-TV Dec. 30, 1951. Staged by Roy Rogers Productions, it became a Sunday evening staple that lasted through June 23, 1957, with only a brief hiatus in the summer of 1952. It was seen in reruns on CBS-TV's Saturday morning agenda between January 1961 and September 1964.

The Roy Rogers Show: (l-r) Dale Evans, Pat Buttram, Roy Rogers, Gabby Hayes. Roy Rogers was billed as the "King of the Cowboys" and staked a personal reputation on honesty and integrity, a shining example to kids of all ages. A Hollywood western legend-turned-radio hero, each week he signed off the air with "from all of us to all of you."

A later TV attempt to capitalize on Rogers' reputation wasn't as successful. *The Roy Rogers and Dale Evans Show*, a musical variety outing, debuted on Sept. 29, 1962, over ABC-TV for an hour on Saturday nights. It included Pat Brady, the Sons of the Pioneers, Cliff Arquette playing his Charley Weaver comedic character, the Ralph Carmichael Orchestra and a handful of lesser knowns. Circus and horse acts were regulars on the show's docket. Authorities have been unable to agree on when the program was withdrawn, some suggesting it was as early as Dec. 29, 1962 while others opt for Dec. 22, 1963. In either case the variety series didn't sustain the interest of the viewers as Rogers' previous show had, but the com-

petition for people's time was probably greater in the 1960s, too. There were also more attractive choices on television by then.

The Saint

On the Air: Jan. 6–March 31, 1945, NBC, Saturday, 7:30 p.m.; June 20–Sept. 12, 1945, CBS, Wednesday, 8 p.m.; July 9, 1947–June 30, 1948, CBS West Coast network, Wednesday; July 10, 1949–Jan. 1, 1950, MBS, Sunday, 7:30 p.m. (*during this interval shows broadcast earlier were repeated*); Jan. 8–May 28, 1950, MBS, Sunday, 7:30 p.m.; June 11–Sept. 24, 1950, NBC, Sunday, 7:30 p.m.; Oct. 1, 1950–June 24, 1951, NBC, Sunday,

4:30 p.m.; July 1–Oct. 21, 1951, NBC, Sunday, 4 p.m. 30 minutes.

Sponsors: Bromo-Seltzer pain and distress reliever (Jan. 1–March 31, 1945); Campbell Soup Co. for a wide line of Campbell's canned soups, Franco-American spaghetti and other foodstuffs (June 20–Sept. 12, 1945); Sustained (July 9, 1947–Jan. 1, 1950, June 11, 1950–Oct. 21, 1951); Ford Motor Co. for Ford automobiles and trucks (Jan. 8–May 28, 1950).

Extant Episodes: 24.

Cast & Credits

Producers—William N. Robson, James L. Saphier.

Directors—Helen Mack, Thomas A. McAvity.

Writers—Jerome Epstein, Dick Powell, Louis Vittes.

Music—Louis Adrian, Vaughn Dexter, Harry Zimmerman (orchestras).

Announcers—Val Brown, Doug Gorlay, Dick Joy, Carlton KaDell, Merrill Ross, Don Stanley.

Leads—Title role played by Edgar Barrier (Jan. 6–March 31, 1945), Brian Aherne (June 20–Sept. 12, 1945), Vincent Price (July 9, 1947–May 20, 1951), Barry Sullivan (alternate for Price), Tom Conway (May 27–Oct. 31, 1951); Patricia Holmes, played by Louise Arthur; Happy, played by Ken Christy; Louie, played by Larry Dobkin; Inspector Fernak, played by John Brown, Theodore von Eltz.

Support Roles—Hy Averback, Tony Barrett, Harry Bartell, Ed Begley, Gloria Blondell, Harry Brown, Bob Clark, Tom Collins, Bill Conrad, Joe DuVal, Stanley Farrar, Joe Forte, Betty Lou Gerson, Jerry Hausner, Lamont Johnson, Peter Leeds, Myra Marsh, Betty Moran, Jack Moyle, Dan O'Herlihy, Ted Osborne, Gale Page, GeGe Pearson, Barney Phillips, Mary Shipp, Jeffrey Silver, Irene Tedrow, Tom Tully, Lurene Tuttle, Peggy Webber.

Dubbed the "Robin Hood of modern crime," the polished, urbane private eye Simon Templar, aka the Saint, was a devil-may-care swashbuckling son-of-a-gun. Too preoccupied solving murders to spend time pilfering from the rich, Templar—who was affluent to excess—dined at posh bistros and indulged himself in the arts. (In listing the career occupations of some of radio's great avocational sleuths, one wag described the Saint simply as an "unemployed do-gooder.") His penchant for helping those in trouble usually raised the eyebrows (and ire) of New York City's men in blue regarding his intentions as well as his modus operandi. He *did* break the law in his resolve to right wrongs, when the situation—to him, at least—warranted it.

Based on a fictional character created by European novelist Leslie Charteris, *The Saint* maintained a love interest, Patricia Holmes, during a portion of the run. His weekly adventures normally included exchanges with his apartment houseboy named Happy, a cabbie named Louie and police Inspector Fernak.

A critic suggested that programs like *The Saint* were presented to radio audiences primarily as entertainment. Citing Templar, the reviewer noted that in one episode he gave an off-the-cuff response when a feminine client thanked him for solving a case: "Don't bother ... it was fun."

In addition to the Charteris novels based on the Saint, the figure was popularized through comic book distribution which was heavily promoted via the radio series.

As of this writing there have been 10 feature-length movies released in which the Saint was the central character. Titles and release dates: *The Saint in New York* (1938), *The Saint in London* (1939), *The Saint Strikes Back* (1939), *The Saint's Double Trouble* (1940), *The Saint Takes Over* (1940), *The Saint in Palm Springs* (1941), *The Saint's Vacation* (1941), *The Saint Meets the Tiger* (1943), *The Saint's Return* (1953),

The Saint (1997). In addition, a made-for-video feature titled *Adventure Video: The Saint* was released in 1986. In some of the early motion pictures George Sanders was cast as the Saint. He was the brother of Tom Conway, the last actor to regularly play the role on radio.

The Saint first appeared on American television between 1963 and 1966 via a syndicated film series produced in England. Actor Roger Moore, a Brit, starred. The program first achieved network status in the U.S. when NBC offered all new episodes starting May 21, 1967, at 10 p.m. Sundays. Roger Moore again played the lead with Ivor Dean, one of three actors who portrayed Scotland Yard Inspector Claude Teal in the syndicated show, reprising that role. *The Saint* aired mainly in spring and summer months over NBC-TV for three consecutive years, permanently leaving that venue on Sept. 12, 1969.

All was not lost, however. The figure made a comeback in 1978 on CBS-TV's *Late Movie* under the banner *Return of the Saint*. In a completely new series, also produced in England, Ian Ogilvy starred. CBS-TV subsequently aired reruns of original Roger Moore episodes during the summer and autumn of 1980. For a while both series were telecast simultaneously, although on different nights of the week, on *The CBS Late Movie*.

Sara's Private Caper

On the Air: June 15–Aug. 24, 1950, NBC, Thursday, 10:30 p.m. 30 minutes.
Sponsor: General Mills Inc. for Wheaties cereal and other foodstuffs.
Extant Episodes: One.

Cast & Credits

Producer/Director—Joe Parker.
Writers—Morton Fine, David Friedkin, Larry Klein, Ken Starr.
Music—Robert Armbruster.

Announcer—Frank Martin.
Leads—Title role played by Sara Berner; Melvin, played by Bob Sweeney; police lieutenant, played by Donald Morrison; Mr. Sacks, played by Frank Nelson.
Support Roles—Ed Fields, Herb Vigran.

In one sense a satire on detective and crime series, in another—although played primarily for laughs—*Sara's Private Caper* was a melodrama. Certainly it was as much a detective feature as many others in which a central character earned a living doing one thing while pursuing investigative criminology on the side. In this instance the individual, Sara Berner—also the name of the actress playing the role—was a clerical worker on a police headquarters staff. She was fascinated by sleuthing; although not equipped for it by training or experience, she never saw that as an obstacle. Berner disobeyed orders from her superior, a police lieutenant, to "leave the crime-solving to my detectives." Instead she donned her analytical cap, often proceeding in total disguise (a la *Mr. Chameleon*, "the man of many faces"), to catch culprits whom the inept detectives about her had missed altogether.

The actress who played her was a masterful dialectician and her transfers between intonations, plus an occasional impersonation of a famous figure, were absolutely priceless. Her unwitting accomplice, a hapless grocery store clerk named Melvin, was also her love interest. His supervisor, Mr. Sacks, at times got pulled into their surreptitious scheming, too.

The Scarlet Pimpernel

On the Air: Sept. 21, 1952–Sept. 20, 1953, NBC, Sunday, 6 p.m. 30 minutes.
Sponsor: Sustained.
Extant Episodes: 52 (complete run).

Cast & Credits

Producer/Director—Harry Alan Towers.
Writer—Joe Murott.

Music—Sidney Torch.

Leads—Title role of Sir Percy Blakeney (aka the Scarlet Pimpernel), played by Marius Goring; Lord Tony Dewhurst, played by David Jacobs.

Based on Baroness Orczy's fictional hero of the epoch of the French Revolution in the 1790s, this imported British entry to American radio featured the exploits of Sir Percy Blakeney and his companion, Lord Tony Dewhurst. The affluent Blakeney, "an English gentleman," dedicated much of his existence to battling social injustice. To accomplish his intents, he adopted the nom de plume of a tiny crimson blossom that dotted the English countryside, dubbing himself the Scarlet Pimpernel. In camouflage, he became the archenemy of madmen responsible for panic attacks among the masses, who threatened the citizenry with imprisonment or a worse fate, the guillotine, during the reign of King Louis XVI. Blakeney/Pimpernel's daring rescues and assorted acts of heroism habitually thwarted the dastardly plans of the would-be evildoers.

Once upon a time the Towers of London Syndicate was the major global supplier of transcribed radio. Harry Alan Towers, producer/director of this series, was behind the operation. Towers initially introduced *The Scarlet Pimpernel* to American listeners in 1952 via syndicated transcription, prior to its network premiere.

In its latter days on the air (1955–56), the famous radio series *Sherlock Holmes* was replayed in the U.S. from a 1954 all-British series. Other imported dramatic features from the London-based British Broadcasting Corp. include *The Black Museum* and *The Third Man*. Crime fighting was a large part of both *Holmes* and *Museum* narratives, and separate entries are included for each.

Scotland Yard

(aka *Scotland Yard's Inspector Burke*)

On the Air: Jan. 21–April 1, 1947, MBS, Tuesday, 8:30 p.m.; April 7–Dec. 29, 1947, MBS, Monday, 8 p.m. 30 minutes.
Sponsor: Sustained.
Extant Episodes: None known.

CAST & CREDITS

Music—Sylvan Levin (orchestra).
Announcer—Phil Tompkins.
Leads—Inspector Burke, played by Basil Rathbone; Sergeant Abernathy, played by Alfred Shirley.
Support Roles—Anne Burr, Philip Clark, Cathleen Cordell, Robert Dryden, Mary Orr, William Podmore, John Stanley.

Unwilling to condone brutality while championing deductive powers in arresting felons, the ingeniously clever Inspector Burke of London's Scotland Yard was assigned to peculiar and esoteric criminal atrocities. Sergeant Abernathy, his partner (note that everybody in Scotland Yard apparently had only one name prefixed by a ranking title), assisted Burke in his challenging pursuits.

At least one prominent radio historiographer suggested that Burke usually caught his criminals through their own mental frailties. This conviction is in opposition to the assertion that the hero was a deductive genius, and a direct contradiction of some others' swaying conclusions.

Scotland Yards Inspector Burke see Scotland Yard

Secret Agent K-7 Returns

On the Air: 1939, Syndicated. 15 minutes.
Sponsor: Dairylea Products Co.

Extant Episodes: 72.
Cast & Credits
Narrator—John Holbrook.
Support Roles—No other credits given on the air.

These were pre–World War II spy stories involving "America's number one adventurer, K-7, former United States secret agent who operated in 22 countries, on land, on sea and in the air." K-7 introduced each tale with background information before John Holbrook narrated the dramatic action. It involved a recurring band of agents who were identified only by letters of the alphabet (e.g. "Agent B-9"). Incidentally, the listener knew the name of people like Rita Drake, B-9's aide, who accompanied him on his missions. Apparently her safety was never in jeopardy. A critic remarked that "the male agents always seemed to have rather dimwitted but resourceful female assistants and the locales were never identified as real countries." While K-7 was occasionally mentioned in the dramas, he played no active role. The plots pertained exclusively to exposing a myriad of spy and espionage villainies.

At least one media authority mentions, without providing a lot of detail, a 1930s transcribed quarter-hour dramatic adventure series called *Secret Agent K-7:* "The serial was patriotic despite its strong pacifist tone, an expression of the public sentiment in pre-World War II America." It would stand to reason that such a show did air, based on the title of this one, *Secret Agent K-7 Returns,* although no tapes from an earlier series are known to exist.

Secret City

On the Air: Nov. 3, 1941–Sept. 25, 1942, NBC Blue, Weekdays, 5:15 p.m. 15 minutes.
Sponsor: Sustained.
Extant Episodes: One

CAST & CREDITS

Leads—Ben Clark, played by Bill Idelson; Jeff Wilson, played by Jerry Spellman.
Support Roles—Franklin Adams (the Mayor), Oscar Brown (Lowell Prior), Sidney Ellstrom, Clarence Hartzell.

In a serialized juvenile thriller, private detective Ben Clark was pitted against mythical figures such as "the stranger in the long-vacant mansion" whom he attempted to explain and subdue. Clark's friend, Jeff Wilson, a mechanic, usually helped him in his conquests of such mysterious, yet intimidating forces.

Secret Missions

On the Air: July 18, 1948–May 22, 1949, MBS, Sunday, 10 p.m.; May 30–Oct. 31, 1949, MBS, Monday, 9:30 p.m. 30 minutes.
Sponsor: Sustained.
Extant Episodes: 12.

CAST & CREDITS

Director—Roger Bower.
Writer—Howard Merrill.
Music—Elliot Jacoby.
Announcer—Bill Hightower.
Host/Narrator—Rear Admiral Ellis M. Zacharias.
Support Roles—Peter Capell, Ivor Francis, Raymond Edward Johnson, Bernard Lenrow, Stefan Schnabel, Luis Van Rooten, Alice Yourman.

Rear Admiral Ellis M. Zacharias wrote a book titled *Secret Missions* in which he brought to life some of the never-before-told episodes involving enemy agent plots against the Allies during the Second World War. On this show he represented the U.S. Office of Naval Intelligence, in which he had served as deputy chief during the conflict, in recreating some of the authentic details from that era through the dramatic action he narrated. It included topics like germ warfare and espionage activity.

Sergeant Preston of the Yukon see The Challenge of the Yukon

The Shadow

On the Air: *Detective Story Hour*, later *Detective Story Program*. July 31, 1930–July 30, 1931, CBS, Thursday, 9:30 p.m.; *Blue Coal Radio Revue*. Sept. 6, 1931–June 5, 1932, CBS, Sunday, 5:30 p.m.; *Love Story Drama*, later *Love Story Hour*. Oct. 1, 1931–Sept. 22, 1932, CBS, Thursday, 9:30 p.m.; Jan. 5–Feb. 2, 1932 (overlapping previous series), CBS, Tuesday, 10 p.m.; *Blue Coal Mystery Revue*. Oct. 5, 1932–April 26, 1933, NBC, Wednesday, 8:30 p.m.; Oct. 1, 1934–March 27, 1935, CBS, Monday/Wednesday, 6:30 p.m.; *The Shadow*. Sept. 26, 1937–March 20, 1938, MBS, Sunday, 5:30 p.m.; 1938, Syndicated (26 episodes); Sept. 25, 1938–March 19, 1939, MBS, Sunday, 5:30 p.m.; summer 1939, MBS, Sunday, 5:30 p.m. (repeats of 1938–39 season); Sept. 24, 1939–April 7, 1940, MBS, Sunday, 5:30 p.m.; Sept. 29, 1940–April 20, 1941, MBS, Sunday, 5:30 p.m.; Sept. 28, 1941–March 22, 1942, MBS, Sunday, 5:30 p.m.; Sept. 27, 1942–March 21, 1943, MBS, Sunday, 5:30 p.m.; Sept. 26, 1943–April 16, 1944, MBS, Sunday, 5:30 p.m.; Sept. 24, 1944–April 8, 1945, MBS, Sunday, 5:30 p.m.; Sept. 9, 1945–June 2, 1946, MBS, Sunday, 5 p.m.; Sept. 8, 1946–June 1, 1947, MBS, Sunday, 5 p.m.; Sept. 7, 1947–May 30, 1948, MBS, Sunday, 5 p.m.; Sept. 12, 1948–June 5, 1949, MBS, Sunday, 5 p.m.; Sept. 11, 1949–Dec. 26, 1954, MBS, Sunday, 5 p.m. 30 minutes, except 25 minutes (Aug. 1–Dec. 26, 1954).

Theme Song: *Omphale's Spinning Wheel* from "Le Rouet d'Omphale," Opus 31 (Saint-Saëns).

Sponsors: Street and Smith Publishing Co. (July 31, 1930–July 30, 1931, Oct. 1, 1931–Sept. 22, 1932); Delaware, Lackawanna and Western Coal Co. for its Blue Coal brand of heating energy (Sept. 6, 1931–June 5, 1932, Oct. 5, 1932–March 20, 1938, Sept. 25, 1938–April 16, 1944—in Northeastern U.S. only from Sept. 24, 1939–March 21, 1943, and Sept. 9, 1945–June 5, 1949, with other sponsors, e.g. Grove Laboratories Inc. for Four-Way Cold tablets, Carrie Salt Co., and elsewhere, Sept. 24, 1944–April 8, 1945 on 28 stations); Perfect-0-Lite bulbs (Jan. 5–Feb. 2, 1932); B. F. Goodrich Co. for Goodrich tires and other automotive products (1938 syndicated show and 1939 summer repeats); Acme-Linex (Sept. 24, 1944–April 8, 1945 on 50 stations); Grove Laboratories Inc. for Four-Way Cold tablets (Sept. 11, 1949–Sept. 3, 1950); Sustained (Sept. 10, 1950–Jan. 14, 1951, Aug. 1–Dec. 26, 1954); U.S. Air Force (Jan. 21–Sept. 2, 1951); Wildroot Cream Oil and other men's hair care preparations (Sept. 9, 1951–Aug. 30, 1953); R. J. Reynolds Tobacco Co. for Camel and other cigarette brands, Procter & Gamble Co. for Tide detergent, plus No-Doz sleep-delay medication (Sept. 6, 1953–July 25, 1954).

Extant Episodes: 223 plus eight from Australian series.

CAST & CREDITS

Producer—Clark Andrews.

Directors—John Cole, Martin Gabel, Harry Ingram, John W. Loveton, Dana Noyes, Bourne Ruthrauff, Bob Steel, Bill Sweets, Wilson Tuttle, Chick Vincent.

Writers—Robert Arthur, Peter Barry, Alfred Bester, Edward Hale Bierstadt, David Bublick, Judith Bublick, Harry Engman Charlot, Alonzo Dean Cole, Stedman Coles, Jerry Devine, Max Ehrlich, Walter Gibson, Gail Ingram, Frank Kane, David Kogan, George Lowther, Jerry McGill, Edith Meiser (script editor), Sidney Slon, Joe Bates Smith, Bill Sweets.

Music—George Earle (orchestra, Sept. 6, 1931–June 5, 1932, Oct. 5, 1932–April 26, 1933), Eugene Ormandy (orchestra, Jan. 5–Feb. 2, 1932), Charles Paul, Rosa Rio, Elsie Thompson (last three individuals organists).

Sound Effects—Al April, Barney Beck, Walt Gustafson, Al Schaffer, Fritz Street.

Announcers—Jean Paul King, Frank McCarthy, Ken Roberts (Sept. 6, 1931–June 5, 1932, Nov. 5, 1934–March 27, 1935, Dec. 5,

1937–April 16, 1944), David Ross (Oct. 1, 1931–Sept. 22, 1932), Ford Bond (Oct. 5, 1932–April 26, 1933), Del Sharbutt (Oct. 1–29, 1934), Arthur Whiteside (Sept. 26–Nov. 28, 1937), Don Hancock (Sept. 24, 1944–June 2, 1946), Andre Baruch (Sept. 8, 1946–June 5, 1949), Carl Caruso (Sept. 11, 1949–Sept. 2, 1951), Sandy Becker (Sept. 9, 1951–Aug. 30, 1953), Ted Mallie (Sept. 6, 1953–Dec. 26, 1954).

Leads—Title role of Lamont Cranston/the Shadow played by James LaCurto (briefly from July 31, 1930, plus substitute in November–December 1934), George Earle (c1930), Robert Hardy Andrews Jr. (c1930–31), Frank Readick Jr. (c1931–March 27, 1935), Orson Welles (Sept. 26, 1937–March 20, 1938, 1938 syndicated run), Bill Johnstone (Sept. 25, 1938–March 21, 1943), Bret Morrison (Sept. 26, 1943–April 16, 1944, Oct. 14, 1945–Dec. 26, 1954), John Archer (Sept. 24, 1944–April 8, 1945), Steve Courtleigh (Sept. 9–Oct. 7, 1945); Margot Lane, played by Agnes Moorehead (Sept. 26, 1937–March 19, 1939), Margot Stevenson (1938 syndicated run), Marjorie Anderson (Sept. 24, 1939–April 16, 1944), Judith Allen (Sept. 24, 1944–April 8, 1945), Laura Mae Carpenter (July 9–Oct. 7, 1945), Lesley Woods (Oct. 14, 1945–June 2, 1946), Grace Matthews (Sept. 8, 1946–June 5, 1949), Gertrude Warner (Sept. 11, 1949–Dec. 26, 1954); police commissioner Weston, played by Ray Collins, Ted de Corsia, Kenny Delmar, Santos Ortega, Ken Roberts, Arthur Vinton, Dwight Weist; Moe (Shrevie) Shrevwitz, played by Mandel Kramer, Alan Reed (aka Teddy Bergman), Keenan Wynn; John Barclay, Blue Coal's alleged "heating expert," played by Tim Frawley, Paul Huber.

Support Roles—Carl Frank, Alice Frost, Gale Gordon, Elsie Hitz, Bill Johnstone, Ross Martin, Barbara Maurel, Bob Maxwell, Jeanette Nolan, Dick Osgood, Adele Ronson, Everett Sloane, Fred Vettel, Ned Wever, Richard Widmark.

In stories copyrighted by *The Shadow* magazine, which first surfaced in April 1931, the identity of the "wealthy young man about town"—Lamont Cranston, aka the Shadow, a well-heeled playboy with a social conscience—was known only by his constant companion, "the lovely Margo Lane." (Miss Lane was added to the cast in 1937 at the suggestion of producer Clark Andrews, whose own sweetheart became her model. For all of Margo Lane's fidelity, however, she was usually granted no more than some peril from which the Shadow could liberate her. In perusing volumes of material on *The Shadow*, this writer found only a single source that questioned the propriety of the relationship between Cranston and Lane, possibly suggesting that they might have fared quite well in contemporary America.)

Cranston used his hypnotic powers "to cloud men's minds" to defeat the forces of evil swirling about them. Each week he left the air with a chilling reminder followed by a mockingly creepy laugh: "The weed of crime bears bitter fruit ... crime does not pay ... The Shadow knows...." Originally a character shrouded in ambiguity who only introduced the mystery tales on *Detective Story Hour, Detective Story Program, Blue Coal Radio Revue, Love Story Drama, Love Story Hour* and *Blue Coal Mystery Revue*, the ominous figure's stature noticeably increased with the passing of time. He was pushed along in the public's consciousness by the pulp publishing efforts of Street and Smith, who placed *The Shadow* magazines on newsstands everywhere. (It was Maxwell Grant who originated the character of Lamont Cranston/the Shadow. Grant was the pseudonym of a prolific author, Walter B. Gibson, who reportedly penned 283 *Shadow* novels. "If ever a mystery character created himself in his own image, that character was the Shadow," said Grant. "To say that the Shadow sprang spontaneously into being would be putting it not only mildly, but exactly," the self-deprecating author allowed.)

By January 1932 the Shadow was

The Shadow: Tense moments occurred for Gertrude Warner and Bret Morrison, the last performers cast in the leading roles of Margot Lane and Lamont Cranston, aka *The Shadow*, during the series' long run. Cranston, "wealthy young man about town," used his hypnotic powers to cloud men's minds so they could not see him as he eavesdropped on their evil plotting, stamping out their "bitter fruit."

clearly entrenched in the varied radio series plots as a major presence. In September 1937 he was firmly recognized as the master of his own aural series, then named for him; and introduced along with him was Miss Lane. It was a feature that caught on with mainstream listeners of all ages and held many spellbound for more than two decades. The Shadow's uncanny, eerie ability to come and go unseen, accompanied by that trademark laugh, set the sinister character apart from most other private eyes operating across the ether. The Shadow's supernatural abilities stemmed from hypnotically conquering the psyche of human beings ("to cloud men's minds," as an announcer faithfully reminded fans).

Under the tutelage of an Indian yogi priest—while spending time in the Orient as a bon vivant—he had mastered the knowledge of making himself invisible. (A reviewer tabbed the phenomenon a "scarifyingly crafted device.") Cranston decided to use that ability to track down evildoers and bring them to justice, devoting "his life to righting wrongs, protecting the innocent and punishing the guilty." One wag noted that, along with Miss Lane, he "confronted the maddest assortment of lunatics, sadists, ghosts and werewolves ever heard on the air."

Freed of certain constraints that limited most adult males in modern society, including having no regular job, no common status and no family, Cranston could contrive on his own to bring criminals to justice. Police commissioner Weston, considered to be Cranston's friend, constantly attempted to trap the Shadow for his own unexplained purposes. Another Cranston crony was a loquacious taxi driver, Moe (Shrevie) Shrevwitz, who offered the wizard and Lane not only immediate transport but a chance to mull over their situations with a third party—when they could get a word in. By the mid 1940s The Shadow may have been but an outline of

himself: the program had grown less ghostly by then, turning into a humdrum cops-and-robbers sequence with a filtered cackling voice that always nabbed the bad guys in the last scene. Staged before a live audience in the 1930s and 1940s, the show played to more than 15 million listeners at home, becoming the highest rated dramatic program on the air in its peak years. Writing in 1967, Jim Harmon may have put the series in its proper perspective: "*The Shadow* has become the chief fictional representative of all that was Radioland. After all, we knew even back then that here was the perfect hero for radio—the man you couldn't see."

"A synonym for 'oldtime radio'" is the distinction critic John Dunning assigned *The Shadow*, lumping it with *Fibber McGee & Molly* and *The Lone Ranger* as the most notable series of the medium. Singling out this one, Dunning cited *The Shadow* as "perhaps radio's most famous fictitious crime fighter." It's possible that legions of fans would agree that, without doubt, the Shadow is one of the most enduring characters of the once popular world of radio drama, having entered contemporary American folklore.

Frank Buxton and Bill Owen provided an instructive account of the series' origin: "[On Street & Smith's *Detective Story* program] a young writer named Harry Charlot came up with the idea of an announcer being 'The Shadow.' Dave Chrisman and Bill Sweets of Ruthrauff and Ryan Advertising Agency carried the idea still further and had him become a narrator—an ethereal, disembodied voice that knew everything…. The program became so successful that … Street & Smith began publishing a new magazine called *The Shadow*. Later the 'Lamont Cranston' character was developed and became the model for such celebrated crime-fighters as 'Superman,' 'Batman' and 'Captain Marvel,' who also lived two lives." (In the meantime, Charlot, who named the mysterious character the Shadow, was the victim of a crime that even his greatest creation couldn't solve. On Sept. 28, 1935, at age 35, Charlot was found fatally poisoned in a run-down hostelry in New York's Bowery section.)

A scholarly, observant Fred MacDonald traced a familiar pattern that ensued when numerous radio detectives, specifically including Lamont Cranston, encountered crime: "At the beginning of a broadcast the hero was usually found peacefully and calmly uninvolved. With the introduction of other characters, he inexorably found himself enmeshed in trouble and was physically and intellectually challenged. Accepting this new reality and eventually solving the dilemma, the detective inevitably ended his weekly adventure with a sense of self-confidence and achievement." MacDonald maintained that this radio blueprint of experience and behavior was one frequently applied by ordinary citizens: "As these champions of justice acted out their formulaic lives, they actually provided a paradigm for effective social existence. Like the challenges which routinely confronted the fictional detectives, the developments which threaten disorder in the personal life of the listener had to be faced and overcome…. The salutary model presented by these sleuths touched the most fundamental aspects of life in the United States."

Entrepreneur Charles Michelson recalled in a 1992 live presentation that the Delaware, Lackawanna and Western Coal Company, distributor for Blue Coal—a longtime sponsor of *The Shadow*—wanted to underwrite the program only in the Northeast, the area of the country that it served. No problem, allowed the enterprising Michelson. "We sold the show to Grove's Four-Way Cold Tablets in the Mid-East and Pacific Coast, and the Carrie Salt Company in the Midwest." Then he illustrated in detail the procedure for airing those commercials simultaneously. The program was broadcast live from New York's Empire Theater. As an announcer stood at center stage, to his left and right were situated soundproof units loosely like telephone booths. When it came time for the commercials, an announcer inside one told about cold tablets while an announcer inside the other spoke of table salt. The announcer in the middle, meanwhile, talked to his listeners about their heating problems, urging them to "order a trial ton" of Blue Coal that day. It was an ingenious early example of a practice that was to become commonplace in radio in succeeding years as networks experimented with selling airtime to multiple organizations simultaneously.

As of this writing there have been four Shadow film productions to reach the silver screen.

In *The Shadow Strikes*, a full-length black-and-white feature released in 1937, Rod La Rocque played both the man of mystery and Lamont Cranston. There was no Margo Lane then—she was initially introduced to radio audiences that same year—and the remainder of the cast included a large number of forgettable thespians. Lynn Shores directed, with writing credits assigned to Walter B. Gibson, the novelist who originated the phenomenon, and Al Martin.

Victor Jory starred and Veda Ann Borg played Margo Lane in a 15-episode black-and-white serialized production, *The Shadow*, in 1940. The feature was directed by James W. Horne and written by Ned Dandy and Joseph O'Donnell.

A third attempt, 1946's full-length black-and-white movie *The Shadow Returns*, was directed by Phil Rosen and written by George Callahan. Kane Richmond portrayed Lamont Cranston/the Shadow with Barbara Read as Margo Lane. A list of unknowns completed the cast.

When 1994's *The Shadow*, shot in color, hit the big screens, it offered the promise of an exciting return to the past for many middle-aged and older theatergoers. But promotional hype gave way to scathing reviews. Some considered it to be a disappointment, although many patrons raved over its campy techniques. Alec Baldwin was in the starring role with Penelope Ann Miller, an unknown, as Margo Lane. A host of obscure supporting players was spiced up with comedian Jonathan Winters. Directed by Russell Mulcahy, the production's writing was credited to Walter B. Gibson.

A lengthy summary of Shadow-related memorabilia, including not only the radio feature but anecdotal details of movies, comics, magazines, books and premiums, may be found in Jim Harmon's discerning volume, *Radio Mystery and Adventure and Its Appearances in Film, Television and Other Media* (McFarland).

The Shadow of Fu Manchu

(aka *Fu Manchu*)

On the Air: *The Collier Hour.* 1929–31, NBC Blue, Sunday, 8:15 p.m., during which several 12-episode installments of Fu Manchu were introduced over the air, running concurrently with similar print tales in sponsoring *Collier's* magazine; *Fu Manchu.* Sept. 26, 1932–April 24, 1933, CBS, Monday, 8:45 p.m.; May 8–Nov. 1, 1939, Syndicated, Monday/Wednesday/Friday; *The Shadow of Fu Manchu.* March 18–Sept. 11, 1940, rebroadcast of the syndicated series. *The Collier Hour* was 60 minutes in length with a portion devoted to the narratives, 30 minutes (1932–33), 15 minutes (1939–40).

Sponsor: *Collier's* magazine (1929–31); Campana skin balm (1932–33); Local underwriters in each market (syndicated run, 1939–40).

Extant Episodes: 86.

CAST & CREDITS

Director—Fred Ibbett.
Writer—Sax Rohmer.
Leads—Title role played by Arthur Hughes (1929–31), John C. Daly, Harold Huber; Nayland Smith, played by Charles Warburton (1932–33), Hanley Stafford (1939–40); James Petrie, played by Bob White (1932–33), Gale Gordon (1939–40); Karamaneh, played by Sunda Love, Charlotte Manson (1932–33).

International terrorists of the twenty-first century could have learned a lot from the exploits of the elusive Fu Manchu in the twentieth century. He shipped a mysterious jade vapor through the mail that, when opened, exterminated all who breathed it. A walking cane was fashioned to include a lethal serpent within its hollow cylinder. Paralyzing flowers, killer coughing spells and fatal fungi were mere child's play for Manchu. Threats, drugs, and torture were among the weapons he used in his bid to eradicate the earth.

This diabolical little fellow—an ingeniously gifted physician who might come along once in every three or four generations, and who could have made incredible advances in medical science for the benefit of mankind—instead unleashed his wicked venom on all the earth's denizens. He was, in fact, determined to destroy the planet as the result of the accidental death of his wife and son. During the Boxer Rebellion the pair was mistakenly slaughtered at the hands of a British officer, Dr. James Petrie. Manchu's intent to avenge their deaths would ultimately annihilate everybody if carried to its final conclusion.

Scotland Yard inspector Sir Dennis Nayland Smith, assisted by Dr. Petrie, set out to stop Manchu at any cost. Their challenge grew out of the tales of British novelist Sax Rohmer, who created the fictional Chinese character for a 1912 short story. The plots of Rohmer's insidious figure and Smith and Petrie's attempts to thwart the archenemy formed a repetitive theme in the story line. A stunningly exotic Karamaneh became the slave girl of the evil doctor; an objective of the combatants was to secure her release. The series, though brief, is memorable, and focused on one of the most effective villains to surface in adolescent radio.

John C. Daly, who appeared as Fu Manchu during some of the run, is not to be confused with John Charles Daly. In succeeding years, the latter Daly was a prominent ABC Radio news reporter and TV anchor and host of the popular Sunday night CBS-TV series *What's My Line?* (1950–67). The actor John C. Daly died in 1936.

Between 1929 and 1980 no less than 10 B-movies with Fu Manchu as the central character were produced in English. Many of these were re-released in foreign dialects: *The Mysterious Dr. Fu Manchu* (1929), *The Return of Dr. Fu Manchu* (1930), *The Mask of Fu Manchu* (1932), *Drums of Fu Manchu* (1940), *Drums of Fu Manchu* (1943), *The Face of Fu Manchu* (1965), *The Brides of Fu Manchu* (1966), *The Vengeance of Fu Manchu* (1967), *The Blood of Fu Manchu* (1968), *The Fiendish Plot of Dr. Fu Manchu* (1980). Christopher Lee appeared in the title role in the 1960s while Peter Sellers starred in 1980.

A pilot film for a Fox Movietone-produced television series in 1952 featuring John Carradine as Manchu and Sir Cedric Hardwicke as Smith never got beyond the audition stage.

Republic Pictures released 39 syndicated episodes of *The Adventures of Fu Manchu* to local television stations in 1956. That firm had acquired the rights a year earlier when Sax Rohmer, then 72, sold them for $4 million. The TV series starred Gale Gordon in the title role with Lester Matthews as Nayland Smith, Clark Howat as John Petrie (instead of *James* Petrie as

on radio) and Laurette Luez as Karamanch (a different spelling of the audio slave girl's name).

There was a similarly styled series of evilmongers running simultaneously over NBC Blue while *Fu Manchu* spread his doom and gloom over CBS. In *The Orange Lantern*, several bad customers attempted to carry out their diabolical schemes, the most notable and persistent being Botak. A crusading district attorney doggedly campaigned to banish the plotters to their just deserts. (See separate entry.)

A partial log of the radio series was compiled by Jay Hickerson.

The Sheriff
(aka *Death Valley Sheriff*)

On the Air: *Death Valley Sheriff.* Aug. 10, 1944–June 21, 1945, CBS, Thursday, 8:30 p.m. *The Sheriff.* June 29, 1945–Sept. 14, 1951, ABC, Friday, 9:30 p.m. 30 minutes.
Sponsors: Pacific Borax Co. for 20 Mule Team Borax and Boraxo cleansers (Aug. 10, 1944–March 23, 1951); Procter & Gamble Co. for a wide line of household cleaning supplies and personal care commodities (April 6–June 29, 1951); American Chicle Co. for Adams brand chewing gums (July 13–Sept. 14, 1951).
Extant Episodes: 13.

CAST & CREDITS

Directors—Florence Ortman, Walter Scanlan, John Wilkinson.
Writers—Milton Lieberthal, Ruth Cornwall Woodman.
Music—Joseph Bonime.
Sound—Bill McClintock.
Announcers—Dresser Dahlstead, John Reed King.
Leads—Title role of Sheriff Mark Chase played by Donald Briggs, Robert Haag, Bob Warren; Barnabas Thackery, played by William Podmore; Jan Thackery, played by Helen Claire; Cassandra Drinkwater (Cousin Cassie), played by Olyn Landick.

This adventure grew out of a couple of progenitor series. The first, in 1930—and easily the best recalled—was *Death Valley Days*. It could be classed as an anthology of narratives about the old West, each one introduced by a familiar, crusty, aging geezer known as the Old Ranger. But in 1944 the series was brought into the modern age under the new moniker *Death Valley Sheriff*. The changes called for lawmen to be propelled into fighting crime by horsepower (e.g. fuel-burning vehicles) instead of on horseback. A year later the series title was revised again, simplified to *The Sheriff*. (It continued to utilize the same morning bugle call that had introduced *Death Valley Days* 15 years earlier. That, and the commercials for the same sponsor, helped put the trilogy under a single umbrella in listeners' minds.)

Mark Chase, about 38, a bachelor and ex-Marine who had come home "from two years of fighting Japs in the Pacific," was elected sheriff of Canyon County, Calif. In the post he railed against lawbreakers of every type in the show's contemporary setting. A law school graduate, he was independently wealthy, having become heir to a relative's private fortune. Seldom toting a weapon, Chase often applied some of his own resources in rehabilitating offenders, and especially the younger ones. A retired psychologist, Professor Barnabas Thackery, helped Chase solve some of his dilemmas. Included in the cast was Jan Thackery, the prof's drop-dead gorgeous daughter. A male actor (actually, a female impersonator) portrayed Chase's feminine cousin Cassandra Drinkwater (aka Cousin Cassie), who was also his blabbermouth housekeeper. She considered it her calling to protect her cousin from the wily advances of amorous women.

Death Valley Days, a return to the radio motif of 1930–44, surfaced as a syndicated television series from 1952 to 1970. It again featured the western anthology thesis hosted by the Old Ranger, successively played by Stanley Andrews (1952–65), Ronald Reagan (1965–66), Robert Taylor (1966–68) and Dale Robertson (1968–70). A failed attempt to revive it in 1974 introduced country singer Merle Haggard in that recurring role.

Jay Hickerson prepared a log for the series.

Sherlock Holmes
(aka *The Adventures of Sherlock Holmes*)

On the Air: Oct. 20, 1930–June 15, 1931, NBC, Monday, 10 p.m.; Sept. 23, 1931–May 4, 1932, NBC Blue, Wednesday, 9 p.m.; May 5–June 23, 1932, NBC, Thursday, 9:30 p.m.; Oct. 5, 1932–May 31, 1933, NBC Blue, Wednesday, 9 p.m.; Nov. 11–Dec. 30, 1934, NBC Blue, Sunday, 4 p.m.; Jan. 6–May 26, 1935, NBC Blue, Sunday, 9:45 p.m.; Feb. 1–March 28, 1936, MBS, Saturday, 10:30 p.m.; April 4–Sept. 26, 1936, MBS, Saturday, 7:30 p.m.; Oct. 1–Dec. 24, 1936, NBC, Thursday, 11:15 p.m.; Oct. 2, 1939–March 11, 1940, NBC Blue, Monday, 8:30 p.m.; Sept. 29, 1940–March 9, 1941, NBC Blue, Sunday, 8:30 p.m.; Oct. 5, 1941–March 1, 1942, NBC, Sunday, 10:30 p.m.; May 7–Oct. 1, 1943, MBS, Friday, 8:30 p.m.; Oct. 4, 1943–May 28, 1945, MBS, Monday, 8:30 p.m.; Sept. 3, 1945–May 27, 1946, MBS, Monday, 8:30 p.m.; Oct. 12, 1946–Jan. 4, 1947, ABC, Saturday, 9 p.m.; Jan. 13–July 7, 1947, ABC, Monday, 8:30 p.m.; Sept. 28, 1947–June 20, 1948, MBS, Sunday, 7 p.m.; Sept. 12–Dec. 26, 1948, MBS, Sunday, 7 p.m.; Jan. 3–June 6, 1949, MBS, Monday, 8:30 p.m.; Sept. 21, 1949–Jan. 18, 1950, ABC, Wednesday, 8:30 p.m.; Jan. 25–June 14, 1950, ABC, Wednesday, 9 p.m.; Jan. 2–June 5, 1955, NBC, Sunday, 9 p.m.; May 1–Sept. 4, 1956, ABC, Tuesday, 7:30 p.m. 30 minutes, except 25 minutes (May 7–Oct. 1, 1943).

Theme Songs: *March of the Ancestors*, based on a theme from *Ruddigore* (Gilbert and Sullivan); *Scotch Poem* (Macdowell).

Sponsors: G. Washington Coffee Co. for G.

Washington coffee (Oct. 20, 1930–May 26, 1935); Household Finance for its personal financial services (Feb. 1–Dec. 24, 1936); Bromo Quinine Cold tablets (Oct. 2, 1939–March 1, 1942); Petri Wine Co. for Petri wines (May 7, 1943–May 27, 1946, Sept. 21, 1949–June 14, 1950); Semler Co. (Oct. 12, 1946–July 7, 1947); Trimount Clipper Craft clothing (Sept. 28, 1947–June 6, 1949); Sustained (Jan. 2, 1955–Sept. 4, 1956).

Extant Episodes: 157 plus 92 shows broadcast in England.

CAST & CREDITS

Producer—Edna Best.

Directors—Joseph Bell, Edna Best, Basil Loughrane, Tom McKnight, Glenhall Taylor.

Writers—Anthony Boucher, Max Ehrlich, Dennis Green, Leonard Lee, Edith Meiser, Howard Merrill, Bruce Taylor (pseudonym for Leslie Charteris).

Music—Albert Buhrmann (organ), Graham Harris, Lou Kosloff, Sidney Torch (orchestras, last three).

Sound Effects—Bill Hoffman, Virgil Reimer.

Announcers—Herbert Allen, Owen Babbe, Harry Bartell, Joseph Bell, Cy Harrice, Knox Manning.

Leads—Title role played (in proper sequence) by William Gillette (1930), Clive Brook (1930–31), Richard Gordon (1931–33, 1936), Louis Hector (1934–35), Basil Rathbone (1939–46), Tom Conway (1946–47), John Stanley (1947–48), Ben Wright (1949–50), John Gielgud (1955–56); Dr. Watson, played (in proper sequence) by Leigh Lovel (1930–35), Harold West (1936), Nigel Bruce (1939–47), Alfred Shirley (1947–48), Ian Martin (1948), George Seldon (pseudonym for Wendell Holmes, 1949), Eric Snowden (1949–50), Ralph Richardson (1955–56).

Support Roles—Grace Braham, Maurice Franklin, Mary Gordon, Junius Matthews, Agnes Moorehead, Harry Neville, Jeanette Nolan, William Podmore, Mary Rimber, Bill Shelley, J. Scott Smart, Lucille Wall, Orson Welles.

Sherlock Holmes, major critics tend to agree, was probably the most universally recognized fictional character in history. One wag claimed he was "the world's most famous detective," calling him "the most revived major character of the airwaves." In 1887 when Sir Arthur Conan Doyle introduced the duo of Holmes and Watson that was destined to become larger than life, no one could have imagined the ultimate implications. The twosome first appeared in a rather inauspicious novel, *Study in Scarlet*. Numerous diversified media triumphs were destined to follow.

For many years the radio detective adaptation would open with an interview between an announcer and Dr. John H. Watson. The setting was Watson's study in the fog-shrouded home he shared with Holmes at 221B Baker Street in London. Watson's function as Holmes' trusted associate was to spin eerie tales of mystery from the late nineteenth century. Was Watson a man of average brains who only came off as dim when compared to the unquestionably clever—although eccentric—Holmes? In his only filmed interview (in 1930, the year he died), Doyle alluded to Watson as Holmes' "rather stupid" companion. Yet Watson was faithful, daring and appreciated by legions of bookworms, comic strip fanatics, film addicts, radio listeners and TV viewers.

For years the aural sequel followed a simple, predictable formula that had been tested by Doyle: Watson narrated the stories and answered queries proffered by staff announcers before and after the play. When G. Washington Coffee Co. underwrote the program, an effusive Watson even turned that dialogue into commercials. While preparing to share another yarn, Watson inevitably found a hot cup of the sponsor's brew to be an extremely satisfying indulgence, especially on bitterly cold nights.

In the mysteries themselves, he often disregarded small hints as insignificant until the deductive genius Holmes suggested their proper import. A master of disguises and dialects, Holmes majored in

Basil Rathbone as *Sherlock Holmes*, **"the world's most famous detective," a marvelously peculiar pipe-smoking intellect whose brainpower invariably facilitated—at times with only diminutive data—his revealing a cold-blooded killer. This transpired to the absolute astonishment of his faithful associate, Watson. Basil Rathbone was a favorite among fans tuning in for the latest exploits of the legendary Sherlock Holmes.**

detail. Calling upon bits of evidence and clues that were infinitesimal in substance, he painstakingly re-enacted whole scenarios. As a result, his reasoning capacities constantly soared beyond those of Watson, to the associate's utter astonishment. "Simply amazing, Holmes!" Watson frequently shouted. With gentle delight, Holmes offered this rejoinder: "Elementary, my dear Watson. Elementary."

Arts historiographer Jim Harmon astutely observed: "Few figures loom larger in the realm of radio mystery than Sherlock Holmes. He was not the first mystery figure on radio; the evil Dr. Fu Manchu and his detective nemesis, Nayland Smith, started in 1929. Holmes may not have even been the detective creation most identified with radio; the Shadow could have a stronger claim. But for class and staying power and universal appeal, ... there was no police like Holmes."

Although at first glance this sleuth yarn appears to have aired for 26 years—making it one of the longest runs in radio detective drama—several wide gaps interrupted its continuous broadcasting. Aside from most summers off, which followed a normal pattern, the show wasn't heard for a year and a half in 1933–34 and for nearly three years from late 1936 to 1939. It was silent for more than a year in 1942–43. For four-and-a-half years between 1950 and 1955 it couldn't be found on the dial. Thus, while Holmes rightly wields a mighty stick among audio investigators, the extent of his influence is diminished by vast periods of time he was off the air (about 10 of the 26 years, in addition to several lengthy summer hiatuses).

In the 1970s a British Broadcasting Corp.-produced radio series of *Sherlock Holmes* was aired in the United States over National Public Radio stations. Sir John Gielgud played Holmes while Sir Ralph Richardson appeared as Watson.

No less than 50 Sherlock Holmes English film productions have made it to the silver screen as of this writing, many of them re-released in foreign languages. They begin with *Sherlock Holmes Baffled* in 1900 and continue through the most recent as of this writing, *Sherlock Holmes*, in 1995. In addition, at least 15 TV movies have been produced in English, the most recent *Sherlock Holmes Returns* and *The Hound of London*, both shown in 1993.

A 1954 syndicated television series of 39 half-hours produced in France proved not all that successful. A critic laid the blame at the feet of casting, claiming Ronald Howard was "too handsome" as Holmes and H. Marion Crawford "too conventional" as Watson. Scripts also appeared to make fun of the aura surrounding Baker Street, diminishing believability. There have been subsequent attempts at TV series but none considered sterling successes.

Gordon E. Kelley authored a comprehensive factual manual that records the infamous mythical sleuth's links to multimedia. *Sherlock Holmes: Screen and Sound Guide* was published in 1994 by the Scarecrow Press, Metuchen, N. J. The volume provides data on Holmes' appearances in silent, sound and animated motion pictures; American and foreign radio and television programs, including animated TV series; media advertising; plus extant radio program recordings and computer programs and games.

Jay Hickerson prepared a log of the radio series.

The Silent Men

On the Air: Oct. 14, 1951–March 9, 1952, NBC, Sunday, 5:30 p.m.; March 19–May 28, 1952, NBC, Wednesday, 10 p.m. 30 minutes.
Sponsor: Sustained.
Extant Episodes: 28.

CAST & CREDITS

Producer/Director—Warren Lewis.
Writers—Warren Lewis, Joel Murcott.
Announcer—Don Stanley.
Leads—Douglas Fairbanks Jr., who assumed a different but clearly identified role in each narrative, in addition to hosting the series; the Chief, played by Herb Butterfield, William Cannon.
Support Roles—Raymond Burr, John Dehner, Paul Frees, Virginia Gregg, Lou Merrill, Lurene Tuttle.

This dramatic anthology offered transcribed tales of undercover operations of special agents of a myriad of federal government branches and their ongoing war against crime. The cases were authentic. In the opening billboard during some of the run, listeners were informed that "daily [they] risk their lives to protect the lives of all of us." Host Douglas Fairbanks Jr. then came on to spell out the circumstances of that week's narrative. He identified the role that he would portray in the drama (always the lead) in the pursuit and capture of the global lawbreakers operating within U.S. borders. "The Chief," who supervised the agents, was the only other continuing character. He regularly provided counsel to the officers.

Although the drama observed that—"to guard our welfare, and our liberties, they must remain nameless"—*The Silent Men*'s title would suggest that it was also an effort to recognize those U.S. law enforcement agents who gained little acclaim or notoriety for their work.

The Silver Eagle

(aka *Silver Eagle, Mountie*)

On the Air: July 5–Dec. 13, 1951, ABC, Thursday, 7:30 p.m.; Jan. 1, 1952–May 28, 1953, ABC, Tuesday/Thursday, 7:30 p.m.; June 1, 1954–March 10, 1955, ABC, Tuesday/Thursday, 7:30 p.m. 30 minutes.
Theme Song: *Winged Messenger.*
Sponsor: General Mills Inc. for Wheaties and other breakfast cereal brands. (The commercials were often identical to those aired by the firm on *The Lone Ranger.* Both shows emanated from Detroit over the same network.)
Extant Episodes: Two.

CAST & CREDITS

Producer/Director/Writer—James Jewell.
Director—Bob Woolson.
Music—Richard Dix.

Sound Effects—Curt Mitchell.
Announcers—Ed Cooper, Ken Nordine.
Narrators—Bill O'Connor, Ed Prentiss.
Leads—Jim West, played by Jim Ameche; Joe Bideaux, played by Jack Lester, Michael Romano; Inspector Argyle, played by John Barclay, Jess Pugh.
Support Roles—Jim Bannon, Paul Barnes, Dan Bivens, Everett Clark, Johnny Coons, Maurice Copeland, Leo Curley, Frank Dane, Harry Elders, Laurette Fillbrandt, Charles Flynn, Don Gallagher, Clarence Hartzell (Doc), Geraldine Kay, Eloise Kummer, Cornelius Peeples, Fern Persons, Alma Platts, Elmira Roessler, Art Van Harvey, Vera Ward, Beverly Younger.

Jim West of the Canadian Northwest Mounted Police was also Silver Eagle, Indian hero, who carried a trademark eagle-feather arrow. He was accompanied by a sidekick, Joe Bideaux, of French Canadian ancestry and who could only be described as a giant of a man, who possessed the strength of a superman and the tenacity to match.

Although Bideaux was impaired in properly enunciating the Queen's English, along with West, the two Mounties formed an impenetrable team that captured escaped cons and tackled more mundane infringements like conservation abuses. They roamed the vast expanses of northwestern Canada, often encountering rugged terrain and bitter climates. Inspector Argyle dispensed their marching orders. To howling wolves and shrill winds, the series opened with: "A cry of the wild ... a trail of danger ... a scarlet rider of the Northwest Mounted, serving justice with the swiftness of an arrow ... the *Silver Eagle!*"

James Jewell, who bore a major hand in producing, directing and writing both *The Lone Ranger* and *The Green Hornet*, carried those same duties for this juvenile adventure thriller. The resemblance to *The Challenge of the Yukon,* aka *Sergeant Preston of the Yukon*, was obvious. The gifted drama troupe and technicians at Detroit's station WXYZ interchangeably appeared in the casts of *Challenge, Ranger* and *Hornet*. When, in 1938, Jewell shifted his allegiance from WXYZ to Detroit's WWJ, he corralled a new team of talented artists. For their program repertoire, they were to collect the regionally aired *Black Ace*, the first running humorous series to present comic Danny Thomas, and the national features *Jack Armstrong, the All-American Boy* (1942–50), the surviving *Armstrong of the SBI* (1950–51), and *The Silver Eagle*. The one discernible difference between *Challenge* and *Silver Eagle* was that—while Preston relied heavily upon wonder dog Yukon King—Jim West put his faith in the burly but handy Frenchman, Joe Bideaux. Each redcoat also had an "inspector" to whom he reported.

Sound specialist Robert L. Mott, discussing gunshot techniques, recalled a hilarious incident in one of his books that involved Jim Jewell. The episode occurred during a live performance of *The Silver Eagle*: "[Jewell] … decided he would do the sound of a screaming eagle. Although this was a sound effect, it was also a vocal effect and therefore could be done by anyone, including Jewell, who had an actor's union card. As his eagle cue approached, Jewell came out of the control room and began warming up for his big moment by running around the studio flapping his arms. Unfortunately, in his zealous attempt for realism, he flew too close to the sound-effects area, and as soundman Curt Mitchell fired his gun, Jewell let out a scream that was a cross between a bald eagle and a deafened producer. But because they were on the air, Jewell couldn't say what was really on his mind. Instead, he fled out of the studio and moments later, despite the studio's sound proofing, the cast and Curt Mitchell heard the muffled howls of a wounded bald eagle."

When Jack Lester was playing the role of Joe Bideaux, he instructed announcer Ed Prentiss to identify him in the closing credits with a French-sounding "Jacques Lestair." Prentiss, meanwhile, himself had concluded a lengthy run as Captain Midnight just 18 months before *Eagle's* premiere. In all he is credited with regular appearances on more than a dozen radio series. Neither was Lester, who was born Jack Swineford, any slouch: By that time he had already played Sky King (1947–49), was featured in a recurring role in the soap opera *Masquerade* (1946–47) and had turned up repeatedly in the casts of several ongoing documentaries and dramatic anthologies.

More than one critic observed that when this series left the air in 1955 it "marked the end of top-flight radio adventures shows." This one was "generally considered the last of the great juvenile shows," wrote one assessor.

Silver Eagle, Mountie see *Silver Eagle*

The Singing Marshall see *Tom Mix*

Six Gun Justice

On the Air: April 22–July 22, 1935, CBS, Monday, 9 p.m.; Aug. 7–Sept. 25, 1935, CBS, Wednesday, 9 p.m.; Oct. 2–23, 1935, CBS, Wednesday, 9:30 p.m. 30 minutes.
Sponsor: No information.
Extant Episodes: None known.

CAST & CREDITS
Writer—Wilbur Hall.
Lead—W. C. Robison.

No further information has been documented on this series. When a request for new data was placed at a popular web site that is read daily by hundreds of radiophiles, no data surfaced.

The Six Shooter

On the Air: Sept. 20, 1953–March 21, 1954, NBC, Sunday, 8 p.m.; April 1–June 24, 1954, NBC, Thursday, 8 p.m. 30 minutes.
Theme Song: *Highland Lament.*
Sponsors: Coleman Heating Co. for its structural warming installations (Sept. 20–Oct. 11, 1953); Sustained (Oct. 18, 1953–June 24, 1954).
Extant Episodes: 39.

CAST & CREDITS

Producers—Frank Burt, Jack Johnstone.
Director—Jack Johnstone.
Writers—Frank Burt, Les Crutchfield.
Music—Basil Adlam (orchestra).
Sound Effects—Floyd Caton.
Announcers—Hal Gibney, John Wald.
Lead—Britt Ponset, "the six shooter," played by James Stewart.
Support Roles—Elvia Allman, Eleanor Audley, Parley Baer, Michael Ann Barrett, Tony Barrett, Harry Bartell, Dick Beals, Ted Bliss, Lillian Buyeff, Ken Christy, William Conrad, Joe Cranston, Ted de Corsia, John Dehner, Sam Edwards, Barbara Eiler, Herb Ellis, Frank Gerstle, Sandra Gould, Virginia Gregg, Robert Griffin, Bert Holland, Lamont Johnson, William Johnstone, Jess Kirkpatrick, Leone Ledoux, Forrest Lewis, Junius Matthews, James McCallion, Del McKennon, Howard McNear, Shephard Menken, Lou Merrill, Marvin Miller, Shirley Mitchell, Gerald Mohr, George Neise, Jeanette Nolan, Sammy Ogg, Dan O'Herlihy, Barney Phillips, Alan Reed, Paul Richards, John Stephenson, Jean Tatum, B. J. Thompson, Russell Thorson, Les Tremayne, Herb Vigran, Ben Wright, Will Wright, Carleton Young.

"The man in the saddle is angular and long-legged" began the epigraph for this short-lived easy-going western series. "His skin is sun-dyed brown. The gun in his holster is gray steel and rainbow mother-of-pearl. People call them both the Six Shooter." Britt Ponset, "the six shooter," was a frontier transient who earned his status from what others said of him, even when he opposed what they believed. Frequently he found himself in the middle of other folks' predicaments and had to figure a way out.

Although normally laid-back, this happy-go-lucky gunslinger often had to rely on his reputation and the hardware he toted. Ponset could be depended upon to try to right wrongs (sometimes those situations didn't pan out) and to be a crime fighter (he was once elected sheriff), but he really preferred to merely help people in need. In a rather corny diatribe, the announcer tagged him a Texas plainsman who "wandered through the Western territories leaving behind a trail of still-remembered legends." Yet the series was considered by many to be a cut above the typical adult western dramatic fare, a critic assessing it as "truly one of the bright spots of radio."

"The Six Shooter" debuted as a one-time folksy western narrative aired on *The Hollywood Star Playhouse* on April 13, 1952. A subsequent audition drama for a separate radio series, based on that script, was recorded on July 15, 1953.

Although Liggett & Myers Tobacco Co. was attracted and indicated strong interest in underwriting this series (as it did for an even more prominent mature western adventure on radio in the 1950s, *Gunsmoke*), star James Stewart demurred. Stewart believed that the identification with a tobacco firm might tarnish his otherwise pure and decent public persona. "Chesterfield [made by Liggett & Myers] begged and begged and begged for months trying to get sponsorship," producer-director Jack Johnstone recounted, "but Jim didn't feel that because of his screen image that it would be fair."

Sky King

On the Air: Oct. 28, 1946–Aug. 29, 1947, ABC, Weekdays, 5:15 p.m.; Sept. 2, 1947–June 2, 1950, ABC, Monday/Wednesday/Friday one week, the following week Tuesday/Thursday, 5:30 p.m., alternating with *Jack Armstrong, the All-American Boy*, then *Sea Hound*; Sept. 12, 1950–June 11, 1953, MBS, Tuesday/Thursday, 5:30 p.m.; Sept. 15, 1953–June 3, 1954, MBS, Tuesday/Thursday, 5:30 p.m. 15 minutes (Oct. 28, 1946–Aug. 29, 1947); 30 minutes—at times reduced to 25 minutes (near end of the run).

Sponsors: Swift & Co. for various meat products (Oct. 28, 1946–Aug. 29, 1947); Derby Foods Inc. for Peter Pan peanut butter (Sept. 2, 1947–June 3, 1954).

Extant Episodes: 15.

CAST & CREDITS

Creators—Robert M. Burtt, Wilfred G. Moore.

Producer/Director—Roy Winsor.

Writers—Abe Burrows, Roy Winsor.

Sound Effects—Curt Mitchel.

Announcers—Pierre Andre, Mike Wallace.

Leads—Title role played by Roy Engel (1946–47), Jack Lester (pseudonym for Jack Swineford, 1947–49), Earl Nightingale (1950–53), Carlton KaDell (1954), John Reed King; Penny King, played by Beryl Vaughn, Beverly Younger; Clipper King, played by Jack Bivens, Johnny Coons; Jim (Uncle Jim) Bell, played by Cliff Soubier.

Support Roles—Viola Berwick (Martha Bell), Stanley Gordon (Sheriff), Norman Gottchak, Charles Hartzel, Art Hern, Jean Mowry ("Peter Pan," commercial spokesgirl), Ken Nordine, Richard Thorne.

"America's favorite flying cowboy," Sky (Schuyler J.) King was the captain of both the Songbird and the Flying Arrow while owning the large spread known as the Flying Crown Ranch near Grover, Arizona. Together with several companions the former FBI agent and Navy pilot went to extraordinary lengths to track down and apprehend evildoers in the modern West.

The menacing Dr. Shade became a particular thorn in King's side, prowling his castle on the nearby Arizona plains (listeners must have pondered: Why on earth would anyone build a castle in an Arizona desert?) and brooding ill will for Sky and his friends.

While Shade was an ongoing archenemy and slipped into episodes now and then, after an initial season of serialized adventures he eventually became merely one of the evil forces that King's crop duster had to quell. Employing aviation as a vehicle to aid in his expeditions, King never refused an opportunity to bring down everybody from cattle rustlers to foreign espionage agents. He was usually accompanied by his teenage niece and nephew, Penny and Clipper King, and his ranch foreman Jim (Uncle Jim) Bell. Bell maintained a crusty exterior but displayed moments of wisdom and humor, coming across to fans as a gentle grandfather. He was married but Martha, his wife, was little more than a presence in most of the story lines in which she appeared.

The show was episodic with cliffhanger chapters during the first few years, and even after it became a half-hour feature. Later it switched to complete-in-one broadcast plot lines. The Songbird took the King family to exotic locales in their quest to fight crime, often far from the western United States, including Asia, Latin America, Europe and Africa. In one sequence they tracked a particularly malicious malcontent to numerous cities across our own nation, in the process giving young listeners a geographic tour of vast areas of their homeland. One reviewer correctly wrote: "Whenever Sky extended himself to capture a villain, he presented a model in responsible adulthood to his audience."

The air itself was an important concept of the world of early radio. A noteworthy crew of fictional pilots filled the skies in an effort to make the universe safer for all mankind. Among them were the heroes of *The Air Adventures of Jimmie Allen, Captain Midnight, Hop Harrigan, Sky King* and *Tailspin Tommy* who starred in their own series. Beyond them were several more who were comfortable behind the cockpit controls as a situation warranted, including Tom Mix, Dick Tracy, Jack Packard (*I love a Mystery*) and yet another Uncle Jim (Fairfield) who was succeeded by Vic Hardy (in *Jack Armstrong, the All-American Boy*). The aviation angle simply added to the thrill of pursuit and capture for the juvenile set addicted to adventure radio. Such heroes inevitably served as positive role models for millions of adolescents of their generation.

The announcer for most of the *Sky King* radio run was none other than Myron (Mike) Wallace, the very same investigative reporter of a contemporary CBS-TV *Sixty Minutes*. Wallace was so caught up in the stock market in those days that— shortly before each live performance of *Sky King*—he was on the phone with his stockbroker, being briefed about the day's activity and making his transactions. So engrossed was he in that pastime that he occasionally squeezed the moments between those phone calls and airtime to virtually nothing.

Actor Jack Lester, then playing Sky, warned Wallace of his peril but obviously to no avail. The day came at last when Wallace *didn't* arrive in the studio by the time the show was on the air. Lester, a true radio trouper, stepped in to fill the void. In high-pitched tones he introduced himself: "And we find Sky in the Flying Crown ranch-house with Penny and Clipper, as he says..." and then, exercising decidedly lower timbre: "Kids, there's something funny about those cattle disappearing from the north range...." In an interview years later, Lester recalled: "The sponsor was so tight with the money, I was afraid they would ask me to do both parts as a regu-

lar thing—for the same money, of course. Maybe Mike thought of the same thing. He was on time after that."

It was probably inevitable that a juvenile radio hero who fought crime by means of such prominent visual elements as a cattle ranch and a squadron of airplanes would be destined for the small screen. *Sky King* took to video air space on Sept. 16, 1951, late on Sunday afternoons over NBC-TV, just after the radio series had probably peaked. The televersion continued on NBC through Oct. 26, 1952. Then it transferred to ABC-TV from Nov. 8, 1952, though Sept. 12, 1954, first on Monday and then on Sunday evenings. Between 1959 and 1966 those network features were rerun more than once over CBS-TV on Saturday afternoons. Kirby Grant played the aerialist-rancher, with Gloria Winters as Penny and Ron Hagerthy as Clipper. There were several other ongoing characters in the Jack Chertok production that weren't included in the radio feature.

Sky King and the Runaway Train, a 16-page comic book produced in 1964 by TV sponsor Nabisco, is the only known illustrated pulp magazine in which the character appeared. An attempt at a newspaper comic strip featuring *Sky King* in the early 1950s, in *The Chicago Sun-Times*, was abandoned after a brief while.

The sponsors of both the *Sky King* radio and television series made optimum use of premiums that were pitched to their adolescent audiences. Today some of those pieces—such as Sky King decoder rings, found in mint condition at contemporary nostalgia shows—command premium prices.

Snoop and Peep

On the Air: May 12–Aug. 11, 1931, NBC, Tuesday, 11 p.m.; Aug. 19–Dec. 16, 1931, NBC, Wednesday, 8:15 p.m. 15 minutes.
Sponsor: Sustained.

Leads—Principals were played by actors Charles Finan and Paul Winkopp.

This was a mystery thriller spoof that was an aberration among an increasing number of serious sleuthing dramas. The central figures were a couple of novice print journalists who appeared in a comical detective sketch awash in cynical melodrama. Their cases included such silly titles as "Phil the Phoney Firebug" and "The Shooting of Dan McGoo."

Somebody Knows

On the Air: July 6–Aug. 24, 1950, CBS, Thursday, 9 p.m. 30 minutes.
Sponsor: Sustained.
Extant Episodes: Two.

CAST & CREDITS

Producer—James L. Saphier.
Writer—Sidney Marshall.
Director/Host/Narrator—Jack Johnstone.
Announcer—Frank Goss.

To the question, "Who knows what evil lurks in the hearts of men?" this feature replied: "Somebody." Inspired by an idea gleaned from *The Chicago Sun-Times*, the series fostered the notion that for every killing there is someone who is aware of who the killer is or has information that could assist in solving the crime. Each week actor Jack Johnstone was host-narrator for a disturbing real-life unsolved murder reenactment that left open the question of whodunit?

Listeners were asked to come forward, using intricate precautions to protect their identities, to reveal what they knew in connection with specific cases. They were requested to submit written details, scribble a half dozen numerals on their material, then to tear off a ragged edge on which they wrote the same six digits. Following a culprit's capture and conviction, whoever turned in the missing edge of the original entry was eligible for a $5,000 reward. Pleas were also addressed directly to the killers, designed to elicit empathetic responses: *You out there … you who think you have committed the perfect crime … that there are no clues … no witnesses … that your identity is unknown: Listen … somebody knows!*

In an attempt toward realism, radio offered a variety of interesting turns to crime story reenactments. *Gangbusters*, for one, provided brief but pointed real-time bulletins with the possibility of monetary rewards for tips from listeners that led to the arrest and conviction of authentic criminals at large. On *Wanted*, names and voices of actual crime victims, their families and acquaintances, perpetrators and arresting officers were aired via the magic of recording tape. And in another twist, the game show *$1,000 Reward* presented a fictional play, then called a fan at home (from a post card submission drawing), offering $1,000 for the identity of the guilty party. There were other diversions, of course; the point is that the phenomenon of series with realistic touches indubitably didn't have its beginnings in television.

Songs of the B-Bar-B see Bobby Benson and the B-Bar-B Riders

The Space Adventures of Super Noodle

On the Air: Oct. 11, 1952–April 4, 1953, CBS, Saturday, 10:15 a.m. 15 minutes.
Sponsor: I. J. Grass Noodle Co. for its brand of soups (hence, the show's title).
Extant Episodes: None known.

Producer—Al Bland.
Director—Gene Dailey.
Writers—Bud Blume, Gene Dailey.
Leads—Title role played by Charles Flynn; Rik, played by Robert Englund.
Support Roles—Everett Clarke, Tomi Thurston.

In a science fiction adventure aimed at the juvenile set, hero Super Noodle and his compatriot Rik were at work some 500 years into the future. There they encountered interplanetary forces of evil that seriously threatened their homeland. The two self-appointed emissaries concentrated all their efforts on combating them, thus preserving a safe environment. (Who hired them and invested millions of dollars in their missions, of course, was never an issue; it probably received merely a fleeting thought and then only from older listeners.)

With television cartoon series based on similar concepts running rampant during this era in American life, it's probably little wonder that some far-out fantasy-like qualities would seep into a few kids' radio series. This one was obviously an attempt to stem the tide of adolescent listeners turning off their radios completely for the new medium.

Space Patrol

On the Air: Sept. 18, 1950–Jan. 8, 1951, ABC, Monday/Friday, 5:30 p.m.; Aug. 18–Sept. 29, 1951, ABC, Saturday, 7:30 p.m.; Oct. 6, 1951–March 19, 1955, ABC, Saturday, 10:30 a.m. 30 minutes, except for the first few shows, 15 minutes.
Sponsors: Sustained (Sept. 18, 1950–Jan. 8, 1951); Ralston Purina Co. for its Checkerboard Square cereals (Aug. 18, 1951–March 27, 1954); the Nestle Co. for a wide assortment of chocolate products (April 3, 1954–March 19, 1955).

Extant Episodes: 132 (including 34 AFRS recordings, some of which may be duplications).

Producer/Directors—Mike Moser, Larry Robertson.
Writer—Lou Huston.
Announcers—Dick Tufeld, Dick Wesson.
Leads—Buzz Corey, played by Ed Kemmer; Cadet Happy, played by Lyn Osborne; Carol Karlyle, played by Virginia Hewitt; Robbie Robertson, played by Ken Mayer; Tonga, played by Nina Bara; Dr. Van Meter, played by Rudolph Anders; Prince Baccaretti, played by Bela Kovacs; Agent X, played by Norman Jolley; Mr. Proteus, played by Marvin Miller.
Support Roles—Joe DeSantis, Robert Dryden, Bob Readick.

The Space Patrol was a thirtieth century police-keeping force based on a man-made planet in the city of Terra. Under the command of chief officer Buzz Corey, it was charged with protecting five worlds from evil that were scattered across the universe—Earth, Jupiter, Mars, Mercury and Venus. Together they were known as the United Planets. One scribe may have correctly dubbed the Space Patrol "a sort of interplanetary Mod Squad."

Corey traveled to far-flung destinations by spaceship. As the series progressed, so did he, moving from flying in the Battle Cruiser 100 to the Terra IV and finally the Terra V. He was usually accompanied by a youthful protégé, Cadet Happy. Happy was a little too free with an annoying penchant to express his emotions by the oft-repeated interpolation: "Smokin' rockets, Commander!" At times he appeared to have little purpose beyond proffering a simplistic inquiry to Corey, allowing the chief to explain some obvious notion to the listeners.

The series was supported by a large cast of recurring characters, including: Corey's romantic interest and the daughter of the secretary-general of the United

Planets, Carol Karlyle (actually, she seemed much sweeter on him than he did on her); security chief Robbie Robertson, called "Major"; a foe who was rehabilitated and who joined the team, Tonga; Space Patrol scientist Dr. Van Meter; and three evil archenemies—Prince Baccaretti, Agent X and Mr. Proteus. Villians didn't die on the series—the worst they got was to be rendered inanimate by Corey's paralyzer ray gun, then shown the error of their ways via the brainograph, a kind of curious contraption that brought them to a conviction of their misdeeds.

Replicas of such devices were offered to the fans as premiums, and they became quite popular. Sound patterns provided special effects for the performances; therefore music was conspicuous by its absence. The opening billboard cited the episodes as "high adventure in the wild, vast regions of space—missions of daring in the name of interplanetary justice."

Many premiums were offered on this show. Besides rings, binoculars, periscopes and cardboard spaceship cockpits, in 1954 Corey's 1,000-pound, 30-foot spaceship toured America (on land), and was then presented to a single supposedly lucky fan.

Virtually paralleling the radio series was a similar one under the same title on ABC-TV. It ran from Sept. 11, 1950, through Feb. 26, 1955. Several of the radio actors reprised their roles in video, or vice versa, including those playing Buzz Corey, Cadet Happy, Robbie Robertson, Carol Karlyle, Tonga, Mr. Proteus and Prince Baccaretti. In addition, Norman Jolley (Agent X on radio) portrayed the secretary general of the United Planets. Only Paul Cavanaugh regularly appeared in a role that was not included in the radio feature, that of Colonel Henderson. Jack Narz, a future game show emcee, announced the TV series. It was produced by Mike Moser and directed by Dik Darley.

Jerry Haendiges prepared a log of the radio series.

Special Agent
(aka *Gentleman Adventurer*)

On the Air: April 17–June 19, 1948, MBS, Saturday, 9 p.m.; June 26–Aug. 28, 1948, MBS, Saturday, 11:30 p.m. 30 minutes.
Sponsor: Sustained.
Extant Episodes: One.

CAST & CREDITS
Producer/Director—Herbert C. Rice.
Writer—Finis Farr.
Music—Chet Kingsbury (orchestra), Morris Mamorsky.
Announcer—Don Fredericks.
Leads—Title role of Alan Drake played by James Meighan; Steve Lawlor, played by John Larkin, Lyle Sudrow.
Support Roles—Margaret Draper, Wendell Holmes, Mort Lawrence, James Monks.

Alan Drake, nephew of Uncle Dan Drake, owner of a well-respected family-run Philadelphia firm that sold marine insurance, was a globetrotting troubleshooter. He probed the often-fraudulent claims filed against Drake and Co. as he pursued modern day pirates on the open seas. Accompanying him was Steve Lawlor, a rather intolerant investigator. Lawlor's penchant for luring the ladies was about as notorious as his intrinsic ability to create discord wherever he went. This twosome's tales of detection were frequently centered in the personal lives of the clients of Drake and Co. Hijacking was but one of the forms of chicanery that preoccupied the villainous types they encountered. The billboard introduced Drake as "the insurance detective whose company protects all comers against all perils anywhere in the world."

Special Investigator

On the Air: May 19, 1946–March 30, 1947, MBS, Sunday, 8:30 p.m.; April 8–June 17, 1947, MBS, Tuesday, 8:15 p.m. 15 minutes.
Sponsor: Commercial Credit Corp. for its money-lending services.
Extant Episodes: One.

CAST & CREDITS

Producer—Herbert Rice.
Music—Chet Kingsbury (organ).
Announcer—Jack Barry.
Lead—Title role of Frank W. Brock played by Richard Keith.
Support Roles—Marion Barney, Ed Begley, Leon Janney, Santos Ortega, Patricia Ryan, Sandy Strauss.

The special investigator, Frank W. Brock, was one of the unsung heroes of American law enforcement whose tasks seldom came under widespread public scrutiny. Brock's assignments were largely to expose confidence games and the practiced swindlers behind them. Returning war service personnel were particularly vulnerable targets upon which both con men and Brock focused their attention. Bogus memorial parks, diploma mills and housing shortage frauds were included in the rip-offs that Brock pursued.

Speed Gibson of the International Secret Police

On the Air: 1937–38, Syndicated. 15 minutes.
Sponsor: Sold in local markets to local time buyers.
Extant Episodes: 178 (complete run).

CAST & CREDITS

Writer—Virginia Cooke.
Announcers—Franklyn McCormack, Ron Rawson.
Leads—Title role played by Howard McNear; Uncle Clint Barlow, played by John Gibson; Barney Dunlap, played by Elliott Lewis.

Support Roles—Sam Edwards, Jack Mather, Hanley Stafford.

If you can imagine "suffering whangdoodles!" as an oft-repeated expletive, a master criminal known as the Octopus and a 15-year-old partially responsible for the fate of the world, you have a pretty good idea of what this serial was about. Aimed at an audience in the sub-adolescent cluster, Speed Gibson of the International Secret Police (ISP) and the global police force behind him battled evil everywhere. Most of their escapades carried them to other continents: In the first 100 episodes, they fought the diabolical Octopus primarily in exotic locales in the Orient; in the final 78 episodes, their focus was on central Africa's Atlantian Syndicate. Two nemeses per drama seemed adequate to those syndicating this one.

Ace pilot Gibson gained his certification by ISP agent Clint Barlow, his uncle. Together with a third party, a literacy-deprived whimsical sidekick, Barney Dunlap—who delivered that timeworn catchphrase given above—the party was ferried to its far-flung destinations on the wings of the Flying Clipper. The show began to the repetitive resonance of a plane's engine and the beseeching cry of an air trafficker: "Ceiling zero—ceiling zero—ceiling zero!" It was, as one critic put it, "one of the corniest, most outrageously enjoyable serials of the 1930s."

Wings, a newspaper that included tales about Speed Gibson and his pals, was routinely proffered to fans as a show-related premium.

Spy Secrets

On the Air: July 31–Sept. 4, 1938, NBC, Sunday, 5:30 p.m.
Sponsor: Sterling Drugs Inc. for Energine cleaning fluid, Energine Shoe-White polish

and a host of additional personal and health care commodities.

Extant Episodes: None known.

CAST & CREDITS

Producer—Himan Brown.
No cast members' names credited on the air.

These narratives featured espionage plots and were aired three years before America's entry into the Second World War when threats to the nation's freedom were uppermost in the minds of many of its citizens.

Squad Car

On the Air: 1954, Syndicated. 15 minutes.
Sponsor: Sold to local sponsors in the markets where it was aired.
Extant Episodes: None known.

CAST & CREDITS

Leads—Peter Finch and James Van Sickle.

These authentic cases were adapted from the files of the metropolitan police department of Louisville, Kentucky. No further details are believed to have been preserved in printed form.

Turning to Louisville is a rare example of radio's reach into the nation's interior to acquire factual information for a detective drama. With few exceptions, most crime series were based in New York, Los Angeles, San Francisco, Chicago, Miami or New Orleans, all on or near the nation's borders. This program offered substance from a region that would have been mainstream to more Americans than the major centers from which the other shows emanated. This probably resulted in the narratives being more typical of the crimes that most audiences were accustomed to hearing about in their real world.

Squad Room

On the Air: Jan. 11, 1953–Jan. 24, 1954, MBS, Sunday, 6:30 p.m.; Feb. 3, 1954–April 6, 1955, MBS, Wednesday, 8 p.m.; Jan. 3–July 17, 1956, MBS, Tuesday, 8:30 p.m. 30 minutes.
Sponsor: Sustained.
Extant Episodes: Seven.

CAST & CREDITS

Producer/Director—Wynn Wright.
Writer—Peter Irving.
Announcer—Phil Tonkin.
Leads—R. J. Scanlon, played by Bill Zuckert; James Grady, played by Charles (Chuck) Webster.

These chilling dramatizations frequently dealt with unsolved murders. Patrolmen R. J. Scanlon and James Grady were featured investigators, their perseverance at last exposing the perpetrators and bringing them to justice.

Stand by for Crime

On the Air: 1953, Syndicated. 30 minutes.
Sponsor: Sold to local sponsors in markets where it aired.
Extant Episodes: 40.

CAST & CREDITS

Producer—Bob Reichenbach.
Leads—Chuck Morgan, played by Glenn Langan; Carol Curtis, played by Adele Jergens.
Support Role—Howard McNear.

On-air electronic newsjournalist Chuck Morgan of L. A. radio station KOP found himself tracking killers, espionage agents, jewel thieves, con artists and syndicates—all in a day's work as a sideline profession for a popular broadcaster. Contributing heavily to the dialogue was Pappy Mansfield, owner of the station. Morgan's attractive blonde fiancée/secretary, Carol

Curtis, whom he dubbed "glamour puss," often aided and abetted him in his sleuthing exploits.

Starr Of Space

(aka *Captain Starr of Space*)

On the Air: June 2, 1953–May 27, 1954, ABC, Tuesday/Thursday, 7:30 p.m. 30 minutes.
Sponsor: Sustained.
Extant Episodes: Five.

CAST & CREDITS

Creator/Writer—Tom Hubbard.
Announcer—Lou Cook.
Leads—Title role of Rocky Starr played by John Larch; Gail Archer, played by Jane Harlan; cadet sergeant Stripes, played by Tom Hubbard.

Captain Rocky Starr of Nova City Space Station and his companions, Gail Archer and cadet sergeant Stripes, combated evil across the universe, flying top-secret spy missions in a futuristic juvenile science fiction thriller. One wag may have aptly described the "starring" trio (no pun intended) as "a space policeman with a wholesome girl friend and a bumbling friend." Yet another reviewer labeled it "a totally forgettable show," complete with "hissing rockets, comets, countdowns and other space trappings" in an "undistinguished" half-hour.

By the time this feature appeared on radio several other established science fiction thrillers were already playing and the airwaves were becoming saturated with them. Possibly that factor, and because the show never attracted a sponsor, contributed to its demise, the "undistinguished" half-hour theory notwithstanding.

Stories of the Black Chamber

On the Air: Jan. 21–Feb. 8, 1935, NBC, Weekdays, 7:15 p.m.; Feb. 11–June 28, 1935, NBC, Monday/Wednesday/Friday, 7:15 p.m. 15 minutes.
Sponsor: Zonite Products Co. for Forhan's toothpaste.
Extant Episodes: None known.

CAST & CREDITS

Writer—Tom Curtin.
Leads—Bradley Drake, played by Jack Arthur; Steve, played by Paul Nugent; Betty Lee Andrews, played by Helen Claire; Paradine, played by Gale Gordon; Thornton Oliver, played by Morgan Farley; Joyce Carraway, played by Rosaline Greene.

Charged with revealing top-secret communications that might guarantee the extension of a free world, Bradley Drake presided over operations of the Black Chamber. Chemicals were employed in the highly advanced facility to decode covert messages issued by nations both friendly and unfriendly to the United States. Drake's aide, called only by his first name, Steve, and his secretary, Betty Lee Andrews, comprised Drake's permanent staff. One of his most urgent challenges was to put global master spy Paradine out of business. Joyce Carraway, Paradine's assistant, helped the unscrupulous villain in his mission to thwart detection by the Black Chamber.

The experiences of Major Herbert O. Yardley, an expert cryptographer for the U.S. War Department during World War I, and a book he wrote about them, formed the basis for this series.

The Story of Sandra Martin

(aka *Lady of the Press, Sandra Martin*)

On the Air: *The Story of Sandra Martin,* May 1, 1944–45, CBS West Coast Network, Weekdays, 4 p.m. (PT); *Lady of the Press, Sandra Martin,* June 11, 1944–45, CBS West Coast Network, Sunday, 7 p.m. 15 minutes (weekdays), 30 minutes (weekly).

Sponsor: No information (weekday series); Miles Laboratories Inc. for Alka-Seltzer stomach distress reliever, Bactine antiseptic, Tabcin heartburn antidote, One-A-Day brand multiple vitamins, Miles Nervine anxiety calmative and "other dependable pharmaceutical products" (weekly).

Extant Episodes: One (*Lady of the Press*).

CAST & CREDITS

Producer—Gordon Hughes.
Writers—Les Edgely, Dwight Hauser.
Announcer—Dick Cutting.
Leads—Title role played by Mary Jane Croft (weekdays), Janet Waldo (weekly); Wilson played by Griff Barnett.
Support Roles—Ivan Green (Hack Taggart), Bob Latting (Eddie Dalton), Howard McNear (Steve Heywood).

Sandra Martin, in love with detective Hack Taggart, was a reporter for the mythical *Los Angeles Daily Courier*. Her investigative exploits led her into some cesspools of moral and ethical depravity and corruption within the confines of her own community. As a crusading journalist, she sought to expose such atrocities, concentrating on real estate scams, the baby black market and a myriad of con games. Other regulars in the cast included her editor, Wilson; cub reporter Eddie Dalton; and racketeer Steve Heywood.

In an unusual twist, both of these series aired simultaneously, one with one lead, the other with another.

Straight Arrow

On the Air: May 6, 1948–Feb. 3, 1949, MBS-Don Lee West Coast Network, Thursday, 8 p.m.; Feb. 7, 1949–Jan. 30, 1950, MBS, Monday, 8 p.m.; plus Feb. 8–June 14, 1949, MBS, Tuesday/Thursday, 5 p.m.; Sept. 15, 1949–June 22, 1950, MBS, Tuesday/Thursday, 5 p.m.; Sept. 19, 1950–June 21, 1951, MBS, Tuesday/Thursday, 5 p.m. 30 minutes.

Sponsor: Nabisco Corp. for Nabisco Shredded Wheat cereal. (Commercials, repeated in singsong style by an announcer while set to the beat of a tom-tom, were some of the most recognizable and easily recalled in juvenile radio: *N-A-B-I-S-C-O, Nabisco is the name to know; for a breakfast you can't beat, try Nabisco Shredded Wheat!*)

Extant Episodes: Six.

CAST & CREDITS

Producer/Directors—J. Neil Reagan (West Coast period), Ted Robertson.
Writer—Sheldon Stark.
Music—Milton Charles (organ).
Sound Effects—Tom Hanley, Bill James, Ray Kemper, Dick Moblo.
Announcers—Frank Bingham, Fred Cole.
Leads—Title role of Steve Adams/Straight Arrow played by Howard Culver; Packy McCloud, played by Fred Howard; Mesquite Molly, played by Gwen Delano.

Steve Adams was a model of "justice, fair play and all good things," owning the Broken Bow Ranch and fighting crime in its varied forms while disguised as Straight Arrow. A Comanche orphan adopted by a white ranching family, Adams never forgot his roots and fulfilled an Indian legend of a warrior who would come to save his people. When overbearing despots or outlaw activity threatened to infringe upon the rights of decent citizens of *any* persuasion, Adams—living as a free American male—became a champion for justice and righteousness on the nineteenth century frontier.

The program's epigraph told the colorful story, painting an image-filled picture that must have enthralled millions of wide-eyed youngsters who faithfully tuned in: "Keen eyes fixed on a flying target ... a gleaming arrow set against a rawhide string ... a strong bow bent almost to the breaking point. And then—[*bowstring released, followed by musical shimmer which Radio Life claimed would 'make shivers tingle down your spine,' and then the thud of the arrow reaching its target, and...*] Stra-a-a-a-ight Arrow! ... To friends and neighbors alike, Steve Adams appeared to be nothing more than the young owner of the Broken Bow cattle spread. But when danger threatened innocent people and when evildoers plotted against justice, then Steve Adams, rancher, disappeared, and in his place came a mysterious stalwart Indian wearing the dress of war paint of a Comanche, riding the great golden Palomino, Fury. Galloping out of the darkness to take up the cause of law and order throughout the West comes the legendary figure of Straight Arrow!" (One wag described the scenario: "When danger threatened innocent people ... he would vanish into a cave at the Broken Bow Ranch and, Clark Kent-style, fling off his dusty ranching duds and emerge as ... Straight Arrow, a bronzed brave atop his golden palomino Fury, crying "Kaneewah!") Normally alongside Adams rode a grizzled, faithful white companion, Packy McCloud, the only individual who knew his *real* identity. A third recurring character was Adams' ranch housekeeper, Mesquite Molly, who must have wondered about that.

Sheldon Stark, who penned *Straight Arrow*, was trained for his task under the tutelage of Fran Striker, creator and head writer of radio's most enduring western epic, *The Lone Ranger*. In effect, in *Straight Arrow* Stark turned Tonto (the Lone Ranger's faithful Indian companion) into the hero of his *own* series. Stark had often written lines for the subservient Tonto; there he had the chance to chronicle the heroic deeds of a full-blooded Comanche warrior, posing under the guise of rancher Steve Adams. The players reversed their roles, with the Indian riding incognito in *Straight Arrow*. This time it was Adams who was to be in disguise. It was a new twist on an old theme popularized by the most visible of all frontier law-enforcers. A reviewer, writing about *Straight Arrow*,

observed that the series "offered the most consistently positive image of Indians" as a people of any radio drama.

The *Straight Arrow 'Injun-Uity' Manual*, a collection of printed cards that dispensed Indian lore, was an imaginative premium offered by the show in 1949. Listeners found one card in each box of the sponsor's cereal. There were 36 inserts in all, delving into such topics as carrying a papoose, Indian bows and arrows, foot bridges, how to make an Indian oven, campfire and grill, how to recognize danger and help signals, poisonous serpents, etc.

During one live episode of *Straight Arrow*, something went terribly haywire. During the aftermath of a great dam exploding, instead of the expected response of rushing water, listeners heard the twittering of birds. It turned out that a soundman had miscued a taped effect.

William and Teresa Harper of North Augusta, South Carolina, two rabid fans of the series, continued in the 1990s to publish a *Straight Arrow* newsletter called *Pow-Wow*—considered the definitive source of memorabilia about the show.

Jerry Haendiges and Terry Salomonson have produced logs on the program.

The Strange Dr. Karnac

On the Air: Feb. 20–April 3, 1943, NBC Blue, Saturday. 30 minutes.
Sponsor: Sustained.
Extant Episodes: None known.

CAST & CREDITS

Music—Bob Hamilton (organ).
Announcer—Fred Cole.
Leads—Title role played by James Van Dyk; Dr. Watson, played by Jean Ellyn.

A medical doctor and neophyte sleuth, Dr. Karnac attempted to solve crimes laced with mystic themes. His professional associate,

Dr. Watson, augmented his efforts in those avocational pursuits. Watson was also Karnac's romantic interest. That relationship could hardly have gone anywhere, however; the series was canceled after only seven weeks into the run.

T-Man

On the Air: July 1–Sept. 2, 1950, CBS, Saturday, 8:30 p.m. 30 minutes.
Sponsor: Sustained.
Extant Episodes: Six plus one of Australian derivation.

CAST & CREDITS

Producer/Director—William N. Robson.
Music—Del Castillo.
Announcers—Bob Lemond, Roy Rowan.
Lead—Title role of Steve Larsen played by Dennis O'Keefe.
Support Roles—Ted de Corsia, Virginia Gregg, William Johnstone, Wally Maher.

"T-Man, the law enforcement agent of the Treasury Department, skilled fighter against crimes, relentless enemy of the underworld," the epigraph for this brief series began. In narratives based on actual cases from the federal agency, mythical officer Steve Larsen championed the public servants representing a bureau with only a heretofore modest public profile. Larsen conducted a relentless search for culprits who could almost always be tied to schemes that resulted in an unlawful financial recompense to themselves.

With slight change in title to *T-Men*, a black-and-white motion picture was released in 1947, preceding the summertime radio series by three years. Directed by Anthony Mann with screenplay by John C. Higgins, the film starred Dennis O'Keefe as treasury agent Dennis O'Brien, who infiltrated a counterfeiting ring. Support came from actors Mary Meade, Alfred Ryder, Wallace Ford, June Lockhart, Charles McGraw, Jane Randolph and Art Smith.

Tailspin Tommy

On the Air: Sept. 5, 1941–c1942, CBS, Friday, then Sunday, in 30- and 15-minute segments. Historical records do not provide comprehensive data on this series.
Sponsor: Sustained.
Extant Episodes: Two (15 minutes each).

CAST & CREDITS

Leads—Title role played by Mark Williams; Betty Lou Barnes, played by Marjorie Reynolds; Skeets Milligan, played by Milburn Stone.

A juvenile thriller, this series featured aerial adventure for the small fry. Simultaneously, ace pilot Tommy Tompkins (aka Tailspin Tommy) of the Silver Streak—flying for airship entrepreneur Paul Smith—frequently found himself landing in lots of criminal activity. He managed to encounter—and solve—a few murders and track down a few other assorted desperadoes along the way. Youthful residents of his town of Three Point, Texas, who were his soul mates were Betty Lou Barnes and Skeets Milligan, who assisted him in his efforts to put lawbreakers behind bars.

An announcer alluded to hero Tompkins' colorful heritage: "Stepping out of newspapers from coast to coast and jumping down from the motion picture screen, Tailspin visits you each week over radio." The characters zoomed across the airwaves "straight from pictures and newspapers, created by Hal Forrest." But alas: *Tailspin*, on radio, turned out to be a fly-by-night affair; he departed from the ether not long after takeoff.

A couple of earlier related motion pictures probably paved the way for the brief radio stint. *Tailspin Tommy* was released in 1934; *Tailspin Tommy in the Great*

Air Mystery followed in 1935. Neither could particularly be considered a box office smash.

Tales of Fatima

On the Air: Jan. 8–Oct. 1, 1949, CBS, Saturday, 9:30 p.m. 30 minutes.
Sponsor: Liggett & Myers Tobacco Co. for Fatima cigarettes.
Extant Episodes: One.

CAST & CREDITS

Producer/Director—Harry Ingram.
Writer—Gail Ingram.
Music—Carl Hoff, Jack Miller (orchestra).
Announcer—Michael Fitzmaurice.
Host/Narrator—Basil Rathbone as himself.
Leads—Lavender, played by Agnes Young; Lieutenant Dennis Farrell, played by Francis DeSales.
Support Roles—Tony Barrett, Ed Begley, Frances Chaney, Betty Lou Gerson.

Actor Basil Rathbone played himself in a series in which he and a supernatural wardrobe woman, Lavender (of all people), attempted to solve absorbing crimes. The complex murder cases they pursued seemed manufactured at times. Listeners, meanwhile, were urged to try to unravel the whodunits along with this pair. At the launch of every episode, Princess Fatima, a sultry-sounding figure—in tones distorted by an echo chamber—proffered an obscure tidbit to the audience (e.g. "Habit is law ... we are, all of us, slaves to a habit").

Such morsels were intended to assist the audience in solving the coming mystery before Rathbone revealed its conclusion. Yet the theatrics compelled radio historiographer John Dunning to unleash a verbal diatribe. Labeling those antics "offensive," the eminent critic wrote: "The maiden Fatima was a flagrant plug for the sponsor [whose name was, not coincidentally, Fatima]. Her filtered voice set the tone of the plays and gave a clue.... The clue was a veiled bit of metaphorical balderdash. Rathbone also read the sales pitch.... Indeed, there were even references to the product planted in the stories." As the finale of the 39-week series approached, Hollywood stars were occasionally added to the casts in an effort to beef up listenership. Among them: John Garfield, Rex Harrison, Bela Lugosi and Lilli Palmer.

Motion picture actor Basil Rathbone established a name for himself in radio mystery drama as the sleuthing genius *Sherlock Holmes*. It was a role he played convincingly between 1939 and 1946 and for which he received almost universal acclaim. He soon debuted in a not-nearly-as-successful copycat version purportedly created just for him, *Scotland Yard's Inspector Burke* (which came and went in 1947). Some critics suggested that the third of Rathbone's mystery trilogies, *Tales of Fatima*, might have been even weaker. Whatever the case, neither of the subsequent series lived up to the near-sterling reputation of the original. (See separate entries.)

Jay Hickerson prepared a log for this series.

Tales of the Texas Rangers

On the Air: July 8–Sept. 30, 1950, NBC, Saturday, 9:30 p.m.; Oct. 8, 1950–May 27, 1951, NBC, Sunday, 8:30 p.m.; Sept. 30, 1951–Sept. 14, 1952, NBC, Sunday, 6 p.m. 30 minutes.
Theme Song: *The Eyes of Texas Are Upon You* (Texas Ranger March).
Sponsors: General Mills Inc. for Wheaties cereal (July 8–Aug. 26, 1950); Sustained (Sept. 2, 1950–Sept. 14, 1952).
Extant Episodes: 107.

CAST & CREDITS

Producer/Director—Stacy Keach.
Writers—Irwin Ashkenazi, Arthur Brown Jr.,

Adrian Gendeaux, Will Gould, Charles E. Israel, Joel Murcott, Robert A. White, Bob Wright.
Technical Advisor—M. T. Gonzaullas.
Sound Effects—Monty Fraser.
Announcer—Hal Gibney, Frank Martin (commercials).
Leads—Jace Pearson, played by Joel McCrea; Captain Stinson, played by Tony Barrett.
Support Roles—Hy Averback, Parley Baer, Joan Banks, Michael Ann Barrett, Tony Barrett, Dick Beals, Ed Begley, Rye Billsbury, Brad Brown, Robert Bruce, Francis X. Bushman, Herb Butterfield, Lillian Buyeff, Ken Christy, Leo Cleary, Bob Cole, Colleen Collins, Whitfield Connor, William Conrad, Tom Cook, Jeff Corey, Leo Curley, Bob David, Don Diamond, Paul Dubov, Sam Edwards, David Ellis, Junie Ellis, Joe Forte, John Frank, Paul Frees, Betty Lou Gerson, Frank Gerstle, Roy Glenn, Tim Graham, Virginia Gregg, Reed Hadley, Stacy Harris, Ken Harvey, Wilms Herbert, Bert Holland, Tom Holland, Bob Israel, Vivi Janiss, Lamont Johnson, William Johnstone, Byron Kane, Earl Keen, Lou Krugman, Jack Kruschen, Harry Lang, Charlotte Lawrence, Peter Leeds, Leroy Leonard, Forrest Lewis, Barbara Luddy, Wally Maher, Hal March, Frank Martin, Edmond McDonald, Tom McKee, Howard McNear, Paul McVey, Shephard Menken, Gerald Mohr, Ralph Moody, Betty Moran, Ernie Newton, Jeanette Nolan, Jay Novello, James Nusser, Nestor Paiva, Barney Phillips, Marion Richman, Dan Riss, Victor Rodman, Henry Roland, Dick Ryan, Jeffrey Silver, Russell Simpson, John Stevenson, Dee J. Thompson, Tom Tully, Lurene Tuttle, Herb Vigran, Peggy Webber, Ernest Whitman, Will Wright.

Texas Ranger Jace Pearson was representative of all members of that elite law-enforcement entity. Although this drama was a compendium of narratives extending from the late 1920s to the late 1940s, the introduction of an ongoing ranger-hero was important to its success. Captain Stinson, Pearson's superior officer, dispensed his assignments. The ranger normally traveled the vast Texas stretches by car (in excess of 260,000 square miles), and sometimes he pulled a horse trailer behind his vehicle. The trailer bore a mighty dark-toned steed, Charcoal. As the situation warranted, Pearson rode Charcoal in the brush land off the main roads—anywhere it would be difficult to drive an automobile, in fact. The true-to-life episodes hinged upon authentic cases of the select 50-member federation known as the Texas Rangers, the "most famous and oldest law enforcement body in North America," with a heritage dating to the 1820s.

Some strategists subsequently noted that there was at least a veneer of similitude linking the series with the better-recalled *Dragnet* police drama. A Lone Star official, operating in Sergeant Joe Friday tradition while applying state-of-the-art measures, trailed the murderers and other desperadoes with methodical approaches that eventually led to their capture. At the end of each chapter—just like on *Dragnet*—the announcer divulged what sentence had been meted out to the fugitives.

A Screen Gems-produced half-hour of *Tales of the Texas Rangers* appeared on Saturday mornings over CBS-TV between Sept. 3, 1955, and May 25, 1957. Willard Parker played Jace Pearson and Harry Lauter was his partner, Clay Morgan. The tales, however, weren't confined to any single epoch on the Western plains. Pearson and Morgan could battle 1950s embezzlers one week and 1850s bank bandits the next. Thus the show became a montage of the Rangers' activities over the first 125 years or so of their existence. This feature was rerun over ABC-TV during three time periods: Sunday evenings, from Sept. 22, 1957, to June 15, 1958; Thursday evenings, from Oct. 2, 1958, to Dec. 18, 1958; and Monday nights, from Dec. 22, 1958, to May 25, 1959.

Tarzan

(aka *Tarzan of the Apes*, aka *Tarzan and the Diamond Of Asher*, aka *Tarzan and the Fires of Tohr*)

On the Air: *Tarzan of the Apes.* Sept. 12, 1932–March 3, 1934, Syndicated by WOR Radio, New York City, three times weekly; May 1–June 22, 1934, Syndicated by WOR Radio, New York City, three times weekly; *Tarzan and the Diamond of Asher.* 1934–35, Syndicated; *Tarzan and the Fires of Tohr.* 1935–36, Syndicated; c1951, Syndication, MBS-Don Lee West Coast Network; March 22, 1952–June 27, 1953, CBS, Saturday, 8:30 p.m. (transcriptions of the 1951 era shows reprised over MBS-Don Lee). 15 minutes, except 30 minutes (1951–53).

Sponsors: Local sponsors in markets where syndicated; General Foods Corp. for Post Toasties cereal and other foodstuffs (CBS).

Extant Episodes: 278.

CAST & CREDITS

Producers—Frederick C. Dahlquist (1932–34); Edgar Rice Burroughs, Hulbert Burroughs, Ralph Rothmund, Fred Shields (1934–36); Walter White Jr. (1951–53).

Directors—James K. Carden (1932–34), Fred Shields (1934–36).

Writers—Edgar Rice Burroughs (1932–34, whose 1914 novel was the basis for adaptations), Rob Thompson (1934–36), Bud Lesser (1951–53).

Music—Albert Glasser (orchestra, 1951–53).

Sound Effects—Jack Brundage and E. Dummel (1934–36).

Announcers—Fred Shields and John McIntire (1934–36), Charles Arlington (1951–53).

Leads—Title role played by James H. (Big Jim) Pierce (1932–34), Carlton KaDell (1934–36), Lamont Johnson (1951–53); Jane Parker, played by Joan Burroughs (1932–34, wife of actor James Pierce and daughter of author Edgar Rice Burroughs).

Support Roles—Dan Davies (Ukah, 1935–36), Thomas Freebairn (Smith and Poltar, 1935–36), Allan Garcia (Vallons, 1932–34), Gale Gordon (Cecil Clayton, 1932–34; O'Rourke, 1935), Fred Harrington (Lord Greystoke, 1932–34; Mitchell, 1934–35), Art Kane (various roles, 1932–34), Cy Kendall (Captain Tracy, 1932–34; Atan Thome, 1934–35; Wong-Tai, 1935–36), Jack Lewis (O'Rourke, 1935–36), Barbara Luddy (Ahtea, 1935–36), Fred MacKaye (Temur, 1935–36), Eily Malyan (Lady Greystoke, 1932–34), Ted Meyers (Kailuk, 1935–36), Dale Nash (Janette, 1935–36), Frank Nelson (Nikolas Rokoff, 1932–34), Jeanette Nolan (Princess La of Opar, 1932–34; Magra, 1), Ted Osborne (Sheik Joseph, 1932–34), Victor Potel (Larson, 1934–35), John Prince (Shahn, 1935–36), Victor Rodman (Wolf, 1934–35; Burton, 1935), Ralph Scott (Lieutenant Paul D'Arnot, 1932–36), Fred Shields (Bill Fraser, 1932–34), Karena Shields (Helen Gregory, 1934–35), Hanley Stafford (Lord Tennington, Count Raoul de Coude and Karanoff, 1932–34), Vernon Steele (Ashleigh and Burton, 1935–36), Lawrence E. Sterner (Professor Porter, 1932–34), George Turner (Brian Gregory, 1934–35), Don Wilson (Lal Taask, 1934–35).

The purists among us will perhaps think of this only as a series of juvenile adventure tales "from the black core of dark Africa, land of enchantment, mystery and violence." It's true that from the Dark Continent emanated "one of the most colorful figures of all time ... the bronzed light son of the jungle" with "a savage cry of victory." There was more to the violence, however, than merely protecting misplaced safari tourists from wild beasts. In truth, the legendary Tarzan, Lord of the Jungle, who was raised by an ape, according to novelist Edgar Rice Burroughs, struggled against evildoers who invaded his territory, much as would any hero found in other preteen thrillers. The jungle milieu simply involved monkey chatter, the roar of an occasional elephant and exotic birds aflutter. To supply those authentic sounds, the show pre-taped background din at several U.S. zoos and inserted the noises at appropriate spots in the dramatic transcriptions.

A young, innocent Jane Parker imbued a bare-chested, longhaired, vine-swinging Tarzan, who possessed the strength of a proverbial ox, with fluent language skills early in the story line. Her own arrival in Africa led her into dangerous encounters with both pygmies and animals, followed by daring rescues by—whom else? When Parker decided to cast her lot with him and remain in the jungle, she and Tarzan became an item (in *The Chimpanzee Chronicle*, no doubt), a liaison present generations might speculate upon more than the fans did in the day it aired. In all fairness, Parker was not only Tarzan's constant companion during the initial run but of assistance in his crusades against malicious plotters. Others have related a charming, not-to-be-missed tale of Tarzan's naissance in the jungle. (See *Tarzan of the Apes* by Burroughs, *On the Air* by Dunning or *Radio Programs, 1924–1984* by Terrace, for brief summations.)

The first *Tarzan* show, produced and recorded by American Radio Features, set a distinct precedent in U.S. radio. It was actually the premier feature prerecorded and distributed to local broadcasters throughout the nation and overseas. By 1933, a few months after the series' inception, 310,748 requests for Tarzan premiums accompanied by 932,244 labels from a sponsor's product were received. Only nine radio stations were carrying the show at the time, impressively testifying to the viability of the radio premium as an advertising model. In *Tarzan's* first six months on the air, a single station—WBBM, Chicago—accepted 75,000 such mail-in requests. Within three weeks after the Signal Oil Co., a Western-based advertiser, formed a Tarzan club, 12,000 lads from the state of California signed up to join. In its first year, in fact, the fraternity boasted a membership of 125,000!

Under a radio contractual agreement, Walter White Jr. and Commodore Pro-

ductions, producer of the 1951–53 audio version, were to be given refusal when *Tarzan* was offered to television. Writer Bud Lesser began preparing a TV series in 1955, however, and a protracted court battle ensued. The outcome was one TV pilot but no *Tarzan* video series at that juncture.

As of this writing, there have been more than 70 full-length or serialized motion picture features produced in English and centered around the fearless figure of Tarzan. They extend from *Tarzan of the Apes* (1918) at least through 1999's *Tarzan and A Circus Season—Travels with Tarzan*. Many of these theatrical productions have also been released in foreign languages, making Tarzan one of the most visible international heroes in filmdom. In addition, there have been at least four *Tarzan* TV movies shown on American television (1964, 1989 and two in 1996), one made-for-video film (1999) and no less than nine TV series between 1966 and 2001. Most versions in the latter category were animated.

Ron Ely played Tarzan in an initial hour-long series on the tube by that title, between Sept. 8, 1966, and Sept. 13, 1968, over NBC, mostly on Fridays at 7:30 p.m. CBS-TV reprised some of the films at the same hour on Wednesday nights from June to September 1969. In the series, Tarzan again appeared without Jane; supporting players included Manuel Padilla Jr., Alan Caillou and Rockne Tarkington. The famous Tarzan yell was dubbed from another actor, Johnny Weissmuller, who portrayed the Lord of the Jungle on the big screen. Banner Productions selected Brazilian and Mexican locales for its background scenes.

Television's second live-action version of the great adventure series was a 1991–92 syndicated half-hour filmed in Yucatan. Wolf Larson starred as Tarzan. Others in the cast were Lydie Denier (as environmentalist Jane Porter—"Me Tarzan, you

Jane"?), Sean Roberge and Malick Bowens. By then musical videos extended more promise to American adolescents than the jungle, and the series was discontinued after one season.

One of comedienne Carol Burnett's audible trademarks was her rendition of a "Tarzan yell." On her weekly CBS-TV variety series in the 1960s and 1970s, she often received appeals from the audience to reprise it. In a single televised comeback shown in late 2001, nearly a quarter-century after Burnett's series left the air, the fans again called for that infamous jungle bellow, a request she was willing and seemed honored to meet.

Jay Hickerson and Peter Ogden both prepared logs for the radio series.

Tarzan and the Diamond of Asher see Tarzan

Tarzan and the Fires of Tohr see Tarzan

Tarzan of the Apes see Tarzan

Ted Drake, Guardian of the Big Top

On the Air: June 20–Sept. 16, 1949, MBS, Monday/Wednesday/Friday, 5 p.m. 30 minutes.
Sponsor: Sustained.
Extant Episodes: None known.

Cast & Credits

Announcer—Bob Larrimore.
Lead—Title role played by Vince Harding.
Support Role—Fred Rains.

When considering your less-than-typical sleuth, be sure to add this one. Ted Drake was a circus detective for a traveling tent show. His involvement in solving mysteries stemmed from the events he encountered both on and off the midway.

Obviously pitched to an adolescent audience, this show was a summer replacement series for *The Adventures of Superman*. Regrettably, not a lot of detail about it survives.

Tennessee Jed

On the Air: May 14, 1945–Nov. 7, 1947, ABC, Weekdays, 5:45 p.m. 15 minutes.
Sponsors: Sustained (May 14–Aug. 31, 1945); Tip Top bread and cakes (Sept. 3, 1945–Nov. 7, 1947).
Extant Episodes: 22.

Cast & Credits

Producer—Paul DeFur.
Director—Bill Hamilton.
Writers—Ashley Buck, Howard Carraway, Tom Taggert.
Music—Elton Britt (vocalist-yodeler, accompanied by harmonica, accordion and guitar).
Sound Effects—Joe Cabbibo, James Flynn.
Announcer—Court Benson.
Lead—Title role played by Johnny Thomas (at inception), Don MacLaughlin.
Support Roles—Court Benson, Jim Boles (deputy), Jeff Chandler, Humphrey Davis (Sheriff Jackson), Juano Hernandez (Indian chief), Raymond Edward Johnson (Masters, a gambler), John McGovern, George Petrie, Barton Yarborough.

Sharpshooter Tennessee Jed Sloan, who fired both rifle and pistol with dead-center accuracy, was initially a simple frontiersman during the post-Civil War era. Eager to put the nightmares of battle behind him, the ex-Confederate warrior roamed the West astride his mighty steed, Smoky. For a while he appeared to have little going for him but an ability to "drill the eye out of a gnat at 500 yards." He could, in fact, ricochet a bullet and continue to nail prey five days a week.

When he gained a reputation for toting "the two deadliest sixguns in all the West," his exploits reached the eyes and ears of the nation's commander in chief. Sloan was requested by the president to become an undercover government agent, fighting for order and justice across the prairie. Reporting directly to U. S. Grant, he rounded up thieves, killers and other desperadoes—assignments most law officers would never expect to get directly from the White House. (He once confounded "the greatest cattle rustler in America," the mythical Sanchez de los Riveros-York.) Earlier, Comanche Indians had taught Sloan how to follow a trail. That wisdom, plus the fact that the "deadliest man ever to ride the Western plains" possessed "an eye like a hawk" and was a "squirrel gun marksman," held him in good stead as he tracked quarry across the old West.

One of the first black non-comedic actors appearing repetitively in radio in this era was Juano Hernandez, who portrayed various Indian characters on *Tennessee Jed*. This versatile dialectician turned up in several other juvenile series, including as the black assistant, Lothar, on *Mandrake the Magician* and as the African, Kolu, on *Jungle Jim*.

One critic of *Tennessee Jed* astutely observed: "Given the frequency of partnerships in the classical/juvenile western, it was a rare series in which the hero operated alone.... Ironically, their failure to gain popularity with listeners rested in part with their inability to generate humor in the personality of a serious hero."

Terry and the Pirates

On the Air: Nov. 1, 1937–June 1, 1938, NBC, Monday/Tuesday/Wednesday, 5:15 p.m.;

Sept. 26, 1938–March 22, 1939, NBC Blue, Monday/Tuesday/Wednesday, 5:15 p.m.; Oct. 6, 1941–May 29, 1942, WGN (Midwest region), Weekdays; Feb. 1–April 30, 1943, NBC Blue, Weekdays, 6:15 p.m.; Aug. 2, 1943–May 26, 1944, NBC Blue, Weekdays, 6:15 p.m.; May 29, 1944–June 20, 1947, NBC Blue (which soon became ABC), Weekdays, 5 p.m.; Aug. 25, 1947–June 30, 1948, ABC, 5:15 p.m. 15 minutes.

Theme Song: *Ambushes Everywhere.*

Sponsors: Dari-Rich dairy and dessert products (Nov. 1, 1937–March 22, 1939); Libby, McNeill & Libby Packing Co. for a wide line of Libby's canned foodstuffs (Oct. 6, 1941–May 29, 1942); Quaker Oats Co. for various breakfast cereals, including Quaker Puffed Wheat and Quaker Puffed Rice (Feb. 1, 1943–June 30, 1948).

Extant Episodes: 179.

CAST & CREDITS

Producers—Anne Hummert, Frank Hummert.

Directors—Wylie Adams, Marty Andrews, Cyril Armbrister.

Writers—Wylie Adams, Robert Hardy Andrews, Cyril Armbrister, Al Barker.

Music—Kelvin Keech (vocalist, who accompanied himself on a ukulele).

Sound Effects—Al Finelli, Walt Gustafson, Walt McDonough, Harry Nelson.

Announcers—Charles Browning, Chuck Leslie.

Leads—Title role played by Cliff Carpenter, Bill Fein, Owen Jordan, Jackie Kelk; Patrick Ryan, played by Lawrence Alexander, Warner Anderson, Clayton (Bud) Collyer, Bob Griffin; Dragon Lady, played by Adelaide Klein, Agnes Moorehead, Marion Sweet; Hotshot Charlie, played by Cameron Andrews; Flip Corkin, played by Ted de Corsia; Connie the Coolie, played by Peter Donald, John Gibson, Cliff Norton; Burma, played by Frances Chaney; Eleta, played by Gerta Rozan.

Support Roles—Charles Cantor, Mandel Kramer, John Moore (Captain Goodhue), William Podmore.

An evil Eurasian, Lai Choi San, aka the Dragon Lady, was the archenemy of U.S.

Air Corps Colonel Terry Lee and his buddies Patrick Ryan (an adult companion), Hotshot Charlie, Flip Corkin, Connie the Coolie, Burma and Eleta. Although they battled pirates in the South China Sea at the series' launch, they fought the Axis powers (a theme pushed intensely by the juvenile thriller) during the World War II years, and still other global villains and crime cartels in the ensuing period.

The serial premiered just as Lee became heir to an abandoned gold mine in the Orient. As soon as he, Ryan and Hotshot launched a search for the mine, the wily, despicable Dragon Lady captured the trio for her own undisclosed purposes. Upon their escape the threesome agreed to remain in the Orient to battle this nemesis and any other menacing threats. They would gain the unyielding support of Flip Corkin, Connie the Coolie and two females, Burma and Eleta.

During World War II, while working on behalf of the Chinese government, the Dragon Lady joined forces with Lee and company and they vented their collective wrath against the Japanese. Yet given her penchant for making life miserable for the Americans during the prewar era, radio fans were never absolutely certain just how far she could be trusted. As soon as the international conflagration ended, Dragon Lady showed her true colors, resuming her diabolical persecution against Lee and his compatriots. With her devilment on the one hand, and a plethora of international evildoers on the other, the Americans had both hands full until the series left the air three years after the end of the war. Despite great odds, they took on all comers, valiantly fighting global evil on behalf of free people everywhere.

Milton Caniff's popular comic strip by the same name became the incentive for this juvenile adventure series. The moguls of matinee, Frank and Anne Hummert, widely recognized for their prolific

melodramas that captured the bulk of daytime radio's quarter-hours in the 1930s, 1940s and 1950s, adapted the cartoon to the air. The Hummerts had earlier transferred *Skippy*, yet another comic strip, to aural format in 1931. By employing the talented services of Robert Hardy Andrews, who penned several of their soap operas (e.g. *Backstage Wife, Just Plain Bill, Ma Perkins*), the pair exploited the potential in Caniff's illustrated story line. For most of a decade the radio chapters closely approximated the pulp drawings, introducing into the audio sequel many of the characters found there. In 1952 Don Sharpe Enterprises produced a half-hour *Terry and the Pirates* video series that was syndicated to local TV stations. The cast included John Baer as Terry Lee, Gloria Saunders as Dragon Lady, Mari Blanchard and Sandra Spence as Burma, Jack Reitzen as Chopstick Joe and William Tracy as Hotshot Charlie.

Terry Regan, Attorney at Law see Attorney at Law

That Hammer Guy
(aka *Mickey Spillane Mysteries*)

On the Air: Jan. 6, 1953–Oct. 5, 1954, MBS, Tuesday, 8 p.m. 30 minutes.
Sponsor: Liggett & Myers Tobacco Co. for Chesterfield cigarettes.
Extant Episodes: 12.

CAST & CREDITS
Producer/Director—Richard Lewis.
Writer—Ed Adamson.
Lead—Title role played by Ted de Corsia, Larry Haines.

Hard-boiled, gritty, rough-and-tumble, yet determined private eye Mike Hammer was the central figure in a drama that carried all the trappings of the same character popularized by Mickey Spillane in pulp fiction. He was hardened into regularly being somebody's target practice ("It's part of my profession," he noted), seldom met a woman he didn't love (especially those "who look like they just stepped out of a pool") and freely admitted, "I get beaten up every day of the week." Obsessed with violence, the radio series was similar in exploitation to the one that appeared on TV in the late 1950s.

Between 1957 and 1959 David McGavin portrayed the title character in a syndicated televersion of *Mickey Spillane's Mike Hammer*, for which 78 half-hour episodes were filmed. In its time it was considered one of the most brutal shows ever aired (stories went by titles such as "Music to Die By" and "Overdose of Lead"). *Variety* panned it as a "mixture of blood, violence, and sex" and *TV Guide* declared that it was "easily the worst show on TV." In a typical episode a couple were tossed down a flight of stairs, a terrible fist fight ensued, a knifing and shooting followed and Hammer made an astonishingly daring pass at somebody else's wife— certainly not kosher by 1950s standards. While both McGavin and Spillane argued in favor of the series, Spillane later confessed that he had almost no hand in its development: "I just took the money and went home," he allowed, although not sounding in the least apologetic.

The same character returned to the tube on April 9, 1983, in a CBS-TV movie with one of the longest titles to that date: *Mickey Spillane's Mike Hammer: Murder Me, Murder You*. Stacy Keach, Lisa Blount and Tanya Roberts starred. That was followed the same year by one of similar lengthy name: *Mickey Spillane's Mike Hammer: More Than Murder*. There have been other made-for-TV movies since: *The Return of Mickey Spillane's Mike Hammer* (1986), *Mike Hammer: Murder Takes All* (1989) and *Come Die with Me: A Mickey Spillane's Mike Hammer Mystery* (1994). Brevity, it appears, was never in the vocabulary of the title writers. In all but the last, Keach played Hammer. Rob Estes portrayed him in 1994, with Pamela Anderson as the costar.

Mickey Spillane's Mike Hammer surfaced as a new CBS-TV series in 1984, running in several broken segments: Jan. 26–April 14, 1984, Aug. 30, 1984–Jan. 18, 1985, May 4–June 6, 1985, April 22–May 6, 1986 and Sept. 20, 1986–Sept. 9, 1987. Stacy Keach still played Hammer, described by one reviewer as a "brawling, womanizing, chain-smoking New York detective." Nothing had really changed in the quarter-century since the first series left the air. Before agreeing to the deal, in fact, Spillane made a number of demands of producer Jay Bernstein, including one that Hammer be "encircled" by stunning females. Certainly there was nothing new there. Supporting actors included Don Stroud, Kent Williams, Lindsay Bloom, Danny Goldman, Donna Denton and Lee Benton.

When Stacy Keach was arrested by British authorities for cocaine possession on April 4, 1984, and subsequently convicted and jailed, production of the show's second season halted temporarily. CBS-TV continued the series under a new moniker, *The New Mike Hammer*, in the 1986–87 season.

Never say die. Continuing a tradition, there was yet another syndicated TV series starring Keach released in 1997 under the title *Mike Hammer, Private Eye*. Directed by Rex Piano, its 26 episodes costarred Shane Conrad, Shannon Whirry, Kent Williams, Peter Jason, Malgosia Tomassi and Rebecca Chaney.

Stay tuned. There could always be a sequel.

Thatcher Colt Mysteries

On the Air: Sept. 27, 1936–Sept. 26, 1937, NBC, Sunday, 2:30 p.m.; Jan. 9–April 3, 1938, NBC, Sunday, 2:30 p.m. 30 minutes.
Sponsor: Packer soap.
Extant Episodes: None known.

CAST & CREDITS

Lead—Title role played by Hanley Stafford (1936–37), Richard Gordon (1938).

This crime drama was based on the stories of Anthony Abbot, the pen name of Fulton Oursler. The protagonist was a New York City police commissioner and these were tales of crimes that he introduced to the audience. The fictional character originally appeared in short stories, syndicated newspaper serials and novels. Some of the details have been lost to history.

The Thin Man *see* The Adventures of the Thin Man

This Is Your FBI

On the Air: April 6, 1945–Jan. 30, 1953, ABC, Friday, 8:30 p.m. 30 minutes.
Sponsors: Equitable Life Assurance Society for its insurance products and services (April 6, 1945–Dec. 19, 1952); Sustained (Dec. 26, 1952–Jan. 30, 1953).
Extant Episodes: 307.

CAST & CREDITS

Producer/Director—Jerry Devine.
Director—William Sweets.
Writers—Jerry D. Lewis, Lawrence MacArthur, Frank Phares.
Music—Frederick Steiner, Nathan Van Cleave (orchestras).
Sound Effects—Joe Cabbibo, James Flynn, Monty Fraser, Virgil Reimer.
Narrators—Dean Carlton, Frank Lovejoy, William Woodson.

Announcers—Milton Cross, Carl Frank, Larry Keating.
Lead—Jim Taylor, played by Stacy Harris.
Support Roles—Parley Baer, Joan Banks, Michael Ann Barrett, Bea Benadaret, Geoffrey Bryant, Whitfield Connor, William Conrad, Georgia Ellis, Herb Ellis, Elspeth Eric, Ed Firestone, J. C. Flippen, Mandel Kramer, Helen Lewis, Paul Mann, Santos Ortega, Victor Rodman, Karl Swenson, James Van Dyk, Lesley Woods, Carleton Young.

While this show, at the top of its billboard, proudly boasted that it was "the *official* broadcast from the files of the Federal Bureau of Investigation"—in contrast to rivals, most notably an eminently better received *FBI in Peace and War*—it also swiftly added a disclaimer: While its tales were "adapted" from FBI files, "All names used are fictitious and any similarity thereof to the names of persons or places, living or dead, is accidental." Some listeners must have pondered that for a while—"So did these events happen or not?" With such gobbledygook up front, who could really be certain?

Top FBI operative Jim Taylor was a continuing character in surprisingly harsh dramatizations, authentic or make-believe; he was just like *Peace and War*'s agent Shepherd. The FBI was hyped in both features. One wag put it like this: "The criminal was a rat: identified, hemmed in, and inevitably tracked down and put away." Meanwhile, real bureau chief J. Edgar Hoover made no bones about which series he liked best, strongly favoring *This Is Your FBI*. He saw that producer Jerry Devine was regularly given VIP tours of FBI facilities and brought up to speed on latest technology so it could be incorporated into story lines. (It was widely understood that the bureau squeezed out all of the public relations value it possibly could from the series, too.)

The show offered portraits of criminal misconduct. Relatively obscure FBI officials ultimately won the battles during the drama's first three years on the ether. Espionage agents, escaped Nazis and the like were the focus in the anthology's 1945 debut. But by 1948 a mythical Jim Taylor, representative of all special agents, appeared, deeply enmeshed in embezzlements, hijackings, con games, heists of many types, fraud and deception of myriad descriptions in each weekly installment. Federal agents came out smelling like a rose.

J. Edgar Hoover was so enamored with the prospect of this series that, at its debut, he offered an effusive discourse in which he lauded the FBI, the U.S. troops fighting overseas and even the show's sponsor. He further emphasized a link between detective radio drama and life: "It is my sincere hope that the broadcasts will enable you to know more about how to cooperate with your local police officials and every branch of law enforcement in your community. I also hope that you will come to know your FBI as a group of men and women who seek no personal glory, and who are part of a great team serving you, your family and the nation."

Seasoned actor Parley Baer had become so used to taping his radio programs that once, while on *This Is Your FBI*, when he accidentally botched a line he didn't give it a second thought. It was Baer's intention to re-record the line later. But in a short while, after reading his portion of the dialog and quietly sitting down, a dose of reality hit him between the eyes: They were *at that moment* on the air live! Sorry, no make-ups that day.

Three Sheets to the Wind

On the Air: Feb. 15–July 5, 1942, NBC, Sunday, 11:30 p.m. 30 minutes.
Sponsor: Sustained.
Extant Episodes: One.

CAST & CREDITS

Creator/Director/Narrator—Tay Garnett.
Music—Edward Ward.
Announcer—Ken Carpenter.
Leads—Joan Lockwood, played by Helga Moray; Dan O'Brien, played by Brian Donlevy, John Wayne.
Support Roles—Lee Bonnell, Sharon Douglas.

Around the world in 180 days on the Empress, a luxury liner, set the parameters for this mystery on the high seas. A couple of the ship's passengers were traveling incognito, however. Joan Lockwood, appearing as a high society matron, was really an undercover agent working on behalf of her employer, British intelligence. Dan O'Brien, meanwhile, who impressed passengers and crew as an inebriated American playboy, was an intelligence agent working on behalf of *his* employer, the U.S. government. Each independently pursued the same goal for a while: They wanted to recover a sultan's priceless pilfered black diamond and expose the thief who was also believed to have committed seven murders in London shortly before the ship embarked on its global voyage out of Southampton. Somewhere at sea Lockwood and O'Brien made important discoveries about one another and decided to combine their efforts to trap the perpetrator and regain the hot rock.

This 21-week series was originally conceived as a theatrical production, never completed, to be called *Three Sheets to the Wind*. The radio drama was originally to be titled *World Cruise*.

Helga Moray, who played Lockwood, was at that time married to director Tay Garnett.

Time for Love

On the Air: Jan. 15–May 28, 1953, CBS, Thursday, 9 p.m.; Sept. 3, 1953–May 27, 1954, CBS, Thursday, 9:30 p.m. 30 minutes.

Sponsors: Sustained (Jan. 15–May 28, 1953); Andrew Jergens Co. for Jergens hand cream (Sept. 3, 1953–May 27, 1954).

Extant Episodes: Four.

CAST & CREDITS

Producer—Marlene Dietrich.
Directors—Murray Burnett, Ernest Ricca.
Music—Alec Wilder (orchestra).
Announcer—Lee Vines.
Leads—Dianne La Volte, played by Marlene Dietrich; Michael Victor, played by Robert Readick.
Support Roles—Joe DeSantis, Guy Repp, Luis Van Rooten.

A mythical, globally famous vocal performer, Dianne La Volte, crusaded avocationally for law and order across the continents. Protecting the innocent and bringing the perpetrators of crime to justice was second nature to La Volte in adventures frequently carrying her long distances from her home base in San Francisco. Such far-flung venues as Venice, Paris, Vienna, Singapore, Rio de Janeiro, Cairo, Casablanca, Nice, Rome and a myriad of other exotic locales were backdrops for her exploits in dogoodism.

She had run-ins with weapons smugglers, counterfeiters, bank bandits and an assorted lot of international spies as she traversed the globe. Wherever she journeyed, La Volte was often in the company of Michael Victor, an American print journalist, who also happened to be her love interest. He had the uncanny ability, with law authorities in tow, to arrive just in the nick of time to rescue La Volte from some menacing fate.

Some reviewers suggested that this drama was an outgrowth of Marlene Dietrich's previous radio adventure feature, *Café Istanbul* (over ABC, 1952). "Sadly," wrote one, "no recordings of *Café* exist to date, leaving us only what was documented in newspapers and magazines to recollect what might have been great performances." Speaking of her singing voice, that youthful critic added: "Those who had the opportunity to hear her [Dietrich] over the radio during the forties and fifties are to be envied."

Tom Corbett, Space Cadet

On the Air: Jan. 1–July 3, 1952, ABC. Tuesday/Thursday, 5:30 p.m. 30 minutes.
Sponsor: W. K. Kellogg Co. for Pep cereal.
Extant Episodes: 40.

CAST & CREDITS

Director—Drex Hines.
Writers—Gilbert Braun, Peter Freedman, Willie Gilbert, Elwood Hoffman, Don Hughes, Richard Jessup, Hal Rine, Palmer Thompson, Jack Weinstock.
Technical Advisor—Willy Ley (space scientist).
Announcer—Jackson Beck.
Leads—Title role played by Frankie Thomas; Roger Manning, played by Jan Merlin; Astro, played by Al Markim; Larry Strong, played by Edward Bryce; Dr. Joan Dale, played by Patricia Ferris and Margaret Garland; Space Academy commander Arkwright, played by Carter Blake.
Support Roles—Joseph Ballow, Sarah Bushel, Peter Capell, Susan Douglas, Elspeth Eric, Paul Ford, Ivor Francis, Leon Janney, William Keene, Richard Keith, Barry Kroeger, Connie Lempke, Gilbert Mack, Ian Martin, James Monks, Maurice Tarplin, Luis Van Rooten.

In the year 2350, Tom Corbett and two male companions, Roger Manning and Astro, the latter from Venus, were students at the Space Academy, a global institution in the West Point tradition. Manning was a cut-up whose favorite expletives were embodied in the phrase: "Aw, go blow your jets!" The youths were in training to become solar guards, a select body of celestial law enforcement officials with peacekeeping responsibilities over Earth, Jupiter,

Mars and Venus, known collectively as the Solar Alliance.

This trio, along with Captain Larry Strong (a rather curious surname), had interplanetary adventures in every episode "as roaring rockets blast[ed] off to distant planets and far-flung stars ... [in] the age of the conquest of space." In their missions, in which they employed advanced technological measures (including the spaceship Polaris, piloted by Corbett), they attempted to eradicate the forces of evil wherever they found them toiling throughout the universe. The show was a soundman's paradise, complete with intergalactic-resonating buzzers, countdowns, innovative hisses and rumbles. A critic wrote: "Tom Corbett was basically Jack Armstrong in a space helmet."

Space Cadet, a novel by Robert A. Heinlein, was the basis for several sequels, including comic books, an illustrated newspaper strip and a televised series that preceded and paralleled the radio drama. Some of the video episodes were adapted to radio. By 1953 *Variety* reported that 100 commodities related to the series—from clothes to toys—were on the market, offered by 30 distributors.

The radio drama was delivered in two-part installments each week. Thus, part one of "Mystery of the Sparkling Meteor" was presented on Tuesday, April 8, 1952, and part two of the same narrative was broadcast Thursday, April 10, 1952. This tactic probably contributed to fans' loyalty—not wanting to miss a single episode—and, of course, would have been heartily endorsed by the sponsor, advertising agency and network as a ploy to increase listenership. Unfortunately, it didn't work that well and the radio experiment was dropped within six months.

Tom Corbett, Space Cadet premiered over CBS-TV at 6:45 p.m. on Oct. 2, 1950, with much of the same cast that was to later be heard on radio. It ran for a quar-ter-hour thrice weekly through Dec. 29, 1950, switching to 6:30 p.m. on ABC-TV, where it was televised in a similar format from Jan. 1, 1951, through Sept. 26, 1952. Meanwhile, simultaneously, it aired in a half-hour version on Saturdays at 7 p.m. over NBC-TV from July 7-Sept. 8, 1951, a most unusual feat. It made it to its fourth network, Dumont Television, on Aug. 29, 1953, and continued as a half-hour series there on Saturdays at 11:30 a.m. through May 22, 1954. Finally, it returned to NBC-TV on Saturdays at 11:30 a.m. from Dec. 11, 1954, through June 25, 1955.

A modern analyst (Gerald Nachman) suggested that the Corbett feature could have contributed to the American lexicon of the present day: "Its half-life continues on in the term *space cadet*, to denote twentieth-century dingalings (whence also *spacey*)," he allowed.

Tom Mix

(aka *Tom Mix And The Ralston Straightshooters*, aka *The Curley Bradley Show*, aka *The Singing Marshal*)

On the Air: Sept. 25, 1933–March 23, 1934, NBC, Monday/Wednesday/Friday, 5:30 p.m.; Oct. 1, 1934–March 29, 1935, NBC, Monday/Wednesday/Friday, 5:15 p.m.; Sept. 30, 1935–March 27, 1936, NBC, Monday/Wednesday/Friday, 5:30 p.m.; Sept. 28, 1936–March 26, 1937, NBC, Weekdays, 5:15 p.m.; Sept. 27, 1937–March 25, 1938, NBC Blue, Weekdays, 5:45 p.m.; Sept. 26, 1938–March 31, 1939, NBC Blue, Weekdays, 5:45 p.m.; Sept. 25, 1939–April 26, 1940, NBC Blue, Weekdays, 5:45 p.m.; Sept. 29, 1941–March 27, 1942, NBC Blue, Weekdays, 5:45 p.m.; June 5–Sept. 1, 1944, MBS, Wednesday/Friday, 5:30 p.m.; Sept. 4–Dec. 29, 1944, MBS, Weekdays, 5:30 p.m.; Dec. 11, 1944–June 21, 1946, MBS, Weekdays, 5:45 p.m.; June 25–Aug. 30, 1946, MBS, Tuesday/Thursday/Friday, 5:45 p.m.; Sept. 2, 1946–June 24, 1949, MBS, Weekdays, 5:45 p.m.;

The Curley Bradley Show, Sept. 26, 1949–June 23, 1950, MBS, Monday/Wednesday/Friday, 5:30 p.m.; *The Singing Marshall*, Aug. 6–Dec. 31, 1950, MBS, Sunday, 8 p.m.; June 11–Sept. 7, 1951, MBS, Monday/Wednesday/Friday, 5:30 p.m.; Oct. 21–Dec. 16, 1951, MBS, Sunday, 8 p.m. 15 minutes, except 25 minutes (Sept. 26, 1949–June 23, 1950).

Theme Song: *When It's Round-up Time in Texas and the Bloom is on the Sage.*

Sponsor: Ralston Purina Co. for Shredded Ralston cereal and other brands (Sept. 25, 1933–March 31, 1939; Sept. 29, 1941–Dec. 16, 1951); W. K. Kellogg Co. for its extensive line of cereal brands (Sept. 25, 1939–April 26, 1940).

Extant Episodes: 29.

Cast & Credits

Producer—Al Chance.

Directors—Charles Claggett, Clarence L. Menser.

Writers—Larry Holcomb, George Lowther, Roland Martini, Charles Tazewell.

Music—Three Ranch Boys.

Sound Effects—Barney Beck.

Announcers—Lynn Brandt, Franklyn Ferguson, Don Gordon, Les Griffith.

Leads—Title role played by Artells Dickson, Russell Thorson, Jack Holden, Joe (Curley) Bradley (1944–51); Mike Shaw, played by Leo Curley, DeWitt McBride, Harold Peary, Willard Waterman; Jimmy, played by Andy Donnelly, George Gobel, Hugh Rowlands; Jane, played by Winifred Toomey, Jane Webb; the "Old Wrangler," played by Percy Hemus.

Support Roles—Joe (Curley) Bradley (Amos Q. Snood and Pecos Williams), Shorty Carson, Patricia Dunlap (Pat Curtis), Sidney Ellstrom (Amos Q. Snood), Templeton Dox, Harvey Hays, Bob Jellison (Calamity), Carl Kroenke (Chris Acropolous), Forrest Lewis (Wash), Phil Lord (Professor Wallace), DeWitt McBride (Sheriff Hank Smith), Vance McCune (Wash), Cornelius Peeples (William Snood), Arthur Peterson (Judge Parsons), Jack Ross, Hugh Rowlands, Gertrude Warner, Bruno Wick (Lee Loo).

This series was initially based on the exploits of "the greatest western film star of the silent era," according to one wag. Not all of what the fans were led to believe about the surreal character was actually true, however. On the air, Tom Mix was a colorful Western plainsman who gained a notorious reputation as a champion of law and order. Operating from the TM-Bar Ranch near Dobie, Texas, he was Sky King on land. Astride "the wonder horse" Tony, he ferreted out bushwhackers and bank bandits, cattle rustlers and stagecoach robbers, murderers and saboteurs—just plain evilmongers of every sort. Enemies of our nation, particularly "Nazis" and "Japs," were in for a vigilant, sustained, punitive time of it during Word War II, even in the Southwest mesas. For them there would be zero toleration.

In serialized fashion, Mix and some companions—dubbed "straightshooters," who "always win"—could be counted on to uphold the laws as they rode with Sheriff Mike Shaw or the Texas Rangers whenever their assistance was needed (often, five days a week). Mix's permanent cohorts included a couple of young buckaroos, Jimmy and Jane, who were his legal wards. A crusty geezer known as the "Old Wrangler" introduced the narrative in its formative years, a duty reassigned to the show's announcer in 1944. The Wrangler appeared within those early tales, too, a kind of Gabby Hayes figure who interjected humor when needed. He'd come out with homilies like "I'll be a lop-eared kangaroo with big black eyes, if it isn't [thus and so]." A large cast of supporting characters showed up to assist Mix and friends in their fight for justice: Pecos Williams, a sidekick during part of the run; Wash, Mix's "colored" cook, later succeeded by Lee Loo, who was Chinese; Amos Q. Snood, local cheapskate, owner of the Cozy Rest Hotel, who dosed himself on "pink pills for pale people"; Calamity, with a proclivity for encountering mild mishaps, and who thus bore an appropriate nickname.

The juvenile thriller was billed as "radio's biggest western-detective program." When it garnered an even larger audience than the established *Jack Armstrong, the All-American Boy*, certainly among adolescent adventurers, there was little room to argue. Straightshooters all over the land, along with Mix, sang the show's opening and closing commercial jingle to the familiar tune of *When It's Round-Up Time in Texas and the Bloom is on the Sage*:

> Shredded Ralston for your breakfast
> Starts your day off shining bright;
> Gives you lots of cowboy energy
> With a flavor that's just right;
> It's delicious and nutritious,
> Bite-size and ready to eat;
> So take a tip from Tom...
> Go and tell your Mom...
> Shredded Ralston can't be beat!

In real life Tom Mix was purportedly a turn-of-the-century soldier of fortune. In a greatly admired volume published in the 1970s, Mix was said to have served with Teddy Roosevelt's Rough Riders in the Philippines, then seen action in the Boer War and during the Boxer Rebellion in China. Returning home, he reportedly became a Kansas lawman before his acceptance into the prestigious Texas Rangers law enforcement agency. On the sidelines, he was a rodeo performer, going on the road in 1906 with the Miller Brothers Wild West Show. Four years later, at age 30, he became an actor, gaining celebrity status in silent films and then in talkies. At 53, having become a millionaire, Mix quit the silver screen to buy a circus and a Wild West show.

In succeeding years, however, some information has come to light that isn't nearly as flattering to the legendary cowboy hero. In a book of memoirs, Mix biographers revealed that he had never been a Texas Ranger and his overseas military record wasn't as impressive as Hollywood press agents had led Americans to think. Not only had he missed action in battle, at 22 he deserted his troops. About the only venue in which he achieved merit beyond films (and much of that due to Hollywood publicity) was as a skilled rodeo performer. "By the time radio got him, he was seldom mentioned in print without a platoon of fantastic adjectives," a critic noted. Still another, discussing *this* radio show, skeptically reminded readers that "most real cowboys had been semiliterate amoral saddle-tramps," and might not be as sterling as they appeared on the air.

The die-hard fans, of course, could never accept such imputations, preferring to be left with their own thoughts and memories, possibly the one expressed by the announcer at the close of the final broadcast: "In the heart and the imagination of the world, Tom Mix rides on, and lives on, forever." Paradoxically, as fate would have it—despite all the danger he had supposedly faced in his life—Mix died on Oct. 12, 1940, in a fatal car crash near Florence, Ariz.

Author Jim Harmon detailed how the broadcast series came about in *The Great Radio Heroes*. The Ralston Purina Co. seized on Mix's glowing reputation from screen and personal appearances and—with an impersonator—turned him into a literal radio legend. Rabid aficionados will find still more incidents from the life of their childhood hero in Harmon's classic volume *Radio Mystery and Adventure and Its Appearances in Film, Television and Other Media*. Details of a 1980s effort to revive the Mix fable, along with information on films, books, comics and premiums linked with Mix, are included in that text.

Joe (Curley) Bradley had been a cowboy in the Sooner State (Oklahoma) and a Hollywood stunt man. He could sing as well as act, having practiced carrying a tune and yodeling since he learned to do it around prairie bonfires. He was a member of The Ranch Boys trio that included Hubert (Shorty) Carson and Jack Ross in addition to himself. The ensemble was regularly featured on Don McNeill's popular daytime network bonanza, *The Breakfast Club*, broadcast from Chicago at the same time that Bradley was performing in the *Tom Mix* cast.

Born Sept. 18, 1910, at Colgate, Okla., he died June 3, 1985, at Long Beach, Calif. In between, Bradley earned radio credits for appearances on *Amazing America, Author's Playhouse, Club Matinee, Headin' South, The Ranch Boys* and *The Road to Danger*. In a 1938 publicity stunt he rode a horse 2,875 miles from Hollywood to Chicago, then appeared in the Windy City broadcast of *The National Barn Dance*.

In a step that would find him pursuing a similar route to that of the movie hero he was to portray, Bradley competed in rodeos and was featured in several movies with the Ranch Boys. That ensemble originally performed singing commercials on *Tom Mix*. Having already filled supporting roles in the drama for a while, Bradley was later tapped for the lead. At that juncture he was asked to lend his golden-throated tones in a solo performance to pitch the sponsor's product, to add credence to the jingle. In 1949 the trade paper *Variety* cited him for his "good range and timber somewhat similar to Gene Autry."

Premiums may have saved the show when, in its second season (1934–35), Ralston Purina offered them for the first time to see if kids were getting its messages. When more than a million responses were received over a 26-week trial, the cereal manufacturer knew it had a winner. A plethora of premiums was issued across the years, most of which could be had for a

dime and one or more boxtops from Ralston cereals. Included were coded comic books, photo albums "containing highly confidential information every straight-shooter should know," decoders of many strains, belt buckles, badges, decals, posters, neckerchiefs, a rocket parachute and a Sheriff Mike whistling badge. A 1946 Tom Mix magnet ring is believed to be one of the most prized items currently in circulation among modern collectors.

Long after the real Tom Mix's demise, his named lived on in Big Little Books, a sportswear line and, of course, Saturday matinees that reprised his talking pictures for new generations.

Tom Mix and the Ralston Straightshooters see *Tom Mix*

The Top Guy

On the Air: Oct. 17, 1951–July 2, 1952, ABC, Wednesday, 8:30 p.m.; July 11–Oct. 24, 1952, ABC, Friday, 8 p.m.; Nov. 6, 1952–May 28, 1953, ABC, Thursday, 8:30 p.m. 30 minutes.

Sponsor: Multiple participation, including American Chicle Co. for Chiclets and Dentyne chewing gums; General Mills Inc. for its cereals and other foodstuffs; and Goodyear Tire and Rubber Co. for Goodyear tires and other vehicle supplies and services (Oct. 17, 1951–Oct. 24, 1952); Sustained (Nov. 6, 1952–May 28, 1953).

Extant Episodes: None known.

CAST & CREDITS

Director—Joseph Graham.
Writer—Richard Ellington.
Announcer—George Petrie.
Leads—Title role of Police Commissioner played by J. Scott (Jack) Smart; Assistant Commissioner, played by Ken Lynch.
Support Roles—Jan Alexander, Jay Jostyn, Danny Ocko, Frank Thomas.

A two-fisted, tough-as-nails police commissioner who was committed to carrying out vigilant law enforcement was at the center of this crime drama.

The role in which J. Scott (Jack) Smart starred virtually reprised one he had just completed after five and a half years. There he was Dashiell Hammett's popular portly radio sleuth, *The Fat Man*, from 1946 to 1951.

Unfortunately, some details of this series remain incomplete.

Top Secret

On the Air: June 12–July 10, 1950, NBC, Monday, 10:30 p.m.; July 23–Aug. 20, 1950, NBC, Sunday, 9:30 p.m.; Sept. 1, 1950, NBC, Sunday; Sept. 18–25, 1950, NBC, Monday; Oct. 5–26, NBC, Thursday, 10 p.m. 30 minutes.
Sponsor: Sustained.
Extant Episodes: 17 (plus six rehearsals).

CAST & CREDITS

Producer/Director—Harry W. Junkin.
Writer—Alan Sloane.
Music—Roy Shields (orchestra).
Announcer—Fred Collins.
Leads—Karen Gaza, played by Ilona Massey; Lord Harland, played by Ian Martin.
Support Roles—Frances Betancourt, Carl Emery, Leon Janney, Connie Lembke, Paul Levitt, Bill Lipton.

Karen Gaza was a drop-dead gorgeous World War II undercover agent for Central Intelligence. These tales dramatized her escapades surreptitiously going behind enemy lines. Simultaneously, she also worked on behalf of Great Britain's MI-2 force. Lord Harland, her superior, touted her as "the cleverest operator MI-2 ever had." Bravely, without fanfare, she fought determinedly for the cause of worldwide peace.

Ilona Massey, the series lead, came to radio from a career as a beautiful Hungar-ian movie star. *Radio Life* claimed this series was "tailor-made for her sultry voice and heavy accent."

Jerry Haendiges has prepared an almost-complete log of the series.

Top Secret Files

On the Air: Oct. 4, 1954–Sept. 12, 1955, MBS, Monday, 8 p.m.
Sponsor: Participating enterprises.
Extant Episodes: One (audition tape from Nov. 11, 1947).

CAST & CREDITS

No information.

Regrettably, no further written detail about this series is known to exist.

Top Secrets of the FBI

On the Air: 1947, MBS. 30 minutes.
Sponsor: Sustained.
Extant Episodes: None known.

CAST & CREDITS

Producer/Director–Roger Bauer.
Writer—Steadman Coves.
Music—Sylvan Levin.
Announcer—Bob Emerick.
Host—Melvin Purvis.
Supporting Roles—Larry Haines, Joe Julian, Bill Quinn, Sidney Smith, Julie Stevens.

In his book author J. Fred MacDonald observed that this postwar series lauded the Federal Bureau of Investigation each week as "the most efficient, the most scientific law enforcement organization in the world." Melvin Purvis, who narrated the weekly dramatizations, was himself a former FBI agent. Purvis carried some personal reputation, too, for he was the deputy in charge of the Chicago office when infamous outlaw John Dillinger, then dubbed Public

Enemy Number 1, was fatally shot outside that city's Biograph Theater in July 1934. (Purvis, incidentally, lent his name to several commercial enterprises following the shoot-out and was reprimanded for it and forced to step down from the agency the next year. He then became involved in the juvenile radio series *Junior G-Men*, included in this volume as a separate entry. Purvis reportedly committed suicide in 1960.)

While *Top Secrets* flaunted the bureau's use of sophisticated technology and professional investigative methods for tracking and apprehending criminals at large, the series wasn't nearly as well known as a couple of its dramatic radio counterparts, *The FBI in Peace and War* and *This Is Your FBI*. Irresponsibly claiming to be "based on actual cases of the FBI," *Top Secrets* maintained no true link with the government department it purportedly represented, according to retired FBI agent and modern day radiophile Jack French.

French termed it "a fairly mediocre crime drama, dressed up with silly quasi G-man stuff." A typical line in one script allowed: "Now, this FBI agent ... let's call him 'Jones' for security reasons, is talking to his chief. Let's call him 'Smith,' also for security reasons."

Nothing remarkably stimulating there, confirmed French.

The Townsend Murder Mysteries

On the Air: Feb. 14–June 17, 1933, NBC Blue, Tuesday/Thursday/Saturday, 7:45 p.m. 15 minutes.
Sponsor: Sustained.
Extant Episodes: None known.

CAST & CREDITS

Lead—Jim Hanvey, played by Thurston Hall.

Detective Jim Hanvey was originally introduced to reading audiences through the fictional works of novelist Octavus Roy Cohen. Hanvey was considered a "hayseed" sleuth, with a persona little more than that of a country bumpkin. Unfortunately, radio historians have not been able to secure and preserve further details of the narrative that went to air so briefly.

The radio feature was pivotal in audio mystery fare in that it may have been the first dramatic detective series where the personality of the central character dominated the action. (There is recorded documentation that the same type of glamorized characterization surfaced in motion pictures by the mid 1930s, resulting in increased financial success for that medium.) "It was inevitable that radio producers and advertising agencies would alter the emphasis in the detective program to develop series [focusing on a key figure]," allowed one introspective radio analyst.

Treasury Agent

On the Air: April 14–July 14, 1947, ABC, Monday, 9 p.m.; July 21–Sept. 22, 1947, ABC, Monday, 8:30 p.m.; Oct. 2–23, 1947, ABC, Thursday, 8 p.m.; Jan. 11–June 6, 1948, ABC, Sunday, 5 p.m.; Oct. 5, 1954–Nov. 26, 1957, MBS, Tuesday, 8 p.m. 30 minutes.
Sponsors: Sustained (ABC); Multiple participation (MBS).
Extant Episodes: Four.

CAST & CREDITS

Producer/Director/Writer—Phillips H. Lord.
Director—Leonard Bass.
Music—Ralph Norman.
Announcer—Carl Warren.
Lead—Joe Lincoln, played by Raymond Edward Johnson (ABC), Larry Haines (MBS).
Support Roles—Frank Barnes, Sandy Becker, Ralph Bell, Tom Holland, Santos Ortega, Alice Reinheart, Everett Sloane, Jimmy

Tansey, James Van Dyk, Chuck Webster, Lewis Whiteman, Lawson Zerbe (Agent Williams), Bill Zuckert.

Joe Lincoln was the fictional chief of the U.S. Treasury Department. He was also the key figure in revealing actual case histories from all the law enforcement entities under that strategic federal agency. Included were tales of the U.S. Secret Service (presidential protection and counterfeiting), Revenue Intelligence (tax fraud evasion), Bureau of Narcotics, Bureau of Customs (alcohol tax unit) and the Coast Guard (border protection and high seas crimes). Having such stories in the "realistic series ... — all dealing with actual criminal events — added a note of authenticity and relevance to radio drama," wrote one reviewer.

Possibly out of budget constraints, a professional actor portrayed Elmer Lincoln Irey, retired coordinator of law enforcement for the U.S. Treasury Department. Irey was introduced weekly to narrate the program. It was a ploy producer Phillips H. Lord had long become accustomed to, having utilized it on his popular *Gangbusters* series, which began in 1935, with actors impersonating local law officers whose stories were featured.

Phillips H. Lord proved extremely successful in introducing a wave of realistic crime dramas to Americans' listening ears. In addition to *Treasury Agent*, he was responsible for the series *Counterspy, Gangbusters, G-Men, Mr. District Attorney* and *Policewoman*. (See separate entries.)

Troman Harper, Rumor Detective

On the Air: Dec. 13, 1942–Feb. 21, 1943, MBS, Sunday, 6:30 p.m.; Feb. 28–Nov. 28, 1943, MBS, Sunday, 6:45 p.m. 15 minutes.
Sponsor: Grove Laboratories Inc. for Bromo Quinine cold tablets.
Extant Episodes: Two.

CAST & CREDITS

Host — Electronic newsjournalist Troman Harper as himself.

"If you believe rumors, you're a sucker; if you repeat rumors, you're one of Hitler's best soldiers," the epigraph for this war propaganda exposé began. It continued: "Learn the truth about rumors. The truth is a banner; with it, you can jab and slice a rumor to ribbons." In one of radio's most unusual and colorful personality-driven sleuthing features, news correspondent Troman Harper ("the rumor detective") attempted to set the record straight about U.S. enemies' boasts. With unhesitating boldness, he'd dispute the untruths that had been disseminated over short wave radio by the Axis powers that week. Then Harper would exclaim: "Horse feathers!" "Pure malarkey!" or some similar epithet intended to ridicule the allegations and those who broadcast them.

This show was similar to one on CBS, *Our Secret Weapon*, which ran virtually concurrently (Aug. 9, 1942–Oct. 18, 1943). For most of its duration it aired on both Sunday and Friday nights. In it Rex Stout, author of the Nero Wolfe detective novels, also refuted current German-Italian-Japanese propaganda broadcasts. CBS staffers collected material actually aired each week. When an announcer read some of the Axis powers' claims aloud, Stout interrupted, offering a response from the Allied powers' point of view. Occasionally major addresses given in other languages were included in brief narratives, in order to make emphatic points. Actors playing Hitler, Hirohito and Mussolini were heard regularly in the dramatic fare. (See separate entry for *Our Secret Weapon*.)

True Adventures of Junior G-Men see Junior G-Men

True Detective Mysteries

On the Air: May 16, 1929–May 8, 1930, CBS, Thursday, 9:30 p.m.; Sept. 8, 1936–Aug. 31, 1937, MBS, Tuesday, 9:30 p.m.; April 5, 1938–March 28, 1939, MBS, Tuesday, 10 p.m.; April 29–June 24, 1944, MBS, Saturday, 10:15 p.m.; Oct. 1, 1944–March 11, 1945, MBS, Sunday, 1:30 p.m.; Jan. 20, 1946–1948, MBS, Sunday, 4:30 p.m.; 1948–1949, MBS, Sunday, 4 p.m.; 1949–April 10, 1955, MBS, Sunday, 5:30 p.m.; April 13–Sept. 14, 1955, MBS, Wednesday, 8 p.m.; Sept. 19, 1955–June 2, 1958, MBS, Monday, 8 p.m. 30 minutes, except 15 minutes (Jan. 3–March 28, 1939).

Theme Song: *Mysterioso #1.*

Sponsors: MacFadden Publications for *True Detective* magazine (May 16, 1929–Aug. 31, 1937); Warner Lambert Pharmaceutical Co. for Listerine oral hygiene products (April 5, 1938–March 28, 1939); Sustained (Oct. 1, 1944–March 11, 1945, 1953–June 2, 1958); O'Henry confectionery bars (Jan. 20, 1946–1953) (clever commercials on the show referred to the candy as "public energy number one").

Extant Episodes: 23.

CAST & CREDITS

Producer/Director/Writer—Peter Irving.
Director/Writer—Murray Burnett.
Music—Chet Kingsbury (orchestra), Paul Taubman (organist).
Sound Effects—Barney Beck, Don Foster, Jim Goode, Bill Hoffman.
Announcers—Frank Dunne, Hugh James, Dan McCullock, Ralph Paul.
Narrator/Host—*True Detective* editor Jack Shuttleworth, played by Richard Keith, who was eventually supplanted by an unidentified editor of the same publication played by John Griggs.
Support Roles—Ralph Bell, Ted de Corsia, Joe DeSantis, Robert Dryden, Elspeth Eric, Mandel Kramer, Alice Reinheart, Johnny Thomas, Gertrude Warner.

This program was based upon stories appearing in *True Detective* magazine, a leading product of one of the feature's early sponsors. Multiple versions were broadcast but the most popular, best recalled and most durable began Oct. 1, 1944 with an actor impersonating John Shuttleworth, the periodical's editor, as he narrated the crime tales. Eventually Shuttleworth's name was discarded in favor of an unnamed editor who carried on in his stead. Pursuing a semi-documentary motif, it employed a strong realism. The show tackled authentic cases, justifying its claim as "a real story of a real crime solved by real people with a real criminal brought to justice."

It was soon airing a postscript to weekly episodes, the description of an actual wanted fugitive. An offer of $500 cash (later upped to $1,000) was proffered to anyone who helped in locating dangerous criminals, provided the thugs were ultimately arrested and convicted. This feature emphatically tied the drama to the world its listeners lived in. These "wanted posters" of the airwaves resulted in apprehending several culprits, setting a precedent for other broadcast series that would carry similar bulletins (notably *Gangbusters* and *America's Most Wanted*). The tales on *True Detective Mysteries*, meanwhile, were frequently presented from the angle of the perpetrators. In this way the slip-ups that were eventually responsible for their capture became obvious to anyone tuning in at home.

A media critic certified this anthology as "the first network detective series of importance." It may have been just that, extending over a three-decade time frame between 1929 and 1958. Certainly it was one of the earliest, and, in spite of some lengthy gaps between segments, it proved it had staying power.

Tune Detective

On the Air: Dec. 9, 1931–1932, NBC Blue, Wednesday; 1932–May 2, 1933, NBC Blue, Tuesday/Thursday. 15 minutes.

Theme Songs: *Der Lauterbach* and *Lohengrin.*
Sponsor: Sustained.
Extant Episodes: One.

CAST & CREDITS

Host—Sigmund Spaeth.

Although no one may have been prosecuted as a result of this unique and authentic investigative feature, it certainly cast the spotlight on an area that was probably widely abused then and may still be now. In real life musicologist Sigmund Spaeth frequently testified in the hall of justice as an expert witness in musical patent and plagiarism disputes. Given that background, on radio he proved composition copyright infringements, exposing tunes that were lifted from older melodies. Some of them were effectively duplicated from existing published works.

Sigmund Spaeth would appear over MBS between Jan. 19 and March 23, 1947, as host of *Sigmund Spaeth's Music Quiz.* From May 12 to Sept. 29, 1940, he had presided over *Fun in Print* on CBS in which studio guests competed with famous authors in question-and-answer rounds.

Twenty-First Precinct

On the Air: July 7–Nov. 24, 1953, CBS, Tuesday, 9:30 p.m.; Jan. 20, 1954–April 20, 1955, CBS, Wednesday, 8:30 p.m.; July 9–Oct. 1, 1955, CBS, Saturday, 8 p.m.; Oct. 7, 1955–Jan. 20, 1956, CBS, Friday, 8:30 p.m.; Jan. 26–July 26, 1956, CBS, Thursday, 8:30 p.m. 30 minutes.
Sponsor: Sustained.
Extant Episodes: 96.

CAST & CREDITS

Producers—John Ives, Stanley Niss.
Program Consultant—Norman Frank.
Director/Writer—Stanley Niss.
Announcers—Arthur Hanna, Bob Hill.
Leads—Captain Frank Kennelly, played by

Everett Sloane (July 7, 1953–Oct. 1, 1955), James Gregory (Oct. 7, 1955–1956), Les Damon (1956); Lieutenant Matt King, played by Ken Lynch; Sergeant Waters, played by Harold J. Stone; Sergeant Collins, played by Jack Orrisa.
Support Roles—George Petrie, Robert Readick, Elaine Rust, Harold Stone, Linda Watkins, Barbara Weeks.

The action in this crime drama, which was produced in conjunction with a 20,000-member New York City Patrolman's Benevolent Association, offered a "factual account of the way police work in the world's largest city." As such it presented a grim, less-than-alluring sketch of law enforcement in an urban context, similar to a few other mature police dramas of its epoch (e.g. *Broadway Is My Beat, The Line-up, Dragnet*). Action took place at the NYPD's 21st precinct.

Under the command of Captain Frank Kennelly, Lieutenant Matt King and Sergeants Waters and Collins performed their duties as crimestoppers in a routine but scrupulous style. Day-to-day events occurring within the confines of a police substation were incidental to the main plots; a single case was pursued in every episode, following the detectives in step-by-step investigation of a specific criminal activity (often quite vivid and brutal) as they soberly sought to resolve it. The description of the surrounding geographical territory and its people, offered at the start of every weekly episode, was a classic: "Just lines on a map of the city of New York. Most of the 173,000 people wedged into the nine-tenths of a square mile between Fifth Avenue and the East River wouldn't know if you asked them that they lived or worked in the twenty-first. Whether they know it or not, the security of their homes, their persons and their property is the job of the men of the twenty-first precinct ... [it included] 160 patrolmen, 11 sergeants, four lieutenants and the captain of the hot-box that is the twenty-first precinct." All of them worked under the command of Kennelly.

Following the model of *Dragnet*, already a huge radio hit, *Twenty-First Precinct* placed the listener directly in the action, from an opening phone call until the final report was completed. At the close of each week's case, Kennelly pronounced: "And so it goes, around the clock, through the week, every day, every year. A police precinct in the city of New York is a flesh-and-blood merry-go-round. Anyone can catch the brass ring—or the brass ring can catch anyone." It was tough-as-nails police work and never for the fainthearted.

While this may have been one of the better adult-oriented police dramas on the air, across a three-year period it never attracted a permanent sponsor. The reason, perhaps, may be that it arrived on radio too late in the golden age to receive much attention from prospective bill-payers; many, by then, were fully enamored with the potential offered by television as America's newest entertainment venue. That did not, of course, prevent *Twenty-First Precinct* from serving up some fascinating tales of hard-core police work.

Twenty Thousand Years in Sing Sing

(aka *Behind Prison Bars*, aka *Criminal Case Histories With Warden Lewis E. Lawes*, aka *Crime Cases Of Warden Lawes*)

On the Air: *Twenty Thousand Years in Sing Sing.* Jan. 22–May 7, 1933, NBC Blue, Sunday, 9 p.m.; Oct. 4, 1933–March 14, 1934, NBC Blue, Wednesday, 9 p.m.; Sept. 19, 1934–April 17, 1935, NBC Blue, Wednesday, 9 p.m.; Sept. 18, 1935–April 8, 1936, NBC Blue, Wednesday, 9:30 p.m.; Oct. 12, 1936–April 5, 1937, NBC Blue, Monday, 9 p.m.; *Behind Prison Bars.* Oct. 18, 1937–April 11,

1938, NBC Blue, Monday, 10 p.m.; *Criminal Case Histories with Warden Lewis E. Lawes.* Oct. 21, 1938–April 21, 1939, NBC Blue, Friday, 8 p.m.; *Crime Cases of Warden Lawes.* Oct. 20, 1946–Jan. 12, 1947, MBS, Sunday, 1 p.m.; Jan. 19–March 30, 1947, MBS, Sunday, 2 p.m.; April 8–Sept. 23, 1947, MBS, Tuesday, 8 p.m. 30 minutes, except 15 minutes (1946–47).

Sponsors: Sustained (Jan. 22–May 7, 1933, Oct. 20, 1946–Sept. 23, 1947); W. L. Warner Co. for Sloan's Liniment muscle healing rub (Oct. 4, 1933–April 21, 1939).

Extant Episodes: One (*Crime Cases of Warden Lawes*).

CAST & CREDITS

Producer—Bernard J. Prockter (1946–47).
Directors—Joseph Bell, Arnold Michaelis, Bill Michaelis.
Writer—Max Ehrlich (1946–47).
Announcers—Ben Grauer and Kelvin Keech (1933–39), Cy Harrice (1946–47).
Host/Narrator—Lewis E. Lawes.
Interviewer—Mr. Stark, played by Joseph Bell.
Support Roles—Tony Berger, Ralph Locke, Alice Reinheart, Cecil Secrest, Ned Wever.

The earliest title of this unique series purportedly referred to an estimated aggregate of time the inmates serving at Sing Sing Prison in Ossining, New York, had been sentenced to for their crimes. Warden Lewis E. Lawes of that facility, author of a book by the same moniker, hosted the narratives that dramatized tales of life in incarceration. Through questions posed by an interviewer identified as Mr. Stark, Lawes related incidents about some of the inmates and what sent them there. The comments added both validity and realism to the show.

When the program title was revised in 1937 to *Behind Prison Bars*, announcer Ben Grauer read crime-related inquiries that had been received from the radio audience. Lawes responded with helpful information and personal advice. By the time the series was reprised in 1946, Lawes had retired from his official duties but continued to narrate the radio dramas.

Arriving on the air as early as it did (in 1933), this show became the impetus for a string of hard-core police dramas to follow, among them *Gangbusters*, debuting in 1935; *The FBI in Peace and War*, 1944; and *This Is Your FBI*, 1945.

Warden Lawes donated most of his income from the radio series to altruistic causes derived from the vices he spoke out against. In his thinking, crime was frequently a result of poverty, or the deprivation resulting from poverty. He dispensed some of his proceeds to ventures like building a fitness center for Sing Sing convicts and providing radios for them. He also supported a welfare fund that benefited the kin of inmates who encountered dire financial straits.

A couple of radio history buffs suggested that actor Guy Sorel stepped in for Warden Lawes late in the run. While that hasn't been corroborated, it is possible that the versatile thespian substituted for Lawes on occasion during an extensive broadcast tenure.

In 1932 Spencer Tracy (as Tom Connors) and Betty Davis (as Fay Wilson) co-starred in a major theatrical production, *Twenty Thousand Years in Sing Sing*, also inspired by Lawes' book. Directed by Michael Curtiz with writing credited to both Lawes and Courtney Terrett, the cast included Arthur Byron as Warden Paul Long with Louis Calhern, Warren Hymer and Lyle Talbot in supporting roles. The widespread acceptance of the book and film would almost assuredly have had a colossal impact on the radio series that subsequently developed.

Two on a Clue

On the Air: Oct. 2, 1944–March 23, 1945, CBS, Weekdays, 2:15 p.m.; March 26, 1945–

Jan. 4, 1946, CBS, Weekdays, 2 p.m. 15 minutes.
Sponsor: General Foods Corp. for LaFrance bleach and Satina laundry starch.
Extant Episodes: Three.

CAST & CREDITS

Director/Writer—Harry Ingram.
Writer—Louis Vittes.
Announcer—Alice Yourman.
Leads—Jeff Spencer, played by Ned Wever; Debby Spencer, played by Louise Fitch; Cornelius Trumbull, played by John Gibson.
Support Roles—Jim Boles (the professor), Ronald Liss (Mickey), Athena Lorde ("the Midget"), Kate McComb (Mrs. Grover).

Jeff and Debby Spencer were a husband-and-wife detective team. Their close confidant was police sergeant Cornelius Trumbull. The Spencers' investigations led them into peeks into authentic case histories.

This program was highly reminiscent of two admired nighttime half-hour man-and-wife detective thrillers, *Mr. and Mrs. North* and *The Thin Man*. (See separate entries.) It was serialized and played to a matinee audience, however, one primarily consisting of homemakers and others who were at liberty during the day. Its sponsor replaced it on Jan. 7, 1946, with what became the very last melodramatic soap opera to air on any U.S. national aural chain during—or since—radio's golden age, *The Second Mrs. Burton*. That series earned its dubious distinction on Nov. 25, 1960, broadcasting the final episode of any serial in a genre that was launched in 1930 and which, over three decades, introduced more than 200 different quarter-hour dramas to matinee listeners. The occasion is traditionally marked as "the day radio drama died" by collectors of old time radio memorabilia.

Under Arrest

On the Air: July 28–Sept. 1, 1946, MBS, Sunday, 5 p.m.; June 8–Aug. 31, 1947, MBS,

Sunday, 5 p.m.; June 6–Sept. 5, 1948, MBS, Sunday, 5 p.m.; Nov. 7, 1948–1949, MBS, Sunday, 9 p.m.; 1950–Dec. 27, 1953, MBS, Sunday, 4 p.m.; Jan. 3–Oct. 3, 1954, MBS, Monday, 8:30 p.m. 30 minutes.
Sponsors: Delaware, Lackawanna and Western Coal Co. for its Blue Coal brand of heating energy (July 28, 1946–Sept. 5, 1948); Dictograph Corp. for its office equipment and supplies (Nov. 7, 1948–1951); Sustained (1951–Oct. 3, 1954).
Extant Episodes: 18.

CAST & CREDITS

Producer—Wynn Wright.
Director—Martin Magner.
Writer—William Wells Jr.
Music—Al Finelli, Milton Ray (organists).
Sound Effects—Al April.
Announcers—Ted Brown, Jack Farren.
Leads—John Drake, played by Joe DeSantis, Craig McDonnell; Jim Scott, played by Joe DeSantis, Ned Wever.
Support Roles—Ralph Bell, Patsy Campbell, Les Damon, Carl Eastman, Betty Garde, Joseph Julian, John Larkin, Craig McDonnell, Kermit Murdock, Eileen Palmer, Bryna Raeburn, Sid Raymond, Vicki Vola.

One reviewer termed this a "space-age cops-and-robbers show" although there seems little to support that assertion. The series dramatized the inner-workings of a local police department. Its initial protagonist was Captain John Drake, its principal figure during the summer runs of 1946, 1947 and 1948. Captain Jim Scott succeeded Drake when the program went to year-round status. The opening billboard promised a waiting audience precious little: "Mutual presents *Under Arrest*. Criminals behind bars—*Under Arrest*, the story of police Captain Jim Scott's fight against crime." A critic called it "an undistinguished show." It's always possible he was right.

United States Postal Inspector

On the Air: Unsubstantiated.
Sponsor: Sustained.

Extant Episodes: One (audition tape, Feb. 26, 1947).

CAST & CREDITS

Producer/Director/Writer—Robert Westerlake.
Lead—Jefferson Black, played by Warren William.

The narrative was based on authentic files of the U.S. Postal Service. Postal inspector Jefferson Black was the central crimes-topper in the drama. Misuse of the mails via confidence rackets, frauds, robberies and other illegal activities was brought from its obscurity by highlighting the work of U.S. postal inspectors. The initiators of a scheme to offer a service without actually providing it were typical of the kinds of offenders brought to justice on the show.

An unidentified, ubiquitous voice boomed out of nowhere at the start of the program, offering this friendly reminder: "Nor rain ... nor heat ... nor gloom of night ... stays these couriers from the swift completion of their appointed rounds." An announcer prompted: "Postal inspectors handle their cases quietly, with dignity, invariably bringing their quarry to justice." It was a comforting thought for a sleepless night.

This was an audition program that just possibly never aired. There is little evidence to support the fact that it became a radio series after its initial outing although that is certainly possible.

Up for Parole

On the Air: March 10–Dec. 8, 1950, CBS, Friday, 9 p.m. 30 minutes.
Sponsor: Sustained.
Extant Episodes: None known.

CAST & CREDITS

Producer/Director—John Dietz.
Writer—Allan Sloane.

Announcer—Lee Vines.
Host—Harry Marble.
Support Roles—Susan Douglas, Rod Hendrickson, Joe Julian, Ed Latimer, Jimmy Lipton, Mary Michael, Chet Stratton, Arthur Vinton.

In this aberrant crime series an inmate appeared before a parole board to plead his case for release from prison. His personal journey in committing a felony, his apprehension, sentencing and rehabilitation were conveyed through a dramatic narrative. At that juncture the audience was given an opportunity to render a judgment as to whether it felt the con's appeal should be granted.

A Voice in the Night

On the Air: May 3–Aug. 16, 1946, MBS, Friday, 8:30 p.m.; Aug. 23–Oct. 18, 1946, MBS, Friday, 8 p.m. 30 minutes.
Sponsor: Sustained.
Extant Episodes: Two.

CAST & CREDITS
Producer—Roger Bower.
Writers—Bob Arthur, David Kogan, Amzie Strickland.
Music—Emerson Buckley (orchestra).
Announcer—Ted Brown.
Leads—Carl Brisson as himself; his secretary, played by Amzie Strickland.

The Golden Oriole, a mythical nightclub, was the venue for this unusual series, featuring owner-vocalist Carl Brisson, a Danish-born established film star in real life. Brisson heisted tunes nominated by club patrons while strolling among the crowd. From that setting—in a contrived, strange turn of events—he departed the club to solve a murder or expose a burglar. The crimes he encountered were often of the violent variety. Inevitably Brisson returned to the Golden Oriole just in time for a tune-filled finale. In a single episode,

he might vocalize a trio of melodies before departing the airwaves. It was one of the most unusual twists in radio dramatic formats ever contrived. Amzie Strickland, who played Brisson's secretary, also penned the scripts. "The result," one wag said, "was laughably corny."

Wanted

On the Air: July 7–Sept. 29, 1950, NBC, Friday, 10 p.m. 30 minutes.
Sponsor: Sustained.
Extant Episodes: 12.

CAST & CREDITS
Producer/Director/Host—Walter McGraw.
Music—Morris Mamorsky.
Announcer/Narrator—Fred Collins.

Here the listeners literally had "the program that brings you *for the first time* on the air a nationwide manhunt in action." Nothing was held back, for an announcer cautioned sternly: "No one is protected." In a realistic crime narrative, names and voices of actual victims, their families and acquaintances, the perpetrators and arresting officers were aired via the magic of recording tape. Producer/director Walter McGraw introduced each case, and host and announcer Fred Collins narrated it.

In spite of its attempt at realism, the series had its flaws. A primary one was that the authentic but rank amateurs who spoke the lines—obviously without much talent as aural thespians—often made little endeavor to hide the fact they were reading from a script. Thus the production frequently came across as a group of neophytes—some of whom had difficulty with words to begin with—trying to read aloud nearly futilely at times. Listeners easily noted the difference in rank amateurs and professionals, and surely missed the practiced speech patterns they were accustomed to hearing.

Wendy Warren and the News

On the Air: June 23, 1947–Nov. 12, 1958, CBS, 12:00 noon. 15 minutes.

Theme Song: *My Home Town* (specifically written for the series by organist Clarke Morgan and popularized in sheet music).

Sponsors: General Foods Corp. principally for Maxwell House coffee but also for Baker's coconut, Gaines pet foods, Post cereals, Jell-O pudding and pie fillings and other food-stuffs (June 23, 1947–Sept. 17, 1954); Procter & Gamble Co. for a variety of household and personal care products (Sept. 30, 1954–1955); Sustained (1955–Nov. 12, 1958).

Extant Episodes: 16.

CAST & CREDITS

Producer—Benton and Bowles advertising agency.

Directors—Hoyt Allen, Allen Fristoe, Tom McDermott, Don Wallace.

Writers—John Picard, Frank Provo.

Music—Clarke Morgan (organist).

Sound Effects—Hamilton O'Hara.

Announcer—Bill Flood (pseudonym for Hugh James).

Leads—Wendy Warren, played by Florence Freeman; Newscaster Douglas Edwards as himself.

Support Roles—Vera Allen, Horace Braham (Charles Lang), Anne Burr (Nona Marsh), Peter Capell (Anton Kamp), Rod Hendrickson (Sam Warren), Lamont Johnson (Mark Douglas), Jane Lauren (Adele Lang), John Raby (Don Smith), Tess Sheehan (Aunt Dorie), Guy Spaull, Lotte Stavisky, Les Tremayne (Gil Kendal), Meg Wylie (Jean).

While some purists might dispute the inclusion of a melodramatic soap opera in the confines of a volume on crime fighting, this daytime serial fully focused its attention on combating evildoing during half or more of its 11 years on the ether. This was not of the cops-and-robbers strain; there were no burglars, spouse-killers and income tax delinquents among the clan. Instead, the targets were almost always enemies of the nation's best interests—specifically, espionage agents, spies, undercover operatives, seditious informants with malice intended and so forth. These global Mafia types would foil the common good of all Americans, and advocated an overthrow of the U.S. government. (Couldn't this have appeared just as authentic if it had aired after international terrorists struck America more than a half-century later? It seemed to foretell what actually occurred that far in the future.)

Protagonist Wendy Warren, a crusading newsjournalist whose credentials were firmly established in both electronic and print media, worked tirelessly alongside U.S. intelligence aides to combat the menacing forces—some recognized, some undetected—that appeared destined to strike against peace-loving people everywhere and to destroy our way of life. While there was definitely room for some domestic conflict within the serial, these supercharged concerns weren't ever far from Warren's thoughts: This was heavy stuff and increasingly gave rise to convoluted plots. Should Wendy and her cohorts fail in their dangerous assignments, the balance of the free world hung in jeopardy.

Professionally, Warren delivered "news from the women's world" daily to a live national radio audience following a brief summary of world news reported by respected CBS newsman Douglas Edwards. From that duty she then entered the fictitious story line as a correspondent for the mythical *Manhattan Gazette*. With Anton Kamp—a pro-U.S. strategist who had emigrated from an unidentified third world nation where trouble was brewing aplenty—Warren sought to expose the diabolical intents of those ruthless hooligans. And while the "cause" for which she and Anton fought was never precisely identified, fans glued to their radios while they gulped down lunch were absolutely certain that, as one wag put it: "If Wendy and Anton weren't successful, all hell could break loose for America."

Such a dramatic serial received popular acclaim for several reasons. Airing as it did at high noon in the East and during the lunch hour for a majority of its radio audience, it easily contended as a primary crowd-pleaser among daytime features. Its subject matter contributed to that, particularly by drawing a large number of male listeners who otherwise normally wouldn't tune in to a soap opera. The audience size was significantly enhanced by the inclusion of a three-minute live news report at the quarter-hour's start. And those news bulletins forced the story line to adapt to the real world by joining it, accepting the fact that a literal new day dawned for every episode, as opposed to three-week intervals for the passing of a single day on many other soap operas. For all of these reasons, this narrative appealed to a widely diversified audience, some of whom followed its spy missions for years.

The serial was one of only three (out of a total of more than 200 aired on daytime radio between 1930 and 1960) to occupy a single quarter-hour time period in runs exceeding a decade. (The other dishpan dramas were *Our Gal Sunday* and *Stella Dallas*.) *Warren* was the only durable soap opera to have cast every role but once. And among all daytime features, including nearly 75 broadcast by network chains on weekdays, by 1950 *Warren* had earned a coveted third spot in the ratings, settling directly behind *The Romance of Helen Trent* and *Arthur Godfrey Time*, respectively.

In my *The Great Radio Soap Operas* (McFarland, 1999), this high noon thriller has been extensively documented in its own chapter.

The Whisper Men

On the Air: Sept. 8–Oct. 6, 1945, MBS, Saturday, 9:30 p.m.; Oct. 13–Nov. 3, 1945, MBS, Saturday, 8:30 p.m.; Dec. 22, 1945–Jan. 5, 1946, MBS, Saturday, 11:30 a.m.; Jan. 12–Feb. 2, 1946, MBS, Saturday, 8 p.m. 30 minutes.
Sponsor: Sustained.
Extant Episodes: Two.

CAST & CREDITS

Director—Anton M. Leader.
Music—Chet Kingsbury (organist).
Leads—Max Chandler, played by Karl Weber, Joseph Curtin; Rod Buchanan, played by Kermit Murdock; Linda Jones, played by Betty Caine.
Support Roles—Betty Caine, Fran Carlon, Ann Shepherd (pseudonym for Sheindel Kalish).

In a global crime melodrama adapted from tales appearing in *Liberty* magazine, Max Chandler—the central figure—was a radio commentator and reporter. The show's billboard informed listeners that Chandler's missions took him "into constant conflict with the 'Whisper Men'—international criminals who plot in secret to further their own sinister interests." In his efforts to quell the disturbances and put their perpetrators out of business, Chandler was assisted by Rod Buchanan. Also regularly appearing in the plots was a feminine reporter for *The Globe* magazine, Linda Jones.

While this series had problems, the main one could have been readily fixed. Someone at Mutual was busy tampering with the time periods, shifting the drama to a new spot on the Saturday agenda far too frequently. After it aired five weeks, it moved; it moved again after four weeks; then after three weeks; then after another four weeks, it was shut down permanently, having totally lost its ability to maintain an audience or attract a sponsor. No continuity there and the potential fans finally gave up.

Two radio historians suggest that popular radio announcer Danny Seymour (recalled for *Aunt Jenny's Real Life Stories* and other programs) produced this series. Other respected authorities name no producer. It is probably a little early in Seymour's career for him to have had such a challenging assignment, although he achieved tremendous upward strides in successive decades. Seymour eventually became a high level executive with two competing advertising agencies, Young & Rubicam and J. Walter Thompson.

The Whisperer

On the Air: July 8–Dec. 16, 1951, NBC, Sunday, 5 p.m. 30 minutes.
Sponsor: Sustained.
Extant Episodes: 13.

CAST & CREDITS

Producer—William Karn.
Writer—Jonathan Twice.
Music—Johnny Duffy (organist).
Announcer—Don Rickles.
Leads—Title role of the Whisperer, aka Philip Gault, played by Carleton Young; Ellen Norris, played by Betty Moran; Lieutenant Denver, played by Jack Moyles; Moran, played by Paul Frees.
Support Roles—Torry Bennett, William Conrad, Betty Lou Gerson, Earl Lee, Janet Scott.

The epigraph for this series succinctly packaged the whole story: "The Whisperer, a brilliant man who—losing his voice in an accident that crushed his vocal chords—worked his way deep within the crime syndicate to help destroy it from within. To the underworld, his familiar rattling hiss is the voice of authority to be obeyed without question. Then a miracle of surgery performed by Dr. Benjamin Lee restored his natural voice, enabling him to resume his real identity. Now, as Philip Gault, brilliant young attorney, he skirts the edges of death living his dual role—for as the Whisperer, he sets in motion the forces of the syndicate; then as Philip Gault, uses his knowledge to fight the organized network of crime which seeks to control the fate of millions in cities and towns across the nation."

Gault was a criminal lawyer in the hamlet of Central City. Other regulars in the cast included Ellen Norris, the nurse in Dr. Benjamin Lee's office—and the only individual to know the Whisperer's true identity (let's face it: every Shadow needed a Margo Lane so the two would have something to talk about); there was Lieutenant Denver of the Central City Police Department; and Moran, the syndicate's honcho in New York City (big towns bred big trouble). When Gault telephoned Moran, he identified himself as "Central City reporting," a fairly precise clue to his identity if any bureaucrats were wiretapping their conversations. (Listeners really didn't consider things like that in those days, or if they did, they soon passed over them. In radio, you could get away with almost anything the censors couldn't object to.)

While Gault luckily never found himself in the throes of being a lawbreaker, he justified his ties with the syndicate thusly: "They obey my voice and I pass along instructions. I never help in their plans for crime." What he did do was to infiltrate plans the syndicate had carefully crafted, then used that information to thwart their nasty schemes. For some reason, as superior as their counterintelligence should have been, they never appeared to catch on to who the stoolie was among them. As a result he never encountered a second "accident." *Variety* thought the whole thing "far-fetched" and said so. A radio historiographer simply allowed that the concept "never reached full potential."

The Whistler

On the Air: May 16–Sept. 5, 1942, CBS West Coast network, Saturday; Sept. 13, 1942–March 28, 1943, CBS West Coast, Sunday, 8 p.m.; May 1–June 26, 1943, CBS West Coast, Saturday, 8 p.m.; July 2–Sept. 24, 1943, CBS West Coast, Friday; Oct. 3, 1943–Sept. 10, 1944, CBS West Coast, Sunday, 8 p.m.; Sept. 18, 1944–June 23, 1947, CBS West Coast, Monday, 8 p.m.; (overlapping with) July 3–Sept. 25, 1946, CBS (full network), Wednesday, 8 p.m.; (West Coast network overlapping with) March 26, 1947–Sept. 29, 1948, CBS (full network), Wednesday, 10 p.m.; Oct. 3, 1948–July 31, 1955, CBS West Coast, Sunday, 9:30 p.m. 30 minutes.

Sponsors: Sustained (May 16, 1942–Dec. 5, 1943; July 3–Sept. 25, 1946, on full CBS network; Aug. 29, 1954–Jan. 30, 1955); Signal Oil Co. for Signal gasoline, oil and other automotive products and services (CBS West Coast network, Dec. 12, 1943–Aug. 22, 1954); Campbell Soup Co. for an extensive line of Campbell soups, Franco-American spaghetti and other foodstuffs (July 3–Sept. 25, 1946, full CBS network); Household Finance Corp. for its financial products and services (March 26, 1947–Sept. 29, 1948, full CBS network); Lever Brothers Co. for its household cleaning and personal care products (CBS West Coast, Feb. 6–July 31, 1955).

Extant Episodes: 502 (approximately).

CAST & CREDITS

Producer/Writer—J. Donald Wilson.
Producer/Director—George W. Allen.
Directors—Sherman Marks, Sterling Tracy.
Script Editors—Joel Malone, Harold Swanton.
Music—Wilbur Hatch, Hunter Taylor (orchestras).
Whistlers—Owen James, Dorothy Roberts.
Sound Effects—Ross Murray, Berne Surrey, Gene Twombly.
Announcers—Bob Lemond, Marvin Miller, Don Rickles, Bob Venables.
Lead—Title role played by Everett Clarke, Bill Forman, Gale Gordon, Bill Johnstone, Joseph Kearns, Marvin Miller.
Support Roles—Hy Averback, Joan Banks, Gloria Blondell, John Brown, Madeleine Carroll, Jeff Chandler, William Conrad, Hans Conried, Howard Culver, John Dehner, Ralph Edwards, Paul Frees, Betty Lou Gerson, Charlotte Lawrence, Cathy Lewis, Elliott Lewis, Frank Lovejoy, Wally Maher, Mercedes McCambridge, John McIntire, Gerald Mohr, Jack Moyles, Jeanette Nolan, Charles Seel, Mary Shipp, Doris Singleton, Barbara Stanwyck, Lurene Tuttle, Jack Webb, Donald Woods.

From his own lips the Whistler explained his function at the start of each weekly episode: "I am the Whistler, and I know many things for I walk by night. I know many strange tales hidden in the hearts of men and women who have stepped into the shadows. *Yes* ... I know the nameless terrors of which they dare not speak!" Spooky. An ebullient announcer then fawned over *The Whistler* being "rated tops in popularity for a longer period of time than any other West Coast program." (He didn't define "period of time," of course.) One wag described it as "mystery presentations that depict the plight of people who were suddenly caught in a destructive web of their own misdeeds."

Accompanied by a mournful wavering warble—the whistling of a dual-octave refrain—the Whistler nevertheless bypassed the direct exposure of wrongdoing in his tales. Instead, this all-seeing, all-knowing fellow expressed his thoughts on the paradoxical situations of the plot lines while the radio audience "tuned in" to his thoughts as the narratives played out. That identifying whistle, incidentally, was accompanied by some echoing footsteps on what reverberated like a damp street.

Ultimately, in the "strange ending to tonight's story," a brief epilogue following the conclusion of a tale, some twist of fortune nailed a killer just when he thought he had gotten away with his transgression. John Dunning stated it eloquently: "The voice was an unforgettable tenor, the message dripping with grim irony. *It all worked out so perfectly, didn't it, Roger*, he would coo, while listeners waited for the shoe to drop.... When the finger of fate struck, some fatal flaw of character or deficiency in the master plan that was so obvious that everyone had overlooked it [unraveled completely]." The killer, so it turned out, had become his own worst enemy, and the fans could distinguish a genial smirk as the Whistler bid adieu.

The whistling melody was considered quite difficult to master. Musical artist Wilbur Hatch was convinced that 19 out of 20 individuals could never perform it correctly. A total of 37 notes comprised the full repertoire—13 at the start, 11 as a tale began, 13 at the end.

One observer dubbed the Whistler "the first of the great omniscient storytellers" of radio. Assessing the medium's eerie aural "presences" (*The Saint, The Shadow*, Raymond of the *Inner Sanctum, The Whistler*, et al), another reviewer summarized: "Many of those menacing voiceovers were read by men whose slithery voices and grim chortles might now seem comically excessive, but when first heard they were frighteningly lifelike and ghoulish."

As of this writing, seven movies have hit the big screen featuring this creepy figure. All were released after the radio series was entrenched. Initially produced in English, they include *The Whistler* (1944), *The Mark of the Whistler* (1944), *The Power of the Whistler* (1945), *The Voice of the Whistler* (1945), *The Secret of the Whistler* (1946), *The Return of the Whistler* (1948) and *The Whistler* (1994). Actor Richard Dix, who appeared in all seven films, played the lead in the early 1940s radio series *King of the Royal Mounties*, based on the exploits of a mythical sergeant in the Royal Canadian Mounted Police. (See separate entry.)

A syndicated television sequel, in which radio star Bill Forman's voice reprised the title role as an unseen narrator, appeared briefly in 1954. It, too, was a half-hour anthology drama.

Jay Hickerson has provided a log for the radio series.

Whitehall 1212

On the Air: Nov. 18–Dec. 16, 1951, NBC, Sunday, 10:30 p.m.; Dec. 23, 1951–Feb. 17, 1952, NBC, Sunday, 5 p.m.; Feb. 24–Sept. 28, 1952, NBC, Sunday, 5:30 p.m. 30 minutes.
Sponsor: Sustained.
Extant Episodes: 44 (complete run).

CAST & CREDITS

Director/Writer—Wyllis Cooper.
Story Consultant—Percy Hoskins.
Support Roles—Horace Braham, Patricia Courtleigh, Lester Fletcher, Harvey Hayes, Winston Ross.

A forerunner of Orson Welles' *The Black Museum*, this intriguing little series preceded *Museum* by only seven episodes. Both were based on a similar motif. On *Whitehall 1212* detectives of London's Scotland Yard solved baffling but authentic cases. Situated on a lower level of New Scotland Yard, the agency's Black Museum held legions of artifacts associated with its cases, including lethal weapons of various descriptions.

The show opened to a distraught female ringing "Whitehall 1212" on the tele followed by a brisk response, "This is Scotland Yard." As the narrative ensued, staff veteran James Davidson, superior over the Black Museum, fawned over a given item and used that as a crutch to reminisce about a related case. Via flashback sequences, a murder and its subsequent police investigation were revisited. Finally, to summarize the details, Davidson reappeared at the conclusion of the drama.

It's unclear why two radio series with

a distinctly similar and unusual theme would air concurrently but that was the case with *Whitehall 1212* and *The Black Museum*. (See separate entry for *The Black Museum*.)

Jay Hickerson prepared a log for this series.

Wild Bill Hickok

(aka *The Adventures of Wild Bill Hickok*)

On the Air: May 27–Oct. 14, 1951, MBS, Sunday, 7 p.m.; Oct. 21–Dec. 30, 1951, MBS, Sunday, 4:30 p.m.; Jan. 4–June 6, 1952, MBS, Monday/Wednesday/Friday, 5:30 p.m.; Sept. 15, 1952–June 12, 1953, MBS, Monday/Wednesday/Friday, 5:30 p.m.; Sept. 14, 1953–June 11, 1954, MBS, Monday/Wednesday/Friday, 5:30 p.m.; Sept. 13–Dec. 31, 1954, MBS, Monday/Wednesday/Friday, 5:30 p.m.; July 17, 1955–Feb. 12, 1956, MBS, Sunday, 5:30 p.m. 30 minutes, except 25 minutes (Jan. 4, 1952–Dec. 31, 1954).

Sponsors: Sustained (May 27–Dec. 30, 1951); W. K. Kellogg Co. for Kellogg's Sugar Corn Pops cereal and other brands (Jan. 4, 1952–Dec. 31, 1954); Multiple participation (July 17, 1955–Feb. 12, 1956).

Extant Episodes: 228.

CAST & CREDITS

Announcer—Charlie Lyon.
Leads—Title role played by Guy Madison; Jingles P. Jones, played by Andy Devine.
Support Role—Curley Bradley.

U.S. Marshal James Butler (Wild Bill) Hickok and his sidekick, Deputy Jingles P. Jones (who added considerable humorous relief), covered the plains, tracking down bad guys and bringing them to justice. The pair exploited the legendary lawman that, a century earlier, had left his mark securing the frontier for newly established settlers from the East. At the start and finish of every episode, a chorus told the story: "When Wild Bill guided those settlers west, he made those wagons roll; over hills and plains he led the wagon trains to their goal. Ride on! Ride on! Wild Bill! Wild Bill Hickok, ride on!"

From one juvenile adventure thrill to another, Hickok and Jones sometimes traveled undercover as federal agents—Hickok astride Buckshot and Jingles atop Joker—both men anxious to rid the Southwest of no-accounts of widely divergent stripes. Hickok was fast with his fists and quick on the draw; a portly Jones, despite his weaknesses as an irrational, inept "fraidy" cat (one reviewer termed him "a slow-witted type who offered little essential help to the star"), he was still an expert marksman. His most common line, delivered in full-throttle, high-pitched screech, was: "Wait for meeeee, Wild Bill!"

John Dunning succinctly summarized the action: "The plots were simple; to hear one is to hear all. Wild Bill and Jingles would encounter some generic owlhoots; there'd be some fisticuffs, some gunplay. Jingles would wield his big belly as a weapon, Wild Bill would punch it out with the ringleader, and the heroes would emerge triumphant. Then it was back on their horses ... and out on the trail for another week."

The central character was undoubtedly not as well known as a few of his western contemporaries such as Gene Autry, Tom Mix and Roy Rogers. Yet Hickok joins that elite group of legendary fighters who actually lived in the West, were considered champions for righteousness, became established as heroes of that territory and instilled into the minds of their youngest listeners a sense of fairness and justice.

The character of Wild Bill Hickok made his way onto the silver screen in four major theatrical productions—three feature-length motion pictures and a serial.

The first effort was a full-length black-and-white silent film released in 1923

Wild Bill Hickok: With Deputy Jingles P. Jones (Andy Devine, left) by his side, Marshal Wild Bill Hickok (Guy Madison) relived some of the feats of a real legendary western hero by that moniker that lived during the previous century. Hickok was said to be "so handsome he might otherwise have been mistaken as a Hollywood matinee idol," which Guy Madison really was.

titled *Wild Bill Hickok*. Clifford Smith directed with screenplay by William S. Hart and J. G. Hawks. Hart, himself, played the hero; a cast of lesser knowns supported him.

The second time out, in 1938, William (Wild Bill) Elliott played the starring role in *The Great Adventures of Wild Bill Hickok*, a 15-episode black-and-white serial with sound. Directed by Sam Nelson and Mack V. Wright, it was written by George Arthur Durlam and Dallas M. Fitzgerald. This cast was also lined with also-rans.

In 1941 *Wild Bill Hickok Rides* appeared on the big screen, another full-length black-and-white production. Directed by Ray Enright with writing credits awarded to Charles Grayson and Raymond L. Schrock, it featured Bruce Cabot in the

starring role. He was surrounded by several names that would make the big time, including Constance Bennett, Howard DaSilva and Faye Emerson.

The final motion picture, *I Killed Wild Bill Hickok*, was issued in 1956 with Tom Brown playing the legendary hero. The film was directed by Richard Talmadge and written by Johnny Carpenter, with Carpenter acting in a co-starring role. Others in the cast included Denver Pyle, Virginia Gibson, Helen Westcott, Roy Canada and Harvey B. Dunn.

In a syndicated *Wild Bill Hickok* television run that overlapped the radio narrative between 1951 and 1958, Guy Madison and Andy Devine played the heroes in white hats. There were 112 half-hour episodes filmed.

Andy Devine acquired his distinctively high-pitched nasal twang from a childhood accident. He suffered a fall while running with a stick in his mouth.

In the 1800s the real Wild Bill Hickok was variously a Pony Express rider, Union scout in the Civil War, scout for Colonel Custer and marshal of Abilene, Kansas. While *this* Wild Bill didn't resemble a celebrity, a critic noted that Guy Madison was "so handsome he might otherwise have been mistaken for a Hollywood matinee idol (which, in fact, he was)."

Wings for America

On the Air: July 5–Sept. 6, 1940, MBS, Friday, 8 p.m. 30 minutes.
Sponsor: Sustained.
Extant Episodes: None known.

CAST & CREDITS

Leads—Riley Davis, played by Phillips Holmes; Lorna Carroll, played by Elissa Landi.

"Pray God that this fantasy may never happen to us." That haunting refrain was repeatedly delivered in this chilling spy reverie that posed the question: "What if?" The central characters were a mythical radio news commentator, Riley Davis, and his aide, Lorna Carroll. The program pursued their exploits, depicting how a Fifth Column—a group of enemy sympathizers or agents working within the nation—could perpetrate subversive acts against our government for the expressed purpose of weakening and overthrowing it, and delivering it ultimately into the hands of our adversaries. There were some scary moments and plenty to contemplate as a result of those dramatizations, aired less than a year after the outbreak of war on the European continent. Such series may have helped Americans maintain their resolve that they would never permit such atrocities to occur.

With Canada's Mounted Police

(aka *Canada's Mounted on the Air*)

On the Air: Jan. 11–April 4, 1932, NBC Blue, Monday, 10 p.m. 30 minutes.
Sponsor: Canada Dry Bottling Co. for Canada Dry Ginger Ale soft drink.
Extant Episodes: None known.

CAST & CREDITS

Leads—Played by Allyn Joslyn and Eustace Wyatt.
No other credits are known to exist.

These dramatizations featured tales focused on Royal Canadian Mounted Police files. Instead of a single hero, as in the more prominent *Challenge of the Yukon*, there were two Mounties as the central figures searching for lawbreakers. "The O'Brien Murders," "The Idaho Kid," "The Island Affair," "The Mad Trapper of Rat River" and "Constable Whaley's First Patrol" were among the titles of the 13-week show.

Following some extensive research on aural dramas about the Royal Canadian Mounted Police, Jack French suggested that this was the progenitor of a dozen or more series in that line (including at least a trio of narratives that were produced by the Canadian Broadcasting Corp.—*Men in Scarlet* [1943–48], *The Queen's Men* [early 1950s] and *The Quiet Force* [1954–55]). The footprints of *With Canada's Mounted Police* therefore loom large for it inspired a wave of successors that enthralled millions of fans young and old in two nations for nearly a quarter of a century.

Martin Grams Jr. prepared a log for this series.

Your Witness

On the Air: 1938, CBS, Wednesday, 10:15 p.m. 45 minutes.

Sponsor: No information.
Extant Episodes: None known.

CAST & CREDITS

Writer—Ashmead Scott.
No actors identified.

This was an audience participation murder mystery. Before the conclusion of a weekly slaying investigation there was a pause in the narrative. The announcer went down into the studio audience bearing a hand-held microphone during the brief intermission. He encouraged some of the guests to reveal who they thought the killer was. In the remaining minutes, the protagonist drew upon clues and deductive ingenuity to trap the culprit after the drama resumed.

Yours Truly, Johnny Dollar

On the Air: Feb. 11–April 22, 1949, CBS, Friday, 10:30 p.m.; July 17–Sept. 25, 1949, CBS, Sunday, 6:30 p.m.; Oct. 1, 1949–Jan. 14, 1950, CBS, Saturday, 7 p.m.; Feb. 3–March 3, 1950, CBS, Friday, 10 p.m.; March 7–May 30, 1950, CBS, Tuesday, 10 p.m.; June 8–Aug. 31, 1950, CBS, Thursday, 10 p.m.; Sept. 30–Dec. 30, 1950, CBS, Saturday, 7 p.m.; Jan. 6–March 3, 1951, CBS, Saturday, 6 p.m.; March 10–June 9, 1951, CBS, Saturday, 7 p.m.; June 16, 1951, CBS, Saturday, 9 p.m.; June 20–July 18, 1951, CBS, Wednesday, 9:30 p.m.; July 25–Aug. 1, 1951, CBS, Wednesday, 9 p.m.; Aug. 8–Sept. 26, 1951, CBS, Wednesday, 9:30 p.m.; Oct. 6, 1951–Jan. 12, 1952, CBS, Saturday, 7 p.m.; July 2–Sept. 3, 1952, CBS, Wednesday, 9 p.m.; Nov. 28, 1952–Jan. 16, 1953, CBS, Friday, 9 p.m.; Jan. 23, 1953, CBS, Friday, 8:30 p.m.; Jan. 30–March 6, 1953, CBS, 9:30 p.m.; March 10–April 21, 1953, CBS, Tuesday, 9 p.m.; April 28–May 5, 1953, CBS, Tuesday, 9:30 p.m.; May 12, 1953–Aug. 10, 1954, CBS, Tuesday, 9 p.m.; Sept. 5–19, 1954, CBS, Sunday; Oct. 3, 1955–March 30, 1956, CBS, Weekdays, 8:15 p.m.; April 2–Nov. 2, 1956, CBS, Weekdays, 9:15 p.m.; Nov. 11, 1956–Jan. 27, 1957, CBS, Sunday, 5:30 p.m.; Feb. 2, 1957–

June 1, 1958, CBS, Sunday, 7:30 p.m.; June 7–29, 1958, CBS, Saturday, 5 p.m.; July 6, 1958–Nov. 27, 1960, CBS, Sunday, 5 p.m.; Dec. 4, 1960–Sept. 30, 1962, CBS, Sunday, 5:10 p.m. 30 minutes, except 15 minutes (Oct. 3, 1955–Nov. 2, 1956), 25 minutes (Jan. 25, 1958–Nov. 27, 1960), 20 minutes (Dec. 4, 1960–Sept. 30, 1962).

Sponsors: Sustained (Feb. 11, 1949–March 6, 1953, Oct. 3, 1955–Sept. 30, 1962); William J. Wrigley Co. for Spearmint chewing gum (March 10, 1953–Sept. 19, 1954). On occasions during some of the latter sustained years there were participating sponsors, including 7-Up soft drink, No-Doz stimulant, Sinclair oil and gasoline, Mentholatum Deep Heating cream and several cigarette brands—Kent, Marlboro, Newport and Philip Morris.

Extant Episodes: 430 minimum single episodes, plus 56 five-part episodes, total minimum 710 episodes.

CAST & CREDITS

Producer/Directors—Gordon P. Hughes, Jack Johnstone, Jaime del Valle, Bruno Zirato Jr.

Directors—Fred Hendrickson, Gordon T. Hughes, Anton M. Leader, Norman Macdonnell, Richard Sanville.

Writers—Les Crutchfield, Jack Dawson, Gil Doud, Paul Dudley, David Ellis, Morton Fine, David Friedkin, John Michael Hayes, Jack Johnstone, Sidney Marshall, Joel Murcott, E. Jack Neuman, Robert Ryf.

Music—Richard Aurandt, Eddie Dunstedter (organ), Wilbur Hatch, Ethel Huber, Amerigo (Rick) Marino, Leith Stevens, Mark Warnow (orchestras except where identified).

Sound Effects—Gus Bayz, Joe Cabbibo, David Light.

Announcers—Dan Cubberly, Art Hannes, Charles Lyon, Roy Rowan, Bob Stephenson.

Leads—Title role played by Dick Powell (1948 audition), Charles Russell (Feb. 11, 1949–Jan. 14, 1950), Edmond O'Brien (Feb. 3, 1950–Sept. 3, 1952), John Lund (Nov. 28, 1952–Sept. 19, 1954), Gerald Mohr (1955 audition), Bob Bailey (Oct. 3, 1955–Nov. 27, 1960), Bob Readick (Dec. 4, 1960–June 18,

1961), Mandel Kramer (June 15, 1961–Sept. 30, 1962); Betty Lewis, played by Virginia Gregg.

Support Roles—Bill Adams, Parley Baer, Harry Bartell, Jeanne Bates, Jackson Beck, Ed Begley, Ralph Bell, Martin Blaine, Jim Boles, Lillian Buyeff, Ralph Camargo, William Conrad, John Dehner, Roger DeKoven, Larry Dobkin, Robert Dryden, Paul Dubov, Sam Edwards, Georgia Ellis, Elspeth Eric, Peter Fernandez, Bernard Grant, Jack Grimes, Ralph Grimes, Larry Haines, Vivi Janiss, Teri Keane, Joseph Kearns, Jack Kruschen, Forrest Lewis, Joan Lorring, Bill Mason, Bob Maxwell, Howard McNear, Bill Meader, Marvin Miller, Ann Morrison, Danny Ocko, Santos Ortega, Vic Perrin, Barney Phillips, William Redfield, Bartlett Robinson, Irene Tedrow, Russell Thorson, Lurene Tuttle, Vicki Vola, Gertrude Warner, Peggy Webber, Lawson Zerbe.

Johnny Dollar was the famous "private insurance investigator with the action-packed expense account." As a mythical figure in radio mystery, the thinly veiled playboy was authoritative, dynamic and charming; in the decades since, he has become an icon of the hero-worshipers among vintage radio enthusiasts. They have put him on a pedestal among celebrated audio sleuths, becoming rabid about their devotion. Without doubt *Dollar* was a radio watershed: It held the dubious honor of featuring the last aural-only detective on the ether, a 13-year veteran who swam upstream against an ebbing tide, pressing for nearly two years beyond the popularly accepted "day radio drama died" (Nov. 25, 1960).

In Dollar's cases—for a portion of the gain turned from repossessed commodities—he pursued both goods and villains with a vengeance. "He had an analytical mind, a nose for trouble, and the brawn to take care of himself when the going got dirty," an analyst stated. Dollar was often impatient, and was adept at blatantly padding his expense account. While he was a confirmed bachelor, he kept a love interest (Betty Lewis) on the string for several years. He respected the police, unlike some of his contemporaries, and called on stoolies and tipsters for information as needed in tracking down misplaced people and merchandise.

Dollar also reported the details of his escapades in the first person, the radio listener "overhearing" his expense summaries, a motif embraced by several on-air investigators. At the end of every episode, he'd total up his expenses for submission to the insurance company paying his fee, then add his signature: "Yours truly, Johnny Dollar." It was a familiar line that the faithful anticipated. On Sept. 30, 1962, he expressed it for the final time and with it vintage radio drew its last breath. Not totally, of course; yet his departure left a void that has never been filled through an ongoing dramatic series focusing on a single character. It was, without apology, the end of the age.

Most critics agree that Bob Bailey was the superior performer as Dollar ("a role he was born to play," said one), although some have allowed that Mandel Kramer was a close runner-up. Others in that part are seldom mentioned by individuals who collect old time radio memorabilia, except on lists for accuracy. During Bailey's drama-by-installment epoch, listeners were given "one of the brightest 15-minute shows on the air," according to one wag. That assessment, almost universally accepted, nearly excludes the drama's earlier and later periods.

According to reliable researcher Terry Salomonson, eight individuals played Johnny Dollar. Their names, with the number of episodes in which each starred, are given in their proper sequence: Dick Powell (one audition, Dec. 7, 1948), Charles Russell (35 including one audition), Edmond O'Brien (105 including six repeats), John Lund (95 including seven repeats

Yours Truly, Johnny Dollar: Edmond O'Brien as "the man with the action-packed expense account," Johnny Dollar, an insurance investigator who frequently found himself knee-deep in trouble while pursuing misplaced people and merchandise. He rode the airwaves to the very end of the age in one of the final dramatic programs canceled. O'Brien was featured as the hard-hitting Dollar early in the show's durable run.

and two auditions), Gerald Mohr (one audition, Sept. 29, 1955), Bob Bailey (548, including 281 quarter-hours, 72 half-hour repeats and one audition), Bob Readick (29), Mandel Kramer (66). There were 801 original broadcasts, 83 scripts aired a second time, two scripts aired thrice, 85 repeat broadcasts and 886 total performances.

Terry Salomonson prepared a log for this series.

The Zane Grey Show

(aka *The Zane Grey Theater*)

On the Air: Sept. 23, 1947–Feb. 24, 1948, MBS, Tuesday, 9:30 p.m. 30 minutes.
Sponsor: Sustained.
Extant Episodes: Two.

CAST & CREDITS

Producer—Stephen Slesinger.
Director/Writer—Paul Franklin.
Director—Emmett Paul.
Music—Harry Zimmerman (orchestra).
Announcer—Bill Forman.
Leads—Tex Thorne, played by Vic Perrin, Don MacLaughlin; Sandy Fletcher, played by Earle Ross.
Support Role—Alvina Temple.

"Strong men lived by the strong law of personal justice" in these tales of the old West, the "rugged frontier of a young nation." Tex Thorne, the central character, was a cowboy-drifter and even-tempered Pony Express rider out of the pages of the inspired novels of Zane Grey. While the narratives were based rather loosely on some of Grey's stories, most owed him little debt.

Sitting astride his faithful horse Topaz, Thorne—with a sidekick, Sandy Fletcher—helped bring some murderers, con artists and cattle thieves to justice, among a diverse quarry. Mature themes relevant to a senior audience were occasionally introduced in these tales. In one episode, a killer was spared hanging when a court found him criminally insane. Such topics wouldn't have surfaced in many other western adventures, if any, in the 1940s.

For all its sophistication (which, by the then standards was a lot), however, a critic observed that the drama never really got past the typical clichés of the juvenile western thriller. Thorne, for instance, was fond of tossing out epithets like: "Don't throw lead at me unless you want your lead back with interest." As someone put it, the more things change, the more they stay the same.

In many ways this program duplicated a far better known predecessor, *Death Valley Days* (1930–44), a derivative of which became *The Sheriff*, aka *Death Valley Sheriff* (1944–51). (See separate entry for the spinoff series.)

Dick Powell's Zane Grey Theater, an anthology of largely original half-hour teleplays hosted by the prominent Hollywood actor for whom it was named, debuted over CBS-TV Oct. 5, 1956. The series was a steady presence there through Sept. 20, 1962. While from time to time Powell starred in an episode, some of filmdom's other big names normally appeared, among them Claudette Colbert, Hedy Lamarr, Jack Lemmon, Ginger Rogers and Esther Williams. Hal Hudson produced the show for Four Star Films, Zane Grey and Pamric Productions. It arrived as Westerns dominated TV.

Appendix:
Series Grouped by
Character and Genre Types

The radio crime fighters included within the pages of this volume were derived from a fairly large number of recognizable types, and the crime fighting series generally conformed to the guidelines of one familiar genre or another. To help the reader identify series with similar characters or characteristics, each program has been classified below by what appear to be its most distinctive features—either its characters or its general type (western, science fiction, etc.). Some of these series could easily be assigned to more groupings than those in which they have been categorized below; for example, one could argue that women sleuths who were also journalists or attorneys belong in more than one category. While the choices below are purely subjective, the intent will hopefully outweigh any potential disagreements the reader might have with the assignments I have given. In any case, I hope that the reader will realize an eye-opening experience in discovering just how many different series (both prominent and obscure) comprise the varied species.

Amateur Sleuths—Full Time

The Amazing Mr. Smith
It's Murder
Johnny Fletcher
The Judge

Anthologies

ABC Mystery Time
The Casebook of Gregory Hood
Crime Classics
Crime Does Not Pay
The Eno Crime Club
In the Name of the Law
Murder By Experts
The Mystery Man
Tales of Fatima
Thatcher Colt Mysteries

True Detective Mysteries
Wanted
The Whistler

Audience Participation

The Adventures of Ellery Queen
Calling All Detectives
Murder Will Out
Somebody Knows
Up for Parole
Your Witness

Avocational Sleuths—Journalists

The Adventures of Christopher Wells
American Agent
The Big Story
Big Town

Box 13
Calamity Jane
Casey, Crime Photographer
City Desk
Confidentially Yours
Deadline Mystery
Douglas of the World
Foreign Assignment
The Front Page
Front Page Farrell
Hot Copy
Mystery Is My Hobby
Stand by for Crime
The Story of Sandra Martin
Wendy Warren and the News
The Whisper Men

Avocational Sleuths—Jurists (et al.)

The Amazing Mr. Malone
Attorney at Law
Attorney for the Defense
Defense Attorney
A Life in Your Hands
Mr. District Attorney
The Orange Lantern
Perry Mason
Roger Kilgore, Public Defender
Terry Regan, Attorney at Law

Avocational Sleuths— Married Couples

The Abbott Mysteries
The Adventures of the Thin Man
Mr. and Mrs. North
Two on a Clue

Avocational Sleuths—Oddities

The Adventures of Father Brown (priest)
The Adventures of Leonidas Witherall
  (schoolmaster)
Alias Jimmy Valentine (reformed con/bank
  clerk)
The Bishop and the Gargoyle (theologian
  and a reformed con)
The Count of Monte Cristo (reformed
  con/aristocrat)
Crime Doctor (reformed con/physician)
David Harum (banker)
Doc Savage (physician)
The Great Merlini (illusionist)
Hollywood Mystery Time (movie producer)
Just Plain Bill (barber)

Meet Miss Sherlock (department store buyer)
Mr. Mercury (circus acrobat)
The Mysteries in Paris (heiress)
The Notorious Tarique (commodities
  collector)
Pete Kelly's Blues (jazz musician)
Raffles (reformed con/chef)
Rocky Jordan (restaurateur)
The Saint (unemployed yuppie)
The Strange Dr. Karnac (physician)
Time for Love (vocalist)
A Voice in the Night (nightclub
  proprietor/vocalist)

Comedy Capers

The Adventures of Detectives Black and
  Blue
Cohen, the Detective
McGarry and His Mouse
Michael and Kitty
Results, Incorporated
Sara's Private Caper
Snoop and Peep

Educational/Informational

Are These Our Children?
Dr. Tim, Detective (juvenile)
The Loser
Our Secret Weapon
Troman Harper, Rumor Detective
Tune Detective

Federal Agents

The Black Chamber
The Border Patrol
Cloak and Dagger
Counterspy
Dan Dunn, Secret Operative 48 (juvenile)
Dangerous Assignment
The FBI in Peace and War
Federal Agent
Forbidden Cargo
Helen Holden, Government Girl
I Was a Communist for the FBI
The Man Called X
Ned Jordan, Secret Agent
Secret Missions
The Silent Men
Special Investigator
This Is Your FBI
T-Man
Top Secret

Top Secret Files
Top Secrets of the FBI
Treasury Agent
Twenty Thousand Years in Sing Sing
United States Postal Inspector

Feminine Detectives

The Affairs of Ann Scotland
Candy Matson
Carolyn Day, Detective
Kitty Keene, Incorporated
Miss Pinkerton, Incorporated
Phyl Coe Radio Mysteries

Insurance Investigators

Here Comes McBride
Special Agent
Yours Truly, Johnny Dollar

Investigators Incognito

The Avenger
The Black Hood (juvenile)
The Blue Beetle (juvenile)
Chandu the Magician (juvenile)
The Green Hornet
The Green Lama
Mandrake, the Magician (juvenile)
Mr. Chameleon
The Scarlet Pimpernel
The Shadow
Three Sheets to the Wind
The Whisperer

Jungle Tales

Jungle Jim (juvenile)
Tarzan

Juvenile Adventures—Aerial

The Air Adventures of Jimmie Allen
Ann of the Airlanes
Flying Patrol
Hop Harrigan
Howie Wing
Sky King
Tailspin Tommy

Juvenile Adventures— Science Fiction

Buck Rogers in the Twenty-Fifth Century
Dantro the Planet Man

The Space Adventures of Super Noodle
Space Patrol
Starr of Space
Tom Corbett, Space Cadet

Juvenile Adventures—Westerns

Bobby Benson and the B-Bar-B Riders
The Cisco Kid
Hopalong Cassidy
Maverick Jim
Red Ryder
The Roy Rogers Show
Straight Arrow
Tennessee Jed
Tom Mix
Wild Bill Hickok

Juvenile Detectives

The Adventures of Dick Cole
Armstrong of the SBI
Billy Swift, Boy Detective
Chick Carter, Boy Detective
Junior G-Men

Juvenile Heroes

The Adventures of Frank Merriwell
Jack Armstrong, the All-American Boy
Speed Gibson of the International Secret
    Police
Terry and the Pirates

Juvenile Troubleshooters—Adults

The Adventures of Superman
Blackstone, the Magic Detective
Captain Midnight
Chip Davis, Commando
Dick Tracy
Don Winslow of the Navy
Flash Gordon
Lady in Blue
Mark Trail
Secret City
Ted Drake, Guardian of the Big Top

Mature Police Dramas

Broadway Is My Beat
Calling All Cars
Confession
Dragnet
The Line Up
Twenty-First Precinct

Mature Westerns

Dr. Sixgun
Gunsmoke
Have Gun, Will Travel
Luke Slaughter of Tombstone
The Six Shooter

Police Detectives

The Adventures of Charlie Chan
Broadway Cop
Bulldog Drummond
Bunco Squad
Call the Police
Crime Fighters
Crime on the Waterfront
D-24
Detective Drama
Detective Stories
Detectives Dalt and Zumba
Gangbusters
Honor the Law
Indictment
The Man from Homicide
Manhunt
Murder is My Hobby
Mystery in the Air
Night Watch
Official Detective
Policewoman
The Private Files of Rex Saunders
Squad Car
Squad Room
The Top Guy
Under Arrest

Police Detectives—Specialists

The Adventures of Nero Wolfe
  (criminologist)
Danger, Dr. Danfield (criminal psychologist)
Dr. Standish, Medical Examiner (coroner)
The Private Files of Matthew Bell (surgeon)

Private Eyes

The Adventures of Bill Lance
The Adventures of Christopher London
The Adventures of the Falcon
The Adventures of M. Hercule Poirot
The Adventures of Michael Shayne
The Adventures of Philip Marlowe
The Adventures of Sam Spade
The Affairs of Peter Salem
Bandwagon Mysteries

Barry Craig, Confidential Investigator
The Big Guy
Boston Blackie
The Cases of Mr. Ace
Charlie Wild, Private Detective
Crime and Peter Chambers
The Crime Files of Flamond
A Crime Letter from Dan Dodge
Danger with Granger
Dyke Easter, Detective
The Fat Man
Hannibal Cobb
I Deal in Crime
I Love a Mystery
I Love Adventure
It's a Crime, Mr. Collins
Jeff Regan, Investigator
Johnny Madero, Pier 23
Let George Do It
The Lone Wolf
Lucky Smith
Man Against Crime
Martin Kane, Private Eye
Matthew Slade, Private Investigator
The McCoy
Mike Malloy, Private Eye
Mr. Aladdin
Mr. Keen, Tracer of Lost Persons
Mystery of the Week
Mystery Theater
Mystery Without Murder
Nick Carter, Master Detective
Pat Novak for Hire
Philo Vance
Private Eye
Richard Diamond, Private Detective
Rocky Fortune
Sherlock Holmes
That Hammer Guy
The Townsend Murder Mysteries

Royal Canadian Mounted Police

Blair of the Mounties
The Challenge of the Yukon
Dangerous Paradise
King of the Royal Mounted
King of the Royal Mounties
McLean of the Northwest Mounted
Red Trails
Renfrew of the Mounted
Silver Eagle
With Canada's Mounted Police

Science Fiction Thrillers

Latitude Zero

Scotland Yard Sleuths

The Black Museum
Dear Margie, It's Murder
Hearthstone of the Death Squad
Inspector Thorne
Inspector White of Scotland Yard
Pursuit
Scotland Yard
The Shadow of Fu Manchu
Whitehall 1212

Specialists in Espionage

The Adventures of Frank Race
The Man from G-2
Mr. Moto
Peter Quill

Secret Agent K-7 Returns
Spy Secrets
Wings for America

State Troopers

Highway Patrol
Tales of the Texas Rangers

Western Adventures

Frontier Town
Gene Autry's Melody Ranch
Hashknife Hartley
Hawk Larabee
Law West of the Pecos
Lightning Jim
The Lone Ranger
The Sheriff
Six Gun Justice
The Zane Grey Show

Annotated Bibliography

BOOKS

Brooks, Tim, and Earle Marsh. *The Complete Directory to Prime Time Network TV Shows, 1946–Present*. Fourth Edition. New York: Ballantine Books, 1988.

This is one of a series of volumes documenting what Americans watched and heard on their television screens during the years covered. It possibly provides more detail about names of cast members than any other published source, and is therefore a functional guide for filling the gaps in faltering memories.

Buxton, Frank, and Bill Owen. *The Big Broadcast, 1920–1950*. Second Edition. Lanham, Md.: Scarecrow, 1997.

A trilogy of Buxton and Owen reference guides (including *Radio's Golden Age: The Programs and the Personalities*, published by Easton Valley in 1967, and *The Big Broadcast, 1920–1950: A New, Revised, and Greatly Expanded Edition of Radio's Golden Age*, by Viking in 1972) may be considered incomplete. Scores of important series that aired before 1950 are totally ignored or their detail is so diminutive as to render it virtually meaningless. None of these texts explore series that debuted after 1950, a period when several of radio's most innovative developments took root (including dramas with mature police, science fiction and western themes, new situation comedies, variety shows and such novel departures as *Road Show, Monitor* and *Weekday*). There is a significant redeeming grace about the works of Buxton

and Owen, however, besides the fact that the pair were among initial researchers to publish extensive program data after the golden age: There are many names included in their cast lists that do not surface elsewhere. Becoming more extensive with each new edition, their works, as a result, make important contributions to the genus.

Castleman, Harry, and Walter J. Podrazik. *505 Radio Questions Your Friends Can't Answer*. New York: Walker, 1983.

For the trivia buff, there's a wealth of recall information here that can be applied in sharpening the senses about almost any avenue of radio programming.

Cox, Jim. *The Great Radio Audience Participation Shows*. Jefferson, N.C.: McFarland, 2001.

Seventeen of radio's most honored, best recalled audience participation series are delineated. Included for each one is the premise it was based upon, the producers, directors, hosts, announcers, vocalists, orchestra conductors, writers, sponsors, ratings, air dates and networks that carried it. Biographical sketches are provided for 177 figures connected with these programs. A guide to more than 400 network audience participation shows is included. The series had crime, mystery and adventure themes. The book is believed to be the first to extensively cover a field that others have missed almost entirely.

_____. *The Great Radio Soap Operas*. Jefferson, N.C.: McFarland, 1999.

Thirty-one washboard weepers are singled out for consideration. Cast lists, broadcast data, premises, sponsors and a heavy dose of anecdotal data help bring those decades of matinee melodrama back to life. There are 158 biographical vignettes on individuals who worked in the serials, photographs of some, plus a list of more than 200 soap operas that aired between 1930 and 1960 and a revealing composite of serial-related superlatives. Hundreds of individuals who worked in dishpan dramas turned up later in the same day in crime, mystery and adventure series and many of their accomplishments are recorded here.

_____. *Say Goodnight, Gracie: The Last Golden Years of Network Radio and Beyond.* Jefferson, N.C.: McFarland, 2002.

This is a complex analysis of many factors impinging on Americans in the decade of the 1950s. It includes major events like the Cold War, the Korean War, an unprecedented prosperity, the inception of racial integration and scams that were perpetrated on an unsuspecting public. Given that environment, the book focuses upon the ebbing tide of radio and the rise of television as millions began to receive their home entertainment and information in the new way. A variety of programming innovations occurring in radio's fading days are explored. In a final chapter, the history of the network chains from the golden age to the present is recounted, including some documentation never widely circulated.

DeLong, Thomas A. *The Mighty Music Box: The Golden Age of Musical Radio.* Los Angeles: Amber Crest Books, 1980.

Tom DeLong has done what apparently no author before him—or since—has: offer readers a comprehensive reflection of the musical programming of vintage radio. The selections range all the way from opera to *Opry,* recalling many of the broadcast tunes of that near-forgotten era. With fresh perspectives and a scholarly, yet easy-to-grasp style, DeLong cites the stars and orchestras, ensembles, vocalists and just about everyone else who brought music to our ears. While a few treatises have been released on specific aural music series, this may be the only volume that addresses all of them. As music was a vital part of much of radio drama, cross-references, while limited, may be discovered.

_____. *Radio Stars: An Illustrated Biographical Dictionary of 953 Performers, 1920 through 1960.* Jefferson, N.C.: McFarland, 1996.

DeLong offers a treasure chest of data on personalities in the industry, including birth and death dates and places, training, experience, honors and achievements in various mediums, outside interests and anecdotes—most never before published. The author's own insights and careful attention to factual detail are particularly refreshing. Written in a lively manner, the book includes representative photos of many of its subjects.

Dunning, John. *On the Air: The Encyclopedia of Old-Time Radio.* New York: Oxford University Press, 1998.

The definitive encyclopedia of American radio from its beginning in the 1920s until the early 1960s, this thick volume has often been referred to by collectors as "the bible of the industry." Its 800 pages contain extensive material, much of it not to be found elsewhere, on hundreds of shows from every species. Researchers rely on it heavily. While the information is extensive and it is generally considered reliable, the work omits dozens of series, unfortunately. The original manuscript was reportedly huge and that may explain some series' absences. Upon its release in 1998, the work was believed to be the most extensive single volume ever published on its topic. It remains a valuable tool and may only be superseded if its author should deliver an expanded update.

_____. *Tune in Yesterday: The Ultimate Encyclopedia of Old-Time Radio, 1925–1976.* Englewood Cliffs, N.J.: Prentice-Hall, 1976.

Another of the "important works" on radio, this one offers vivid details behind the scenes of most of the major series of the golden age and beyond. Programs are described with essays, some fairly brief but others quite liberal. Both the nostalgia buff and the serious student will gain helpful information here. A large number of these entries were absorbed into Dunning's newer work but some of the detail didn't make that transfer so this "companion" book remains a viable part of radio historiography.

Goldin, J. David. *The Golden Age of Radio: The Standard Reference Work of Radio Programs and Radio Performers of the Past.* Larchmont, N.Y.: Radio Yesteryear, 2000.

This work purports to include the airing dates and networks of 61,160 different broadcasts taken from 13,097 separate program titles. It also offers 233,680 radio air credits for 21,942 individual performer names. Despite the fact that the information is offered in easy-to-find style, it skims over protracted subject areas. Critics have noted that much of the book's content exists in print elsewhere, but it does corroborate such data and sometimes offers additional facts.

Grams, Martin, Jr. *Radio Drama: American Programs, 1932–1962.* Jefferson, N.C.: McFarland, 2000.

This is a compendium of information that would not be easily acquired without going to an awful lot of web sites. Even then, many of these shows would be missing. There's a mix of both prominent and obscure features, most with titles and dates of individual episodes for entire runs, many of the mystery variety. A brief history accompanies many of the series logs.

Harmon, Jim. *The Great Radio Heroes.* Garden City, N.Y.: Doubleday, 1967.

This early but highly readable text has since been updated (*The Great Radio Heroes*, Revised Edition, McFarland, 2001) and indexed, probably its greatest innovation. Harmon offers an affectionate portrait of a wide range of juvenile adventure and detective programs. There are some choice morsels here based on his personal impressions growing up during that era.

_____. *Radio Mystery and Adventure and Its Appearances in Film, Television and Other Media.* Jefferson, N.C.: McFarland, 1992.

In many ways this is a continuation of *The Great Radio Heroes* but it covers the subject in greater depth. Harmon gives considerable attention to such deviant matters as comic strips and books, pulp fiction, TV, movies, series-related clubs and organizations one could join and a full list and description of premiums offered by juvenile adventure shows. The title is somewhat misleading for the book doesn't capitalize on the popular nighttime dramas and thrillers (at least, those targeted primarily to adults); it zeroes in on the late-afternoon adolescent adventures. A number of actors who appeared in mystery programs are briefly profiled, however.

Hickerson, Jay. *Necrology of Radio Personalities.* Original document and four supplements. Hamden, Conn.: Jay Hickerson, 1996, 1997, 1998, 1999, 2000.

This is simple but important documentation on the death dates and places of hundreds of performers and others associated with network and syndicated radio.

_____. *The New, Revised Ultimate History of Network Radio Programming and Guide to All Circulating Shows.* Second Edition. Hamden, Conn.: Jay Hickerson, 1996.

Most serious radio researchers would be hopelessly lost without this indispensable resource on their shelves. The spiral-bound log, updated every four or five years, contains more than 6,000 golden age programs—not all, to be sure, but quite likely more information on more shows of all types than is available in any other published or electronic format. The softbound book includes sign-on and sign-off dates, stars, networks, sponsors, days and broadcast times. Updates in the form of supplements are available annually.

_____. *The Second Revised Ultimate History of Network Radio Programming and Guide to All Circulating Shows.* Third Edition. Hamden, Conn.: Jay Hickerson, 2001.

Same as previous listing but updated considerably.

Hyatt, Wesley. *The Encyclopedia of Daytime Television: Everything You Ever Wanted to Know About Daytime TV But Didn't Know Where to Look!* New York: Billboard Books, 1997.

This inspired, delightfully written manual of TV, past and present, details hundreds of shows, with illustrations. In addition to cast lists, dates, times and networks, there are meticulous accounts of plots and series backgrounds. Radio aficionados can trace careers of radio personalities into TV and shows that transferred from an audio to a visual medium during the hours of sunshine.

Lackmann, Ron. *Same Time ... Same Station: An A–Z Guide to Radio from Jack Benny to Howard Stern.* New York: Facts On File, 1996.

With brief essays on hundreds of personalities and programs, and with more than 100 excellent photos, this book received the wrath of critics for scurrilous contradictions and scores of errors, which substantially diminished it as a reliable source. The author subsequently made a commendable overhaul, correcting most of those flagrant errors in *The Encyclopedia of American Radio: An A–Z Guide from Jack Benny to Howard Stern*, co-written with Ronald W. Lackmann (Facts on File, 2000).

MacDonald, J. Fred. *Don't Touch That Dial! Radio Programming in American Life from 1920 to 1960.* Chicago: Nelson-Hall, 1991.

This is one of the better texts (if not *the* best) for scholarly-minded hobbyists. Separate chapters on detective programming and westerns are filled with keen observations on how these genres influenced society. The likelihood is great that Mac-Donald examined most series pertaining to each form, including many rare and obscure titles. Sensibly, he covers the full parameters of the length of the golden age.

Maltin, Leonard. *The Great American Broadcast: A Celebration of Radio's Golden Age.* New York: Penguin Putnam, 1997.

An impressive gift book for the nostalgia lover, this one attempts to cover it all yet has a hard time concentrating on programming produced away from the West Coast. That's probably because most of the actors, directors and writers who were the subjects of poignant interviews conducted by the author lived there. Anecdotal material is absorbing, although some of it appears in other places. The text includes illustrations.

McNeil, Alex. *Total Television: The Comprehensive Guide to Programming from 1948 to the Present.* Fourth Edition. New York: Penguin Books, 1996.

A student of the genre cited this volume as probably the single best text on the market in what it does—providing coverage of TV shows and personalities since 1948. While it probably contains more entries (and therefore, more series) than similar compendiums, on the surface it doesn't appear to contribute the intricate details stored in the works of Tim Brooks and Earle Marsh. (See separate listing.)

Mott, Robert L. *Radio's Sound Effects: Who Did It, and How, in the Era of Live Broadcasting.* Jefferson, N.C.: McFarland, 1993.

A man who spent his career behind the microphone vividly describes the scene for his readers. Mott introduces most of the professional network radio sound specialists and tells of the shows they worked on while listing another group of obscure artists: the organists and other musicians. Heavy doses of anecdotes are right out of the pages of life.

Nachman, Gerald. *Raised on Radio: In Quest of The Lone Ranger, Jack Benny, Amos 'n' Andy, The Shadow, Mary Noble, The Great Gildersleeve, Fibber McGee and Molly, Bill Stern, Our Miss Brooks, Henry Aldrich, The Quiz Kids, Mr. First Nighter, Fred Allen, Vic and Sade, The Cisco Kid, Jack Armstrong, Arthur Godfrey, Bob and Ray, The Barbour Family, Henry Morgan, Joe Friday and Other Lost Heroes from Radio's Heyday.* New York: Pantheon Books, 1998.

This is one of the most delightfully readable and joyously written volumes attempting to cover the entire spectrum of old time radio. While it fails to do that, and isn't error-free, the author takes his readers on a venturesome trip that makes one long for a return to the pages of yesteryear. It's a fantastic introduction for OTR beginners and a nostalgic treat for more seasoned enthusiasts.

Settel, Irving. *A Pictorial History of Radio.* New York: Grosset & Dunlap, 1967.
Excellent illustrations make this a poignant walk down memory lane. Beginning with the invention of radio and proceeding by decades from the 1920s through the 1960s, this is a loving portrait of an era that entertained and informed.

Sies, Luther F. *Encyclopedia of American Radio, 1920–1960.* Jefferson, N.C.: McFarland, 2000.
As of this writing, Sies' book is believed to be the largest single volume ever published on the subject of radio. In excess of 900 pages at an oversized 8.5" × 11", it includes nearly 29,000 separate entries. The preponderance of them pertain to obscure local market radio performers in far-flung rural areas and cities of all sizes across America during the 1920s and 1930s. It does include personalities featured throughout the golden age and beyond, however. A percentage of the weighty volume is devoted to broadcast series and therein Sies gives his readers valuable cast lists (alas, some with misspelled names) that researchers might never otherwise have access to. Some limited extraneous data is included with most write-ups, but not the extensive commentary supplied by several other authors in volumes with similar intents.

Slide, Anthony. *Great Radio Personalities in Historic Photographs.* Vestal, N.Y.: The Vestal Press, Ltd., 1982.
Celebrity-focused and alphabetically arranged, these 235 black-and-white photographs and their captions chronicle the old-time radio years. The photos are generous-sized close-ups of those individuals featured.

Stedman, Raymond William. *The Serials: Suspense and Drama by Installment.* Norman: University of Oklahoma Press, 1971.
The most insightful, accurate and authoritative chronicle published between the end of the golden age and nearly the turn of the century, this priceless volume long set the standard for serious exploration of the soap opera. A scholarly approach by an educator who devoted much of his life to discovering the true story, it provides valuable analysis and commentary on virtually all of radio's daytime network serials.

Summers, Harrison B., Editor. *A Thirty-Year History of Programs Carried on National Radio Networks in the United States, 1926–1956.* New York: Arno Press and the *New York Times,* 1971.
The amount of effort that went into this reference is incalculable; nowhere has it been duplicated. The wealth of data it provides on programs, times, days and years on the air, sponsors and ratings is absolutely phenomenal. This could be the most important single reference work on radio.

Swartz, Jon D., and Robert C. Reinehr. *Handbook of Old-Time Radio: A Comprehensive Guide to Golden Age Radio Listening and Collecting.* Metuchen, N.J.: Scarecrow, 1993.
This volume is a highly readable collection of short narratives on hundreds and hundreds of programs. Importantly, it contains several other sections of merit, including a radio history, program category logs and emphasis on old-time radio collecting. The serious student and the nostalgia buff will love it.

Terrace, Vincent. *Radio Programs, 1924–1984: A Catalog of Over 1800 Shows.* Jefferson, N.C.: McFarland, 1999.
More shows may be listed here than in any other single published source—1,835 of them, to be exact. The work includes 517 program openings and 243 closings, making it even more distinctive. Photos are limited but text is insightful.

PERIODICALS

References from issues published in the 1920s, 1930s, 1940s and 1950s of the following magazines were freely adapted for this book: *Billboard, Broadcasting, Newsweek, Radio Guide, Radio Life, Radio Mirror* (and the subsequent *Radio-TV Mirror* and *TV-Radio Mirror*), *Time, Variety.*

TAPE RECORDINGS

Collections of shows owned by several individuals, involving thousands of hours of recorded programming, provided irrefutable evidence of premises, cast members' names, sponsors and other extraneous, pertinent detail.

WEB SITES

A plethora of web sites are related to one or to several crime, juvenile adventure and detective radio series. The people behind these valued repositories have worked diligently to provide accurate, concentrated data that is available to users with a diverse range of intents. Authoritative documentation for this volume was realized by exploring a wide band of web sites. Meanwhile, the source consulted most frequently in gathering information electronically was, without question, a daily discussion forum aimed at vintage radio adherents located (as of this writing) at *old.time.radio-request@oldradio. net.*

Index